PROVIDENCE ISLAND, which lies off the coast of Nicaragua, was colonized by English puritans in 1630. Although they envisioned creation of a godly society very much like that being constructed in contemporary Massachusetts Bay, the puritan settlers on Providence Island became hopelessly factionalized. They began large-scale use of slaves, and they moved heavily into privateering – licensed piracy. The backers were drawing on the legacy of the great Elizabethans, Drake and Ralegh, in arguing that striking at the great enemy, Spain, was necessary to the defense of Protestantism and that a plantation in the Indies would make England rich and strong enough to be the true leader of the reformed religion. The Providence Island adventurers were the greatest puritan political leaders in England. They included men such as John Pym, who led parliament into Civil War in the early 1640s. Providence Island failed because these same leaders did not provide the basic institutional arrangements found in all successful colonies, whether in New England or the Chesapeake: private property in land, control of taxation, and civilian control of the military establishment. The settlement was "extinguished" by the Spanish in 1641 without ever achieving success.

Providence Island, 1630–1641

Providence Island, 1630–1641

The Other Puritan Colony

KAREN ORDAHL KUPPERMAN

University of Connecticut

CAMBRIDGE
UNIVERSITY PRESS

Published by the Press Syndicate of the University of Cambridge
The Pitt Building, Trumpington Street, Cambridge CB2 1RP
40 West 20th Street, New York, NY 10011-4211, USA
10 Stamford Road, Oakleigh, Melbourne 3166, Australia

© Cambridge University Press 1993

First published 1993
First paperback edition 1995

Printed in the United States of America

Library of Congress Cataloging-in-Publication Data is available.

A catalogue record for this book is available from the British Library.

ISBN 0-521-35205-3 hardback
ISBN 0-521-55835-2 paperback

Contents

Maps

Preface

When I first discovered the puritan colony on Providence Island, it seemed to offer the possibility of answering one key conundrum of early colonial history: Which is more important in shaping new American societies, culture or environment? The standard examination question goes something like this: What would their communities and economy have looked like if the puritans had gone to Virginia rather than to the unproductive land of New England? Providence Island, just off the coast of Nicaragua, was settled at the same time as Massachusetts Bay by the same kind of substantial puritans. Instead of creating classic New England towns based on subsistence agriculture, these puritans seemed to emulate their West Indian neighbors by pursuing plantation agriculture with slaves as their source of labor. Moreover, they indulged heavily in privateering. It seemed to be a clear and rather simple case of nature overwhelming nurture.

What I found was a far more complex and more interesting story. Because Providence Island was backed by the most substantial lay puritans in England, it was a colony that received consistent support and was the focus of great interest. Many in England believed that New England would prove to have been no more than a holding station from which the settlers would all eventually move to found a great English colony in Central America. Providence Island was to be the first beachhead of this effort. Working on the history of Providence Island made me see that we have artificially cut up the early English colonial effort into hermetically sealed little units, New England (usually only Massachusetts Bay) and the Chesapeake, and have ignored massive evidence of an integrated colonial vision that was widely shared on both sides of the Atlantic. The backers of Providence Island were also involved in Virginia, Bermuda, Massachusetts, Connecticut, and Maine settlements, and they advised on others. They saw all these efforts as interrelated; we have allowed the unusually parochial vision of John Winthrop to dominate anachronistically.

Moreover, because Providence Island was founded by men who had studied earlier colonies intensively and who believed that they had evolved the best plan for creation of a godly English society in America, this plantation's experience offers us the opportunity to understand what made for success (or failure). Looked at from the vantage point of this failed colony that should have succeeded, we can see that all the successful colonies have much in common with one another. Thus, analysis of Providence Island can help to break down inflated views of the differences between the Chesapeake plantations and New England's communities.

This comparative treatment was not the book I intended to write; the sources forced it on me. The problem in writing about Providence Island was that the colonists spent much of their time in seemingly pointless, self-defeating wrangling. More energy was spent on settlers' resistance to company demands that they contribute their and their servants' labor and supplies to construction of the public works, particularly the fortifications, than on any other issue. Because the island was in the heart of the Spanish empire and was sure to be attacked, this seemed simply incredible.

To understand the issues that exercised the planters, I looked at the experience of contemporaneous English settlements and found that every English colony, puritan or not, experienced the same arguments and problems. They also shared the same problems of retarded economic development that plagued Providence Island. Every colony before Massachusetts Bay limped through about a decade of economic drift and settler discontent before finding the crop and arrangements that led to its success. Closer examination showed that economic establishment followed the granting (or seizure) of land ownership. Owning the land gave planters the security without which they would not emigrate. Because taxation for the public works could threaten that security by preempting property, land ownership was accompanied by a representative assembly, at least for the larger planters, to authorize levies for joint concerns. Finally, the settlers, many of whom were moved to emigrate because of their experiences with Stuart upgrading of the military and attendant billeting of soldiers on civilian populations, refused to allow a professional military establishment. Most of the colonies began with military veterans in charge, but they quickly moved to make such men unnecessary. Citizen control of the militia was essential to success, and no colony survived without this step.

Providence Island failed because it took none of these steps. The backers, all puritan grandees and many of them veterans of the Virginia and Bermuda companies, believed that all previous colonies had degenerated because they had been run by merchant interests in England that had not exercised systematic control. They restricted their company to a handful of leading gentlemen and aristocrats who, they believed, would always keep their eyes on lofty goals. For the same reasons, they insisted that settlers remain tenants, and they appointed all governors and councilors from London. Because of the ever-present threat of Spanish attack, professional soldiers were a looming presence in Providence Island. They were doubly necessary because the demands of the unfamiliar environment required old Caribbean hands, many of whom were military men. The venture was doomed by faulty design backed up by genuine commitment on the part of its backers; ironically, other colonies circumvented design flaws because their investors were less consistently faithful.

The saga of Providence Island is also important for English history because company members were, in the next decade, to lead the nation into civil war. John Pym was company treasurer, and Lords Saye and Brooke were key investors, as were the Earls of Manchester and Warwick. They were linked by a deep religious commitment; their colony, like their decision to oppose the king, derived from the heartfelt belief that the reformed religion was in grave danger. Historians of seventeenth-century England recognize the genuineness of this conviction. But construction of new puritan societies created unprecedented problems for traditional leadership. These grandees confronted their misunderstanding of the fundamental underpinnings of English society in their experiment in the Indies; they would repeat many of the same errors in the coming two decades at home.

Many colleagues have helped me immeasurably in developing the background and understanding to write this book. David Harris Sacks gave me the benefit of his expertise in Anglo-American history as I was beginning the project. Valerie Pearl, Cynthia Herrup, Christopher Thompson, John Morrill, John Reeve, John Adamson, John Walter, Christopher Hill, David Ransome, and D. M. Fiennes have also generously helped me clarify the issues as seen by seventeenth-century English people and have shared knowledge of sources. On the American side, I have benefited by assistance from John Demos, John Murrin, Jack Greene, Russell Menard, Stephen Foster, Joyce Lorimer, Michael McGiffert, David Beers Quinn, William Sorsby, William Warner, and Charles Cohen. Roy Ritchie read and commented on the entire manuscript.

My research and writing were supported by a travel grant from the American Philosophical Society, fellowships from the American Council of Learned Societies and at the National Humanities Center in 1984–5, grants from the University of Connecticut Research Foundation, and a

xii   *Preface*

National Endowment for the Humanities Fellowship at the John Carter Brown Library in 1989.

I began writing the manuscript while a Rockefeller Foundation fellow at the Villa Serbelloni in Bellagio, Italy. Lisa and Miguel A. Arbués translated documents from the Archives of the Indies in Seville. Robert and Mary Naeher offered ready assistance in many ways. The two original maps were drawn by Tracy Smith of the University of Connecticut Cartography Lab; seventeenth-century locations on the Providence Island map are drawn from A. P. Newton, *The Colonising Activities of the English Puritans* (New Haven, 1914). I wish to thank the *William and Mary Quarterly* and the *Historical Journal* for permission to reprint portions of work previously published in those journals.

As always, my deepest debt of gratitude is to my husband, Joel Kupperman, for his interest and support throughout this long project.

Author's Note

In quotations from seventeenth-century writers, I have modernized spelling except for proper names and names of commodities from the Indies. Punctuation and capitalization have been retained as in the original.

I have not capitalized the word *puritan* because puritanism was a broad stream in early seventeenth-century England, and those who were designated or who called themselves puritans shared some but not necessarily all of the attitudes or beliefs within that extended movement. When puritans began to found new societies in America they discovered the great variety covered by the single term *puritan*. Many historians have argued that the term is so inexact, and its use implies such a spurious unity, that it should be given up. Presenting the term in lowercase form indicates its lack of precision without losing the reality of the movement.

The Records of the Providence Island Company, two large folio volumes, are in the Public Record Office at Kew, CO 124/1,2. Volume I contains copies of all letters sent from London to the colony, as well as to Association Island. Volume II contains detailed minutes of company meetings. Footnote references to these volumes are by date of meetings, or date and recipient of letters – for example, PIC Gen. Ct., 2–14–31 or PIC to Gov. Bell, 2–31.

The following abbreviations are used in footnotes and appendixes.

Add. MS	Additional Manuscript
B. L.	British Library
Bod. Lib.	Bodleian Library
H. M. C.	Historical Manuscripts Commission
M. H. S.	Massachusetts Historical Society
P. R. O.	Public Record Office
S. I.	Somers Islands (Bermuda)

1

The Providence Island Company and Its Colony: The Program

PROVIDENCE ISLAND is a small volcanic island off the coast of Nicaragua. A colony was planted there in 1630 by a small joint-stock company composed of the most prominent lay puritans in England. This venture, the exact contemporary of the Massachusetts Bay Colony, was intended to be *the* great puritan colony. Providence Island Company members were also intimately involved in helping Massachusetts to get started, but they expected the disappointed New Englanders eventually to leave their cold, rocky refuge for the far more promising Caribbean location.

John Pym, Lord Saye and Sele, the Earl of Warwick and his brother the Earl of Holland, their cousin Sir Nathaniel Rich, Lord Brooke, Lord Mandeville (the Earl of Manchester from 1642), Sir Benjamin Rudyerd, Oliver St. John, Sir Gilbert Gerard, Sir Thomas Barrington, Richard Knightley, Henry Darley, Sir William Waller, Lord Robartes, John Gurdon, and Christopher Sherland made up the core of the company membership; William Jessop was the company secretary. These men drew on the traditions of the great Elizabethan imperialists such as Ralegh but represented broad experience of recent, less individualistic, and more successful ventures through having had leading roles in the Virginia and Bermuda (Somers Islands) Companies. They are well known to history because of their centrality in the resistance to Charles I and in the English Civil War. Their Providence Island venture preoccupied them during the period of Charles I's personal rule and the long interval between the parliaments of 1629 and 1640, and it helped to cement the working relationship that allowed them to move easily into military and parliamentary command as war came to England in the early 1640s.

The Providence Island colony attracted many colonists of the same middling puritan stripe as did New England; backers and settlers alike expected to create a solid godly community in the Indies. In this their hopes were disappointed. There were many reasons for their failure: Some derived from the island's location in the Indies, others related to economic problems. But the colony's struggles also revealed problems at the heart of contemporary attempts to create godly communities as replications of an idealized English society, problems echoed in New England and in interregnum England. For puritans, the proper relationship between Christians and civil authority was filled with ambiguity, and this ambiguity was revealed by the process of society building in America.

Providence Island was a puritan colony, but it confronted problems not faced by mainland plantations, especially the ever-present danger of attack, a danger made acute after the Providence Island adventurers received a patent for privateering in 1636, halfway through its decade of life. Its location made the presence of professional military men imperative. Many of these veterans were godly men but, like John Underhill and John Endecott in New England, were disruptive in their godliness. In the end they were also ineffective. After repelling two attacks, in 1635 and 1640, the plantation was overrun by Spanish invaders in 1641, at a time when its sponsors' attention was diverted by the increasing pace of events at home.

As a West Indian settlement, the island created a plantation economy. Its principal crop was tobacco, which failed to bring satisfactory returns, and it never succeeded in developing a commodity of greater economic power. For ideological reasons, the investors denied Providence Island planters ownership of their lands, and uncertainty of tenure fed economic failure. Refused private property in land, the planters defied instructions and moved heavily into property in human beings, buying slaves at a rate unparalleled at this early date in any other English colony, puritan or not. Providence Island was the site of the first slave rebellion in an English colony, and the settlers were confronted by the realities surrounding reliance on perpetually bound labor defined by race earlier than any other colonists.

At its extinction in 1641 the puritan settlement on Providence Island, with its economy fueled by privateering and slavery, looked much like any other West Indian colony. Yet to the end the company and the leading planters strove to create a godly society and to externalize the effects of these economic choices. Company members continued to try to attract the right kind of effective preachers and godly colonists, and the planters remained true to their quest for a purer society. So convincing was their struggle that even at its end the Providence Island colony was capable of attracting a contingent of several hundred New Englanders willing to go to this alternative puritan venture. It was the vanguard of this remigration that found the Spanish in possession of that island and took back the news that this other puritan colony had come to an end.

The Providence Island Company adventurers were a remarkable group of men, all aristocrats or leading gentry, drawn together first and foremost by their deeply felt religious beliefs.[1] Interrelated by marriage and profoundly conscious of the leadership position conferred by their high rank – though for many of them their family's elevation had been relatively recent – they formed a "class within a class" in English society. They saw no conflict between their religious concerns and their class interests; puritanism, for them, was an empowering, focusing force that endowed them with energy and direction.

Testimony abounds to the adventurers' great seriousness about religion in their private as much as their public lives. They were, as Henry Parker wrote of Saye and Brooke, "singularly devote." John Humphrey wrote of Saye and Manchester that both had "the deep dye of Christ's blood," just as Edmund Calamy said of Warwick in his funeral sermon that the earl was "not only under the awe of Religion, but that he had the substance and power of it in his heart." The evidence comes not only from official biographers. John Dane, who settled among the puritans of New England, had been a butler in the household of Sir Thomas Barrington: "That was a very Religious family as ever I came in." All were known for their great appetite for sermons; Brooke's contemporary biographer wrote that he preferred ministers "whose preaching was not with enticing words of man's wisdom, but in demonstration of the spirit and of power." There was nothing feigned or "politic" in their religious commitment.[2]

---

1. The term *Adventurers* is used here as it was used in the seventeenth century: to denominate those who adventured their money in ventures. The term was not used to refer to people who actually emigrated (adventured their persons) in colonial enterprises.
2. Henry Parker, *A Discourse Concerning Puritans* (London, 1641), 53; John Humphrey to the Earl of Manchester, March 27, 1641, Historical Manuscripts Commission, Eighth *Report* (1884), no. 424; Edmund Calamy, *A Patterne for All* (London, 1658), 1, 33–7; John Dane, "A Declaration of Remarkabell Provedenses in the Corse of My Lyfe," *New England Historical and Genealogical Register* VIII (1854), 152; Thomas Spencer, "The Genealogie, Life and Death of the Right Honourable Robert Lorde Brooke," ed. Philip Styles, *Publications of the Dugdale Society* XXXI (Oxford, 1977), *Miscellany I*, 173–4.

Some dissented from this picture. The Reverend Ralph Josselin, invited in 1640 as chaplain to Lord Mandeville, refused: "I durst not accept lest I should lose my self in a loose Family," Alan Facfarlane, ed., *The Diary of Ralph Josselin, 1616–1683*, British Academy *Records of Social and Economic History* n. s., III (London, 1976), 8–9. Thomas Shepard, brought to preach in the home of Sir Richard Darley, and his sons Richard and Henry, found it a "profane house," but Shepard was able to work a

These puritan grandees worked to spread reformation, making the preached word available wherever they had influence.[3] They sought out the company of other godly men; they were renowned for preferring the company of clergymen to that of frivolous gentry. John Pym lived with Richard Knightley at Fawsley in Northamptonshire for a time in the later 1630s. The circle that gathered there, which Clarendon called "that Classis," included Saye, Sir Nathaniel Rich, John Hampden, John Pym, John Crew, and Christopher Sherland. Clarendon pointed out that Fawsley was conveniently near "the place where the Lord Mandeville lived."[4] When the plague struck London, the Providence Island Company met at Fawsley.

These men apparently lacked the dour strictness many associate with puritanism. Reports attesting to their good humor and liberality abound. Their biographers show them at games, the theater, and dancing.[5] The Earl of Manchester was known for his "meekness and sweetness of disposition," and Warwick's reputation for joviality led some to question his religious pretensions. Edmund Calamy's remark that all who knew Warwick loved him seems borne out by his daughter-in-law Mary Rich's account of her conversion in his household. Moreover, they are remarkable for their marriages to strong, independent, godly women.[6] Puritanism, rather than causing them to constrict their outlook, seems to have given them a zest for life and endeavor.

For leading puritans, religious commitment meant empowerment. Charles Cohen argues that puritans were obsessed with the limits of human ability. But regeneration, a sense of personal election, conferred power through focusing of one's energies and attention combined with a conviction of the correctness of one's goals. The humility all puritans

reformation there; Michael McGiffert, ed., *God's Plot: The Paradoxes of Puritan Piety, Being the Autobiography and Journal of Thomas Shepard* (Amherst, 1972), 51–3.

3. For the work of Lord Robartes, see Mary Coate, *Cornwall in the Great Civil War and Interregnum, 1642–60: A Social and Political Study* (Oxford, 1933), 327–31. For others see Chapter 8.

4. Edward Hyde, Earl of Clarendon, *The History of the Rebellion and Civil Wars in England*, 3 vols. (Oxford, 1707), I, Pt. I, 182–85. Conrad Russell has determined the composition of the group; see "The Parliamentary Career of John Pym," in *The English Commonwealth, 1547–1640*, ed. Peter Clark, Alan G. R. Smith, and Nicholas Tyacke (New York, 1979), 148 and n.

5. See Martin Butler, *Theatre and Crisis, 1632–1642* (Cambridge, 1984), chap. 5; J. T. Cliffe, *The Puritan Gentry: The Great Puritan Families of Early Stuart England* (London, 1984), 143–4.

6. On Manchester, see Simeon Ashe, *A True Relation of the Most Chief Occurrences* (London, 1644), 10; on Warwick, see Calamy, *A Patterne for All* (London, 1658), 37; on Mary Rich, see Sara Heller Mendelson, *The Mental World of Stuart Women* (Amherst, 1987), 79–87; see also Butler, *Theatre and Crisis*, 91–2.

sought became "purposeful self-criticism," part of the focusing process.[7] Providence was the key. The puritan grandees' belief in their capacity to read God's providence in events and to align themselves with revealed divine purpose gave them a sense of control; the godly were nothing less than God's agents in this world.[8] This conviction conferred tremendous self-confidence; it also led the adventurers to take great risks in service of the task they had assumed. Naming their colony Providence Island was enormously significant. Not only did they believe they were responding to divine will in founding the settlement; the grandees also knew they were casting themselves wholly on God's providence in venturing into the heart of the Spanish Indies. The project would succeed only with God's approval.

These investors differed from other godly men in that providence had endowed them with positions of power and concomitant wealth and responsibility. Conscious of their high rank, godly grandees transformed the nobleman's leadership role. In preparing for command, they added a new emphasis on humanistic education to the traditional stress on military training. Humanism, which taught wholehearted commitment to the public good, intensified and channeled their inherited view of themselves as leaders.[9]

Providence Island Company members believed theirs was a time of both great danger and great new possibilities for true religion. If they failed in their duties, the reformed religion could be all but extinguished. At the same time, men such as Lord Brooke believed that their era would see new understanding of the Bible's meaning. Both fear and promise gave them a sense of urgency. Like-minded men came together to meet the challenge during the 1620s and 1630s, conscious of their selection for key roles in the world-historical drama.

The grandees' project for a puritan colony on Providence Island has always provided a minor footnote in the prehistory of the English Civil War. The venture has never been seen as having been important in itself, even to the men who backed it. When it has been noticed at all, it

---

7. Charles Lloyd Cohen, *God's Caress: The Psychology of Puritan Religious Experience* (Oxford, 1986), 5, 7, 37–46, 101, 111–33.
8. On the role of providence in puritan leadership, see Blair Worden, "Providence and Politics in Cromwellian England," *Past and Present* CIX (1985), 55–99. See also Barbara Donagan, "Understanding Providence: The Difficulties of Sir William and Lady Waller," *Journal of Ecclesiastical History* 30 (1988), 433–44.
9. See Mervyn James, *English Politics and the Concept of Honour, 1485–1642, Past and Present, Supplement 3* (Oxford, 1978); Quentin Skinner, *The Foundations of Modern Political Thought*, 2 vols. (Cambridge, 1978), I, *The Renaissance*, 175–7, chap. 8, 246–7; Valerie Pearl, "Oliver St. John and the 'middle group' in the Long Parliament: August 1643–May 1644," *English Historical Review* LXXXI (1966), 501 fn.

has been treated as a rather cynical cover for other activities. One was privateering – legalized piracy on Spanish ships – which was allowed to the company after the colony was attacked in 1635.

The other practice supposedly hidden in seemingly innocuous activities of the Providence Island Company was plotting resistance to the king. Company courts and committees, which brought together many of the great names associated with defiance of Charles I, have been seen as the venue for meetings of the growing opposition during the crucial decade of Charles's personal rule. This interpretation began during company members' lifetimes. As Mercurius Civicus wrote to Mercurius Rusticus, rebellion was "conceived (some say) near Banbury, and shaped in Gray's Inn Lane, where the undertakers for the Isle of Providence did meet and plot it. . . ." *The Rebel's Catechism* also asserted that the civil war was the result of long plotting: "For what Purpose else did Sir Arthur Haselrig and Mr. Pym sojourn two Years together with Mr. Knightly so near the Habitation of the good Lord Saye?"[10]

The same sentiments were also expressed positively. Arthur Wilson in his *History of Great Britain* included Saye and Warwick among the few "gallant Spirits" who "aimed at the public Liberty more than their own interest." As the Long Parliament opened, a government informer reported sentiment that Warwick, Saye, and Brooke were "the best men in the kingdom."[11]

Our interpretation of the causes of the Civil War and of the aspirations of national leaders in the 1620s and 1630s has now begun to change. The idea of an organized puritan opposition with origins stretching back to the early years of James I's reign seems less convincing today than it did when A. P. Newton wrote *The Colonising Activities of the English Puritans*, the only previous book-length study of this venture.[12] At the same time, the outbreak of war in 1642 is coming to seem more the result of political failure and miscalculation than a deliberately sought outcome. With varying degrees of certainty, historians have

10. Anon., *A Letter from Mercurius Civicus to Mercurius Rusticus, 1643, Somers Collection of Tracts*, ed. Walter Scott, 2nd ed. (London, 1810), IV, 581–82; Anon., *The Rebel's Catechism, 1643*, in *The Harleian Miscellany* (London, 1747), VII, 446. See Valerie Pearl, *London and the Outbreak of the Puritan Revolution: City Government and National Politics, 1625–43* (Oxford, 1961), 133n. on the authorship of *Mercurius Civicus*. Sir Arthur Haselrig, Lord Brooke's brother-in-law, was not a company member but was involved with them in New England ventures.

Anthony à Wood's story that the famous tower room in Lord Saye's Broughton Castle was used for secret meetings is not borne out by Providence Island Company records, which record no meeting at Broughton; *Athenae Oxoniensis*, 4 vols. New ed. with additions by Philip Bliss (London, 1817), III, 546.

11. Arthur Wilson, *History of Great Britain* (London, 1653), 161; "Report on Daniel Brinckley," *Calendar of State Papers. Domestic, 1640*, 377.

12. New Haven, 1914.

pushed the beginning of opposition closer to the actual outbreak of the Civil War and have stressed the accidental qualities of that conflict's causes.[13]

On the other hand, a civil war did take place, and the Providence Island Company investors took the lead when opposition erupted. The Providence Island Company members are best known as the core of the Long Parliament's Middle Group; their political and military activities in the Civil War years have left an indelible stamp on the record.[14] But they were involved in many activities throughout the two decades preceding that upheaval; common causes first brought them together in the 1620s.[15] They worked together in projects for educational reform; their commitment to protect threatened divines meant common efforts to find safe positions for their clients. When necessary, they contrived to spirit some leading clerics out of the country. On a more mundane level, they turned to one another's families for marriage partners for themselves and their children, firmly cementing their relationships.[16]

Most important, they were heavily involved in politics, both in the 1620s when parliament was meeting and in the 1630s when it was not. They were assiduous in working for their localities; ordinary men and women perceived leaders such as Warwick, Brooke, Saye, and Barrington as their allies, willing to intervene at home and in London in defense of their constituents. Concern for the poor was one keynote, particularly in times of dearth; another was the need to revive the failing textile industry to bring employment to their regions. When war came, these leaders were able to draw men to the cause through loyalty to themselves.[17]

13. Conrad Russell presents this case forcefully and cogently in his *The Causes of the English Civil War* (Oxford, 1990). For review essays discussing recent interpretations of the upheaval and its causes, see Richard Cust and Ann Hughes, "Introduction: after Revisionism," in their *Conflict in Early Stuart England: Studies in Religion and Politics, 1603–1642* (London, 1989), 1–46; Blair Worden, "Revising the Revolution," *New York Review of Books*, Jan. 17, 1991, 38–40; and Thomas Cogswell, "Coping with Revisionism in Early Stuart History," *The Journal of Modern History* 62 (1990), 538–51.
14. J. H. Hexter, *The Reign of King Pym* (Cambridge, MA, 1941); Pearl, "St. John," *English Historical Review* LXXXI (1966), 490–519.
15. Christopher Thompson, "The Origins of the Politics of the Parliamentary Middle Group, 1625–1629," *Transactions of the Royal Historical Society* 5th ser., 22 (1972), 71–86.
16. For such relationships, see Appendix I.
17. William Hunt, *The Puritan Moment: The Coming of Revolution in an English County* (Cambridge, MA, 1983), 169, 187, 240–52, 270; Clive Holmes, *The Eastern Association in the English Civil War* (Cambridge, 1974), 34–41; Anthony Fletcher, *The Outbreak of the English Civil War* (London, 1981), 363; Ann Hughes, *Politics, Society and Civil War in Warwickshire, 1620–1660* (Cambridge, 1987), 88, 112–13, 122, 153; Hughes, "Local History and the Origins of the Civil War," in Cust and

Most were members of parliament, and many were very active; their speeches ring through the proceedings of the 1620s. When Charles I, outraged at attempts to impeach the Duke of Buckingham, dissolved the Parliament of 1626, he attempted to recoup the subsidies he thought parliament should have granted him by levying a forced "loan" on his subjects. This attempt at unparliamentary taxation, in which assessments were laid on counties, set off alarm bells all over the country, and resistance to payment was widespread. Future Providence Island Company members were in the lead in this resistance. Richard Knightley "as unmoveable as a rock" in Northampton and Lord Saye in Oxfordshire, with Christopher Sherland and John Preston, formed one network of refusers, according to Richard Cust. And Warwick, Rich, and Barrington in Essex led another. Sir Francis Barrington, father of Sir Thomas, although old and sick, was imprisoned; his cell became the focus of daily pilgrimages from the countryside that included John Winthrop. These sessions provided a clearinghouse for information about resistance elsewhere. Saye's son-in-law, the Earl of Lincoln, led the resistance in Lincolnshire. Government punishment of the localities for this refusal and for resistance to another irregular tax in billeting of soldiers on the population fed disaffection.[18]

From the beginning of the personal rule of Charles I at the end of the 1620s and through the next decade, the men who formed the Providence Island Company in 1630 had become, according to Conrad Russell, "fundamentally disillusioned with Charles's regime."[19] They were far out in front of their peers in this judgment and were prepared to act on it. Investment in the Providence Island Company and encouragement of the New England colonies, like protection of their clients at home, were one set of actions. Another was resistance to innovations that seemed destined to free the king of reliance on parliament.

During the 1630s, the royal government was financed largely through the collection of customs – with important effects on the development

Hughes, ed., *Conflict in Early Stuart England,* 243–47; Richard Cust, "Politics and the Electorate in the 1620s," ibid., 157–58; Cliffe, *Puritan Gentry,* 120–24; John Blankenfeld, "Puritans in the Provinces: Banbury, Oxfordshire, 1554–1660," unpub. Ph.D. diss. Yale University, 1985, 222–35, 418–46; John Gruenfelder, "The Election for Knights of the Shire for Essex in the Spring, 1640," *Transactions of the Essex Archaeological Society* 3rd ser., II (1969), 143–6.

18. Richard Cust, *The Forced Loan and English Politics, 1626–1628* (Oxford, 1987), 102–5, 152, 166–70, 208, 223, 231–4, 270–1; Simon Adams, "The Protestant Cause: Religious Alliance with the West European Calvinist Communities as a Political Issue in England, 1585–1630," unpub. D. Phil. diss. Oxford University, 1973, 395–7. Cust alleges that Saye was later tricked into paying his assessment; 102–5.

19. Russell, *Parliaments and English Politics, 1621–1629* (Oxford, 1979), 424. See also Hughes, *Politics, Society and Civil War in Warwickshire,* 100.

of colonies – and supplemented by the extension of old half-forgotten fines and taxes. These included fines for property holders who had failed to come forward to be knighted and fines for encroachment on royal forests. Ship money, a tax collectible in emergencies to supplement the royal navy, was extended to all the counties and the amounts required were high. Once again the Warwick–Barrington connection raised resistance in Essex. Warwick, Saye, Mandeville, Brooke, and William Jessop, all Providence Island Company men, met in London early in 1638, and the Venetian ambassador reported that leading men were holding meetings to discuss "bringing the forms of government back to their former state." Lord Saye attempted to force a judicial judgment on the legality of the levy. When a test case was mounted in the trial of John Hampden, company member Oliver St. John conducted the defense.[20]

Although they were alarmed by these attempts to tax without recourse to parliament, none of this was sufficient in itself to bring English grandees to the point of war against their king. Only one thing – religion – could do that. Men and women throughout England, and preeminently the great puritans of the Providence Island Company, were absolutely convinced of a plot against the reformed religion in England. Moreover, they believed that the king was a willing supporter of this "popish plot." It was in defense of the true Protestant religion that opposition gathered.

John Morrill has called the English Civil War "the last of the Wars of Religion."[21] Certainly for these leaders the tie between religion and resistance was clear; Providence Island Company members who took the lead in 1640 did so because of their intense commitment to the reformed religion and their belief that it was in great danger in England.

Many labeled Saye and Brooke particularly as religious radicals who sought separation from the Church of England. Moreover, this perception stretched far back in time. As early as 1608, Lord Saye, father of the Providence Island Company member, wrote to the Earl of Salisbury

20. The meeting in London was for the marriage negotiations on behalf of Charles Rich, Warwick's son. On resistance to ship money, see V. A. Rowe, "Robert, Second Earl of Warwick and the Payment of Ship-Money in Essex," *Transactions of the Essex Archaeological Society* 3rd ser., I (1968), 160–3; Esther Cope, *Politics Without Parliaments, 1629–1640* (London, 1987), 106–21.

    Kenneth R. Andrews points out that although the ship money campaign was constitutionally and politically unwise, it did fulfill an important goal: the creation of the first modern navy, comparable to those of other European powers, in history; *Ships, Money and Politics: Seafaring and Naval Enterprise in the Reign of Charles I* (Cambridge, 1991), chap. 6.

21. "The Religious Context of the English Civil War," *Transactions of the Royal Historical Society* 5th ser., 34 (1984), 155–78, quote p. 178.

of his "greatest grief" that his son had fallen under the influence of men of "as well spiritual as temporal distracted humours," in whose company "some of no learning but tradesmen or mechanical fellows will take upon them to know who shall be saved or condemned."[22] The anonymous pamphlet *Vox Veritatis* said that Lord Saye was "a Brownist always in his Opinions, and ever guilty of separation." He was "The first, and chiefest plotters [*sic*] of the Nobility, in this Treason." The "Protestants Protestation" of September 1641 pictured "Lord Saye the Anabaptist" leading "a pack of half witted Lords" and tutoring the leadership of the Commons. And Richard Baxter wrote that "in the beginning of the Parliament there was scarce a noted gross Sectary known but the Lord Brooke in the House of Peers, and young Sir Henry Vane in the House of Commons." Clarendon's judgment was that Saye and Brooke were the only peers who were "positive Enemies to the Whole Fabric of the Church."[23]

Saye and Brooke and their associates, especially John Pym, saw matters very differently; they believed they were defending the true English reformed church against a dangerous and increasingly open campaign to return the nation to Roman Catholicism. Moreover, the perception that the reformed religion was in jeopardy was widespread throughout the nation. And the threat, in the form of unwelcome innovation, was seen as coming from those whose responsibility it was to protect the church. Two dangers threatened English Protestantism in their minds. One was the pressure emanating from the royal government to force the church in the direction of Arminianism and away from its Calvinist traditions with their primary emphasis on preaching and Bible reading.[24] The dissolution of parliament in 1629 and the beginning of Charles I's personal rule coincided with the campaign to enforce religious conformity in England.

Puritan laymen, and preeminently those involved in the Providence Island venture, had bought up advowsons and bestowed these clerical

---

22. Saye to Salisbury, Feb. 8, 1608, *H. M. C., Salisbury Manuscripts at Hatfield House* XX, 47–8. William Fiennes, who succeeded his father as Baron Saye in 1613 and was raised to the peerage as a viscount in 1624, was twenty-five years old when this letter was written.

23. *Vox Veritatis* (n. p., 1651), 6–7; "Protestants Protestation," *H. M. C. Salisbury Papers* XIV, 277; Matthew Sylvester, ed., *Reliquiae Baxterianae* (London, 1696), 63, 75; Clarendon, *History of the Rebellion*, vol. I, pt. I, 233–34. See also A. G. Matthews, ed., *Walker Revised* (Oxford, 1948), 369 on the reported remarks of Robert Albright; and *Mercurius Aulicus* (Week of Jan. 20, 1643). On the religious opinions of Saye and Brooke, see Chapter 8.

24. On the Calvinism of the English church and the threat of Arminianism, see Nicholas Tyacke, *Anti-Calvinists: The Rise of English Arminianism, c. 1590–1640* (Oxford, 1987), esp. chaps. 6–8.

livings on puritan clerics who had been deprived of pulpits because of their beliefs. These laymen thus made good preaching available. Increasingly during the 1630s, this avenue was closed as the government inquired ever more closely into the actual religious practices throughout the land and proscribed ministers who refused to conform. The government seemed determined, having shut down parliament, the main venue for expression of the people's grievances, to close such avenues for dissemination of godly teaching.

Arminians, those advocating a theology of free will, which held that salvation could to some extent be achieved by good works and through the sacraments, now came to ascendancy in the church, capped by the appointment of William Laud as Archbishop of Canterbury in 1633. Directives from the top called for restoration of ceremonies, railing off the altar as a specially sacred space, and deemphasis of preaching. The people's experience of God was to be through ritual and the recitation of set prayers. Charles I and his ministers mistrusted Protestant emphasis on study and exhortation, its insistence that each individual approach God unaided by the hierarchy and its ceremonies.

John Pym saw the danger as early as the middle of the 1620s. In the Parliament of 1628, he and Christopher Sherland linked the rise of Arminianism to the growth of arbitrary government, particularly the unpopular billeting of troops, including many Irish Roman Catholics, on the people. They pointed to the Catholics around Charles I, in his government and his household, and, joined by Knightley and Rich, gave voice to popular fears of a popish plot.[25] As the king became more isolated from the country in the 1630s and anti-Arminians were stripped of office, these suspicions grew. The London puritan artisan Nehemiah Wallington believed that throughout the 1630s there was a consistent plot to bring in "popery little and little."[26]

The popish goals of the Arminian trend connected very neatly in the puritan grandees' minds with the other great source of danger: international Roman Catholicism and its leader, Spain. Charles I's government seemed insensitive to the danger and at times sought rapprochement with Spain, a nation the puritans saw as brutally attempting to force

25. Russell, *Parliaments and English Politics*, 31–32, 345, 379–84; Tyacke, *Anti-Calvinists*, 130–4, 165.
26. Paul S. Seaver, *Wallington's World: A Puritan Artisan in Seventeenth-Century London* (Stanford, 1985), 158, 165–8. For the context and structure of these fears, see Caroline Hibbard, *Charles I and the Popish Plot* (Chapel Hill, 1983); Peter Lake, "Anti-Popery: The Structure of a Prejudice," in Cust and Hughes, ed., *Conflict in Early Stuart England*, 72–106; Robin Clifton, "The Popular Fear of Catholics during the English Revolution," *Past and Present* no. 52 (1971).

fellow Protestants back to the Roman Catholicism they had rejected.[27] Puritan leaders saw the nation apparently deserting the cause while European Protestants were hammered by Spain in the increasingly destructive Thirty Years' War (1618–48). Puritan preachers graphically painted the horrors suffered by French and German Protestants as they were pounded by rapacious Catholic armies.[28] Puritan laymen regretted that England was a weak, faltering country that could do little on the international scene. Spain had tried to force England back to Roman Catholicism in 1588; once successful on the continent, it would try again.

England was shirking its historic role as the great Protestant leader. Puritan ministers thundered about the curse placed by God on the people of Meroz for refusing to contribute to a just war (Judges 5:23), and they pointed to the hard times of the 1620s, which were marked by harvest failure, growing poverty, and the resurgence of plague – all taken by them as evidence that God was withdrawing his favor from England.[29]

All these causes were intertwined in the minds of the puritan grandees. Religious persecution had driven many valuable citizens away, thus weakening England's productive capacity. John Pym pointed to the "great many," especially "divers Clothiers" who had been driven by the "innovations in Religion and rigour of Ecclesiastical Courts" to "set up the manufacture of Cloth beyond the Seas, whereby this State is like to suffer much by the abatement of the price of wools, and by want of employment for the poor, both which likewise tend to His Majesty's particular loss."[30] Thomas Hooker, client of the Earl of Warwick, who became one of the great New England leaders, painted vividly the horrors through which Germany was living and warned that England could be next to suffer: "for England hath seen her best days, and the

---

27. John Reeve asserts that the court "allowed England to become a satellite of Spain during the 1630s"; L. J. Reeve, *Charles I and the Road to Personal Rule* (Cambridge, 1989), 180–8.

28. On the "extraordinary state of mind" of England at the end of the 1620s, see Stephen Foster, *The Long Argument: English Puritanism and the Shaping of New England Culture, 1570–1700* (Chapel Hill, 1991), 108–14.

29. Gouge, *Gods Three Arrowes: Plague, Famine, Sword* (London, 1631). On the curse of Meroz, see Hunt, *The Puritan Moment*, 199–202.

30. John Pym, *A Speech Delivered in Parliament, by a Worthy Member Thereof, and a Most Faithful Well-Wisher to the Church and Common-weale, Concerning the Grievances of the Kingdome* (London, 1641), 35. This speech was delivered to the Short Parliament, April 5, 1640. See also the 1636 complaint of Norwich merchants that persecution had caused a slump in the cloth industry; Holmes, *Eastern Association*, 7.

reward of sin is coming on apace." Hooker pictured God on the threshold saying "farewell, or rather fare-ill England!..."[31]

Belief in the popish plot prevented rapprochement between parliament and king between 1640 and 1642 when war actually broke out. Pym, Saye, and Brooke all explained in print after the outbreak that, despite the appearance of rebellion, they really fought in defense of the king, to free him of "those Papistical Malignants" and bring him back to the true English course: "'tis for the King we fight, to keep a Crown for our King...." The opponents were papists who had captured the court. Those who did not see the danger were dupes, who did not understand that Roman Catholics operated by first seeking an opening and then little by little crushing any who differed from them, ultimately emerging as the sole religion.[32]

Thus, even though many historians of the English Civil War no longer see a long-standing organized opposition movement, the leaders of the Providence Island Company still stand out. Their intense religious commitment caused them to believe, far earlier than their peers did, that the country had embarked on the wrong course and that the consequences could be enormous. Ironically, as the older interpretation is revised, the Providence Island venture assumes new importance. Rather than serving as a cynical cover for assemblies of an already existing opposition group, the company activities themselves provided these Long Parliament leaders with an invaluable education in administration and finance, as well as forging a strong working relationship among themselves.

The Long Parliament's first great issue was disestablishment of the episcopacy, and its prosecution was forced by company members. Clearly, their long and close association in company affairs bred in them experience and mutual trust that allowed them to work together to reach common goals when the need arose. Associations forged in the

---

31. Thomas Hooker, *The Danger of Desertion*, 1631, in Alan Heimert and Andrew Delbanco, eds., *The Puritans in America* (Cambridge, MA, 1985), 64–9. See also Hunt, *The Puritan Moment*, 176, 235–45.

32. Brooke, *A Worthy Speech Made by the Right Honourable the Lord Brooke, at the election of his Captaines and Commanders at Warwick Castle* (London, 1643), 3–6; John Pym, *A Declaration and Vindication of John Pym, Esquire* (London, 1643), 4–7; Pym, *A Speech Delivered in Parliament... Concerning the Grievances of the Kingdome*, 8–9; notes of Pym speech in Wallace Notestein, ed., *The Journal of Sir Simonds D'Ewes* (New Haven, 1923), 8; Saye, speech of Oct. 27, *Eight Speeches Spoken in Guildhall* (London, 1642), 18–19; Sir Benjamin Rudyerd, *Two Speeches in the House of Commons* (London, 1642), A3v. See also Tyacke, *Anti-Calvinists*, 242–44.

Providence Island Company were carried over into the war and inter-regnum years and formed the basis for effective partnerships on the national scene.[33]

Moreover, their experience in trying to work through cumbersome Stuart administrative tangles or in borrowing money in the London money markets, as well as their discouraging attempt to defy the Spanish servant of Antichrist without proper support, led them earlier than most to see that fundamental changes were required if the government was to function effectively.

No one who has read the records of Providence Island Company meetings and correspondence can believe that this venture was a sideshow in members' minds. They poured their energies and fortunes into the project with an impressive wholeheartedness; the success of this venture was essential in their minds. No discouragement could deter them. Some members fell off, and others attended only intermittently, but the core, particularly Warwick, Saye, Brooke, Mandeville, and Pym, remained fully committed to the end. No detail escaped their notice, and no obligation was shirked.

Therefore, it is time to retire the other contention about the alleged cynicism of the venture: that the investors were little interested in building a godly society and were really concerned only to create a base for privateering. Even the most superficial investigation of the Providence Island Company as a business demonstrates the falsity of that assumption. The adventurers poured their personal fortunes into the project, going to great lengths to try to shore up the little godly settlement and to found it securely. All this was far beyond what they would have had to do if privateering had been their only intention.

Establishment of an English presence in the West Indies was one avenue to a solution of the nation's problems, both religious and economic. Spain had become the greatest power in the world through the riches its American colonies brought to it. Why could England not repeat that achievement? In looking west for solutions to national problems, leaders were restoring a traditional stance. The great Elizabethans, such as Drake, Hawkins, and Ralegh, had been granted power to carry on English foreign policy by private enterprise. In 1585 Elizabeth had authorized a privateering war in the Atlantic and Caribbean that lasted to the end of her reign. Joint-stock companies sent out expeditions to prey on the fleets carrying American treasure to Seville; in some years the take contributed as much as 10 percent of England's gross national

33. John Reeve points to the key role of the Providence Island Company; *Road to Personal Rule*, 210–14.

product. Privateering between 1625 and 1630 had also brought in great rewards.[34]

West Indian ventures seemed to offer the ideal solution to England's problems. Here was a way of striking at Spain, the enemy of both England and the reformed religion, but without any governmental outlay. Not only would the government not have to spend any money, but such expeditions would actually make a substantial contribution to the royal revenues and enrich their backers at the same time. Thus, the crown would not have to turn to the extraparliamentary taxation that aroused resistance. Choking off some of the stream of wealth to Spain would weaken Habsburg ability to continue wars designed to force European Protestants back into the Roman Catholic fold.

Parliamentary leaders who combined love of Protestantism, hatred of Spain, and a desire for a strong, active English nation had first hoped to regularize privateering and give it an independent status through the creation of a West Indies Company. Holland, a people coming to rival Spain, had created such a company, and English leaders sought to emulate that country – in the words of Sir Benjamin Rudyerd to make King Charles "safe at home & feared abroad."

War against Spain in the latter half of the 1620s offered the necessary opportunity. In the Parliament of 1626, these men put forward a proposal for a West Indies Company that, in return for substantial government incentives, would have taken the war to the Spanish colonies and weakened that nation's war effort in Europe. John Pym suggested a huge fleet of sixty vessels, half of which would be ships of 300 to 500 tons. It would have been paid for by contributions (actually investments) from across the country, in which it would have emulated the Virginia Company, with its large number of small investors. Rudyerd, speaking in favor of the project, promised that many English people would "bring in large and liberal contributions, towards so noble, so profitable an enterprise."

Essential to the argument was the notion that England was weak in international affairs only because of its failure to become sufficiently involved in the new enterprises, not because of any inherent defects. Spain, according to Rudyerd, was "weak in men and barren of natural commodities," and he went on: "No sir, they are his mines in the West Indies, which minister fuel, to feed his vast ambitious desire of universal

---

34. On the sixteenth century, see Kenneth R. Andrews, *Elizabethan Privateering: English Privateering during the Spanish War, 1585–1603* (Cambridge, 1964); for the 1620s see J. C. Appleby, "English Privateering during the Spanish and French Wars, 1625–1630," unpub. Ph.D. diss., University of Hull (1983); and Andrews, *Ships, Money and Politics*, 109–10.

monarchy" and to keep Spain's neighbors in danger. Choking off the supply of riches to Spain would weaken its power to threaten European Protestants; diverting some of it to England would allow that nation to lead the defense of Protestantism. Rudyerd ended his speech by confronting any who might speak against the proposal: "I must entreat him to pardon me, I do scarce think him to be a good Englishman."[35]

Parliament's dissolution and the ensuing eleven years meant that the main theater in which concerned men confronted England's problems was closed. Most returned to their offices in county and local government in the 1630s and carried on much as before.[36] But those who had sought a fundamental solution to the nation's weakness and misdirection did not return to business as usual. They continued their campaign to find an income for the country that would allow it to rival the great powers, and they worked to make sure that a stronger England would also be a Protestant nation.

A truce with Spain also marked 1629 as a time of changing national policy. The peace made colonization more imperative for those who believed that England must have a presence in the heart of the West Indies capable of bringing some of that region's riches home and simultaneously denying them to Spain. Only the wealthiest and most committed could even consider such a task; it was surely a venture for puritan grandees.

Some puritans, seeing early warnings of a terrible judgment coming to England, fled to New England. Members of the Providence Island Company, particularly the Earl of Warwick, used their positions in the New England Company to secure a patent for settlement of Massachusetts Bay for these emigrants. Yet there was a strong feeling that those who went to New England were selfishly seeking their own safety, "a shelter and a hiding place," as John Winthrop promised his wife, rather than the country's good. As John Cotton, himself an emigrant from Boston in Lincolnshire to Boston in Massachusetts, reported, the New Englanders

35. For the debate on the creation of a West Indies Company in 1626, see the manuscript diary of Bulstrode Whitelock, Cambridge University Library MS Dd 12.21, 128v–131v. Rudyerd's speech was printed in 1641 and reprinted in Leo Francis Stock, ed., *Proceedings and Debates of the British Parliaments respecting North America* (Washington, DC, 1924), I, 61–2, but with a date of 1623/4?. On plans for a West Indies Company throughout the 1620s, see John C. Appleby, "An Association for the West Indies? English Plans for a West India Company," *Journal of Imperial and Commonwealth History* 15 (1987), 213–41, esp. 220–7; note 31 discusses the dating of Rudyerd's speech. This proposal was revived in 1637 and again in 1641; see Chapter 11.

36. See Russell, *Parliaments and English Politics*, 425–6.

were accused of having "fled from England like mice from a crumbling house, anticipating its ruin, prudently looking to their own safety, and treacherously giving up the defense of the common cause of the Reformation."[37]

Massachusetts Bay drew heavily on the "middling sort" of puritans; even the colony's leadership came from the lower gentry. For puritan grandees such as the Providence Island adventurers, a different, more heroic, course was necessary.[38] No mere refuge in America, although it might protect a "saving remnant" of the reformed religion, would fulfill their conception of England's needs and their duty. Colonies must do that, but they must also make England able to play its proper role in world affairs. If the nation would do nothing, they would stake their own fortunes and reputations on the job.

West Indian ventures, it was hoped, could help to rebuild the English economy. That was why this settlement must be placed in the "heart of the Indies." Many of the Providence Island investors lived in the hard-pressed cloth-producing regions of England. The English textile industry, outclassed by technically innovative clothworks in Europe, was in decline. Textile manufacture was the country's most important industry, woolen broadcloth comprising up to 87 percent of total exports, so the problem was of national significance.[39] Ironically, much of the materials, especially dyes, fibers, and fixatives, that went into cloth manufacture were produced in warm regions. Therefore, England was dependent on actual or potential enemies for essential supplies. Colonies such as Providence Island, it was hoped, could produce these exotic materials, thus giving England a domestic source. New sources of supply would provide increased, and diversified, employment for the English poor; therefore, the beneficial effect of such ventures would reverberate throughout the national economy.

Like many of their contemporaries, the puritan grandees believed they lived in a society that was breaking down and that the king and his advisers did not seem to care. Fate had distinguished these men from most in that they had the resources and training to design and attempt

37. Winthrop to Margaret Winthrop, May 15, 1629, *Winthrop Papers* II, 91–92; Cotton, "The Foreword Written in New England: An Apologetical Preface for the Reader of Mr. Norton's Book," in John Norton, *The Answer to the Whole Set of Questions of the Celebrated Mr. William Apollonius* (1648), trans. Douglas Horton (Cambridge, MA, 1958), 10.
38. T. K. Rabb points out the ways in which the Massachusetts Bay Company and the Providence Island Company shared goals that made them differ markedly from earlier colonizing companies; *Enterprise and Empire: Merchant and Gentry Investment in the Expansion of England, 1575–1630* (Cambridge, MA, 1967), 88, 146.
39. Derek Hirst, *Authority and Conflict: England, 1603–1658* (London, 1986), 4.

to carry out a program. Their plans began with tiny Providence Island, but they expected this venture to be only the first step on a course that would result in the development of a mighty English empire in Central America. There was no tension in their minds between the genuine patriotism and religious concern that motivated them and the personal enrichment they hoped would flow to them from the project's success. In this they concurred with another puritan leader. The Pilgrim Edward Winslow had praised this double promise when he wrote in 1624: "In America, religion and profit jump together."[40] God, understanding the cost of such massive commitments, would reward those who took up his call. Success, even riches, would surely come to an enterprise so clearly marked out to do God's work. The providence of God would shine on the island named Providence.

Because it was an intensely puritan colony and a failure, Providence Island offers a unique yardstick by which to measure the accomplishment of those colonies that succeeded. On one level, its example allows us to test accepted wisdom about Massachusetts Bay as the prime example of a puritan planned society. Historians have assumed that the characteristic New England Way is simply the best expression of puritanism, the pattern all puritans would have followed if given the chance to design their own society. The Providence Island example demonstrates that this is not true, that the Massachusetts course represented a series of choices among possible paths and that many English puritans thought of the New England regime as unacceptable. Thus, the true radicalism of the Massachusetts experiment stands out sharply when it is viewed against the program of the Providence Island Company.

Examination of Providence Island also offers an avenue for understanding that the successful English colonies actually had much in common. Many historians in recent decades have treated the Chesapeake and island colonies as if they were utterly different from the New England settlements in every respect. Thus, we have a bifurcated, and unsatisfying, approach to the foundation and development of the early English presence. Study of a well-developed failure offers illumination of the fundamental grounds of colonial success, the elements without which no English settlement in America thrived. Only through looking at what failed ventures lacked can we understand the ingredients of stability and growth. If the vital components are isolated, then it becomes clear that

40. *Good Newes from New England* (London, 1624), 52, 64.

all successful colonies shared key attributes, and the regional differences are less fundamental.

English colonization, although conducted under royal patents, was always pursued by private companies. Such projects faced immense economic problems from their inceptions. All soaked up almost inconceivable amounts of money, and all had to find ways of paying for supplies and settlers' passage. Therefore, plantations were inevitably forced to focus in the first instance on the problem of returns. Everyone involved in such ventures knew that all English colonies had been plagued by this quest. What was not clear in 1630 when two puritan colonies, Massachusetts Bay and Providence Island, were planned was how to meet this need, which had made the beginnings of all previous ventures so difficult and uncertain.

No colony became successful without finding a solid economic base. This was an obvious requirement. But none was economically successful unless it also solved key social and political problems by hitting on the right combination of institutions that made experimentation with crops and other products feasible. Virginia, Plymouth, Bermuda, and Barbados all went through the same general experience in their early years: a decade or so of dismal failure and poor production, at the end of which, with the proper arrangements in place, the plantation settled into a comfortable established pattern or even in some cases wild success. Failures such as Providence Island never emerged from this early period of discouragement.

What were the proper arrangements? Each of these colonies was the subject of some kind of experimentation with novel forms of organization in its beginning phase. Each became successful when, either through the colonists' own initiative or by direction from England, the plantation established three key institutions: private property in land; a representative assembly for the purpose of handing out obligations for public works and other general tasks; and civilian control of the colony's military establishment. In most cases, these developments occurred together. These three institutions usually emerged simultaneously because they signified the transfer of control and planning from the hands of backers in England to those of people on the scene; therein lies much of the reason for their centrality.[41] If any of the three was lacking, regardless of what else the men and women involved might do, colonies failed; when all were present, success followed.

---

41. Jack P. Greene points out that colonists emigrated for personal independence, which entailed institutions that would protect and enhance that independence. *Pursuits of Happiness: The Social Development of Early Modern British Colonies and the Formation of American Culture* (Chapel Hill, 1988), 197.

Takeoff of a colonial economy required an entrepreneurial spirit on the part of planters; only after prolonged experimentation would crops and their attendant techniques be mastered. The crucial institutions provided an environment in which settlers would undertake such risks. Providence Island never emerged from the normal early period of failure and confusion because its backers were firmly committed to the idea that only by keeping all control in their own hands in London and by restricting their membership to a small number of the right sort of godly grandees could they keep their experiment in transplantation on track, never swerving in the direction of the short-term thinking they believed had irrevocably perverted other colonial ventures. Settler empowerment, the transfer of control to America, which we can see was the key to success, they viewed with horror as the surest road to chaos.

Company members, men already famous as champions of parliament and the future great parliamentarians of the Civil War years, had every reason to know that people's control over their lives, in the form of some kind of representative government and security of tenure, were the keys to a fundamentally strong and vigorous society. Each English colony had, sometimes after bitter failure, made some provision for a representative assembly; none had been successful without such innovation, which often came at the same time as private property in land. Moreover, many Providence Island investors had participated in this transition in other companies.

Colonial assemblies were crucial because only they could levy taxes in the form of obligations to contribute, either in supplies or labor, to the settlement's public works. Just as in England, where unparliamentary taxation was bitterly fought in campaigns that ultimately ended in civil war, English settlers in America would not accept levies, however necessary, unless the levies were authorized by an assembly.[42]

Therefore, during the time that they chafed under Charles I's personal rule and pointed out the dangers of government based on the prerogative rather than parliamentary action, these great parliamentary leaders were the only colonial investors who as late as the 1630s denied their settlers both private property in land and a representative assembly to assign responsibilities in America. This denial, rendered even less understandable by the participation of many Providence Island investors in settler empowerment in other colonies, constituted the fatal flaw that doomed their plantation to failure. Planters were not free to take the enormous risks involved in experimenting with products. Lacking a secure economic

---

42. See Edmund S. Morgan, *Inventing the People: The Rise of Popular Sovereignty in England and America* (New York, 1988), 43 ff., 123–24.

role, substantial settlers also lacked the attributes of leaders and were therefore crippled in attempting to make government effective in the island. Providence Island was extinguished by the Spanish in 1641, but it was a failure long before that date.

The Providence Island Company had initially envisioned a relationship of total dependence on the settlers' part. In the original design, the colonists were tenants at halves, holding their land at the pleasure of the company: sharecroppers with no security of tenure. This system, already discarded in other colonies, was slowly and reluctantly dismantled over the course of the ensuing decade, but the planters were never given the control and security that would have made real success possible.

It has become a commonplace that the New England puritans were motivated above all by communitarian values and that the appearance of economic individualism spelled retreat from the original utopian quest.[43] The experience of Providence Island calls this conception into question and suggests that, far from being antithetical, economic individualism and religious fervor were mutually supportive.[44] Emigrants poured out of England into Massachusetts Bay during the decade when Providence Island attracted only a few hundred precisely because New England offered the ground of economic individualism: land, and the power to protect it. Security of tenure involved not only ownership but a representative system of government to forestall unwarranted seizure of property. Massachusetts Bay's location also meant relative freedom from the fear of expropriation through Spanish attack.

Land ownership and control over appropriations in America gave beleaguered puritans the promise of security, the ability to support the reformed religion without fear. Emigration alone was insufficient, as the Providence Island investors discovered; independence through economic individualism, the possession of a competency, was crucial.[45] Only the independent landowner and his family could boldly stand up to pressure. That security for themselves and their religion made emigration, despite its hardships, worthwhile. And, as Stephen Foster argues, a highly developed commercial system was necessary to make the New Englanders' program a reality.[46]

43. This position and the literature supporting it are discussed in Greene, *Pursuits of Happiness*, chaps. 1 and 3.
44. See Virginia DeJohn Anderson, "Migrants and Motives: Religion and the Settlement of New England, 1630–1640," *New England Quarterly* 68 (1985), 339–83, and *New England's Generation: The Great Migration and the Formation of Society and Culture in the Seventeenth Century* (Cambridge, 1991).
45. On the concept of competency, see Daniel Vickers, "Competency and Competition: Economic Culture in Early America," *William and Mary Quarterly* 3rd ser., XLVII (1990), 3–29.
46. Foster, *Long Argument*, 16, 76, 288.

The association of economic individualism and protection of the reformed religion, puritanism, comes through with exceptional clarity in the case of Providence Island. At several points in the colony's history the company debated reorganization of their relationship to the settlers, including the idea of allowing security of tenure, even private property in land. These discussions were forced by prominent ministers who at various times offered to lead a migrating band to Providence Island but only if the adventurers met their terms on property and self-government. Demands never centered primarily on congregational direction of religious observance, always on property relations and political control. These ministers believed religious integrity could not be ensured without guaranteed independent property rights. These clergymen and their congregations thus echoed the stance of prominent Forced Loan refusers in England for whom their resistance to unparliamentary taxation was "an extension of their religious experience."[47]

The Providence Island investors had great faith in their settlers, and they were committed believers in representative government. What they could not countenance was the creation of separate societies in America; in their view the colonies were extensions of England, somewhat like an English county. Richard Ligon in Barbados and John Winthrop in Massachusetts Bay both described their assemblies, using precisely the same words, as "in the nature of a parliament."[48] John Pym and his associates knew this formulation could never be anything but false. Only one parliament existed, that in Westminster.[49]

The Providence Island experience offers modern readers the same lessons it offered the men and women who dedicated their lives and fortunes to it: the difficulties of replicating English society in a new setting and the special problems in attempting to create a godly society. Analysis of the reasons for its failure allows us to appreciate the achievement of the successful colonies, although their lessons were unwelcome to the company's godly grandees. Many of these unwelcome lessons

47. Cust, *Forced Loan*, 171–2, 220–1, 230–2.
48. Richard Ligon, *A True and Exact History of The Island of Barbadoes*, (1st pub. 1657; repr. London, 1673), 100–1; John Winthrop, *Winthrop's Journal: History of New England, 1630–1649*, ed. James Kendall Hosmer, 2 vols. (New York, 1908), I, 74. See the illuminating discussion of the implications of the early colonial assemblies in Jack P. Greene, *Peripheries and Center: Constitutional Development in the Extended Polities of the British Empire and the United States, 1607–1788* (Athens, GA, 1986), 8–12.
49. On the constitutional status of the colonies, see Russell, *Parliaments and English Politics*, 94; and Warren M. Billings, "The Transfer of English Law to Virginia, 1606–1650" in K. R. Andrews, N. P. Canny, and P. E. H. Hair, eds., *The Westward Enterprise: English Activities in Ireland, the Atlantic, and America, 1480–1650* (Liverpool, 1978), 243.

would be reinforced at home in the decade following the extinction of their colony. Although they led the nation into civil war in 1642 and enthusiastically championed the challenge to Charles I and Archbishop Laud, company members who survived to its end dropped out one by one as events progressed to their climax in regicide. The puritan grandees' goal all along, in America and at home, had been rectification of England's shortcomings within the basic system of inherited social structures. The challenge of colonization, as well as of civil war, offered English men and women the opportunity to redesign those structures and to think about their bases. The stresses experienced by puritan leaders in the English Civil War could have been anticipated by thoughtful consideration of their first experience in the building of a godly society.

2

Founding a Colony on Providence Island

Successful establishment of a colony was an enormously difficult and expensive enterprise. Most of the Providence Island investors, veterans of the Virginia, Somers Islands (Bermuda), and New England Companies, knew this and knew many of the pitfalls by 1630. In creating their own enterprise, they attempted to overcome the problems they had encountered with earlier ventures. New England had seen the Sagadahoc colony, planted by the western merchants' Virginia Company in 1607, fail in less than a year, and the 1620 Plymouth colony still struggled mightily to pay off its backers a decade after its founding. Sir Walter Ralegh's Virginia colony, Roanoke, settled in 1585 and resettled in 1587, disappeared because of national preoccupation with the challenge posed by the Spanish Armada and Ralegh's subsequent neglect. It became the famous Lost Colony. Jamestown, England's first permanent settlement, was founded by the Virginia Company of London in 1607 and had struggled on the edge of disaster for its first decade and a half. The Virginia Company had suffered the disgrace of charter revocation in 1624. By 1630, the now-royal colony prospered but through growing tobacco, a disgraceful product in many English eyes. Bermuda, an offshoot of the Virginia colony, was firmly established by 1630, but many feared that its fertility was exhausted. In any case, it also produced tobacco, and attempts to diversify economically had met with little success.

None of these English plantations offered an acceptable model of proper empire building. Two puritan corporations formed colonies on radically new lines in 1630, one in Massachusetts Bay and the other on Providence Island.[1] Armed with experience of all these previous ventures, each aimed to create a society of godly men and women working in

---

1. John Rous connected the two ventures in his diary, noting in February 1630 that ships had set to sea for New England and for a plantation near Mexico. See Mary Anne Everett Green, ed., "Diary of John Rous," *Camden Society* LXVI (London, 1856), 47.

unity to satisfy both individual and common goals. The Providence Island adventurers in London were prepared to invest enormous sums of money in the expectation that their rich tropical island would produce enough wealth to enrich backers and settlers alike. Ultimately, they hoped their colony would serve as the nucleus for settlement of Central America, which would benefit the entire English nation. None would have believed that their enterprise would fold in a decade after absorbing a fortune, whereas its fellow puritan colony on the cold, rocky shores of Massachusetts Bay would go on to become the model for many later expeditions.

The adventurers' first instructions appointing a governor and council for their new colony emphasized shared goals and the promise that success for one would mean enrichment for all. They promised to listen carefully to those who were on the spot: "That so by our mutual Care of each other's good this Noble Work the foundation whereof is already through Gods blessing so happily laid, may daily thrive and prosper."[2] This hope for a mutually beneficial partnership of like-minded souls was never to be realized.

Providence Island was settled on Christmas eve 1629, just before the truce between England and Spain became effective.[3] Charles I had authorized a privateering war against Spain after his accession in 1625, and puritan grandees, happy to combine the search for profit with a chance to strike at the enemy of Protestantism, had participated enthusiastically. Preeminent among them was Robert Rich, second Earl of Warwick, who followed in his father's footsteps in maintaining a veritable private navy for his manifold ventures.[4] Two of his ships, "the Bark *Warwicke & Somer Ilands*" under Captain Sussex Camock and the *Robert* under Captain Daniel Elfrith, discovered two islands separated by fifty miles off the coast of Nicaragua, Santa Catalina (Providence) and San Andreas. Captain Camock stayed on San Andreas with thirty men to hold and explore it, and Elfrith rushed home in the *Warwick* to report.

Some of the essential ambiguity of Providence Island's promise comes through in the initial announcement of its discovery. Elfrith's homeward

2. PIC Instr. to Gov. and Coun., 2–30/1.
3. PIC to Capt. Daniel Elfrith by the *Seaflower*, 2–30/1.
4. Wesley Frank Craven, "The Earl of Warwick, A Speculator in Piracy," *Hispanic American Historical Review* 10 (1930), 457–79; John C. Appleby, "English Privateering during the early Stuart Wars with Spain and France, 1625–1630," unpub. Ph.D. diss., University of Hull (1983), 206.

journey took him by way of Bermuda, where he held estates and where his son-in-law Captain Philip Bell was governor. Bell included a persuasive argument for colonization of Santa Catalina in a letter about Bermuda affairs to Sir Nathaniel Rich, cousin and man of business to the Earl of Warwick. The island's attraction for Bell and Elfrith also presented its main problem, "it lying in the heart of the Indies & the mouth of the Spaniards." This location meant that it would be a good base for privateering but would be vulnerable to attack. Bell assured Rich that the island, once fortified, would be "invincible." San Andreas, lower and more suited to plantation agriculture, could never be made "half so strong."[5]

Providence Island, 110 miles from the Central American coast, is volcanic in origin; present-day inhabitants refer to it affectionately as "the Rock." Dominated by a peak 1,190 feet high from which radiate spines, "rather fantastically formed," going down to the sea, its fertile land is found in the valleys between the spurs. "By anyone's standards ... Providencia must be accounted utterly beautiful." It is surrounded by coral reefs, which make approach extremely difficult for the newcomer and which enhanced its appeal to the adventurers. The climate is considered mild for the region. Temperatures are in the eighties year-round, and the island is refreshed by the near-constant easterly trade winds. Rain is heaviest in autumn, and summers can be dry for as much as five months.[6]

Bell, trading on his years of experience in the Indies, assured Sir Nathaniel that the tobacco and other commodities produced on the island would "double or treble any mans estate in all England," even if

---

5. Capt. Philip Bell to Sir Nathaniel Rich, March, 1629, in Vernon A. Ives, ed., *The Rich Papers: Letters from Bermuda, 1615–1646* (Toronto, 1984), 319–21. Infant English plantations on Nevis and St. Kitts were expelled by Spanish attack in 1629, but the islands were quickly resettled; Kenneth R. Andrews, *Trade, Plunder, and Settlement: Maritime Enterprise and the Genesis of the British Empire, 1480–1630* (Cambridge, 1984), 302.

6. Captain Richard Owen, *A Nautical Memoir, Descriptive of the Surveys made in H. M. Ships "Blossom" and "Thunder," from 1829 to 1837* (Dublin, 1840?), 101–5; Peter J. Wilson, *Crab Antics: The Social Anthropology of English-Speaking Negro Societies of the Caribbean* (New Haven, 1973), 44; James J. Parsons, *San Andrés and Providencia: English-Speaking Islands in the Western Caribbean* (Berkeley, 1956), 1–3. The detailed sailing directions in the *Nautical Memoir* demonstrate the treachery of the waters around Providence Island. The author wishes to thank Commander Andrew David of the Hydrographic Department of the Ministry of Defence, Taunton, England, for copies of the relevant pages of the rare *Nautical Memoir*.

In 1783 Thomas Jeffreys, Geographer to the King, lamented that Providence Island, one of the best of the West Indies, had been left "forsaken and desolate." He wrote that not only did it abound with valuable woods, and pigeons, turtle, and fish for eating, but it was "watered by four streams, two only of which are dry in summer," *The West-India Atlas* (London, 1783), 16–17.

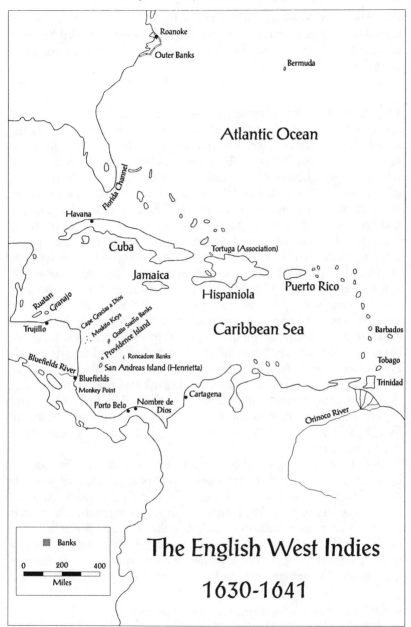

Roanoke

Outer Banks

Bermuda

Atlantic Ocean

Florida Channel

Havana

Cuba

Tortuga (Association)

Jamaica

Puerto Rico

Hispaniola

Caribbean Sea

Ruatan

Granajo

Cape Gracias a Dios

Moskito Keys

Quito Sueño Banks

Providence Island

Trujillo

Roncadore Banks

San Andreas Island (Henrietta)

Barbados

Bluefields River

Bluefields

Tobago

Monkey Point

Trinidad

Porto Belo

Nombre de Dios

Cartagena

Orinoco River

Banks

0   200   400

Miles

The English West Indies

1630-1641

the anticipated gold and silver failed to appear.[7] Word of the find spread quickly as investors were sought; John Rous included "news of an island" discovered "In the west ocean" by Warwick's ships in his diary for 1629.[8]

The island's first settlers came from Bermuda with Philip Bell, who was appointed governor. Daniel Elfrith also removed to Providence Island, as did Captain Samuel Axe, a fortifications expert who immediately set about constructing Warwick Fort overlooking the main harbor, near where the city of New Westminster was to be built. In February 1631, the *Seaflower* left London filled with just under 100 passengers and the hopes of the Providence Island investors.[9] The first shipload of colonists had been hastily assembled, but was such as to give the investors heart.

England had not yet solved the problem of stimulating the "poorer sort" to work hard in their callings. Consumer goods were few, and wages did not extend much beyond necessities. Therefore, most men and women preferred a life of underemployment, with leisure hours to spend in conviviality. The comfort bought with their small discretionary incomes was temporary but real. Gentry increasingly saw their role as organizing the poor, molding them into an effective work force. All colonies faced the challenge of creating habits of industry, but the Providence Island investors believed that their colonists, because they sought a common goal, would all work hard together, each making a significant contribution. The incentives were double: the creation of a society in which godly men and women could live happy and productive lives, and in which their efforts would be rewarded by the creation of substantial estates.

Each of the investors had been warned to look out for fit men and boys ready to go. Freemen would go as tenants at halves; they would be allotted as much land as the investors thought they could manage and would keep half their profits, with the other half going to the adventurers. The oath they took acknowledged that the investors were the "true owners" of the plantation. Families were the basic unit of English society; anyone living outside a family structure was seen as threatening good order. The settlers were to be distributed into artificial families of

7. Bell to Rich, March 1629, in Ives, ed., *Letters From Bermuda*, 320.
8. Green, ed., "Diary of John Rous," *Camden Society* LXVI, 43. See also Joseph Mead to Sir Martin Stuteville, January 31, 1629/30, B. L. Harleian MS 390, f. 492.
9. For varying estimates of the number of passengers, see PIC Gen. Ct., 2–14–31; Ct. 12–3–31; and Commission to Capt. Wm. Rudyerd, 2–31. New Westminster is the present-day Old Town. See Parsons, *San Andrés and Providencia*, 7.

about seven men, and only the head of each family could receive goods from the company magazine. The family head was responsible for the "well ordering" of his people. Morning and evening prayers would set the tone, and family heads would stamp out drunkenness, swearing, and all behavior that might bring the adverse judgment of God onto the endeavor. They must especially punish idleness, "the Nurse of all Vice."

Families were to be distributed over the land, close enough together for mutual protection but not for encroachment on one another. Although the colonists were tenants dependent on the will of the company, they were assured they would not lightly be moved from land after even one month's occupation. The land was not to be divided up in any permanent way but to be "manured in common." Planters should be thickly situated at the most vulnerable areas even if the land was less productive there, "Safety being to be preferred before profit." Once profits began to appear, those who accepted inferior land would be compensated for sacrifices to the public weal.

All planters were expected to contribute to the public works: the fortifications, churches, governor's and ministers' houses, and roads. They were also to turn out for regular militia training and to contribute to the minister's provisions. The company contributed materials and ordnance for the fortifications; the colonists were to contribute labor. These public works were necessary to the safety and productivity of the colony; certainly, the company reasoned, they would benefit primarily the settlers themselves. Shared benefits would accrue from shared responsibility.[10]

Servants' inducements to emigrate emerge less clearly in the company records because each freeman–emigrant was encouraged to make his own bargain with servants. Most served for three years, although some recruited by company members directly were promised only two years of servitude.[11] Servants could expect to receive land at the expiration of their terms. Therefore, in theory, servants were offered economic opportunity beyond their wildest expectations at home.

Attracting able "artificers" was a more difficult problem. The company hoped to offer them the same inducements of land and servants at half profits that other freemen received, but skilled workers could command more. Additional wages from London were not ruled out, but the adventurers thought each family should make its own contracts and pay for the skilled work it required. Early discussions of compensation for

---

10. This conception of the colony occurs in the company's initial instructions to the Gov. and Coun. sent in the *Seaflower*, 2–31, and in PIC to Gov. Bell, 2–31.
11. PIC to Gov. Bell, 2–31; PIC to Elfrith, 2–31.

all categories of colonists floated on the premise that rich commodities would soon flow from the island, and therefore vague promises of future special recompense abounded.[12]

Opportunities could only increase because the company agreed not only to supply the colonists with magazines and armaments but also to seek out the best commodities that could be grown or processed on the island to enrich everyone involved in the venture. The adventurers took on the job of acquiring seeds, plant slips, and samples, and of learning about the culture of rare tropical commodities that grew in similar zones all over the world. This crucial contribution would be the linchpin of the whole enterprise.

In the meanwhile, the most important concern was to establish the colony in plenty and safety and to build a secure foundation for the future. Settlers were to plant corn and other food crops immediately, twice as much as they thought they needed. As soon as the company was reliably informed that food surpluses existed, they would send large supplies of colonists. The next step was to begin to experiment with tropical commodities already available, especially vines, olives, oranges and lemons, pomecitrons (citrons), sugarcane, ginger, and oil-producing plants. They also hoped that settlers would find sources of "Fustique" and other dye woods.

The investors' main concern was that colonists not fall into the tobacco trap that had ensnared both Virginia and Bermuda. Although they realized that tobacco might temporarily occupy an important role in the island's economy because it was one commodity for which sure marketing paths existed and because the Bermuda emigrants would know how to raise and process it, no family was to be allowed to plant any tobacco until substantial food crops and some experimental tropical crops were growing on their land.

Short-term thinking must be avoided at all costs: "We fear nothing more than that the earnest intending to plant Tobacco thereby to raise present Commodity should (as it hath done in the Summer Islands and Virginia) cause you to neglect things necessary and useful, which if it do, it will cause us wholly to forbid it." Better commodities, to be found by the adventurers, might take a little longer to develop but would in the long run "more enrich both yourselves and us in one year than Tobacco shall do in seven and that with far less pains." For their part, the company promised "not to stick at any charge, trouble or pains so that we may enrich that Island with the most precious commodities that that earth and climate will produce which we consider

12. PIC Ct., 11–22–30; 12–3–31; 2–9–32.

will be as rich as are in any part of the world." They also promised liberal rewards to any who introduced a viable crop.[13]

In their private letter to Governor Bell, the adventurers spoke more frankly and harshly, making it clear that they intended to retain ultimate control over the island's economic development. Saying that he should remember "that you deal for gentlemen who do more prize honor than profit," they went on: "But we shall attain neither if men should do in this as they have done in other Plantations, apply themselves so to the planting that Scurvy weed of Tobacco thereby to raise present Commodities as that they neglect not only Staple Commodities but worse in that kind than brute beasts, forget to provide for their own bellies and lodging." Bell was to keep track of each family's attention to instructions and to inform the company of what each was planting.

The other great immediate need was attention to the fortifications, already begun by Captain Samuel Axe. Each family was first to build a strong house double the size needed for accommodation of its members, which the company directed should be covered with the good slike (mud) that they were informed the island afforded. Then the colonists were to turn immediately to the fortifications. Captain Axe had built his plantation near Warwick Fort even though it put him far from fresh water; his sacrifice for the public good should be emulated by others.

Warwick was the fort "of greatest Consequence." Following the survey and plan Axe had sent them, the company directed construction of two further forts: Fort Henry in the southern part of the island and another east of Fort Warwick overlooking the harbor. A large amount of ordnance, fourteen pieces, was sent; the captains were to decide amongst themselves how these guns should be distributed, the company saying they did not wish to be "peremptory."

Defense was not a concern for the captains alone. Elaborate instructions were given for a set of signals to be relayed throughout the island on the approach of any doubtful ship, and every man was to know when to repair to the forts. All were to be trained at least once a month by Captain William Rudyerd, the Muster Master General of Providence Island, "for we would not have one person in the Island who should not be able to know how to demean himself as a good soldier ought to do." Certainly no opposition to training or to contribution to the forts either in goods or labor was anticipated; the colonists must be the first to realize how their safety depended on these preparations. Even though peace had been concluded with Spain (the peace articles were sent to Captain Bell with his instructions), "it seems there is no peace between

13. PIC Instr. to Gov. and Coun. by the *Seaflower*, 2–31.

us in that Latitude wherein you are." Hostile acts on the colonists' part were forbidden, but defense was still essential.

As the company waited for the *Seaflower*'s return, they found their expenses mounting alarmingly. The ship and its supplies had cost more than anticipated: Ship hire had been £130 per month for a minimum of ten months, plus £4 each for victuals for passengers. All adventurers were called to pay the remainder of their initial investments in two installments; meanwhile, John Pym borrowed money at interest to meet the company's "urgent occasions." Concern grew steadily as the ship failed to reappear. It had sailed in February 1631; by November, Pym was gravely concerned because every month beyond the ten contracted for added £130 to the bill. In the event, the *Seaflower* arrived back in London only in March 1632. At the same time, the investors were confident that they need never borrow money at interest again. Their "husbandly concern" to load the *Seaflower* fully with provisions and passengers in order to get the colony off to a good start had resulted in unusual expenses that would never be repeated.[14] They believed the colony would soon be self-supporting.

Meanwhile, some good news trickled back to England to reinforce the adventurers' optimism. In December 1631, letters from Providence Island dated about July were carried into England by a "stranger" ship, the *Whale*. Excerpts from the letters ecstatically praising the island and its products were circulated among the investors and other interested parties.[15] Colonists, each writing to his own patron among the investors, avowed the island capable of nurturing any rare commodity. Governor Bell's report to the company at large claimed that the land and climate were capable of "great and excessive fertility." Food crops and domesticated animals were all "by God's blessing as plentiful as we could expect or desire." He reported a great variety of fruits already planted, many native to the island, and predicted that "this your little Spot of Land will grow one of the gardens of the world."[16]

Other letters echoed these themes. Not only did precious plants grow well, but they bore fruit over an extraordinarily long period. One plot of land could bear double or triple plantings of corn in the same year. Those settlers already in the island before the arrival of the *Seaflower* had stockpiles of food ready for the new colonists, and, according to

14. PIC Gen. Ct., 2–14–31, 5–19–31, 11–24–31. On costs of ship rental, see Kenneth R. Andrews, *Ships, Money and Politics: Seafaring and Naval Enterprise in the Reign of Charles I* (Cambridge, 1991), 191–92.
15. Sir Thomas Barrington's copy of these excerpts can be seen in the Essex Record Office, Hatfield Broad Oak MS DDBa 02/8.
16. Modern Providencia does provide abundance of fruits and vegetables; see Wilson, *Crab Antics*, 44 and chaps. 3–4.

Captain Axe, the food was so "good and dainty" that no place in the world could compare. Modesty alone prevented him from comparing his victual to a lord's table. Many writers rhapsodized about the beauty of Providence Island, the fragrance of the air, and beautiful birdsongs, "double and treble resounding Echoes." Lewis Morgan, the plantation's first minister, frankly compared the island to "the Eden of god," and wrote that they had found "all things according to our heart's desire." The island, he wrote, abounded "with fish Parrots, Tobacco, Cedars, Lig[num] vita, Fustick, wild vines, fig trees. Oranges, Lemons, Vines, figs Pomegranates, Rhuberb we have planted and they prosper. Indigo, Cochineal, Cloves, pepper, Mace, Nutmegs, raisins, Currants, and I doubt not but the Land will bear as well as any Land under heaven."

Morgan and other writers reported their great satisfaction in the spiritual state of the colony as well, particularly noting that Governor Bell was a serious and religious man, as were most of those who had come from Bermuda and in the *Seaflower*. Morgan heaped praise on Bell: "[A] man whose countenance proclaims him grave, his words Eloquent, his deeds religious. He's all a Christian." In a letter to a friend who was not an investor, Morgan summed up his responses, saying he wished his friend, John Reeve, an apothecary, could come and see "that peace, unity, religion, and sweet contentation that our hearts enjoy etc. I doubt not but you would most willingly spend an Age in this same Eden."

On a more practical level, Bell wrote that not only had the colonists begun to stockpile food but a brick works was already making very good brick for the governor's house and the church. There were some slightly disturbing notes among the general joy. Bell mentioned that drought conditions had partly reduced the corn crop. Although focusing most heavily on the tropical fruits abounding in the island, he also praised its tobacco, saying he hoped "we shall not come much if at all behind the best Spanish that's brought into England." With his Bermuda background, he argued that tobacco would be a good income-producing commodity "till we can be furnished with some better and more staple commodities." Experienced investors might have seen a warning sign in this contention.

Finally, although this information was not included in the excerpts circulated, somewhere in the letters was a hint that the colonists had begun to feel that the system of tenancy at halves was unjust. The investors did not take the issue very seriously at this point. In the company court, the adventurers justified the policy by saying first that it was done in other plantations, which was not strictly true. The Virginia and Somers Islands companies had both begun with such a scheme but had largely or completely backed away from it by 1631. Little Plymouth colony had also begun with a plan of manurance in common but had given it up. Whether other companies used such a plan or not, the reason the Providence Island adventurers thought it would work for them was their belief in the boundless riches that would flow from their island. In this early discussion, they reiterated this article of faith: All will become wealthy, therefore none has a grievance. Certainly the colonists' paeans of praise for their tropical paradise lent color to this belief.

At the beginning of 1632, then, the Providence Island investors had reason to be pleased with their colonization scheme. A plantation was established without the initial high death rate that all colonies, including the contemporaneous Massachusetts Bay settlement, had experienced.[17] Buildings were up, food was plentiful, and no extraordinary sickness had attended its founding. The enemy was at bay and the colonists optimistic. Moreover, the settlement was a *godly* colony, led by a man of virtue and high seriousness.

It may have sounded too good to be true, and it was. Nothing had prepared the backers for the storm of invective that broke over their heads with the return of the *Seaflower* in March 1632, when all the promise of Providence Island seemed to turn against them.

As time had passed and the *Seaflower* had failed to appear, the investors had discussed what should be done. Although their costs were already much larger than anticipated, the adventurers decided by February 1632, one year after the *Seaflower*'s departure, that they would commence planning for a larger ship carrying 150 colonists and a large magazine of supplies sufficient for the needs of old and new settlers alike. They reasoned that whatever news the *Seaflower* brought their resolution could not change; good news would make them liberal, bad would make them eager to relieve the plantation so as not to lose their investment. This time they would hire a ship, the *Charity*, and victual it themselves, thus avoiding exorbitant costs and "the hazards of the passengers' ill usage" through a covetous master's stinting of supplies.[18]

---

17. For a vivid description of widespread sickness and mortality following the arrival of the Winthrop fleet, in which "there is not an house where there is not one dead, and in some houses many," and in the Plymouth colony the preceding decade, see Thomas Dudley to the Countess of Lincoln, March 12 and 28, 1630/1, in Everett Emerson, ed., *Letters from New England: The Massachusetts Bay Colony, 1629–1638* (Amherst, 1976), 67–83.

18. PIC Mtg 12–31–31, Prep. Ct. 2–6–32; Ord. Ct. 2–1–32; Gen. Ct. 2–14–32.

In the midst of their planning, the *Seaflower* returned. A committee of those in town met to read the letters it brought but, in distinct understatement, wrote that they found them "long, and containing variety of matter," and suggested that the *Charity*'s sailing be delayed until the entire company could meet to compose their replies. What the letters revealed was a situation little short of mutiny on Providence Island.[19]

Even more shocking was the identity of the rebellion's leader: the minister, Lewis Morgan. The man who should have been a pattern of godliness and the support of good order was instead the fomenter of rebellion. The company had sent Morgan, a recent Oxford M.A. and the son of an Oxford clothier, on the *Seaflower* with some misgivings. As the adventurers explained privately to Governor Bell, they had hoped to send "a more grave and experienced man" but had found that for various reasons, especially the company's decision not to allow families to emigrate yet, more settled ministers had been unwilling. Morgan, although young (he was twenty-two or twenty-three when the *Seaflower* sailed), was a "studious and sober man" who "seems to be of a meek and humble spirit."[20] The company wrote that they expected him to be "very industrious in teaching, and catechising the people, and in monthly administering the Sacrament." The company advised Bell to make it his responsibility to see that the sacrament was administered regularly. They wrote that they expected Morgan would "peaceably comply with those of more eminent gifts which we may send hereafter." In the meanwhile he would live in the governor's house, thereby enhancing the governor's status, and Bell would be in a position subtly to encourage and mold Morgan.[21]

Lewis Morgan's father outfitted his son lavishly for the voyage, spending an amount equivalent to Morgan's annual salary of £40 to see that he lived in the proper state. In view of that, the company allowed Morgan a free gift of £20 worth of books on condition that if he left the island the books were to remain and he was then to be compensated for them in London. As a further guarantee of proper state, Morgan was to be attended by Ralph Walcott, a nephew of Lord Brooke.[22] The young preacher could continue his scholarly studies in Providence Island and grow up with the colony.

Instead of a harmonious partnership with Governor Bell and a generally beneficial order flowing from the godly example of the minister, the

19. PIC Ctee. 4–2–32.
20. John Foster, *Alumni Oxonienses, 1500–1714* (Oxford, 1891–92), III, 1030.
21. PIC to Bell, 2–31.
22. PIC Gen. Ct., 2–10–31; PIC Instr. to Gov. and Coun., 5–10–32, Pt. 23.

company now found Lewis Morgan to be the "Author, at least the fomenter" of "a Revolt from the Company Government." The planters sent home a petition describing their grievances. In addition, Morgan sent Sir Nathaniel Rich a letter "stuffed with bitter expressions, savoring a Spirit inclined to Sedition and Mutiny."[23] The company moved to deal with Morgan, providing secretly for his removal from the colony; their intention was not to be made known to him until the ship was ready to leave. They then surveyed the damaged relationship between them and their colonists.

Mr. John Essex, sent to the island as "ancient" under Captain William Rudyerd at Fort Henry, had apparently been Morgan's co-leader of the incipient revolt.[24] He had returned on the *Seaflower* without permission to bring the colonists' complaints in person. The company strongly suspected that he intended to publish some of the letters he carried, because they had been delivered to him unsealed. The *Seaflower* had been attacked by a Spanish warship in the Florida channel on the homeward voyage, and Essex had been killed in the action, which, from the company's point of view, prevented the disaster that might have come with publication. As it was, they believed they could contain the damage, especially because their plans for renewed efforts were well under way.[25]

Although insisting that they took the petition "in good part," the adventurers pointed out their own enormous expenses, and "therefore they see no Cause why the repining and murmuring of some of them should secretly charge them with disregard of their liberty security or profit, or with too much looking to themselves as from their letter they cannot but gather."[26] They were especially incensed to find in Morgan's letters the "Imputation of so dishonorable an End as Covetousness, gilded and covered with the Hypocritical pretense of Godliness as is most impudently cast upon us."[27] Some colonists wrote letters to individual adventurers containing "infamous libels," not what would "beseem one Christian man to write to another."[28]

In their answer the investors affirmed that each adventurer was at

23. PIC Ctee. 4–11–32.
24. On Essex, see PIC Instructions to Gov. and Coun., 2–7–31.
25. PIC, Instr. to Gov. and Coun., 5–10–32. The attack on the *Seaflower* was listed as one of the grievances leading to Cromwell's Western Design; see *A Declaration of His Highness, by the Advice of His Council; Setting Forth, on the Behalf of this Commonwealth, the Justice of their Cause Against Spain*, 1655, in *The Works of John Milton*, gen. ed. Frank Allen Patterson (New York, 1937), XIII, 539–41.
26. PIC Ctee. 4–11–32.
27. PIC, Special Instr. on Morgan, 4–10–32.
28. PIC Instr. to Gov. and Coun., 5–10–32.

least £600 out of pocket, whereas the settlers had a comfortable subsistence "which many of them wanted at home." Company members
saw their reputations at stake; the colonists might accuse them of being
hypocrites, but their peers would call them fools. "Some of you know
that in the other Plantations £25 or £50 a man was a whole Adventure.
And if any man were out £100 before return of profit, he was accounted
a great Patriot but scarce a wise Adventurer." Colonists were warned
against comparing adventurers' investments to their estates in England
because of the many possible dangers in adventuring in colonies.

The colonists, like the investors, had been given a great opportunity
to serve their nation and to preserve the true Christian religion, a
mission not to be taken lightly. Maybe the planters would prove to be
unworthy. Some of them were perhaps like the Israelites

> who were not satisfied with the promise of that good Land which
> God provided for them, but still were murmuring and repining
> because they were not put into the possession of all that their heart
> could presently desire. This gave God occasion to deprive them of
> that good Land which he intended to bring them unto, and to let
> their Carcasses fall in the Wilderness as men most unworthy to
> enjoy so great blessing.

The company could only hope, for the sake of the Calebs and Joshuas
among them, that God would continue his blessing. The Providence
Island Company promised continued commitment on their part as long
as they or their posterity lived, regardless of "all green foolish conceits,
and histrionical expressions of frothy and ill affected persons to the
contrary."

In sending a petition to the Providence Island Company, settlers were
behaving as they would have done in England. Hard-pressed subjects
who felt their rights were violated and their subsistence threatened
traditionally petitioned the royal government for redress, sometimes
even carrying their lists of grievances in person. If their just complaints
were ignored, then riot or other threats to public order might result.
Those in authority reacted to such increased pressure in two ways: by
calling for punishment for leaders of the disorders and by taking steps
to redress the people's grievances. Both in strictly limiting retribution
and in seeking to correct the underlying problems, the government
"implied recognition of the legitimacy of the complaint."[29]

29. John Walter, "Grain riots and popular attitudes to the law: Maldon and the crisis of
    1629," in John Brewer and John Styles, ed., *An Ungovernable People: The English*

Many Providence Island Company members had built strong county followings by acting as mediators between local constituents and the royal government, transmitting and focusing grievances and enforcing government policies meant to conserve food supplies and protect wages. Now the adventurers reacted to the settlers' petition as the Privy Council might respond to a county grievance carrying a threat of rebellion. The first step was to remove the ringleaders. John Essex was already dead; Morgan was to be removed by a decisive stroke kept secret until the moment of its execution. Petitioners who could be co-opted, like Mr. Edward Gates, were forgiven. Having provided for exemplary punishment, the adventurers proceeded to look at the planters' grievances.

Despite their indignation, the company attempted to deal conscientiously with the fundamental complaints of the colonists. The most serious was the one they already knew about: The planters objected to the terms of their contract. They believed the company was gouging them by requiring that they give half their profits to the investors. It did no good for the company to tell the settlers that they had known the terms before they went, although they tried that approach. The adventurers said, in effect, you had nothing before. If you return with nothing after two or three years, you have at least had a good place to live whereas we are out a small fortune.

In attempting to deal seriously with the colonists' challenge, the company reiterated the article of faith on which the entire endeavor was founded: The land is so rich that even half profits will enrich the colonists beyond their dreams. The main fault was in the settlers' failure to experiment with commodities as directed. If they could produce even good tobacco,

> half of [what] one man can make in a year will be a far greater profit to him than any man's handy labour can yield him in England in 7. Ah but you will say Our Tobacco will not yield any such price. At least you should have tried this ere ever you complained.

And tobacco was the least of the products they could expect:

> But we pray you remember we have written unto you, and you may easily believe it, That we have already sent even to the furthest part

and their law in the seventeenth and eighteenth centuries (London, 1980), 66–84, quote p. 82; John Walter and Keith Wrightson, "Dearth and the Social Order in Early Modern England," *Past and Present* 71 (1976), 22–42, esp. 32; Hunt, *Puritan Moment*, 40–8. The right of petition for redress of grievances became a major issue for the New Model Army in the Civil War; Mark A. Kishlansky, *The Rise of the New Model Army* (Cambridge, 1979), chaps. 7–8.

of the world for the richest Commodities, to enrich that as yet poor Island.

Seeds of some of these rich commodities were actually being sent in the *Charity*.

The planters' second contention was that the island was "unfortifiable." In response to this, the company wrote that they had been assured of the invincibility of Providence Island not "by any slight or improbable Rumours, but by the view and Plot of some skillful men now resident amongst you." The target here was Captain Daniel Elfrith, as the company wrote to him privately. Fears about the island's safety were bound up with growing friction between the military men and the island's civilian population, tension that grew worse as time passed.

Elfrith had been in the Indies since 1607 and had served the Earl of Warwick in command of the famous privateering ship *Treasurer*, interpreting the earl's orders broadly. His piratical activities had brought a crisis in the Virginia Company when he attempted to use Virginia as a base in 1618–19, thereby endangering the entire colony.[30] He was out of tune with the goals of Providence Island, and many colonists wrote home in alarm about his recklessness, through which they believed he deliberately risked their safety. On an unauthorized voyage to Cape Gracias a Dios on the Central American mainland, he had seized a Spanish frigate and left his pinnace in return, opening Providence Island to revenge before the fortifications were in good order. At one stroke, Elfrith announced to the enemy that an English colony was planted in their midst and gave them a good excuse for attack, an act for which the company said they "must pity [regret] his rashness." Elfrith may have hoped that a Spanish attack would lead to a royal grant of letters of reprisal authorizing privateering.

He also jeopardized both his own reputation and the safety of the colony by inviting into it "a Mulletto as you call him, by too freely entertaining him there, and by carrying him back again, against the advice of the Council." The "Mulletto" was Diego el Mulato, a privateering captain who had sailed with the famous Dutch privateer Piet Heyn.[31] El Mulato, although born in Havana, had turned renegade

30. Wesley Frank Craven, *Dissolution of the Virginia Company: The Failure of a Colonial Experiment* (New York, 1932), 127–35; and Craven, "The Earl of Warwick, A Speculator in Piracy," *Hispanic American Historical Review* 10 (1930), 463–65.

31. Piet Heyn, that "ever renowned Hollander (whom like unto our Drake the Spaniards to this day fear and tremble at, calling him Pie de Palo, that is, wooden leg)," captured virtually the entire Spanish treasure fleet just outside of Havana in 1628, the most spectacular prize of the time; Thomas Gage, *The English–American his Travail by Sea and Land: Or, A New Survey of the West India's* (London, 1648), 80. On the

against the Spanish and had earned the esteem of the Dutch, but the colonists and company feared allowing any privateer to see the weakness of the new plantation.[32]

Dutch privateers had long operated in the Bay of Honduras and had often called at Providence Island before its occupation by the English.[33] A small number of Dutch men were already living on the island, and the colonists had been warned to treat them with care while monitoring their "carriage" and religious opinions. The governor's council hired one as a carpenter and bought up tobacco raised by the others in the English colony's first year. Their expertise could be useful as long as they were made part of the plantation; any hint that the new settlement was opening its doors to privateers could bring the wrath of the Spanish upon them. These Dutch entrepreneurs, who included William Blauvelt, known to the English as Bluefields, remained and entwined their activities with those of the colonists throughout the settlement's life.[34]

Daniel Elfrith and the Dutch presence both linked the island to the world of Caribbean adventuring that the colonists found so threatening. Elfrith attempted to repair his damaged reputation with the company by sending them an elaborate manuscript describing the coastlines and giving navigation directions for the Caribbean. His rutter (navigation guide) is described by its modern editors as "remarkably precise." Elfrith wrote that he had gathered this information through many years in "discovery" as well as "in Man of War affairs" and had kept it private for his own use. He was moved "to present these my Labours unto your Lordships view" by his realization that the "Ancient Seamen" who knew these parts were now all dead and because "all the drafts and platts which are made in England are very false."

Added to the rutter, which is in a clerk's hand, is Elfrith's own handwritten description of Providence Island and the adjacent mainland. He omitted the approaches to Providence Island, where company ships would find willing pilots, but gave detailed directions for approaching the Moskito Coast and Trujillo Bay. The Providence Island investors' plans for the future required such information.

capture of the treasure fleet, see Cornelis Ch. Goslinga, *The Dutch in the Caribbean and on the Wild Coast, 1580–1680* (Gainesville, FL, 1971), 176–92.

32. Gage, *English–American*, 188–90.

33. E. O. Winzerling, *The Beginning of British Honduras, 1506–1765* (New York, 1946), 29–31.

34. PIC to Bell by the *Seaflower*, 2–31; Instr Gov. and Coun., 5–10–32, Pt. 25; PIC to Bell, 4–10–33. Bluefields in Jamaica and Bluefields on the Moskito Coast are both named after the Blauvelts, who continued activities into the later seventeenth century; see William Dampier, *A New Voyage Round the World, 1697*, ed. Sir Albert Gray (London, 1937), 32.

Elfrith ended with his humble submission: "Thus far I have formerly proceeded and would have gone further if I might have had where with all and also liberty: but Seeing it is your pleasures to the Contrary I am Contented to rest." He suggested that he had not yet explored the shoals to the north, west, and southwest, as well as the coast southward from the Moskitos. Knowledge of all these "in my Judgment it were Expedient should be perfected And if it please your Lordships to Send any man whom you shall think more fitter than my self to make these discoveries I will be ready to give him the best advice I can for the performance thereof."[35]

Company members walked a very fine line with Captain Elfrith. Their reply to him began by chastising him for his adventures, saying they "could but marvel" that a man of such experience "should hazard the reputation of your discretion" by such escapades. They went on to excuse his previous errors in describing the island's natural security, which they attributed to lack of time to acquire knowledge, a situation now rectified. Thanking him for his efforts to acquire commodities and plants from the mainland and praising his exploration, they offered vague hope of future employments to come while laying down the law on the exercise of his office of admiral. Elfrith was specifically authorized to pursue his exploration of the outlying shoals.[36]

Security was uppermost in everyone's mind. Clearly, the fortifications had to be strong enough and Elfrith had to be restrained. The company wrote the governor and council that they believed Captain Axe, together with a highly skilled workmaster they were now sending, could make the island's defenses sufficiently strong. Thus, the adventurers recognized and answered the petition's second grievance.

The company was frankly amazed by the colonists' third major complaint, which related directly to the second, their sense of insecurity: They objected to the requirement that they contribute materials and labor to the public works, the fortifications. The settlers asked that the company send servants of its own to work exclusively on the public works, thus freeing the planters to devote themselves to developing the crops everyone agreed were essential to success. The company, although pointing out that the public works were for the colonists' own good, did agree to start sending servants for that role. Servants already signed up were diverted to that endeavor, thus, as the adventurers wryly pointed out, making it impossible for them to augment the number of

35. This manuscript is printed as "Daniel Ellffryth's Guide to the Caribbean, 1631," ed. Stanley Pargellis and Ruth Lapham Butler, *William and Mary Quarterly* 3rd ser., I (1944), 273–316. Elfrith's late addition to the rutter is ibid., 310–16.
36. PIC to Elfrith, 5–10–32.

servants held by individuals, particularly those involved in the petition. Any servants currently in the island whose time was up could sign on for an additional two years on the public works, at the end of which time each was to have land and two servants of his own.

The colonists also objected to their uncertainty of tenure; they feared dispossession of land laboriously cleared by them. The company promised that when they received full information about how each family was situated, they would begin to grant leases for years or even for life. The artificial family structure also seemed to the colonists to involve a kind of dispossession, especially for those who had already cleared their land. The company wrote that it had seemed the safest organization to them but that they would now decree no set pattern, "but leave them to sort themselves as they shall see good Only requiring that they be orderly and industrious," and allotted two acres per head.[37]

Settlers also objected to the economic arrangements set up by the company, both in the cost and quality of magazines of supplies sent out to them and in the requirement that they consign all their tobacco to the company for sale. In Providence Island as in other colonies, the markup on supplies was 25 percent. The colonists argued that this was too high, that the supplies were not of good quality and were not distributed fairly in the island. Investors blamed the poor quality on former company husband John Dyke's maladministration and reported that Dyke had been bought out and was "now none of our company."[38] The adventurers argued that 25 percent was a modest profit in view of the expense of compiling a magazine and the long wait for returns. They would gladly be rid of the burden of having to send magazines. Until some other way of supplying the island was established, they decreed that on the arrival of any ship a table be set up displaying the magazine with prices of the items, and that the governor and council oversee distribution according to need. They also remitted their requirement that planters pay for goods from the stores out of their first proceeds; longer times would be allowed, especially for the poorest.

Flexibility was also the keynote in reply to the colonists' wish that they need not consign their tobacco to the company. Although the investors thought the planters would find that consignment was in fact the most beneficial system, they were happy to have the tobacco divided into company and planters' shares in Providence Island and to have the settlers' tobacco sold by their friends in England, thus lessening the company's burdens. For the time being, trade with other than company

37. PIC Instr. Gov. and Coun., 5–10–32, Pt. 16.
38. PIC, Divers Mtgs. after 4–13–32.

ships was forbidden, "(that we may not suffer in our right)," although the adventurers promised to remove this prohibition when the "Island be thoroughly peopled and well Fortified."[39]

Shortly after this answer was sent off, the new company husband, John Hart, was directed, upon release of the tobacco brought in the *Seaflower* from the customs, to remove the company tobacco first, after which the planters' tobacco was to be sold.[40] This was the kind of treatment the colonists feared. Many abuses could creep in – all the best tobacco could be assigned to the company, or the planters' share could be sold in a glutted market. It was no wonder they felt happier having their "particular friends," who were concerned only with the settlers' interests, handling the sale, even though freight charges were subtracted from the profits.

All these complaints over economic arrangments were of crucial importance to both sides, but they were overshadowed by a far more fundamental grievance emanating from Providence Island: The colonists longed for something approaching a normal life, or at least as close to English normality as they could achieve on a semitropical island. Whether settlers could experience conventional social relations in a godly setting would be the single most important determinant of success or failure. Both the company and the planters were very clear on this point and treated it with the utmost seriousness.

This desire for customary life revolved partly around easily resolvable issues such as the island's sex ratio. The company assured the colonists that they were now sending women and that they would send a midwife by the next ship. Other concerns, such as oppressive or destructive weather, were more problematic, but the colonists could learn what crops to grow and how to dry and store them to prevent rot or insect attacks, or so the company thought.

Even more serious was the mixed nature of the island's population, a problem that itself could be subdivided into several related problems. One part, that some "ill disposed persons" had entered the island, especially among those who had accompanied Captain Bell from Bermuda, could be concluded simply by sending them away again. Unruly practices could be prevented. "Strong waters" were to be locked up and doled out by those in authority except for private stores sent by friends to "persons well qualified with Temperance." At the last minute before the *Charity* sailed, the company heard that some colonists had

39. PIC, Instr. Gov. and Coun., 5–10–32.   40. PIC, Ord. Ct. 6–25–32.

sent privately for cards, tables, and dice. Bell received a special letter directing that all were to be burnt on arrival. The colonists should indulge in lawful recreations, "as Chess, shooting, etc." As in the case of alcohol, so with gaming, a class bias entered into the gentry's abhorrence. Cards and dice were seen as particularly corrupting for the young and the "poorer sort" of people. Providence Island Company investors allowed gaming in their own homes; in their island colony such activities could only lead the vulnerable into idleness and vice. Small supplies of alcohol were regularly sent by friends to colonists of the "better sort" throughout the colony's life; only the poor were apt to be seduced by it.[41]

One disruptive element in the population could not be sent away: the military men. Providence Island's location meant that soldiers, especially those who had spent time in the Indies, would necessarily be of the utmost value to the colony, both for their skills in combat and their knowledge of the environment and its products. They were in some ways beyond discipline. Their power drew on a source not controllable by traditional English methods, and they demanded deference beyond what the other planters were willing to give.

Despite everything, the Providence Island Company saw grounds for hope in 1632 as they prepared the *Charity* for its voyage. Nothing had dampened the investors' belief that their island was a potentially rich land, far above Bermuda or any other English colony. They wrote to Governor Bell that all "great works in their Infancies" suffer from "intervenient difficulties." If Bell would go on with cheerfulness and make the cause of true religion and the cherishing of peace and justice his chief goals, then he could safely "leave the issue to God who will undoubtedly give you a desired End, if you conscionably Serve him in the use of his own means." At about the same time, a well-wisher wrote to Governor John Winthrop of Massachusetts Bay in a similar vein. Mr. James Hopkins, vicar of Great Wenham, Suffolk, advised Winthrop to ignore criticism and not to be discouraged by his colony's "hard beginnings," which represented God's testing, his urging to "cleave the closer unto him." Hopkins asserted that all plantations were "mean at

41. David Underdown, *Revel, Riot, and Rebellion: Popular Politics and Culture in England, 1603–1660* (Oxford, 1985), 47–8, cites a 1541 act prohibiting "Tables, tennis, dice, cards, bowls" and other "unlawful games" for people below yeoman status [33 Henry VIII, C. 9: *Statutes at Large*, ed. Danby Pickering, V (Cambridge, 1763), 85]. For gaming in the homes of gentlemen, see Cliffe, *Puritan Gentry*, 141–2; and Butler, *Theatre and Crisis*, 91–3, 150–1.

the first," so New England's apparent failure at that early stage need not erase all hope.[42]

The Providence Island adventurers' conviction of the richness of the soil and the inevitable blessing of God on their actions made them confident, so much so that they directed the governor and council to set aside twenty lots of twenty-five acres each "in the most commodious and Fertile places of the Island." These would be distributed among the adventurers by lot in case they decided to emigrate or to send over "a Son kinsman or near Friend."[43]

In the colonial context, the Providence Island Company showed remarkable flexibility and goodwill when faced with the challenge of the colonists' mutinous petition. In similar circumstances of disappointment with a newly planted colony, the Virginia Company, arguing that the debacle of Jamestown's beginning stemmed from diffusion of power, had moved in 1609 from a mixed to a frankly military organization supported by laws threatening the harshest punishments for even minor infractions. In the original charter, government had been by an appointed council, which elected its own president, but under this "equality of governors," the settlement had degenerated "from civil Propriety to Natural, and Primary Community," confirming the worst fears about what might happen in the colonial setting.

So in 1609 the Virginia Company determined that during Virginia's "infancy" command was to reside in their soldier-governor armed with "sole and absolute" power, and the council was reduced to an advisory role. Their instructions to Governor Sir Thomas Gates constituted "a magna carta for baronial tyranny." All colonists, civilian as well as military, were to begin and end their workday "upon the beating of the Drum"; anyone resisting such regimentation was in the first instance "to lie upon the Guard head and heels together all night, for the second time so faulting to be whipped, and for the third time to be condemned to the Gallies for a year." Malfeasance brought harsh penalties. A gardener who was seen to "willfully pluck up therein any root, herb, or flower, to spoil and waste or steal the same" could be executed. Cooks, bakers, or laundresses who cheated their customers could expect exemplary punishment, and private trading with mariners carried the death penalty.[44]

42. PIC to Gov. Bell, 5–10–32; James Hopkins to John Winthrop, Feb. 25, 1633, *Winthrop Papers* III, 105–7.
43. PIC, Instr. to Gov. and Coun., 5–10–32, Pt. 39.
44. Virginia Company, *A True and Sincere Declaration of the Purpose and End of the Plantation Begun in Virginia* (London, 1610), 6–12; William Strachey, *For the Colony in Virginea Britannia. Lawes Divine, Morall and Martiall, etc.* (London, 1612), 2, 13–15, 17, 32. Strachey says the laws were established in early summer of

The Providence Island Company resisted the temptation to meet disappointment with similar regimentation. Armed with strong faith in the revitalizing and focusing power of godly men and women led by sufficient ministers, the adventurers turned away from military-style control toward infusion of the right sort of settlers and commitment to English law. The soldiers' influence was to be diluted, as the company added a substantial civilian element to the council. At last, they were sending a large company of the right kind of colonists, led by Mr. Henry Halhead of Banbury and Mr. Samuel Rishworth, whom company members held "in much esteem for their piety and Judgment," because they had "right hearts to God and to the good of the Plantation." Both came with "great Families and many Children."

Halhead and Rishworth were to be placed on the council immediately, along with Mr. Edward Gates, already resident in the island. Although he had signed the petition, Gates had indicated his dedication to the project. He was the only resident to receive new servants by the *Charity* because of his steadfastness, his new position of dignity, and consideration of his birth and "parts." The strategy was to overrule the "passions" of dissidents "by the presence and power of such as be obliged to the Company by the bonds of religion and fidelity."[45]

These substantial colonists were recruited on their shared faith in the enterprise and in the nobility of the adventurers. The *Charity*'s estimated 150 passengers were recruited by company members, mostly from near London, from East Anglia, Devon, Warwickshire, and Oxfordshire. Henry Halhead was in his mid-fifties when he sailed with his wife, Elizabeth (forty-eight years old), and his youngest children, teenaged Patience and Grace and eight-year-old Samuel. Halhead was a substantial merchant and recent mayor of Banbury, and his family had long been associated with Lord Saye and Sele in local affairs. Henry, a younger

---

1610 and were "exemplified and enlarged" by Sir Thomas Dale on June 22, 1611. David Konig, "Colonization and the Common Law in Ireland and Virginia, 1569–1634," in James A. Henretta, Michael Kammen, and Stanley N. Katz, eds., *The Transformation of Early American History: Society, Authority, and Ideology* (New York, 1991), 70–92, characterized Gates's instructions, 83. See also Darrett B. Rutman, "The Virginia Company and Its Military Regime," in Rutman, ed., *The Old Dominion: Essays for Thomas Perkins Abernethy* (Charlottesville, 1964), 1–20. On reasons for the institution of military rule, see Warren M. Billings, "The Transfer of English Law to Virginia, 1606–1650," in K. R. Andrews, N. C. Canny, and P. E. H. Hair, eds., *The Westward Enterprise: English Activities in Ireland, the Atlantic, and America 1480–1650* (Liverpool, 1978), 217. A particularly illuminating discussion is offered by Stephen Greenblatt, "Martial Law in the Land of Cokaigne," in *Shakespearean Negotiations: The Circulation of Social Energy in Renaissance England* (Berkeley, 1988), 129–63, esp. 148–55.
45. PIC Prep. Ct., 2–4–33; PIC Instr. to Gov. and Coun., 5–10–32.

son, had been hit hard by the great Banbury fire of March 1628, but he nevertheless sold three houses, two shops, and a barn when he emigrated in 1632. Halhead offered just the right kind of determination. While he was mayor, fines paid by the disorderly and disruptive had relieved the poor, and he boasted that "rogues and vagabonds" soon left town.[46] Henry Halhead was intended to move symbolically into the position of leadership formerly held by the dangerous John Essex. Halhead and Rishworth were to occupy his plantation, and eventually Halhead was allowed to buy rights to it, paying Essex's debt to the company stores and sending the surplus to his executors.[47]

Halhead led a contingent recruited by Lord Saye and Sele. Banbury was famous throughout England for its puritanism. The English edition of Camden's *Britannia* in 1608 portrayed the town as noted for zeal, cakes, and ale, and this was repeated in Fuller's *Worthies*. Banbury was burlesqued by Ben Jonson in his *Bartholomew Fair*, in which the character listed as "Banbury Man" is appropriately named Zeal-of-the-Land Busy, and this was the first of many witty satires on that town's religious seriousness. Banbury became emblematic in literary circles of the self-important, somewhat hypocritical, dour puritan. Certainly the town took its religion seriously, and its citizens were prepared, like Henry Halhead, to put themselves on the line for it. Many had suffered from the depression in the area's textile industry and from the Banbury fire.

Samuel Rishworth's background is unknown. Like Halhead, he would have found a comfortable home in Massachusetts Bay; had these men emigrated to New England, their names might be among those known by every American schoolchild. Rishworth's actions in Providence Island prove him to have been a committed puritan who upheld his own notion of the moral law regardless of what others might say or do.

During January and February 1632, Sir Thomas Barrington solicited volunteers in his Essex neighborhood to go as servants. Indentures written in Barrington's own hand are in the Essex Record Office, most signed with a mark. These men agreed to hold themselves ready when Sir Thomas should call them to go to the Island of Providence. John Beecher, Richard Howcomer, John Larkin, and Nathaniel Cophand, all of Braintree, "do promise and agree with Sir Thomas Barrington to go under his name and as of his family into the Island of Providence."

---

46. D. E. M. Fiennes and J. S. W. Gibson, "Providence and Henry Halhed, Mayor of Banbury 1630/31," *Cake and Cockhorse* 7 (1978), 199–210; Barton John Blankenfeld, "Puritans in the Provinces: Banbury, Oxfordshire, 1554–1660," unpub. Ph.D. diss., Yale University, 1985, 42–50, 98, 136, 194–6, 213–50, 362–5; Richard Cust, *The Forced Loan and English Politics, 1626–1628* (Oxford, 1987), 233. On regions from which new colonists were recruited, see PIC Instr. to Gov. and Coun., 5–10–32.

47. PIC to Gov. and Coun., 7–20–33.

Another, shorter indenture of "Braintree men for Providence" was signed with a mark by Thomas Maynard, Henry Neale, Martin Cofeild, and John Wilbord. One man, Andrew Cowland of Raine, received 12 pence in return for his promise to go, and his indenture stipulated that he would be a servant under the island's governor.[48]

Braintree was an unincorporated industrial town formed to produce the "new draperies," lighter-weight cloth that was supposed to transform England's position in the international textile market. By the end of the 1620s, the Essex textile industry had fallen into a disastrous slump; huge stockpiles of unsold cloth meant no work for many. Hard times were combined with bad harvests and dearth, creating such misery that, according to a government report, "their poverty is exceeding great, and lamentable is the being of all this Multitude of people which live by these Manufactures." In their distress, Braintree men and women petitioned the government for relief, and when help was not forthcoming, their anger twice boiled over in riots in 1629. Emigration must have seemed a grand alternative to Sir Thomas's clients.[49]

Colonists who were recruited by company members occupied a special status; they were in a sense extensions of the grandees' families. Lord Saye expected Henry Halhead to watch over the men and women recruited from Oxfordshire. On the basis of Halhead's reports, Lord Saye would supply his own recruits with supplies and servants. In 1634 he sent word inquiring about those for whom he felt responsible and asking Halhead to explain to them why he could not send additional servants immediately.[50]

Not only were solid colonists of the right puritan stripe being sent but also three new ministers to replace the inadequate Lewis Morgan. Arthur Rous, John Pym's stepbrother, coming with a large family, was to preach a weekday lecture in New Westminster; Ralph Walcott, Lord Brooke's nephew who had formerly attended Mr. Morgan, was to be his servant. Hope Sherrard was to be the minister of New Westminster; and Mr. Ditloff, a refugee from the Palatinate whose first name never appears in the records, was to minister to the other side of the island, although temporarily he was to be placed in the governor's house. When Mr. Halhead and Mr. Rishworth were settled, Ditloff was to be

48. Essex Rec. Off., DDBa 02/5, 02/6, 02/10.
49. John Walter, "Grain riots and popular attitudes to the law: Maldon and the crisis of 1629," in John Brewer and John Styles, ed., *An Ungovernable People: The English and their law in the seventeenth and eighteenth centuries* (London, 1980), 49, 65–6, 71–2; Hirst, *Authority and Conflict*, 47. The 1629 report, *A Briefe declaraton Concerning the state of the Manufacture of Woolls in the Countie of Essex*, is in the Bodleian Library, MS Firth, c. 4, pp. 488–91.
50. Jessop to Halhead, 8–34, Jessop Ltrbk, No. 47, B. L. Add MS 10615.

in their care. Ultimately, the ministers were to have land and servants of their own; until that time, their maintenance was to be supplied by the planters.

Colonists came and went throughout the life of the Providence Island colony, but in many ways the core of the cast was complete when the *Charity* arrived. Henry Halhead, Samuel Rishworth, and Hope Sherrard would be principal actors in the settlement's drama; their departure brought down the curtain on the godly experiment. The tempestuous captains came and went, but Axe, Elfrith, Bell, and Rudyerd were intricately intertwined in the colony's affairs throughout its life. Most often it was they who forced the pace of action through dramatic confrontations. The strained relationships formed within this company of settlers determined much of the future of Providence Island.

3

Contested Authority:
The Governorship
of Captain Philip Bell

THE GOVERNOR OF PROVIDENCE ISLAND was handed a job made impossible by the plantation's very design. Colonists and investors thought of the settlement as similar to a unit of local government in England, but the implications of such an assumption were not at all clear. The island was settled at a time when the relationship between central and local government was changing and developing in England, a process in which many of the investors, as county and national leaders, were deeply involved. Such change grew partly out of the widespread sense of crisis in England, which excited puritan leaders; it involved both consolidation of gentry control over local affairs and strengthening of their partnership with central government. Stuart local government rested on a web of loyalty, mutual obligation, and clientage. These networks were forged in small increments over time. They were fragile, resting on the ability of leaders to command respect in the county and in London and on the willingness of local men to give loyalty and support.[1] No colony would succeed until it found a way to replicate these relationships or devised another web to take their place. Government would not function by mere fiat, particularly when separated by thousands of miles of water and several months from the locus of power in London.[2]

1. This process is described in Anthony Fletcher, *Reform in the Provinces: The Government of Stuart England* (New Haven, 1986). On local relationships on which government rested, see idem, "Honour, Reputation and Local Officeholding in Elizabethan and Stuart England," in Anthony Fletcher and John Stevenson, eds., *Order and Disorder in Early Modern England* (Cambridge, 1985), 92–115.
2. Networks of loyalty and cooperation were essential because even in England communications from the Privy Council might take months to arrive in the provinces. See Thomas Garden Barnes, *Somerset, 1625–1640: A County's Government During the "Personal Rule"* (Cambridge, MA, 1961), 87–8.

Surprisingly little understanding of the nature of such relationships is reflected in the design of Providence Island's government. The adventurers were obsessed with the dismal failure of other colonial ventures, such as Bermuda and Virginia, to forge and sustain orderly, well-governed societies, and they traced such failure to the presence of divided councils in America and the shortsighted greed of merchants and lesser gentlemen in England. Their solution was to keep power in their own hands in London, while restricting company membership to a small group of like-minded grandees.

The contemporaneous Massachusetts Bay Company also sought a radical solution to the same problems: The New England puritans, less intimately acquainted with the corridors of power at home, took the opposite tack and cut their colony off from English control by taking the charter with them and converting company meetings into the colony's government. Massachusetts Bay's unchecked authority created some problems, particularly when political and congregational authority became linked after the mid-1630s, but Providence Island's need to refer every important decision to London was utterly unworkable.

Captain Philip Bell, the first governor, went directly to the island after relinquishing the governorship of Bermuda. Although several of the Providence Island Company members were investors in Bermuda, Bell, a client of the Earl of Warwick, was known to only some of company. In their commission creating him "Governor, Captain general, and chief Commander of the said Island of Providence," the adventurers assured Bell of their confidence in his qualities: "sincerity, wisdom, courage, fidelity." Bell should take satisfaction, the company wrote him, in receiving the post without having thrust himself forward; his selection was an act of providence, directly from God's "overruling hand," and therefore he could expect God's blessing.

As governor, Captain Bell was the chief administrative, judicial, and military officer in Providence Island. Theoretically, all decision making was subject to his control. The company strengthened this illusion by urging him to use his power in a "large and ample manner." The adventurers thought of his office in terms of analogies; they compared him to the lieutenants of the counties in some contexts, in others to the chief justices of England. Both were the representatives of the central government to the localities.

The lieutenants, operating under the royal prerogative, carried out royal directives and maintained the peace. They were the link connecting the king and his Privy Council with the counties; information and opinions were gathered and disseminated by them and their deputies. Many English leaders were ambivalent about increasing royal reliance on the lieutenancy. Several Providence Island investors were, or were of sufficient importance to be, chosen lieutenants or deputy lieutenants, and they therefore saw the relevance of the office as a model for colonial government. But gentlemen throughout England viewed the Stuarts' increasing reliance on the lieutenancy as usurping the local government roles of the gentry and as symptomatic of the growth of prerogative government. Like Providence Island's governor, the lieutenants were authorized to impose martial law in case of rebellion or invasion.

In many ways it was natural for the adventurers to visualize government of their colony in terms of analogies to the lieutenancy. They conceived of the governor as their link to the colonies who would function just as the lieutenants did, as a two-way conduit of information and policy considerations. Like the lieutenants, he was to serve at pleasure; although stressing their esteem and confidence, the company declined to give Bell a definite term at the outset. Their analogizing the governorship to the lieutenancy, though, shows the confusion and wishful thinking in their planning. The lieutenancy was becoming a focus of discontent by the time the colony was founded, and the office, requiring close and continuing ties with both the locality and the Privy Council, rarely functioned well. A man who was assiduous in maintaining the relationships necessary to make himself effective in the county lost his connections at the center, and vice versa. The system was inadequate in England, but its exportation to the Indies was a disaster.

Governor Bell and his successors were hopelessly crippled by their intermediary position between colonists and company. Although theoretically a governor had enormous power, and therefore great responsibility, no decision of his was final, and many colonists had powerful friends in England who would help them overturn any unwelcome judgment. The investors' lengthy first instructions to the governor and council gave the governor an absolute veto even in the face of a unified council but stipulated that any such divisive issue must be referred to London for final decision. No positive action could be taken without the governor's approval backed by at least half the council.[3] The governor's veto, conferring ability to stop plans from going forward, was often the most controversial of his powers in every colony. The adventurers stipulated that it would not extend to one

3. PIC Commission to Gov. Bell, and letters to Bell and council by the *Seaflower*, 2–31. Captain John Smith wrote that the Jamestown colonists also argued that "the authority here is but a shadow," *Generall Historie of Virginia, New-England, and the Summer Isles,* 1624, in *The Complete Works of Captain John Smith,* ed. Philip L. Barbour (Chapel Hill, 1986), II, 208.

temporarily appointed by the council if their own designee should die.[4]

The justices also seemed an apt parallel to the governorship of Providence Island. The king's main constitutional role was as the fount of justice. The chief judges represented him throughout the land as they made their twice-yearly circuits to hear important cases. The assizes over which they presided were the "high point of the political and administrative year" in the counties. Like the lieutenants and their deputies, the judges gathered information and were expected to write reports of their activities. They stood for the royal presence and carried national justice to the entire land.[5]

In Providence Island's system, the governor's council corresponded to the justices of the peace, leading local gentlement selected for their probity and status in the community to serve as magistrates. The company saw no reason why English judicial practice could not be transported to their island. The initial instructions to the governor and council laid out a basic system. In a capital case, a jury composed of men of "unspotted fame and most observable for their just and conscionable dealing and course of life" was to be impaneled. The sheriff was to present the names of thirty-six such candidates, of whom the governor would choose twenty-four, allowing "the delinquent... his just challenges as here in England." The jury so impaneled would be judges of fact only, with the governor and council supplying the place of justices, "and accordingly to pronounce sentence agreeable to the laws of England."

In important civil or criminal cases, the governor and council might proceed in the same way, but "for more satisfaction of the people," the company recommended it would be better "in this Infancy of the plantation" to bring such matters before a large public hearing of all the parties and witnesses, with the decision rendered by the governor and council. Anyone condemned to death could, on the motion of the governor and three of his council, be reprieved until the company had an opportunity to review the case. In all judicial proceedings, equity and impartiality were to be the watchwords.[6]

The stately course of justice outlined in these first instructions foundered on the disorders endemic in the colony's first year. The company apologized for the quality of some immigrants, citing their

4. PIC to Gov. and Coun., 2–31. The negative voice claimed by the governor and magistrates in Massachusetts Bay proved a perennially disruptive issue; see Andrews, *Colonial Period*, I, 450–2; Morgan, *Puritan Dilemma*, 156–60. Parliamentary leaders in England, led by Lord Brooke, attempted to deny the king a negative voice in 1642; see Russell, *Causes of English Civil War*, 142.
5. Hirst, *Authority and Conflict*, 33–5; Fletcher, *Reform in the Provinces*, 6, 47–55.
6. PIC, Instr. to Gov. and Coun., pts. 27–29.

care in selecting settlers, "their demeanour being such here whilst they were under our eye that we might well conceive them to be civil men."[7] It was notoriously difficult to prejudge how young English men would react to American conditions, especially in a plantation's beginning. John Winthrop in Massachusetts echoed the Providence Island Company when he complained in a letter to his wife Margaret about the behavioral changes in his colonists: "I think here are some persons who never shewed so much wickedness in England as they have done here." Even after five years of settlement, Reverend Nathaniel Ward of Ipswich, Massachusetts, wrote despairingly to John Winthrop, Jr., of the "multitudes of idle and profane young men, servants and others" that plagued the colony so that many said "with grief we have made an ill change, even from the snare to the pit."[8] In the unsettled conditions attendant on all new plantations, magistrates in Massachusetts, not bound by the careful procedures the Providence Island Company outlined, executed summary justice, possibly even in capital cases; the Massachusetts deputies' challenge to the magistrates' rule in the 1640s partly concerned this broad area of discretionary powers the latter had assumed.[9]

In the face of unruliness and disorder, the Providence Island Company decided to act quickly, fearing any implication that they might "connive" at toleration of disorders from "too much Indulgence and sinful neglect." In 1632 the investors ordered the governor and council "not to be partial or sparing in the punishment of all disorders according to their quality and demerit." On the other hand "a just moderation" was also required. Therefore, the adventurers issued the kind of divided counsel that made governance of Providence Island so difficult. Murder, "open insurrection, rebellion, or wickednesses of a more abominable nature not fit to be named of Christians, (which God forbid should ever be committed amongst you)" were to be punished with death "according to the laws of England." Inferior felonies were to be punished by hard labor and the wearing of a badge until company members reviewed the evidence and passed sentence. By this instruction, they diminished the

---

7. PIC, Instr. to Gov. and Coun., 5–10–32.
8. John Winthrop to Margaret Winthrop, July 23, 1630; *Winthrop Papers* II, 303; Nathaniel Ward to John Winthrop, Jr., Dec. 24, 1635, ibid., III, 215–17.
9. John M. Murrin, "Magistrates, Sinners, and a Precarious Liberty: Trial by Jury in Seventeenth-Century New England," in Hall, Murrin, Tate, eds., *Saints and Revolutionaries*, 161–5; 183–6.
　　Prosecutions for offenses against community and for disorder were also increasing in England in the 1620s and 1630s. See Cynthia Herrup, *The Common Peace: Participation and the Criminal Law in Seventeenth-Century England* (Cambridge, 1987), 38–41, 62–3, and Keith Wrightson, "Two Concepts of Order: Justices, Constables and Jurymen in Seventeenth-Century England," in Brewer and Styles, ed., *An Ungovernable People*, 24–5, 32.

autonomy of the island's government, and therefore its ability to act quickly and decisively. In the event many sentences were overturned, reinforcing the paralysis.[10]

Administration of justice dominated the council's concerns, as in most colonies, and took up enormous amounts of time.[11] In England justices of the peace attempted to settle disputes by arbitration before they escalated into court cases. As leading gentlemen, they commanded the respect necessary to make them effective in the role of mediator.[12] The factionalization of Providence Island's leadership made such intervention ineffective; nor could the government overawe potential troublemakers. Prosecutions were so frequent that in 1633 the company decreed that the most common crimes, "swearing, drunkenness, sabbathbreaking, and such other crimes as the people are most inclined to and do therefore most usually commit," could be punished with predetermined sentences by any councilor on the oath of two sufficient witnesses, reserving the right of appeal to the full council on a double-or-nothing basis. These hearings would correspond to petty sessions in England, in which a minimum of two justices of the peace would sit on minor offenses. Other colonies also allowed justices, alone or in pairs, to try small cases.[13]

In 1634, as they refined their experiment, the Providence Island Company, using the single institution of the governor and council, recreated the two-part system of England in their island colony: quarter sessions, conducted by leading local men as justices of the peace to

10. PIC to Gov. and Coun., 5–10–32.
11. Lois Carr argues that it is difficult to distinguish the administrative and judicial functions of the Maryland governor and council in the 1640s, "The Foundations of Social Order: Local Government in Colonial Maryland," in Bruce C. Daniels, ed., *Town and Country: Essays on the Structure of Local Government in the American Colonies* (Middletown, CT, 1978), 73–4. On the same phenomenon in the New England colonies, see John M. Murrin, "Political Development," in Jack P. Greene and J. R. Pole, eds., *Colonial British America: Essays in the New History of the Early Modern Era* (Baltimore, 1984), 417.
12. Herrup, *Common Peace*, 54, 85–8.
13. PIC to Gov. and Coun., 7–20–33. Petty sessions, though they had existed informally for some time, were formally instituted in the early 1630s; see Barnes, *Somerset*, 81–5. On the practice in other English colonies, see Timothy H. Breen, *The Character of the Good Ruler: A Study of Puritan Political Ideas in New England, 1630–1730* (New Haven, 1970), 84–5; Bruce H. Mann, *Neighbors and Strangers: Law and Community in Early Connecticut* (Chapel Hill, 1987), 7fn; Billings, "Transfer of English Law to Virginia," in Andrews, Canny, and Hair, eds., *The Westward Enterprise*, 223, and John M. Murrin and A. G. Roeber, "Trial by Jury, The Virginia Paradox," in Jon Kukla, ed., *The Bill of Rights: A Lively Heritage* (Richmond, 1987), 112–14. New Haven colony brought all cases, however small, to formal trial. See Gail Sussman Marcus, "'Due Execution of the Generall Rules of Righteousnesse': Criminal Procedure in New Haven Town and Colony, 1638–1658," in Hall, Murrin, and Tate, eds., *Saints and Revolutionaries*, 101, 111.

preserve order in the community; and the assizes, presided over by representatives of the central law courts and the monarch. Those accused of assaults and batteries were to be bound over to the council as to a sessions, where small offenses could be handled by the suit of the injured parties, as was typical in England. But "great batteries, mixed with contempt and riots," being offenses against the common weal, must be brought to the council through a formal indictment. The adventurers instructed Bell to add his own account in cases where he was a witness, to enhance their ability to judge the evidence in London.[14]

As they refined the judicial system in the colony, the investors also increased their own role in its operation, but secretly, in a way that tied the governor's hands. Factionalization and defiance had driven Governor Bell and his council to excessive measures. The company had heard reports that for some offenses "which you apprehend to be of a high nature," planters, even men "of parts or quality," had been put into the bilbowes, which they wrote was never to be used on free men, and never on land, except in case of mutiny.[15] This reprimand was delivered in a letter to Bell alone "lest the publication thereof should open a gap to more liberties."

Similarly "mutilation of a member" as a punishment for any crime was not to be carried out until approved from London, but "in regard of the forementioned inconveniency" only Bell was to know of the company's order. He could forestall action through use of his veto, a power beyond that of judges in England who could not simply free a convicted person.[16] Reinforcing the ambiguity of Governor Bell's attributes of apparent power but shrinking personal autonomy, the investors closed their 1634 directions on judicial procedures by urging moderation in punishments, "especially towards men of Art, that may be otherwise deserving."[17]

A fundamental fallacy lay at the heart of the grandees' thinking about the government of Providence Island. Although they thought of their colony as analogous to a county of England, they wanted the settlers never to forget that it was the private property of a group of investors

14. PIC to Bell by the *Long Robert*, 7/8–34; Herrup, *Common Peace*, chap. 3.
15. The bilbowes, a punishment used at sea, was an iron bar bolted to the floor at one end to which ankle shackles were attached.
16. On the powers of English judges, see Herrup, *Common Peace*, 142, 161.
17. PIC to Bell by the *Long Robert*, 7/8–34. The company's treatment of Nicholas Goodman (see Chapters 7 and 8) is a good example of the damage done by such ambiguity.

in England. It was to be governed according to the laws of England, but it was not a fully realized unit of English society. When the investors heard that the governor and council were taking recognizances in the king's name, the company found it "very strange," saying that such procedures were done only by "a Judge of Record." Courts of Record were the common law courts, which kept formal records that were considered to be infallible; Providence Island's judicial system was to operate according to the common law but not as a common law court.[18] Recognizances were bonds to observe some condition, such as keeping the peace on pain of a fine or imprisonment, and were a key means used to reduce conflict in England. In future the governor and council were to record bonds to the company only.[19]

Inconsistencies at the project's core were not alarming to the grandees because they believed that the sense of common purpose, the goodwill, and the hopes of everyone involved in the venture, especially in a settlement made up of godly men and women, would preclude the disorders and challenges that kept other colonies in turmoil. The key thing was that the colony's leaders act as patterns of virtue and unity for the entire plantation: "[W]e command unto you that you labor by all means to maintain love and unity as between yourselves that are Magistrates so through the whole colony."

Proper carriage was deemed essential to maintainance of respect. Only councilors were allowed to cover their heads in the presence of the governor, and even they must uncover before speaking. Acknowledging that "even ceremonies of honor in civil affairs" enhance the dignity of officers, the company sent as an "Ensign of honor and Jurisdiction . . . a

18. David Konig argues that the common law was sufficiently inconsistent and ambiguous in the early seventeenth century, particularly in the "interpretive latitude" it gave to those operating under charters, that its transplantation to the colonies was problematic; "Colonization and the Common Law in Ireland and Virginia, 1569–1634," in Henretta, Kammen, and Katz, eds., *Transformation of Early American History*, 70–92.

19. PIC to Gov. and Coun. by the *Long Robert*, 7–34. Recording recognizances, taken in the name of the proprietor rather than the king, was the most important function of the justices in early Maryland; Carr, "Foundations of Social Order," in Daniels, ed., *Town and Country*, 78; see also David Konig, "English Legal Change and the Origins of Local Government in Northern Massachusetts," ibid., 21–2. On Courts of Record, see W. S. Holdsworth, *A History of English Law*, V (London, 1924), 157–61; for the definition of recognizance, see Herrup, *Common Peace*, 88, and Walter, "Grain riots and popular attitudes to the law," in Brewer and Styles, ed., *An Ungovernable People*, 61. For a contemporary discussion of recognizances, see William West, *Symbolaeographia* (London, 1590), book II, sect. 40. Massachusetts Bay stopped issuing writs in the king's name in 1641; G. B. Warden, "The Rhode Island Civil Code of 1647," in Hall, Murrin, and Tate, eds., *Saints and Revolutionaries*, 140.

Tipstaff of the same form that is carried before our chief justices of the courts in England which when ever you go either to church or council, or other place of judicature we would have always borne before you." The staff had a plate of silver on one end with the company seal: "vizt Three Islands and the words written about it *Legemejus expectabunt* taken out of Isaiah 42.4 The islands shall wait for his law which prophecy we hope may in some sort be fulfilled by planting the Gospel in those Islands."[20] The silver plate on the other end bore the words "*Innocens liberabit Insulam,* taken out of Job 22.30 The innocent shall deliver or preserve the Island."

The Providence Island adventurers were lords and leading gentlemen, and they knew the importance of the trappings of power. From the beginning, they acknowledged that officers' dignity and respect would rely in great part on the state in which they lived. A "commodious" brick governor's house was to be built near the church, "somewhat large, and spacious for the honor of the place, for public resort, and for entertainment." They asked officials for advice on their own recompense but made only vague promises to Bell that his would be sufficient to "maintain you in a fashion suitable to the dignity of your place." The investors wanted at all costs to avoid paying salaries in sterling in England; the preferred method was to send servants to colonial officials, the fruits of whose labors would be shared equally by the company and the men for whom they worked. Governor Bell and Captain Daniel Elfrith, the island's admiral, were each sent six at first, and Captain Samuel Axe, fortifications expert, councilor, and commander of Warwick Fort, five. Captain Elfrith was assured that the Providence Island Company "is composed of persons that will by no means Suffer the care or Industry of those we employ to be either unregarded or unrewarded."[21]

Despite frequent similar promises, the backers were never able or willing to supply the full number of servants intended. From the outset, the company acknowledged to Governor Bell that, although his six servants should give him a "competent maintenance," some men now coming, "whose friends have been at a great particular charge with them, have a few more Servants for the present." Thus, men theoretically inferior to the governor would be able to maintain a greater state than he.

20. PIC Instr. to Gov. Philip Bell, 2–31. Columbus also found this passage prophetic of European colonization of the West Indies; Delno C. West and August Kling eds., *The Libro de las profecias of Christopher Columbus* (Gainesville, FL, 1991), 171, 251.
21. PIC, Instr. to Gov. and Coun., 2–31. For the brickworks, see Essex Rec. Off., HBO MS DDBa 02/8. The governor's house was not built during Captain Bell's tenure; see the PIC to the Council, May, 1636.

This anomaly points to a fundamental problem the importance of which was slowly realized by the gentleman–adventurers of the Providence Island Company. Reasoning by analogy, they believed that they could erect something similar to English county government, but their experience revealed profound problems inherent in such a program. As in English counties, the political structure in the island was always reflective of and influenced by patron–client relationships. Nothing settled in Providence Island was ever truly settled; only round one could take place there. Moreover, even within Providence Island there was more than one power structure, and the seemingly innocuous statement that some with important and determined friends at home might live in greater state than the governor covered an explosive reality.

The man with the greater number of servants was probably Captain William Rudyerd, younger brother of Sir Benjamin Rudyerd, a leading figure in the Providence Island Company as in puritan political circles. Captain Rudyerd, "a Gentlemen that hath served long and commanded in the wars," was an abrasive figure packed off to the colony to put his continental military experience to use. Philip Bell had been commissioned not only governor but "Captain general, and chief Commander of the said Island of Providence." Captain Rudyerd, third in the official precedence behind Bell and Captain Elfrith, was Muster Master General and was to be commander of Fort Henry, defending the south of the island, when it was built.

The captains and lieutenants of the various forts formed a governing framework parallel to and interlocking with the civil government. They were normally on the governor's council, and the governor was always a captain. This was part of the price paid for "lying in the heart of the Indies & the mouth of the Spaniards." Again and again throughout the colony's life, captains and their underlings defied the governor and his council, and they often found support in London. In 1636, after Bell had been relieved of command, his successor was told to treat the "soldiers and persons of like quality" sent by the company with "mildness and gentleness, though you be over them in authority." Others who would have been "very useful" had left the company's service because of "ill or unkind usage breeding discontent."[22]

In practical terms, this meant that the military men's expertise gave them a position outside of and immune to the settlement's constituted authority and that if their defiance was kept within very broad limits, the company in London would back them up. The civil society, as in the puritan colony founded simultaneously to the north, was led by solid

---

22. PIC to Gov. and Coun., 2–31; PIC to Gov. and Coun., 5–36.

"middling" rank planters who must have expected to hold the same kind of sway in the south as their counterparts did in New England. Residence in the Indies worked against this expectation. In dealing with the unfamiliar environment, with its alien crops and labor systems, the expertise of men such as Elfrith and Bell, who had spent much of their lives in the islands, gave them a dominant position. Their conception of land use and the relations dictated by it necessarily dominated. Captain Axe, as a fortifications expert, and Captain Rudyerd, with his experience in the continental wars, were seen as invaluable and were conciliated by the adventurers.

Moreover, their connections with leading gentry, even noble families, bred in some of the military men a need to dominate socially and politically. They were steeped in the system of honor relations inherited from the knightly tradition, which prized autonomy and the esteem of colleagues above all. Anything that diminished a man's status struck at the heart of his being; the smallest slight could be devastating if allowed to go unpunished. Until a clear hierarchy emerged, men of honor would compete for dominance; humiliation of his rivals enhanced a man's status. Mervyn James has demonstrated how even in England gentlemen would continually strive for preeminence over their fellows, relaxing only in the presence of clear inferiors or superiors.[23]

Within county government in England, status competition was generally kept in bounds by the need for the gentry to present a relatively united front, and by networks built up over generations. The incoherent relationships with which Providence Island began its life called forth such challenging behavior with a vengeance. The stakes were enormously high for those who had gambled their lives and reputations by coming to the island, and the social and political hierarchy was so indeterminate that everything was contested. The captains distributed patronage among their allies, doling out exemptions from duties and supplies sent for the general good from England to the chagrin of the company; they thus used their offices to build personal followings. Captain Rudyerd, with his grander lifestyle and solid connections in England, constantly challenged the pretensions of Governor Bell to control and respect. Rudyerd kept the colony's life in an uproar as long as he was there.[24]

Governor Bell, although less explosive, shared Captain Rudyerd's outlook. He was a grandson of Sir Robert Bell, Chief Baron of the

23. James, *English Politics and the Concept of Honour,* 5–6, 28–30; Fletcher, "Honour, Reputation and Local Officeholding," in Fletcher and Stevenson, eds., *Order and Disorder,* passim.
24. PIC to Gov. and Coun. by the *Long Robert,* 7/8–34; PIC to Bell by the *Elizabeth,* 4–10–33; William Jessop to Thomas Flory, 8–11–34 in his letterbook, B. L. Add. MS 10615, no. 17.

Exchequer and Speaker of the House of Commons under Queen Elizabeth, brother-in-law of another speaker, Sir Heneage Finch, and kinsman of company member Sir Edmond Moundeford of Norfolk as well as of Sir John Hobart and Sir Edward Dering. He had left the service of the Bermuda Company partly because he believed it beneath his dignity to serve a body tainted by the concerns of merchants. He no longer wished "to live in such a slavish subjection to such mean & base minded men as the citizen part of the Company are & do show themselves," considering such submission a violation of "my nature."[25]

The Providence Island Company regarded Bell as a man of status and dignity. When company secretary William Jessop wrote to him privately in 1634, he thanked Bell for his invitation to address him as a friend, Jessop saying he would "place your friendship among that highest rank of favour which my correspondents in the world have yet afforded me." Yet in the same letter he apologized for the company's failure to show their esteem in the tangible ways Bell demanded.[26] What the company refused to see was that their parsimony helped to cripple the governor in the quest for predominance and that by helping to keep the order of

25. Bell to Sir Nathaniel Rich, March, 1628/29, in Ives, ed., *The Rich Papers: Letters from Bermuda*, 314–16. "Citizen" here meant merchant or townsman in distinction to the landed gentry. Samuel Johnson defined citizen as "A townsman; a man of trade; not a gentleman," *A Dictionary of the English Language* (London, 1840), I, 314. See also PIC to Bell, 2–31.

Philip Bell was the son of Sir Edmund Bell, MP. On his family connections, see the family tree in Maurice F. Bond, ed., *The Diaries and Papers of Sir Edward Dering, Second Baronet, 1644 to 1684*, House of Lords Record Office Occasional Publications, no. 1 (London, 1976).

Providence Island held other men who had reached similar conclusions about the merchant element in the Bermuda Company. Captain Sussex Camock also left Bermuda resolved never to deal with such a mixed company again; Bell to Rich, Ives, ed., *Letters from Bermuda*, 319. Capt. Nathaniel Butler, who preceded Bell as governor of Bermuda and would later be governor of Providence Island, carried a petition to the "Lords of the Company" for the Somers Islands when he left office there. The petition complained of the company's gouging the colonists and assumed that the noble members would set things right; Butler, *History of the Bermudaes or Summer Islands*, ed. J. Henry Lefroy (London, 1882), 291–97. Lefroy erroneously attributed this work to Captain John Smith.

26. Jessop to Bell, 8–16–34, B. L. Add MS 10615, no. 48. Later the deposed Bell complained about materials sent him for a suit. Jessop's long reply demonstrates the enormous importance of such marks. He wrote that he was "very sorry that the materials for your suit were such as deserve not your acceptance," and that he was "very tender of distressing one whom I value." Jessop thought the company should have taken on the task of getting the materials, but the investors pushed the job off on him. Jessop, overloaded with business, had ordered his tailor to assemble the materials and had sent them without checking. Taking "the fault" wholly on himself, Jessop asked forgiveness, "there being no purpose in me to mock or lessen you or my esteem of you, though I have thereby lessened my own discretion," Jessop to Bell, 4–17–37, ibid., no. 158.

relationships in doubt, they fueled constant challenges to the political order. Their repeated efforts to ordain a hierarchy from London had little effect.[27]

William Jessop praised Governor Bell for his cultivation of a humble heart in the face of adversity, referring to a confrontation with Captain Nathaniel Axe. Humility is an important Christian virtue, but it made for a poor governor of an English colony in the heart of the Spanish Indies. Company members blamed Bell for failing to command respect, but they did not realize that they contributed heavily to that failure. In an effort to strengthen his authority, the adventurers had given Bell a definite term, a further three years, in 1632. They had settled a plantation of 100 acres to be permanently attached to the post of governor and had allocated thirty-two servants to the position. But Governor Bell never received his full allotment of servants and therefore did not achieve the economic position the company thought appropriate for his place.

Bell's repeated requests for compensation and the trappings of power received inconsistent replies. In 1633 the company offered to enlarge his plantation, but at the same time they curtly told their governor that he was to be allotted £20 for supplies for himself and his wife: "To which sum the Company were willing to contract themselves out of a desire that he being Governor may be an example of frugality to the rest of the inhabitants." If he needed more, he was referred to their magazine, where he could purchase his requirements. The next year they praised Bell's "good husbandry" in forgoing the expensive guard of honor, the cost of which was "so great in the beginning that we could not conveniently have permitted the continuance thereof," although he was still authorized to use it on "any special occasion." Again praising his frugality, the company thus urged a sober simplicity on their governor while they also expected him to maintain a grand authority.[28]

Company instructions held Governor Bell responsible for maintaining good order, for peace and unity in the council, and for getting the colonists moving on productive agriculture to make the plantation an economic success. Many of their specific instructions were far beyond the capability of any governor in a new settlement. He was to see that no one who overcharged for commodities was allowed to remain on the

27. See for example PIC to Gov. and Coun., 5–10–32, pt. 40.
28. PIC Ctee., 5–22–33; PIC to Bell, 4–10–33, 7–33, and 8–34. John Winthrop of Massachusetts Bay considered his guard of honor essential to the dignity of the governorship and was outraged when it was removed, *Journal*, ed. Hosmer, I, 216, 220. Winthrop also stressed his great expenditures to maintain himself in a governor's state; *Winthrop Papers* III, 173–4.

governing council, as well as to oversee each man's use of his servants. He was expected to audit the productivity of each plantation on the island, on a monthly basis if possible, rewarding industry and reproving indolence. Captain John Smith, in Jamestown's darkest hour, had instituted a policy of "he that will not work shall not eat." Captain Bell was also to impose the Apostle's rule.[29]

In Providence Island, as previously in Bermuda, Bell was a stickler for carrying out the letter of his orders. In Bermuda he had stood against the united council, refusing to allow the desperate colonists to buy food from an English merchant unconnected with the Somers Islands Company, "though his heart yearned with compassion for the poor inhabitants," because of "his fear of your displeasure for breaking your instructions."[30] The Providence Island investors must have been drawn by his literalism, knowing he would follow their instructions scrupulously. But many situations called for a flexibility and judgment of which Bell, who when he met opposition and criticism in Bermuda compared himself to Jesus and St. Paul, was not capable.[31] Company records are filled with complaints about the governor's opening and reading planters' letters and about his attempts to restrain free men from leaving the island, forcing the company to remove ambiguity from previous instructions that had allowed some leeway.[32]

The adventurers' shifting priorities undercut Governor Bell's campaign for control as their attention veered in the direction of other projects. The company commended the assiduousness of the governor and council in dealing with "scandalous offenders," tolerance of whom could lead to a general judgment against the settlement by God, but at the same time in 1633 they urged Sussex Camock, leader of their promising expedition to establish trade on the Central American mainland, to send any disorderly person who troubled his venture to Providence Island, where the malcontent was to be kept safely until the company had time to deliberate about him. Such men would surely add to the disorders that threatened that settlement's existence.[33]

29. PIC to Bell, 8–34 and 2/3–35. Smith, *Generall Historie*, in *Complete Works*, ed. Barbour, II, 208. See 2 Thessalonians 3: 10.
30. Bermuda Council to Bermuda Co., March 1628/29, in Ives, ed., *Letters from Bermuda*, 304–5. See also Gov. Philip Bell to Sir Nathaniel Rich, March, 1628/9, ibid., 323.
31. Bell to Sir Nathaniel Rich, March, 1628/9, ibid., 314–15.
32. PIC Ct., 6–9–34; PIC to Gov. and Coun., 5–10–32 and 8–34; PIC to Bell 5–10–32, 7–1–33, and 2/3–35; PIC to Collins, Master of the *Long Robert*, 8/9–34.
33. PIC to Gov. and Coun., 7–20–33; PIC to Bell, 7–1–33.

Governor Bell's literalism and inflexibility made him a poor player in the fluid world of the Caribbean, and the company gently chided him for following their instructions too closely. The adventurers had forbidden their settlers to participate in local Caribbean trade because such commerce would rob the company of the products that should be stockpiled for their ships, and it might produce "a greater Envy of the Spaniards drawn upon you for being a receptacle and a relief to their Enemies." In 1633, in the face of the colony's failure to develop a valuable product, the investors wrote "herein we are not so curious" that an occasional transaction with a friendly Dutch ship should not be allowed. In a postscript to their private letter to Bell, the members were more direct, indicating that he should have realized that the offer made by a Dutch captain for their tobacco was good enough, considering its relative worthlessness in England, to allow him to disregard company orders and sell.[34]

Bell was chastised for failing to control his increasingly factionalized council. Leaks of council business were a constant problem that the governor was powerless to stop. More serious were the "private dissensions and secret heartburnings" that rent the council, preventing the colony's leaders from getting on with building a secure economic foundation.[35] So clever were the factions in presenting their cases through friends in London that "the truth of things is now obscured and the guiltless may lie under an undeserved prejudice."[36]

By 1634 constant council meetings were so burdensome that the company was forced to order set times from which the colony's leaders were to diverge only in emergencies. They also reiterated their insistence on strict secrecy in council proceedings. The adventurers' initial instructions had directed that the most important civil and criminal issues be heard in public assemblies, but early in 1635 they wrote "it suits not with the gravity of councilors to discuss their affairs of counsel in the audience of the country," especially when they disagreed. They had expected a level of discretion in Governor Bell of which he was not capable.

Early in 1635, when the Providence Island Company was already

---

34. PIC to Bell, 4–10–33. The company was later angry about trade with Dutch ships; see PIC to Gov. and Coun., 5–36. Bell's ridigity can be seen in his refusal to allow Richard Read to come home because Read's name had been misspelled on the warrant. See Jessop's criticism of Bell's "scruple ... considering that the name must necessarily point to your person, there being none other of the same name in the Island," Jessop to Read, 3–15–35, B. L. Add MS 10615, no. 122.

35. PIC to Gov. and Coun., 5–10–32, 4–10–33, 7–20–33; PIC to Bell by the *Expectation*, 2/3–35.

36. Jessop to Bell, 8–16–34, B. L. Add MS 10615, no. 48.

seeking a replacement for Bell, members sent a new set of instructions once again urging him to "keep a fair correspondency with the Councilors," and to remember that they were to work together on almost all issues: "And for the word Absolute power we do utterly dislike the language and therefore would not have it once named, the same tending to the discouragement of men's stay and coming thither."[37] The investors ordered Bell to govern according to their commission and instructions. Company members apparently conveniently forgot their own command sent in the previous September that Bell use his veto without explanation to forestall punishments decreed by the council. Their instructions added to his natural inflexibility to destroy Bell's effectiveness.

Records of official proceedings in Providence Island were so ineptly kept, the company complained, that the adventurers often had difficulty understanding them. They found many procedural errors in judicial proceedings, such as allowing witnesses to testify without oath or letting parties to cases participate in decision making. They considered most transcripts woefully incomplete. Investors suspected that such lack of clarity was partly strategic to protect councilors' particular interests; they constantly reiterated their standards for adequate record keeping and for certification of records by the entire council.[38]

But on some occasions company members considered the colony's reports too complete, especially in transmitting unfavorable information about investors' kin. In July 1634 a four-man committee, which included John Pym and Sir Benjamin Rudyerd, two men who felt shamed by too-full disclosures about their relatives, was appointed to meet each returning ship, read the records it carried, and prepare an extract, "that what is unfit may be taken away and the rest new written to remain in the Company's hands as a Record." These four would decide what had and had not happened in Providence Island.[39] As their desire to keep close control over the development of their island colony was increasingly frustrated, the adventurers moved to plug loopholes rather

37. Hope Sherrard wrote Sir Thomas Barrington in February 1635 that Bell had reduced the colonists to "his absolute slaves and vassals" by requiring that all his commands be obeyed without question or hesitation; Sherrard to Barrington, B. L. Egerton MS 2646, ff. 76–77v.
38. PIC to Gov. and Coun. by the *Long Robert*, 9–34, and by the *Expectation*, 2/3–35; PIC to Bell about Axe, 5–32, and by the *Expectation*, 2/3–35. On the available guides to judicial procedure, especially Michael Dalton's, *The Countrey Justice: Contayning the Practice of the Justices of the Peace Out of their Sessions* (London, 1618), see Warren M. Billings, "English Legal Literature as a Source of Law and Legal Practice for Seventeenth-Century Virginia," *Virginia Magazine of History and Biography* 87 (1979), 403–16.
39. PIC Gen. Ct., 7–2–34. These extracts do not survive.

than seeing that opening the way to flexibility and discretionary powers in the island might provide better chances of success.

Governor Bell, hamstrung by company orders and his rigid temperament, and condemned by the adventurers to frugality and humility, was faced with the swaggering of powerful personalities, each competing for dominance and each convinced that another's gain in status diminished him. In these fluid circumstances, the smallest provocation could explode into a major confrontation while different claimants jockeyed for position. Attention ultimately focused on London, where colonists' "friends" would take care of their interests. Connections at home not only determined how well one lived in Providence Island; they also intervened in company proceedings to see that their clients were spared humiliation and loss. Any planter was only as powerful as his friends in London.

Captain William Rudyerd was a constant source of trouble as long as he remained in the island. He quarreled violently with the Reverend Lewis Morgan, the colony's first minister, largely because he thought Morgan had not given him due respect. William Rudyerd's servant had lent some of the captain's books to Morgan, apparently before Rudyerd himself was on the island. Rudyerd sent "so often I am ashamed to relate" to Morgan for the books because he wanted to check all his possessions against the inventory of the things he had shipped. He claimed he told Morgan that he could have them all again after the checking was complete. Instead of returning the books, Morgan sent word to Rudyerd, delivered in front of the governor, "that I were best mend my manners; or else I should be *mala.*"

Such an insult, delivered in such circumstances, was intolerable from anyone but especially from Morgan, Rudyerd's social inferior. Rudyerd, son of a great gentry family, would be extremely sensitive to any public slight; that it occurred in front of the governor intensified his need for retribution.[40]

He wrote to Morgan about his "sluttish; and unbeseeming message; which relishes you in every part." Morgan's claims to gentle status he treated with scorn: "[K]now your foul mouthed answer deserves rather sharp retribution than any equal respect from A gentleman; I have given you too Much respect; which has begot so much incivility." He warned Morgan that "your Carriage here shall be recorded; and a just Account

40. Fletcher, "Honour, Reputation and Local Officeholding," in Fletcher and Stevenson, eds., *Order and Disorder*, 101, 110–15; Lawrence Stone, *The Crisis of the Aristocracy, 1558–1641* (Oxford, 1965), 42.

seriously sent for England." Rudyerd's rebuke to Morgan claimed that what bothered him most about the altercation was that "your Carriage have been such that you have made both my Lieutenant; & my self forbear that sacred religious duty of the Sacrament." In the end, Rudyerd wrote that he had received all his books except two, "but they I look not for."[41]

Both men were springs of trouble in Providence Island during Governor Bell's administration, but they were treated very differently. Rudyerd's rebuke to the minister was dated May 28, 1632. Morgan's recall was already on its way aboard the *Charity* by the time it was sent, but Rudyerd was to stay a further two years as a constant focus of trouble.

While debating Morgan's recall, the investors discussed complaints against Rudyerd: The council had charged him with "drunkenness, swearing, ill carriage towards the Governor, and other misdemeanors, since he came into the Island." The horrified company at first decided that if on trial sufficient proof of the charges existed, he should be returned to England "with a certificate of the particular depositions, and the whole manner of their proceedings thereupon." Two days later the resolution was read out and amended to read that if Rudyerd showed signs of reformation he should be allowed to remain in Providence Island and the trial should be suspended.[42]

A further two days later a letter arrived from the perpetually absent company governor, the Earl of Holland, asking for "a friendly accord of the difference arising from the complaint made against Captain Rudyerd." The company, apparently pleased to have this chance to reconsider, deputized Sir Nathaniel Rich to draw up a reply, which he presented the following day. In their final deliberation on the matter, in a meeting attended only by Saye, Brooke, Rich, and Pym, the adventurers made their prime consideration the preservation of "peace and unity among themselves." The order for Rudyerd's trial was revoked and replaced by a general instruction for sequestering and trying anyone who was "factious, opposite to government or a hinderer of religion."[43]

Sir Benjamin Rudyerd wrote a long, painful letter to Governor Bell objecting to his brother's treatment in Providence Island.[44] Saying he was "not Patron of any mans fault," Rudyerd wrote that he did not wish to uphold his brother in anything he had done but that he objected to what he saw as the governor's unjudicial proceeding in which wit-

41. Bermuda Archives, Accession 51, no. 6.
42. PIC Ctee., 5–3–32, 5–5–32.
43. PIC Ctee., 5–7–32, 5–8–32; PIC to Gov. and Coun., 5–10–32, pt. 45.
44. Sir Benjamin Rudyerd to Gov. Philip Bell (?), 1633, sent by the *Falcon*, Bermuda Archives, Acc. 51, 5.

nesses went unsworn and the accused was not heard. He was particularly incensed that Bell had upheld his procedure "with a show of Scripture."

Sir Benjamin then went on to describe life in Providence Island from his brother's point of view. William's injuries began when he was left behind by the departing *Seaflower*. Then, almost as soon as he arrived, accusations were written to England about him, and he found himself "damnified by the irrecoverable embezzling of a great part of his goods, so that he was continually galled and kept in such a perpetual rawness and vexation, as would have made a better tempered man than he to wince in his harness."

What really outraged Captain Rudyerd was that secretary Thomas Hunt, a man inferior in social status (Sir Benjamin called him "that precious Pettifogger Hunt"), was "countenanced and valued above him." The elder Rudyerd felt that his brother's indignation was absolutely justified. William was censured for "words spoken to Hunt at the Council," but no account was taken of the fact that he was "rudely and snappishly provoked." Worse yet, Hunt was allowed to remain at the council table, even to vote on the sentence: "You know that to sell Cheese by a false Weight is an Abomination, then what is it to misweigh Persons and Causes."

The subject of William Rudyerd's quarrel with Hunt was innovations in the worship service, particularly in the singing of psalms. Sir Benjamin appealed to Governor Bell to keep the peace. He referred to the tension between a gentleman's need for respect and the claims of Christianity on its adherents. Pointing out that both Bell and his brother William were gentlemen, he hoped for "a fair and Civil Correspondence between you." He then went on: "but because a New-man in Christianity, is better than an ancient Gentleman in Heraldry," he hoped that when his brother should again "fall into any fault, that you seek to restore him with the Spirit of meekness," adding ominously, "Lest you also be tempted some other way."

In Rudyerd's case, peace and unity in the colony were sacrificed to achieve harmony in the company in 1632. No one wished to offend Sir Benjamin Rudyerd, even at the cost of deeply offending Governor Philip Bell. Company members may also have been sympathetic to William's position. Many of his quarrels were with godly men who, although inferior to him in social and occupational status, thought their religious commitment bestowed a kind of superiority on them. Company members, all godly men and convinced puritans, were committed to the notion that the claims of godliness and of hierarchy were perfectly compatible. They may have read challenges to the established order as danger signs, indicating the possibility that the cause of religious reformation might open the door to those who wished to take advantage.

Moreover, the adventurers still believed in Captain Rudyerd's usefulness. His roughness might be a small price to pay for his role in the island's defense. After all, manners suitable to a gentleman in society were not much use in the heart of the Spanish empire, and tradition allowed greater freedom of speech to military men than to others.[45] Some of Rudyerd's quarrels with other councilors concerned his vigorous action to complete Fort Henry and to challenge ships that came too near.[46] He could easily have been considered too valuable to lose. And his value would have been decisively diminished if he were forced to bend the knee and accept censure by the council. A gentleman's honor lay in the esteem he could command from others. Take that away and he was stripped of his personal vigor. Even in England, aristocrats and leading gentlemen would accept extreme punishments, including imprisonment, rather than be forced publicly to admit error or guilt before their peers.[47] The Providence Island Company grandees would have imposed such humiliation on Sir Benjamin's brother most unwillingly. Captain William Rudyerd's tenure culminated in the death of his servant two years later after a beating ordered by him.

Such problems were not limited to Providence Island. Massachusetts Bay, although it was self-governing, saw a very similar rivalry between its two greatest men in the early decades. John Winthrop and Thomas Dudley vied for control in the infant colony, each on occasion assuming the deputy governor's role in the other's administration. Dudley, like William Rudyerd, had served in the European wars and held chief military command in New England. Winthrop wrote that he was "one that would not be trodden under foot by any man." Dudley accused Winthrop of trying to make himself "popular," of currying favor with the crowd, thereby endangering their entire enterprise. When Winthrop accused Dudley of setting a bad example and overtaxing the public treasury by bestowing "such cost about wainscotting and adorning his house, in the beginning of a plantation," among other things, Dudley resigned from the government. Thomas Dudley had grown up in the household of the Earl of Northampton. He had served as steward and

---

45. See the testimony of John Underhill before the Massachusetts General Court, October, 1637, reported by John Winthrop, *Antinomians and Famillists condemned by the Synod of Elders in New-England*, in Thomas Weld, *A Short Story of the Rise, Reign, and Ruin of the Antinomians, Familists, and Libertines* (London, 1644), 41–2.
46. PIC to Gov. and Coun., 4–10–33; PIC to Bell, 4–10–33.
47. Stone, *Crisis of the Aristocracy*, 42; Fletcher, "Honour, Reputation and Local Office-holding," in Fletcher and Stevenson, eds., *Order and Disorder*, 101.

confidant to the Earl of Lincoln to whom he had been introduced by, among others, Lord Saye and Sele. Like William Rudyerd, he expected to live in a style befitting his station, with the respect due him, and he reacted violently to any challenge to his dignity.[48]

Such conflicts occurred repeatedly during the Bell administration. The 1634 case of Lieutenant William Rous, John Pym's stepnephew, demonstrates the same difficult mix of priorities between London and Providence Island, and between the demands of order and of honor, as that of Captain Rudyerd two years earlier. Lieutenant Rous had struck Thomas Forman, the island's smith, in the governor's presence. The council suspended Rous from their table and from his offices in militia training and as second in command at Fort Henry under Captain Rudyerd. Dismissal of a gentleman from office involved deep humiliation and disgrace; Lieutenant Rous could erase his dismissal only by the greater humiliation of public confession of guilt. In a similar case in Massachusetts Bay, Captain John Endecott did admit that he had been "too rash" in striking "goodman Dexter"; only later, he argued, did he learn that it was "not lawfull for a justice of peace to strike." But, he wrote Governor Winthrop, "if you had seen the manner of his carriage, with such daring of me with his arms on kembow etc. It would have provoked a very patient man." Godly captains reacted violently when challenged by their inferiors.[49]

Lieutenant Rous, like Captain Rudyerd, could not bear the slightest humiliation. Several years later, when Rous, now embarked on privateering in the service of the Providence Island Company, was a captive in Cartagena, he met Thomas Gage, an English Dominican who traveled with the Spanish. "That gallant Captain Rous" complained to Gage of "some affronts" offered by the Spanish in the ship that captured him, that he refused to bear, "though a Prisoner unto them." Rous wished to repair his honor by challenging "his contemners" to meet him in a duel, "(a brave courage in a dejected and imprisoned English man to challenge a Spaniard in his Country, a cock upon his own dunghill)." Gage dissuaded Rous, warning him of cowardly treachery from his captors.[50]

In 1634 Governor Bell removed Lieutenant Rous's humiliation. He restored Rous, his ally on the factionalized council, to all his offices

---

48. Winthrop, *Journal,* ed. Hosmer, I, 75–9, 84–8, 113–14, 169–72; II, 48; Cotton Mather, "The Life of Mr. Thomas Dudley," Mass. Hist. Soc. *Proceedings* II (1871 for 1870), 207–22.
49. On the humiliation of dismissal see Fletcher, "Honour, Reputation, and Local Office-holding," in Fletcher and Stevenson, eds., *Order and Disorder,* 95–6; Endecott to Winthrop, April 12, 1631, *Winthrop Papers* III, 25.
50. Gage, *English-American,* 332–33.

without the acknowledgment of error the council had demanded as the price of readmission. The company was outraged, particularly as Bell claimed his "prerogative" allowed him to do so. The company chastised Governor Bell, not privately and discreetly, but humiliatingly with a "sharp reproof" in their public letter to the governor and council, informing him that there was no such thing as the governor's prerogative. Lieutenant Rous was not to come to the council table until he had met the council's terms, although the company acknowledged the usefulness of having him continue in his other posts.

Company letters to Bell and to the entire council were sent in the *Long Robert* in September 1634. William Jessop, the company secretary, wrote privately to Rous at the same time. John Pym had appealed to the company to take off the censure because of his kinsman Rous's "usefulness in these times of danger, and the remitting of other faults," which they at first agreed to with the stipulation that it was done only at the special request of their treasurer and should not encourage the lieutenant "to run into the like miscarriage in time to come." Then, according to Jessop, the adventurers decided that the remission could not be sent "for some reasons which were apprehended to be very weighty." Pym had left town but had asked Jessop, if the censure were not removed, to write Lieutenant Rous and advise him to save himself embarrassment by staying away from the council table.[51]

Just before the *Long Robert* sailed, the *Elizabeth* returned from Providence Island with further news. Jessop wrote another private letter to Lieutenant Rous saying that the "large letter" he had prepared was now irrelevant. He thanked the lieutenant for his expressions of love sent by the *Elizabeth*: "I can also wish myself able to make acceptable return, but I am sure that your wisdom and goodness will entertain my affection though it be alone and not strong enough to draw after it suitable expression." Rous's remission was included by Jessop in the copies of letters sent in the *Long Robert*; it apparently indicated that his offense was "freely remit[ted]" without requiring "any public acknowledgement."[52] The public humiliation of the governor in the company's open letter traveled in the same ship.

Thus, Governor Bell's friends in the island caused him as many problems as his enemies. His greatest ally and embarrassment must have been his father-in-law, Captain Daniel Elfrith. In their instructions of May 1632, the company had set out specific guidelines for Elfrith: no

51. PIC Ct., 7–30–34. Jessop to Rous, 8–18–34, B. L. Add MS 10615, no. 44.
52. PIC, "The Company's Remission of Lt. Rous's public acknowledgement sent by the *Robert*," 1634; Jessop to Rous, 9–9–34.

act of hostility without specific direction from London unless the island was attacked; and no voyages from the island "on what pretext soever without the consent of you the Governor and Council." Captain Elfrith's energies were to be confined within the island, subject to control by a council whose authority he barely recognized, but the company declined to punish him for his defiance of the council.[53] In his own way Elfrith was to be as explosive a force as Captain Rudyerd was, and his support of his son-in-law must have been at best a mixed blessing.

Captain Elfrith immediately wrote the company asking forgiveness for his actions and that he be allowed to function as admiral in terms that made sense to him. In chafing under his new restricted role, he apparently quarreled even with his chief ally, Governor Bell. The company replied, thanking him for his goodwill and praising his usefulness. They agreed that exercise of his office "belongs solely to your self," yet he was to undertake nothing without the explicit instruction of the governor and council. Dropping hints of privateering to come in the future, they made him captain of Black Rock Fort and added to his number of servants.[54]

By mid-decade investors were wondering whether Elfrith's vaunted expertise was genuine. The company's formal letter sent in the *Long Robert* in September 1634 began with the hope that his expressed intention of finishing Black Rock Fort would lead to "a real performance." The Earl of Warwick wrote him privately, thanking Elfrith for revised estimates of Providence Island's hopefulness but remarking that he wished "your former information had as fully discerned the nature of the soil as the Company's experience and your present information do now represent; for by that means much expectation had been saved." Warwick wrote that Elfrith's proposals for "regaining of those expectations," perhaps through privateering, were out of "season" for discussion. Warwick and the company advised Elfrith to concentrate on transplantation of commodities from the mainland as the surest avenue to wealth and honor.[55]

Elfrith had quarreled with Captain Samuel Axe over the state of the fortifications, Axe's area of expertise and responsibility. Warwick wrote to Axe that his "sufferings" proceeded not from the company's intention "but rather from the mistakes and ignorance of those under whom you suffer."[56] When Axe was driven to defy the governor and council,

53. PIC to Gov. and Coun., 5–10–32; PIC to Elfrith, 5–10–32.
54. PIC to Elfrith, 7–3–33.
55. PIC to Elfrith by the *Long Robert*, 7/9–34; Warwick to Elfrith, 8–18–34, Jessop Letterbook, B. L. Add MS 10615, no. 42.
56. Warwick to Axe, 8–18–34, ibid., no. 43.

the company tried to be evenhanded: They told Axe that he was right about the fortifications and that their instructions never intended to place him "under the exemplary command or direction of any our other officers in the things whereof them selves are ignorant" but that defiance of legally constituted authority was never justified, therefore he was also wrong.[57]

By the time the adventurers wrote, Axe and his valuable skills had left Providence Island to work on company projects on the mainland. The investors urged Captain Axe to return to Providence Island, where he would be restored to all his offices "provided only that for the honor of the government you make an acknowledgement of your former mis-carriage in so directly opposing the Governor's order." Although the company had worried about irreparably damaging the honor and effec-tiveness of Captain Rudyerd and Lieutenant Rous, they told Axe that his submission would not lessen him; indeed, by giving "testimony of a discreet and humble spirit," he would put himself in line for greater rewards. Captain Axe was keenly aware that he had been poorly recompensed and had complained about the unjust and unequal way the magazines sent from London had been distributed. A humble posture served a soldier badly in the Indies.[58]

Charges of partiality in distributing magazines of supplies sent from England, by friendship rather than necessity, made peaceful relationships impossible.[59] There was "a great falling out" when Bell demanded that the clerks of the stores present him their books immediately for his inspection. They refused ("discreetly and modestly," the company thought) and begged time to make them up properly, especially as it looked as though "an advantage was sought for against them." The company overturned Bell's imprisonment of the clerks, calling it "unlawful, and unreasonable," although they did endorse his rejection of an illegal judicial judgment against Daniel Elfrith in a suit brought by Thomas Jenkes, Clerk of the Stores. Elfrith, incensed by the clerks' defiance, had refused to perform any of his duties, and the company blamed not the admiral but Governor Bell for countenancing such behavior, "the safety of the Island being more considerable than his own satisfaction in a private and but supposed injury."

Samuel Rishworth and Captain Elfrith had been given responsibility

57. The company did remove a fine of 500 pounds of tobacco levied on Axe, apparently for supporting Nicholas Goodman, the workmaster under him, when Goodman was charged with attempting to poison Governor Bell's servants. See PIC Gen. Ct., 5–15–34, 5–16–34; PIC to Axe, 7/9–34.
58. PIC to Gov. and Coun. by the *Long Robert*, 9–34; PIC to Bell, 7–1–33; PIC to Axe, 7/9–34.
59. PIC to Gov. and Coun., 4–10–33, 9–34.

for getting in the debts owed to the company within the island. Bell blamed Rishworth for the improperly conducted proceedings and charged him with partiality in judgment, disrespectful language to the governor "in the face of the Country," with pride and violence, and with wilfull record-keeping omissions in his office of secretary of the council.[60]

The company's working assumption combined exaggerated notions of their governor's power to command respect as their voice on the island with policies and personnel that consistently undermined whatever natural regard attached to his office. When Governor Bell wrote that the councilors failed to pay him the proper respect, the company responded angrily. Part of their anger was directed at the governor, who seemed "modestly willing to deny your own particular interest therein." They were indignant that he was willing to overlook the wrangling and public defiance of Rishworth, who fought the introduction of slavery into Providence Island, Bell writing that Rishworth's actions were "bare weaknesses only, and compatible [?] with right ends in the main." Bell was wrong; Rishworth's actions were "faults of a high nature and most of them punishable in a high degree." The weakness was Bell's, and the company blamed him for it bitterly.[61]

Throughout the company's dealings with Governor Philip Bell and his councilors, the pull between the demands of a gentleman's honor for autonomy and the right to dominate and command esteem, and the puritan citizen's duty to be humble and submissive, surfaced periodically in explosive outbursts that demonstrated the tension constantly seething just below the surface. The grandee adventurers had not thought through the problems of government in a puritan society, although they acknowledged the experimental nature of the venture in their initial instructions to the governor and council, saying that they would delay writing a constitution and laws "until we again hear from you and receive full advertisement of the state of the Colony and your affairs there, and how you find the Temper and disposition of the People, and what vices you perceive them most inclinable unto that upon advice we may apply remedies accordingly."[62] Still less had they considered how placing such a polity in the Spanish Indies would add to those problems. Governor Bell was to set an example of frugality and humility, forgoing the trappings of his office, yet he was to exercise unquestioned authority

---

60. PIC to Bell by the *Expectation*, 2/3–35.
61. PIC to Bell by the *Long Robert*, 7/9–34, and by the *Expectation*, 2/3–35; PIC to Axe, 7/9–34.
62. PIC to Gov. and Coun., 2–31.

over the military men of high social rank who lived more grandly under the protection of more powerful friends than he did.

Everything hinged on the power of the substantial men of the godly sort to transform society. In 1632, when the company softened its censure of Captain William Rudyerd to a general instruction against dissension, the same batch of letters carried news that substantial civilian leaders, newcomers Samuel Rishworth and Henry Halhead and already-resident Edward Gates, were to be added to the council. The adventurers must have hoped that these godly men would provide a counterweight to the explosive captains and would place harmony and hard work at the center of the leadership's concerns while diluting the captains' power to create dissension. At the same time, they also set up an order of precedence among the captains and lieutenants to stop wrangling over that issue. Together with a secure three-year term for Governor Bell, these changes would place Providence Island on its intended track.[63] The promised transformation did not take place. The civilian leaders themselves became sources of friction, and the logic of the plantation's design and location carried it in another direction.[64]

By 1634, in the face of numerous complaints about dissension, the company was already looking ahead to the end of the Bell era in Providence Island. They closed their long letter to the governor and council sent in the *Long Robert* in September 1634 with the bare statement that Bell, whose term would expire before the next ship, should continue in office "till other order do arrive there with you."[65] After four years of experience, the qualities they sought in a governor were modesty, wisdom, good birth, and being "well disposed to religion."[66] Captain Robert Hunt was chosen and sent with a new commission in the *Blessing* in May 1636.

Providence Island was placed on a new footing, not only by its change of governor but also because the settlers had successfully repelled a Spanish attack in July 1635, news of which had come to the company

---

63. PIC to Gov. and Coun., 5–10–32, pts. 34, 40, 43, 45; PIC to Bell, 5–10–32.
64. On Halhead and Rishworth, see Chapters 2 and 5. Gates was back in England by 1634 seeking forgiveness for an unspecified fault and offering to return to the island even as a servant if necessary. The company allowed him to return but not to be a councilor. PIC Ct., 6–9–34; PIC to Gov. and Coun., 9–34; Jessop to Jo. Purdy, 8–11–34, B. L. Add MS 10615, no. 23.
65. PIC to Gov. and Coun., 9–34. For complaints, see PIC Ct., 6–21–34, 2–5–35; and PIC to Camock, 9–34, and to Axe, 9–34.
66. PIC Ct., 5–2–35. These were orthodox qualities; see Breen, *The Character of the Good Ruler*, 8.

in December. The investors were overwhelmed by God's "gracious . . . deliverance" and rededicated themselves to the venture. They decreed that all fines, imprisonments, and suspensions "for matter of crime, and misdemeanor that stood upon record at the day whereon your deliverance was through God's mercy obtained" were to be freely remitted, although the company still intended to examine them.

The company admonished the colonists to obey and assist Captain Hunt by their oaths to "this government" and "the allegiance that you owe to his Majesty," thus indicating continuing ambiguity over whether Providence Island was a unit of government under the Crown or simply company property. In a parenthetical expression, the investors wrote that Captain Bell was to remain on the council and that they would "hereafter further consider his former services." Hunt's own instructions urged him to give his predecessor "all the respect to his own person that may be convenient." The adventurers privately sought to reassure Captain Bell that they would respect good service and would be "very moderate and willing to hear your defense in any thing which hath been or shall be objected against you where we cannot deny but there have been many particulars." Rather than being "transported with any jealousy," they hoped Bell would carry on cheerfully.[67]

In their own deliberations, company members, appalled by the many accusations against Governor Bell, had considered removing him "as a delinquent" and had been forestalled only by consideration of the implications of appearing to prejudge a case unheard, especially after such a dramatic sign of God's favor on the island under his governorship.[68] Instead, they decided to weaken his position by removing his principal allies. The adventurers spoke vaguely of finding some "sea employment" for Captain Elfrith, but he remained a further two years and never received a privateering commission from them. William Rous was to captain the *Blessing*, the ship carrying the company's letters, in privateering as long as its supplies held, and then was to return with it to England to inform the company of the state of the island. Hunt was advised to keep watch in case Captain Bell should nevertheless attempt to "make a dangerous party in the Island."[69]

Philip Bell's world collapsed around him with his replacement by Robert Hunt. Governor Hunt was prepared to countenance any and all complaints against his predecessor and allowed Bell's enemies to hound

67. PIC to Gov. and Council, 5–36; PIC to Bell, 5–36; PIC Instr. to Hunt, 5–36.
68. For a time in early 1636, when it appeared that Captain Hunt would have to delay his departure, the investors considered sending an interim governor so as to be able to remove Philip Bell, PIC, mtgs. 2/3–36.
69. PIC Gen. Ct., 3–2–36. Privateering had been authorized by the government in retaliation for the Spanish attack.

him mercilessly, even removing his servants and slaves from his service. The governor allowed men to testify against Bell without taking an oath, "which we do by no means allow to be claimed or received as a privilege, annexed to any man's place, in any case whatsoever."[70] The council tried to force Bell to show them letters sent to him alone.[71] The company responded indignantly that these attacks on Bell's conduct of his office amounted to attacks on the company and that they created discord where Hunt had been commanded to sow the seeds of peace. Proceedings under Hunt smacked of using public justice to settle private differences, an offense compounded by denial of the respect due a man of Philip Bell's status.[72]

Company support quickly eroded when Bell returned to England in 1637 and demanded recompense for his years of service. In 1634 the Earl of Warwick himself had urged Bell to "expect all noble wage from the Company which have employed you." In 1635 Jessop wrote the obviously anxious Bell that "if the whole work do not dissolve into nothing, your former pains and merit will not pass away without recompense answering their own worth and former engagement."[73]

In accordance with their decision to avoid paying salaries in England, the company had promised Bell thirty-two servants and 100 acres of land, but he had never received the full complement of men.[74] On June

70. Some puritans considered oath taking, invoking God's name, to be dangerous as a routine practice. An oath was an act of worship, and many of the godly sort resisted oath taking with the ungodly. Increase Mather later denounced "Solemn Oaths upon trivial differences," *An Earnest Exhortation to the Inhabitants of New-England, 1676,* in Richard Slotkin and James K. Folsom, eds., *So Dreadfull a Judgment: Puritan Responses to King Philip's War, 1676–1677* (Middletown, CT, 1978), 180. On oaths and their significance, see E. Brooks Holifield, *Era of Persuasion: American Thought and Culture, 1521–1680* (Boston, 1989), 114–18, and Stephen Foster, "The Godly in Transit: English Popular Protestantism and the Creation of a Puritan Establishment in America," in David D. Hall and David Grayson Allen, eds., *Seventeenth-Century New England,* Col. Soc. of Mass. Pubs., vol. 63 (Boston, 1984), 234.

New Haven colony normally conducted judicial proceedings without requiring oaths; Marcus, "Criminal Procedure in New Haven," in Hall, Murrin, Tate, eds., *Saints and Revolutionaries,* 112–14, 120. See also Murrin, "Trial by Jury in Seventeenth-Century New England," ibid., 175.

71. Wm. Jessop to Ens. Fitch, 4–7–36, B. L. Add. MS 10615, no. 155.

72. PIC to Gov. and Coun. by the *Mary Hope,* 3–37. See the testimony of Samuel Rishworth to the company, PIC Ct., 6–22–37. See also William Jessop's letters of support to Bell 4–5–36 and 4–17–37, B. L. Add. MS 10615, nos. 154, 158.

Contrast Bell's experience under Captain Hunt with his own account of his tender treatment of his predecessors in Bermuda; Bell to Somers Islands Company, ca. 3–27, in Ives, ed., *Letters from Bermuda,* 283–93.

73. Warwick to Bell, 8–15–34; Jessop to Bell, 4–6–35, B. L. Add. MS 10615, nos. 41, 80.

74. Company commitments appear in PIC to Bell, 5–10–32, 4–10–33, 9–34.

14, 1637, he appeared before a committee consisting of Lords Saye and Brooke, John Pym, and company husband William Woodcock and described the state of the island. He presented "certain propositions" which were read only after his withdrawal.[75] Captain Bell renewed his request at the general court of November 27, "offering to refer the same to indifferent men if the Company shall please or to themselves in assurance of their nobleness." On December 11, the general court discussed his demands, which Bell based on the argument that for much of his five-year term he had lacked as many as twenty-five of the promised servants. Figuring the value of a servant at £10 per annum, the amount owed him came to £1,250; if the value of a servant was figured at 200 pounds of tobacco a year, then he was owed £1,046.14.2.[76]

The company argued that the promise of thirty-two servants was not made until May 1632 and that Captain Bell himself had suggested at various times that they delay sending many servants until the island was ready for them. Some servants they had sent had run away or died. Moreover, the company had remitted many of the governor's debts to them in partial compensation for their failure to send him men, and they had given him additional allowances. Finally, Bell had drastically overestimated the value both of a servant's labor and of the tobacco exported from Providence Island. Company members used some of his own letters to argue their case.[77]

The following month the exchange became heated. Bell answered the company's exceptions before a committee, using "some expressions, which the Company interpreted to be unfit to be offered." Once more citing their reluctance to pay money in England for service in the Indies, the committee members offered Bell a loan of £50. At this point, he held a trump card: The company's suit in the Admiralty Courts concerning Spanish attacks on Providence Island required his testimony.[78] In February 1638, dissatisfied with further exceptions drawn up by John Pym, Bell asked that the matter be referred to arbitration and suggested his brother Sir Robert Bell, London merchant and Virginia

---

75. PIC, Ctee. at Brooke House, 6–14–37.
76. Contemporaneous Virginia estimates placed the production value of a servant much higher. In the 1620s colonists put the number of plants a worker could tend at 2,000 to 3,000, with each four plants producing one pound of tobacco. A servant tending 2,000 plants would make 500 pounds of tobacco. See Russell Menard, "The Tobacco Industry in the Chesapeake Colonies, 1617–1730: An Interpretation," *Research in Economic History* 5 (1980), 145–46.
77. PIC Gen. Ct., 11–27–37, 12–11–37.
78. PIC, Ctee. at Brooke House, 1–22–38.

investor, for his side. The committee chose John Hampden as their arbitrator, allowing the two men to choose an umpire if necessary. The adventurers refused to promise to abide by the award, arguing that a committee of five men (Darley, Mandeville, Saye, Brooke, and Pym were present) could not bind the entire company. The arbitrators set to work immediately, with the company delaying its general court to receive the results.[79]

In the event, Bell refused to accept the arbitrators' award and, now demanding payment of a £500 annuity, petitioned the king to refer the case to the Lord Keeper, Sir Thomas Coventry. Late in 1638 the Lord Keeper ruled that individuals could not be bound by promises given under the company's seal and that in any case there was "no Color" for the demand of a £500 annuity or for any recompense other than the value of the crops that thirty-two servants could have raised during Bell's term. Coventry asked for a commission to examine witnesses and decide the true value of thirty-two servants, but again rehearsing all their arguments, the company refused to participate, saying that evidence contained in the correspondence already submitted was more reliable than the "witness of any particular person." The letters affirmed that 100 pounds of tobacco was the normal product of one servant's annual labor, with 200 being possible in some circumstances. Captain Bell, sensing the end of his hopes, then approached the company to ask that the Earl of Holland, governor of the Providence Island Company, decide the matter.[80]

Captain Bell began to shore up his eroding position by demanding payments for cattle and equipment sold in the island. In the middle of 1640, he finally offered simply to take the award determined by the arbitrators. John Pym offered him £20 for his cattle, and Bell, who dropped out of the company records at this point, went away to consider.[81] Late in 1640 he was given permission to lead a party to settle on the West Indian island of St. Lucia, but by June of 1641 he was in Barbados, where he became governor (but with the title of deputy governor). Mrs. Bell, who had remained in Providence Island after her husband left, asked the company for 800 pounds of tobacco for her husband's plantation, as well as £10 "in part of what's due to her." The company promised to consider her request.[82]

79. PIC Ct., 2–5–38; Ctee., 2–6–38; Gen. Ct., 2–8, 9, 12, 13, 14, 22–38.
80. PIC Ct., 5–30–38; 6–6–38; Gen. Ct., 11–22–38; Ct., 1–28–39; 2–12–39.
81. PIC Ct., 5–23–39; 7–5–39; 5–7–40; 6–20–40.
82. PIC Ct., 6–26–40. Philip Bell was granted a license to lead 140 colonists to St. Lucia, November 29, 1640; *Acts of the Privy Council*, Colonial Series, I (London,

The fate of friendless Captain Bell's demands symbolizes the relationship of the entire project to its London adventurers with their manifold connections and diverse projects. As the grandees had undercut his governorship, they then devalued his service. At the same time, Philip Bell recognized that he was more at home in the Indies than in England and once again cast his lot in with a colonial venture.

1908), 290. On Bell's governorship of Barbados, see J. Scott, "Description of Barbados," ca. 1667, B. L. Sloane MS 3662, fols. 56–62; Gary A. Puckrein, *Little England: Plantation Society and Anglo-Barbadian Politics, 1627–1700* (New York, 1984), 52, 92–4; Dunn, *Sugar and Slaves*, 17, 79.

4

Frustrated Hopes for Economic Development

COLONIES WERE VASTLY EXPENSIVE ENTERPRISES, always soaking up sums far greater than the original investors ever imagined. Plantations were begun in exaggerated hopes of rich commodities; expectations of fabulous returns were particularly elevated in the case of southern regions. The correspondence between planters in the early English colonies and their backers in England always took on a semihysterical tone in consequence, as the investors urged the settlers to send them products of value, and quickly. Planters were caught in a classic bind: They praised the richness and fertility of their land to keep backers committed to the project; but when the promised products failed to appear and adventurers' costs mounted alarmingly, recriminations against the settlers inevitably followed.

Much of the mythology of development focused on the engendering power of heat. Not only rich crops but minerals as well were thought to be generated by the sun's rays in the hot regions of the earth. Minerals such as gold and silver were thought to grow or form in the earth and then to be drawn to the surface by the magnetic power of the sun.[1] Moreover, analysts argued that hot climates were most fruitful and the crops produced in them most rich; the "Sun with his masculine force" fructified the "teeming" feminine earth.[2]

---

1. Gabriel Plattes, *A Discovery of Subterraneall Treasure, viz. Of all manner of Mines and Minerals, from the Gold to the Coale; with plaine Directions and Rules for the finding of them in all Kingdomes and Countries* (London, 1639), 2–3, 35–9; Roger Barlow, *A Brief Summe of Geographie* (1540–1541), ed. E. G. R. Taylor (London, 1932), 179–80.
2. Ligon, *True and Exact History of Barbadoes*, 84; Virginia Company, *A True declaration of the Estate of the Colonie in Virginia*, 1610, in Force, comp., *Tracts*, III, no. 1, 12–13; John Hagthorpe, *Englands Exchequer. Or a Discourse of the sea and navigation, with somthing thereto coincident concerning plantation* (London, 1625), 28–33.

   For a fuller discussion of these issues, see Karen Ordahl Kupperman, "Fear of Hot Climates in the Anglo-American Colonial Experience," *William and Mary Quarterly* 3rd ser., XLI (1984), 217–19.

Many writers whose credibility was fortified by firsthand experience argued that lucrative trades could be set up with southern regions almost from the very beginning of plantation. For example, Robert Harcourt, whose experience in Guiana dated back to 1609, wrote *A Relation of a voyage to Guiana* (London, 1613), which was republished in 1626. In it he argued that a colony there would cost nothing to maintain and that valuable cargoes of precious woods and spices, brought to the settlement by the Indians, could be sent home immediately.[3] No gap caused by awkward beginnings need occur.

Those on both sides of the Atlantic who were interested in Providence Island had additional reasons to seek enrichment. Return on investment was obviously necessary to continued support of the venture. Not even the wealthiest grandee could pour in money forever. But the adventurers were also convinced that they were doing God's work in establishing a godly community in the Indies to help solve England's problems. Economic success was essential to the kind of stability and harmony that would allow true religious values to prosper. If colonists could eliminate fears about providing for themselves and their families and about handing on a settlement to their children, then they could focus their attention on what really mattered: cooperation in fostering the worship of God and, through helping England, protection of reformed religion.

Providence, the name of this colony in the Indies, was not invoked lightly. All involved in the venture saw clearly that they had indeed cast themselves on the providence of God by venturing into the heart of the territory of Spain, enemy both to England and to true religion. Because the stakes were so high, the project could prosper only through God's intervention. Success in their island of Providence would be the result of God's favor shining on them. Failure would mean that God had found them wanting in their actions and had not favored them. John Winthrop's warning to the puritans who chose Massachusetts Bay could just as well have been addressed to the Providence Island emigrants: "[I]f we shall deal falsely with our god in this work we have undertaken and so cause him to withdraw his present help from us, we shall be made a story and a by-word through the world...."[4] For this reason, the quest to find and establish a suitable selection of tropical commodities in the colony was crucial to the godly experiment.

---

3. Harcourt, *The relation of a voyage to Guiana, now newly reviewed and enlarged* (1613; 2nd ed. 1626), 48–50, 80–81.
4. Winthrop, "A Modell of Christian Charity," 1630, *Winthrop Papers*, II, 282–295, quote 295.

Southern locations presented particular problems because colonists were unfamiliar with their environments and crops. Some plantations were successful; many failed. Examination of the successes reveals a similar trajectory: Colonies such as Barbados and Virginia limped through about a decade of discouragement, producing little or nothing. After this initial period of failure, those plantations destined for prosperity developed a staple crop of such economic power that they took off financially. Other problems facing colonies that survived were solved as part of this fruition. What was required for such a culmination? In successful colonies, some planters took on the task of finding and experimenting with crops that would grow in their environment. These planters absorbed repeated failure, sometimes over many years, but kept testing different seeds and techniques until the right combination was discovered. The Providence Island Company constantly urged such a course of action on their colonists but were as constantly disappointed. This chapter examines why the planters in Providence Island failed to take up that challenge.

Providence Island began like its near-contemporary, Barbados. Although early letters promised a wide range of products, especially grapevines, citrus fruits, ginger, sugarcane, and dyewoods, only poor-quality tobacco came from the plantation in its early years. The adventurers, veterans of the Virginia and Somers Islands Companies, had warned against reliance on tobacco, and early in 1631 the Privy Council had tried, through directives and taxes, to command the American plantations to diversify by planting "real commodities." The government ordered severe limitations on tobacco planting to avoid the "speedy ruin" that threatened the colonies and the "danger to the bodies and manners of the English people" carried by this popular weed that Lord Brooke called "that killing-saving Indian herb, Hen-man-bane."[5] Tobacco was an unworthy as well as an unreliable product in an easily glutted market, but it was the only crop the experienced settlers knew well.

Colonists were hit with a veritable barrage of advice and instructions about the products they should grow. The range and variety of directions are the best indicators of the investors' woeful ignorance of the West Indian environment, its agriculture and products, a condition that persisted throughout the colony's life. The instructions sent out in 1632 commanded settlers, already pressed by the requirement that they contribute labor to the public works and worried about basic subsistence,

5. C. S. P. Col., 1574–1660, 124–25; Lord Brooke, *The Nature of Truth* (London, 1640), facs. ed. with intro by V. de Sola Pinto, n.p. 1969, 129–30.

to experiment with a bewildering variety of plants and semiindustrial processes. Silk grass was expected to be a good commodity. The adventurers approved of colonists' resolution to try to get some from the mainland. The colonists were urged to plant a large quantity and send some home for experimentation. The investors accepted the planters' report that, of the two kinds of cotton growing naturally on the island, the fibers of one were too short for spinning. But had they thought it might be good for some other uses? Send some home for trial. Meanwhile, better cotton seeds were being sought in the other islands.

The company also accepted colonists' claim that the island was not fit for large-scale sugar plantations but ordered them to plant some for their own use and "for the island's ornament."[6] They should also procure and plant mulberry trees, taking great care that goats and cows be kept on a small outlying island to protect the valuable plants.

The company sent directly to the governor a sealed box filled with seeds, "which we suppose to be the seeds of Palma Christi," to be "tenderly regarded" by him. Palma Christi, *Ricinus communis*, also called the castor oil plant, bears an oil-producing seed. John Josselyn reported that it "was thought to be the plant that shaded Jonah the Prophet." It was introduced into the Indies by the Spanish from Africa in 1520 and spread widely. At the time in the 1630s when it was being urged on the Providence Island settlers, it was also brought to the Leeward Islands, including St. Kitts and Barbados. Livestock find it unpalatable, and it spreads easily; by 1645 there were "infinite numbers of those shrubs" in St. Kitts.[7] Such a product could be of immense value to the English economy, because the textile industry used large quantities of soap that had to be made with a sweet-smelling oil. Soap made from the only sure domestic source of oil, fish oil, imparted an ineradicable odor to the finished cloth. Thus, a secure supply of a sweet oil from an English possession would help to rebuild the English textile industry.

The Providence Island Company, proud of having obtained the seeds, was very enthusiastic about Palma Christi:

> By the little experience made of them in other parts it appears, That they will grow eight Foot high in Three Months. That one acre will bear 300 Trees, That one tree will bear a bushel of seeds, That this

6. Contemporary Providence Islanders do grow a small amount of sugar for their own use and for distilling into rum. See Wilson, *Crab Antics*, 83–4.
7. John Josselyn, *An Account of Two Voyages to New-England*, 1674, ed. Paul J. Lindholdt (Hanover, NH, 1988), 53; Father Andrew White, "A Briefe Relation of the Voyage unto Maryland," 1634, in C. C. Hall, ed., *Narratives of Early Maryland, 1633–1684* (New York, 1910), 35; David Watts, *The West Indies: Patterns of Development, Culture and Environmental Change Since 1492* (Cambridge, 1987), 114–16, 162.

bushel of seed will make 3 Gallons of oil, so generally useful, That there is no Fear of glutting by its Quantity nor of meanness of price in its Sale. So that if it shall please God to second his good Providence in their procuring with a blessing on your Industry in planting them, we doubt not but they will lay a Foundation of profit sufficient to repay our expences, And to recompence your Labour (which in this will not be great) within short Time, though the Island were able to produce no other staple Commoditie.

The adventurers promised to send equipment soon for extracting the oil.

In the same shipment, the investors sent two rhubarb roots, one to be entrusted to Governor Bell, the other to Captain Rudyerd. Like the Palma Christi plants, once flourishing, the rhubarb was to be dispersed throughout the island. They also sent seeds in case the roots failed to take hold.[8] They also sent canary vines, which they urged the planters to cherish. It was thought that the vines would thrive best on the north or northwest side of the island, but the planters were urged to try all ways. Two pots of "scorsonra roots" were included for the settlers to put in the ground; further instructions would be forthcoming by the next ship. Scorzonera, black salsify, was used as a root vegetable. It was also thought to have medicinal properties. Sometimes called viper's grass, it was believed to cure snakebite. Finally, the company simply said: "There be other seeds sent of several sorts whereof we require your care."[9]

Thomas Punt, master of the *Seaflower*, which carried these instructions, was commanded to stop at St. Kitts, Nevis, or Barbados to take on fresh water and also cotton seed and pomegranate slips. On the way he was to stop at the island of Association (Tortuga, just north of Haiti), whose English planters had voluntarily come under the adventurers' protection. He was to pick up good tobacco seeds, guinny pepper for planting and use, and any other fruits he thought might be useful in Providence.[10]

The next year, 1633, the company sent another barrage of commands. The colonists' tobacco was so poor it yielded only 1 groat profit per

---

8. Rhubarb was valued as a medicine for its purgative effect. *Rheum rhaponticum*, the rhubarb used in cuisine today, was introduced into Europe in the late sixteenth century. The investors may have sent Chinese rhubarb, whose root produced a valuable drug, or *Morinda Citrifolia*, native to the West Indies, whose roots also produce a purgative effect. See Samuel Eliot Morison, ed. and trans., *Journals and Other Documents on the Life and Voyages of Christopher Columbus* (New York, 1963), 141 n.
9. PIC, Instr. to Gov. and Coun., 5–10–32, pts. 30, 46.
10. PIC, Instr. to Punt, 5–8–32.

pound, "which may justly slack your pace in the pursuit of that commoditie." Stocks in their warehouse in 1633 were first offered for sale at 16 pence per pound. Within a week company agents had dropped the price to 14 pence, and finally to 13.[11] Tobacco had brought high prices in the early 1620s, but the boom ended by 1624; when Providence Island was founded in 1629, prices were at their lowest. In 1633, when the Providence Island investors were trying to discourage their colonists from growing tobacco, there was the beginning of a short-lived recovery in prices, but it was over by 1637 because tobacco imports into England had risen dramatically in the 1630s.[12] Cotton was far more promising in the short run. Settlers were urged to concentrate on cotton "till better things may be obtained and brought to perfection which will in Time be greater profit."[13]

Governor Bell was directed to send men to Henrietta Island (San Andreas), which also belonged to the adventurers, to gather "Mechoacan commonly called wild potatoes, to the value of a tunne if so much may be had." The company had sent a piece, dried, which was to serve as a pattern; colonists must slice and dry the plants in the sun, pack them in dry casks, and return by the next ship, "it being a drug of value."[14]

Meanwhile, the company had not forgotten its promise to introduce lucrative commodities and the equipment to process them. In 1633 the adventurers sent an "engine" to help process cotton and a mill to extract oil from oilseeds.[15] They also sent Mr. Richard Lane, a godly man and protégé of Lord Brooke, to supervise the planting of the valuable dye madder and to teach the colonists its care. Governor Bell was warned to assign Lane land of his choice immediately; the madder plants must not be out of earth any longer than absolutely necessary.[16]

Madder was a dye widely used in the English textile industry, second only to woad. All were imported, woad and indigo usually from England's enemies, and madder generally from the Low Countries. During the

---

11. PIC, Ctee. 5–28–33; 6–3–33; 6–7–33. A groat was worth four pence.
12. Russell R. Menard, "A Note on Chesapeake Tobacco Prices, 1618–1660," *Virginia Magazine of History and Biography* 84 (1976), 401–10; Menard, "The Tobacco Industry in the Chesapeake Colonies, 1617–1730: An Interpretation," *Research in Economic History* 5 (1980), 109–77. A witness in an equity case before the High Court of Admiralty concerning tobacco brought home in a ship named the *Charity* said that vessels carrying tobacco from Virginia or St. Christopher's usually carried the cargo to Holland if the price in England was low; Peter Wilson Coldham, *English Adventurers and Emigrants, 1609–1660: Abstracts of Examinations in the High Court of Admiralty with Reference to Colonial America* (Baltimore, 1984), 39.
13. PIC to Gov. and Coun., 4–10–33; 7–20–33; PIC to Bell, 4–10–33.
14. PIC to Bell, 7–1–33. Mechoacan was used as a purgative.
15. PIC to Gov. and Coun., 7–20–33.
16. PIC to Bell, 4–10–33.

1620s, the price of madder rose dramatically, and projectors tried to encourage its culture in England. Madder produced by English servants on Providence Island could be a major boon to the textile industry. It was less controversial and considered more reliable than logwood and the other dyewoods the adventurers hoped to import. In different combinations, madder could produce colors from true reds through purples, light blue, and even black. At the other end of the spectrum, it could color cloth orange or yellow. Its drawback was a long period to maturity; three years were required before the first harvest.[17]

All through these early years, negative reports filtered back to individual investors; these are referred to in company correspondence, but most are now lost. One, a letter from Captain William Rudyerd, Lieutenant William Rous, Roger Floude, and John Brigham, possibly addressed to John Pym in October 1633, was calendared by the Historical Manuscripts Commission. These men began negatively: "We do not find here the largeness that was reported." They reported drought conditions, which had brought "hardness' to many, and remarked that Providence Island would never glut the tobacco market. In emulating Spanish practice of storing the tobacco a year before sending it home, they found that "worms eat our rafters, and the dust falling on our tobacco hinders the burning, and makes the taste bitter." Tropical fruit trees flourished but did not bear, and their main food was potatoes. "Whatever others may relate, this is the truth."[18]

Providence Island Company members were deeply distressed by such reports and their venture's continuing failure. Would God's providence not shine on it? The company was in continuous session, meeting every few days throughout May, June, and July 1634 in long, searching discussions desperately seeking better direction for the future. Attention now focused on a kind of silkgrass discovered growing on the mainland near Cape Gracias a Dios by a company expedition led by Sussex Camock. The investors directed that it be transplanted to Providence Island. Henceforth, it was to be known as Camock's flax. This fiber, for whose development the adventurers received a monopoly patent, was lauded as the answer to all the island's problems.[19]

17. Eric Kerridge, *Textile Manufactures in Early Modern England* (Manchester, 1985), 166–68; Joan Thirsk, gen. ed., *The Agrarian History of England and Wales*, V, vol. II; *1640–1750: Agrarian Change* (Cambridge, 1985), 341, 538. On the controversy over logwood, see Russell, *Parliaments and English Politics*, 63, and Arthur M. Wilson, "The Logwood Trade in the Seventeenth and Eighteenth Centuries," in Donald C. McKay, ed., *Essays in the History of Modern Europe* (New York, 1936), 1–15.
18. Historical Manuscripts Commission, 19th *Report*, Appendix, Part VI (1887), Bouverie MSS, 85.
19. See Chapter 10.

Like its predecessors, the letter carrying this news also brought commands to find, grow, and experiment with a huge list of products. Captain Camock would be sending slips of many drug plants to the island; even though no one knew their prospects, they "may be a foundation of future Advantage." The company suggested that, because the new plants would only replace other trees, "the experiment cannot be very troublesome, nor at all prejudicial." Settlers were urged to continue to work on the tomarin, a red dye of which Captain Elfrith had sent samples that had been found to be worth 2 shillings a pound.[20] It would be a good commodity if not too time-consuming to produce. If indigo could thrive, the colonists were not to neglect it. "There is also a sort of long pepper growing about Captain Rudyerd's fort (as we are informed) we would have it preserved, and whatsoever grows upon those trees to be sent to us for a pattern, it being likely to prove itself worthy of respect." Planters were also to send "good quantity" of the red pepper called Guinny pepper.

The mechoacan brought from Providence Island by the surgeon "is as good as ever came into England," therefore more was to be sent. He had also mentioned a drug he called jallop, and the company wanted some sent home. The investors still hoped that the cotton growing wild in the island, of which the company had received a sample, could be made "serviceable." Therefore, they would like 500 pounds or more to be shipped home "if you shall not spend too much time in the gathering of it."[21] Noting the upward price curve in 1634, the adventurers removed their prohibition on tobacco; with it and cotton the plantation could at least be maintained until something better was developed. At the same time, following the advice of Governor Bell, they set prices (6 pence per pound for cotton and 10 pence for tobacco) at which they would accept planters' produce in exchange for goods from the stores. These prices, at which the company expected to lose money, were to be continued for one year only.[22]

At the end of all these orders, the company accepted the colonists' evidence that the island was too hot for the oilseeds from which they had earlier hoped so much and allowed them "to let the further trial

---

20. The company had written about tomarin in their Instr. to Gov. and Coun., 5–10–32, pt. 47.
21. Cotton, annotto (*bixa orellana*), and indigo were cultivated by West Indian natives before the arrival of the Europeans; Watts, *West Indies*, 65.
22. In 1636 company secretary William Jessop wrote to Ensign Fitch that he had sold as much of his tobacco as he could for 17 pence; "If I had kept it longer by me, I might have gained 1d or 2d more in the price and have lost 3d or 4d in the shrinkage." B. L. Add MS 10615, no. 153.

thereof fall."²³ Clearly, many of these newly recommended commodities would also fail. The adventurers offered no suggestions about how responsibility for these myriad products was to be divided up, nor on compensation for those colonists who put their energies into unfeasible ventures.

These directions were written in the summer of 1634; the company had not communicated with their settlers formally for a year, during which discouragement had become rampant on the island. In July 1633 the investors had commanded the colonists to demonstrate their industry by stockpiling commodities, particularly cotton, and promised to send vessels to pick up such products when they would be ready. During the ensuing long wait for news and supplies, the planters came to feel, as they wrote the adventurers in December 1633, "like forsaken Indians."

Saying that the colonists "might well have spared" that term, the company explained the situation as they saw it. They wrote of their enormous expenses without any shred of recompense. How long could they continue to put money into a losing enterprise? Convinced as they were of the rich fertility of Providence Island, they asserted again and again that the problem was human failure. Every letter from the colony detailed the wrangling and conflict among the settlers, and particularly among the leadership; if planters put some of that energy into working on their crops, then success would come. The adventurers were amazed that the colonists seemed to have so little grasp of the stakes involved in the enterprise.

Everything was circular. The *Long Robert*, sailing in the autumn of 1634, carried fewer servants than the colonists were expecting. This meant that not only would gentleman–planters be stinted ("we hope that they have learned to wait with patience as well as we"), but servants whose time was expiring and who had been attracted to Providence Island partly by the promise of a servant and land upon their freedom would just have to wait. And whose fault was that? There was little point in sending servants if no established crops existed for them to work on; they would only be a drain on the island's food supplies. Moreover, no one wanted to come anymore, largely because the complaining letters of the settlers had put intending emigrants off.²⁴

So great was colonists' discouragement that many had written requesting permission to come home. The company tried to dissuade

23. PIC to Gov. and Coun. by the *Long Robert*, 9–34. Oilseed cultivation also failed on Bermuda; Henry C. Wilkinson, *The Adventurers of Bermuda*, 2nd ed. (London, 1958), 219.
24. Secretary Hunt testified that he lost £20 plus all his labor in three years on Providence Island, PIC Ctee 6–27–34.

them, arguing that the island was finally on the verge of financial success, particularly from the Camock's flax, and that it would be foolish to abandon their efforts now after enduring all the hardships. They looked for a "new courage" in the settlers and for renewed commitment to the joint task. Nonetheless, acknowledging that free men had the right to remove, they directed the governor and council to allow those who had satisfied their debts to the stores to leave. No one was to hold a plantation on Providence Island as an absentee, however; those who left must sell their interest because the adventurers were determined "to preserve the Island from coming wholly into the hands of servants and factors."[25] Many planters did leave, including Captain William Rudyerd, who testified before the company's general court that "the Island in respect of itself is not worth keeping."[26]

Hopeful official letters were written in July and August 1634 when many company members were in London. Unfortunately, by the time the *Long Robert* actually sailed in September, the instructions and the expectations underlying them had become largely irrelevant, as can be seen in the shorthand notes of private letters kept by company secretary William Jessop. Jessop wrote to men who were particular clients of Providence Island investors with special encouragement and instructions. His constant refrain was that fulfillment depended on two elements: godly harmony and economic success. Neither could come without the other. He urged each of his correspondents to redouble efforts to transplant Camock's flax from the mainland.

Then, at the very end of August 1634, the *Elizabeth* arrived from Providence Island with news that silk grass did not thrive there: "[T]he great hopes of the Camock's flax in the Island have disappeared and come to nothing." Because the investors were scattered in the country, Jessop had no choice but to send the letters already prepared and to urge his correspondents to try again with the flax.[27] The planters, who had waited for more than a year for a response from home, received letters that were obsolete even before they left England, and they were once again left to their own devices. Given largely useless new instructions from the adventurers, many colonists did leave Providence Island in 1634, although some of these were to return later. Those who remained took advantage of the company's grudging permission and largely devoted themselves to tobacco.

25. PIC to Gov. and Coun., and to Bell by the *Long Robert*, 9–34.
26. PIC, Gen. Ct., 6–21–34.
27. Jessop Letterbook, B. L. Add MS 10615, items 23–62; quote in postscript to letter to Lt. Hugh Price, item 62.

Company members had little conception of what it would take to establish a viable cash crop in a new plantation whose environment differed so much from that which the settlers were used to. Nor did they understand the degree of expertise involved in the cultivation and processing of each plant. Drawing on their fallacious assumption that rich soil and tropical heat equaled unparalleled fertility, they apparently assumed that the colonists could merely put seeds or slips in the ground and wait for valuable commodities to grow. Most of the plants they suggested were labor-intensive; many would require attention at the same time of year. Crops such as madder had only recently been introduced into England, and expertise was strictly limited even in that familiar setting. Yet, the investors directed Richard Lane, their expert in madder cultivation sent out in 1633, to plant his slips, instruct his servants in their care, and then leave the island on another mission. While he was gone, his servants "shall clear ground, plant provisions, take care of the madder, and do all other things according to the usual custom of servants for their own maintenance and the profit of our selves and their said Master."[28] Thus, while this important new crop was first tried, no one who knew about its culture would be there to confront problems as they arose. Too many avenues of enterprise were being pursued simultaneously for any of them to succeed.

Even tobacco, a crop whose needs and characteristics some of the colonists knew well, required broad experience and constant attention for successful production. In 1632 the company directed the governor and council, in order to maintain the island's reputation, to have all tobacco inspected and to allow only "merchantable" leaves shipped home. The adventurers thought that "the badness of your tobacco arises from the illness of your seed" from the Somers Islands, so they undertook to get better. The island's leaders must then see that planters cut off all but the "principal leaves," because too many leaves "suck out the virtue of the plant. And make the tobacco weaker and worse." Poor-quality tobacco was to be kept for a year to see if it could become merchantable.[29]

All this was good advice, but it required experience to follow. Tobacco was so notoriously difficult to produce well that throughout the colonial period successful planters took great pride in their skill.[30] They expected

28. PIC to Bell, 4–10–33; PIC to Lane, 4–15–33.
29. PIC, Instr. Gov. and Coun., 5–10–32, pt. 33.
30. Lois Green Carr, Russsell R. Menard, and Lorena S. Walsh, *Robert Cole's World: Agriculture and Society in Early Maryland* (Chapel Hill, 1991), 55–65; T. H. Breen, *Tobacco Culture: The Mentality of the Great Tidewater Planters on the Eve of the Revolution* (Princeton, 1985), 46–58.

only one in ten of the seedlings they planted to survive. Each plant received weekly attention, keeping weeds at bay and removing the flowering top and suckers, or side-growth. Knowing when to perform these operations, or the more crucial one of harvesting, was crucial: "[E]xperience alone can enable a person to judge when tobacco is fully ripe."[31] Once cut, the tobacco had to be cured or dried, an even more delicate operation; much tobacco was lost during this process or became unsalable.[32]

Like the many ostensibly more valuable crops urged on their colonists by the Providence Island Company, tobacco required an enormous investment in time and effort before it could be produced confidently and reliably. The barrage of instructions emanating from London with each ship denigrated the colonists' effort and time by assuming that planters could simultaneously acquire, plant, and master a myriad of crops, eliminating those that would not thrive. The investors put considerable effort into acquiring the best seed, but they seemed relatively blind to the need for skill and experience in cultivation and processing.

Such blindness may have stemmed from unwillingness to saturate the population with old Caribbean hands who would pollute the substantial godly pool sent from England. Occasionally, the records allow glimpses of company efforts to gain the fruits of expertise without allowing the expert to take over. The drug mechoacan was seen as being potentially very valuable. The company's early instructions had simply directed the colonists to find and process a ton of it. Later, realizing that as with all West Indian commodities, experience was essential to its production, the company told Governor Bell "in our name to command Trippett the gunner to discover to you the true way of making Mechoachan." He was to "make it before you" and other men selected by Bell. Trippett was to be held on the island until he complied.[33] Licensing individuals to produce and market mechoacan might have produced better results, but the price in diverted profits would have been higher than the Providence Island Company was willing to pay. As it was, mechoacan was abandoned by 1636 as unprofitable; whether, like so many other

31. "The Method of Cultivating and Curing Tobacco in that part of Virginia which borders upon Maryland, as practised by Judge Parker, and communicated to the American Museum in 1798," in William Tatham, *An Historical and Practical Essay on the Culture and Commerce of Tobacco* (London, 1800), 118–29, esp. 125.
32. In 1637 William Jessop complained that tobacco in Bermuda was "freshly made up" in the casks, and most arrived in England "rotten" and unsalable; B. L. Add MS 10615, nos. 172, 173.
33. PIC to Bell by the *Expectation*, 34/5.

commodities taken up and quickly dropped, it could have been developed into a rewarding crop would never be seen.[34]

The adventurers (and their settlers) were in a double bind. Everyone agreed that economic success was essential to the godly aims for which the colony was founded, but none wanted to develop the social relations seen in other West Indian islands. The real question lay in the degree to which plantation societies were structured around the commodities they produced and the rhythms and relationships dictated by those crops. As long as the island was not dominated by Europeans with long Caribbean experience, that question could be seen as still open.

By 1634 the Providence Island colonists felt like "forsaken Indians" partly because they saw themselves slipping in the company's concerns; increasingly, the adventurers looked to trade with Indians on the mainland for the economic return to sustain their company. In investors' minds, these areas of endeavor were two parts of the same whole, with Providence Island serving as "a Refuge and Retreat upon all occasions, and the place to secure our Trade," but the settlers naturally feared that the island's role would be a subsidiary one.[35]

One of the great sustaining themes of English imperial strategy was the notion that the Indians of Spanish America looked upon the countrymen of "Don Francisco Draco" as liberators. The Black Legend of Spanish cruelty and exploitation drawn from the work of Bartolomé de las Casas richly supplied English Protestants brought up on Foxe's *Actes and Monuments* with vivid images of the suffering of the Indians and the welcome they would give to English ships.[36] Drake was a powerful symbol: a man who won the everlasting affection of the exploited by his good treatment, while keeping the Spanish in terror. Sir Walter Ralegh expected a liberator's welcome from the Indians in Guiana, and he was delighted that "my name hath still lived among them" on his long-delayed second visit. Robert Harcourt also reported that Ralegh's name was remembered by the Guiana Indians.[37]

The Duke of Buckingham reported an interview he held in Madrid in 1623 with "Don Fennyn, a Spanish Secretary," saying that the people

34. In 1636 Jessop advised Aaron Butcher to give up labor on mechoacan; B. L. Add MS 10615, no. 146.
35. This formula occurred in PIC to Gov. and Coun., 4–10–33.
36. For a particularly vivid rendition of the Black Legend, see Lewes Roberts, *The Merchants Mappe of Commerce* (London, 1638), 54–5, 62.
37. See Ralegh to Bess Throckmorton Ralegh, November 14, 1617, *The Works of Sir Walter Ralegh, Kt.* (Oxford, 1829), VIII, 630–2; Harcourt, *Relation of a Voyage to Guiana*, 2nd ed., 11–13.

of the Indies withheld from the hated Spaniards the secret locations of rich mines of gold and precious gems. Don Fennyn described the Indians as "besotted with a prediction, how that there shall come a nation unto them, with flaxen hair, white complexion, grey eyes, that shall govern them." They would gladly accept English sovereignty to be freed of Spanish tyranny. Robert Harcourt's *Relation of a voyage to Guiana*, republished in 1626, renewed the belief that the Indians would rise up to greet and aid the English and that God himself had, through repeated Spanish failures, reserved lands for them.[38]

The adventurers' plans were based on these assumptions. They expected to establish trading stations to which Indians would bring the valuable commodities of the Central American mainland to exchange for English manufactured goods. Providence Island could then be used as a safe storehouse for these products until they could be carried home. In addition, good crops could be transplanted to the island, thereby creating a healthy economy for the colonists.[39] In 1633, after a brief flurry of interest in finding and colonizing the mythical island of Fonseca, two trading ventures were begun. One was near Cape Gracias a Dios, the other at Darien. These trading ventures were clearly the focus of company hopes.

The Darien expedition, sent out in April, had been suggested by Captain Anthony Hilton, governor of Association Island. Hilton, whose island base had become an international trade center, declined to head up the Darien venture, so Richard Lane, having planted his madder on Providence Island, was to lead it, aided by an Indian who had been taken to London. The destination, the "Bay of Dureren [Darien] ... lies Southeast and by South from cape Catina not far from Porto Bello upon the continent of the West Indies." If the party perceived danger from Spanish ships or foul weather, their instructions vaguely said, the ship could hide in a "harbor lying thereabout (as we are informed between the maine and an Island called the Islea de Pinas)."[40]

Once landed, Lane was to seek out the "principal commanders" among the Indians and, mentioning "Don Francisco Draco," attain their friendship by judicious distribution of gifts. "You shall as much as you shall be able conceal the end of your coming, that the Inhabitants

38. "The Secret Discovery which Don Fennyn, a Spanish Secretary, made to the Duke of Buckingham, in the year 1623, at Madrid," *State Papers Collected by Edward Earl of Clarendon*, 3 vols. (Oxford, 1767–68), I, 14–15; Harcourt, *Relation of a voyage to Guiana*, B3v–B4, 11–13, 48–50, 82–3.
39. For a description of the Moskito Coast environment and products, see Robert A. Naylor, *Penny Ante Imperialism: the Mosquito Shore and the Bay of Honduras, 1600–1914* (Cranbury, NJ, 1989), chap. 1.
40. PIC, Gen. Ct., 2–15–33; 3–4–33; Instr. and Secret Instr. to Lane, 1633.

may conceive it to be out of a desire of renewing friendship with them, the ancient favourers of the English name . . . and to assist them against their enemies, rather than to make advantage of them by a trade for gold, or other commodities." While restraining his men from "boisterous carriage" toward the Indian women, particularly "mocking, pointing, or laughing at their nakedness," Lane was to find out what commodities of value the Indians possessed and what English goods they most prized. He was authorized to leave men behind to manage the trade in his absence.[41] This trade promised both riches and danger. In 1634 a Dutch ship captain who called at both the Bay of Darien and Providence Island testified that he had seen gold "about the Natives' necks," but the vice admiral of their little fleet, trying to force the pace of trading, was shot dead by an Indian dart.[42]

The trade at Cape Gracias a Dios was established under the command of Captain Sussex Camock, client of the Earl of Warwick and one of the Bermudian party that brought Providence Island to his attention through Sir Nathaniel Rich.[43] The Providence Island Company looked forward to establishment of a permanent English presence along the Moskito Coast. So seriously did they take this new area of enterprise that the investors applied for and won a new patent giving them exclusive rights to trade on the coast with "divers heathen people" between 6 and 24 degrees of latitude and 290 and 310 degrees of longitude. The patent also gave them sole rights to manufacture thread and cloth of "a kind of flag or grass brought from those parts and not in common use in this kingdom, which is by them called Camock's flax," or any other new materials imported by them from this region.[44]

Camock was seconded by men already employed by the company, Nathaniel Marston and Edward Williams, "who are acquainted with the Several natures and languages of the Indians, have received courteous usage in many parts of their Country, have had large promises of future

41. PIC Secret Instructions to Lane, April 15, 1633.
42. PIC, Ctee., 12–24–34.
43. Sussex Camock's brother Thomas had married Frances, daughter of the second Lord Rich and aunt of the Earl of Warwick. Thomas was prominent in Bermuda and had received 1,500 acres at Black Point in Maine arranged by Warwick through the Council for New England. Sussex Camock had long served the Earl of Warwick as a privateering captain; he was "grievously wounded" as commander of the *Little Neptune* in the earl's 1627 privateering fleet. The Camock name is written Chaddock or Chadwick in the Bermuda records. See William Ball, "Might and Would Not, or The observation of the Right Honourable the Earl of Warwick's voyage made upon the coast of Portingale in the year of our Lord Anno Domini 1627," ed. Nelson P. Bard, in N. A. M. Rodger, ed., *The Naval Miscellany*, V, Navy Records Society (London, 1984), 26, 41–53, 58, 61, 71, 76; Wilkinson, *Adventurers of Bermuda*, 2nd ed., 89; Newton, *Colonising Activities*, 141.
44. PRO Signet Office Docquet Book 11, 1634–1638, March 1634/35; PIC Ct. 2–4–35.

entertainment, and Commerce, and are engaged to return unto them."
Williams had already been expelled from Providence Island for drunkenness, impiety, and disorderliness.[45] Nonetheless, the company admitted
that they could not set up the mainland trade without such knowledgeable men. Thus, the pressing need for economic returns forced the
investors to compromise their principles. Camock was urged to treat
Marston and Williams with "moderation," so that by winning their
affection he could learn what they knew. At the same time he was to
restrain "to your utmost power all sins and disorders as swearing,
drunkenness, uncleanness and the like, which will render the name of
Christians odious to the very heathen."[46]

Although the adventurers may have believed they could separate the
trade and the island colony into mutually beneficial but discrete entities,
the planters feared that their interests would necessarily suffer. Separation
was not possible. Williams missed the *Golden Falcon* carrying Camock
and Marston, so the company shipped him on a later vessel; he was to
remain on Providence Island until he could get passage to the cape.
Thus, a man expelled by the governor and council was set up to return
with the title of company agent.[47] Moreover, Camock was directed to
send anyone who was a source of dissension and disorder to Providence
Island to be held there so they would not disturb his trading.

These instructions seemed clearly to indicate the relative importance
of the two ventures in the company members' minds; the next was
even more devastating. Camock was authorized to remove men from
Providence Island to replace any he left behind or to fill out his complement. In the event, many men, including the island's fortifications
expert Captain Samuel Axe and Workmaster Nathaniel Goodman, chose
to go with Camock, as did Albertus Bluefield. Hope Sherrard, complaining of the danger in which the island lay at the beginning of 1634,
wrote that "fifty of our Ablest and skilfullest men are gone from us of
late." Some had returned to England, but many had gone to the mainland. Faced with bitter recriminations from the governor and council,
the company could say only that they had not foreseen such a massive
outflow.[48]

Further evidence of the relative esteem of the mainland project and
Providence Island lay in company orders that colonists were to plant
provisions for Camock and his men so that they would not be "diverted

45. PIC, Instr. to Gov. and Coun., 5–10–32, pt. 21.
46. PIC, Ctee., 5–22–33; Instr. to Camock, 7–1–33.
47. Apparently Williams actually was left at Association Island and waited there. See PIC
to Bell about Williams, 7–29–33; to Camock by the *Long Robert*, 9–34; Instr. to
Joseph Collins, Master of the *Long Robert*, 7–34.
48. Hope Sherrard to Sir Thomas Barrington, January 6, 1634, BL Egerton MS 2646, f.
58; PIC to Gov. and Coun. by the *Long Robert*, 1634; PIC Ctee., 12–24–34.

from our trade." And, although the company continued to urge settlers to stockpile goods for its ships, Camock was also authorized, if he could fully load their ships with valuable trade items from the mainland, to ignore Providence Island's more humble products, except for samples.[49] The company also told Captain Bell to forget about setting aside plots for each of the twenty investors for the time being. Rumors began to circulate that the company was considering sale of the island, which the investors absolutely denied.[50]

All difficulties were submerged in the investors' high hopes for rich commodities. Even though they expressed the utmost confidence in Camock's ability, the company reiterated the goods they expected him to find and send to them:

> Silk-grass, Gum of pine Tree, Lignum vitae, and other Gums. Anotto or Tomarin. Skins of all Beasts that have any Furre, or may seem vendible. Cassia Fustula, Sarsaperilla Guacum, Mecoachan or wild potatoes. Red oil, Wax and honey. Contra Yerva which is an Antidote against poison of Serpents and arrows, and by that means it may be discovered. Or what other Antidotes you shall find in the Country. Bezar stone, Manatee stones, the stone in the Alligator's head. And if you shall meet with any things upon the main that may be useful in Providence we desire you from Time to Time by all opportunities to furnish that Island.

Camock was also authorized to purchase black slaves for the colony. Bell had requested such a move, and the company, although arguing that too many slaves would endanger the vulnerable settlement, agreed that 20 to 40 would be a good idea.[51]

Firm alliances with Indians living on the Moskito Coast were among the few long-lasting successes of the Providence Island venture. The colonists apparently convinced the "king" of the Moskitos to send his son to England in 1633 or 1634, where he remained for three years. In return, Governor Bell sent a young company servant named Lewis Morris to live among the Indians with the additional goal of setting up a turtling station. The Providence Island records are strangely silent about this exchange and about the settlers' relationship with the natives. At a committee meeting in May 1633, the investors decided, on application of his guardians, Mr. Roope and Mr. Hartley, to release Morris from his contract with the disreputable Edward Williams. The company agreed to pay Williams £6, and Morris engaged himself to serve the company for three years. The investors promised to place Morris under

49. PIC to Bell by the *Expectation*, 2/3–35; Instr. to Camock, 7–1–33.
50. PIC to Bell, 4–10–33; Ct. 3–9–35.
51. PIC, Instr. to Camock, 7–1–33; PIC to Bell, 4–10–33.

Joseph Collins, who commanded the *Golden Falcon* in 1633 and the *Long Robert* in 1634; Collins was to teach Morris the art of navigation.[52]

Morris's later career demonstrates that he did indeed learn seamanship, but the chronology of his assignments is unclear. In 1634 he was apparently on the coast among the Indians under the general command of Sussex Camock. William Jessop wrote him, addressing him as "Honest Lewis," that the company would not send his requested supplies but that "your captain" was instructed to furnish him out of his own shipment. Jessop suggested that Morris show him this letter. In March 1635, Jessop responded to Morris's wish to come home, saying that the company would either grant his request, despite the fact that his contract was not up, or send him servants by the next ship in May. By this time Morris was apparently in Providence Island. In the event no ship was sent until the following year, but Morris apparently stayed in the colony. In 1639 the investors referred to him as "having been long in our service."[53]

Sir Hans Sloane, who spent time in the islands in the later seventeenth century, wrote of the visit of the Moskito king Jeremy to Jamaica in 1687. Jeremy came claiming English protection because his people had submitted to them under King Charles I. He told Sloane that the Providence Island colonists persuaded "them to send home the King's Son, leaving one of his People as Hostage for him, which was Colonel Morris, now living at New York." The prince returned when his father died, and he became king of the Moskitos. Sloane described the Moskitos as "wholly unlearned . . . only some that have been at Providence, have learned the Lord's Prayer, the Creed and Ten Commandments which they repeat with great devotion." He described them as affable and hospitable, "especially endear'd to those of the English Nation. The Men generally speak broken English," and they would allow only English colonists to settle among them.[54]

Lewis Morris's stamp remained on the Moskito Coast. Nathaniel Butler, Providence Island's last governor, remarked that during his 1639 privateering voyage his ships passed a small island near the shore

---

52. PIC Ctee., 5–27–33. An extremely cryptic reference to "the Indian" occurs in minutes of a company court of March 4, 1633. Nicholas Roope was a shipowner and privateering entrepreneur of Dartmouth. He commanded a pinnace accompanying the *Elizabeth* to Providence Island in 1633. He was connected to John Pym; his daughter married the Reverend Anthony Rous. Navigation training would have made Morris very valuable to him; see Newton, *Colonising Activities*, 119, 136–37.

53. Jessop Letterbook, B. L. Add MS 10615, 37, 119; PIC to Butler by the *Mary*, 7–39; PIC, Articles of Instruction to Capt. Butler, Capt. Axe, and Capt. Carter, 7–39.

54. PIC Ctee. 5–27–33. Sir Hans Sloane, *A Voyage to the Islands Madera, Barbados, Nieves, S. Christophers and Jamaica* (London, 1707, 1725), I, lxxvi–lxxviii.

"called by our English Morris his Island, so called of the name of one of their men who formerly had been left there with two Indians to turn Hawks-bill Turtle." The privateer Captain William Jackson, on his most famous voyage under a Providence Island Company commission between 1642 and 1645, stopped at Cape Gracias a Dios, where the "Indians in their Canoes came aboard of our Vice-Admiral, to visit their old acquaintance, Captain Axe, & Lewis Morris, the Master, who had formerly lived among them. These Cape Indians are our friends, & divers of them speak & understand our Language, by reason of the great correspondence they held with the islanders of Providence, before it was taken up by the Spaniards."[55]

The Moskito prince who went to England in the 1630s was the beginning of a long line of native rulers who maintained ties to the English; many of them made journeys to England or to English possessions and some received an English education. This succession, all apparently within a single family, continued up to the 1850s. Oldman, the king at that time, went to England after the capture of Jamaica by the English in 1655.[56]

Lewis Morris went on to a distinguished career. He moved to Barbados, where he and his brother owned a sugar plantation. He served in the parliamentary armies in the English Civil War, participating in the taking of the Scilly Isles and attaining the rank of colonel in the assault on Barbados; he also took part in Cromwell's Western Design that captured Jamaica. He was converted to Quakerism by Henry Fell in 1656 and became one of the most prominent and fervent Friends in the islands; he corresponded with George Fox and William Penn. In the early 1670s, he bought the property he named Morrisania in New York and became a partner in the Tinton Manor (corrupted from Tintern, for his birthplace) Ironworks in New Jersey. He survived to become the sole owner of Tinton. His nephew, also named Lewis, inherited in 1691. He became chief justice of New York and founded the dynasty

55. Butler Diary, Sloane MS 758, 6–1–39; Anon., "Mercurius Americanus. A Briefe Journal of a Succinct and True Relation of the most Remarkable Passages observed in the Voyage undertaken by Captaine William Jackson to the Westerne Indies or Continent of America," in *The Voyages of Captain William Jackson (1642–1645)*, ed. Vincent T. Harlow, *Camden Miscellany*, XIII (London, 1923), 25–6. This manuscript was collected by Sir Hans Sloane. That Morris commanded the vice admiral, the ship second only to the flagship in Jackson's company, shows the skill and status he had achieved as a seaman.

56. On the Moskito Indians and their relationship to the English, see Parsons, *San Andrés and Providencia*, 10–12; Michael D. Olien, "The Miskito Kings and the Line of Succession," *Journal of Anthropology Research* 39 (1983), 198–204, and "E. G. Squier and the Miskito: Anthropological Scholarship and Political Propaganda," *Ethnohistory* 32 (1985), 111–33; and William Sorsby, "The Mosquito Coast of Nicaragua and Honduras," unpub. ms., 166–68.

that produced Gouverneur Morris and the Lewis Morris who signed the Declaration of Independence.[57]

The Providence Island Company's long-range planning now centered on the mainland. Camock's expedition was to look out for a good site for permanent settlement. Each group of traders was to carry one man able to read and write who, supplied with pen, paper, and ink, was to keep a journal recording "the several natures and numbers of people, their government, Commodities, Countries Soils Rivers." All journals were supposed to be collected into one ledger book, but if such records were kept, they have not survived.

Unlike many other colonizing enterprises, Providence Island left no scientific legacy, nor did the company evince any interest in scientific information beyond the specifically commercial. When Nathaniel Marston wrote asking for a book by Edward Topsell, author of *The Historie of Foure-footed Beastes. Collected out of all the volumes of C. Gesner, and all other writers to this present day* (1607) and *The Historie of Serpents. Or, the second booke of living creatures. Collected out of divine scriptures* (1608), the company refused to send it on the grounds of expense unless they were sure the expedition was to be a success, "though the book in itself be very useful." William Jessop wrote Marston that only two copies were to be had in London, both commanding great prices, and commented: "A terrible rule, and I dare not send it being contrary to the Company's express desire, which I would not willingly contradict." Jessop did send along the requested "strong water."[58]

Although the Darien trade project failed quickly, with Richard Lane coming home in less than a year, initial reports of the Moskito Coast trade, and the Indians' reception of the English, were very encouraging.[59]

57. William Warner first made the connection between Lewis Morris, the Barbados sugar planter and New York gentleman, and Lewis Morris, the Providence Island Company employee. I thank him for sharing his unpublished paper "Puritans and Privateers" with me. Lewis Morris is the subject of a biography by Samuel Stelle, *Lewis Morris: Anglo-American Statesman, ca. 1613–1691* (Atlantic Highlands, NJ, 1983), but this book is somewhat inaccurate on the Providence Island phase of Morris's career. Morris is also briefly profiled in Eugene R. Sheridan, *Lewis Morris, 1671–1746: A Study in Early American Politics* (Syracuse, 1981), 1–4. On his conversion, see Barbara Ritter Dailey, "The Early Quaker Mission and the Settlement of Meetings in Barbados, 1655–1700," *Journal of the Barbados Museum and Historical Society* XXXIX (1991), 25, 28.

58. Jessop letterbook, B. L. Add MS 10615, no. 27, August 11, 1634. We do not know which book Marston asked for. The Providence Island Company did authorize very large sums for theological books for the island's ministers.

59. See PIC to Bell by the *Expectation*, 2/3–35.

Camock gratifyingly sent home samples of many products, and the company urged him to continue his searches but to concentrate on the Camock's flax (for "some inconveniencies known to our selves" they wished to avoid calling it *silk* grass) and on annotto. The company's experiments with silkgrass found it "a very excellent staple commodity, vendible in greater abundance than you shall be able to send it to us, and at such a price as will exceed our former hopes, and in a very large manner answer your desire and industry." The adventurers sent exact instructions for boiling the stalks to separate the threads without breaking them; they also suggested that the colonists experiment with different methods of preparing the fiber.[60]

Silkgrass was a blanket term for many products. The English textile industry eagerly sought a fiber with the qualities of silk, and all colonizing ventures looked out for such a plant. Thomas Hariot had found a silkgrass, probably the yucca plant, in Ralegh's Roanoke colony on the Outer Banks of North Carolina. The colonists wove a piece of grosgrain of it, which so impressed Hariot with its possibilities that he listed it first among the "marchantable commodities" of the area. He argued that the same plant grew in Persia and that much of the silk imported from there was made of this fiber.[61] In Bermuda and Virginia, colonists also looked out for silkgrass. In some areas, it was identified as the milkweed plant, in others Indian hemp, *Apocynum cannabinum*. The Massachusetts Bay colonists hoped for production of "silk grass . . . hemp and flax."[62]

Camock's flax was probably a bromeliad, *Aechmea magdalensis*, although *Agave barbadensis* and *Furcraea tuberosa* have also been identified as the silkgrass of West Indian colonial records.[63] In 1626, Robert Harcourt had republished a list of promising mainland com-

60. PIC to Gov. and Coun., and to Camock, by the *Long Robert*, 9–34. In the sixteenth century, linen cloth was the single most expensive import into England, almost double the expenditure for wine, the second commodity. In addition, linen fiber and thread were also expensive imports, and developers insistently called for development of a domestic source of linen; Joan Thirsk, *Economic Policy and Projects: The Development of a Consumer Society in Early Modern England* (Oxford, 1978), 68–75.

61. Thomas Hariot, *A Briefe and true report of the new found land of Virginia* (Frankfort, 1590), 7.

62. Smers Islands Company, Instr. to Moore, in Lefroy, ed., *Memorials*, I, 58–64; Sir John Eliot's copy, "The grounds of settling a plantation in new England," 1629, *Winthrop Papers* II, 147; Thomas Gorges to John Winthrop, 12–23–41, ibid., IV, 322–23. On the identity of the silkgrass in Virginia, see Helen Rountree, *The Powhatan Indians of Virginia: Their Traditional Culture* (Norman, OK, 1989), 65.

63. Parsons, *San Andrés and Providencia*, 10; David Watts, *Man's Influence on the Vegetation of Barbados, 1627–1800*, University of Hull Occasional Papers in Geography, 4 (1966), 74.

modities very similar to the list in the Providence Island Company's instructions to Camock. He argued not only that silkgrass made a fine silk or linen cloth but also that the English now knew "the best way to order it."[64] Company husband William Woodcock reported after conference with experienced tradesmen that the flax was suited to many kinds of manufacture and would fetch at least 4 shillings a pound, maybe much more, and that the market could not be glutted. At the same time, investors' hopes were raised by reports that Camock would be ready to freight a ship of 200 tons; the flax grew so abundantly that only "want of hands" would stint the cargo.[65]

Annotto (*Bixa orellana*) was a plant whose seeds produced an orange or yellow dye. Harcourt wrote that it fetched 12 shillings a pound in Holland; its presence was first noted in Barbados in 1627. It was difficult to produce, however, and never became an important crop, although its promise was so great that it was repeatedly introduced. As late as 1667, John Scott wrote in his "Description of Barbados" that it was "a rich Dye (A Commodity the English never yet knew how to manage)."[66]

In these commodities as in their instructions to the Providence Island colonists, the adventurers cut the margin too thin. The peculiar organization of the company with its small membership created economic pressures for returns that inexperienced colonists could not answer. The emphasis on control from London but compensation from products developed in the field severely limited planters' willingness to experiment with and invest their energies in possible but not assured commodities. The investors saw themselves as offering colonists a kind of partnership in which all would participate in profits, but they did not see that new economic ventures required backing, seed money, so that a variety of paths could be pursued with the assumption that inevitably some would fail.

After the Providence Island Company achieved a separate charter of incorporation for the mainland trade in Central America, frustration was high in the island, not only because the colonists saw the company's priorities shifting, but because they were cut out of this far more promising endeavor. The sense of isolation and neglect was far from uniform, however. Those men with firm connections to company grandees were repeatedly reassured that they would have access to the profits.

---

64. Harcourt, *Voyage to Guiana*, 2nd ed., 41–7, 80.
65. PIC, Prep. Ct., 6–9–34, 6–16–34. Expectations that silkgrass would thrive on Providence Island had already been overturned. Hopes for silkgrass from the Moskito Coast continued into the eighteenth century; see Jeffreys, *West-India Atlas*, 16.
66. Harcourt, ibid., 44; Scott, "Description of Barbados," B. L., Sloane MS 3662, 56–62; Watts, *Man's Influence on Barbados*, 46–7, 51, 71, 88.

Company secretary William Jessop, writing privately to adventurers' particular clients, stroked his correspondents and assured them that, should Providence Island prove a failure or if a new and better plantation were initiated, places would be found for them. Men lacking a particular friend in the company courts, or whose friends lacked influence, must have been frustrated indeed as the rumors and promises flew around their heads.

Jessop's correspondents received all manner of special treatment. He handled the sale of their cargoes, bought special things for their comfort, got news of their friends and relations, sought out special servants for them, and arranged their business affairs. Those for whom he reserved his warmest greetings, mostly men with military titles, received his firmest assurances. Jessop wrote Ensign Thomas Fitch in September 1634 that if he were to find the island "unanswerable to the company's hopes and your labour and shall conclude that a removal to the Main[land] may advance you," the secretary would fix it. Meanwhile, Jessop had arranged for Fitch to receive more servants than the company intended and had assigned to him George Phillips, a long-time servant of the Countess of Warwick and the best of those servants now sent out. A similarly warm, though veiled, promise was sent to Lieutenant Hugh Price.

Mr. Thomas Jenkes, clerk of the stores with Ensign Fitch, received two letters from Jessop by the *Long Robert*. The first, written in mid-August 1634, sympathized with Jenkes over the island's lack of profit but said that the promising trade from the mainland "cannot but now conduce to the flourishing of the Island." In September, after the return of the *Elizabeth*, Jessop acknowledged Jenkes's claims both of the impossibility of profit from Providence Island and of the great profits to be expected from the mainland, and he promised "more speedy access" for those who had labored unprofitably for the company.[67]

At the same time, the *Long Robert* carried orders absolutely forbidding Providence Island colonists to involve themselves in trade with the mainland. The adventurers had heard "that some were resolved to go thither whom we intended not to that employment." This restriction was taken very seriously. William Jessop provided John Bartlett with a variety of goods he had ordered, except for two pounds of beads, private trading goods forbidden by company order, "which I dare not infringe."[68]

---

67. Jessop Letterbook, B. L., Add MS 10615, nos. 31, 40, 52, 53, 62.
68. PIC to Gov. and Coun. by the *Long Robert*, 9–34; Jessop Letterbook, 32; but see Jessop's letter to Thomas Heath, 1635, no. 79, to whom he sends a "few beads", saying "the use that you mean to make of them I know not."

The pattern set in the early years continued on Providence Island through-out the life of the colony. Exaggerated hopes for products foundered on the realities of inexperience and lack of focus. Sussex Camock had left his post at Cape Gracias a Dios early in 1635, leaving Samuel Axe in charge of the Indian trade. Hopes for an expanding relationship between Providence Island and the mainland were in abeyance. Camock's flax never proved to be successful, probably because its processing was so labor-intensive, but the company continued to seek out new methods, saying "we would not have it wholly cast aside."[69] John Pym had consulted "Mr. White of Dorchester" who, after trials with Camock's flax, reported that it "makes a very fine thread and spins much better than ordinary flax." Pym again described several methods of separating the fiber from the stalk, and the company suggested that the soil of Henrietta Island (San Andreas) might be better for growing it.[70]

Expeditions sent to the mainland for Camock's flax could at the same time bring a new crop, dette, to Providence Island. Dette was probably vanilla, a plant known to the Moskito Indians as *diti*. The company had been informed "by men of understanding" that it would be "very valuable." Therefore, the colonists were to "cherish" it, and the company was chagrined to hear that cattle had been allowed to eat dette planted in the island. Like the Camock's flax, its growth, production, and marketing were to be entirely in the hands of company agents or those holding company license.[71]

Even after privateering opened other avenues of profit, the adventurers continued to hope for returns from Camock's flax. Captain William Rudyerd, back in the Caribbean and in company employ in 1637 as a privateering captain, was directed, if he failed to fulfill his hopes of prizes, to go to the Cape, taking the advice of Captain Elfrith and other knowledgeable men, and, going on shore "in your own person," find the great fields of flax growing near Monkey Bay. Rudyerd was to try several ways of clearing the fiber, including boiling, drying, and beating, for which he had been provided instruments. Most important, they wanted evidence from his trials of how much flax a man could process in a year. The investors reckoned that four or five pounds of cleared fiber a day per man would make the flax a profitable commodity; they were considering sending men for that purpose.[72]

69. PIC to Gov. and Coun. by the *Blessing*, 3–36.
70. PIC to Gov. and Coun. by the *Blessing*, 3–36; PIC, Ct. 2–12–36, 2–19–36.
71. PIC Ct., 2–19–36; PIC To Gov. and Coun. by the *Blessing* 5–36, and by the *Happie Return* 6–36. On the identification of dette, see John A. Holm, "The Creole English of Nicaragua's Miskito Coast," unpub. PhD. diss. London University, 1978, 40. On earlier confusion over dette's identity, see Narda Dobson, *A History of Belize* (London, 1973), 50.
72. PIC, Instr. to Rudyerd by the *Mary Hope*, 1–37.

* * *

Perception of Providence Island's economy changed dramatically in the middle of the 1630s. Successful repulsion of the first Spanish attack in 1635 and the subsequent issuance of letters of reprisal to the company meant that the privateering for which many of the settlers and some of the adventurers had yearned was finally possible. When they conferred command of a ship on Lieutenant William Rous, the investors frankly informed him that they expected privateering to "supply the defects of the Island, which we conceive will not alone yield profit answerable to our disbursements."[73]

Now the island was expected to serve as a base for privateers and a source of supplies and revictualing. In a letter of May 1636, the colonists were warned to expect an influx of 500 to 600 men within a few months. The planters would be expected to have provisions ready for them, especially corn and cassava, "if there be any in the Island." They were instructed to take special care in planting fruit trees and gardens and in tending the cattle the company believed thrived on the island.[74]

Conflicts between the interests of the privateers and those of the colony were inevitable and quickly began to surface. Captain Thomas Newman, who offered to take a privateering ship in the company's name in 1636, was appalled when told that the adventurers also expected him to carry passengers to Providence Island. Newman argued that he would be forced off "his intended course for prizes, the victual of the ship will be thereby wasted, the ship pestered and the certain charge increased, because seamen will not go forth in her in that case without wages."[75] Privateers were also authorized to take men from Providence Island to serve with them, always with the advice and consent of the governor and council.[76]

At the same time, privateering was expected to open new avenues for Providence Island's development. Company letters continued to show the same mixture of hopeful enthusiasm and ignorant underestimation of the specialized skills necessary to raise tropical crops. Privateering captains were instructed to interrogate prisoners about the valuable commodities of the Indies with an eye to transplanting them to Providence

---

73. PIC to Rous by the *Blessing*, 3–19–36.
74. PIC to Gov. and Coun. by the *Blessing*, 3–36; and by the *Happie Return*, 5–36.
75. PIC Ct., 5–16–36; PIC Instr. to Newman by the *Happie Return*, 6–36. Seamen on privateers normally served for a percentage of the take rather than set wages. John Smith provided a chart showing how the booty should be divided up; Smith, *An Accidence*, in Barbour, ed., *Complete Works*, III, 26–7.
76. See, for example, PIC Instr. to Rous, 3–20–36.

Island, and they were to raid gardens near the coast for plants – "fruits, drugs, or other useful commodities" – which were to be kept in earth on shipboard for transplantation.[77] Captains were instructed to attempt to capture African slaves skilled in pearl diving to enrich the colony.[78] Privateering would make the island's planters far more vulnerable to renewal of the kind of attack endured in 1635; the prospective trade-off for increased danger would be enlargement of the population and new attention to the colony's economic development backed by sustained company interest in its future.

During Providence Island's second half-decade, the company studied their project's prospects. Systematic reports allowed investors to develop a rounded picture, and what they learned was discouraging. Secretary of State Sir John Coke drew up a report for the Privy Council to use in discussing the company's application for letters of reprisal after the first Spanish attack. He wrote that the island contained 3,000 to 4,000 acres of "low good ground," and another 4,000 of hilly land where corn or cattle could be raised; "the rest is all sheer and rocks." Although water was lacking in hot weather, the island "beareth all kind of provisions for sustenance as corn, potatoes, Casada [cassava], planting [plaintain], pines [pineapples], oranges, lemons, and all Indian fruits as Melons exceeding good." Peas did extremely well, and the land sometimes yielded two or three corn crops a year, although plantings after the first were subject to blasting. "In sum it will yield provision sufficient for 1,000 men besides women and children. Now there are of able persons about 500, women about 30 or 40."

Coke reported flatly that the island had no trade "with any place." He described company efforts to establish trade on the mainland rivers but said that the Indians had no commodities until they were planted especially for trade. He wrote that company ships had brought home some gums and perfumes, "and they hope for flax." As for the island itself, "Cottons bear well. Tobacco prospereth not." Providence Island, Coke argued on behalf of the adventurers, must be abandoned unless the company won the right to recoup their losses through privateering and, eventually, through trade on the mainland. No benefit could be expected from the island itself beyond the considerable role it would

77. PIC Instr. to Rous in the *Blessing*, 3–20–36, Instr. to Newman in the *Happie Return*, 6–36.
78. PIC, ibid.; PIC to Gov. and Coun. by the *Blessing*, 5–36. For a description of the "great human cost" involved in the "cruel" pearl fishing industry, see Kenneth R. Andrews, *The Spanish Caribbean: Trade and Plunder, 1530–1630* (New Haven, 1978), 26–9, 33–34. The first slaves brought into Bermuda were pearl divers; Craven, "Introduction to the History of Bermuda," *William and Mary Quarterly*, 2nd ser., 17 (1937), 359.

play as a safe refuge and storehouse, able both to protect and to revictual English ships. The investors alleged that they had spent £30 for every man sent to the island and that it would take £8,000 a year to keep the colony going, a sum they could no longer pay in the absence of any return.[79]

Coke's report did not necessarily reflect fully the company's beliefs about their island. Obviously, they wanted to paint as grim a picture as possible while their application for relief was before the Privy Council. Early in 1636, two months after Coke's memorandum, John Pym proposed a new scheme for dividing the island's 3,000 good acres into plantations at annual rents. Each plantation would be expected to produce a set amount of cotton and tobacco to be taken up by the company at a fixed price. He expected a "convenient profit" to flow into company coffers from this scheme, with enough extra to pay for public works and company officers on the island.

At the same time Pym proposed sending ten men to the mainland to cut flax near Monkey Bay south of the Bluefields River. Pym must have been acting on written reports similar to the one Albertus Bluefield was to deliver in person in June 1637, when he said of Monkey Bay that it was easily fortifiable by virtue of islands in the bay, and "that he was two miles up in the Maine and found the Country all overgrown with silk grass, and hath a river in it of about eight or ten feet deep, and thirty foot broad." Pym suggested that the flax be sent to Providence Island for "fuller dressing." As much as ten or twelve tons of Camock's flax could be produced, he thought, through "profitable manufactures." Dette for Providence Island could also be obtained there.[80] When the price of tobacco again slipped after 1638, the company urged the planters to abandon it utterly and plant cotton. Two weavers and a woman skilled in spinning cotton were sent out to help the islanders develop their own industry, even to manufacturing their clothing.[81]

Slowly, however, the more pessimistic assessments came to seem irresistible. Returning planters brought discouraging reports of the land and its promise. Philip Bell and Samuel Rishworth both returned to England in the *Expectation*, arriving in June 1637. Rishworth carried a letter detailing the planters' grievances; the company's answer would determine whether the settlers would stay or abandon the island. When

79. Sir John Coke, Draft Memorandum, December, 1635, Public Record Office CO 1/8 (Colonial Papers, VIII, 83). The adventurers were granted letters of reprisal authorizing them to attack and seize Spanish ships.

80. PIC Gen. Ct., 2–19–36; PIC to Gen. Ct. by the *Blessing*, 5–36; PIC Ctee., 6–14–37.

81. PIC to Gov. and Coun. in the *Expedition*, 4–23–38; in the *Spy* and *Swallow*, 7–38. Earlier the company had chastised Captain Elfrith for failure to make use of the expensive cotton engine they had sent; PIC to Elfrith by the *Blessing*, 3–36.

questioned about the meaning of this threat, Rishworth answered that he knew only of a widespread desire to found a colony on the mainland, "the Island offering no quantity of Tobacco or Cotton though it will produce good quantity of provisions and for strength may be fit to resist all the power of Spain."

Captain Bell's report, delivered at the same meeting where the company heard Albertus Bluefield's glowing report of Monkey Bay, confirmed Rishworth's with a good deal of circumstantial evidence. Bell estimated that Providence Island could support 1,200 settlers if they concentrated on provisions but only 600 to 700 if they were expected to raise commodities.[82] He pointed to the enormous labor demands of cotton: "[T]wo men with very great labor night and day and upon good ground, made in one year 1100 wtt."

Bell's portrait of the land was discouraging indeed. Progress was impossible because cleared land was invaded by coarse grass far more difficult to deal with than the original cover. (Captain Samuel Axe told the company the next year that the grass could grow a finger's length in a single night.) More servants were needed just to keep the existing plantations operable. When servants' time ran out, settlers deserted their old land for new. The soil cover on the hills was $1\frac{1}{2}$ feet deep, and crops grew well under the shelter of the trees, but

> The soil is hard and apt to retain the rain which sometimes falls three months together whereby the ground is made Chillish and Commodities die, specially tobacco, That the Corn is subject to be blasted with winds, and if there be not want of providence there's no cause to fear famine. That the Rats increase exceedingly through the people's negligence. That the children thrive well, the cattle give not the quantity of milk as in other places, are fat but only in the Rain time. And the poultry thrive much better at first then now. That there is good water all the year long, and salt may be made in the Island if the pits can be kept whole.[83]

In March 1638 Captain Samuel Axe's "Relation of the Isle of providence" reiterated Bell's points. The clay of the valleys and the invading grass made "the getting of victual . . . difficult." Nonetheless, if the island grew only provisions, it would maintain 1,500 men. Axe testified that the settlers "have great store of hogs, the Corn growing reasonably well, but will not keep above four months. Cassava grows very well also pease, plantains and Muskmelons, pine apples. Also cattle thrive

82. Modern Providence Island has a population of about 2,000. See Wilson, *Crab Antics*, 91.
83. PIC Ctee., 6–14–37.

well and all poultry but Turkies, good oranges and lemons, but the vines thrive not well." At the same time Captain Nathaniel Butler, under consideration for the post of governor of Providence Island, flatly insisted on a salary; he believed that the labor of twenty servants would produce "small profit" in the island.[84]

All reports stressed two things: (1) Providence Island was a natural fortress, and the fortifications made it impregnable, and (2) the Moskito Coast offered everything in the way of commodities that the island lacked. Captain Axe praised the "good store of victuals" at the Cape, where the grass was not troublesome and the climate was healthful for English bodies. The sugarcane was as fair as any in the world, two crops of flax grew in a year, and the annotto, cotton, and tobacco were excellent.[85]

Axe's report avoided the simple enthusiasm of earlier praise; he pointed out dangers and difficulties as well as promise. The overall effect of his relation, however, was to reinforce the company's assumptions. Everything told the investors that Providence Island's destiny was as a fortress storehouse and garden. In the short run, it would supply the adventurers' privateers and play a key role in the war against the Roman Catholic enemy. Its greater importance would lie in its role of supporting the colonization of the Central American mainland, where the company's men would process the commodities already growing there, "which may by the industry of many hands be brought home in great quantities" and where they would develop new products in that "soil capable of the richest drugs and merchandise which come from America."[86]

Letters sent out to the colony urged the settlers to plant provisions for the refreshment of ships coming into their harbors and ordered the governor to see that each plantation sowed crops sufficient for themselves and many others. "Riotous feasting" that wasted provisions was absolutely forbidden.[87] Despite the advice of all their experts, however, the company's command to grow commodities was not given up. In 1638 the investors directed the governor and council to "prevent the disorderly removing from old plantations," allowing no exceptions, and to require the head of every plantation to plant a set amount of cotton. The

84. For Capt. Axe's testimony, see PIC Gen. Ct., 3–7–38; for Capt. Butler's negotiations, see PIC Ctee., 3–26–38.
85. PIC Gen. Ct., 3–7–38; see also Bluefield's report, 6–14–37.
86. PIC Ctee., 6–24–37.
87. PIC to Gov. and Coun., 4–23–38; Letters in the *Spy* and *Swallow*, 7–38; Instr. to Commission for Grievances, 7–38.

tobacco boomlet of the mid-1630s was over and that crop was to be avoided.[88]

Such advice, commands, and cajoling were no more effective at the end of the decade than they had been in the colony's beginning. Tobacco was the primary crop all through the island's life. In 1639, as so many times before, the investors reiterated that the colony's tobacco was "little or nothing worth" in England and that cotton would be sure to repay their effort. They sent more equipment and skilled workers to help the settlers develop their manufactures, which they still hoped would bring "prosperity." Yet at the same time they admitted that tobacco, although of "base value," was "the commodity of the island."[89]

Should the development of Providence Island have taken a different course? Why did that assemblage of solid men and women with their godly aims and substantial backing not duplicate the success of mainland puritan colonies where settlers worked hard and produced steady growth of population and economy? Much of the answer lies in the organization of the colony and the company's land distribution policies, combined with the military demands of its location; economic problems also grew from ignorance and wishful thinking. Easy assumptions about the rich soil and climate of the tropics and the rapid growth possible in such an environment masked enormous problems: Tropical crops required expertise, and most were voracious consumers of labor. All were vulnerable to the vagaries of the weather and pests, and many were unsuited to the island's conditions. It is little wonder that the colonists stuck to the tobacco that at least some of their number knew and understood, despite the constant pressure of the London adventurers.

The trajectory of Barbados's development offers an important and instructive comparison to Providence Island's dismal track. Barbados was settled by English colonists in 1627, just two years before Providence Island. Both colonies limped through the 1630s with a mixed tobacco and cotton economy. Barbados, whose soil is also predominately clay, produced tobacco of notoriously poor quality. Yet throughout the decade Barbadian planters, as in the puritan colony, feared the consequences of abandoning tobacco. Peter Hay, agent for the Proprietor's trustee, wrote home: "[Y]ou desire us all to plant cotton, which is a thing the planters

---

88. PIC to Gov. and Coun., 4–23–38, and 7–38; Menard, "Note on Chesapeake Tobacco Prices," *Virginia Magazine of History and Biography* 84 (1976), 401–10.
89. PIC to Butler by the *Mary*, 7–39; Instr. to Gov. and Coun., 6/7–39; to Woodcock, 7–39.

can hardly do, because they are indebted, that if they leave planting of tobacco they shall never be able to pay their debts. . . ."[90]

Barbados settlers did try to diversify into cotton as the Providence Island settlers had worked with cotton and Camock's flax. When Sir Henry Colt visited Barbados in 1631, he found the planters filled with hope over "the trade of Cotton." By 1634, when Father Andrew White stopped en route to Maryland, he described the cotton bolls and the "invention of wheels" by which planters extracted the seeds from the fibers. In the late 1630s, as the price of tobacco plummeted, these colonists ended their dependence on that crop. Barbados entered into agreement with St. Christopher's and Virginia to cut production, and Barbadians planted little tobacco after 1638. But they found that cotton, like tobacco, faced an uncertain and rapidly changing market.[91]

Neither crop offered the kind of sustained profits planters looked for, and the colony's first decade of life was as unsettled as that of Providence Island. In 1640 the cotton crop failed and, with no tobacco to sell, colonists feared famine. Throughout the 1630s, planters had lived "wholly upon pone (that Indian bread) and homine, and potato root." The party bound for Maryland in 1634 found meat so scarce and the price so high that Father White wrote "it Cost us our eyes." Nicholas Foster wrote that at the end of the decade Barbados "was in a very low condition," and "small hopes appeared of raising any fortunes there for the future."[92]

Up to this point, the economic development of Barbados and of Providence Island looks almost identical. Then, at the end of the 1630s in Barbados, "some of ingenious spirits set their wits at work to consider which way the desolation of the Plantation might be prevented," a feat that required finding "some richer Commodities." Barbadians turned to new crops, indigo and sugar, and the latter soon predominated. With sugar, Barbados went from the margins of the British empire to center stage. The first crop was marketed in 1643, and within little more than a decade the colony was the wealthiest of all England's possessions. J.

90. Quoted in J. Harry Bennett, "Peter Hay, Proprietary Agent in Barbados, 1636–1641," *Jamaican Historical Review* 5 (1965), 16.
91. On the collapse of the cotton market at the end of the 1630s, see Hilary McD. Beckles, "Plantation Production and White 'Proto-Slavery': White Indentured Servants and the Colonisation of the English West Indies, 1624–1645," *The Americas* 41 (1985), 25–6.
92. Sir Henry Colt, "The Voyage of Sr Henrye Colt Knight to ye Ilands of ye Antilleas," in V. T. Harlow, ed. *Colonising expeditions to the West Indies and Guiana, 1623–1667* (London, 1925), 69; White, "Briefe Relation of the Voyage unto Maryland," Hall, ed., *Narratives of Early Maryland*, 35–7; Nicholas Foster, *A Briefe Relation of the Late Horrid Rebellion Acted in the Island Barbados, in the West-Indies* (London, 1650), 1–2; Bennett, "Peter Hay," *Jamaican Historical Review* 5 (1965), 16, 23.

Scott, looking back from 1666, believed that Barbados was "seventeen times" richer than it had been before the sugar revolution.[93]

The shift to sugar was delayed partly because of the temporary high prices for tobacco in the 1630s but more because of the enormous demands for capital outlay and extremely sophisticated technical knowledge necessary for its cultivation and processing. First attempts to produce sugar were dismal failures; only a time-consuming and expensive learning process studded with reverses ultimately led to success.[94] The planters' willingness to admit Dutch entrepreneurs, who brought knowledge, equipment, and credit, was essential. Scott praised the "Hollanders" as "great encouragers of Plantations," and he wrote that the disruptions of the English Civil War gave them the opportunity to manage "the whole Trade." Ironically, the Barbados sugar revolution was presided over by Philip Bell, who was governor throughout almost all the 1640s.[95]

Richard Ligon, who came to Barbados in 1647 and found sugar cultivation "newly practised there," described the process by which sugar became established:

> Some of the most industrious men, having gotten Plants from Pernambock, a place in Brasil, and made trial of them at the Barbadoes; and finding them to grow, they planted more and more . . . till they had such considerable number, as they were worth the while to set up a very small Ingenio. . . . But, the secrets of the work being not well understood the Sugars they made were very

93. Foster, *Briefe Relation of the Late Horrid Rebellion*, 2; J. Scott, "Memoir of Barbados," B. L., Sloane MS 3662, 56–62. Barbados was by far the single greatest destination for English servants (70 percent of men and 65 percent of women) in the 1650s; see David Galenson, *White Servitude in Colonial America: An Economic Analysis* (Cambridge, 1981), 82.

94. The transformation of the Barbados economy can be followed in Robert Carlyle Batie, "Why Sugar? Economy Cycles and the Changing of Staples on the English and French Antilles, 1624–54," *Journal of Caribbean History* 8 (1976), 1–41; F. C. Innes, "The Pre-Sugar Era of European Settlement in Barbados," ibid., 1 (1970), 1–22; Puckrein, *Little England*, chaps. 3, 4; Richard S. Dunn, *Sugar and Slaves: The Rise of the Planter Class in the English West Indies, 1624–1713* (Chapel Hill, 1972), 59–67; Carl and Roberta Bridenbaugh, *No Peace Beyond the Line: The English in the Caribbean, 1624–1690* (New York, 1972), 56–61, 76–100; and John J. McCusker and Russell R. Menard, *The Economy of British America, 1607–1789* (Chapel Hill, 1985), 149–51.

95. Scott, "Memoir of Barbadoes," ff. 59–60. On the larger context, see Jonathan I. Israel, *Dutch Primacy in World Trade, 1585–1740* (Oxford, 1989), 237–40; Sidney W. Mintz, *Sweetness and Power: The Place of Sugar in Modern History* (New York, 1985), 37–9; and Philip D. Curtin, *The Rise and Fall of the Plantation Complex: Essays in Atlantic History* (Cambridge, 1990), 81–5. I have benefited from discussion of this point with Professor Israel.

inconsiderable, and little worth, for two or three years. But finding their errors by their daily practice, began a little to mend; and, by new directions from Brazil, sometimes by strangers, and now and then by their own people, who . . . were content sometimes to make a voyage thither, to improve their knowledge in a thing they so much desired. . . . And so returning with most Plants, and better Knowledge, they went on upon fresh hopes.

Ligon's account represented the sequence of the Providence Island investors' dreams. Again and again they urged their planters to seek out valuable commodities from the mainland and experiment with their culture and processing. They expected the tenacity Ligon saw in the Barbados planters who returned after failure for new advice and different techniques and seeds. Once begun, this experimentation and learning continued. In 1647 Ligon said the planters made only "muscavadoes" of poor quality, but by 1650 when he left the island they had learned to make good white sugar.[96] The key to Barbados's economic take-off was commitment to this crop in preference to all others, combined with flexibility in accepting Dutch influence and ability on the part of the "most industrious men" to ride out a considerable period of experimentation.

In Providence Island "ingenious spirits" never came forward. The investors' relationship to their plantation seemed to preclude such entrepreneurial activity. The adventurers believed that they could develop products beneficial to the English economy and to themselves and their colony through centrally controlled programs. By insisting that their planters remain tenants of the company, they removed incentives for taking initiative. Planters were saddled with debts that the company pressured them to repay quickly, so they were forced to plant crops that promised a certain return even though that return was poor. When the investors made plans to develop promising commodities such as Camock's flax or dette, they retained complete control of the process, sending out employees with military backgrounds to take charge and seeking to keep the trade in these products for the company. Company insistence that colonists trade only with company ships at fixed rates quashed the entrepreneurial impulse. Individuals who came forward with development

96. Ligon, *True and Exact History of Barbadoes*, 84–6. Lewis Morris was one of the Barbados planters who became rich in sugar production and marketing; Stelle, *Lewis Morris*, 28–9.
   See also William Bradford's account of the transformation of Plymouth with the introduction of individual land holdings there; *Of Plymouth Plantation, 1620–1647*, ed. Samuel Eliot Morison (New York, 1953), 120–1.

schemes were put off while the company waited for solid proof of their projected returns.[97]

Above all things the Providence Island Company wanted to avoid the short-term mercenary thinking they associated with merchants, and which they believed had perverted earlier colonizing ventures. Ironically, their experiment in entrepreneurial organization produced a classic case of limited goals crowding out long-range development. The Providence Island planters, directed to try a plethora of crops, discarded many at the first sign of failure. They could afford to do little else. The post-1640 experience of Barbados and other West Indian colonies suggests that feasible as well as unrealistic prospects were dropped; the organization of the colony was such that no one could afford to gamble and invest the time necessary to overcome problems with any one commodity. Nor was the capital equipment necessary to process the most lucrative crops sent out to the island because the company's program was not sufficiently focused.[98] Centralized control and ownership from London, which were meant to avoid the problems seen in Virginia and Bermuda, retarded the island's development by cramping colonists' capacity and incentive for innovation.

Could success have come to this venture with a different sort of commitment? The United States Agency for International Development (AID) sponsored an analysis of more than 100 post–World War II attempts at "new lands" colonization in tropical and semitropical regions all over the world. The accumulated evidence demonstrates that all such projects follow a similar path of development. Moreover, if the recent evidence is applied retroactively to the Providence Island venture, it suggests that the attempt may have been given up just as it neared the stage at which success was possible. Modern projects share many characteristics with early modern, including the propensity not only to underestimate the time and support necessary before settlements become self-supporting but to underestimate as well, after a long and discouraging start-up period, the long-range potential of the settlements. Thus, very promising ventures may be given up as hopeless just as they reach the stage at which they could achieve success. Economic success began to come to Barbados two years after the dispersion of the Providence Island settlers.

Analysts have isolated four distinct stages in modern "new lands"

---

97. See, for example, William Jessop's answer to Captain Hooke, April, 1935, B. L. Add MS 10615.
98. Richard Ligon gives a vivid picture of the elaborate "ingenios" for processing sugar on Barbados; he estimated that an investment of £14,000 was necessary to set up a fully functioning sugar plantation; *History of Barbadoes*, 86–96, 108.

projects. The first, and crucial, one is that of planning and the generation of feasibility studies. Many ventures fail because of inadequate information, especially about the demands of the environment. The second stage, and the one from which Providence Island never emerged, is the settling period, during which colonists are "risk-averse." Having moved to a new and unfamiliar habitat, planters "adopt a conservative stance, their first priority being to meet their subsistence needs." Faced with an alien setting, colonists "try to transfer area-of-origin house types, farming practices, and other skills even though they may not be suited to the new habitat." During this phase, which often lasts from five to ten years, colonists do well just to feed themselves and build shelter. Pressure to build ambitious infrastructure projects results in low morale and a high dropout rate. As in the early colonies, AID advises that major setbacks can occur with adverse environmental change (such as the coarse grass that invaded cleared land in some West Indian colonies) or through havoc wrought by imported animals, such as rats, that infested the islands.[99]

In successful settlements, according to AID's analysis of modern attempts, the second phase ends with a sensational psychological shift. The third stage, economic takeoff, occurs when the same people who have been risk-averse now change dramatically and rapidly into active risk-takers. Settlers now diversify their agriculture and employ "a wide range of investment strategies." Stage four is the handing over of control to the planters and the formation of institutions to incorporate them into the local political structure. Stages three and four may proceed together; in some cases four precedes three.[100]

This analysis is very suggestive for the history of Providence Island and its contemporaries among English colonies. It is possible that the company nursed the plantation through the discouraging years of stage two and then missed the transition to the settlers' seizing of the initiative that would have led to successful commodity development. Virginia and Barbados both went through about a decade of discouragement before each found, through extensive experimentation, the crop that became its gold. In each, stages three and four progressed together.

Virginia was granted both private property in land and a representative

99. Ligon, *True and Exact History of Barbadoes*, 96–7; Captain Philip Bell, testimony before Providence Island Company, June 14, 1637, PIC Records, P. R. O., CO 124, 1/2; Captain Samuel Axe, "Relation of the Isle of Providence," P. I. C., March 7, 1638.

100. Thayer Scudder, *The Development Potential of New Lands Settlement in the Tropics and Subtropics: A Global State-of-the-Art Evaluation with Specific Emphasis on Policy Implications*, U. S. Agency for International Development Evaluation, Discussion Paper No. 21 (np, 1984).

assembly to marshal planters' opinions at the end of the 1610s just as tobacco culture began to flourish, and the great Indian attack of 1622 helped to free leading planters of company control.[101] The Barbados Assembly, organized by dissident planters, first met in 1638 when the "ingenious spirits" began to investigate the demands of sugar production. The assumption in both colonies of local control, even with a proprietors' veto always possible, was emblematic of planter elites' taking control of their settlement's economic life. Such control was offered only to the last group of emigrants to Providence Island, those recruited by John Humphrey. This move to stage four was too late; Providence Island had become Providencia by the time the New England vanguard arrived.

Massachusetts Bay, founded at the same time as Providence Island, offers a case in which the stages were telescoped. Its environment was far less alien and its agricultural routine more familiar; adequate subsistence was achieved rapidly.[102] Because the colonists brought their charter with them, they moved to stage four immediately and controlled their own subsistence development, which required far less experimentation than in any of the southern colonies. The first decade saw an economy built on meeting the needs of the annual large influx of new colonists; only with the outbreak of the English Civil War did Massachusetts face the need for diversification. New England's failure to develop a staple crop meant that it ceased to be attractive as a magnet for servants, and the colony saw the effective end of inmigration after 1640. The depression of the 1640s caused profound unease in Massachusetts, but the colony was already well founded when it struck. Both New England and Virginia were able to ride out the difficult years of the 1640s.[103]

Whether Providence Island, like the other English West Indian plan-

101. J. Frederick Fausz, "Merging and Emerging Worlds: Anglo-Indian Interest Groups and the Development of the Seventeenth-Century Chesapeake," in Lois Green Carr, Philip D. Morgan, and Jean B. Russo, eds., *Colonial Chesapeake Society* (Chapel Hill, 1988), 52–3, 56.

102. On the agricultural history of New England during the seventeenth century, see Howard S. Russell, *A Long, Deep Furrow: Three Centuries of Farming in New England* (Hanover, NH, 1976), 39–45, and Karen Ordahl Kupperman, "Climate and Mastery of the Wilderness in Seventeenth-Century New England," in David D. Hall and David Grayson Allen, eds., *Seventeenth-Century New England*, Col. Soc. of Mass. *Pubs.*, 63 (Charlottesville, 1984), 3–38.

103. On the depression of the 1640s, see McCusker and Menard, *Economy of British America*, 93–9, and Menard, "British Migration to the Chesapeake Colonies in the Seventeenth Century," in Carr, Morgan, and Russo, eds., *Colonial Chesapeake Society*, 104. On Massachusetts's crisis of confidence in the economic downturn, see Karen Ordahl Kupperman, "Errand to the Indies: Puritan Colonization from Providence Island through the Western Design," *William and Mary Quarterly* 3rd ser., XLV (1988), 84–8.

tations on St. Christopher's and Montserrat, would have followed Barbados's lead and moved successfully into sugar production can never be known. Its later history suggests that the appropriate model was Bermuda, similar in size to Providence Island, which continued to grow tobacco and increasingly moved to livestock pasturing, all on relatively small plantations. Its success was modest but steady.[104]

Providence, occupied briefly by the Spanish after its seizure, served intermittently as a buccaneering and privateering base throughout the colonial period; it was not continuously occupied in the seventeenth century. In the eighteenth century its economy was based on cotton, tropical woods, and stock raising, with fruits added in the nineteenth. In 1835 a British expedition conducting a nautical survey of the region called at Providence Island. Mr. C. F. Collett, a member of the expedition, praised the island's fertility and the tropical fruits that appeared in "abundant luxuriance." Woods such as cedar, ironwood, and manzanilla flourished, the cedar squaring off "from twenty to twenty-four inches." Turtling, both for meat and shells, played a major role in Providence Island's trade; the British report called it a "delicious article of food." In 1835, according to Collett, the estimated 342 inhabitants, of whom half were slaves, exported 30,000 pounds of cotton and 170 pounds of tortoise shell annually. In a curious echo of the earlier colony's plight, he asserted that the English-manufactured goods they purchased with their cotton from Jamaica were priced so high that the islanders were perpetually in debt, a situation in "the traders' interest." They grew a little sugar and coffee for their own use. Association Island became a coconut plantation in the nineteenth century; for a time it was the major United States source of this product.[105]

Modern San Andreas (Henrietta) is a free port and resort; both it and Providencia belong to Colombia. Providence Island's contemporary society and economy are vividly brought to life in Peter J. Wilson's anthropological study *Crab Antics*, which portrays a life of "competency" based on the land and sea. A modest prosperity was apparently possible, then, for Providence Island, but nothing of the magnitude that would have satisfied the adventurers.

---

104. Riva Berleant-Schiller, "Free Labor and the Economy in Seventeenth-Century Montserrat," *William and Mary Quarterly* 3rd ser., XLVI (1989), 540, 544; Charles M. Andrews, *The Colonial Period of American History*, 4 vols. (New Haven, 1934–1938), I, 237.
105. C. F. Collett, R. N., "On the Island of Old Providence," *Journal of the Royal Geographical Society* 7 (1837), 203–10; Owen, *Nautical Memoir*, 101–6; Parsons, *San Andrés and Providencia*, 18, 28–34.

5

Land and Society:
The Middling Planters

ENGLISH MEN AND WOMEN who emigrated to Providence Island were immediately thrust into a bewildering world over which they had little control; all the inherited and learned responses and expectations appropriate to their former lives were of little value on the voyage or in their new homes. For the vast numbers who went to all the colonies as indentured servants, this experience must have been disorienting indeed, but for those who had occupied substantial and important positions in England, their sudden loss of control and status must have been savage in its impact.

Henry Halhead, leading merchant and former mayor of Banbury, and associate of Lord Saye and Sele, whose home at Broughton Castle was near Banbury, and Samuel Rishworth headed the 1632 contingent of godly settlers for Providence Island. On paper their command over the passengers on board the *Charity* was impressive, as was their promised status in the colony. What they found was that the plantation's inability to develop economically at the level and rate looked for created an adversarial relationship between company and settlers where both had anticipated partnership. Each party felt aggrieved. The substantial civilian planters lost not only money and security; they also were deprived of recognition and status.

Henry Halhead and Samuel Rishworth got a taste of the hardships awaiting them even before they got to Providence Island. Their wait at Plymouth was so long that the company was forced to give them £16 to tide them over. Once they were on board ship, their nightmare really began. The passengers on the *Charity*, despite the efforts of the adventurers to prevent such exploitation, experienced a crossing far worse than those on the *Seaflower*. A "dangerous Infection" ran through the passengers. In the midst of their suffering, the master of the ship, Thomas Punt, ordered the food to be scanted drastically, even though, as the cook testified, plentiful good food was available. Sailors who complained about the food were badly treated. The surgeon testified that sick passengers were denied comfort and relief, and he showed a certificate signed by many of the passengers. Punt took on bad water at Nevis against the advice of the ship's mates, although good water was available nearby at St. Christopher's.

Most grotesque of all, Punt persecuted Halhead and ordered him committed to the bilbowes, an iron bar bolted to the floor at one end to which ankle shackles were attached, because Halhead had forbidden one of his own servants to go ashore without his permission. Punt acted despite the fact that he, Rishworth, and Halhead jointly held the commission for government of the passengers on the voyage. References to this incident in the company records are extremely cryptic. The Reverend Arthur Rous, Pym's stepbrother, was involved; he was accused of having attempted to "inveigle" one of Halhead's servants. The company complained that the documents sent them were so defective that they were unable to judge the case. Mr. Rous died after a short time in the settlement; two years after the event, the company decided that "all passages concerning that business shall be utterly blotted out and taken off the record, so far as they concern Mr. Rous, that no memory of them may remain."[1]

Almost as soon as he was in the island, Halhead found himself at odds with Mr. Ditloff, a second minister, who was a refugee from the Palatinate. Ditloff had borrowed money from Halhead and Rishworth while all three awaited the *Charity* in Plymouth.[2] Once they were in Providence Island, Ditloff suspended Henry Halhead from the sacrament, an act effectively moving him from the center to the extreme margins of that infant society. Ditloff alleged two reasons. The first was that Halhead had failed to return a stone to the apothecary, although Halhead thought he had. He said he did not know where it was but would make "any honest satisfaction." The second reason was that, according to Ditloff, Halhead had affirmed to him privately that John Wells, Mate on the *Charity*, was a "carnal man, and would sometimes swear." He then publicly called Wells honest and religious and denied that he had used the word carnal.

Ditloff's tenure on Providence Island was brief and turbulent. He later defended himself before the company's courts against charges that he had sung profane songs on the sabbath by arguing that his command of English was imperfect. The earlier dispute over what Halhead had or had not said may have derived from a misunderstanding. In any case,

1. PIC, Prep. Ct., 11–21–32; Ctee., 3–21–33; PIC to Gov. and Coun., 7–20–33, 9–34.
2. PIC, Prep. Ct., 11–21–32.

the causes were trivial. The Providence Island Company, horrified at such treatment of a leading colonist, wrote that it was not fitting to suspend a man for such causes and that they could not "imagine that any Minister will be so indiscreet as to do the like hereafter and therefore in such cases we absolutely forbid it to be done."[3]

With their kinship connections to leading families in England and their expectations of reward from that wider world, the captains appear constantly in the correspondence between London and Providence Island. Henry Halhead and Samuel Rishworth, mentioned infrequently, were far more active in the settlement's daily life, attempting to erect the kind of good order and shared community that was the ideal in England, especially among the puritans from whom they sprang.[4] English parishes traditionally tried to maintain such orderly relations without reference to central authority; the leading civilians of Providence Island must have aimed at a similar level of agreement and shared purpose among the men and women they led. Halhead, Rishworth, and their fellow civilian councilors occupied the key status of mediators and arbitrators in disputes between settlers. They would naturally have expected to act in concert with the ministers in achieving harmony.[5]

Henry Halhead, an honest, substantial puritan man seeking the opportunity to do himself, his God, and his country good, must have wondered whether he had made the right choice in emigrating. Samuel Rishworth was dismayed at his first experience of Providence Island, and he wrote frankly of the ways in which the island fell short of his expectations. When he wrote again to Sir Thomas Barrington after more than a year in the colony, he said little, "seeing I perceive by my Last Letters, I gave Some Distaste to some of the honourable company." Although he was sorry for that, he had written "that which in conscience I thought I was bound to write." Realistic "better encouragements" would be welcomed by him. Rishworth's concern in this letter of December 1633 was not with the island's failure to develop economically; he was disturbed about its disorderly society. Both Halhead and Rishworth disappear from the records for long periods, but occasional glimpses show them

---

3. PIC to Bell by the *Elizabeth*, 4–10–33.
4. The Providence Island Company recognized Halhead's contribution in 1636 when they allowed him 100 pounds of tobacco for his services in overseeing the "public employments" of the island; PIC to Gov. and Coun., 5–36. Similarly, they had thanked Rishworth for taking over the secretary's role temporarily when secretary Thomas Hunt had left the island; PIC to Gov. and Coun. *Long Robert*, 1634.
5. See Keith Wrightson, "Two Concepts of Order: Justices, Constables and Jurymen in Seventeenth-Century England," in Brewer and Styles, ed., *An Ungovernable People*, 21–46, esp. 24–6.

striving to live proper lives in the godly society for which they had emigrated.[6]

Halhead and Rishworth, along with Mr. Edward Gates, the other civilian added to the council in 1632, expected to occupy positions of leadership on the island as the colonists attempted to create comfortable and productive plantations in a recognizably English social setting. Their basic problems were those of all new lands settlements: They had to clear land and build houses, roads, and fortifications, and they had to begin immediately producing crops for sustenance and export. Even experienced planters would have found this program difficult. For English gentlemen and servants, many unfamiliar with agriculture in any form, much less cultivation in the tropics, it was impossible.[7] Psychologically disarrayed by the traumatic voyage, the gentlemen would have found their claims to authority undercut by their own ignorance of the project before them, especially as the captains and the Bermudians could claim exactly the expertise the crippled leadership lacked. The company's requirement that the planters remain tenants sharing half their proceeds with the investors must have seemed like a cruel joke.

Throughout the colony's existence, the planters' complaints revolved around the same basic issues as those in the petition of 1632. The planters wanted control of their economic lives. They wanted secure tenure of their land, and they wanted to market their crops as advantageously as they could. In the fluid world of the Caribbean, colonists who waited for company ships, as they were commanded to do, often lost opportunities to sell their commodities at good prices. Company ships arrived erratically, especially when investors were convinced that the settlers were failing in their duty to stockpile rich products. As a consequence, both sides could lose out. Uncertain arrival of ships meant that the magazines of English goods on which the colonists depended were also only intermittently available. None of these problems was unique to Providence Island. Settlers in all English colonies complained bitterly about insecurity of tenure, inadequate and overpriced magazines, and demands for contributions of their labor to public works. Free trade was an issue in every early colony.

Every colonizing company felt that these complaints were unjust. The companies invested enormous sums of money in establishing colonies,

6. Samuel Rishworth to Sir Thomas Barrington, December, 1, 1633, B. L. Egerton MS 2646, fol. 52.
7. Such lack of farming experience was not unusual. Massachusetts Bay also drew few settlers with agricultural background. One in three colonists in the 1630s was from a town of over 1,000 inhabitants; six in ten came from towns. See Anderson, *New England's Generation*, 28–31.

and the demands for increased spending never seemed to end. Meanwhile, returns from newly founded plantations were small or nonexistent. Adventurers thought that the colonists should understand that they could not continue putting money into a venture indefinitely without returns; certainly, settlers' demands for freedom from company magazines and for free trade with all comers seemed irresponsible. Planters should not on one hand complain that supplies were short, implying that the company should send magazines more frequently, and then insist that they could trade with anyone they pleased so that company magazines went unsold and expensively hired ships returned empty. Investors found settlers' resistance to contributing labor to the public works – roads, churches, and fortifications – bizarre; as every colonizing company pointed out, public works benefited no one so much as the colonists. The anticipated partnership between planters and investors quickly became adversarial as the stresses inherent in the situation came to the fore.

Everyone involved wanted the same outcome: a securely established settlement sustained through the early years until planters could find the product that would bring steady returns. The Virginia and Bermuda companies evolved a formula that was widely used with variations, and many Providence Island investors had had ample experience of their program. Virginia was founded on the principle that every emigrant became a stockholder. Initially, the adventurers "in purse and person" were to form a joint stock that would be divided up seven years after the company's reorganization in 1609. As terms of servitude ended, freedmen were placed on small plots of land as tenants. During this period of common work for the joint stock under the harsh regime of martial law, the little colony barely held on.[8] Then, between 1616 and 1618, the Virginia Company embarked on a major reorganization of its colony. Investigations proved that the company had little to show either in America or in England for the estimated £75,000 invested so far.

At this point, the company elected to separate the problems of sustaining the colony, recompensing individual investors, and developing the overall prospects of the plantation. Four great boroughs, Jamestown, Charles City, Henrico, and Kecoughtan (Elizabeth City), were set up as company lands. These were to be farmed by men sent over at company expense who would be tenants at halves. The company's half of their proceeds would go to the common needs of the colony, such as government and public works, and to replenish the company's joint stock. The rest of the land would be offered to investors as "Particular

8. See Chapter 2.

Plantations," which adventurers could populate with servants and run for their own benefit. Everyone already in the colony in 1618 was to receive 100 acres of land, all but those who had paid their own way before 1616 agreeing to payment of an annual quitrent of 2 shillings. Subsequent colonists who came on their own were to receive 100 acres, with a 2-shilling quitrent. Settlers transported at company expense were to receive fifty acres requiring a 1-shilling annual rent at the end of their seven years of tenancy at halves on the company lands.[9]

Particular plantations were given wide economic freedom and encouragement. One hundred acres would go to the proprietors for every colonist imported; tying land acquisition to the importation of servants meant that the estates would actually be cultivated. Moreover, the plantations were granted free trade in magazines and in the commodities they produced themselves. If Virginia Company investors were to profit from the colony, their recompense would come from such independent ventures under the company umbrella. Servants who had filled their time on such plantations, like company servants, were eligible for fifty acres of their own. Despite opening the door to free trade, the company did not cut off its own magazines. Rates were set for acceptance of tobacco in exchange for goods from the store, and the company markup was restricted to 25 percent.[10]

The Somers Islands, or Bermuda, Company, chartered in 1615 as an offshoot of the Virginia enterprise, allowed proprietorial development of independent plantations, called "tribes," almost from the beginning; investors could know that most of the money and effort they invested would go directly to develop their own property. Lands reserved to the company for common costs, as in Virginia, were worked by tenants at halves for terms of five years, a system that became generalized and fixed in law throughout Bermuda by 1620.[11]

Both colonies thrived by allowing investors, through privatization of their property, to recompense themselves. But company and colony expenses were met by placing tenants at halves, sharecroppers on company lands. Tenancy at halves thus was seen by backers in England as the most reasonable way of sustaining a colonizing company and

9. Puritan merchants such as Matthew Cradock, who were nonemigrating members of the Massachusetts Bay Company, similarly made money from separate ventures conducted under the company umbrella; see Andrews, *Ships, Money and Politics,* 90–1.
10. These arrangements are described in Craven, *Dissolution of the Virginia Company,* chap. 3, and in Edmund S. Morgan, *American Slavery – American Freedom: The Ordeal of Colonial Virginia* (New York, 1975), chap. 5. The quitrents were rarely collected; see Billings, "Transfer of English Law to Virginia," in Andrews, Canny, and Hair, eds., *Westward Enterprise,* 237.
11. Craven, *Introduction to the History of Bermuda,* 53–9, 75.

meeting common costs. It was universally hated by those forced to work under the system; many observers also argued that it was short-sighted. George Sandys, treasurer in Virginia and brother of one of the most influential men in the Virginia Company, wrote home against "that so absurd Condition of halves," saying that tenants were unable even to feed themselves, much less to satisfy their halves. They could build no secure foundation for the future while struggling just to keep up with their obligations. Too many ran into debt and lost heart.[12]

In Bermuda also the colonists objected bitterly to this arrangement, where none had "any land at all of their own, but live all as tenants, or as other mens poor servants."[13] Ironically, it was Sir Nathaniel Rich who first experimented in Bermuda with a more straightforward arrangement using indentured servants and, finally, slaves instead of tenants. Tenancy at halves ultimately disappeared; attempts to introduce tenancy into Maryland, founded shortly after Providence Island, were almost completely unsuccessful.[14]

Plymouth colony, founded in 1620, offers another variation on the same themes. The Pilgrims were equal partners with their investors in London, and all assets were held in common at first; the joint stock was to be dissolved in seven years after which the property would belong in equal shares to the English investors and the colonists. Many of the Pilgrims objected to the latter condition. In 1626 the planters were able to buy out the discouraged investors and transferred control of their affairs to America. All the assets, land and livestock, were divided, each settler receiving twenty acres. Contrary to the Virginia experiment, servants had no right to land unless a master chose to give it. The eight men who took on responsibility for discharging the debt to the investors, a heavy obligation, were given a monopoly of the colony's trade. Thus, the Pilgrims voluntarily took on a burden – monopoly control of their trade – that settlers in other colonies resented.[15]

Barbados, founded shortly before Providence Island, offers a confused

12. George Sandys to Sir Samuel Sandys, March 30, 1623 in Susan Myra Kingsbury, ed., *The Records of the Virginia Company of London*, 4 vols. (Washington, DC, 1906–35), IV, 73–5; George Sandys to Samuel Wrote, March 28, 1623, ibid., 64–8.

13. John Smith, *The Generall Historie of Virginia, New-England, and the Summer Isles*, 1624, in Barbour, ed., *Complete Works*, II, 374.

14. On Rich's experimentation, see Wesley Frank Craven, *An Introduction to the History of Bermuda* (Williamsburg, 1940; rpt. from *William and Mary Quarterly* for 1937–38), 90. On the disappearance of tenancy at halves, see Andrews, *Colonial Period*, I, 238. On Maryland see Lorena S. Walsh, "Community Networks in the Early Chesapeake," in Carr, Morgan, and Russo, eds., *Colonial Chesapeake Society*, 204–5, 213; James Horn, "Adapting to a New World: A Comparative Study of Local Society in England and Maryland, 1650–1700," ibid., 147–8; and Carr, Menard, and Walsh, *Robert Cole's World*, 7–12.

15. Andrews, *Colonial Period*, I, 264–67, 283–90.

picture. The settlers were required by the proprietor to pay rents, although they considered themselves freeholders. The rent, initially 5 percent of proceeds, was changed to a set amount of cotton per member of household. Rents were always difficult to collect. Peter Hay, the proprietor's receiver, complained that members of the council took the lead in refusal to comply. Early in the 1640s Philip Bell, now governor of Barbados, acceded to the assembly's demand that rents be suspended. The assembly then proceeded to pass an act that decreed outright ownership of their property in land. The proprietorial relationship continued to be troubled through the Civil War and Interregnum years.[16]

Representative government, which also implied civilian control of the military establishment, joined secure land tenure as the basic grounds of colonial success. When Providence Island was settled, general assemblies had already played a role in government of most other English plantations for a decade; sponsors recognized the contribution to stability made by giving colonists a voice in policymaking. The Virginia Company had ended its experiment with military rule and had recognized the utility of popular participation in government by 1619. The Virginia Assembly, according to David Konig, tied the Virginia Company to the interests of the most powerful local landowners; thus land ownership and representative government were two aspects of the same movement.[17] Plymouth, lacking a legal patent, elected governors and assistants from its foundation in 1620 and formed a representative general court in 1636.

In 1620 the Bermuda Company directed the colony's new governor, Captain Nathaniel Butler, to call an assembly, which in addition to the governor, his council, and the bailiffs of the tribes, consisted of two burgesses from each tribe "chosen by plurallitie of voice." Butler's instructions acknowledged that "every man will more willingly obey laws to which he hath yielded his consent." Even though all legislation was subject to a proprietorial veto – Butler warned that the assembly's work could be "annihilated" by the adventurers "but with holding up their hands only, and a dash or two of a pen" – the empowerment that was offered to substantial planters by this degree of control everywhere seems linked to a colony's entry into a new phase of commitment and development.[18]

Assemblies were common practice at the time of Providence Island's founding. Massachusetts Bay had transformed its corporate charter into

16. Bennett, "Peter Hay," *Jamaican Historical Review* 5 (1965), 12, 14–15, 19; Hilary McD. Beckles, *White Servitude and Black Slavery in Barbados, 1627–1715* (Knoxville, TN, 1989), 15–18, 27; Puckrein, *Little England*, 48–51.
17. Konig, "Colonization and the Common Law in Ireland and Virginia," in Henretta, Kammen, and Katz, eds., *Transformation of Early American History*, 87–92.
18. Butler, *History of the Bermudaes*, ed. Lefroy, 189–92.

a government that included an assembly and an elected governor and council. Lord Baltimore's charter for Maryland, issued in 1632 when the Providence Island Company first reconsidered the government of its colony, provided for a general assembly (although Calvert did not recognize it as a law-making body initially) as well as a governor and council appointed by the proprietor.[19] The authority of the assembly organized by dissident Barbadian planters in 1638 was recognized by Governor Philip Bell in 1641 when he agreed to accept his salary directly from them. As in Virginia, the assembly made possible the planter elite's seizure of control.[20]

Thus, even before Providence Island was settled, the essential meaning of the American experience was plain for those capable of reading it: Private property in land, combined with a degree of political devolution, was the key to success. Even those colonies with some sort of rent arrangement on the books operated in practice as if settlers owned the land they worked. Tenancy and sharecropping were not only hated, but more important they did not work. All emigrants came to the colonies looking for the same thing: a competency for themselves and their families. Land ownership represented stability and independence, the ability to fend for themselves and be threatened by no one. An assembly, by handing out public obligations in an acceptable way, protected that security. The tens of thousands who emigrated during the decade through which Providence Island struggled, a decade of great uncertainty and looming threats in England, came for this great goal of security. Religious convictions as well as economic health were protected by the independence offered by possession of competency.[21] Providence Island, with its constant fear of attack and its denial of land ownership, flew in the face of this basic lesson that colonists demanded security.[22]

19. Andrews, *Colonial Period*, I, 180–8, 220–5, 290–8, 431–46; David W. Jordan, *The Foundations of Representative Government in Maryland, 1632–1715* (Cambridge, 1987), 1–2, 17, 28–9, 35–6. Barbados planters organized their own assembly in 1638, shortly before Philip Bell became governor of that island; Puckrein, *Little England*, 41.
20. Puckrein, *Little England*, 41, 94. In 1783 Thomas Jeffreys, geographer to the king, praised the Barbados constitution as a model for other islands and credited Philip Bell with creating "all these political advantages." Jeffreys, *The West-India Atlas* (London, 1783), 20.
21. So evocative was this language that Samuel Sewall, writing of sanctified Christians, pictured them as having been granted "a most beneficial and inviolable lease under the Broad Seal of Heaven, who were before only Tenants at will," *The Selling of Joseph: A Memorial*, in *The Diary of Samuel Sewall, 1674–1729*, ed. M. Halsey Thomas (New York, 1973), II, 1117.
22. On the term *competency*, see Daniel Vickers, "Competency and Competition: Economic Culture in Early America," *William and Mary Quarterly* 3rd ser., XLVII (1990), 3–29, and Anderson, *New England's Generation*.

None of this was as clear to contemporaries as it is to us. The colonies in existence in 1629–30 when the new puritan settlements were being planned looked distinctly messy and haphazard. Puritan leaders looked with distaste on the examples of existing plantations as they contemplated the establishment of two American colonies during 1629. John Winthrop put the problem well in his "Reasons to be considered for justifying the undertakers of the intended Plantation in New England." In countering those who pointed to "the ill success of other Plantations," he delineated three fundamental errors they had made: (1) "their main end was Carnal and not Religious"; (2) "They used unfit instruments, a multitude of rude and misgoverned persons the very scum of the Land"; and (3) "They did not establish a right form of government." The Providence Island investors agreed wholeheartedly with Winthrop's analysis.

Advocates of the northern colony argued that problems faced by earlier ventures could be avoided if all authority were located in the settlement. The lesser gentlemen, including Winthrop, who headed the Massachusetts Bay Company agreed to emigrate, but they made their commitment conditional on taking the company charter with them.[23] Thus, control, and the basis of a system of self-government, was transferred to America. Correspondence and the flood of books written in Massachusetts but printed in London during the 1630s and 1640s show that the New Englanders were deeply concerned about how their actions were received in England, but they were actually answerable to no one short of the royal government, whose attempts to investigate were stymied.

The Massachusetts Bay Company had originally envisioned a headright system: Every immigrant who paid his own way became a stockholder by adventuring his person, and every stockholder was to be entitled to land, fifty acres per head of household and more for those of better quality. In America the plan was soon transformed. Towns were laid out by companies created for the purpose, and the shareholders were allotted land within the town. Massachusetts became wildly successful with its promise of security of tenure from the beginning. By this single stroke it cut through the problems that had plagued all other colonies. While Providence Island struggled to attract a few hundred settlers of the right godly type, English men and women went to New England in their thousands.[24]

23. Winthrop, "Reasons to be Considered," *Winthrop Papers* II, 142–3; "The true coppie of the Agreement of Cambridge, August 26. 1629," ibid., 151–2.
24. Rutman, *Winthrop's Boston*, 40–6, Anderson, *New England's Generation*. For a different view see John Frederick Martin, *Profits in the Wilderness: Entrepreneurship*

Although the Providence Island investors agreed with Winthrop's analysis of the poor record of earlier colonies, they disagreed fundamentally with the Massachusetts leadership on how to avoid similar failures in the new puritan colonies. The adventurers interpreted the cautionary examples as demonstrating that divergent goals and disruptive elements would necessarily pollute any foreign venture. Merchants and their short-range thinking had played a particularly baleful role in earlier companies, focusing attention on immediate gain and not on sound foundations. The Providence Island backers believed that the way to avoid repetition of earlier failure was to keep all control concentrated in their hands in London, where corrupt influences could never enter.[25] In their desire to prevent the subversion of purpose they saw in other ventures, they disastrously misjudged the avenues to the establishment of a strong and well-knit society.

Charles I has been criticized by historians for his increasing reliance on the lieutenancy and prerogative government and for failing to understand the bases of English local government and of the partnership between the center and the counties. The implication is that his opposition understood better the fundamental relationships on which order stood. In designing a government for their colony, however, the Providence Island investors, key opposition leaders in the 1640s, demonstrated their own lack of such comprehension. The adventurers thought that they could recreate merely by fiat the sources of status and the web of relationships on which they rested by sending the right kind of people and dictating relationships. They sent substantial godly men and women but undercut their capacity for leadership and their effectiveness as examples by denying them the degree of freedom of action enjoyed by

---

     and the Founding of New England Towns in the Seventeenth Century (Chapel Hill, 1991).

25. The notion that merchants' concerns had ruined the Virginia and Bermuda ventures was widespread. On leaving the governorship of Bermuda, Captain Nathaniel Butler carried a petition from the planters against the company's practice of voting by head rather than by share, which allowed the merchants to predominate; similarly Captain Philip Bell cited the merchants' role in the company as his reason for leaving Bermuda for Providence Island in 1629. George Donne, son of the poet, blamed Virginia's problems in part on its direction by "Men of Trade." In 1634, as its financial problems became acute, the Providence Island Company discussed the dangerous consequences of accepting merchants into their number; PIC Ctee. 5–17–34, Gen. Ct., 5–19–34. On Bermuda see Butler, *History of the Bermudaes*, ed. Lefroy, 291–7; Petition from the Council in Bermuda, ca. October 1622, and "The Grievances instanced, proved and perticularized," ca. October 1622 in Ives ed., *Letters from Bermuda*, 235–9; Philip Bell to Sir Nathaniel Rich, March 1629, ibid., 313–25; and Craven, *Introduction to the History of Bermuda*, 163, 198. On Virginia see George Donne, "Virginia Reviewed," ed. T. H. Breen, *William and Mary Quarterly* 3rd ser., XXX (1973), 460.

local gentry in England. Not only did these putative leaders lack governmental independence, but as tenants whose economic activities were directed by the company, they also lacked the attributes of leaders. The squabbling and divisiveness on the council about which the company constantly complained were results of the leadership vacuum.

In answer to the colonists' 1632 petition, the company had offered vague promises of changes in the prescribed pattern of landholding in Providence Island, meanwhile arguing disingenuously that the system of halves had worked well in other plantations. Over the next four years, they slowly and grudgingly retreated from this position. The example of Massachusetts Bay with its widespread land ownership was always before the Providence Island Company as the two plantations competed for immigrants. Providence Island Company members were among the greatest of puritan lay patrons of godly ministers in England; they formed a partnership with their ministerial clients and friends in the effort to make England a truly godly society. But this partnership did not translate well into colonial ventures, where the clerics became leaders of a different constituency. Each of the several confrontations between intending colonists and the adventurers was provoked by a minister who, as the settlers' leader, demanded outright ownership of land. Lewis Morgan, Providence Island's first minister, was the "fomenter" of the initial challenge to tenancy at halves in the colony. At crucial points throughout the colony's history, prospective minister-colonists who could promise to bring substantial followings with them forced company members to reconsider their policy. Land ownership and reformed religion were seen as mutually reinforcing.

Land tenure was not the only source of colonists' grievances; settlers also chafed under their dependence on the company for their essential supply of servants and magazines. Settlers' grievances about the land system were paralleled and reinforced by complaints over stinting of men and supplies. Unkept promises on both sides led to the adversarial relationship between planters and adventurers that neither had foreseen. The colonists were keenly aware of their helplessness; ultimately, their situation depended on what the company decided to do. Even if the investors had kept to a strict schedule in sending supplies, many other agents, from plague to pirates, could intervene to cripple their plans.[26] Planters were left with an overwhelming sense of insecurity.

26. The investors blamed their failure to send servants in 1636 and 1637 on the plague; PIC to Gov. and Coun. by the *Happie Return*, 6–36, and by the *Mary Hope*, 3–37.

In April 1633 the adventurers had written that, although they were not able to send a supply by this ship, the *Elizabeth*, they would fulfill their promise and send a full complement by the next one. When the *Golden Falcon* was sent in July 1633, however, the company declined to load it with supplies and servants. The investors wrote that their promise had been conditional on the expectation that the *Charity*, the ship that had carried Halhead and Rishworth in 1632, would return filled with staple commodities. That ship's empty return made them "seriously lay to heart the vastness of their expenses and the little fruit that hath accrued unto them thereby," all of which they blamed on the colonists' wrangling in "private quarrelings" to the neglect of planting and experimentation.

Because of the settlers' "small Providence," the company were determined "not to proceed in such vast expenses as formerly until we see that the planters do addict themselves to the planting of some staple commodities." By this time, the company argued unrealistically, the colony should no longer be dependent on magazines from home. The colonists also received word by the *Golden Falcon* that the company was developing its project for the mainland under Captain Sussex Camock. Thus as the adventurers diverted their attention to other prospects, the colonists were unexpectedly forced to wait an entire year for the infusion of supplies and men they needed. The *Long Robert* would not sail before September of 1634.[27]

The settlers complained not only that magazines were stinted by the company but also that much of the merchandise was of poor quality or spoiled. Moreover, goods were not distributed fairly within the island; those with powerful friends and influence were favored and others found that even their own stores were not safe from confiscation.[28]

In May 1634 the Providence Island Company first faced the challenge of competing directly with the terms offered by New England. A substantial minister, Reverend Henry Roote, who had actually been to see Providence Island for himself and had won the support of the godly planters there, promised to emigrate with a company of 100 settlers who would pay their own way if he and his flock were allowed control over life in Providence Island comparable to their prospects in Massachusetts. Their main demands were the removal of unsuitable people

---

27. PIC to Gov. and Coun. 4–10–33; PIC to Gov. Bell 4–10–33; PIC to Gov. and Coun. 7–20–33. Compare John Winthrop's statement to Sir Simonds D'Ewes in July 1635 that thirty ships had already come to Massachusetts Bay that summer; *Winthrop Papers* III, 200.
28. PIC, Ctee. 5–22–33; PIC to Gov. and Coun., 4–10–33, 7–20–33; PIC to Bell 7–1–33; PIC to Elfrith, 9–34; PIC to Axe 9–34.

to be named by Roote and "to have the government in their own hand."

The investors initially agreed to these conditions; with the development of their enterprises on the mainland, those expelled from Providence Island could be compensated for their plantations and allowed new opportunities in Central America. They were "constrained to yield" on the demand for self-government "to preserve the island from desertion." Governor Bell and the council and the Reverend Hope Sherrard wrote the company, urging the investors to agree to Roote's conditions. Sherrard indicated that he would be so discouraged if Roote did not return that he might not be able to continue on the island. Samuel Rishworth wrote to Sir Thomas Barrington, indicating in the strongest terms that Roote, "my ancient acquaintance and worthy friend," spoke for the colonists of the right sort. The substantial godly men on whose partnership the company had based its enterprise were pointing the way to the kind of orderly, committed society everyone had hoped for.[29]

In their reorganization of 1634, the investors held a series of intensive debates about what to do. Although the colonists were dependent on the company for supplies, they also held a trump card that the adventurers believed they might now play: The planters could simply give up the project and leave the island. With their new hopes for Camock's flax and the promise of Providence Island as a safe storehouse, the investors wanted to protect their investment and save the colony. Even when Henry Roote and his promised followers decided against emigrating, the adventurers determined to go on.

Over the summer of 1634 and relying on an extensive analysis laid out by John Pym, the company decided to send clothes and equipment for the 300 men they thought were currently on the island and to send further servants with their own supplies. Pym's investigations had revealed that a large ship cost little more to hire than a smaller one, and a capacious vessel could pick up the quantities of flax they hoped to find with Camock on the Moskito Coast. In their debates members also reasoned that if the planters were determined to leave, this ship could bring them home and save further expense; certainly the company was obligated to offer that opportunity in order to save "scandal and complaint."

Pym initially suggested sending 200 men, with supplies valued at £8 to £10 per man, together with a magazine worth £1,500 in ammunition

29. Rishworth to Barrington, December 1, 1633, B. L. Egerton MS 2646, f. 52; PIC Ctee 5–25–33; PIC Ct 5–19–34; PIC to Gov. and Coun. 7–20–33; PIC to Gov. and Coun. by the *Long Robert*, 1634; PIC to Gov. Bell, *Long Rob.* 1634; PIC to Sherrard, *Long Rob.* 1634.

and clothes for the colonists already on the island. He calculated the cost, added to the fortune already invested, at £5,500. The proposal was scaled back over the course of the debates to a commitment of £3,300, including ship rental, a magazine of £600 for the settlers, and the sending of 100 equipped men.[30]

When the *Long Robert* sailed with the new supplies, it also carried instructions for their fair distribution. The company apologized for the negligence of the company husband, saying they had been deceived as well as the colonists. The new husband, William Woodcock, would see that no poor quality goods were sent, and company members would supervise their acquisition. In the island, the goods were to be distributed in return for cotton and tobacco at set rates: cotton at 6 pence per pound and tobacco at 10. These were generous terms, they wrote, and they expected settlers to pay off their massive debts to the company store at these easy rates. Company members resented being made to look bad by the partisan actions of private men in Providence Island and directed that their invoice be posted publicly. Goods were to be distributed at an open market held weekly like a fair, and councilors were to supervise. On the other hand, if private men brought in commodities at their own expense, they could sell them, always providing the goods were wholesome contributions to island life.[31]

Servants, men to work the land, constituted the other great need of the planters. Colonists went to Providence Island on the understanding that they would be supplied with men to work at halves. In the supply of men as on all others the company reneged on early promises. This meant that planters whose servants were finishing their time would be bereft of men to work their crops, and officers would not receive the servants that constituted their salaries. The investors argued they had been informed that the island was not yet ready to receive large numbers of men who would only constitute an additional burden until staple commodities were established.[32] The pattern of promise and retreat would continue throughout the colony's life.

Although the adventurers recognized that they were breaking their own commitments, they reasoned that the promises had been made on the basis of an implied contract that the planters had broken first. The

---

30. PIC, Ctee. and Ct. 5–17–34; Ct. 5–19–34, 6–13–34, 6–16–34, 6–21–34, 6–26–34.
31. PIC to Bell by the *Long Robert*, 9–34; PIC to Gov. and Coun., *Long Rob.*, 9–34; PIC to Elfrith, *Long Rob.*, 9–34. Early in 1635 company members wrote to Governor Bell that men who sold commodities at excessive rates were to be barred from the island's government; PIC to Bell by the *Expectation*, 2/3–35.
32. The pattern had begun even before 1634. See PIC to Gov. and Coun., 7–20–33; PIC to Bell 7–1–33.

company had agreed to their huge initial outlays of money on the assumption that within a few years the returns from the island would repay their investment and would pay for future supplies. No one could have assumed that company members had shouldered an open-ended and ever-growing burden with no hope of retreat. Because the dismal performance of Providence Island was the clear result of planters' negligence, some members argued, any promises made to them could "justly be evaded." Settlers' own complaints had made it impossible to recruit godly colonists, and sending more of the wrong sort would only make the situation worse.[33]

The *Long Robert*'s supplies did little to assuage colonists' discontent. The company wrote of their incredulity at complaints about the clothes in the cargo. They had sent three suits, three shirts, and three pairs of shoes and stockings for every servant, "and proportionally of other things," with higher-quality clothes for planters of the better sort. The fault must lie in unequal distribution. Persistent reports that leading settlers were engrossing goods and selling them at exorbitant rates were profoundly disturbing, as was news that the colonists were trading away their products to Dutch ships in exchange for supplies.

Such behavior not only cheated the investors out of the goods that should repay them – the planters were chronically and deeply in debt to the company stores by this time – but too much of the island's produce was exchanged for alcohol, increasing disorder, and pulling the settlement steadily away from the shared goals of investors and substantial planters. Investors were outraged to learn that in one instance the island's entire crop had been traded to Dutch ships for the wine known as sack while the company's own ship was actually in the harbor. At the very same time, planters were allowed to take goods out of the company stores on credit; Mr. Hooke came home in 1635 owing £92.6s.6d. The company was also sure that colonists' debts were manipulated, traded from hand to hand when planters left the island, to evade their just obligations to the adventurers.[34] Modern new lands experience replicates that of Providence Island and other colonies. Investigators find that repayment of loans is most effectively accomplished when settlers are forced to market their crops through the investors or authorities. At the same time, however, such marketing is inefficient, and private traders offer much better services to planters than "official" ones.[35]

The Providence Island Company had relied too heavily on colonists'

33. PIC, Prep. Ct. 6–16–34.
34. PIC to Bell by the *Expectation* 2/3–35; PIC, Ctee. 7–8–35, 6–24–35, 6–26–37; PIC to Gov. and Coun. by the *Blessing* 5–36 and by the *Mary Hope* 3–37.
35. Scudder, *Development Potential of New Lands Settlements*, 37, 40.

dependence to bring them around to proper behavior, but planters were not without alternatives. Left without support from England, settlers found their salvation in the lively Caribbean trade scene, where Dutch traders moved freely carrying goods throughout the region. Such contacts were common; it was through their Dutch connections that Barbados planters received their first instruction in sugar cultivation and processing. Providence Island investors explained to their planters that the Dutch, with their low customs rates, could always compete unfairly with company ships, which were bound by law to carry their cargoes to England where customs were high. Robert Harcourt claimed that Dutch ships always gained at least "cent per centum" on cargoes carried to the West Indies. The investors stipulated that a tax comparable to English customs be collected from Dutch ships; this revenue could help defray public costs in the island.[36] But the company increasingly allowed members to send private magazines for colonists' supply.[37]

None of these problems over magazines was unique to Providence Island; every other colony experienced them. When Captain Nathaniel Butler was governor of Bermuda in 1620, he wrote to Sir Nathaniel Rich about the colonists' outrage at the rule that they trade with none but the company magazine ships at "cutthroat" prices. Nor did the magazines contain the supplies the colonists needed. Complaints continued throughout the decade; in 1629 the Bermuda council was still complaining about the inadequacy and excessive prices of the company's magazines, as they explained why they had, against orders and in defiance of Governor Philip Bell, traded with a well-equipped private ship.[38] In Virginia and Barbados, planters also felt victimized by the company's magazine policies, believing that they were paying high prices for inadequate supplies and that their tobacco was undervalued by the company. Analysts blamed the problem on the greed of merchants,

---

36. PIC to Gov. and Coun. by the *Mary Hope*, 3–37, and by the *Swallow* and *Spy*, 7–38; Harcourt, *Relation of a Voyage to Guiana*, 1626 ed., 81–2. Throughout the 1630s, the government made strenuous efforts to force English ships to bring their cargoes to England rather than to Holland; Andrews, *Ships, Money and Politics*, 102–3.
37. PIC to Gov. and Coun. by the *Blessing* 5–36 and by the *Mary Hope* 3–37.
38. Nathaniel Butler to Sir Nathaniel Rich, Oct. 23, 1620 [H.M.C. Manchester Papers 284], in Ives, ed., *Letters From Bermuda*, 190–1; Lefroy, ed., *Memorials of the Bermudas*, I, 230–3; Bermuda Council to the Bermuda Company, March 1629 [HMC 415], ibid., 303–11. Bell was soon to become governor of Providence Island; his father-in-law, Daniel Elfrith, was among the letter's signers. Such complaints continued in Bermuda. See William Golding, *Servants on Horseback: Or, A Free People bestrided in their persons, and Liberties, by worthlesse men: Being a Representation of the dejected state of the Inhabitants of Summer Islands* ([London], 1648), 1–5, 22.

a prejudice that fed the Providence Island Company's desire to have all control in their own hands.[39]

Nor was Massachusetts Bay free of the problem. The Reverend John White wrote in 1636, distressed by news of shortages and high prices for clothing in Massachusetts. He had discussed with friends in England investing in a magazine of supplies that they proposed to sell at a 25 percent markup, the same as that charged by the Providence Island Company. These investors would, he wrote, of course insist that colonists trade with no one else. These problems persisted; in 1641 Thomas Gorges of Maine wrote that "they very much want" clothing in Massachusetts.[40]

Henry Roote's decision not to return to Providence Island in 1634 had occasioned an ambivalent response, disappointment tempered with relief, from the investors. Freed of pressure from Roote's godly substantial colonists, they delayed making policy changes. In 1635 the company again faced a minister, George Burdett, who sought conditions comparable to those of New England. Burdett demanded competency for "some godly families and persons now intending to return to New England" whom he expected to persuade to accompany him. The company offered to give the prospective colonists a "competent" portion of land and to allow them to keep everything they raised for their own sustenance. In place of the hated system of halves, they would keep two-thirds of their tobacco and cotton. When richer commodities were established, the settlers would be allowed to keep a portion worth at least as much as two-thirds of the tobacco and cotton. This provision was to be extended to all planters once their debts to the company store were settled.[41] George Burdett declined the adventurers' offer and emigrated to New England a few months later; he stayed for six years as a restless and abrasive figure.[42]

In 1636 the investors were filled with confidence over Providence Island's successful repulsion of the Spanish attack and their own plans for the coming governor, Robert Hunt. Having put the company on a sounder footing with a new joint stock, they proposed a dramatically

39. Hagthorpe, *England's Exchequer*, 25; Smith, *The True Travels, Adventures, and Observations of Captaine John Smith*, 1630, in Barbour, ed., *Smith Works*, III, 216–17; Foster, *Late Horrid Rebellion*, 1–2; Butler, *History of the Bermudaes*, ed. Lefroy, 290–7.
40. John White to John Winthrop, November 16, 1636, *Winthrop Papers* III, 321–2; Thomas Gorges to Sir Ferdinando Gorges, September ? 1641, in Moody, ed., *Gorges Letters*, 57. See also Thomas Dudley to the Countess of Lincoln, March 28, 1631, in Emerson, ed., *Letters from New England*, 81.
41. PIC, Ctee., 2–20–35.
42. See Chapter 8.

changed relationship with their colonists that they expected would draw some of the freemen going to New England. At the General Court on February 19, John Pym proposed that the island's 3,000 acres be divided into farms of 50 and 30 acres, the former to be worked by fourteen men, the smaller by eight, with the stipulation that each farm plant a certain amount of tobacco and cotton as directed by the governor.[43] The planters would renew their own complement of servants as terms ended paying for the passage of new servants in tobacco and cotton taken up at set rates. Pym proposed that planters pay a small tax for "public charges" and set aside a fifth of proceeds for the company, which he reckoned would bring in £2,500 each year.

Company members agreed, but they suggested that the colonists be asked to stipulate a rent they thought fair in "consideration of the company great charge." They also suggested a delay in settling leases until those "not fit" were weeded out of the island. But even as the adventurers moved to meet colonists' demands for security of tenure and means of profit, they still did not allow for the kind of entrepreneurial leap about to happen in Barbados. In the same meeting, they specified that if the product on which they currently focused their hopes, dette, were introduced into the island, it would be reserved to agents acting for the company.[44]

Company letters written in May 1636 informed the colonists of their new initiative. First, as the planters had requested in a petition transmitted by Governor Bell, halves were to be remitted for the past year and, "of our own bounty" the company allowed settlers to keep all proceeds for 1636 as well, providing only that the colonists not evade company rules about trade and debts to the magazine. Captain Elfrith had also advised this abatement, and the company thanked him for his advice. They then announced the new terms for disposition of land. As in other colonies, public lands were to be set aside to support officers, after which the land was to be divided into plantations "that every man may know his own, and have a certainty of term and estate."

The Providence Island "plantations or tenements" were to be compact, not scattered pieces, and all small holdings were to be enlarged because experience showed that undersized units were unproductive. Rent terms

43. Fifty acres was considered the minimum feasible plantation size in the Chesapeake, of which an eighth or a tenth would be cultivated in any year, Gloria L. Main, *Tobacco Colony: Life in Early Maryland, 1650–1720* (Princeton, 1982), 41; Jean Butenhoff Lee, "Land and Labor: Parental Bequest Practices in Charles County Maryland, 1732–1783," in Carr, Morgan, and Russo, eds., *Colonial Chesapeake Society*, 328n. In modern Providence Island, holdings of twenty acres provide a surplus for the market; most islanders hold fewer than ten acres; Wilson, *Crab Antics*, 48, 69.
44. PIC, Gen. Ct., 2–1–36, 2–19–36, 2–20–36.

were to be variable, according to the value of the land and how much tobacco and cotton it might bear, but the planters should expect to give the company about one-fourth of marketable proceeds.[45] The investors might be satisfied with less if the planters shouldered the burden of the public works without expense to the company. Planters were to covenant to plant good commodities in reasonable amounts and to pay for transportation of servants to keep the labor supply large enough for the colony to be truly productive. The company vowed not to look to profits more "than shall stand with the comfortable and plentiful subsistence of the tenants."[46] No date was set for the issuance of leases.

These new arrangements reflected the changing nature of leases in England, where, with the demand for land rising, leaseholds were increasingly common. Long-term leases were for shorter periods, usually twenty-one years, but tenancy at will was on the decline. Providence Island investors were landlords over numerous tenants in England – the Earl of Warwick alone owned sixty-four manors in Essex in 1630 – and they were known as conscientious landlords attentive to their clients' needs. Lord Saye presided in person over his manor courts, exhibiting a remarkable grasp of the detail of local affairs, and his attention to duty was typical of this group. They saw themselves as responsible owners administering land for grateful tenants whose interests they represented in encounters with representatives of the central government when necessary. They naturally assumed that such a relationship would best support the transplantation of English society to the Indies.[47]

The adventurers must have expected gratitude; what they received was news of another mutinous petition and conflict within the governor's council. The investors, whose 1636 promise to supply the island fully was not met because the plague kept them away from London in 1636 and 1637, were astounded to learn that through "some evil disposition" the planters had been led to set a time by which they would all desert the island if supplies had not arrived. Such a resolution was "full of weakness in them, of injustice to us, (which is worst of all) unthankfulness to God who had so wonderfully preserved them." Because the

---

45. Mr. Paul Amirant [Amyraut], who said he was willing to go to the colony as minister, thought he could encourage others to go on condition of sufficient land at a rent of one-fourth of clear profits, PIC Ct., 6–14–36. The Providence Island Company tried twice without success to recruit Amyraut; see Chapter 8.
46. PIC to Gov. and Coun., 5–36; PIC to Elfrith, 3–36. See also PIC Agreemt. with Hunt, 3–1–36.
47. Hunt, *Puritan Moment*, 14–15, 36; Nelson P. Bard, Jr., "William Fiennes, First Viscount Saye and Sele: a study in the Politics of Opposition" (unpub. Ph.D. diss., University of Virginia, 1973), 58–60. On the changing nature of English leaseholds, see Thirsk, ed., *Agrarian History of England and Wales*, IV, 304–5, 680–7.

royal government had taken notice of the island and found it valuable to England, they warned that no deserter would escape punishment if he came home.[48]

Once again the company felt betrayed by the very men who should have been its firmest allies; Samuel Rishworth now fulfilled his intended leadership role at the head of the petitioners rather than as the adventurers' advocate. When called home to explain the colonists' resort to such a "turbulent" proceeding and to enlighten investors about the island's prospects, Rishworth answered mildly. Planter John Symons had written privately to Lord Saye that Rishworth was empowered to speak for the colonists and would put their case strongly, but Rishworth in person merely referred the company to the settlers' written words. Asked specifically about threats of deserting the plantation, he said they meant only that many settlers hoped to participate in the new venture on the mainland when that became possible.[49]

Asked by the company about malfeasance of their officers, particularly the clerks of the stores, Rishworth answered that their actions could not stand scrutiny. Some adventurers then recited charges of engrossing scarce goods made against Rishworth himself, which he answered in detail. He stated that before leaving the island he had asked whether anyone had objection to make against him, which challenge went unanswered. Nonetheless, he avowed before the company that if anyone could charge him with having done £5 worth of wrong he would not only make restitution but would "humble himself for it."[50]

Samuel Rishworth was returned to Providence Island and the position of councilor in 1638; the company wrote that they would not have restored him "but that he hath acknowledged before us his offence about the petition." His position in the island's government depended not on the leadership role he had obviously assumed within the island but on his humility before the company in London. His son Samuel was appointed clerk of the council.[51] But, though they labeled the petition mutinous and the petitioners turbulent, the investors as in 1632 moved to confront the colonists' demands. They set up a commission to hear grievances, which was to be inaugurated at the same time as their new

48. PIC, Ct. 5–14–36; PIC to Gov. and Coun. by the *Blessing* 5–36, by the *Happie Return* 6–36, by the *Mary Hope* 3–37; PIC to Rudyerd by the *Mary Hope* 1–37, PIC to Hunt by the *Mary Hope* 3–37.
49. PIC, Ctee. 2–11–37, 6–14–37; Ct. 6–22–37; PIC to Gov. and Coun. by the *Mary Hope* 3–37.
50. PIC Committee, 6–26–37. Thomas Dudley in Massachusetts Bay was also accused of taking advantage of scarcity to enrich himself; Winthrop, *History*, ed. Hosmer, I, 77.
51. PIC to Gov. and Coun. 4–23–38.

governor, Captain Nathaniel Butler. English tradition did not allow them to ignore such a statement of their clients' wishes.[52]

Convinced that they had been grievously wronged by the neglect and insufficiency of those they had sent, company members increasingly came to feel that nothing but the presence of truly great men could overcome the wrangling and purposelessness of their planters. They did not understand that only the emergence of an indigenous leadership with a firm stake in the colony's future could make such a transplanted society function properly. Instead, they continued to think, as the Virginia Company had in its early failing years, of authority as the product of inherited traits.[53] In 1637 and 1638 company members discussed the possibility of emigration by some of their own number, a prospect made more attractive by the possibility of privateering, which provided a suitable sphere of action for a gentleman. In 1638 the Earl of Warwick, Lord Brooke, and Mr. Henry Darley all declared their resolution to go to the island; surely the commanding presence of such men would turn the colony around.[54]

And finally they agreed to offer prospective colonists who transported themselves, their families, and six servants the opportunity to become freeholders with a modest annual payment of twenty pounds of tobacco per head or its equivalent in cotton. Freeholders were promised a voice in election of the governor and in making laws. As before, the concessions came in negotiations with a godly minister who represented a body of intending immigrants. Competition with Massachusetts Bay again forced investors to offer substantial gains in property ownership and self-government. The Reverend Ezekiel Rogers owed much to Providence Island Company member Sir Thomas Barrington, who had favored and protected him. Despite the obligations Rogers may have felt and the terms he extracted from the Providence Island Company, however, he declined to go the Caribbean. In the summer of 1638, shortly after the company presented him these terms, he and a significant number of

---

52. PIC, Commission and Instructions for hearing of grievances sent in the *Swallow* 7–2–38. At the same time, some indication of a degree of prosperity among the planters began to emerge. The company agreed to compensate Rishworth, Governor Hunt, Captain Rous, and Ensign Fitch for their investments of 500 pounds of tobacco worth £12 10s each in a pinnace that accompanied Rous's ship, the *Blessing*; PIC, Ctee. 6–26–37, 4–18–38. See also the ship *Providence*, John Pinkard master, and its cargo of tobacco and cotton that was entangled in several lawsuits: P. R. O., H. C. A. 24/100 f. 322, 24/101 f. 326. 24/102 ff. 51–52, 13/56 ff. 416–17, 421–2.

53. Bernard Bailyn, "Politics and Social Structure in Virginia," in James Morton Smith, ed., *Seventeenth-Century America: Essays in Colonial History* (Chapel Hill, 1958), 90–118.

54. PIC, Ctee. 6–24–37, Ct. 2–14–38.

followers left Rowley in Yorkshire, into whose church he had been placed by the Barringtons, to found Rowley, Massachusetts.[55]

Despite their failure to lure Rogers and his godly band, the company did extend some of these concessions to colonists already on the island. Rents were lowered to twenty pounds of tobacco per head, with the requirement that planters plant and set aside a plot producing cotton or tobacco worth 150 pounds per head so that they could pay for goods from the stores as well as their rent and "improve their own estates." The plantations were to be surveyed. Once the company received the results, leases for years or for lives would be made according to the settlers' desire, a promise first given in May 1632 and renewed in May 1636. Such long-term leases offered far more security; they were inheritable and could be sold, giving much of the protection of ownership in fee simple.[56] The surveys would ensure that no one had engrossed more than his allotted fifty acres; those who had been encroached upon were to be restored to their full acreage.

Once again, as with their courting of Henry Roote in 1634, the adventurers, having made a promise of self-government in an unsuccessful attempt to lure an emigrating godly band, dropped the idea once the "constraint" was gone. No mention was made of self-government in these letters; the company merely informed the colonists that a new governor, Captain Nathaniel Butler, was coming to take charge of the island's affairs. Butler, who had instituted the representative assembly in Bermuda, was not to repeat that innovation in Providence Island, although he did come armed with a special commission to investigate the colonists' grievances.[57]

Throughout the rest of the colony's life the company tried to bring order to the company stores and the system by which they were allotted. Reports of partiality in distribution continued, as did colonists' complaints about the company's 25 percent markup. On their part the adventurers continued to believe that the settlers were manipulating their debts to avoid just payment. Finally, as company members' attention was increasingly diverted to events in England, they told the planters

55. PIC, Ctee. 3–1–38. On Rogers's career, see David Grayson Allen, *In English Ways: The Movement of Societies and the Transferal of English Local Law and Custom to Massachusetts Bay in the Seventeenth Century* (Chapel Hill, 1982), 21, 195; and Stephen Foster, *The Long Argument: English Puritanism and the Shaping of New England Culture, 1570–1700* (Chapel Hill, 1991), 28–32.

56. On the differences between types of leases, see Russell R. Menard, "From Servant to Freeholder: Status Mobility and Property Accumulation in Seventeenth-Century Maryland," *William and Mary Quarterly* 3rd Ser., XXX (1973), 37–64.

57. PIC, Ctee. 6–24–37; PIC to Gov. and Coun. 5–10–32, by the *Blessing* 5–36, 4–23–38; Instr. Com. for Grievances 7–38.

to trade with whomever they pleased in lieu of magazines, and they authorized London merchant Maurice Thompson to send stores privately for sale in Providence Island.[58] The promised assignment of secure longterm leases for plantations never took place.

Providence Island's English colony was destroyed by the Spanish in 1641 without ever having become successful. Poor, unfocused economic development and failure to develop a strong, vigorous leadership went hand in hand. The investors' basic premise, that only keeping control in their own hands would prevent the kind of perversion of aims seen in other colonies, forestalled development of the integrated, purposeful society led by godly men that had been anticipated by settlers and adventurers alike. The company's denial to planters of private property in land and control of the island's economic life may have been more serious in colonists' eyes than the company's failure to institute some form of representative government. The colonists' complaints centered on the former, but the experience of other colonies demonstrates that having taxing power in their own hands would have been necessary. In neglecting planters' desire for certainty of possession and entrepreneurial control, the investors refused access to the kind of status and expertise on which leaders in other colonies built their legitimacy. Indigenously derived leadership, not directives from London, ultimately spelled success.

The adventurers understood all this when they thought about England's problems. In the Commons debates over the forced loan in 1628, Sir Nathaniel Rich made a famous speech, notes of which lay out this formula: "No propriety [property], no industry; no industry, all beggars; no propriety, no valor; no valor, all in confusion." In 1628 and when parliament finally met again after its eleven-year hiatus in 1640, John Pym also firmly associated industry and commitment with certainty of ownership of the fruits of one's labors: "[F]or who will contend, who will endanger himself for that which is not his own?"[59] But their faith in the shared purpose of themselves and the Providence

58. PIC to Gov. and Coun. 4–23–38, by the *Swallow* and *Spy* 7–38, by the *Mary* 6/7–39, 3–29–41; PIC to Butler by the *Mary* 7–39; PIC, Instr. Com. of Grievances, 7–38; Agreemt. with John Peck 6/7–38; Agreemt. with Thompson, 2–25–40; PIC, Ct. 12–26–40, 2–25–41.
59. Rich, Speech of March 26, 1628, B. L. Stowe MS 366, ff. 20v–21. The Pym quotation is from his Speech on the Impeachment of Roger Manwaring, June 4, 1628, in J. P. Kenyon, ed., *The Stuart Constitution, 1603–1688: Documents and Commentary*, 2nd ed. (Cambridge, 1986), 15–16; see also Pym, Speech to the Short Parliament, April 5, 1640, *A speech delivered in parliament, by a worthy member thereof, and a most faithfull well-wisher to the church and common-weale; concerning the grievances of the kingdome* (London, 1641), 36 (incorrectly numbered 26).

Island colonists, combined with the island's status as company members' own possession, blinded the investors to the overseas application of the same reasoning.

Other colonizing companies were not so blinded, or, divided as they were, had less capacity for holding firm against settlers' demands, as virtually absolute property ownership, at least for the substantial planters, became the general rule in practice throughout the colonies whatever the charters may have stipulated. Establishment of the principle of private property in land as the foundation of society was a stunning innovation of the early English colonies.[60] Its absence proved to be the great stumbling block for Providence Island as time after time the investors lost out to Massachusetts for the right kind of settlers while their own colonists, lacking a leadership with the marks of status and legitimacy derived from mastery of life within the island, endlessly wrangled and quarreled.

The sources of legitimacy were not really different in England. Except for the greatest magnates, most leaders drew authority from their mastery of local affairs and their centrality in a web of relationships, vertical and horizontal, that promised mutual support and aid. They were involved in the economic life of the county and proudly displayed knowledge of its demands. The problem faced by all colonies was replication of such a network and the necessary mastery of economic relationships. One element in success could be combined religious zeal: In a controlled form, shared puritanism certainly provided Massachusetts Bay with a network on which to found a tightly integrated society.[61]

As Providence Island's settlers discovered, however, puritanism was not enough. Land ownership was equally crucial to New England's success.[62] After the middle of the first decade, access to church member-

60. Billings, "Transfer of English Law," in Andrews, Canny, and Hair, eds., *Westward Enterprise*, 236–7. See the divergence of the English and American definitions of "fee simple" (under the heading "fee") in the *Oxford English Dictionary*. For illuminating discussion of the issues involved, see Vickers, "Competency and Competition," *William and Mary Quarterly* 3rd ser., XLVII (1990), 3–29, and Stephen Innes, "Fulfilling John Smith's Vision: Work and Labor in Early America," Introduction to *Work and Labor in Early America* (Chapel Hill, 1988), 45–6.

61. Fletcher and Stevenson, "Introduction," to *Order and Disorder*, 2–3; Timothy H. Breen and Stephen Foster, "The Puritans' Greatest Achievement: A Study of Social Cohesion in Seventeenth-Century Massachusetts," *Journal of American History* LX (1973), 5–22; John Murrin and Gary Kornblith, Paper delivered to conference on Anglo-American social history, Williamsburg, VA, September 1985, 11–12, 16.

62. Virginia Anderson asserts, as have many before her, that land ownership was virtually universal among adult white men in early Massachusetts Bay. John Frederick Martin agrees that land ownership was a crucial element in that colony, pointing out that the founders of Dedham, long considered one of the classic communitarian New England towns, organized a land corporation two years before the church covenant was formed. On the other hand, he argues that tenancy was always present in New

ship and to a role in the northern colony's political life could be gained only by those judged "visible saints" by a congregation. Full church members, who were the only colonists with the right to vote and hold office, very quickly became a minority of the population. Yet the decline of church members and voters as a percentage of population had little effect on the region's burgeoning towns. As landowners, families possessed the badge of membership in the community, and the most important guarantee of security.[63]

Colonists, actual and prospective, were keenly aware of what the colonies offered. Land ownership was the magnet that drew some 10,000 settlers to the Chesapeake during the decade through which Providence Island struggled, and as many to New England. Emigrants to the Chesapeake accepted a significantly lower standing of living than in England in order to own land. When land was no longer readily available, they left at the end of their terms of servitude, braving the rigors of the newly opened regions in order to own farms. The primacy of land ownership in the colonists' concerns can be seen in the document the first Virginia Assembly dubbed the "great Charter." Historians long sought in vain a document prescribing a liberal political order consonant with such a label until Wesley Frank Craven established in 1932 that the colonists' Magna Carta was the document that set forth the new principles of private property in Virginia in 1618.[64] In 1635 when Governor John Harvey threatened the Virginia councilors' title to their lands, as well as their trade, he was expelled from office and shipped back to England.[65]

England. See Anderson, *New England's Generation*, and Martin, *Profits in the Wilderness*.

63. On the extent of church membership and the franchise, see Rutman, *Winthrop's Boston*, 156–7; Francis Bremer, *The Puritan Experiment: New England Society from Bradford to Edwards* (New York, 1976), 95–6; Stephen Foster, "The Massachusetts Franchise in the Seventeenth Century," *William and Mary Quarterly* 3rd ser., XXIV (1967), 613–23, and appendix of the same name to his *Their Solitary Way: The Puritan Social Ethic in the First Century of Settlement in New England* (New Haven, 1971); and Richard C. Simmons, "Freemanship in Early Massachusetts: Some Suggestions and a Case Study," *William and Mary Quarterly* 3rd ser., XIX (1962), 422–8. J. F. Martin suggests that historians, through misunderstanding of the word "inhabitant," have dramatically overestimated the town franchise in Massachusetts Bay; *Profits in the Wilderness*, 218–24, 277–85.

64. James Horn, "Adapting to a New World: A Comparative Study of Local Society in England and Maryland, 1650–1700," in Carr, Morgan, and Russo, eds., *Colonial Chesapeake Society*, 148; Craven, *Dissolution of the Virginia Company*, 52–8. See the "Instructions" from the Virginia Company to Governor George Yeardley, November 18, 1618, in Kingsbury, ed., *Virginia Company Records*, III, 98–109.

65. Bailyn, "Politics and Social Structure in Virginia," in Smith, ed., *Seventeenth-Century America*, 95–7, and Fausz, "Merging and Emerging Worlds," in Carr, Morgan, and Russo, eds., *Colonial Chesapeake Society*, 71–2.

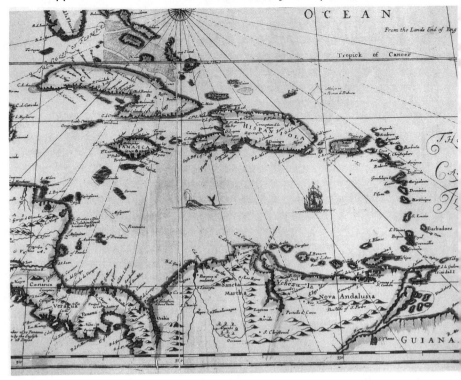

New map of the English plantations in America. (Robert Morden and William Berry, London, 1673; courtesy of the John Carter Brown Library at Brown University.)

In the West Indian islands, the promise of land ownership drew colonists in the early years. The Barbadian Assembly complained in 1675: "In former times We were plentifully furnished with Christian servants from England ... but now We can get few English, having no Lands to give them at the end of their time, which formerly was their main allurement."[66]

In colonies lacking strong proprietorial control, practice often outran legal niceties. In 1620, before the division of property in Plymouth, colonist William Hilton wrote home: "We are all free-holders, the rent

---

66. Barbados Assembly petition to the king, reprinted in Galenson, *White Servitude in Colonial America*, 137. For Galenson's argument that throughout the colonies land was essential for drawing colonists, see, in addition, 144–5, 176.

day doth not trouble us." Similarly, the Barbadian planters assumed the rights of freeholders. Once Massachusetts Bay had instituted widespread freehold land ownership, that became the rule throughout New England. George Fenwick, agent for the lords and gentlemen (many of them members of the Providence Island Company) who had planted Saybrook in Connecticut, wrote of his difficult negotiations for selling the abandoned plantation to the Connecticut towns. When they could not agree on a lump sum, Fenwick suggested a small annual rent per acre and disgustedly reported its refusal: "[T]his I proposed but it would not be borne; and must all here be independent and supreme lords of our own land."[67]

The connection of successful colonization with individual land ownership and the development of native commodities that naturally followed had been forcefully and cogently pointed out by Captain John Smith, early governor of Virginia and America's most informed and thoughtful colonist–promoter. Smith wrote the first full history of all the English colonies and drew the most important lessons of forty years of colonization in his *Generall Historie of Virginia, New-England, and the Summer Isles,* published in 1624. Well before the foundation of Providence Island, he warned that "the vain expectation of present gain in some, ambition in others, that to be great would have all else slaves, and the carelessness in providing supplies, hath caused those defailements in all those Plantations."

Already disappointed by Virginia's concentration on that unworthy product, tobacco, Smith focused his hopes on New England. He wrote of America's lure for those "that have great spirits and small means," but he also warned that "no man will go from hence to have less freedom there than here." In advocating colonization of New England he made his meaning clear: "Here are no hard Landlords to rack us with high rents, or extorting fines, nor tedious pleas in Law to consume us with their many years disputation for Justice . . . as here every man may be master of his own labour and land. . . ."[68]

John Smith died in 1631; his last book, *Advertisements for the Unexperienced Planters of New England, Or Any Where,* was written

67. William Hilton to his cousin, in Captain John Smith, *New Englands Trials,* 1622, in Barbour, ed., *Smith Works,* I, 430–1; George Fenwick to Sir Gilbert Gerrard and Sir William Masham, November 10, 1643, B. L. Egerton MS 2648, f. 1. On freehold property in Massachusetts, see Foster, *Their Solitary Way,* 37–8. In modern Providencia, owning a piece of land is the single most important aspect of identity; land ownership confers a sense of equality among the island's inhabitants; see Wilson, *Crab Antics,* 45–6, 67.
68. Smith, *Generall Historie,* in Barbour, ed. *Smith Works,* II, 410, 420–2, 462, 467.

just as Providence Island and Massachusetts Bay were being established. In it he predicted the success of Massachusetts and correctly analyzed the grounds of that success. He urged the Massachusetts Bay company "not to stand too much upon the letting, setting, or selling those wild Countries, nor impose too much upon the commonalty either by your magazines, which commonly eat out all poor men's labours, nor any other too hard imposition for present gain." The way to success, and gain, was to encourage commitment by giving each man as much land as he could cultivate "to him and his heirs for ever," and he warned that no one would leave England to be worse off in the colonies. He wrote approvingly of the company's first settlement at Salem, in contrast to the disorder and purposelessness of Virginia's early years. In Salem planters were "overseers of their own estates."[69] John Smith's voice carried weight because of his experience, but few, with or without experience, equaled him in his capacity to reflect on its meaning. Captain Daniel Elfrith and the other American veterans who advised the Providence Island Company offered less compelling insights.

The Providence Island investors ultimately came to concede the position set forth by Smith. At the end of the colony's life, the company finally offered terms that attracted settlers from Massachusetts, which was now suffering an economic depression with the falling off of immigration from England. As the 1640s opened, Captain John Humphrey accepted the post of governor and recruited several hundred New Englanders to go to the West Indies. His defection was keenly felt because he was one of the most prominent men in Massachusetts and had been an officer in the venture from its beginnings in England. Like many people, Humphrey had worried about the colony's prospects in the cold, rocky North; the economic downturn at the end of the first decade seemed, to men and women steeped in providentialist thinking, an indication that God did not intend them to stay there.[70]

Humphrey warned his patrons, Lord Saye and the Earl of Manchester, that his colonists would expect the same control that they had had in New England, and he warned against imposition of economic hardship in requiring repayment of transportation and other costs of planters who were selling their New England property at a loss.[71] In a meeting at the end of June 1641 that was devoted largely to the reckoning up of

69. Smith, *Advertisements*, ibid., III, 275, 287.
70. Humphrey to Isaac Johnson, December 9, 1630, *Winthrop Papers* II, 329; Humphrey to John Winthrop, December 12, 1630, ibid., 331–4; Winthrop, *Journal*, ed. Hosmer, II, 25–26.
71. John Humphrey to Earl of Manchester, March 27, 1641; H.M.C. Manchester Papers, 424.

the company's enormous debts, investors agreed that Captain Humphrey would be the colony's governor and that the emigrants from New England "shall have fit freedom and encouragement." This cryptic phrase apparently referred to assurances convincing enough to draw experienced colonists from the North, but the concessions demanded throughout the colony's life by its planters were granted too late. The vanguard of this remigrating band found Providence Island in the hands of the Spanish, and the colonists dispersed.[72]

Henry Halhead, leader of the substantial civilian colonists, appears only once more in the historical record. At the end of his life he wrote a book that must have been partly inspired by his attempt to make a success of the transplanted English society of Providence Island. His book, published apparently posthumously in 1650, was an impassioned attack on enclosures that deprived English people of land and the nation of productive citizens. *Inclosure Thrown Open: or Depopulation Depopulated, not by Spades and Mattocks, but by the Word of God* opened with a quotation from Ezekiel 4:1: "So I returned and considered all the oppressions that are done under the Sun; and behold the tears of such as were oppressed, and they had no comforter. And on the side of their oppressors there was power; but they had no comforter."

Halhead's book was published by his friend Joshua Sprigge, whose father had been Lord Saye's steward. Sprigge wrote that Halhead had been a magistrate and shopkeeper in Banbury "until Providence snatching him thence, made him Governour of the only Island called by her name."[73] Although Halhead was "fresh and green" in old age, Sprigge wrote, his opposition to enclosure was of long standing. Halhead wrote that enclosure enriched the few at the expense of the settled lives of the many, creating poverty by removing men and women from their customary land. One of the ways that enclosers worked, according to Halhead, was to convince common people that they would be three times better off once the land was enclosed. The people did not realize the truth until they had lost their rights.

Halhead argued that parliament ought to rectify these wrongs; instead, that body, now under puritan control, was full of enclosers. Parliament

72. PIC Ct. 6–28–41. Several New England historians wrote with satisfaction about tne sad return of the Humphrey colonists. See Winthrop, *Journal*, ed. Hosmer, I, 334, II, 33–5; William Hubbard, *A General History of New England*, 2nd ed. (Boston, 1848), 375–85: J. Franklin Jameson, ed., *Johnson's Wonder-Working Providence, 1628–1651*, 1654 (New York, 1910), 207–8.
73. Sprigge was a prominent clerical supporter of the new regime in England. By 1650 he was fellow and senior bursar of All Soul's. In 1673 he married the widow of James Fiennes, who had succeeded his father as Lord Saye and Sele. See Greaves and Zaller, eds., *Biographical Dictionary of British Radicals*.

had attacked enclosure in the Grand Remonstrance of 1641, but by 1643 it had begun to support the practice. Halhead, comparing himself to a man ringing the fire bell because he has "seen and felt the danger of it," suggested that neighborhoods organize to take testimony from ancient men about how many people and animals and what crops the land had supported at the opening of the century in comparison to its present yield and that they offer the evidence to parliament.

Joshua Sprigge portrayed Halhead as staying on Providence Island "until the Isle of Great Britain, being about to be born again into a new and free state, might deservedly be christened The Isle of Providence." Whatever hopes Halhead had had of the parliamentary cause, he had lived to see them dashed, as his hopes had been shattered in the Indies. Enclosers, he wrote, lived in cities, remote from their properties, and set bailiffs, like the taskmasters of Egypt, over the poor who remained on the land. Resistance was impossible; if wrongs were not rectified, then the people must wait for God to punish the oppressors. Halhead had learned that placing faith in human agency, regardless of professed aims, led only to disappointment.[74]

74. Halhead, *Inclosures Thrown Open*, with preface by Joshua Sprigge (London, 1650), A2, 1, 4–6, 8, 11–12, 15–17. Sprigge erred in writing that Halhead had been governor of Providence Island; his assumption is instructive about expectations for such a man in the colonial setting. D. E. M. Fiennes and J. S. W. Gibson point out that the Halheads and Lord Saye, on behalf of a client, had been associated in fighting enclosures by Sir Thomas Chamberlayne; "Providence and Henry Halhead," *Cake and Cockhorse* 7 (1978), 199–200. On parliament's role, see J. S. Morrill and J. D. Walter, "Order and Disorder in the English Revolution," in Fletcher and Stevenson, eds., *Order and Disorder*, 140. Company member Richard Knightley had been fined for depopulating enclosures in the 1630s; Cliffe, *Puritan Gentry*, 111.

6

Servants into Slaves

O N JULY 19, 1634, the Earl of Warwick wrote to Hugh Wentworth, his agent in Bermuda, about management of his plantations there. One concern was the use planters made of slaves belonging to the earl. He wanted "my negroes" best placed "with regard to my profit" and requested details of their distribution and the terms on which tenants acquired their labor. Like his land, they were property, their role to enrich the earl and to develop his estate. The logic of this position stumbled on the fact that the slaves were also human beings who could make a claim on his Christian sensibilities. In the same letter he wrote of a complaint received from "Sander, one of my negroes," against a planter named Winter for selling Sander's child. Sander also asked that his wife be allowed to live with him. Warwick, cautious because he admitted he did not know all the "particular grounds," asked Wentworth to investigate and to help "the poor man in all lawful office of favour." He especially hoped man and wife could be together, "it seeming to me a request full of reason." His letter concluded by conceding Wentworth's superior knowledge of the facts and acquiescing in whatever decision he made. Warwick stipulated that Sander should be informed of his interest in the case. Thus, Wentworth was placed in the classic overseer's bind: he was commanded to maximize profits while communicating the owner's fatherly concern for the slave's welfare.[1]

This letter encapsulates a problem slowly worked out over the succeeding two centuries in American history. The independence offered planters by their acquisition of land in America ultimately meant loss of freedom and individuality for other men and women who were themselves defined as property and who thus contributed to freeholders' status. After the tremendous growth of population throughout Europe in the sixteenth and seventeenth centuries, England was seen as being overpopulated; land was in short supply, and people were plentiful. In America the situation was just the reverse. The land that settlers sought

1. Wm. Jessop Letterbook, B. L. Add MS 10615, no. 8, 50.

so eagerly could be worthless without labor to develop it. Access to labor became a major issue throughout the colonies, and brokers soon came forward to organize the trade in labor.

Indentured servitude, the device that made servants available to all the colonies, was an extension of a long-established English practice. Most young English men and women left home at about the age of fourteen or fifteen and became servants, working on a series of annual contracts devised at hiring fairs throughout the country. During the year's term, the master's control over the servant was similar to that of a father; therefore, the young men and women were still under a form of parental control. Servitude was a stage of life, offering a chance to learn the basic skills that would allow one eventually to set up on one's own. Each party was obligated to honor the contract throughout the year. Servants who were found away from their masters would be sent back with a whipping, and masters had to keep their charges even if some disaster made it financially onerous. Theoretically, servants were free only during the one day each year when they attended the annual hiring fair, where they could meet with others in their situation and compare notes on masters. Masters with bad reputations might find it difficult to attract good servants, so the system gave both parties some control over the mutual obligations for which they contracted.[2]

The system changed in the colonial setting. Masters paid for a servant's passage, so the latter's obligation was for a longer term to work off the initial investment. Servants had much less leverage in this situation, because contracts were forged in England, and, through a master's death or chicanery, newcomers' assignments might be different from what had been agreed.[3] The promised rewards were what lured English men and women to the colonies. In England servants would traditionally work for as much as a decade in a series of annual contracts before saving enough to marry and set up a home, usually as a tenant. Increasingly, even such limited independence was beyond reach, for the numbers seeking leases exceeded the supply of holdings. In America freedmen (servants who had served out their terms) were offered land of their own, something beyond their reach in England.

In expanding regions such as the Chesapeake, the process could be repeated endlessly, or so promoters thought. Land clearly was the lure

2. On servitude in England, see Ann Kussmaul, *Servants in Husbandry in Early Modern England* (Cambridge, 1981).
3. On the transformation of servitude, see Warren M. Billings, "The Law of Servants and Slaves in Seventeenth-Century Virginia," *Virginia Magazine of History and Biography* 99 (1991), 45–62; and Beckles, "Plantation Production and White 'Proto-Slavery'," *The Americas* 41 (1985), 21–45.

for those who took up indentures. Providence Island was not blessed with abundant land, but the company looked forward to offering freedmen tenancies on the mainland. Thus, servitude would be a stage of life rather than a condition in the colonies as in England; those who had passed through it would be eligible for full membership in the society. The labor needs of the colonies could be satisfied without unrequited exploitation, and settlers who had contributed to a colony's economic development as servants could reap the benefits of such development as full planters.

Temporary servitude was the linchpin of the Providence Island Company's plans, as they analyzed and drew on their previous experience in the Virginia and Bermuda Companies. So crucial was labor to the entire scheme that the company decreed that their officers in the island should be paid in servants. This system would make the island's economy a self-reinforcing economic unit. Only through commitment and attention to detail would company representatives get the full benefit of their servant–salaries, and such commitment would lead to rapid development of valuable commodities, making the entire venture profitable more quickly.[4] Thus, not only would company members' pockets be preserved from the drain of supplying their officers with salaries in sterling in England, but their own investment would soon be crowned with rewards. As servants were transformed into freedmen, they would take their places as planters with servants of their own while new men and women came to supply the colony's labor needs.

This was the theory on which indentured servitude was based in all the early colonies. In Providence Island the gap between theory and practice in the supply of labor, as in most matters, was large. Two sets of promises were made at the outset. Substantial planters, especially company officers, were promised specific numbers of servants, and servants were promised land and servants as they became freedmen. Investors quickly began to retreat from these promises, partly because they had not reckoned on colonists' determined resistance to providing free labor for the island's public works: the fortifications, roads, and public buildings. The adventurers felt justified in sending planters fewer servants than promised because they believed colonists were showing a shocking lack of regard for their own duty in refusing labor to the public works. When the investors were forced to divert servants to that endeavor, planters' rosters were shortened. Although they adopted a scolding tone in their letters, company members must have realized

4. See PIC to Gov. and Coun., 4–23–38.

that such punitive deprivation also retarded the colony's economic development, thus shortchanging everyone, including themselves.

Because sending sufficient servants was a considerable problem, the investors hoped that freedmen might fill the gap temporarily. In 1632 the company wrote Governor Bell that servants who had completed their terms (three years – longer if they were young) would be invited to serve the company on the public works with all provisions free for a further two years, after which they would be supplied with land and two servants at halves. Those who chose to work independently would be free to do so, but the 1632 letter pointed out that by the time they had served these further two years the island would be flourishing and producing rich commodities; with land and servants they could enter that world of "greater profit." "And at the expiration of their terms of years we assure them of kind usage, and real performance of all conditions. Yea that we shall do something of bounty and reward according to their industry and merit."[5]

The intertwined problems intensified as the venture continued. By 1633 and 1634 servants' terms were coming to an end. When the company failed to supply new workers in the numbers promised, planters lacked sufficient labor to keep plantations clear of weeds and to tend still-experimental crops. Company officers would not receive their full salaries regardless of whether they were attentive to duty, and recent freedmen would be unable to develop new plantations. Without a critical mass, the investors realized, everyone's time would be taken up with merely growing provisions.[6] On the other hand, the company reasoned that more bodies to be fed and maintained could constitute a burden if the island was not ready for them. In 1633 the investors made large paper assignments, with the governor leading the list at thirty-two, saying that the men to fill them would come in due time. For the moment, the company saw the withholding of servants as a way of forcing renewed efforts on the planters' parts: "And for such planters as went over upon hope of servants from us, as soon as we shall see means of profit raised, that servants may be beneficial unto them we shall take care to furnish them."[7]

The colonists' inability to find any clear path to success, any commodity that would enrich themselves and the investors, created discouragement and fed the distortion of the island's system of government. Perhaps

5. PIC to Gov. and Coun. 5–10–32, pts. 23, 24, 43, 4–10–33; PIC to Bell 5–10–32.
6. PIC to Gov. and Coun. by the *Blessing* 5–36.
7. PIC to Bell 4–10–33, 7–1–33; PIC to Gov. and Coun. 7–20–33. Instead, the company compensated officers by remitting their debts, or halves; PIC to Bell 5–10–32; PIC to Gov. and Coun. 7–20–33.

because labor was in short supply, many planters worked their servants too hard, and persistent reports of maltreatment filtered back to England. By 1634, the company wrote that their efforts to recruit servants met with little success because of all the discouraging letters arriving from Providence Island. Godly and experienced men could not be attracted, and sending a hundred of the wrong sort would not either secure or develop the island. When, after long and painful discussion, investors decided to hire a large ship in 1634, they found that they could not fill the *Long Robert*. Servants and freedmen were a major source of grievances. Complaints of ill treatment of servants, particularly in stinting their supply of food and clothing, run through the records; there are also indications that servants who emigrated on the expectation of serving one master were sometimes put to work on other service.[8]

Some colonists, particularly those who had been recruited from among investors' clients, had "friends" who brought their complaints before the company; these usually got redress. The need for a "friend at court" was a staple feature of life in early modern England. Everyone depended on "friends," patrons who could put your case before those in authority. The Providence Island Company itself relied on the Earl of Holland, who held the post of company governor despite his failure to invest a penny. He alone among the adventurers had the connections at Charles I's court that were necessary to get sympathetic hearings on requests for patents, tax concessions, and letters of reprisal. Men in the island's governing ranks all negotiated their demands through patrons. Anyone who came alone to the company's court to present his own suit, in person or by letter, fared much less well. At no level did one assume that simply having a good case without a friend to argue it would lead to success.[9]

Men with powerful and committed friends won out in the competition for servants. Promises of workers were most often made to men when they were recruited; the company often guaranteed that the servants would come on the ship immediately after the one carrying the prospective master. Sometimes, inevitably, these allotments were stinted when the time actually came, although the company did apparently strive to fulfill its obligations, particularly at the change of governors in 1636 and

8. For instances of maltreatment, see PIC to Gov. and Coun. 5–10–32, by the *Long Robert*, 9–34, and by the *Blessing*, 5–36; PIC to Bell 4–10–33; PIC Prep. Ct. 6–16–34, Ct. 6–21–34, Ctee. 6–27–34.
9. See request for servants for planters made by "particular friends," PIC to Gov. and Coun. 5–10–32, pt. 43.

1638.[10] For those on the island already, connections were essential. When unassigned servants were sent, their distribution depended on the governor's estimate of planters' industriousness or usefulness.[11] To obtain preassigned men, a friend in England was essential.

Company members who had recruited clients as colonists continued to watch out for their interests; Lord Saye kept in touch with the Banbury group through Henry Halhead, who communicated their needs. In 1634 and again in 1635, Jessop wrote to Halhead about Saye's efforts to recruit servants for "his countrymen." In March 1635, Jessop was forced to correct Saye's own letter. Saye had written that Goodman Wyatt and Goodman Millner were to receive eight servants each, but the company had shortened that allotment to four apiece in order to accommodate "other useful persons now sent and other industrious planters in the Island."[12]

Throughout his shorthand record of private letters sent to Providence Island, William Jessop's care for the interests of those with whom he had a particular connection runs as the major theme. In 1634 he set out to place a planter, Mr. Acton, and his wife in the proper style of life. Mr. Acton, as Jessop wrote repeatedly, was closely connected through his marriage to a noble family and was therefore deserving of consideration. Acton's friends had requested a place for him on the council, which the company, not wanting to make changes at present, did not grant. However, "it being implied that you want a maid," Jessop did his best. In August the company directed that no women were to go on the *Long Robert,* but when they relented in September, Jessop "made bold," despite the lack of a direct request from Acton, "to furnish you with a maid." Elizabeth Jones was to serve for four years for maintenance and twenty pounds of tobacco. Jessop knew little of her, having just met her the day before the ship sailed, but hoped she would do well. It was at the same time that he selected George Phillips from among the new servants for Ensign Thomas Fitch, "because I like the honest simplicity of the man and his seeming willingness to take pains, as also because he has been a long time a servant to the Second Countess of Warwick, and is recommended to the Company by my Lord himself."[13]

10. See PIC to Gov. and Coun. by the *Blessing* 5–36, 4–23–38; PIC Instr. Hunt 5–36; Assignments of servants sent in the *Expedition,* 4–38; Passenger list in the *Swallow* and *Spy,* 7–38.
11. See John Brigham's complaint to a company committee that his offer of 2,000 pounds of tobacco for the labor of twenty servants for a year was denied by Governor Bell, PIC Ctee. 7–1–35.
12. B. L. Add MS 10615, no. 47, 114.
13. B. L. Add MS 10615, no. 25, 52, 63.

When writing to his correspondents with news that they were to get servants, Jessop almost always indicated that only through his intervention was the assignment made. Sometimes he claimed to have personally recruited the immigrants; at others he said he had influenced company allotments of the newcomers. Certainly, those in the island would have believed that his friendship was absolutely necessary. In 1635 he told Jeffrey Maymouth, addressing him simply as "Jeffrey" in contrast to the fulsome salutations to some of the well-connected military men, that he could not expect to receive servants because the supply was going either to newcomers or to men long committed to the project. He suggested that Maymouth work hard and thereby induce others to further his cause. In 1637 in a letter to Ensign Fitch, Jessop thanked Jeffrey Maymouth for some turtle shells "and shall endeavour his reciprocation by the next to procure him some servants." Ties of patronage and good will, in the colonies as in England, lubricated the machinery and allowed it to operate as well as it did.[14]

Inevitably, allotments of new labor went to the more well-connected men on the island. Newly freed servants were often slighted. In 1634 when the *Long Robert*'s complement was so disappointing, freedmen received no servants. Investors were aware that men had signed indentures and undertaken "that voyage" because of the company's promise of servants of their own when their terms expired, and they were mindful of their own promises of "bounty." But they asked the freedmen to think of "the great burden which we have already undergone" and the present hopes of commodities from the mainland. Servants' own discouraging letters had dissuaded others from emigrating.[15]

Servants and freedmen were not always friendless, however. Many times the company courts saw friends, sometimes parents, of servants coming in to try to alter the servants' situation. Occasionally, the flow went the other way, with colonists writing to William Jessop asking him to inform their relatives of their needs. Sometimes friends were able to get servants released from service before their terms were actually up, especially if they were prepared to send the freedmen servants of his own. William Tidd was released from company service on such an arrangement.[16] George Phillips, who left the service of the Countess of Warwick to go to Providence Island in 1634, wrote Jessop that his "present employment" did not bring him "contentment"; Jessop won his freedom from service early in 1635, apparently with the concurrence

14. B. L. Add MS 10615, no. 131, 164.
15. PIC to Gov. and Coun. by the *Long Robert*, 9–34. In 1636 two freedmen were sent two servants apiece; see PIC to Gov. and Coun. by the *Blessing* 5–36.
16. PIC to Bell 5–10–32.

of his master, Ensign Fitch, who received six new servants in 1636.[17] William Harman was freed because of "very hard usage" by his master Charles Toller, but others were freed without explanation.[18] James Gardiner's father's petition won James, a chirurgeon, the right to come home.[19]

Throughout the plantation's life, the Providence Island investors apparently always recruited at least some colonists from among their own circle; many servants were connected to company members. Thomas Grimsditch wrote William Jessop of his dissatisfaction in his employment under his captain. Jessop informed Grimsditch's uncle, Sir Nathaniel Rich, who wrote to Hope Sherrard and the captain about "better employment" for Grimsditch in 1635. A year later Jessop wrote Grimsditch that his father had intervened and asked that he be sent home, which had been ordered. Jessop sent him a fur coat to keep him warm at sea; once in England Sir Nathaniel would find him a more attractive situation.[20] Similarly, Lewis Morris's connections prompted Jessop to help look out for his interests.[21]

There is some indication in the records that being assigned to the company's service gave an easier life than serving an individual master, and contracts could be manipulated in the island. William Russell complained to company husband John Dyke that he had been forced to serve private men despite going to the island on a company servant's contract. Mr. Thomas Danners's (or Danvers) friend, probably his father, brought Danners's complaint before the company: Two of his servants, John Waford and Luke Bazelie, had been taken for the public works. He also alleged that some of Danners's private stores had been seized for the general magazine. The company directed that he be given one man from the public servants and Thomas Trenener, a new immigrant.[22]

Friends sometimes brought more fundamental complaints of mistreatment. Governor Bell was ordered to look into the complaint of William

17. B. L. Add MS 10615, no. 120, 153.
18. B. L. Add MS 10615, no. 136, 137, 138; PIC to Gov. and Coun. by the *Blessing* 5–36.
19. PIC Ct. 6–9–34.
20. PIC to Gov. and Coun. by the *Blessing*, 5–36; B. L. Add MS 10615, no. 83, 118. Sir Nathaniel Rich died in 1636; in his will he gave "Thomas Grimsdich, the eldest son of my brother Grimsdich, who is now in the Isle of Providence, the forty pounds per annum annuity which my Lord of Warwick is to pay during the life of the said Thomas." For Sir Nathaniel's will, see Henry F. Waters, *Genealogical Gleanings in England*, 2 vols. (Boston, 1901), II, 871–3.
21. See Chapter 4.
22. PIC to Bell, 4–10–33, 7–1–33.

Rowliff that was brought in by William's father in 1632.[23] In 1634 the parents of Edward Bragg, the servant the Reverend Arthur Rous had been accused of "inveigling" from Henry Halhead in 1632, complained of his suffering, even to the point of nakedness, under an unnamed master.[24] Investors expected company officers to investigate and order amendment.

One case was so appalling that the company was informed of it by indignant colonists: The death of Captain William Rudyerd's servant following a beating. When he returned to England in 1634, Rudyerd was called before the general court to be questioned; his brother and former earnest defender Sir Benjamin was absent from the meeting. When asked about his "cruel usage" of his servant, Rudyerd argued that the man was falling into scurvy and his correction was designed to prevent that. Scurvy, caused by lack of vitamin C, plagued all the colonies. The first symptoms of the disease are lethargy and a degree of anorexia; pains in the joints set in later. Movement becomes difficult, which intensifies the lethargy. Contemporaries saw a progression from "laziness" to full-scale scurvy; therefore, it was easy for them to believe that it was the lethargy, a moral defect, that caused the scurvy.[25] Rudyerd testified that he had used "all fair means to prevent the Scurvy which through laziness was seizing upon him." When those failed, he "gave him a blow that he might set himself to his business." The servant, named Floud, complained to Governor Bell, who sent him back to his master. On Floud's return, Rudyerd commanded Sergeant Whitehead to tie his hands around a tree. Captain Rudyerd said he had his three boys whip Floud with rods, "and about fourteen weeks after the Servant died."[26]

Sergeant Whitehead testified to a company committee a week later. He made light of the whipping, saying that Rudyerd had gotten two little boys to give Floud "a few lashes on the shoulder to shame him," and that he bled little. He said no salt was applied and that although sea water was brought to frighten Floud, Whitehead did not remember any being thrown on him. His memory was that Floud had lived six weeks after the whipping and had stayed with Rudyerd during that time. Not only had the man never been whipped before, but, reported Whitehead ominously, "some in the Island had suffered many degrees beyond him." No one in the colony said that Rudyerd had killed Floud

23. PIC to Bell 5–10–32.
24. PIC to Gov. and Coun. by the *Long Robert* 9–34.
25. See Karen Ordahl Kupperman, "Apathy and Death in Early Jamestown," *Journal of American History* 66 (1979), 24–40.
26. PIC Gen. Ct. 6–21–34.

with whipping, he said, and many wondered how he had put up with the man so long.

Symon Harris, whom Rudyerd had specifically recommended as a witness, testified before the same meeting. He said that he had no direct knowledge of the affair, not having seen the whipping. He had not heard "fame" in Providence Island that Floud had been killed by it. What was said was that he had refused to work a long time before, "And that through laziness he had got the Scurvy and further he could not say." Samuel Symonds gave similar testimony.[27] Although the company's first response had been to emphasize the seriousness of the charges and the need for intensive investigation in the island, the committee was apparently satisfied. Captain Rudyerd would later return to Providence Island with renewed status as commander of a company privateering ship.

Most company attention focused on male servants, whose hands and backs would supply the labor to develop the plantations and the commodities everyone hoped for. Colonial promoters were aware, however, that women were crucial to the long-term success of any English colony. Even in modern new lands settlements with advanced technology, the presence of wives committed to the project is vital. In a seventeenth-century "new plantation," wrote the Virginia planters to their sponsoring company in London, "it is not known whether man or woman be more necessary."[28] Women brought essential skills of food preservation and preparation and clothing production and maintenance. Their presence also provided stability and commitment to the settlement; energies were focused on building for the family's future. Men lacking wives were much less apt to stay on the island and were far less productive while there.

The Providence Island Company recognized the importance of sending women and moved in that direction early. William Hurd, whose experience was considered important to the new settlement's successful launching, was promised that his wife could come, for he was reluctant to go without her. She did not go with Hurd in 1631 but was in the colony by 1634.[29] John Waymouth and Maurice Boynes, experienced gunners and therefore among the most highly prized colonists, both demanded that their wives be sent to the island; the company hoped they could force

27. PIC Ctee. 6–27–34.
28. Scudder, *Development Potential of New Lands Settlement*, 2, 26, 33; John Pory, "A Reporte of the Manner of Proceeding in the General Assembly convened at James City," July 31, 1619, in Kingsbury, ed., *Virginia Company Records* III, 160.
29. PIC to Bell 2–31; PIC Gen. Ct. 5–19–31; B. L. Add MS 10615, no. 38.

Waymouth's wages down if they complied. Boynes asked that his brother accompany his wife.[30]

Many times men were recruited on the promise that their wives and children would be sent to them as soon as they requested it.[31] Sometimes wives did not answer the call. Jessop informed William Painter and Price James in 1636 that, despite careful conveyance of their letters by John Pym, no answer had been received from their wives. In 1638 the investors wrote the governor and council that they wanted Painter and James to stay in the island because their skills would be important as the company moved to develop ores believed to exist in Providence Island. The company offered to "take care to send their wives to them by the first opportunity if they do desire it." Price James ultimately went home to get his wife; in 1639 the adventurers agreed to send him, his wife, and child back to Providence Island at company cost.[32]

John Randall and Robert Francis were similarly disappointed. Francis urged Jessop twice to look out for his wife. Several of these men were offered servants when their wives failed to appear.[33] When wives did not come to the colony, men were apt to want to leave, and wives frequently performed the function of "friends"; the company often heard requests from wives in England asking that their husbands be allowed to come home.[34] Wives came before the company regularly to collect the salaries of those men whose skills were so much in demand that they could command sterling salaries.

Ordinary servants sometimes migrated with their families. The company directed that wives and children of public servants should be put to work "in setting of ground, making provision of victuals, washing, and the like for the use of the public servants that the men may wholly employ themselves in the works."

Unattached female servants were also sent to Providence Island as early as 1632.[35] In 1634 the adventurers directed that women who were

30. PIC Ct. 12–3–31, Ctee. 6–26–33; PIC to Gov. and Coun. 5–10–32, pt. 35.
31. PIC Ctee. 3–26–36, Ct. 6–30–39.
32. PIC to Gov. and Coun. by the *Swallow* and *Spy* 7–38; PIC Ct. 6–30–39; B. L. Add MS 10615, no. 135. John Winthrop was outraged at the "weakness" of trader John Gallop's wife who refused to emigrate to Massachusetts Bay. He wrote that if she could not be persuaded, Gallop's children should be sent without her, remarking that it would cost him £40 to come for her; Winthrop to the Rev. John White, 7–4–32, in Emerson, ed., *Letters from New England*, 99.
33. B. L. Add MS 10615, no. 36, 117, 123; see also PIC to Gov. and Coun. by the *Blessing* 5–36.
34. See, for example, the wife of Richard Feild, gunner, who got company approval for him to come home; PIC Ct. 6–9–34.
35. PIC to Gov. and Coun. 5–10–32, pt. 37. In 1633 the Widow Bunberry was discharged from company service, and she and her children were to be free to shift for themselves; PIC to Bell by the *Elizabeth*, 4–10–33.

to be married would have the cost of their transportation remitted, and early in 1635 they arranged to send a midwife and her two children.[36] When Philip Bell testified on the state of the island in 1637, he reported that English children were thriving in Providence Island.[37]

Twenty-seven women were among the seventy-two passengers of the *Expectation* in 1635, one of the few ships whose passenger list survives; four traveled with their husbands, and two with children. Dorcas Horsham, a woman of forty who traveled with Elizabeth Horsham, sixteen, and Edward Horsham, fourteen, may have been the island's promised midwife. Most of the unattached male servants were young, ranging from fourteen to twenty, although there were a few older men. The single women were older; only three were in their teens, and the rest ranged between twenty and thirty. Some of these and a few who were considerably older may have been traveling to join husbands. Elizabeth and Dorothy Lawrence, twenty-six and twenty-eight, may have faced the trip with greater equanimity because of the companionship of a sister. Two sets of brothers also traveled on the *Expectation*, Leonard and William Smith, twenty-two and twenty, and Andrew and John Leay, twenty-four and twenty-six.[38]

Female servants not only brought essential skills and allowed free planters to form families; they also enhanced the lifestyle of substantial planters. From the middle of the decade, planters whose wives were in the island wanted maids among their servants, and the company did its best to comply. Mr. Richard Lane was induced to return to Providence Island in 1635, and he traveled on the *Expectation* with his wife and three young children, aged seven, four, and three, accompanied by a maid; at the same time, Hope Sherrard's intended wife went out with a maid and two servants.[39]

Although most of these women remained mere names in the company records, the unfortunate Elizabeth Jones, recruited hastily by William Jessop for Mr. Acton when he heard that other families of Acton's station were to have maids, became a center of controversy. In 1636 at the "earnest request of her friends," Elizabeth Jones was authorized to come home. William Jessop described her as "dumb;" she was accused of "meddling" with William Davis (or Danyes). Acton had sold her for 300 pounds of tobacco; he hoped to get out of paying for her transport,

36. PIC to Bell by the *Long Robert* 9–34.
37. PIC Ctee. 6–14–37.
38. Two passenger lists for the *Expectation* are included in John Camden Hotten, ed., *The Original Lists of Persons of Quality . . . Who Went from Great Britain to the American Plantations* (London, 1874), 67–9.
39. PIC Ctee. 3–5–35.

but Jessop told him he must pay, especially in view of the prospect of other servants from the company.[40] Samuel Rishworth, to whom Davis owed money, had also written to Jessop about her plight. In reply, the secretary wrote that he had procured company permission for her to come home. He went on, "I am sorry that I had a hand in sending of her, considering the friends she has in England, and am sorry for the accident befell her there; yet hold myself not at all blameworthy, she being to me a mere stranger and offering herself for the voyage."[41] A friendless servant would have been less troublesome.

Many anonymous colonists were without friends; they had been recruited by agents working on behalf of the company. All colonies used recruiters to provide English servants to meet their new settlements' labor needs. Although the puritan plantations preferred to import only men and women known to those in authority, none was able to jettison completely use of such impersonal agencies. William Bradford complained about men who "began to make a trade of" recruiting and transporting servants, and Massachusetts Bay's leaders resented the disorderly element such men brought them.[42] Although many of even its most humble colonists were closely connected to investors, the Providence Island Company paid recruiters all through the colony's life, taking colonists from St. Christopher's as well as from the English ports.[43] Company member Henry Darley suggested that able boys be put out to learn trades at company expense and that they then be sent to practice their crafts in Providence Island. The investors appropriated £20 for the scheme, but it never came to fruition.[44]

40. Elizabeth Jones's price can be compared to the mean price of 500 pounds of tobacco that newly arrived servants fetched in Virginia and Barbados early in 1637, and the offer of up to 600 pounds from Barbados in 1645; see Galenson, *White Servitude*, 100, 134. Three hundred pounds of tobacco was also the cost of transportation for the wife of carpenter William Smith to Providence Island in 1638; see PIC to Gov. and Coun., 7–38. The investors reluctantly agreed to charge Association planters only 250 pounds of tobacco for servants when the colonists said they could not pay more; Ctee 5–21–36. Servants with four years to serve commanded 1,100 pounds of tobacco in the Chesapeake, 1641–43, and 1,375 pounds, 1644–46; see Menard, "From Servants to Slaves," *Southern Studies* XVI (1977), 372.
41. PIC to Gov. and Coun. 5–36; B. L. Add MS 10615, no. 25, 63, 111, 147, 152.
42. Bradford, *Of Plymouth Plantation*, ed. Morison, 321; John Winthrop to Margaret Winthrop, July 23, 1630, *Winthrop Papers* II, 303; Nathaniel Ward to John Winthrop, Jr., December 24, 1635, ibid., III, 215–17.
43. PIC Ctee. 3–21–33, 4–6,8,10–33; Ct. 7–14–34, 5–23–36, 3–13–38, 3–6–38, 3–9–41, 3–25–41, 6–28–41; PIC to Bell 4–10–33; PIC Instr. to Collins in the *Long Robert*, 9–34.
44. PIC Ctee. 2–22–35.

As labor increasingly came to be viewed as a commodity, servants found themselves treated as such; reports of servants being sold from hand to hand filtered back to the disturbed company. The adventurers were mainly concerned about the implications of such sales for the colony's social order. They stipulated that no planter was to remain on the island who had divested himself of his plantation and servants; no one could be there who was not involved in productive work. Nor could one depart leaving an overseer in charge of his plantation; their colony was not to become a settlement of agents and servants.[45] Frequent repetitions of the command against selling servants in order to live idly indicate that the practice continued. The adventurers were particularly unhappy when councilors divested themselves of servants, rendering them unable to maintain the style of life appropriate to their station.[46] By 1641 masters who left the island were allowed to remove their English servants with their other property, although the company that had recruited the servants would then have no jurisdiction over them.[47]

Terms and conditions of servitude reflected labor's status as a commodity of great importance; in Providence Island as in Virginia, "our principal wealth ... consisteth in servants."[48] An indentured servant's term was theoretically set by an estimate of the length of time he or she must work to repay the cost of transportation to America, usually £6. The Providence Island Company, believing in the great productivity of their island, initially set the normal term at the low figure of three years.[49] In 1637 the company calculated that a servant could raise 100 pounds of tobacco each year. With tobacco selling at 6 pence per pound, that would amount to £2 6s, from which the servant's maintenance must be deducted. Thus, barring accident or disease, both ever-present possibilities, a servant could just about pay off his cost in three years; whatever happened, the planter was obligated to pay for the servant's transportation.[50]

45. PIC to Gov. and Coun. by the *Long Robert* 9–34.
46. PIC to Gov. and Coun. 7–20–33, by the *Blessing* 5–36, 4–23–38; PIC to Bell by the *Expectation* 2/3 35.
47. PIC to Gov. and Coun. 3–29–41; PIC to Dep. Gov. Fitch 3–29–41.
48. John Pory to "My Singular Good Lorde," September 30, 1619, *Virginia Company Records* III, 221. Richard Dunn estimates that in the 1630s English servants constituted 40 percent of colonists in the Chesapeake and over 50 percent in Barbados; at the same time servants were about a third of the workforce in New England; Dunn, "Servants and Slaves: The Recruitment and Employment of Labor," in Pole and Green, eds., *Colonial British America*, 159–60.
49. On terms of servitude, see Galenson, *White Servitude*, 8, 98–102.
50. PIC Ct. 12–11–37. These figures come from the investors' salary negotiations with Bell and may represent a low estimate. Hilary McD. Beckles estimates that a servant's

In the first flush of enthusiasm after the colony's successful repulsion of the Spanish, the company decided in 1636 on a change of government and wrote that they expected soon to send 500 men; they urged the planters to forge their own contracts with the new servants. Transfer of negotiations to the island was overtaken by unexpected developments in England, however. Mr. William Woodcock, Providence Island Company husband, recruited servants for a projected venture on the company's island of Henrietta (modern San Andreas). When that project was deferred, the men were left at Providence Island. Woodcock's contract had called for the servants to receive £10 in the commodities of the country on the expiration of their terms. In 1637 the company wrote that it had now become impossible to recruit servants "upon more easy conditions." Although they argued that such terms were usual in other plantations and were not onerous considering that the freedom dues were to be paid in commodities the men themselves would raise, the investors acknowledged that some planters might refuse servants on these terms. If so, the newcomers were to be organized into families. The company directed an elaborate scheme of overseers to see that they worked hard, with officers to observe the overseers.[51]

Terms were extended to provide for the new concessions. Servants sent in 1638 had contracted for terms of four years, with the company accepting ultimate responsibility for the £10 freedom dues. The adventurers directed that masters set the servants to work at halves for their final year to raise their £10 of commodities; otherwise, masters must discharge the company of the contracted obligation some other way.

Freedmen often did not get the most important form of compensation they had been promised, however. Company failure to meet commitments to those who had served their time, promises that had been the chief attraction of Providence Island, constituted a keenly felt grievance. Such defalcation distorted the island's society, pulling it away from the goal of replicating English society and rendering servitude more exploitative. It was therefore disturbing to some of the colony's substantial planters. Samuel Rishworth objected to the treatment of servants, as did Mr. Samuel Symonds, formerly a planter in Bermuda. Before he would emigrate, Symonds presented a list of demands based on his survey of conditions in Providence Island. One demand was his insistence that freedmen who joined themselves into families be given land immediately even if they could not yet have servants of their own, to which the

cost was normally paid off in two years in Barbados in the mid-seventeenth century; *White Servitude and Black Slavery in Barbados*, 2.
51. PIC to Gov. and Coun. by the *Blessing* 5–36, about Henrietta, 4–7–36, by the *Mary Hope* 3–37, 4–23–38.

company agreed.[52] The company's agreement with new governor Robert Hunt in 1636 promised tenancies for freedmen on the island or the mainland, but Samuel Rishworth's 1637 testimony in the company court demonstrated that freed servants were still unsupplied with promised servants. Again in 1638 in letters to new governor Captain Nathaniel Butler, the company acknowledged the presence of "poor men" who had served their terms but lacked servants.[53]

On the other hand, servants could also constitute a terrible burden. If freedmen or others who received men did not make a success of their plantations, the servants could become a hated anchor keeping them in Providence Island. The company stipulated that no one should be allowed to return home unless he had paid off his own and his servants' transportation, as well as his debts to the company store.[54]

One group of colonists was at least partially freed from the circular trap servitude represented for masters and poor immigrants alike: workers with necessary skills. They and the ministers alone commanded wages paid in England. Wages were paid regularly on demand; thus, this group was the only one to which the company fully kept its promises of recompense. Gunners, essential to the island's defense, were among the most highly paid; still the colony failed to keep most of them for very long. Some of the gunners had apparently spent time in the Indies and therefore offered a variety of important skills. Maurice Boynes attracted company support when he undertook to raise a piece of brass ordnance sunk at sea; he was promised wages and servants and that his wife and brother would come by the next ship.[55] Philip Trippett, gunner, won investors' attention for his reputed skill in processing mechoacan.[56]

Other categories of skilled workers commanded wages, payments collected regularly for some of them by their wives in England. Sawyers, carpenters, bricklayers, millwrights, and coopers hammered out favorable contracts, usually involving a combination of wages and servants. These men could also expect to collect payments from individual planters who employed their expertise. Few colonists apparently possessed sufficient skill to build their own plantations without such aid. Throughout the colonial period, planters called for men adept in the building trades;

52. PIC Ct. 7–2–34; PIC to Gov. and Coun. by the *Long Robert* 9–34; PIC to Bell by the *Long Robert* 9–34, by the *Expectation* 2/3 35.
53. PIC Agreement with Hunt 3–1–36; PIC Ct. 6–22–37; PIC to Butler by the *Swallow* 7–3–38.
54. PIC to Gov. and Coun. by the *Mary Hope* 3–37, by the *Mary* 6/7 39.
55. PIC Ctee. 5–18–33, 6–26–33, 6–28–33.
56. PIC to Bell by the *Expectation* 2/3–35.

their skills were literally golden.[57] Competition was stiff. In 1638 "divers that were going to New England," including carpenter John Arrat and his wife, children, and two helpers, and Peter Talbot, sawyer, declared their "willingness to go to Providence" to the company's great satisfaction.[58]

In a similar category were the health professionals: apothecaries and barber–surgeons, or chirurgeons. The skills of apothecaries and barber–surgeons were seen as being far more relevant to the colonial scene than those of university-trained physicians. Physicians based their treatment on the theory that disease resulted when a patient's four humors were out of balance; thus, purging excessive or corrupted humors through bleeding, emetics, or laxatives constituted their major treatment. Apothecaries, originally a sideline of grocers, treated diseases with herbs and drugs, many recently imported from newly discovered lands. Their analytical skill at matching drugs with diseases endemic to alien environments was highly prized. Barber–surgeons were also tradesmen. Their particular area of expertise was treatment of fractures, wounds, and sores, including syphilitic lesions. Thus, they rather than physicians accompanied military expeditions, and their presence in the colonies seemed natural.

As the Providence Island Company pulled away from its promise to recompense servants with land and servants of their own and transferred responsibility for freedmen's rewards to the planters, settlers increasingly exercised other options. African slaves were present in the island from the beginning; Philip Bell brought his slaves from Bermuda. As the struggle over the supply of English servants intensified, Providence Island's colonists increasingly supplemented the labor supply with slaves who quickly became a major part of the population. Slavery was the underside of the self-reinforcing concept of English servitude. As a stage-of-life phenomenon, servitude was seen as leading to intensified development of the island's economy while making all emigrants participants in the fruits of that development. Slavery shored up the promise of full membership in the society for all English colonists; gaps in

57. For many examples of such calls, see Galenson, *White Servitude*, 107, 134–5, and 255–6, fn. 29. For skilled workers collecting wages from planters, see PIC to Gov. and Coun. by the *Long Robert*, 1634, by the *Blessing* 5–36, and Ctee, 6–26–35.
58. PIC Gen. Ct. 4–6–38. Talbot soon left Providence Island; he sailed on the ship *Providence* and left it at Galway in Ireland in the summer of 1639. See P. R. O., H. C. A. 24/101 f. 326.

the system were supplied by the absolute denial of rights to Africans.[59]

The Providence Island Company was deeply disturbed by the presence of slaves but not because of any moral objections to slavery as an institution. Some members already owned slaves on their Bermuda plantations. Investors were convinced of slavery's acceptability on environmental determinist grounds. As early as 1632, they had discussed providing slaves as the labor supply of the settlement on Association Island (modern Tortuga), because "they conceive English bodies not fit for that work."[60] Their reluctance to see Providence Island heavily supplied with slaves stemmed from their hopes for the colony as a godly settlement replicating the best features of English communities; a heavy presence of outsiders permanently excluded from the society would mar that development. Moreover, as the population of African slaves grew, the company worried about the island's safety; runaways could reveal the colony's weaknesses, and disaffected slaves could open it to invaders. Like the promoters of all the southern colonies, they constantly worked and pleaded for a balance of permanent and temporary servants.[61]

Enslavement of Indians had been absolutely forbidden to the colonists. No Indians lived permanently on Providence Island at the time of its settlement; the island was visited seasonally by Moskito Coast Indians for the rich turtling. The adventurers, eager to establish ties with these Indians and to initiate a mission to them, authorized the governor and council to import a small number of men and children for education. The colonists were to treat the children "as tenderly careful as if they were your own in the nearest relation," and the men were to work voluntarily and return home at will; men who chose to stay would be laborers perpetually. No women should be brought "for fear of some inconveniencies depending thereon."

Any colonist committing a scandalous act was to be punished in the presence of the Indian who had witnessed it so that they could be brought to understand "that though it be practised by the professors yet it is not allowed by the profession." If the Indians could not be restrained from their idolatrous worship, they must be removed from the island, "so there may be no mixture of paganism with the pure religion of Almighty God." Their labor was to be devoted to the public works, and the company took responsibility for their maintenance. They were to be paid with "beads, glasses or such other Trifles."

---

59. Russell Menard argues that freedmen's demands for high wages accelerated the turn to slavery in the Chesapeake, "From Servants to Slaves," *Southern Studies* XVI (1977), 374–5.
60. PIC Ct. 6–25–32.
61. On the quest for balance in other colonies, see Galenson, *White Servitude*, 101–2.

Hatchets, knives, and other things "they do most esteem" were to be kept for trade on the mainland.

Not only would such Indians be valuable contacts as the mainland trade was established; the natives might voluntarily ask for "some of our nation to go over to them," which would be very advantageous when the company was ready to establish a colony there. In the event the investors discovered what its agents already knew: The Moskito Coast Indians were shrewd and experienced traders who knew what Europeans had to offer and how to select the best. The company's reiterated horror at colonists' transfers of weapons to coastal Indians shows that the settlers also quickly learned about native trading acumen. The Americans would not be satisfied with "trifles." Early in 1635, the company forbade the colonists' plan to "forcibly restrain" Indian access to the failing turtle fishing at the Moskito Cays. So fearful were investors of breaking "the good correspondency that is betwixt us and them" that they wrote they would rather increase the colonists' supply of victual from England to make up for their own losses of turtle. At the same time, they again forbade bringing Indian women into the island; despite this prohibition Governor Bell had an Indian woman among his servants in 1638.[62]

Africans, unlike Indians, lacked leverage over their fate, and the international trade in slaves was brisk in the Caribbean. Slavery began slowly in Providence Island, mostly as a spillover from Association Island or as a by-product of the mainland trade. The adventurers, following Governor Bell's suggestion, thought between twenty and forty slaves might be imported in 1633 to ease the problem of labor for the public works. They instructed Sussex Camock to attempt to buy some slaves from Dutch ships at the mainland for a good price, preferably in local commodities, although they would accept bills of exchange to be paid in England if necessary. At the same time, investors went into partnership with Captain Anthony Hilton on Association Island in a project to use slaves to cut logwood, authorizing Hilton to acquire as many slaves as he could use there or on other islands.[63] By 1634 they were also seeking slaves to supplement Providence Island officers' complements of servants. Soon female slaves were added.[64]

62. PIC to Gov. and Coun. 5–10–32, pt. 31, by the *Long Robert* 9–34, 4–23–38; PIC to Bell 5–10–32, by the *Expectation* 2/3–35; PIC to Camock 4–10–33.
63. PIC Instr. to Camock 7–1–33, PIC to Bell 4–10–33; PIC Gen. Ct. 2–18–33.
64. PIC to Bell by the *Long Robert* 9–34, by the *Expectation* 2/3–35; Instr. to Collins in *Long Robert* 9–34.

Despite company efforts to keep the number of slaves low and their insistent advice that they be distributed with discretion and treated well, the experiment with slavery faltered in 1635. On Association Island the slaves were said to be out of control and the planters dispersed because of fraud and mismanagement, but on Providence Island slavery first foundered on the rock of Samuel Rishworth's puritan conscience. Mr. Rishworth had been outspokenly critical of the settlement's failure to develop as a godly society from the beginning. He abhorred slavery and believed holding human beings as slaves was forbidden to Christians. As early as 1633, he began to challenge the turn toward slavery. As the number of slaves began to mount, he spoke to the Africans, promising to attempt to win their liberty, after which some ran away into the island's interior. The company was incensed, arguing that slavery was lawful for "such persons . . . during their strangeness from Christianity." Rishworth should, they wrote, have discussed his intentions with the slaves' particular masters "before any overture touching their liberty." They worried that the entire affair "may be of very ill consequence."[65]

In the same papers, Governor Bell had informed the company of "heavy charges" against Rishworth that involved defiance of the governor and malfeasance at the council table. How much of Rishworth's actions stemmed from his attempt to end slavery in Providence Island is unclear; one of Bell's charges was that Rishworth had sold commodities to servants without their masters' knowledge, "which is unjust and of very mischievous consequence."[66] As with Elizabeth Jones, Rishworth made the case of anyone suffering under servitude his business. William Jessop wrote Rishworth a long letter to accompany the official missive, which made clear that Rishworth was attacked because he had taken a stand for conscience's sake. "It will be a constant comfort and an impregnable fortress to experience suffering from the direction of injustice. God's people stand on a hill, and their actions are more obvious and public than others, and therefore it concerns them to look unto their feet lest by their stumbling God's enemies should be occasioned to prevail."

65. Lifelong, inheritable servitude as the accepted status of Africans in the colonies was still in the future. In 1638, company member Lord Mandeville wrote as Sir Nathaniel Rich's executor to Thomas Durham in Bermuda. In answer to Durham's questions about the Africans on Rich's holdings, Mandeville wrote, "For the negroes I see no reason why they should deserve freedom from their service, though I hope and pray that you do not over-use them with intemperate labour, which as they be men ought to be avoided. If you shall find it necessary to bind them for a certain number of years, it may possibly be done hereafter, and I adduce it may be done if you shall show cause." Lord Mandeville to Mr. Thomas Durham, May 24, 1638, B. L. Add MS 10615, no. 177.
66. PIC to Bell by the *Expectation* 2/3 35.

Jessop hoped God would help Rishworth "so to walk and maintain your way that the cost of your Christian profession may be accepted entire." A year later, saying they had not had time to review the case, the adventurers restored Samuel Rishworth to his place of councilor.[67] The planters obviously looked to Rishworth for leadership throughout this period; he was chosen spokesman for their petition and went to England in 1637 to present their grievances in person. He may have been less successful as a planter, however. In 1635 Francis Grissell came to the company asking that the cost of his transportation be remitted. He had gone to Providence Island on a contract with Samuel Rishworth "with whom he spent his time without profit."[68]

Rishworth's challenge caused the company to reconsider, not the legal and moral foundation of slavery, but its wisdom; their instructions henceforth were filled with advice about how to distribute the slaves so that they had no opportunity to plot rebellion or flight together.[69] Some of the earliest slaves imported were bought at Cape Gracias a Dios for "bills, lances, hatches, lances, beads, canvas clothes and shirts," and knives. These commodities, staples of the Moskito Coast trade, indicate that the Africans may have been escapees from Spanish slavery captured and resold by the Indians. These slaves, having already rebelled against slavery once, would have made an explosive element in the confined plantations of Providence Island.[70]

By 1637 the company prohibited further importation of slaves unless they were possessed of special skills. The investors pointed to their own experience on Association Island, deserted by its planters following a slave mutiny that they attributed to "the great number of Negroes." Providence Island had already fended off one Spanish attack; in future crises, the slaves would increase the island's danger.

Not only was increased importation of Africans "prejudicial" to the colony's safety, but it also made importation of English servants impossible "by bringing down the bodies and labors of men to such cheap rates." Therefore, the company directed that for each slave a

67. B. L. Add MS 10615 no. 70; PIC to Gov. and Coun. by the *Blessing* 5–36.
68. PIC Ctee. 7–1–35; Ct 2–12–36.
69. PIC to Gov. and Coun. by the *Blessing* 5–36.
70. PIC Ctee. 6–26–37, 7–4–37. A committee of 1–31–38 agreed to pay William Bluefield for procuring slaves at "the Cape."

There is a bitter irony in Thomas Gage's account of hundreds of runaway slaves in nearby Guatemala, perhaps some of them among those taken to Providence Island: "These have often said that the chief cause of their flying to those mountains is to be in a readiness to join with the English or Hollanders, if ever they land in that Gulf; for they know, from them they may enjoy that liberty which the Spaniards will never grant unto them", *The English-American*, 130.

family contained, it must contribute one man's labor per week on the public works, "which we suppose they may allow without murmuring, considering the Negroes cost them so little."[71] In the company's private letter to Governor Hunt, the adventurers went further, directing him to put some of the island's Africans aboard any of the company ships bound for London; these slaves were to be sold in Virginia or Bermuda. They reiterated the prohibition against buying slaves, "considering how dangerous a multitude of them may be, to your safety, by siding with an enemy, or standing out in rebellion against your government; or depriving you of the means of livelihood and defense, which they may do secretly, or more publicly in case of distraction or assault."[72]

Planters and adventurers knew how serious these threats were. There was a steady leaching of slaves out of servitude and into the sanctuary of the island's mountainous interior, where they apparently created alternative communities. Expeditions to recover runaway slaves were partially successful, as allotments of the "Negroes taken in the woods" show, but many could not be recaptured. In 1638 the company, recommending "all fair means" to entice them back, directed that if they remained recalcitrant "and thereby seem to seek their own destruction we would have one or two of them apprehended and executed that the rest may take warning."[73] As the tensions mounted, an abortive slave rebellion, the first in any English colony, erupted on May Day, 1638.[74]

71. PIC to Gov. and Coun. by the *Mary Hope* 3–37.
72. PIC to Hunt 3–37. All colonies worried about defense as they moved to slavery for their labor force. One concern was staffing the militia. In the later seventeenth century, concern lessened and mainland militias were increasingly manned by landless laborers or even, in some cases, dependent Indians. In Barbados tenants were imported specifically to serve in the militia. See Lois G. Carr and Russell R. Menard, "Immigration and Opportunity: The Freedman in Early Colonial Maryland," in Tate and Ammerman, eds., *The Chesapeake in the Seventeenth Century*, 231; Richard R. Johnson, "The Search for a Usable Indian: An Aspect of the Defense of Colonial New England," *Journal of American History* 64 (1977), 627–32; Beckles, *White Servitude and Black Slavery*, 114.
    When Providence Island was attacked in 1640, the Spanish delayed, waiting for runaways to come out to them. In the event, however, slaves participated in the island's defense both in 1640 and 1641 by throwing rocks, and, in 1640, by hunting down and capturing escaped Spaniards hiding on the island. See Henry Halhead, Richard Lane, Hope Sherrard, and Nicholas Leverton to the PIC, June 17, 1640, Finch MSS, Leicestershire R. O., ff. 4–14; General Francisco Díaz Pimienta to Philip IV, September 11, 1641, Archive of the Indies, Seville, *Audiencia de Santa Fe, legajo* 223.
73. PIC Ct. 12–11–37, 6–22–37; PIC to Gov. and Coun. 4–23–38; PIC to Elfrith 4–23–38.
74. PIC to Gov. Butler by the *Mary*, 7–39. Governor Butler recorded Hope Sherrard's service commemorating the colonists' delivery from the rebellion on May 1, 1639; B. L., Sloane MS 758. Father Andrew White, whose ship called at Barbados on the way to Maryland in 1634, reported an abortive revolt by English servants on that island,

Governor Butler's diary recorded colonists' runaway-hunting "sport" on March 27, 1639: "Upon this day we had a general Hunting after our rebel negroes, but they were so nimble as we could scarce get a sight of them: only one of their cabins was found upon the top of a high Hill, and burned." On other occasions, his "tame Negroes" captured escapees and brought them back. Butler put one recaptured slave to work in irons; others, he wrote without elaboration, were punished according to the company's instructions. The governor seems to have placed complete trust in his own slaves; several times he records sending them in teams without supervision to cut timber for the fortifications.[75]

Despite their own warnings and the planters' knowledge of the risks (both to the colony's safety and to the godly enterprise on which they were embarked) of reliance on slavery as a labor system, the number of slaves in the island steadily mounted. The company had found irresistible the temptation to use African slaves on the public works when English labor failed and had steadily acquired slaves for that purpose; Governor Nathaniel Butler was authorized to buy up to 100 in April 1638.[76] Investors also made use of the flexibility the island's slave population gave them; they could take back English servants from planters when some special need arose, supplying slaves in their place. When they could not send English servants, they authorized the governor and council to make up planters' allotments with Africans, whom they expected to buy from Dutch traders for 150 pounds of tobacco, as opposed to the 300 to 500 pounds of tobacco an English servant might cost.[77] Some of the island's slaves were captured from the Spanish by Providence Island privateers.[78]

Slavery freed planters of the reliance on company goodwill and constancy that had so frustrated them in the early years. Outright ownership

A Briefe Relation of the Voyage unto Maryland, 1634, in Hall, ed., *Narratives of Early Maryland*, 34.

75. B. L., Sloane MS 758, letter 33; diary entries for March 7, 27, April 30, May 7 and 13, 1639; January 12, 1640. Philip Bell also seems to have had a close and trusting relationship with at least some of his slaves. He directed in his will that after his wife's death his slave Arbella be freed with Mango "who used to run along with me." See Puckrein, *Little England*, 151.

76. PIC to Gov. and Coun. by the *Mary Hope* 3–37, 4–23–38; PIC to Butler 4–23–38, by the *Swallow* 7–3–38.

77. PIC to Gov. and Coun. by the *Swallow* and *Spy* 7–38; PIC Instr. to Coun. of War 7–38; Instr to Axe for the *Swallow* 7–38.

78. John Winthrop reported the privateers' capture of "many negroes," *Journal*, ed. Hosmer, I, 260, as did Captain Don Torivio de Palacio y Sierra in his "Relación de Meritos," Archive of the Indies, Seville, *Audiencia de Santa Fe, legajo* 223.

of labor made up for their status as tenants on the land and gave them independence, freedom that was bought at the expense of the slaves' utter loss of rights. Soon the island had acquired several hundred slaves, making enslaved Africans a larger percentage of the total population than in any other English colony for decades to come. Governor Nathaniel Butler warned in a letter to Lord Brooke that was probably written in late 1639 or early 1640 that "The Negroes [increase much upon] over-breed us."

In 1641 the victorious Spaniards captured 381 slaves "of both sexes including children and youths" and about 350 English people. Barbados would not reach such a high proportion of slaves in the total population until the 1660s and St. Kitts not until the 1680s. Even then, the Spanish had expected to find more slaves. On inquiring, General Francisco Díaz Pimienta found that their number had recently been reduced; as fears for their own safety mounted, the English colonists had sent many Africans to St. Kitts and Bermuda, "having before killed fifty for conspiracy against them." Some of these dispersed slaves were sold in New England, brought by Captain William Peirce on his return from carrying seventeen Pequot boys and women to slavery in Providence Island.[79]

Historians have discovered a degree of hesitancy in other English colonies in their plunge into construing slavery as a total, lifelong, inheritable condition. In Providence Island there was no doubt that the Africans were set apart by their lifelong service and their meaner care. The company laid out the reasons for their attractiveness as a labor source in mid-1638: "Negroes being procured at cheap rates, more easily kept, and perpetually servants." Although the large number of slaves had been imported against the company's express instructions, the investors wrote, "considering that their coming into the Island hath been advantageous we are more inclinable to excuse it."[80]

Investors attempted to mitigate the effects of this opening to heavier reliance on slavery by laying down certain conditions, terms partly designed to restore company control of the plantation's development

---

79. B. L., Sloane MS 758. The words in brackets were crossed out. The conquest of Providence Island is described in General Francisco Díaz Pimienta to Philip IV, Sept. 11, 1641, Archive of the Indies, Seville, *Audiencia de Santa Fe, legajo* 223. In 1640 one Spanish estimate had written of 1,600 slaves on Providence; see the "Relation of Captain Don Torivio de Palacio y Sierra," n. d., ibid.

   For estimates of population percentages, see Galenson, *White Servitude*, 119–20. John Winthrop noted the sending away of the captive Pequots and the arrival of "cotton, and tobacco, and negroes, etc.," *Journal*, ed. Hosmer, I, 227–8, 260.

80. PIC to Gov. and Coun. by the *Swallow* and *Spy* 7–38. The previous year Samuel Rishworth had testified that the restraint on buying slaves had been observed by everyone except Philip Bell; all others who bought had authorization; Ct. 6–22–37.

and to ensure investors' share of its returns. Settlers were to pay the company forty pounds of tobacco annually for each slave, whereas the payment for servants was only twenty pounds. Families were to donate sixteen days' labor per year to the public works for every African "servant" (down from the one day a week decreed in 1637) because of the relative cheapness of acquiring slaves; this was double the contribution for an English servant. A family of fourteen was to have no more than six slaves (soon raised to one slave for every two English servants); excess slaves were to go to the public works or to poor freedmen unable to buy slaves of their own. Any owner who objected to relinquishing Africans over the allotted number should be reminded, they wrote, that "they have no reasons considering that we might take them all away for breaking of our Instructions." Those "turbulent spirits" who had objected to the governor's temporary suspension of the "taking in" of slaves should be banished, and the company chastised its officers for diverting public slaves to their own plantations. Finally, no settler was to make a profit out of the slave trade; masters who left Providence Island were to sell Africans for no more than they had paid for them.[81]

The company's long-range plan was to replace the worrisome slaves with English servants, who could then be supplemented by new slaves brought in carefully in small numbers. By 1638 the company accepted that planters would always choose African slaves over English servants if given a free choice; the investors' task was to make them take servants in lieu of their slaves. The scheme was announced in July 1638 with the arrival of the new governor, Captain Nathaniel Butler. The company did not prohibit the buying of slaves even at this juncture but stipulated that everyone acquiring a slave "shall be bound to take off two English servants at the common cost of transportation or otherwise." All importation of slaves was to rest on Governor Butler's judgment of its effect on the island's safety.

The Providence Island Company undertook a separate joint stock organized by company husband William Woodcock with some London merchants for the recruitment and transportation of 200 English servants to be exchanged for 200 slaves. They hoped to send the men in August 1638, just a month after the *Swallow* and *Spy* left London with news of the plan. They expected slaves belonging to the company to make up half the number removed, with the other 100 coming from the number planters had imported over the limit set by the company. The company was to receive £15 for each slave. Planters would have the 200 English

81. PIC to Gov. and Coun. 4–23–38, by the *Swallow* and *Spy* 7–38; PIC to Butler by the *Swallow* 7–38.

servants distributed among them and with Butler's permission could acquire new slaves. "And when the families are filled up with convenient number of Negroes we shall every year send English to exchange for Negroes that we may be the better able to support the charge."[82]

As happened so often in the history of Providence Island, settlers told to prepare for immediate and radical change experienced nothing but silence. The company's next letters were sent, not the next month, but a full year later in July 1639. In a hastily composed letter the adventurers explained that the contract to remove the Africans had fallen through because of the death of William Woodcock, which had occasioned great losses to the investors. Now they had decided against selling the slaves unless the governor and council thought there were more than the island could manage. If there was an immediate need to remove some Africans as an aftermath of the island's slave rebellion, they suggested that Maurice Thompson's factor could take them for sale in New England or Virginia.[83] As for those kept in the plantation, the company suggested that the colonists "keep them harder to work."[84]

Men who left the island were stripped of their slaves, who remained in the colony's labor force. Two skilled men, Peter Gates and Robert Woodfall, both smiths, were to have two slaves restored to each of them when they returned to Providence Island in 1639. John Randall (or Randle) and Price James, whose wives had failed to answer their calls to emigrate in 1636, had both gone home. Now James was prepared to return to Providence Island with his wife and child; the company agreed to pay their passage and directed that he receive again the two slaves and three servants taken from him when he left. Randall, apparently returning alone, was to have his two slaves. The company approved Governor Butler's contract for acquiring Captain Elfrith's slaves when he left but were indignant that the bargain made on their behalf was very unfavorable compared to those between individuals. Company slaves were all to be put to work growing victuals to supply the privateering ships, either under overseers or on contract to private men.[85]

82. PIC to Gov. and Coun. by the *Swallow* and *Spy* 7–38, 6/7–39; PIC to Butler by the *Swallow* 7–3–38; PIC Instr. to Coun. of War 7–38. On organization of the joint stock see PIC Ctee. 6–10–38, 6–17–38; Ct. 11–29–38.

83. Maurice Thompson, who had lived in Virginia, is the preeminent example of the rising group of merchants who built their trade on American commerce; 1638 was the year he began to break the Guinea traders' monopoly on the West African slave trade. See Andrews, *Ships, Money and Politics*, 56–7, and Puckrein, *Little England*, 70.

84. PIC to Gov. and Coun. by the *Mary* 6/7–39; PIC to Butler by the *Mary* 7–39.

85. PIC to Butler by the *Mary* 7–39; PIC Ct. 6–30–39.

Nineteen blank pages follow the 1639 letters in the company records; the next recorded letters are of 1641. By this time the island had survived a second Spanish attack, the aftermath of which was disruptive to that infant society. The interim governor had shipped the colony's civil and religious leaders home in chains. But momentous changes were also occurring in England. Citing "the many public occasions now lying upon us in respect of the sitting of the Parliament and the important affairs now depending," the adventurers again wrote hastily to their governor and council on Providence Island. They now acceded to planters' requests to remove both English servants and African slaves when they left the island, provided the colony was not put in jeopardy by such removals and only after ownership of slaves was proven. They were most concerned that the new deputy governor, Captain Thomas Fitch, examine the accounts, taking testimony on oath. They were sure that they had been defrauded both on the debts owed to the company and on the distribution of slaves, and they were determined to get reparations.[86]

Providence Island was very close to the end of its life as these hasty arrangements were made, but the adventurers did not know that. They hoped for a new beginning with the first shiploads of settlers from New England who would revitalize their godly community in the Indies. They did not expect the influx of New Englanders to change the island's slave economy. Their agreement with Emmanuel Truebody to send two ships from New England to Providence Island and to transport 100 men called for Truebody to receive twenty-five slaves on completion. It was to be business as usual on Providence Island.[87]

Providence Island's easy and massive turn to slavery as a principal labor system for cultivation of tobacco makes the colony an anomaly among English plantations. No other English colony moved so quickly into reliance on slaves, nor was tobacco readily seen as a crop fitted for slavery. In Barbados, which was after Providence Island the colony with the highest concentration of slaves, importation of Africans in large numbers was associated with sugar cultivation, a labor-intensive crop well suited to regimented gang labor. Historians have argued that the crop thus dictated the labor system. Barbadians apparently did not employ slaves extensively while the island's economy was devoted to

---

86. On events following the second Spanish attack see Chapter 9. PIC to Gov. and Coun. 3–29–41; Instr. to Dep. Gov. Fitch 3–29–41; Fitch Commission to Examine Accts. 3–29–41; PIC Ct. 3–25–41, Mtg 3–24–41.
87. PIC Ct. 6–28–41.

tobacco and cotton as Providence Islanders did but began importing African slaves in large numbers once sugar cultivation and processing were perfected in the 1640s. Even then the Barbadians' turn to slavery was somewhat slow; five years elapsed after the establishment of sugar before Africans were imported in large numbers.[88] In the Chesapeake colonies, although Africans were introduced as early as 1619, their numbers grew very slowly until the end of the century and initially their servitude was not necessarily a lifelong sentence.

Slowness among English settlements to use slaves has been attributed both to Africans' higher price and to a preference for English servants who shared colonists' language and customs – as long as the English servants came in large numbers. Neither consideration applied in Providence Island, where slaves were said to be both cheaper and preferable. Modern scholars generally hold that slaves were more expensive to acquire than English servants in the early seventeenth century. This is directly contradicted by the frequently reiterated assertion in the Providence Island Company records that slaves were far cheaper than servants, which is borne out by the price of 150 pounds of tobacco at which the investors expected to buy them.

The relative expensiveness of slaves in Barbados as that island moved to large-scale importation in the 1640s is disputed, with most historians arguing that they cost more than English servants.[89] It is possible that Providence Island's proximity to the Moskito Coast and Dutch traders made slaves more available and less expensive than in islands to the east. Certainly, Africans were easier to obtain there than in the Chesapeake at this time, and the preference of early seventeenth-century mainland planters for English servants, whom they could acquire in

88. See Beckles, *White Servitude and Black Slavery in Barbados*, 6.
89. In 1645 New Englander George Downing wrote to John Winthrop, Jr., that a slave's purchase price could be paid off in a year and a half; *Winthrop Papers* V, 43. Gary Puckrein argues that slaves were more expensive to purchase than servants' contracts in the 1630s, *Little England*, 70; see also Galenson, *White Servitude*, 175, and Beckles, *White Servitude and Black Slavery*, 3, 117–18. Richard Dunn asserts that slaves cost £25 in the early 1640s, but the price soon dropped to £15 as against the cost of £12 for a servant. See *Sugar and Slaves*, 72, 237. These prices can be compared to the £10 each paid for Peter and Christopher, two slaves owned by the Providence Island Company, by Mr. Lewis Ford in Bermuda in 1637, or the £100 paid for ten slaves bought from a Dutch man of war in 1636; PIC Gen. Ct., 6–24–37, Ctee. 3–26–36. Carl and Roberta Bridenbaugh assert that slaves were less expensive, both at purchase and in the long run; see *No Peace Beyond the Line*, 266. See the discussion of relative prices and the timing of the transition to slavery in Richard N. Bean and Robert P. Thomas, "The Adoption of Slave Labor in British America," in Henry A. Gemery and Jan S. Hogendorn, eds., *The Uncommon Market: Essays in the Economic History of the Atlantic Slave Trade* (New York, 1979), 377–98.

large numbers, evidently played a large part in delaying the introduction of slavery there.[90]

With its healthy environment and large supply of family labor, New England moved most slowly of all into the use of slaves, and enslaved Africans never formed more than 3 percent of the population. Economic historians link a low rate of servitude to the region's failure to find a staple crop, but many scholars would also argue that the raw exploitation of human beings under slavery was repugnant to puritanism.[91] Except for Samuel Rishworth and the few he was able to convince, the puritan planters and investors in Providence Island had no such qualms. The company devoted elaborate discussions to many aspects of the colony's society and development, but their justification of slavery on environmental and religious grounds seems almost casual.

Environmental determinism as a justification for enslaving Africans is an example of the underside of providentialist thinking. Puritans were poised to examine every occurrence and condition for the hand of God within. Everything had meaning, and the godly could read the judgment of God on their actions in the unfolding of events. Providence was a stern master and Christians often saw warnings in its judgments, but it could also be used to justify a terrible narcissism. Providence might make use of the ungodly merely as agents to test or aid the saints. When the Massachusetts Bay General Court sought the causes of King Philip's War in New England, colonial leaders saw no need to ponder the Indians' grievances. The natives were only God's instruments in warning the settlers against the war's real causes: the colonists' immodest behavior, long hair, and straying from the path of the founders.[92] Thus, the Indians could be put down, and the colonists could turn to examining

90. For a discussion of theories concerning the transition from servitude to slavery in English colonies generally, see Menard, "From Servants to Slaves," *Southern Studies* XVI (1977), 355–90; Galenson, *White Servitude*, 149–68; Richard S. Dunn, "Servants and Slaves: The Recruitment and Employment of Labor," in Greene and Pole, eds., *Colonial British America*, 157–94; and Alden T. Vaughan, "The Origins Debate: Slavery and Racism in Seventeenth-Century Virginia," *Virginia Magazine of History and Biography* 97 (1989), 311–54.
91. For the economic argument, see Galenson, *White Servitude*, 156, 176; and Menard, "From Servants to Slaves," *Southern Studies* XVI (1977), 380–1. Menard argues that slaves numbered fewer than 5 percent even in the Chesapeake population in 1680. The young puritan governor of Maine asserted that solving his colony's servant problem with African slaves would be unlawful; Thomas Gorges to Sir Ferdinando Gorges, May 19, 1642, in Robert E. Moody, ed., *The Letters of Thomas Gorges: Deputy Governor of the Province of Maine, 1640–1643* (Portland, ME, 1978), 94–5.
92. Act of the General Court, November 1675, reprinted in Edmund S. Morgan, ed., *Puritan Political Ideas, 1558–1794* (Indianapolis, 1965), 226–33.

their behavior *within* their own society. Outsiders need have no claim on their attention.

The same inward-turned logic allowed the company dedicated to Providence to assume that God had provided perfectly acclimated heathens to work in tropical fields. If God had not intended their use, why did he make Europeans ill-suited to such labor conditions, while Africans worked so well under the hot sun? Because the whole enterprise was a venture to advance true religion, the answer could not have been that God intended Europeans to stay in Europe. Slavery was a potent rhetorical conceit in England during the years of Charles I's personal rule and the Civil War, but the English were capable of perfect compartmentalization in their thinking. Lifelong servitude, horrifying for one of themselves, was acceptable for people whom God had set apart physically and psychologically.

It was easy to move from the environmental determinist position to the assumption that those exploited, through some viciousness of character, invited their condition. The company authorized slaughter of runaways, who "seem to seek their own destruction." Similarly, Nathaniel Butler, while expressing his concern for Indian victims of Spanish cruelty, thought nothing of stealing corn forcibly from "Cannibal Indians." The Pequots sold into slavery on Providence Island appeared in the company records only once as "the Cannibal Negroes brought from New England." No doubt existed about the nature of the "special care" stipulated for the fifteen boys and two women.[93]

Two legal justifications for slavery were current when the English colonists began to import Africans.[94] One held that because the slaves were captives in just wars – those conflicts on the continent of Africa in which they had been seized – the slaves' lives were forfeit. Such captives could be killed if the conqueror chose; therefore, a prisoner lost ownership of his or her own life and could be enslaved. The other justification, relied on by the Providence Island Company, was that heathens may be enslaved "during their strangeness from Christianity."[95]

Grounding slavery on that doctrine created a terrible burden of hypocrisy because it meant that any effort to teach the slaves about Christianity would, if it led to their conversion, render them unfitted for slavery. Company members were in no doubt that the slaves were

93. B. L. Add. MS 758, diary entries for Oct. 15, Nov. 4, Nov. 8, 1639, March 16–17, 1640; PIC to Gov. and Coun. by the *Swallow* and *Spy* 7–38, July 1638.
94. See Winthrop D. Jordan, *White Over Black: American Attitudes Toward the Negro, 1550–1812* (Chapel Hill, 1968), chaps. 1 and 2, esp. pp. 20–4, 68–70, 91–5.
95. See David Brion Davis, *The Problem of Slavery in Western Culture* (Ithaca, 1966), esp. chap. 7.

human, but they forgot that fact as well as their avowed intention of bringing true religion to the heathen in seeking economic development.[96] Nowhere in their letters, formal or informal, does any discussion of religious education for slaves occur. These staunch puritans thus turned their backs on human beings in need, men and women who were in their power.

John Smith's last book, written just as Providence Island was founded, predicted that, so great were opportunities for freedmen in America, "the very name of servitude will ... become odious to God and man."[97] Without knowing it, he pointed to one of the deep ironies of early colonial history. The greater opportunity some colonies afforded young English men and women to end their servitude by setting up on their own ultimately turned planters in the direction of unending servitude for African men and women who were set apart and therefore forced to accept an odious condition.

As the colonial period progressed, European servants gained a measure of rights in distinction to the Africans, who had no rights as slaves. A wedge was thus driven between the two types of servitude, and servants insisted on their distinction from slaves. In the relationship between servants and slaves, however, as on so many other aspects of the transformation of servitude, the brief experience of Providence Island distinguishes it from other English colonies. The records offer glimpses of a solidarity between servants and slaves, a consciousness of their shared condition, that was unusual in the colonial setting.

Nathaniel Butler's diary of the decade's last year is filled with notations of escapes, or tries at escapes. He especially delighted in noting attempts against his opponents among the colonists, Mr. Richard Lane and the Reverend Hope Sherrard. Sometimes the runaways, who often stole their master's boat to make good their escape, were bands of slaves or servants, but often the groups were mixed, African and English fleeing their mutual servitude together.[98] In his notes of his letters to the

96. For seventeenth-century condemnations of the Barbados planters for their denial of Christian teaching to their slaves, see Ligon, *A True and Exact History of Barbados*, 82; and John Berkenhead to Secretary John Thurloe, February 17, 1654, in Thomas Birch, ed., *A Collection of State Papers of John Thurloe, Esq.* (London, 1742), III, 159.
   Ultimately the colonies dealt with the problem by decreeing that baptism would not free a slave; Jordan, *White Over Black*, 67–8, 74, 91–5; Vaughan, "The Origins Debate," *Virginia Magazine of History and Biography* 97 (1989), 329.
97. Smith, *Advertisements*, 1631, in Barbour, ed., *Complete Works of Smith*, III, 287.
98. Many slaves escaped to the Moskito Coast during the 1641 capture of Providence Island by the Spanish, where they joined with the region's native population; see John A. Holm, "The Creole English of Nicaragua's Moskito Coast," unpub. Ph.D. diss., University of London, 1978, 179, 315.
   For the fear of joint action by servants and slaves on Barbados, see Jack P. Greene,

company, Governor Butler wrote of the "desperate runaways out of the Island both English and Negroes. . . . And I find that the over harsh and rigorous dealing of the masters mainly occasioneth this. But I am afraid that if I should name some of the masters unto you and the manner how you would not believe me. I pray to God there fore that this Incredulity cost you not dear at some time or other. . . ."[99] Although its experience differed from other English colonies, Providence Island shared this one key characteristic with those plantations that relied on bound labor – increasingly exploitative conditions of servitude.

"Changing Identity in the British Caribbean: Barbados as a Case Study," in Nicholas Canny and Anthony Pagden, eds., *Colonial Identity in the Atlantic World, 1500–1800* (Princeton, 1987), 221–4; Beckles, *White Servitude and Black Slavery*, 8, 98–105.

99. B. L., Sloane MS 758, letter 33; diary entries for May 16, 17, 22, Oct. 13, 20, 29, Nov. 26, 1639; Jan. 28, 1640. See also the escape of slaves and servants together reported by Samuel Rishworth, PIC Gen. Ct. 6–22–37. The company sent directions for dealing with runaways in PIC to Gov. and Coun. in the *Blessing* 5–36, and in the *Swallow* and *Spy* 7–38.

7

Military Requirements
and the People's Response

MANY CAUSES CONTRIBUTED to the great outpouring of English men and women to America in the 1630s. Economic hardship impelled numerous emigrants to seek a better life, but many, especially puritans, were also fleeing new and unwelcome intrusions of the central government into the country's life. The drive toward a new Arminian religious conformity formed one area of intrusion, and large numbers chose America in order to worship as they believed God directed. Another was the government's push to create a "perfect militia" and to force the country to support a misconceived war effort against both Spain and France in the late 1620s.

These wars placed heavy strains on the relationship between king and parliament that was the heart of the English national political system. War also laid bare stresses in county and local government as it had developed under Stuart rule. And the demands of war placed intolerable burdens on the people in towns and countryside, who were already weighed down by inflation, harvest failure, and industrial depression.[1] These problems helped men and women make the decision to emigrate to the new puritan colonies in the 1630s, but they also raised difficulties in the new settlements when colonial governments seemed to be making the same sort of demands as the Stuart monarchy. Defense, as seemed obvious to company investors in London, was a major concern for Providence Island, which was a sure target for Spanish attack. Company members could never understand settlers' reluctance to contribute time and effort freely to the fortification and defense of the island. They saw no link between colonists' experiences in England and the grievances they articulated in the Indies.

In calling on their colonists to muster and train for their own defense, as well as in expecting them to build and maintain fortifications, the

---

1. See Russell, *Parliaments and English Politics*, 81, 323–6.

Providence Island investors were extending a controversial English tradition to their new society. Company orders and the adventurers' scorn for recalcitrant colonists evoked responses conditioned by bitter experience in the England of the 1620s, where the government had tried to force the country onto an adequate war footing. Although war and invasion scares kept problems of defense before the public eye, the counties resisted Whitehall's call to create a "perfect militia" capable of mounting an expert resistance to England's enemies.

Defiance rested on several foundations. One was the government's vesting of control of the militia in the lieutenants of the counties. The gentry disliked the office of Lord Lieutenant, which had been created by the Tudors to settle the country and carry the central government's influence into the localities. Justices of the peace, who saw many of their functions, such as control of the militia, assumed by the lieutenancy, dragged their feet when ordered to tax constituents and draw up lists of obligations. The justices objected that, although lords lieutenant might be necessary in time of war, the gentry could perform their functions quite well in ordinary times.[2]

The legal basis of the militia was also problematical. An act of 1604 in the beginning of James I's reign repealed a number of inherited statutes, including the militia act of 1558. Repeal made sense because the Elizabethan wars with Spain had demonstrated the inadequacy of the earlier distribution of responsibilities among the counties. The old statute was not replaced, however, probably because the process of establishing new, more realistic rates and commitments would have aroused a public outcry as the assessments of those who had previously been undertaxed were raised.[3] Henceforth, until the beginning of the Civil War, the right to call the militia for training or defense rested solely on the royal prerogative, the king's right to act on his own initiative for the common good.

When Charles I came to the throne and began to call for increased efforts, revitalizing the office of the lieutenancy in the process, hostility to the lieutenancy and its control of the militia showed in the systematic resistance of many counties, where justices of the peace were uneasy about unforcing so unfair a system with only the royal prerogative to

2. See Fletcher, "Honour, Reputation and Local Officeholding," in Fletcher and Stevenson, eds., *Order and Disorder*, 106–8.
3. On the reasons for the repeal of the earlier militia act, see Robert Ashton, *The English Civil War: Conservatism and Revolution, 1603–1649* (London, 1978), 55. On the legal position, see Richard Tuck, " 'The Ancient Law of Freedom': John Selden and the Civil War," in John Morrill, ed., *Reactions to the English Civil War, 1642–1649* (London, 1982), 145–6; see also Russell, *Parliaments and English Politics*, 274–5, 386.

justify it.[4] Extending the prerogative to cover areas where the law was inadequate could lead only to enlargement of the king's and shrinking of parliament's role. Many would have followed John Selden in arguing that new and better laws were the only way to deal with such a crisis.[5]

So crucial was the problem of the militia and its legal basis that both Charles and the parliament moved to ensure control of the institution as tensions increased in the late 1630s, producing the sparks that ignited the war. Charles I acknowledged this in his final speech from the scaffold at his execution: "And I call God to witness, to whom I must shortly make an account, that I never did intend for to encroach upon their privileges. They began upon me; it is the militia they began upon."[6]

It had been clearly apparent that Charles I's government was responding to genuine needs in the drive to perfect the militia during the later 1620s, a period when England was at war with the two greatest powers in Europe. The nation's military capacity was woefully out of date. The Earl of Warwick found the Essex militia "very raw" when they were mustered to meet a feared invasion in the mid-1620s; and the coastal defenses were crumbling, falling into the sea.[7] But being so backward meant that the campaign to catch up would be expensive. And failure to reform the old assessment standards based on traditional obligations meant that the burden would fall very unequally. Even royal proclamations pointing to an imminent invasion in the summer of 1625 failed to stir the people to contribute to fortification rebuilding and militia training.[8]

Innovations in weaponry, particularly the introduction of the flintlock musket early in the century, vastly increased the costs to those men with feudal obligations to equip one soldier. The government argued that military expertise was as outmoded in the counties as the soldiers'

---

4. T. G. Barnes has presented a classic case of such resistance in Somerset; see his *Somerset*, 98–123.
5. On Selden, see Tuck, "Ancient Law of Freedom," in Morrill, ed., *Reactions to the English Civil War*, 145–7. See also M. J. Mendle, "Politics and Political Thought, 1640–1642," in Conrad Russell, ed., *The Origins of the English Civil War* (London, 1973), 219–45, esp. 223.
6. Reprinted in Kenyon, ed., *Stuart Constitution*, 2nd ed., 293–4. On the issues raised by the Militia Bill and the pamphlet war surrounding it, see Lois G. Schwoerer, *"No Standing Armies!" The Antiarmy Ideology in Seventeenth-Century England* (Baltimore, 1974), chap. 3. Control of the militia continued to be an issue throughout the Civil War; see Kishlansky, *Rise of the New Model Army*, 76.
7. B. W. Quintrell, "Towards a 'Perfect Militia', Warwick, Buckingham and the Essex Alarum of 1625," *Essex Archaeology and History* 3rd ser., 15 (1983), 96–105, quotation on 102.
8. Cust, *The Forced Loan and English Politics*, 95.

equipment. One of the most costly elements of the program to rebuild the militia was the use of veteran soldiers as muster masters. These men, "Low Countries Serjeants" who had served in the continental wars, were sent to the counties to further the perfection of the militia.[9]

Gervase Markham, a prolific writer of practical books, wrote a handbook called "The Muster Master" about 1630, the year of Providence Island's foundation. Although it was never published, there is evidence that copies circulated widely. Markham wrote of the importance of the office and the need for conscientious attention in filling it. The muster master "ought to be a man of fair virtue, good Birth, temperate, & mild Nature; of great skill, high valor, and deep Judgement. The first that he may give good example; the second to Defend him from Contempt; the third, because he hath to do with Rudeness; the fourth that he may expound the mysteries of the Wars; the Fifth, that he may not be scard [scared] with Greatness; and the Last, that he may distribute, all Jointly together, equally, honestly, and Justly."[10]

Muster masters were rarely seen as combining these qualities. Grievances over their swaggering disregard for the norms of civil society and their contempt for the dignity of local notables had a long history in some counties. They were seen as tremendously expensive, and the office was castigated as "venal," representing a patronage plum for the lieutenant.[11] The muster masters were resented as outsiders interfering in local affairs, possibly even as spies seeking to report on local laxness in administration. Counties expressed their displeasure by failing to collect the sums required to pay the muster master's salary. Some counties fell many years behind.

The campaign for an exact militia and the appearance of the "Low Countries Serjeants" as muster masters in the counties coincided with large-scale billeting of troops returned from the ill-fated 1627 expedition against France on householders in many parts of the country. All the veterans seemed foreign because of their experience in brutal wars abroad; the soldiers had suffered terribly in the seige of the

---

9. Quintrell, "Towards a 'Perfect Militia', *Essex Archaeology and History* 3rd ser., 15 (1983), 101–3, argued that Warwick first introduced the idea of using Low Countries serjeants to try to whip the Essex militia into shape to meet the feared invasion of 1625–26; he also used Low Countries engineers on the fortifications. On the introduction of the new muskets, see Hirst, *Authority and Conflict*, 123.
10. Gervase Markham, "The Muster Master," ca. 1630, ed. Charles L. Hamilton, *Camden Miscellany XXVI* Camden Fourth Series, Vol. 14 (London, 1975), 56–62.
11. See, for example, E. S. Cope, "Politics Without Parliaments," *Huntington Library Quarterly* XLV (1982), 271–84. For one particularly obnoxious muster master in 1604, see W. P. D. Murphy, ed., *The Earl of Hertford's Lieutenancy Papers, 1603–1612, Wiltshire Record Society* XXIII (1969 for 1967), 38–9, 62–4.

fortress on the Isle of Rhe. Some were Irish Roman Catholics, "papists, Redshanks, and Archduchess's captains . . . fitter to die in ditches . . . than to be employed in any hope of good success," according to Richard Knightley.[12] Not only were English towns forced to entertain Catholic troops, but many puritan leaders came to believe that the Duke of Buckingham had deliberately betrayed European Protestants in the ill-fated French venture, opening the country to the adverse judgment of God.

Billeting not only constituted an irregular tax; it also subjected civilians to victimization by unruly soldiers.[13] In the 1628 Commons debate on billeting, Sir Walter Erle gave a vivid picture of the soldiers' conduct: "They disturb markets and fairs, rob men on the highway, ravish women, breaking houses in the night and enforcing men to ransom themselves, killing men that have assisted constables that have come to keep the peace." Their presence caused many to fear that some kind of permanent military presence in the counties was planned. It was widely believed, as Knightley alleged, that the government used billeting as a punitive measure, placing troops in areas where resistance to extraparliamentary taxation had been strong. Many held billeting to be, as Christopher Sherland frankly said, "against the fundamental liberty of the kingdom."[14] The Commons debate culminated in presentation of a petition against billeting to the king; Sir Nathaniel Rich headed the committee for drawing up the petition.[15]

Although many of them favored the campaign to make England militarily strong, Providence Island Company adventurers fought

12. For popular fears of Irish Roman Catholics, see Robin Clifton, "The Popular Fear of Catholics during the English Revolution," *Past and Present* no. 52 (1971), 49. Conrad Russell portrays Providence Island Company members Rich, Pym, and Knightley as "weaving . . . a coherent fabric of terror" in 1628; *Parliaments and English Politics*, 381–2.

13. On popular fear of soldiers, see Barbara Donagan, "Codes and Conduct in the English Civil War," *Past and Present* 118 (1988), 70–3.

14. *Commons Debates 1628*, ed. Robert C. Johnson, Maija Jansson Cole, Mary Frear Keeler, and William B. Bidwell, 4 vols. (New Haven, 1977), 360–71. See Simon Adams, "The Protestant Cause" (Oxford D. Phil. diss., 1973), chap. 11, esp. 408, 421.

15. *Commons Debates 1628*, 391, 449–52. On the militia and related problems of the lieutenancy, muster masters, and billeting, see Lindsay Boynton, *The Elizabethan Militia, 1558–1638* (London and Toronto, 1967), 225–6, 239–41, 244–47, 269–75, 287–91; Fletcher, *Reform in the Provinces*, 302–8; Hirst, *Authority and Conflict*, 123, 156, 345; Kenyon, *Stuart Constitution*, 2nd ed., 2; A. Hassell Smith, "Militia rates and militia statutes 1558–1663," in Clark, Smith, and Tyacke, *English Commonwealth*, 93–4, 99–100, 104–5; and Esther S. Cope, *Politics Without Parliaments, 1629–1640* (London, 1987), 94–106.

billeting and related issues on the national stage of parliament, and men and women who later became their colonists were touched by the reality of billeting in their home localities. The county of Essex and the town of Banbury, both of which contributed settlers to Providence Island, saw incidents over billeting so outrageous that they were brought before parliament in 1628, a body already filled with apprehension over the presence of the soldiers. Even before the violent incidents, Sir Henry Marten reminded the parliament, "in what passion and distemper many members of the House arrived thither, what bosoms, what pockets full of complaints and lamentable grievances, the most part brought thither, and those every day renewed by letters and packets from all parts and quarters."[16]

T. H. Breen has pointed to the "Witham Affray" as an event that helped to predispose men and women of Essex to emigrate to New England.[17] Witham, a town that because of past compliance with royal demands thought itself exempt from billeting, was saddled with a company of Irish soldiers in 1628. On St. Patrick's Day townspeople showed their dissatisfaction and their sense of the alien nature of the Irish by fixing red crosses to the whipping post and tying a red cross to the tail of a dog. The soldiers responded angrily to the insult both to their religion and their patron saint, and the argument soon led to violence, with shots being fired. About thirty people, including Captain Cary (or Carew), were wounded. Wild – and inaccurate – rumors of widespread deaths at Witham circulated, and the troops were ultimately withdrawn.[18] The servants recruited for Providence Island by Sir Thomas Barrington early in the 1630s were from this troubled region.[19]

The violence in Witham attracted far less attention than contemporaneous events in the puritan town of Banbury, where billeting was imposed as a frankly punitive measure for past resistance to unparliamentary taxation, resistance led by Lord Saye and Sele.[20] Disaffection between troops and townspeople built up over days and

16. Sir Henry Marten (with John Glanville), *The Copies of two Speeches in Parliament* . . . *At a Generall Committee of both Houses, the 22 of May. 1628* (London, 1628), 4, 9.

17. T. H. Breen, "English Origins and New World Development: The Case of the Covenanted Militia in Seventeenth-Century Massachusetts," *Past and Present* 57 (1972), 80–1.

18. On the nature of the Witham Affray and its propaganda uses, see G. E. Aylmer, "St. Patrick's Day 1628 in Witham, Essex," *Past and Present* 61 (1973), 139–48, and B. W. Quintrell, "Gentry Factions and the Witham Affray," *Essex Archaeology and History* 3rd ser., 10 (1978), 118–26. Quintrell points out that Witham had been caught in competition between the Earl of Warwick and other Essex gentry.

19. See Chapter 2.

20. Cust, *Forced Loan and English Politics*, 58; Blankenfeld, "Puritans in the Provinces," unpub. Ph.D. diss., Yale University, 1985, 213–50.

finally culminated in the burning of much of the town in a fire thought to have been set deliberately by the troops.

Henry Halhead and his followers may have accepted the call to emigrate in 1632 in part because of heavy losses in the great fire of Banbury in 1628. Halhead was identified among the four men who suffered the largest damage.[21] William Whately, the renowned puritan minister of Banbury, described the great fire in his sermon *Sinne No More*. The fire began on Sunday morning, March 2, 1628, during services. In four hours it burned 103 dwellings and twenty kiln houses and other outbuildings – about a third of the town Whately thought, along with grain and other commodities to the value of £20,000. Whately saw the fire as a judgment against the sin of drunkeness, always present with the soldiers. Great significance was attached to its beginning in a malt kiln "the proper instrument of making that thing, which is the next and immediate worker of drunkenness, that huge sin, that fertile broody big-bellied sin, which is ... apt to take the forms of all sins." Not only was that kiln destroyed but all kilns within its path: "[I]t leaped from one side of the street to the other, to fetch in kilns, it spared none it came near, it spoiled more malt, then of any other goods of one kind."

Although Whately was prepared to see the fire as punishment for sin, he warned onlookers not to mock at his congregation in this time of trial: "[L]et there be none, no not one amongst you that out of a malicious desire to scourge piety so nick-named, upon our sides, shall mock at Puritanism, upon occasion of this hand of God which he hath stretched out against us, whom the world hath pleased, but falsely, to call Puritans." He argued that God corrects those he loves and uses such correction as a warning to others.[22]

Citizens of the town had a more concrete explanation: The forty soldiers billeted on the town had set the fire. In petitions to the House of Lords, the constable and others, including Henry Halhead, testified that the soldiers had committed "divers outrages" and had attacked Constable George Phillips "in his own shop." The soldiers claimed to be answerable only to their own officers and attacked Phillips when he tried to commit one of them on the order of the magistrate. The soldiers had been heard to threaten to burn the town, "wishing only that the

---

21. Fiennes and Gibson, "Providence and Henry Halhed," *Cake and Cockhorse* 7, (1978), 200–1. William Whately may have had Halhead in mind when he wrote: "How many rich men are become poor, and poor men beggars? How are the labors of many a father, Grand-father, great Grand-father, suddenly converted into smoke and rubbish, in the space of a day and night?", *Sinne No More* (London, 1628), 5.
22. Whately, *Sinne No More*, 2–3, 12–14, 20, 30–2 [32 is mislabeled 36], 45.

poor Men were out, and then they would quickly fire out all the rich men." When the town burned, the citizens knew whom to blame.[23]

Such incidents brought billeting and the attendant problem of martial law before the Parliament of 1628. Were the soldiers under the control of the local civil authorities, like all other subjects? In the House of Commons, Sir Edward Coke argued that martial law could not function in time of peace, "which is when the courts of Westminster are open." To those like Sir Henry Marten, who argued that common law and martial law could exist together, one for the civilian, the other for the soldier, he answered, "It is impossible: . . . If the soldier and the judge should sit both of one bench the drum would drown the voice of the crier."[24] The House of Lords debated the question of the relationship between the soldiers and the townspeople of Banbury; Lord Saye, whose seat at Broughton Castle was near Banbury, pressed the case of the civilians. The debate culminated in a ruling by the Lord Keeper on the vexed question of martial law in a civilian community: "The soldiers . . . are not to be governed by a distinct lawe, but by the Law of the Kingdom and [he] charge[d] them to live Orderly according to the Law."[25]

Each of the issues involved in the national military effort reinforced the hostility generated by the others. Billeting and the commissions of martial law that sometimes accompanied it strengthened the hand of the lord lieutenant and reminded subjects that the entire structure, all of which seemed directed toward centralization of power, rested on the royal prerogative rather than on laws made by parliament. In summing up the nation's grievances in 1628, the Petition of Right focused on four wrongs: forced loans, arbitrary imprisonment, billeting of soldiers on citizens, and the use of martial law.[26] Of these, according to Conrad Russell, billeting was much the most important to the country.[27]

23. Petition of George Phillips, Constable of Banbury, March 26, 1628; Examinations of George Phillips, John Haynes, Henry Halhead, March 26, 1628; House of Lords MSS. *Banbury, A History*, abstracted from *The Victoria History of the County of Oxfordshire*, ed. Alan Crossley (Oxford, 1984; orig. pub. London, 1972), 8–9.
24. *Commons Debates 1628*, ed. Robert C. Johnson et al., 449–50, 545, 554–5, 558–60.
25. *Lords Debates, 1621, 1625, 1628*, ed. Frances Helen Relf, *Camden Society* XLII (London, 1929), 72–8; Russell, *Parliaments and English Politics*, 335–7, 359. See also Cust, *Forced Loan*, 57. These issues would surface again during the Interregnum; see Underdown, *Revel, Riot, and Rebellion*, chap. 8.
26. The Petition of Right is printed in Kenyon, *Stuart Constitution*, 2nd ed., 68–71.
27. Russell, *Parliaments and English Politics*, 344–6, 380. See also Lindsay Boynton, "Martial Law and the Petition of Right," *English History Review* LXXIX (1964), 255–84; Schwoerer, *"No Standing Armies!"*, chap. 2; and Cope, "Politics Without Parliaments," *Huntington Library Quarterly* XLV (1982), 272. These issues would continue during the 1640s when the alternatives of maintaining soldiers through

Certainly the citizens of Banbury had reason to know not only how great a grievance billeting constituted, but also that the government would impose it as punishment for those who resisted any part of its program.

All these struggles were played out anew in Providence Island, where the uneasy relationship between civilian authority and the essential military men always balanced on the edge of explosion into outright conflict. Many on both sides were puritans, but the stresses could not be submerged in a shared religious outlook. The price paid for the colony's location was very high. Although the need for effective defense in the heart of the Spanish empire was clearly great, the Providence Island Company was evoking memories of hated impositions in its calls for military training, contribution of time and goods to the fortifications, and especially in entrusting training to abrasive veterans of the continental wars such as their Muster Master General, Captain William Rudyerd.

John Pym presented the military impositions on English counties, including specifically the muster master's wages, as grievances in his opening speech to the Short Parliament in April 1640, and his parliamentary colleagues had pointed to the unsatisfactory system in the Petition of Right and the Grand Remonstrance.[28] Throughout the 1630s, however, company members, including Pym, expressed outrage when Providence Island colonists objected to the company's military impositions. To their colonists in the Indies, although the investors could point to the iron law of necessity and the near certainty of Spanish attack, the company's commands constituted no less a grievance. In Providence Island as in counties throughout England, impositions necessitated by preparation for war violated the ideal and expectation of local self-government.[29]

Civilian colonists drawn from troubled counties in England thus brought with them a horror of military occupation and a sense of alienation from the swaggering demands of veterans who saw themselves as set apart from normal civil procedures. Providence Island Company members, although they represented their constituents' grievances in parliament, had difficulty seeing the deep gulf between military and

heavy taxation or accepting their living off the land caused great bitterness that came to a head in 1646–47. An associated problem was the army's demand for indemnity for wartime acts. Great paranoia was generated by the army's presence in the country. See Kishlansky, *Rise of the New Model Army*, 146–57, 186–7, 208–12. Lord Brooke apparently paid the militia in his own army himself; Strider, *Brooke*, 47.

28. Pym, *A speech delivered in parliament . . . concerning the grievances of the kingdome*, 26–8.

29. Russell, *Parliaments and English Politics*, 76–81.

civilian roles; they expected to combine both kinds of leadership in their own lives. The puritanism of these lordly men combined the humanist's doctrine of service to society with the godly person's commitment to duty. Their reinterpretation of the knightly tradition in the light of their educations and their religious conversions produced an unparalleled level of energy in work for the public good as they saw it. The adventurers, risking huge amounts of their own time, money, and energy on the project, expected colonists to contribute on the same level, especially because settlers would be primary beneficiaries of all work. Colonists' resistance to demands for contributions to the fortifications and militia training seemed merely churlish to them. If the colony succeeded as all hoped, the nation and the Protestant religion would be secured, a goal toward which everyone could work whole-heartedly. They did not foresee the tremendous resentment the colony's military impositions would generate.

Providence Island brought together an explosive combination of English settlers and military men whose assumptions were derived from field experiences in the Indies or in Europe's religious wars. Although many of them were closely connected to gentry or aristocratic families, the veterans' choices had set them apart from the ideal of English life shared by other colonists. Many had been away from England for a long time. Captains Daniel Elfrith, Sussex Camock, and Samuel Axe represent one group of these men. They had been in the Indies for years, and most had been involved in privateering. They were at home with the cooperative international character of Caribbean life and were willing to pay the price it could exact in conflict and double-dealing. Their knowledge made them indispensable, if often highly abrasive, settlers.

The West Indian veterans were an alien element in the puritan settlement not only by their experience but because they occupied a different mental universe. English puritans gained a sense of power and control by learning to read and align themselves with Providence; their entire venture in the Indies was committed to the Providence for which it was named. The humanistic learning of the grandees and the piety and Bible study of the rank and file contributed to their sense of being in touch with the providential working out of history, in which God's will could be seen and followed.

Puritan leaders in England believed that all events could be read for signs of God's intent and that every happening had meaning in the grand scheme. Fate, Oliver Cromwell declared, was a "paganish" concept. Yet the outlook of the West Indies captains was entirely fatalistic; fortune, not Providence, ruled their lives, and it was an utterly capricious, even irrational, force. They were tossed to and fro by its whims, and their conduct accommodated such uncertainty.

Thomas Gage, who left the Roman Catholic priesthood and service in Spanish America to become an associate of Oliver Cromwell in his native England, encountered such reasoning when the Spanish ship on which he returned to Europe was captured by Diego el Mulato, the renegade from Havana who sailed with the Dutch and whose 1631 visit to Providence Island had caused so much trouble for Daniel Elfrith. Gage met privately with his captor and, pointing out that he was really English and out of sympathy with the Spanish, implored Diego to return his property seized with all the rest. "The Mulatto" replied with "that common proverb at Sea, Oy por mi, mañana por ti, to day fortune hath been for me, to morrow it may be for thee: or to day I have got what tomorrow I may lose again." The luck of the draw dominated in the Indies; today's ally might be tomorrow's enemy.[30]

The West Indian captains, accustomed to the fluid world of the Caribbean, could never be committed to a single project as the other colonists could. When the opportunity came to leave Providence Island for the mainland with Sussex Camock, these men took it. Samuel Axe not only went to the mainland but twice applied to Dutch sources for letters of marque, once in 1639 after the Providence Island Company had obtained exclusive English rights to privateering.[31] Like the fate that governed them, these men were used to operating on a stage of constantly shifting commitments and liaisons.

The other group of military recruits, soldiers who had served on the continent, was composed of men such as Captain William Rudyerd, Governor Robert Hunt, and probably William Rous and Thomas Fitch. For these men foreigners, especially Roman Catholics, were irrevocably the enemy, and the wars in which they fought were exceptionally brutal. Virginia governor Captain John Smith, one of the few veterans who reflected in print on his experiences in Europe, found himself "both lamenting and repenting to have seen so many Christians slaughter one another."

Service in Europe was brutalizing, but it could also impart a level of

---

30. Oliver Cromwell, Speech to the First Protectorate Parliament, January 22, 1655, *Oliver Cromwell's Letters and Speeches with Elucidations by Thomas Carlyle*, ed. W. A. Shaw (London, Everyman, n. d.), III, 81; Gage, *English-American*, 189. At Diego's request Gage visited the privateer's mother in Havana after he resumed his homeward journey; ibid., 199. On the contrast between fate and providence, see James, *English Politics and the Concept of Honour*, 7–8, 43–58; Skinner, *Foundations of Modern Political Thought*, II, 175–6, 236–43; Thomas, *Religion and the Decline of Magic*, chap. 4.
31. PIC to Axe by the *Mary*, 7–39.

cosmopolitan sophistication lacking in both the West Indian captains and the civilian colonists. Some of these military men had traveled widely throughout Europe and had absorbed a broader outlook. Cotton Mather wrote of Captain Thomas Dudley of New England that in his early life he had served in the Low Countries, "which was then an Academy of Arms, as well as Arts." John Pory, secretary in Virginia, called the Netherlands "that university of war." Men such as John Smith and Captain Nathaniel Butler learned French and Italian, and Butler's endeavors showed his understanding and appreciation of Italianate architecture. Venice was a magnet that drew many of these men; Captain Philip Bell, like Lord Brooke, looked back with pleasure on his time there. In a period in which style counted heavily, these continental veterans may have been the most sophisticated men on the island.[32]

The captains of both traditions expected all hands to set to work on the fortifications under their direction immediately on arrival. Like the swaggering Low Countries Serjeants whose presence was so hated in England, they expected to give orders and be obeyed. The planters, especially those who had suffered from military impositions at home, reacted angrily to their demands and craved time to build houses, plant fields, and prepare for an orderly life in the tropics. As John Winthrop, Jr., wrote, in new plantations everything had to be done "as in the beginning of the world."[33] The settlers thought the company should provide servants who would work exclusively on the public works. No issue occasioned more bitterness on all sides than this one.

32. For Smith's autobiography, see *The True Travels, Adventures, and Observations of Captaine John Smith*, 1630, in Barbour, ed., *Complete Works of John Smith*, III, 153–203, quotation from 157. On Dudley's early life, see Mather, *Magnalia Christi Americana*, Book II, 15–16. John Pory wrote to "the Right honorable and my singular good Lord," September 30, 1619, in Kingsbury, ed., *Virginia Company Records* III, 219–22.

Philip Bell mentioned his time in Venice in his letter to the Bermuda Company in Ives, ed., *Letters from Bermuda*, 283. Lord Brooke's Venetian year is recounted in Spencer, "Genealogie of Robert Lorde Brooke," ed. Styles, in Dugdale Society *Publications* XXXI (1977), 171.

Continental experience, which imparted a broader outlook, could also make one an object of suspicion. New England's Edward Winslow, in answering Dr. Robert Childe's demand for wider religious toleration, pointed out that he had traveled extensively in Italy and held a degree from the University of Padua. Perhaps he had ceased to be thoroughly English; Winslow, *New Englands Salamander, Discovered*, 1647, Mass. Hist. Soc. *Collections*, 3rd ser. II (1830), 117–18.

33. John Winthrop, Jr., to Henry Oldenburg, Nov. 12 1668, M.H.S. *Colls.*, 5th ser., VIII (1882), 133.

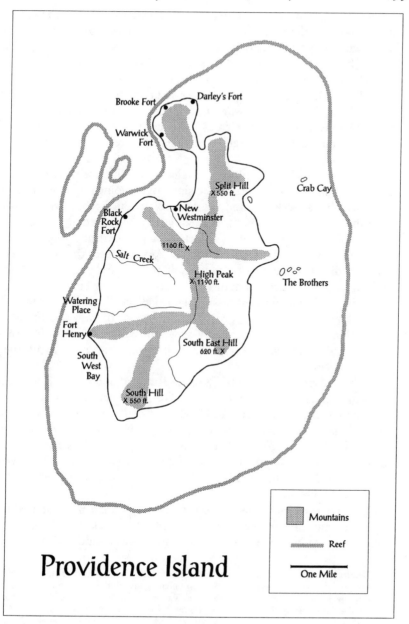

Providence Island

In their first instructions the adventurers set out a program: The settlers were to focus their attention on the fortifications and on building houses and preparing fields for planting. As soon as possible, they were also to build a church and a "commodious" governor's house spacious enough to entertain "persons of quality" if such should come out from England. Peace had recently been concluded between Spain and England, but the company warned in sending a copy of the articles, "It seems there is no peace between us in the Latitude wherein you are, and therefore you must be as careful and vigilant to prevent their Attempt as ever."

Captain Samuel Axe, placed in charge of the fortifications, had already begun Warwick Fort on the small island joined to Providence at the north by a neck of land; it overlooked the harbor where New Westminster was to be built. The company suggested that a second fort be placed eastward of Warwick Fort on the same small island. Eventually, Brooke Fort and Darley's Fort studded this coast. The investors directed that a fort also be built at the island's southwest point and named Fort Henry in honor of company governor Henry Rich, Earl of Holland. Ultimately a fifth fort, named Black Rock Fort, was built overlooking the southern approach to the harbor of New Westminster. In the first shipment the company sent fourteen pieces of ordnance – six demiculverins, six sakers, and two saker drakes with all their appurtenances.[34]

By the end of 1633, Captain William Rudyerd and his officers wrote to John Pym, impatient that the fortification proceeded so slowly as "we are environed with enemies." They said that the island was well peopled along the seven miles of coast from Fort Henry to Fort Warwick. They suggested that twenty-nine pieces of ordnance then on the island be placed on the west and said twenty ordnance were required to defend the uninhabited northern shore, which was partly protected by breakers.[35]

The company's initial instructions repeatedly emphasized the need for vigilance and preparedness. Food should be stockpiled in case of emergency; readying the fields for planting was as essential to defense as

34. Demiculverins were 4 1/2-inch, ten-foot guns that fired nine-pound shot. Sakers fired five-pound shot, and saker drakes were small guns of the same bore as sakers. Captain John Smith included tables of the varieties of ordnance in his *An Accidence or The Path-way to Experience. Necessary for all Young Sea-men* (London, 1626) and *A Sea Grammar* (London, 1627); see Barbour, ed., *Complete Works*, III, 26, 109. See also Andrews, *Spanish Caribbean*, 102, 160.

35. William Rudyerd, William Rous, Roger Floyde [Floud?], John Brigham to John Pym?, Oct. 28, 1633, H.M.C. Tenth *Report*, Appendix Pt. VI (1887), Bouverie MSS, 85.

building the fortifications. Plantations must be sited with an eye to rapid manning of the forts in time of crisis, with promises of compensation for those who were placed on poorer land as a result. And all colonists must turn out for military training once a month under the muster master general, Low Countries veteran William Rudyerd. Everyone was to hasten to his assigned place when any ship approached the island.[36]

In the early correspondence, the company sought to calm colonists' fears about their vulnerability. In May 1632 the company sent ten additional pieces of ordnance (fewer than the colonists had requested in their petition) and workmaster Nicholas Goodman, hired at the extraordinary salary of £80, to assist Captain Axe. The adventurers repeated their mariners' judgment that the island was already well fortified. Pointing to the recent "extraordinary losses" and manifold commitments of the Spanish, the company urged the settlers to think of "the Almighty Arm of that God who is a sure rock of defense to all that trust in him" and calmly go about their business.[37]

Investors marveled that, even while the planters were so afraid, they complained about exactions for the public works. They objected to feeding and clothing their servants while they labored on the fortifications and implied that the assignments had been unfairly handed out. The company responded with ridicule but gave in on some points, allowing food and supplies out of the stores for those doing public labor. They replied to settlers' demand that several hundred servants be sent to work exclusively on public works by diverting those recruited to recompense officeholders. Pointing out that public servants could only free planters from public labor, which was for their own "safety and conveniency," investors could see "no motive" for it "but love to ease and liberty, against which humanity and care of their own reputation" should prevail.[38]

This circular wrangling continued throughout the colony's life. Added to this was contention among the island's military leaders. Daniel Elfrith and Samuel Axe quarreled over the usefulness of Warwick Fort. Their animosity had begun over division of a share of the island's first tobacco crop, which the company had vaguely said should be apportioned among Axe, Elfrith, and Bell for their efforts in its first settlement. The company tried to settle the dispute over the forts by

36. PIC Instructions to Gov. and Coun., 2–7–31.
37. PIC, Instructions to Gov. and Coun., 5–10–32; Ctee 4–11–32, and 4–24–32.
38. PIC Ctee 4–25–32; Instructions to Gov. and Coun., 5–10–32; PIC to Bell, 5–10–32; PIC to Elfrith, 5–10–32; PIC to Gov. and Coun. by the *Golden Falcon*, 7–20–33.

stipulating that Axe and Workmaster Goodman were to be supreme in matters of fortification, but both escaped the continuing conflict by leaving the island to accompany Sussex Camock to the Cape, while Elfrith worked on finishing Black Rock Fort.[39] Goodman had been a source of disorder and dissension on Providence Island; both he and Axe were involved in a cryptically reported "poisoning business" whose intended victims had been Governor Philip Bell's servants.[40]

As the experts wrangled, the gun carriages and ropes rotted and the powder sent from England was spoiled by the rain. "It seems strange to us," the company wrote, "that powder so chargeable to us, and so useful to you should perish for want of boards, than which nothing may be more easily had." The investors could not send sawyers and suggested if colonists had servants with that skill they should be employed to make sheds for the ammunition. They asked for measurements of the muskets presently there so that ones sent in the future could be of the same length to facilitate militia training. Meanwhile, sending additional ordnance and gunners and further directions for construction of gun carriages, the company relayed rumors of planned Spanish action against the colony and begged colonists to put the collective interest of the entire project first.[41]

Although deeply divided among themselves, colonists were keenly aware of their own danger. The Reverend Hope Sherrard wrote to Sir Thomas Barrington at the beginning of 1634 saying that the island had ammunition for only one day's fight. More important, fifty "of our Ablest and skilfullest men are gone from us" (many with Captain Camock to the Cape) "so that we have not able men half enough to man our forts, nor any power of men to speak of, to repel an enemy from landing." The settlers had word that St. Martins had fallen to the Spaniard "that would engross the world to himself," and that other islands inhabited by the English were targets: "[A]nd who knows how soon our turn may be if God divert not?" The precariousness of life in Providence Island was perverting the entire godly experiment. The Reverend Henry Roote had refused to stay in part because of feared

---

39. See Chapter 4.
40. PIC Ct., 5–17–34; 5–30–34; PIC to Axe by the *Long Robert*, 1634; PIC to Camock ibid.; PIC to Elfrith ibid.; PIC to Bell by the *Expectation*, 2/3–35.
41. PIC to Gov. and Coun. 4–10–33, 7–20–33, by the *Long Robert*, 1634; PIC to Bell 4–10–33, 7–19–33; Instructions to Jo. Collins of the *Falcon*, 7–1–33; Ctee. 3–26–33, 6–6–33, 6–26–33.
   In all colonies colonists were suspicious of the supposed expertise of fortifications experts. See Richard Ligon's description of the damage done by one swaggering but ill-informed "expert," a Captain Burrows; *History of Barbadoes*, 100.

Spanish attack, Sherrard wrote, and he himself wanted permission to come home.[42]

In June 1634 Captain William Rudyerd, now back in London, came into the company's court to answer charges of having caused his servant's death. When that interrogation was over, the investors asked him for an assessment of Providence Island. Rudyerd bluntly declared the island was worthless; it could be valuable only as a privateering base. He said that "if some industrious and knowing men may be employed about it," the island could easily be fortified; with 600 men it could be held against any force. The present forts, he argued, could not keep out flat-bottomed boats, and he suggested building a series of small timber and sand forts at the water's edge to shelter musketeers. He also suggested cutting the neck of land to make the small northern island a secure retreat, which was done by buccaneers later in the seventeenth century, and said 100 ships could ride safely under the ordnance.[43]

Letters sent out by the *Long Robert* in 1634 reflected the company's sense that work on the fortifications was finally reaching a satisfactory state, and they directed colonists to use Rudyerd's ideas. This impression was strengthened by the report of a Dutch ship captain, Richard Pagett, "alias Eversten," who told the company's committee on December 24, 1634, that not only were the island's fortifications "handsome, and their ordnance fit to prevent the approach of ships," but there were only two safe approaches and the coast was very dangerous for "strange ships."[44]

When the feared attack came, in July 1635, this optimism seemed to be borne out. Association Island had been attacked first, so the colonists had warning. Captain Samuel Axe, left in charge of the Cape trade by Sussex Camock, returned to Providence Island to help with preparations when he heard of its danger. On the other hand, hostile acts by men like Axe may also have helped to bring on the attack; the company learned that Axe had accepted Dutch letters of marque authorizing privateering. The Spanish felt justified in wiping out a colony that sustained a nest of English pirates.[45]

The Spanish ships, under the command of Captain Gregorio de Castellar y Mantilla, first anchored outside the harbor of New Westminster while an emissary carried a demand for the island's surrender.

42. Hope Sherrard to Sir Thomas Barrington, Jan. 6 1634, B. L. Egerton MS 2646, f. 58–59v.
43. PIC Gen. Ct. 6–21–34.
44. PIC to Gov. and Coun.; PIC to Bell, 1634; Ct. 5–20–34; Ctee. 12–24–34.
45. PIC to Samuel Axe, 3–26–36.

When Governor Bell refused, citing his responsibility to the government of Charles I, the Spanish determined to attack on the eastern side of the neck connecting the small island to the larger. The English colonists had never expected an assault at this very difficult point, which required sailing against the prevailing winds and currents, so it was unfortified. Nonetheless, they were able to drag heavy guns to the cliffs overlooking the inlet and repel the threatened invasion. The "torn and battered" Spanish ships "went away in haste, and disorder."[46]

The Spanish attack changed everything. Now that the enemy had made the first hostile move, the company could approach the king with a demand for letters of reprisal. Providence Island could then sponsor and sustain privateering, as many of the captains had wished from the beginning. Although the investors repeatedly stressed their firm commitment to the goal of creating the foundation for a godly English presence in Central America, the civilian colonists must have seen their island move ever deeper into military rule with grave misgivings. The rift between the godly civilians and the military men, some godly and some not, grew constantly wider and more profound through the rest of the settlement's life.

Spain and England were nominally at peace, although as the investors had pointed out in their first instructions, the truce did not extend to the Indies. In December 1635 the governments of each country held detailed discussions about the new instability in the Caribbean. The Providence Island Company first heard of the repelled Spanish attack in December, and the investors then immediately applied for relief through their governor, the courtier Earl of Holland, whose free company membership and office were sustained for just such emergencies. Through him they informed Charles I of "the extraordinary importance of the place, able to give his Majesty a great power in the West-Indian Seas, and a profitable Interest in the Trade of the richest part of America."

In dealing with the company's application for letters of reprisal, Secretary of State Sir John Coke drew up an analysis of the island's present state and promise. Sailing ships that entered the Caribbean had to steer a course that would take them around the western end of Cuba and out through the channel south of Florida. Thus, Coke declared, Providence Island "lieth in the high way of the Spanish fleets" carrying treasure from Cartagena and Portobelo. Coke stressed that the island

---

46. PIC, "A Declaration made the 21st of December 1635 To the right Honorable the Earle of Holland," PRO CO 1/8, 81. These events are recounted in William Sorsby, "Puritan Corsairs, 1629–1641," unpub. ms., 1987.

was naturally strong, approaching ships facing extreme danger of "rocks and shoals," and he also repeated claims it was very well fortified, with thirteen or fourteen fortified places throughout. The military establishment consisted, he wrote, of three captains, three lieutenants, and thirteen or fourteen gunners. Although there were about forty pieces of ordnance presently on the island, they would need eighty big guns (drakes were most useful) and fifty or sixty boats or shallops to carry musketeers for adequate defense.

Coke reported that all the planters were "trained and armed" but argued that the island needed 1,000 "good men" to defend it. At the same time he declared, echoing the opinions of men such as William Rudyerd, "other benefit from that Island is not to be expected but what may be gotten by trade, or by prizes. The trade is not yet settled." Coke's informants told him that they could not keep the project going for under £8,000 per year, and he passed on to the king the company's claim that they could not meet their commitments without his "speedy" authorization of reprisal. The colonists had threatened to desert the island unless they were reinforced by May 1636. There were also hints of Dutch interest in acquiring the plantation.[47]

After inspecting two maps of Providence Island and the adjacent mainland, the king was impressed with "the considerableness of the place," and on December 21, 1635, he signified his willingness to authorize the Providence Island Company to engage in privateering.[48] In so doing the court began a significant turn in foreign policy. As the decade of the 1630s opened, England had made peace with both Spain and France, and Charles I adopted a pro-Spanish stance. As a Habsburg power, Spain was heavily involved in the Thirty Years' War against Protestants in Germany and in the Netherlands. Although many English men and women hated their country's alignment with the hammerer of Protestants, Charles and his Lord Treasurer Richard Weston believed it made sense. Spain's war would weaken the Dutch, already emerging as trade rivals to England, and Charles hoped to convince the Spanish to restore his brother-in-law Frederick, married to his sister Elizabeth, as

47. PIC, "Declaration to the Earl of Holland," PRO CO 1/8, 81; Sir John Coke, draft memorandum on the Isle of Providence, PRO CO 1/8, 83; PIC Gen. Ct., 5–26–36.
48. Declaration at Whitehall, Dec. 21 1635, PRO CO 1/8, 86; PIC Ct. 1–29–36. Captain Samuel Axe sent the company a "plat" of the Moskito Coast in 1634, and Mr. Thomas Heath sent another. The Dutch sea captain Richard Pagett "alias Eversten" sent the adventurers a map of the Darien region. See PIC to Axe by the *Long Robert*, 7/9–34; PIC Ctee., 12–24–34; William Jessop to Heath, 3–30–36, B. L. Add MS 10615, no. 149.

Elector of the Palatinate. Frederick had been removed by conquering Habsburg forces.[49]

Charles's beloved queen, the French Roman Catholic Henrietta Maria, was the center of a group of courtiers who favored an anti-Spanish and pro-French policy. They included the Earl of Holland. When the earl was reelected governor of the Providence Island Company in May 1636, the general court decided to send some emissaries to administer the oath of office to him "for more solemnity, and validity."[50] Holland almost never attended a meeting, but members wanted to ensure that he could legally act for them. These courtiers in the queen's circle looked to a French alliance as the best way to restore the Elector Palatine, thus gaining a role for England on the continent, and they hoped for a vigorous campaign against Spain in the West Indies. In 1635, at the same time as the Spanish attack on Providence Island, France had entered the Thirty Years' War against Spain. Between 1635 and 1637, the English government considered the possibility of an anti-Spanish campaign, perhaps in concert with the French and Dutch, and Charles I's grant of letters of marque to the Providence Island Company was that policy's first (and only) step.[51]

As Charles I considered what to do about Providence Island, the Spanish government pondered the same issue. During December 1635, the Spanish Council of War for the Indies discussed what could be done about what they saw as an infestation of pirates. The councilors agreed that the English had no right in the region and could be eliminated under international law. With so many islands in the Caribbean, however, the English would just reappear elsewhere unless the over-extended Spanish crown was prepared to commit a major force to sweep them from the Indies. Despite this urgent discussion, it would be another five years before the depredations of Providence Island Company privateers became so taxing that the commander of the plate

49. See Simon Adams, "Spain or the Netherlands? The Dilemmas of Early Stuart Foreign Policy," in Howard Tomlinson, ed., *Before the English Civil War: Essays on Early Stuart Politics and Government* (New York, 1984), 79–101.

50. PIC Gen. Ct., 5–26–36.

51. R. M. Smuts, "The Puritan Followers of Henrietta Maria in the 1630s," *English Historical Review* XCIII (1978), 26–45, esp. 40; Barbara Donagan, "A Courtier's Progress: Greed and Consistency in the Life of the Earl of Holland," *Historical Journal* 19 (1976), 317–53, esp. 342–4. Martin Butler points to the queen's involvement in court masques of the period that urged this war strategy; *Theatre and Crisis*, 33. On Spain's terms for restoration of the Elector Palatine, see L. J. Reeve, "Quiroga's Paper of 1631: A Missing Link in Anglo-Spanish Diplomacy during the Thirty Years War," *English Historical Review* CI (1986), 913–26.

   Kenneth R. Andrews argues that ship money was used during this period to create the first modern navy so that England could play a key role in international politics; see *Ships, Money and Politics*, 11, 22–3, 75, 131–7.

fleet allowed diversion of his ships to this task. And even then the Spanish nightmare of the scattered settlers regrouping in other locations and carrying on privateering came true.[52]

Letters of reprisal theoretically gave the Providence Island Company the right to redress losses through capture of Spanish shipping, but in reality they were a license for legalized piracy. In its turn the company could issue licenses to others; they were the only English agents who could legally do so at that time. The adventurers formed partnerships with merchants such as Maurice Thompson. The merchants, who shared 20 percent of their take with the company, could then field ships and use Providence Island as a base.[53] Through this means, the investors could recoup some of their massive outlay, keep the colony going, and strike at the sources of Spanish power. They assumed that they could keep their godly experiment somehow sealed off from the unfavorable effects of the privateers; both projects were linked in the adventurers' minds by the common thread of their commitment to the preservation of the Protestant religion, which necessarily involved defiance of the power of Spain.

Privateering linked the Providence Island investors with the great men of the Elizabethan period – Drake, Ralegh, Hawkins. Those heroes had, with government authorization, carried on a virulent sea war against Spain. They sought to deprive the leader of the Roman Catholics of Indian treasure that allowed it to harry European Protestants. Ralph Lane, governor of Ralegh's Roanoke colony, wrote Sir Francis Walsingham that through their efforts they hoped the Church of Christ might "find a relief and freedom from the servitude, and tyranny that by Spain (being the sword of that Antichrist of Rome and his sect) the same hath of long time been most miserably oppressed with." Between 1585 and 1603, Elizabeth's government sanctioned a war pursued by private enterprise for profit, and huge fortunes were made from it.[54]

The privateering war ended with Queen Elizabeth's death. The Stuarts who replaced her followed a policy of amicable relations with

---

52. B. L. Venezuela Papers, Add MS 36323, fs. 297–300. The plate fleet annually carried treasure from the West Indies to Spain.
53. These London merchants would rise to prominence in the navy under the Earl of Warwick's command after 1642; see Andrews, *Ships, Money and Politics*, 13, 30–3, 37.
    For a description of this mechanism and its workings, together with a journal of the dramatic 1642–45 voyage of Captain William Jackson under such a commission, see Vincent T. Harlow, ed., *The Voyages of Captain William Jackson (1642–1645)*, Camden Miscellany XIII (London, 1923), v–xxvi, 1–39.
54. Ralph Lane to Walsingham, August 12, 1585, in *Roanoke Voyages*, ed. Quinn, I, 203. On the privateering war, see Andrews, *Elizabethan Privateering*.

Spain, a perversion of England's historic destiny in the minds of many. Ralegh, executed on orders of Charles I's father, James I, to conciliate Spain just eleven years before Providence Island's settlement, was symbolic of what the investors worked for: defiance of Spain, greatness for England, security for the Protestant religion. Pym recorded his impressions of Sir Walter's death at the hands of the public hangman in his *Memorable Accidents*: "A.D. 1618: Sir Walter Raleigh 'had the favour to be beheaded at Westminster, where he dyed with great applause of the beholders, most constantly, most christianly, most religiously.'" Ralegh's thoughts echo through the works of the men who saw themselves as carrying on his quest.[55]

The assumption that colonization and privateering could proceed together also had a long history in English adventuring. Sir Walter Ralegh's Roanoke colony, the first English attempt at settlement of America, was designed in the first instance as a privateering base. Ralegh's men chose a southern site, close to the route Spanish ships must use in exiting the Caribbean. Roanoke Island, sheltered within the Carolina Outer Banks, was close but hidden away. The colony planted in 1585 under the governorship of Ralph Lane came home discouraged with Sir Francis Drake's fleet in 1586. After many months of adventuring in the Indies, Drake had hoped to inaugurate it as a privateering base. Instead, he reluctantly presided over its dismantling.

Much had been wrong in the first Roanoke colony's design – the site was very poor, and the colony's composition exclusively of soldiers militated against orderly development. Ralegh was quick to identify the design errors and planned the second expedition quite differently. This was to be in a better site (on Chesapeake Bay) and was to be composed of families who would aim in the first instance at self-sufficiency; the colony was not to be an adjunct to other ventures. This second attempt also failed, its planters becoming the famous Lost Colonists, and much of the reason for its failure lay in the hangover of the association of privateering with colonization. Investors ultimately learned in the sea war between 1585 and 1603 that the expense and trouble of a base was not necessary; privateering proceeded well without such support.[56]

The Providence Island Company would relearn many lessons through bitter experience. Their colony was composed of families almost from

55. H. M. C. 10th *Report*, App., Pt. VI (1887), Bouverie MSS, 85. On Ralegh's influence, see Christopher Hill, *Intellectual Origins of the English Revolution* (Oxford, 1965), 208–11.
56. On Roanoke see David Beers Quinn, *Set Fair for Roanoke: Voyages and Colonies, 1584–1606* (Chapel Hill, 1985) and Karen Ordahl Kupperman, *Roanoke: The Abandoned Colony* (Totowa, NJ, 1984).

the beginning, thus avoiding the first mistake of Roanoke, but the commitment to privateering after 1636 and the increasingly heavy pressure of military interests led to ever-greater tensions within the island. Once the path of privateering was taken, there was no turning back. Many of the colonists had been waiting for this opportunity; the rest more and more withdrew into a separate closed society. The intrusion of a military presence that had helped to drive some colonists from England created great bitterness in Providence Island's last years, as it would do in England under military rule during the Interregnum.

In May 1636 the Providence Island Company sent out massive letters describing the changed situation and their plans and expectations. The letters carried news both of a new governor, Captain Robert Hunt, and of the company's authorization for privateering. The island's deliverance meant that God exercised a special care for the project. Henceforth, the government of Charles I took an official interest in Providence Island. No longer did its fate concern only the investors and colonists and their friends; all England was watching their activities.

In announcing the beginning of privateering, the investors sought to allay settlers' fears. Such adventuring would begin slowly until they were convinced Providence Island was fully protected; large numbers of men trained in military pursuits would soon come for that purpose. Meanwhile, no one among the planters was to set out without company authorization. On the other hand, ventures against the Spanish would now have high priority. The masters of the *Blessing* and the *Expectation* were authorized to take shallops and twenty men each to man them from Providence Island. Lieutenant, now Captain, William Rous was singled out for praise and reward. He was to be captain of the *Blessing* and was to return home after its "sojourn" to inform the company of the state of the island. Daniel Elfrith's son John (or Jeremy) was also to join the ships, but his status was less clear. Captain Daniel Elfrith and Captain Samuel Axe were promised employment in the future but in vague terms. Axe had not yet committed himself to return to Providence Island to stay. Elfrith's request for a salary to be paid in England was refused, but he was promised favorable employment.

At the same time, the colonists themselves were to be whipped into shape. All inhabitants were to be exercised in military pursuits twice a week "sometimes with false fires, and some times by shooting at a mark," until they possessed "a perfect knowledge of the use of arms." Several skilled military men were sent to oversee that training; three had been removed from Landguard Fort, built by the Earl of Warwick to defend the Essex coast, "purposely for the service of the Island." The company paid for their transportation and provided them servants but expected "the charge thereof be duly reimbursed to us with all convenient expedition." Settlers were to swallow their resentment at the soldiers' manner and attitude. The governor and council were directed "on all occasions to show mildness, and gentleness, though you be over them in authority. Ill or unkind usage breeding discontent, whereof we have had experience in others, that have left our service, (out of some distaste) wherein they might otherwise have been very useful." Five or six hundred more men would be coming soon, and the settlers were to have provisions planted for them, as well as for ships that might call in "from time to time."

The investors were in no mood now to countenance grumbling about the public works. The colony could not afford to neglect the fortifications as long as the Spanish were alerted; privateering from the island would only increase their enmity. At the beginning of their general letter to the governor and council, the investors outlined the settlers' faults as their information painted them:

> [O]mitting to exercise the men for many months together, the not appointing of a constant guard upon the storehouse, whereby the powder, arms, and other requisites for your safety have been too much endangered; the not keeping of arms in good repair, the suffering of ordnance to remain unmounted, the leaving of the forts unfurnished with necessaries, for the entertainment of our enemy upon a sudden assault. And the not providing to keep the ordnance and carriages covered with sheds to preserve them from the weather; which argue a great Inconsiderateness and such as might have brought the whole colony into a strange confusion and hazard, if God's wise and gracious Providence had not watched over you.

Such neglect not only violated planters' obligation to the company whose expenses were so great but also their duties to their own reputations and their country. Only Henry Halhead was singled out for reward for his service in overseeing the public works. Not only would colonists now repair and maintain the forts and ordnance; they were also commanded to build a large house for the new governor, and a good minister's house.[57]

Next month, in June 1636, the investors sent out privateer Captain Thomas Newman in the *Happie Return* under the company's own

---

57. PIC, letters, instructions, and agreements sent in the *Blessing*, May 1636; PIC Ct., 3–2–36. The company had asked planters to contribute forty pounds of tobacco per head, comparable to the contribution in other island colonies, but the colonists argued it was too much considering their situation; PIC Ctee. following Gen. Ct., 5–21–36.

On the building of Landguard Fort, see Quintrell, "Warwick, Buckingham, and the Essex Alarum of 1625," *Essex Archaeology and History* 15 (1983), 96–105.

commission. Captain Newman was to review the island's fortifications, and the colonists were directed to accept his advice. The adventurers added to their former instructions the advice that colonists should be vigilant in keeping the watch. The promised large number of new colonists could not now be sent, they wrote, because of the visitation of the plague in England, which hit in full fury immediately after the *Blessing* had cleared its coast.[58]

Civilian colonists reacted to these directives sullenly. Investors were astounded when they demanded that their debts to the stores for the last year be remitted in return for work on fortifications that were, as the company never tired of pointing out, for the settlers' own safety. In March 1637 the adventurers wrote of their disgust at hearing that the fortifications were almost in ruins, that essential gunpowder sent the previous year had lain out in the rain until it spoiled, and that the watches were so ill maintained that William Bluefield had come into the harbor in his boat and proceeded to his house without being challenged. They wrote sarcastically of information that the church was also in disrepair that, on care of God's house, the planters might learn from "the very pagans themselves."[59]

Such apparently irrational behavior on the settlers' part can be at least partly explained. They may have believed that the company owed them compensation for work on the fortifications, because it was now necessitated by the privateering from which adventurers would profit directly. Reports of the poor quality of colonists' work often came from private sources, and may as much reflect power struggles among military men, as in the case of the dispute over the usefulness of Warwick Fort, as genuine neglect. In June 1637, just three months after these letters were sent, both Samuel Rishworth and Philip Bell testified in person before company committees that the fortifications were sound and well tended.[60] Moreover the planters may have felt that too much emphasis and faith were being placed on fortifications. David B. Quinn has recently argued that the 1607 Sagadahoc colony in Maine was killed and the Bermuda economy retarded in part precisely because of overconcentration on fortifications.[61] With the increasing commitment of slaves to work on the fortifications, the issue receded in the company's

---

58. PIC to Gov. and Coun., 6–36, 3–37; Instr to Newman, 6–36.
59. PIC to Gov. and Coun. by the *Mary Hope*, 3–37.
60. PIC Ctee. 6–14–37, 6–22–37.
61. Quinn, "Bermuda in the Age of Exploration and Early Settlement," *Bermuda Journal of Archaeology and Maritime History* I (1989), 19. Professor Quinn points out that Sagadahoc and Bermuda each prepared for attacks that never came. Providence Island was attacked three times in its decade of life.

correspondence with the colonists, although calls on settlers' servants and slaves for labor were always a source of friction.[62]

Conflict over government calls for free labor on the public works was a constant feature of life in all the colonies and in England as well. Throughout England, as in Providence Island, horror was frequently expressed at the state of the harbors, roads, bridges, and coastal fortifications. At the same time that the Providence Island Company was directing its colonists to build a brick powder house, the English government commanded the county of Norfolk to get its gunpowder out of storage in churches and church porches and into a proper magazine. Obligations to keep up roads, harbors, and dikes attached to some forms of leasehold; in other areas they were more evenly distributed over all landholders. Much of the problem seems to have stemmed from the way the impositions were levied. Householders increasingly resisted demands that were perceived as coming directly from the royal government rather than determined, as taxes ought to be, by parliament.[63] "Obligation enforcement," prosecutions of individuals or communities for failing to maintain their roads and bridges, formed the second largest category of prosecutions at the local level in the early seventeenth century.[64]

Problems over forced contributions of money or labor to the public works were seen in all the colonies. Governor Nathaniel Butler found the Bermuda fortifications in sad condition on his arrival in late 1619 and immediately set about rebuilding them. Butler's great accomplishment as governor was his reconciliation of the settlers to impositions on their time and money for public needs. His hand was greatly strengthened by the new Bermuda Assembly through which colonists consented to contribute. Captain Nathaniel Butler tied English traditional rights and preparation for war tightly together in his first speech to the assembly. Not only were strong fortifications crucial, but each planter must be trained in defense, "that is to say, to be soldiers." There was no point in planting tobacco unless one could be sure of keeping it, and he warned fathers that only through military preparedness could they ensure that their sons would grow up freemen.[65]

62. PIC to Gov. and Coun., 4–23–38.
63. Fletcher, *Outbreak of the English Civil War*, 214–15; Boynton, *Elizabethan Militia*, 260; Barnes, *Somerset*, 62–4; Thirsk, ed., *Agrarian History*, IV, 681; Russell, *Parliaments and English Politics*, 59.
64. Wrightson, "Two Concepts of Order," in Brewer and Styles, ed., *An Ungovernable People*, 34–5. See also Carr, "Foundations of Social Order," in Daniels, ed., *Town and Country*, 74.
65. Butler, *History of the Bermudaes*, ed. Lefroy, 148–66, 194–7; Craven, *Introduction to History of Bermuda*, 132–7.

New Englanders were concerned over arbitrary taxation for public works from the beginning. When ordered in 1632 to help pay for the fortifications at Cambridge, the inhabitants of Watertown, led by their minister, refused, saying "it was not safe to pay moneys after that sort, for fear of bringing themselves and posterity into bondage." John Winthrop, on probing their reasons, found that they had not understood that the government over which he presided was "in the nature of a parliament," with the assistants chosen by the freemen. Watertown then agreed to pay. William Pynchon of Springfield was chastised by Connecticut because he refused to "press" an unwilling man's canoe for Indians who were transporting badly needed corn to English colonists. Pynchon's answer was that if he, as a magistrate, were to seize a man's property without legal order, "how long would Tyranny be kept out of our habitations?" He pointed to the men in England, including many Providence Island investors, who had resisted unparliamentary taxation and chose to suffer thereby, and concluded, "[T]o lose the liberty of an English subject in N. E. would bring woeful slavery to our posterity."[66]

Impositions for the public works were taken very seriously. When Massachusetts Bay in 1641 drew up its law code, the Body of Liberties, fifth among the ninety-eight points was the following: "No man shall be compelled to any public work or service unless the press be grounded upon some act of the general Court, and have reasonable allowance therefore."[67]

Once again Providence Island, as the one colony utterly lacking in machinery for popular participation in government, occupied a wholly anomalous status. Pynchon footnoted his defense, "See Sir John Fortescue in his treatise of Rights." Fortescue, writing in the middle of the fifteenth century, argued that the English legal tradition, with the people's representatives in parliament at its center, had developed from ancient times in perfect accord with English needs. Englishmen

---

66. Winthrop, *Journal*, ed. Hosmer, I, 74–5; Pynchon, "Statement," Mass. Hist. Soc. *Proceedings*, 48 (1914–15), 47–8; Andrews, *Colonial Period*, II, 95–9.

67. The Massachusetts Body of Liberties, drawn up by the Reverend Nathaniel Ward, is reprinted in Morgan, ed., *Puritan Political Ideas*, 177–203; point five is on p. 180. See the similar stipulations that taxation for public works must be levied only by the assembly in the Fundamental Orders of Connecticut, passed early in 1639, and in the Bermuda Orders and Constitutions of 1622. The Fundamental Orders are reprinted in Mary Jeanne Anderson Jones, *Congregational Commonwealth: Connecticut, 1636–1662* (Middletown, 1968), 178–83, esp. 182. The Bermuda Orders and Constitutions are in J. H. Lefroy, *Memorials of the Bermudas* (London, 1877), I, 209–10.
    J. F. Martin argues that at the town level in New England taxation was by shares in the land corporation and were thus subscriptions on investments; *Profits in the Wilderness*, 161–7.

"brought up on Sir John Fortescue, as most of them were," believed that England, unlike the rest of Europe, was prosperous and secure precisely because property, especially land, was safe from taxation except by the people's representatives in parliament. Providence Island Company members such as Pym, Rich, Knightley, and Saye cited the Fortescue tradition as they argued against the king's unparliamentary exactions in ship money, billeting, and the forced loan, but none could see the parallel in their own colonists' resistance to demands for contributions to be spent as the company saw fit.[68] The company disgustedly dealt with colonists' recalcitrance by introducing ever larger numbers of company-owned slaves. Absolute loss of freedom for Africans was the answer to settler resistance to infringement of their English rights.

No one on either side of the Atlantic harbored any doubts about the danger in which Providence Island lay. Every set of instructions to ships' masters and privateering captains from 1636 on included directions about what to do if they found the island in Spanish hands. They were not to counterattack but to take their men and supplies to the Moskito Coast to look for scattered colonists and to attempt to hold the company's interest there. Company ships were always directed to interrogate any prisoners they took and to watch for signs of Spanish preparations for attack. In January 1638 members in London, hearing of "great preparations in Spain for the West Indies," renewed their own efforts and warned their emissaries. The Earl of Holland, whose connections at court again proved valuable, had obtained permission for John Pym to remain in London over the winter season so that he could react instantly to news from the island.[69]

The Providence Island Company again made plans for massive changes in their colony, including the introduction of a much larger military presence to balance the investors' growing involvement in privateering. Colonists' resentment at the perversion of the godly community for which they had emigrated was to be mitigated by the

68. Pynchon, "Statement," M.H.S. *Procs.* 48, 47–8. See Pym, *A speech delivered in parliament . . . concerning the grievances of the kingdome*, 13–14; Skinner, *Foundations of Modern Political Thought*, II, 54–6; Russell, *Parliaments and English Politics, 1621–1629*, 53, 336–7, 357; Cust, *Forced Loan*, passim.; Morgan, *Inventing the People*, 153–5. Morgan argues that colonies found that they could not operate without assemblies, even when authorized to do so. Ibid., 43 ff., 123–4.

69. The Earl of Holland to Attorney General John Bankes, Jan. 2, 1638, Bod. Lib., Bankes MS bundle 65, piece 16.

presence of some of the company grandees who intended to emigrate. Could the personal presence of company leaders have succeeded in reconciling the warring factions on Providence Island? The lords and gentlemen combined the traditions of the knight, the scholar, the public servant, and the godly man within themselves. They never understood why various groups among their colonists rejected one or other of these ways of thought, which they saw as completely compatible. Men such as Lord Brooke prided themselves on being utterly at home with military pursuits in a way that the ordinary civilian colonists could not. He participated in the "military vogue" of the 1630s, which saw artillery gardens erected in the cities where young men trained in martial arts. Brooke spent time in these exercises when he was in London, perfecting his form. His biographer told how Brooke, to avoid "profusion of blood" before the Civil War battle of Edgehill, offered to engage in single combat with the Earl of Northampton. Northampton refused, for "good reason," as "he was gross and corpulent...But the Lord Brooke had both an agile body, and also an all-daring and undaunted spirit."[70]

Many of the Providence Island investors took up commands in the Civil War; they saw such commands as a natural extension of their place in society. The Earl of Warwick and Lords Saye and Brooke were exceptionally energetic in militia training as they became lords lieutenant.[71] Machiavelli, arguing that the magistrate's place was at the head of a strong citizen militia, wrote that training in war was essential for the virtuous prince, and Machiavelli's influence was widely felt. After his first taste of the continental wars, Captain John Smith returned to Lincolnshire to prepare himself for a life of command. In attempting to ape the manners and training of the lords and gentlemen

70. Boynton, *Elizabethan Militia*, 263–5; Pearl, *London and Puritan Revolution*, 172; Spencer, "Genealogie of Lorde Brooke," ed. Styles, Dugdale Soc. *Miscellany* XXXI (1977), 178–9. Brooke took command of the combined armies of Warwickshire and Staffordshire in 1642; Strider, *Brooke*, 66.

 The New England minister John Wise pictured Harvard as an artillery garden and its students as soldiers of Christ; *The Churches Quarrel Espoused*, 2nd ed. (New York, 1715), 100–1.

71. Fletcher, *Reform in the Provinces*, 302–8; Fletcher, *Outbreak of English Civil War*, 350–3; Hirst, *Authority and Conflict*, 228. The Self-Denying Ordinance of 1644 excluded all members of the House of Lords from command and was an attack on the hereditary military rights of the aristocracy. Providence Island Company members, the Earls of Warwick and Manchester, were on the committee to compose objections to it; see Kishlansky, *Rise of the New Model Army*, 34–5.

 In the colonies, military titles carried high prestige; see Norman Dawes, "Titles as Symbols of Prestige in Seventeenth-Century New England," *William and Mary Quarterly* 3rd ser., 6 (1949), 78–9; Morgan, *Inventing the People*, 170.

he had seen in Europe, he built "a Pavilion of boughs" where he sat studying "Machiavills Art of war, and Marcus Aurelius."[72]

In promising to come to Providence Island in person, grandees were offering the only leadership that might have been able to fuse the concerns of the military men, the privateers, and the civilians in one grand campaign against Spain and for Protestantism and England. As early as 1636, the Earl of Warwick had delighted adventurers by his "noble petition" for a voyage to Providence Island. With his large fleet and his extensive experience in privateering, Warwick was naturally attracted to the new opportunities in the Indies. The company drew up a special commission making Warwick governor in chief of the plantation and "Captain General and Chief Commander by sea and land of all forces" under the company. When he was away from the island, his deputy governor would command in his place.[73]

Warwick's intended voyage did not take place, but company members continued to discuss personal emigration, believing that only their own presence could save the colony. Their belief had been reinforced by a royal promise of special favors to those who went. The adventurers made plans to prepare the island by sending a large force to perfect the fortifications and to plant food. And each pair of grandees would be accompanied by a large and fully stocked fleet.

In their March 1637 letter to Governor Robert Hunt, the adventurers pointed to the hope of a vigorous anti-Spanish foreign policy in which Providence Island "may be very serviceable to some designs that are now thought on in this kingdom," and hinted that company members "or others of very good quality" would soon emigrate. The hope that Charles I would commit the nation to a great effort against Spain had faded by the next year, but company members continued to plan for emigration. They believed that, given such distinguished company, the eminent ministers Ezekiel Rogers and Charles Chauncy would divert their flocks from New England to Providence Island. Compensation was promised if they did so and the grandees failed to emigrate.[74]

Events in England soon drew the attention of Providence Island Company members and none emigrated, but the colony did experience a great change in 1638 with a huge influx of professional military men

72. Skinner, *Foundations of Modern Political Thought*, I, 129–31, 173; Smith, *True Travels*, in Barbour, *Works of Captain John Smith*, III, 155–6.
73. PIC Gen. Ct., 2–20–36. On Warwick's career as a privateer, see Craven, "The Earl of Warwick, A Speculator in Piracy," *Hispanic American Historical Review* 10 (1930), 457–79; and Andrews, *Ships, Money and Politics*, 110, 117.
74. PIC to Gov. Hunt, 3–37; PIC Ctee. 1–31–38; Ct. 2–14–38; Ctee. 3–1–38; Ct. 30–20–38.

under a new regime. The new governor was Captain Nathaniel Butler, "an ancient soldier at sea and land," who had rebuilt the fortifications on Bermuda, reconciled the Bermuda colonists to exactions for the public works, and calmed the religious controversy raging on those islands. Providence Island's new order included a separate Council of War and a Commission for Grievances. Butler's instructions carried news that the system of halves was henceforth abated, but, unlike his commission for Bermuda, the new regime did not involve a representative assembly to normalize assignment of public works obligations.

Butler sailed on the *Expedition* in April 1638; he was to be admiral as well as governor and was authorized to privateer when he felt it was safe to leave the island. His principal care as governor was to be the fortifications and exercising the men in use of arms. Governor Robert Hunt was now to be commander of Black Rock Fort, replacing Daniel Elfrith. Captain Thomas Scott was to command the men on the island's west side and to be commander of Fort Henry, with John Foster as his ensign. Mr. Coleborne was to be lieutenant of one of the windward forts, where the governor thought he would serve best. All but Hunt were new to Providence Island. Soon Lieutenant William Woodcock also agreed to go.[75]

In their eagerness to send experienced military commanders, the investors entertained men whose records in puritan colonies were already problematic. Captain William Rudyerd had been sent back to the island in 1637 as commander of a company privateer, notwithstanding the cloud under which he had left. John Pym had earlier suggested that he be made governor of Association Island. The discussion of whether he was fit to be made a privateering captain did not mention his servant's death and concerned only charges made against him of selling company goods and wasting gunpowder. Pym successfully defended Rudyerd against the complaints; the large sum of £10 was allowed for "provisions extraordinary" for his ship's "great cabin." The colonists were admonished to offer Rudyerd "advice, respect, and friendship."[76]

Captain Samuel Axe was lured back to stay in Providence Island; his

75. PIC Letters, Instructions, Commissions sent by the *Expedition*, 4–38; Ctee. 4–12–38, 4–18–38, 5–4–38.
76. PIC Ct., 5–14–36; Mtg. at Warwick Castle, 1–20–37; Ctee. at Preston, 2–24, 26, 27; PIC to Gov. and Coun. by the *Mary Hope*, 3–37, Instr. to Captain William Rudyerd, 1–37. Henry Darley's brother, who had been in Providence Island since 1634, was given permission to join Rudyerd's expedition if he wanted to; PIC to Gov. and Coun. by the *Mary Hope*, 3–37; see also PIC to Bell by the *Long Robert*, 9–34, and PIC Ctee. 4–18–38.

expertise was too valuable for investors to balk at his record. When the company had written Axe in 1636 to thank him for his care in returning to help the colonists prepare for the Spanish attack, they also chastised him for "the slaughter of divers Indians by the English under your command, during your abode upon the Maine." The adventurers were deeply disturbed, saying they had labored to find out the facts, and they concluded, "[W]e are not able to clear you from a sin of a very high nature. We know the law will not take notice of it, yet the Lord is the avenger of blood, and wheresoever it is shed in an undue way, his justice will certainly require it." Nonetheless, Axe was back in Providence Island to stay in 1638, and the company paid his price: He said he would not consent to go there if Captain Elfrith remained. The company accepted Elfrith's often-expressed wish to leave, and Axe, who, though he was a councilor, was not required to attend council meetings except "when his own occasions will conveniently permit," became the constant companion of Governor Butler when both were present in Providence Island.[77]

Captain Andrew Carter, the man who would eventually dismantle the entire godly experiment, came to Providence Island in 1637. In 1638 the company put him on the governing council, and by 1639 they were offering him further rewards and promises of favor. He took on the important and controversial post of muster master general.[78] The rash of military appointments in 1638 extended to confirmation of Alexander Bryan in the post of marshall; his sentence of death for "mutinous words" against Governor Bell had been lifted by the company in 1637.[79]

The Providence Island Company also sought in 1638 to attract experienced men who had suffered under ideologically defective regimes in English colonies to the north. The investors offered the very large stipend of £100 plus free transportation and food in the colony to Captain John Underhill of Massachusetts for one year; his New England salary had been £31 4s plus housing and a stipend of £6 4s for maintenance.[80] John Underhill, a hero of the Pequot War of 1636–7, was in England publishing his book on the war and on the prospects of

---

77. PIC Ct. 3–6–38, 4–20–38; Ctee. 3–26–38; PIC to Elfrith, 4–23–38; PIC to Gov. and Coun., 7–38. Company secretary William Jessop wrote Captain Axe a long, conciliatory letter that was full of praise and promises and showed great care for Axe's profits, in March 1636; B. L. Add MS 10615, no. 148.

78. PIC to Gov. and Coun. by the *Mary Hope*, 3–37, by the *Swallow* and *Spy*, 7–38; PIC to Captain Carter by the *Mary*, 7–39.

79. PIC to Gov. and Coun. by the *Mary Hope*, 3–37, by the *Swallow* and *Spy*, 7–38.

80. PIC Ctee. 3–24–38. On Underhill's salary in Massachusetts, see Rutman, *Winthrop's Boston*, 174.

New England, *Newes from America*. Underhill was descended from a distinguished gentry family. He was expelled from Massachusetts Bay as a follower of Anne Hutchinson. Although deeply religious and an experienced soldier, Underhill would have added to Providence Island's disruption, as he did wherever he went. Massachusetts leaders had accused him of seducing a young woman in the guise of seeking religious experience and of saying that he found the spirit of God in a pipe of tobacco. Underhill did not accept the invitation to Providence Island. He emigrated to New Hampshire, where many of Hutchinson's followers had gone, and became for a time governor of Dover, which had been acquired in 1633 by a group of gentlemen headed by Lords Saye and Brooke. Later he advised the Dutch in New Netherland.[81]

Captain William Claiborne, a Virginia leader whose trading domain on Kent Island in Chesapeake Bay had been taken over by the recently founded Roman Catholic refuge of Maryland, received a grant of incorporation for himself and his associates for Ruatán Island in the Bay of Honduras. Ruatán was to be renamed Rich Island in honor of the Earl of Holland. Although subject to the general laws passed by the Providence Island Company, the patentees were to choose their own government and ministers, and they were to give the company a quarter of their proceeds for the first three years and thereafter to reserve a twentieth of the commodities and land for the company. Although Claiborne himself never emigrated there and soon returned to the Chesapeake, the associates did send colonists who remained until they were evicted by the Spanish in 1643; remains of their buildings were said to have been visible into the twentieth century.[82]

Providence Island's new council of war, authorized to oversee fortifications, military training, and privateering including the judgment

---

81. John Underhill, *Newes from America* (London, 1638). See Winthrop, *Journal*, ed. Hosmer, I, 275–7. For Underhill's letters and petitions to Winthrop, see Mass. Hist. Soc. *Collections*, 4th ser., VII (1865), 170–94. On Underhill's life, see L. Effingham de Forest and Anne Lawrence de Forest, *Captain John Underhill: Gentleman* Soldier *of Fortune* (New York, 1934). On Dover see Charles E. Clark, *The Eastern Frontier: The Settlement of Northern New England, 1610–1763* (Hanover, NH, 1983), 39–41.

82. PIC Ct. 6–6–38. Although Claiborne's (spelled Claybourne in the Providence Island records) associates were not named, he was related to Nathaniel Butler and had been associated in other ventures with the prominent London merchant Maurice Thompson. On Claiborne's importance, see Fausz, "Merging and Emerging Worlds," in Carr, Morgan, and Russo, eds., *Colonial Chesapeake Society*, 47–98, and Nathaniel C. Hale, *Virginia Venturer: A Historical Biography of William Claiborne, 1600–1677* (Richmond, VA, 1951).

and disposal of prizes taken, was composed of Governor Butler and Captains Hunt, Axe, and Carter. The functions of government were increasingly taken from the council and relegated to the captains. The contemporaneous commission to investigate grievances was also under the military interest; its members were Captains Butler and Axe and Mr. Elisha Gladman, the keeper of arms, ammunition, and all war materiel.[83]

Civilian colonists reacted strongly against this growing martial emphasis. Privateering not only brought into their midst English captains with their different values; it also exposed their society to the international culture of privateering in the Indies. All Providence Island Company privateering commissions included provisions for consortship agreements – that is, partnerships with Dutch or other English ships met in the Caribbean if such were deemed beneficial by the captain. In privateering as in other fields, the Dutch were the most knowledgeable operators in the region, and such cooperation was common in the early seventeenth century.[84] Captain Thomas Newman, who sailed under a company commission in the *Happie Return* in 1636, formed a partnership with the same Diego el Mulato whom Captain Elfrith had brought to Providence Island to the company's outrage in its early days. Diego took their rich prize for disposal in Holland, and the company was forced to sue for its share of the proceeds.[85]

A European presence had always been part of life in Providence Island, but now a different element was introduced, as colonists were forced to rely on the expertise of men such as a high German named Van Botten, who claimed fortifications skill.[86] The foreigners wooed by the privateers were always much more casual about the island's security than colonists or the company thought good. Investors wrote in fury on hearing that the governor and council had allowed some Spaniards into the island and allowed them "to acquaint themselves with the strength and situation thereof." When Samuel Rishworth was questioned about

83. PIC Commissions and Instructions by the *Swallow* and *Spy*, 7–38.
84. On consortship see Andrews, *Spanish Caribbean*, 186–7. Captain Butler was chagrined to find that the Dutch mariners he met on his privateering voyage consistently had information far superior to his own; Butler Diary, B. L. Sloane MS 758, 7-2-39, 7-5-39, 8-14-39. For an example of Dutch-derived detailed knowledge of the Indies and Spanish sailing patterns, see New Sweden Company, "Secret Instructions for Peter Minuit," 1637 in C. A. Weslager, *Dutch Explorers, Traders, and Settlers in the Delaware Valley, 1609–1664* (Philadelphia, 1961), 173–7.
85. PIC Ct. 1–28–39, 5–23–39. Thomas Gage described one of Diego's conquests from the Spanish point of view; see *The English-American*, 314–17.
86. PIC to Gov. and Coun. by the *Blessing* 5–36, by the *Mary Hope* 3–37; PIC to Butler 4–23–38.

this breach, he said that the Spanish were from a Dutch ship. When the Dutch, contrary to their promise, allowed the Spaniards on deck and even allowed them to go fishing, the governor decided it would be better to imprison them on the island, where they could be held for future use as pilots. "And if the Spaniards were suffered to go abroad in the Island the fault was in the Marshall who had Command to the contrary."[87]

Captain Thomas Newman so angered the colonists by allowing Spaniards to "view the passages" that he was imprisoned on Providence Island. The company was outraged, pointing to the trust the investors reposed in Newman and saying that such "offensive carriage" on the part of the governor and council would jeopardise the entire "design" by bringing "an ill report upon the place." Captains of "our men of war" were to be treated with respect and forbearance of "all personal restraints" unless they actually endangered the island. The company's unrealistic response to colonists' complaints was that the issue should be referred to London; the investors would inform Newman of their displeasure.[88]

Foreigners who could be useful were supposed to come into the settlement as prisoners. Privateering ships were ordered to bring not only skilled pilots but any high-ranking Spaniards they captured to Providence Island, where they could be held for eventual exchange for company officers who might be captured. Captain William Rous was already a prisoner by 1638; Thomas Gage interviewed him in Cartagena. He was eventually taken to San Lucar in Spain where he languished in great "want and misery" until he was finally released with the help of the English ambassador.[89]

All the side effects of privateering and the military buildup in Providence Island combined to pervert the experience of civilians there. The reluctance of privateers to carry passengers, especially women, and the danger in which such passengers traveled meant that peopling the island with a normally mixed population became increasingly difficult.[90] Planters, like investors, were convinced that a heavy concentration of English servants was essential to an effective militia; yet the very developments that made the militia so important increasingly pushed settlers in the direction of relying on slavery.

87. PIC to Gov. and Coun. by the *Mary Hope* 3−37; PIC Ctee. 6−14−37.
88. PIC to Gov. and Coun. 4−23−38, 7−38; PIC to Butler 4−23−38; PIC Instr. to Council of War 7−38.
89. PIC Ct. 1−29−38, 7−1−39, 11−19−39, 2−20−40.
90. Travel became increasingly dangerous as the decade progressed. In 1639 the *Mary* was seized by Algerian pirates on its outward voyage; PIC Ct. 2−20−40, 2−25−40.

Governor Nathaniel Butler kept a diary of his governorship from February 1639 to February 1640 that gives a vivid picture of life in Providence Island near the colony's end. From his point of view the island was now a privateering base; his attention focused on the fortifications, and much of his time was spent entertaining and commissioning ship captains or disposing of their prizes. "Old Hallyhead" rarely appeared in Butler's story, and Richard Lane, controversial civilian councilor and protégé of Lord Brooke, entered only as Butler's opponent. Axe and the other captains were his chosen companions.

The inevitable concomitant of such activity was heightened vulnerability for the colonists, who lived in constant fear of attack. During the little more than nine months he actually spent among the colonists, Butler recorded twenty-five alarms.[91] No month failed to produce at least one attack scare; two months saw five apiece. All twenty-five were false alarms, but each required colonists to drop other employments and respond, and each contributed to their sense of insecurity. The day after Butler's return from privateering, September 13, 1639, the company's pinnace *Swallow* arrived with news that Warwick's pinnace the *Robert* had been captured and all its crew sent prisoners into Spain. The colonists also learned that the governor of Cartagena had importuned the commander of the Spanish treasure fleet to attack Providence Island, which the galleons' commander refused because he had no such commission.[92]

Governor Butler's diary also shows how the civilian colonists responded by increasingly withdrawing into their own separate community. To the extent that they could, the settlers simply ignored the military men and their activities. Puritan planters joined together in a gathered church whose exclusiveness was emblematic of their overall rejection of alien authority and its priorities. Butler reported with disgust the colonists' elation when privateers failed; "some of them shewed as much Joy as if they had been Spaniards" when Butler's own expedition found the captured town of Trujillo empty. He was furious that the Reverend Hope Sherrard proclaimed a day of thanksgiving for the recovery of a shipwrecked man who had lived for more than two years on a rocky outcrop, the Roncadores shoals. Although such thanksgiving was "very commendable in itself, and a course fully approvable," Butler pointed out that Captain Axe's delivery from the Spaniards had occasioned no such celebration. Butler himself was "never publicly

91. Butler was away from the island on a privateering mission from the end of May to mid-September 1639.
92. Captain Nathaniel Butler, "A Diary, from Febrary 10th 1639 of My Personal Employments," B. L. Sloane MS 758, 9–13–39 and passim.

prayed for, otherwise than in general terms, during my absence" by Mr. Sherrard.[93]

Butler singled out Halhead, Lane, and Mr. John Francis as councilors who were particularly disruptive. They tried secretly to undermine every act of the council of war "so ill they who never were soldiers take it that you have left them out from being councilors of war [though (God knows) they have not the least insight]."[94]

Despite Captain Butler's scorn, the Providence Island councilors were acting in the best tradition of English colonization. Successful company-sponsored settlements moved quickly to downplay the authority of professional military men, as in Virginia's discarding of its experiment with martial law.[95] In the aftermath of the great Indian attack of 1622, the Virginia Assembly organized a militia based on the eight counties into which the colony was organized; the captains were planters and traders without professional military experience. An elaborate system of compensation made the system acceptable to the rank and file.[96]

The New England colonies preferred to train their own people in a citizen army rather than to employ disruptive continental veterans such as Captain John Underhill. Massachusetts originally imported experts with Low Countries experience and even employed a German/Dutch surveyor of ordnance as Providence Island did, but the colony quickly moved to make such men unnecessary. John Winthrop, Jr., stayed behind in England for a time to study fortification; he was aided by Providence Island Company member Sir Nathaniel Rich in his efforts to

93. B. L., Sloane MS 758, notes of letters to Lord Saye, pts. 6, 39; diary 2–17–39. The preservation and deliverance of the shipwrecked man from the Roncadores was included by Increase Mather in his book *An Essay for the Recording of Illustrious Providences* (Boston, 1684), 71–2.

94. B. L., Sloane MS 758, notes of letter to Lord Brooke, pt. 42. Material in brackets crossed out in original. John Francis had been made a councilor when he emigrated in 1636. At that time the company wrote that he had been involved in England in training men "and may thereby be fitted for Martial services." He was given "charge and oversight" of Trippett's fort, which was renamed Brooke Fort; PIC to Gov. and Coun. by the *Blessing*, 5–36.

95. On Virginia's early reliance on professional soldiers, Low Countries veterans, and its subsequent turn toward civilian control, see Craven, *Dissolution of the Virginia Company*, chaps. 2 and 3; Rutman, "Virginia Company's Military Regime," in Rutman, ed., *Old Dominion*, 1–20.

96. William L. Shea, *The Virginia Militia in the Seventeenth Century* (Baton Rouge, 1983), 39–44, 47–52. See also Fausz, "Merging and Emerging Worlds," in Carr, Morgan, and Russo, eds., *Colonial Chesapeake Society*, 47–93. Sir Francis Wyatt, Virginia's governor in 1622, received a long letter of advice on how to conduct the colony's warfare from his father, George Wyatt, who had the professional military experience his son lacked; J. Frederick Fausz and Jon Kukla, eds., "A Letter of Advice to the Governor of Virginia, 1624," *William and Mary Quarterly* 3rd ser., XXXIV (1977), 104–29.

provide the colony with that essential knowledge.[97] By 1634 the trained
bands, composed of every able-bodied man above the age of fourteen,
nominated their own captains who were generally approved auto-
matically by the General Court. Like the Israelites, wrote the younger
Winthrop's friend Edward Howes, the settlers would "fight with one
hand, and build with the other." Captain John Underhill reacted to
citizen control of the militia as Nathaniel Butler did to civilian demand
for places on the council of war in Providence Island. He heaped scorn
on this "disordered practice," saying it "never was heard of in any
School of war; nor in no Kingdom under heaven." Similarly, professional
soldier George Donne, second son of the poet, argued that both
Virginia and New England had fallen into disorderly practices that
endangered the colonies.[98] Jack P. Greene points out that Ireland
was the only English colony that retained a professional military
establishment.[99]

John Underhill was wrong. In casting off a professional military
establishment, the New England colonies reflected the sentiments of
their native England, where the ideal of defense by trained amateurs
and aversion to professional soldiers were deeply entrenched. Providence
Island Company members who took up commands in the Civil War
responded as virtuous magistrates called to lead the citizenry; their
humanist training had taught them that the prince must be as prepared
to lead his people in war as in civil life. The Civil War armies drew on
old noble-gentry networks, drawing bitter reproach from passed-over
continental veterans.[100] Lord Brooke warned against employing
gentlemen who had been commanders in the German wars, saying that

97. Isaac Johnson to John Winthrop, Dec., 1629, Massachusetts Historical Society
    Collections, 4th ser., VI (1863), 30–2; Edward Howes to John Winthrop, Jr., 1633,
    Winthrop Papers III, 112–3; John Winthrop to John White, 1632, ibid., 87.
98. Edward Howes to John Winthrop, Jr., 1633, *Winthrop Papers* III, 124; Petition of
    John Underhill to the Governor and Assistants of Massachusetts, 1637, ibid.,
    503–4; T. H. Breen, ed., "George Donne's 'Virginia Reviewed': A 1638 Plan to
    Reform Colonial Society," *William and Mary Quarterly* 3rd ser., XXX (1973),
    449–66. Composition and training of militia companies is described in William
    Wood, *New Englands Prospect* (London, 1634), 52–3. On the rejection of profes-
    sional soldiers and the creation of a citizen-led militia, see Breen, "The Covenanted
    Militia in Seventeenth-Century Massachusetts," *Past and Present* 57 (1972), 74–96,
    esp. 82–6. Breen also discusses the controversy over creation of private artillery
    companies in Boston and other towns, and John Winthrop's fear of "a standing
    authority of military men," ibid., 88; Winthrop, *Journal*, ed. Hosmer, I, 260, II,
    254. See also Robert E. Wall, *Massachusetts Bay: The Crucial Decade, 1640–1650*
    (New Haven, 1972), chap. 3.
99. Greene, *Pursuits of Happiness*, 38.
100. On humanist doctrines and the rejection of a professional military that accompanied
    them, see Schwoerer, *"No Standing Armies!"*, 15–18. On gentry domination of the
    armies, see Kishlansky, *Rise of the New Model Army*, 5–6.

he "cannot so well approve of the aid of foreign and mercenaries auxiliaries." Their cause needed men "whose hearts go with their hands," not soldiers who fought in any war that offered employment. He also took the very unusual step of allowing volunteer companies to elect their own officers.[101]

After his death, Brooke's biographer listed his virtues in hopes of convincing those who thought military men were not religious. Nonetheless, many in England on both sides saw with grave misgivings their country overrun by troops. The presence of armies constituted a pervasive and dire threat, and they feared that even the godly would become tainted by the soldiers' perverse outlook.[102]

Even more fundamental for Providence Island colonists than antipathy toward the military men and their alien values in the Indies was the feared consequences of perversion of their godly experiment. Deeply imbued as they were with providential thinking, the godly men and women of Providence Island believed that military preparations were powerless to protect them if God had withdrawn his blessing. Conversely, with the protection of God, no enemy could prevail. In withdrawing into a separate covenanted community, the godly civilians were working to protect their little colony just as surely as was Governor Butler with his attention to the fortifications. While their struggle continued, the island repelled yet another Spanish attack in 1640. And the colony finally fell the next year when Captain Carter, left in charge by Nathaniel Butler, had disbanded the little congregation and sent its leaders home. The judgment of Providence was surely clear.

In his 1650 pamphlet against enclosure, Henry Halhead tried to warn England of God's punishment to come and of the uselessness of purely material preparations:

> Therefore, let none of us make to ourselves any vain confidences, or put our trust in any arm of flesh, or the strongest Fortifications that can be made by any of the sons of men: For Jerusalem was a famous City, and very strongly fortified; so that it would hardly have been believed, that should have befallen it, that did. But we

101. Lord Brooke, *Worthy Speech*, 7; Ann Hughes, *Politics, Society and Civil War in Warwickshire, 1620–1660* (Cambridge, 1987), 153, 196–7.
102. Spencer, "Brooke Genealogie," ed. Styles, *Pubs.* Dugdale Soc, XXXI, 192. On the pervasive fear of armies in England, see Nehemiah Wallington, *Historical Notices of Events in the Reign of Charles I*, 2 vols. (London, 1869), I, 276–9; Seaver, *Wallington's World*, 101; Russell, *Parliaments and English Politics*, 380; Christopher Hill, *Some Intellectual Consequences of the English Civil War* (Madison, WI, 1980), 19–20; and Stephen Saunders Webb, *The Governors-General: The English Army and the Definition of Empire, 1569–1681* (Chapel Hill, 1979), chaps. 1 and 2, esp. pp. 25–31, 78.

see (as aforesaid) that, for the sins of the Prophets, and for the iniquities of the Priests, the Lord laid it waste.[103]

The professional soldier's skills were irrelevant unless they served a godly society; those who trusted in them risked both their religious life and their safety.

103. Halhead, *Inclosure Thrown Open*, 18. See the similar sentiments in John Smith's treatment of Governor Nathaniel Butler's departure from Bermuda, *Generall Historie*, in Barbour, ed., *Complete Works*, II, 389.

8

The Turbulent Religious Life
of Providence Island

IN PROVIDENCE ISLAND as in all puritan colonies religion functioned both as a binding force and as a source of disruption and controversy. Like its contemporary, Massachusetts Bay, the colony was founded as the nucleus of a great colonial experiment in the protection and extension of reformed Protestantism in the face of a hostile English government seemingly intent on returning the nation to some form of Roman Catholicism. Religious goals continued to play a major part in the founders' thinking throughout the settlement's existence until the grandees were distracted by ecclesiastical issues at home with the meeting of the Long Parliament. The leading figures among the settlers were always concerned to achieve a fulfilling Christian life in their little island. This quest led them by a tortuous path through the same issues that troubled old and New England: toleration of dissent, the role of the laity in church governance and worship, and the relationship of religious and civil authority.

These were troubling issues because colonization offered unprecedented opportunities for free expression and for unfettered construction of religious societies. Historians of colonial America have assumed that Massachusetts Bay's New England Way, which strictly controlled religious expression and conferred church membership only on those judged to be "visible saints" by the congregations while restricting voting and office holding to church members, represented the fullest expression of the system all puritans would have chosen. The experience of Providence Island offers evidence that not only did mainstream English puritans not choose such a link between sainthood and political rights, with the enormous power it conferred on the religious arm, but many saw the Massachusetts experiment as dangerously deviant.

Mainstream lay puritans at home argued that placing such power in the hands of congregations and the ministers who led them would replicate the perilous situation where the Church of England establishment, linked with the government of Charles I, sought to control every aspect of the people's lives and consciences. The first issue taken up by the Long Parliament was disestablishment of episcopacy because of the bishops' role as temporal lords.[1] For religious leaders to have a role in government threatened the very foundations of the state because such power could not be effectively limited; John Pym accused Archbishop Laud of seeking "an arbitrary power without limitation . . . a papal power."[2] The danger lay in the fact that it was in the nature of the clerical profession to seek power; unless carefully controlled, *all* ministers would augment their own power.[3]

1. Sir Benjamin Rudyerd, alone among the Providence Island investors, supported episcopacy but only if the bishops were stripped of their temporal powers. In a speech to parliament in 1641 he said, "[I]n my opinion they govern worse then they preach, though they preach not at all; for we see to what pass their government hath brought us. . . . Mr. Speaker, It now behooves us, to restrain the Bishops to the duties of their functions." "Another Speech of Sir Benjamin Rudyer[d] in the High Court of Parliament," 1641, in *Speeches of Sir Benjamin Rudyer[d] in the high Court of Parliament* (London, 1641), 16–17. But Rudyerd also argued that the condition of church and state "exacts," even "extorts" a "thorough reformation," ibid., 9–10. See D. R. Barcroft [David L. Smith], "The Political Career of Sir Benjamin Rudyerd," unpub. undergrad. diss., Cambridge University, 1985.
   Richard Baxter thought the Earl of Manchester was also "conformable to Episcopacy," see J. S. A. Adamson, "The Peerage in Politics, 1645–49" (unpub. PhD diss., Cambridge University, 1986), 75.
2. Pym, parliamentary speech of Feb. 26, 1640, notes of John Moore, in Wallace Notestein, ed., *The Journal of Sir Simonds D'Ewes* (New Haven, 1923), 413. D'Ewes rendered the same phrase "arbitrary power without bounds," ibid. I thank William Abbott for bringing this speech to my attention.
3. A wide range of opinions about church government was represented in the Providence Island Company. Saye, Brooke, St. John, Darley, Knightley[?] favored the independents. Warwick, Manchester, Gerard, and Gurdon were associated with the presbyterians, though Warwick also kept up his ties with many independents. Company members Saye, Rudyerd, Pym, and Barrington were among the lay members of the Westminster Assembly of Divines. See Cliffe, *Puritan Gentry in Conflict*, 95–96, 101, 104–5, 110, 152–4; Adamson, "The Peerage in Politics," 106–7; Valerie Pearl, "The 'Royal Independents' in the English Civil War," Royal Hist. Soc. *Transactions* 5th ser., XVIII (1968), 71; Pearl, "Oliver St. John and the 'Middle Group' in the Long Parliament," *English Historical Review* LXXXI (1966), 491, 494–8, 500–1, 512, 514; and Andrews, *Colonial Period*, I, 235, fn.
   On the danger presented by the bishops' power, see Lord Brooke, *A Discourse Opening the Nature of That Episcopacie, Which is Exercised in England*, 2nd ed. (London, 1642), facs. repr. William Haller, ed., *Tracts on Liberty in the Puritan Revolution, 1638–1647*, II (New York, 1934), 5–8, 11–12, 14–17, 39–41, 61; William Fiennes, Lord Saye and Sele, *Two speeches in parliament* (London, 1641), 2; *The Journal of Sir Simonds D'Ewes*, ed. Willson Havelock Coates (New Haven, 1942), 133; and *The Substance of a Conference at a Committee of Both Houses, in the Painted Chamber October 27. 1641 Managed by John Pim Esquier, And Oliver Saint-John His Majesties Sollicitor Generall, on the behalfe, and by the Command of the House of Commons. Concerning the Excluding of the thirteene Bishops* (London, 1641); William W. Abbott, "The Issue of episcopacy in the Long Parliament" (unpub. D. Phil. diss. Oxford University, 1981), 69–71, 79, 107. Hatred of bishops was a recurrent theme in popular plays of the 1630s; see Butler, *Theatre and Crisis*,

Lord Saye opposed establishment of Presbyterianism on the same grounds: It was a form of church government "serving to ensnare and enslave the Brethren under the priests." The clergy, according to Saye, "always had an itching humor" for "a coercive power."[4] When power came to these lay puritans in England, they broke connections between religious and civil power. During the summer of 1641, parliamentary leadership removed members of the clergy from any role in local government, and in 1646 parliament refused to allow presbyteries the power of suspension from sacraments, which was to be in the hands of lay commissioners appointed by parliament.[5] As Cromwell said of efforts to impose doctrinal uniformity, "We look at ministers as helpers of, not lords over, the faith of God's people."[6]

The issues were far deeper and more important than mere forms or even distribution of power; the Providence Island Company fraternity looked forward to a broad toleration of religious opinions and practices when parliament seized power. The ideal of these puritan grandees was a state religious settlement, where government would have powers over the social and moral context in which the church functioned. This state church would offer broad toleration, so that no tender consciences would need to seek new havens. In this Erastian system, differences in religious practice could pose no threat to the social and moral order and therefore could be allowed. Not only would painful believers find protection in such a scheme, but the entire Christian community would benefit from their search for religious truth.

Many puritans, including prominent figures on both sides of the Atlantic, believed that they lived in a time of extraordinary apprehension of God's truth, when new understanding would become possible. Thus, they sought to create an environment in which no possible avenue to understanding God's revelation would be prematurely cut off. The

235–41. See also William M. Lamont, *Godly Rule: Politics and Religion, 1603–60* (London, 1969), chapter 3, esp. 67–8, and Hunt, *The Puritan Moment*, 217.

4. For Saye's warning on the dangers of Presbyterianism, see *Vindiciae veritatis. Or, an answer to a discourse intituled, truth it's manifest* (London, 1654), 124, 128. Saye's religiosity was praised in Anon., *A Letter Touching the Lord Saye* (London, 1643), 2. Valerie Pearl, in her "The 'Royal Independents' in the English Civil War," *Transactions of the Royal Historical Society* 5th ser., XVIII (1967), 69–76, attributes this tract to a joint venture of Lord Saye and his second son, Nathaniel Fiennes, but J. S. A. Adamson offers convincing evidence that Saye wrote it alone between 1646 and 1648. See "The *Vindiciae veritatis* and the political creed of viscount Saye and Sele," *Bulletin of the Institute of Historical Research* 60 (1987), 46–51.

5. Fletcher, *Reform in the Provinces*, 11; Kishlansky, *New Model Army*, 99.

6. Cromwell to the Governor of Edinburgh Castle, September 12, 1650, in Wilbur Cortez Abbot, ed., *The Writings and Speeches of Oliver Cromwell* (Cambridge, MA, 1937–45), II, 337; James Fulton Maclear, "The Making of the Lay Tradition," *The Journal of Religion* XXXIII (1953), 113–36; Hirst, *Authority and Conflict*, 281.

times were filled with possibilities and to restrict any would be defiance of God. As Lord Brooke wrote, "The light still, will, must, cannot but increase."[7] And the heart's apprehension of the truth of the spirit mattered far more than the "Critical, Cabalistical, Sceptical, Scholastical Learning" sponsored by the bishops. Lord Brooke thought that women made up the largest proportion of the "Chorus of Saints," because women, being more capable of affection, were "most apt to make knowledge real."[8]

As the adventurers emphasized over and over again in their letters to the colonists, religion was in their view a matter of inward truth rather than strict adherence to outward forms. Focusing on that which could be perceived by others led to the sin of pride, against which Sir Benjamin Rudyerd warned Governor Bell:

> There are many who think That no Sins are so great as those that break out into visible botches and sores, whereas the subtle unperceivable sins which infect the spirit are far more incurable and deadly, as Pride, Envy, Malice, Falseness ——— [sic], which being spiritual wickednesses, do hold more of the Devil. . . . Many believe, If they frequent Sermons diligently, repeat them when they come home readily, keep the Sabbath formally, use family Exercises constantly, though all this make no change at all in their dispositions and affections, yet they believe I say, That they are more religious than their Neighbours, carrying themselves proudly and Contemptuously towards them, when in truth they do but take great Pains to meet Popery round about the other way, believing that the work wrought hath wrought their Salvation.

Rejecting "petty Professors" who "do commonly agree in little snips and outsides of Religion," Rudyerd testified, "But God requires Truth in the Inward parts, sincerity and uprightness of heart, a total, thorough, real conversion, rectifying our thoughts, words, and deedes, by an

7. *Discourse of Episcopacy*, 116. On the theme of the increase of light, see Theodore Dwight Bozeman, *To Live Ancient Lives: The Primitivist Dimension in Puritanism* (Chapel Hill, 1988), 124–7.
8. On the bishops' learning, see Lord Brooke, *Discourse of Episcopacy*, 9; and on women's spirituality, see Brooke, *The Nature of Truth* (London, 1640), facs. repr. ed. V. de Sola Pinta (n.p., 1969), 68–9. Brooke even put forward tentatively a proposal for preaching by laymen, which proliferated in the New Model Army before it was prohibited by Parliament in 1645. Providence Island Company member Godfrey Bosvile, Lord Brooke's stepbrother, was elected preacher by the battalion he commanded as colonel. On lay preaching, see Brooke, *Discourse of Episcopacy*, 104–15, and Kishlansky, *New Model Army*, 72. On Godfrey Bosvile, see Alexander Stephens, *Memoirs of J. H. Tooke* (London, 1813), II, 309.

effectual working of the Spirit, not by a fantastical over-weening apprehension of our own."[9]

As a neoplatonist, Brooke believed that all truth was unitary regardless of its various sources. For him and his fellow puritans of the Providence Island Company, religious toleration, allowing the unveiling of the light, would ultimately result in unity among Protestants through recognition of the fundamental truth. The goal was not acceptance of endless variety; rather, these leaders sought the avenue to essential truth through ending conflict over nonessentials. Company members Brooke, Pym, Warwick, Barrington, and St. John sponsored and supported Samuel Hartlib, John Dury, and Jan Comenius, emigrés from Eastern Europe who advocated a reconstruction of society through a new philosophy of education and who sought to create a model community from which the ideal of world reformation could be spread. In the heady promising days of 1641, Brooke wrote that truth was broken up into shallow "particular rivulets" but "that learned, that mighty man Comenius doth happily and rationally endeavour to reduce all into one."[10]

John Milton praised Lord Brooke, "a right noble and pious lord," for his "mild and peaceful" arguments, which Milton compared to the last words of Jesus to his disciples. Brooke "exhorts us to hear with patience and humility those, however they be miscalled, that desire to live purely, in such a use of God's ordinances, as the best guidance of their conscience give them, and to tolerate them, though in some disconformity to ourselves."[11] As the creation of new puritan societies became possible, however, patience and humility were in short supply. When, after the Antinomian Crisis of 1636–7, Massachusetts Bay moved to restrict free

---

9. Rudyerd to Gov. Bell, 1633, Bermuda Archives, Acc. 51. See also PIC to Gov. Bell, 2/3–35.
10. Brooke, *Nature of Truth*, 124, 143–5; John Dury to Brooke, B. L., Sloane MS 654, f. 250–1; Strider, *Lord Brooke*, 135–7. On the connections of Providence Island Company members with Hartlib, Dury, and Comenius, see Blair Worden, "Toleration and Cromwellian Protectorate," in W. J. Sheils, ed., *Persecution and Toleration* (Oxford, 1984), 199–233, esp. 210–13; Webster, *Great Instauration*, 29–47; G. H. Turnbull, *Hartlib, Dury, and Comenius: Gleanings from Hartlib's Papers* (London, 1947); H. R. Trevor-Roper, "Three Foreigners: The Philosophers of the Puritan Revolution," in *Religion, the Reformation and Social Change*, 2nd ed. (London, 1972), 237–93. New Englanders were also interested in the work of these men; John Winthrop, Jr., is reported to have attempted to recruit Comenius for the presidency of Harvard. See Samuel Eliot Morison, *Builders of the Bay Colony* (Boston, 1930), 273.
11. *Areopagitica* (1644), in John Milton, *Areopagitica and Other Prose Works*, ed. K. M. Burton (London and New York, 1927), 35–6. On the close correspondence between Lord Brooke and Milton, see Christopher Hill, *Milton and the English Revolution* (New York, 1978), 149–53, and Strider, *Lord Brooke*, passim.

and open expression of religious ideas, many puritans responded with dismay. Many left the Bay Colony to found other New England settlements, and the Providence Island investors redoubled their own efforts to make their southern colony prosper.

The Protestant doctrine of the priesthood of all believers placed responsibility on each Christian, while the translation of the Bible and the proliferation of devotional manuals broke the clerical monopoly of access to God. For many puritans, the center of the reformed community was the godly head of household presiding over family devotions, not the minister. Protestantism carried within it a tension between the claims of godly men and women touched by the spirit, the lay saints, and those of their educated leaders, the ministers. The congregational system instituted in New England and as far as possible by Providence Island Company members in the livings they held in England, theoretically gave all power to the saints. Ministers were created by the congregation's call. In practice the ministers soon began to exert a strong hand of guidance in Massachusetts Bay, forming extracongregational professional organizations that enhanced that role.[12] Many puritans on both sides of the Atlantic viewed such developments with alarm. Anticlericalism, opposition to lodging of power in the clergy, was a strong and recurring thread in the thinking of godly men and women from all walks of life as it was for the Providence Island grandees.

Claims for lay authority, even anticlericalism, did not involve contempt for the ministry. Providence Island Company members surrounded themselves with groups of ministers with whom they spent their time in preference to county society. They also accepted ministers' strictures on their private lives. They avidly sought sermons and lectures, and they accepted advice on their personal spiritual states. The Earl of Warwick, whose appetite for sermons was said to be enormous, submitted to an examination by the minister and elders of St. Mary Aldermanbury before his first communion there. Because he had been sick during the assessment, he offered to return if they felt they needed to examine him further, an offer they declined.[13]

12. Stephen Foster compellingly charts the way in which ministerial authority was enhanced by emigration to New England; *Long Argument*, chap. 4, esp. 152, 170–1. On the centrality of the household in puritan spirituality, see Charles E. Hambrick-Stowe, *The Practice of Piety: Puritan Devotional Disciplines in Seventeenth-Century New England* (Chapel Hill, 1982), 47–9, and Seaver, *Wallington's World*, 188.
13. Calamy, *Pattern for All*, 36. On Warwick's appetite for sermons, see Donagan, "Clerical Patronage of Warwick," *Proceedings of American Philosophical Society* 120 (1976), 405.

Providence Island Company members were unusual among English gentlemen in fostering a degree of congregational control in the livings they held. Each protected and patronized a circle of puritan ministers but did not impose them on unwilling congregations; the laity chose the man who could best guide and exhort them. The Earl of Warwick, described in a funeral sermon by his client Edmund Calamy as ". . . one of the greatest friends that the godly and painful Ministers had in England," owned twenty-two advowsons. Warwick responded to requests for particular preachers, but after he had also heard the man preach, Warwick overruled the minister of the town of Warwick of which the earl was recorder when the burgesses wanted Samuel Clarke for their lecturer. Warwick summoned Clarke to London to hear him preach, after which he agreed with the burgesses that Clarke should become assistant to the unwilling vicar.[14]

Lords Brooke and Saye similarly took pains over the consciences of Christians in parishes whose livings they controlled. As master of the Court of Wards, Lord Saye presided over many livings, and he confirmed the congregations' choice of ministers. He believed, however, that it was essential that no congregation have coercive power; loving persuasion was their only arm. Where the peace was disturbed or blasphemous conduct was a problem, the magistrate must enforce good order.[15]

Lord Brooke's Warwick Castle became a center of puritan ministers, and Brooke was a "dear Foster-Father" both to those who "went his way" and to those who conformed. All of "small means" were his beneficiaries as long as they were "laborious in their places." His biographer wrote that Brooke preferred the company of such men to that of the "Jesuited Gentry" of the county. When Brooke offered the living of Alcester to Samuel Clarke, Clarke went to preach to the congregation, after which he recorded, "I was freely and unanimously chosen by them for their Pastor."[16]

14. Edmund Calamy, *A Patterne for All* (London, 1658), 33–7; Samuel Clarke, *The Lives of Sundry Eminent Persons in the Later Age* (London, 1683), 6; Hunt, *Puritan Moment*, 104, 163–5; Holmes, *Eastern Association*, 19; Pearl, *London and Outbreak of Puritan Revolution*, 166.
15. On Saye's belief that the congregation's power should be strictly limited, see *Vindiciae veritatis*, 22–5, and Adamson, "The *Vindiciae veritatis*," *Bulletin of the Institute of Historical Research* 60 (1987), 58–9.
16. Spencer, "Genealogie of Lord Brooke," ed. Styles, Dugdale Society *Publications* 31 (1977), 173–4; Clarke, *Lives of Sundry Eminent Persons*, 6. Clarke had been protected by Providence Island Company member Richard Knightley at Fawsley as well as by the Earl of Warwick and Lord Brooke; see Clarke, *Lives of Sundry Eminent Persons*, 7.
   Those who disapproved also identified Saye and Brooke as central actors. In the mid-1640s a parishioner informed against his minister, "Mr. Paige," who said parliament "went to put down the book of Common Prayer." When its use by

Under Brooke's influence, Warwickshire's godly created a network supporting clergymen and offering lectures and services that gave those within it a degree of independence of the demands of the hierarchy. This "alternative church structure" gave ministers the support of like-minded men; ministers heard each other's sermons and exchanged notes and comments. Many ministers dined regularly at Warwick Castle with Brooke and through him were introduced to national figures.[17] Nehemiah Wallington's friend James Cole wrote him from Warwick in 1634 of the unheard of degree of freedom allowed in worship there:

> With us where I do now sojourn there be two congregations that is in two great men's hands, where is neither crosses, nor surplices, nor kneeling at the Sacrament, nor the Book of Common Prayer, nor any other behavior but reading the Word, singing of Psalms, prayer before and after sermon with catechism, which I did think it had not been in any congregation in this kingdom, if I had not seen it and, through God's mercy, have been partakers with them in the use of God's ordinances.

Cole soon emigrated to New England; the worship service he described in Warwickshire was very similar to the congregational practice he found in Connecticut.[18] Such a system was made possible in Warwick only by the powerful patronage of interested men.

The religious sentiments and preferred forms of worship of the Providence Island investors, particularly Lords Saye and Brooke, fit closely with those of the founders of Massachusetts Bay. Not only had the grandees supported and aided the New England colonies, following their progress with great interest, but some even considered emigrating there. As Providence Island and Massachusetts Bay progressed through their first decade, however, the lords and gentlemen found that a profound gulf separated the two experiments in godly society building.

The religious leadership of the puritan colony on Providence Island was extremely poor; none of the ministers who emigrated there was adequate to the task. Company leaders had strong ties to many of the greatest clerical puritans in England, including those who sailed to New England.

members of parliament was pointed out, Paige answered, "there was a proverb, that though there were 10 honest men in a Jury, and two knaves, those 2 knaves might do more than the 10 honest men, and is not Saye and Brooke in the house"; B. L. Add MS 22084, f. 133.
17. Hughes, *Politics, Society and Civil War in Warwickshire*, 73–9.
18. For James Cole's testimony, see Seaver, *Wallington's World*, 98. On Brooke's patronage of ministers, see Hughes, *Politics, Society and Civil War in Warwickshire*, chap. 3. Paul Seaver firmly identifies one of the "great men" referred to by Cole as Lord Brooke and suggests that the other might have been Lord Saye.

The company grandees had been zealous to protect and find employment for ministers persecuted by the royal campaign to enforce conformity in the church.[19] Yet these ministerial clients resisted calls to serve the beleaguered colonists in the Indies. Many did emigrate but to Massachusetts rather than to Providence. Their protectors' effort to establish the nucleus of a godly English presence in the Indies was left bereft of the leadership and support it so badly needed.

Ministers' unwillingness to accept the call to Providence Island demonstrates their own perception of the opportunities offered by colonization. In choosing emigration, puritan ministers like their flocks sought autonomy, control over their own lives. In England they achieved position only as clients of gentlemen with access to power. Some of their energies were necessarily bent in the direction of courting such laymen, and patronage could always be withdrawn. Emigration to Providence Island would have involved an extension of such dependence. Freedom from oversight by bishops there was more than balanced by greater vulnerability to decisions taken 3,000 miles away by the puritan grandees. What the investors saw as a great partnership, their ministerial clients more realistically visualized as renewed submission.[20] New England, on the other hand, offered genuine independence, not only of the episcopal hierarchy but also of the gentlemen whose patronage was such a mixed blessing. Despite the most strenuous and continuous efforts, the adventurers had no success in diverting any of the clerical stream flowing toward Massachusetts Bay in the 1630s.[21]

Ministers who did emigrate to the island colonies often became the nuclei around which discontented settlers formed interest groups. They represented a pole of authority equivalent in the planters' minds to the colonial government, particularly as that government was constituted wholly from England. Puritanism demanded virtue, especially in those entrusted with command, and it required each Christian to act for the

19. Among the more famous of these were Simeon Ashe, Jeremiah Burroughs, Edmund Calamy, Samuel Clarke, John Davenport, John Dod, William Gouge, Thomas Hill, Thomas Hooker, Stephen Marshall, Philip Nye, Hugh Peter, John Preston, Ezekiel Rogers, Thomas Shepard, Richard Sibbes, Peter Sterry, Nathaniel Ward, Thomas Weld, Roger Williams, and John Wilson. See Donagan, "Clerical Patronage of Warwick," *Proceedings of the American Philosophical Society* 120 (1976), 388–419.
20. See the extreme humility with which Thomas Twisse, the future Prolocutor of the Assembly of Divines answered a rebuke by Lord Saye, his protector. He apologized for writing in such a way as to offend "my betters[,] and they in authority too." B. L., Add. MS 4276 f160.
21. I thank Stephen Foster for his advice on this issue; he points out that New England's puritans rejected lay patronage of the kind practiced by the English grandees; see *Long Argument*, 167. On the tensions between clients and patrons, see Barbara Donagan, "Puritan Ministers and Laymen: Professional Claims and Social Constraints in Seventeenth-Century England," *Huntington Library Quarterly* 47 (1984), 81–111.

general good. Where ministers and their flocks saw men in civil authority falling away from virtue, they were required by their faith to act for the public weal. Congregations must have expected to dominate interpretation of events in Providence Island as their counterparts did in New England. The ministers must also have expected a role in regulation of social relations. In parishes throughout England ministers served as mediators and arbitrators. Quarrels and disputes were traditionally taken to them for resolution.[22] Emigrating ministers and company investors had radically different ideas about the ministers' roles in the island, but neither side was sufficiently aware of the gap to hammer out their differences in England beforehand.

In their earliest deliberations, the adventurers decreed separation of the religious and civil spheres. The first minister, Lewis Morgan, was to enhance the governor's status by living in his house and conducting family services, but he was not to be on the governor's council.[23] The principle of separation of spheres was fundamental in Providence Island's design and was amplified in 1632 when three ministers were sent. The advice of the ministers was to be solicited on major issues, but they had no right to speak, symbolized by their removing their hats when addressing the council. And the civil government was forbidden to meddle in ecclesiastical issues. The ministers were to be treated with honor and freed from burdens so that they could "spend their Times and pains in the Service of your souls, and that God may make their Endeavours effectual to the Confirming of those that Stand, to th'increase of Grace, and to the converting of others which are yet Strangers from God, to the knowledge of his Grace."[24] Properly done, their jobs would take up all their time.

The Providence Island plan envisioned structures working in parallel, all united by a shared concern for the plight of England and of the "true and sincere Religion and worship of God, which even in the Christian world is now very much opposed."[25] Although different men brought

22. Fletcher, *Reform in the Provinces*, 66–7.
23. PIC to Gov. Bell, 2–31; PIC, Ct., 12–3–31. The idea that attention to governmental functions necessarily led to neglect of ministerial duties was a major argument against episcopacy urged by Providence Island Company members in the Long Parliament. See Lord Brooke, *A Discourse of Episcopacie*, 7–9.
    Veterans of the Somers Islands Company among the Providence Island investors may have been drawing on experience in Bermuda, where ministers were initially on the council but were later withdrawn from it. See Wilkinson, *Adventurers of Bermuda*, 2nd ed., 199, 225, and Andrews, *Colonial Period*, I, 235.
24. PIC to Gov. and Coun., 5–10–32, point 42.
25. This statement appeared in the Providence Island Company's first letter to Gov. Bell, 2–31. This vision was remarkably similar to the ideal society imagined by the London puritan Nehemiah Wallington. See Seaver, *Wallington's World*, 181.

various forms of expertise, everyone could recognize that they worked for the same goals and that the success of one required the success of all.

Lewis Morgan, a fresh young Oxford graduate, had been hastily substituted for the more substantial (unnamed) man who had been unable to go with the first group from England. Although he had been judged "meek and humble" and a good scholar, Morgan was led through his youth and inexperience to head the mutiny against the company's initial plans for the plantation, even to labeling the grandees hypocrites. His leadership of the remonstrants shows that some colonists regarded him as a fit guide, but that role resulted in his ignominious recall.[26] A suitably sobered Morgan came to the company on his return to England and begged their forgiveness. His distress, and the pleading of his father-in-law, Mr. Morris, dissolved the grandees' anger. On Morgan's submission of a written statement of his error, they not only forgave him but agreed to his request for more money. The company reimbursed him for books left in Providence Island and gave him £5 for the pains he took with the passengers on the return voyage.[27]

The adventurers were outraged by the political role played by Lewis Morgan, but far more disturbing news of conflict over *religious* issues emanated from the colony. Like other puritan settlements, Providence Island's population contained godly men and women with very strong, and differing, ideas about worship and church organization. Inevitably, forms of worship became a subject of controversy.

Lewis Morgan's religious leadership brought confrontation, notably with the explosive Captain William Rudyerd. The nasty dispute between Morgan and Rudyerd over Rudyerd's borrowed books and the captain's rejection of the minister's claims to gentility overlay a more profound controversy over the use of psalms in the worship service. Rudyerd and his lieutenant William Rous, both related to important company members, were constrained to absent themselves from the sacrament because of Rudyerd's disagreements with Morgan.[28]

Sir Benjamin Rudyerd, writing on behalf of his brother to Governor Philip Bell, described the Providence Island congregation's practice:

26. At least one colonist attempted to defy the governor when he implemented the company's recall of Morgan, defiance which the investors were prepared to excuse, saying that loyalty to the minister was an error capable of "favorable interpretation." PIC to Gov. Bell, 4–10–33, point 10. See also point 19 on Bell's censure of Jeremy Elfrith for opposing Mr. Morgan. The company had decided to forgive Elfrith on his promise of amendment.
27. PIC Ctee. 3–15–33; 3–21–33; 3–26–33.
28. The position taken by these military leaders may be compared to the "belligerent precisionism" of John Endecott and Thomas Dudley in Massachusetts; Morgan, *Puritan Dilemma*, chap. 8, quotation on p. 103.

[P]icking here a Verse, and there a Verse to be sung after the
Sermon, wherein two Reverend Preachers were cited for Examples:
this is a Course I never heard, nor heard of, and I am sure that in
London congregations it is not used, neither can it be conveniently
performed, where the Clerk doth publicly direct what Psalm, or
what part, or what parcel by itself, is to be sung; And although it
be no ill nor unlawfull thing, to sing the scattered collected pieces
of a Psalme, yet certainly It is no discretion to be unnecessarily
singular.[29]

In objecting to Lewis Morgan's use of psalms, a practice approved by
members of the congregation judging by Secretary Hunt's vociferous
defense, Captain Rudyerd sought to challenge a radical puritan direction
being taken by the minister and his supporters.[30] Psalm-singing was one
badge of puritan congregations; it was emblematic of the godly challenge
to the church hierarchy.[31] Captain Rudyerd sneered at Lewis Morgan's
claim to gentility; the captain's rejection of the congregation's claim to
control in the choice of psalms and an active part in the worship service
may have stemmed from his concern to preserve the outward forms of
good order. Both Rudyerds disliked tinkering with the established order
of worship and church governance by those whose place made them
more fit to be followers.

Most of the godly sort gloried in the congregational role in psalm-
singing. As in Providence Island, so in New England, puritan congregations enthusiastically took up psalm-singing, despite the fears of some
that it was no longer proper in New Testament times. The *Bay Psalm
Book* was first published in 1640 in an edition of 1,700, and the 1651
edition ran to 2,000 copies. Psalms were commonly sung before and
after the sermon in Massachusetts. John Cotton, refuting those members
of "Antichristian Churches" who referred to psalms as "Geneva Jigs,"
asserted that psalm-singing was "a moral duty."[32]

29. Rudyerd to Bell, sent by the *Golden Falcon*, 1633, Bermuda Archives, Acc. 51, 5.
   Many London congregations with ties to foreign reformed congregations in the
   Netherlands and elsewhere were more independent and radical than others throughout England; see Abbott, "The Issue of Episcopacy in the Long Parliament," unpub.
   D. Phil. diss., Oxford University, 1981, 158; and Murray Tolmie, *The Triumph of
   the Saints* (Cambridge, 1977), esp. chap. 2.
30. Secretary Hunt and Captain Rudyerd came to blows at the council table over the
   issue of psalm singing. See Chapter 3.
31. In 1633 Joseph Haworth, the vicar of Batley, Yorkshire, was presented for singing
   psalms after the lessons rather than hymns. See Allen, *In English Ways*, 167.
32. *The Whole Booke of Psalmes Faithfully Translated into English Metre* (Cambridge,
   MA, 1640); John Cotton, Teacher of the Church at Boston in New-England, *Singing
   of Psalmes a Gospel-Ordinance* (London, 1647), 2, 14–17, 23, 34, 40–3, 62–3, 71.
   On the role of psalms in New England, see Hambrick-Stowe, *The Practice of Piety*,
   49, 111–16 and Bozeman, *To Live Ancient Lives*, 139–50.

Opponents of metrical psalm-singing associated it with lewdness, especially when both men and women sang. Reformers had indeed advocated psalms set to music as a substitute for popular tunes whose impact could be questionable. The title page of the *Whole Book of Psalmes*, published in London in 1561 and reprinted in many editions, suggested they be sung in worship services before and after prayer and sermons, as well as in private homes, "laying apart all ungodly songs and ballads; which tend only to the nourishing of vice, and corrupting of youth."[33] That psalms could provide some of the emotional impact of ballads indicates the ambiguity of their appeal.

In New England where psalm-singing developed under the strict scrutiny of leading ministers respected in England for their learning, its effect could be seen as wholly salutary. In Providence Island, the emotional association with other forms of vernacular song and the ambiguous meaning of singing drifted to the surface. The Providence Island Company heard alarming stories of the shipboard activities of the three ministers sent to replace Lewis Morgan in the *Charity* in 1632: Arthur Rous, Hope Sherrard, and Mr. Ditloff, refugee from the Palatinate.[34] When Ditloff left Providence Island and passed through England in returning to his own country, the company examined him on reports that the ministers had sung songs called catches. Ditloff replied that Arthur Rous had taught him these songs, whose meaning he did not understand; "the matter of the songs was the motion of Creatures as the Nightingale and the like." Ditloff alleged that Sherrard joined in the singing, which continued after their arrival in the island but never took place on the sabbath. He steadfastly clung to his story when Lord Saye said that he had a letter showing that Sherrard had reproved him for singing catches on the sabbath; Ditloff answered that that was impossible, since Sherrard had sung with him. "In conclusion he desired the Company to convince him of his error or else to receive satisfaction in his denial."[35]

With Hope Sherrard and Mr. Ditloff ministering to the population centers on opposite sides of the island and Arthur Rous delivering the weekday lecture as teacher with Sherrard in the capital, New Westminster, the grandees had designed a puritan paradise: plenty of sermons and

33. *The Whole Booke of Psalmes: Collected into Englysh Metre by T. Starnhold [Sternhold], J. Hopkins & others* (London, 1561), tp.
34. The Earls of Warwick and Holland and their kinsman Sir Nathaniel Rich had firm connections with the Palatinate. See Barbara Donagan, "A Courtier's Progress: Greed and Consistency in the Life of the Earl of Holland," *Historical Journal* 19 (1976), 342–3; and Donagan, "Clerical Patronage of Earl of Warwick," *Proceedings of American Philosophical Society* 120 (1976), 399–400. See also Michael Strachan, *Sir Thomas Roe, 1581–1644: A Life* (Salisbury, 1989), 361–2.
35. PIC Gen. Ct., 6–19–34.

easy access to them. In partnership with the substantial godly men and their families, the ministers should have wrought a reformation. But expectations were disappointed when the ministers instead attacked and crippled the very godly men who should have been their main support. Rous died within months of his arrival, but repercussions of his dispute with Henry Halhead over Rous's attempt to "inveigle" servant Edward Bragg on the outward journey outlived him and finally were expunged from the record by order of the company. The adventurers could not expunge colonists' feelings about Rous, however.

Arthur Rous, John Pym's stepbrother, was perceived as an unfit teacher by the godly congregation on Providence Island; his singing of profane songs was only one manifestation. Henry Halhead and Samuel Rishworth were disappointed in Rous before their ship left England. While awaiting the arrival of the *Charity*, they spent a day with Rous at his lodgings near Plymouth. On their return they confided to Ditloff, who waited with them, that "Mr. Rous was insufficient, that he was not able to pray extempore, and that he would soldier-like beat his men." Ditloff then wrote to the influential puritan minister Philip Nye that Rous was "fitter for a buff coat than a cassock," that his manner was more like a soldier's than a minister's. With his customary agility, Ditloff assured the company when they interviewed him after his return from Providence Island that he changed his opinion as soon as he got to know Rous, and he blamed the negative view on Halhead and Rishworth.[36]

It is hard to avoid the implication that John Pym was obliging his adopted kin by giving Arthur Rous, with his large family, a post in Providence Island. Certainly, Rous did not have Lewis Morgan's youth and inexperience to explain his behavior; he must have left a pattern of failure behind him when he emigrated. Just as Sir Benjamin Rudyerd foisted his difficult brother William on the settlement, so Pym helped out a faltering stepbrother. In both cases the plantation suffered by such fraternal charity.[37] A minister like Rous, having been judged unfit by

36. PIC Gen. Ct., 6–19–34.
37. Company secretary William Jessop's brother Constant or Constantine also apparently disgraced himself in Providence Island. In the batch of private letters sent early in 1636, William Jessop thanked Captain Bell, Mr. Jenkes, and Ensign Fitch for their care of his brother, including Fitch's loan of £70. Secretary Jessop attributed Constant's trouble to "disaffection to his person" by envious colonists and reported that Constant occupied a "place of trust" in England. William Jessop to Thomas Jenkes, 3–30–36; to Ensign Thomas Fitch, 3–30–36; to Captain Philip Bell, 4–5–36, B. L. Add. MS 10615. Constant Jessop was appointed to the lucrative living owned by the Earl of Warwick at Fyfield in 1643. See Donagan, "Clerical Patronage of Warwick," *Proceedings of American Philosophical Society* 120 (1976), 398, 417.

the lay leaders of an emigrating band, would not have been taken to the puritan colonies in New England, but the Providence Island planters were not free to make such a judgment, particularly in the case of the near relation of an influential investor. Henry Halhead and Samuel Rishworth must have been deeply troubled as they set sail.

Ditloff soon left Providence Island but first caused tribulation of a different, and far more troubling, sort; he claimed a sort of power for his ministerial office that the Providence Island investors were loath to countenance. Like Arthur Rous, Ditloff approached Henry Halhead in a confrontational spirit; shortly after their arrival he excommunicated Halhead on grounds that the company deemed trivial. Halhead was the substantial godly leader in whom the investors placed their hopes; for the ministers to cripple his effectiveness and deny the anticipated partnership of the lay and ministerial leaders was wholly unacceptable. The adventurers wrote that they "absolutely forbid" such excommunications and affirmed that they could not imagine any other minister being so "indiscreet."[38]

Ditloff claimed far greater powers, declaring in the island that the company had orally given him and his congregation complete self-government over their own parish. Hope Sherrard, the other minister remaining after Rous's death, opposed Ditloff's claims and was highly commended by the investors for "his discreet and orderly carriage." The company affirmed to the governor and council that "no authority belongs to the ministers or parishioners of themselves to do an act of that nature." As for Ditloff's allegation that they themselves had authorized it, "we do utterly disclaim it." Ditloff had departed into "his own country," having been paid £25 owing for his salary and £35 for the books he left behind in the island, before the company read the reports of his actions in the colony. Otherwise he would have been called to account for "the pride and insolency of his carriage."[39]

Third among the ministers sent in 1632 was Hope Sherrard, who had attended Emmanuel College, Cambridge, in the humblest rank of sizar. Sherrard was to remain until the very end, ministering in his fashion to the settlement, and he apparently finished as the leader of a very small separated congregation. For much of the time he was the only minister

38. PIC to Gov. Bell, 4–10–33. For the excommunication of Henry Halhead, see Chapter 5. In their campaign against the bishops in the Long Parliament, one of the charges brought by Providence Island company members was that bishops excommunicated people for trifles. Lord Brooke argued that excommunication must "very warily and but rarely be used," *Discourse of Episcopacie*, 30. See also Abbott, "The Issue of Episcopacy in the Long Parliament" (unpub. D. Phil. diss., Oxford University, 1981), 74, 122.
39. PIC to Gov. and Coun., 9–34.

on the island, though not for lack of effort on the company's part. The records are filled with their futile attempts to get the right sort of man to emigrate.

The lords and gentlemen of the Providence Island Company would find that substantial puritan ministers made far more sweeping demands for power than ever Ditloff did. Each time the company sought to attract a minister of the right godly stripe, the negotiations faltered on the stumbling block of control. Ministers with leadership qualities and strong puritan credentials refused to emigrate without the company's clear commitment to control by the godly sort, not only of the colony's religious life but also of its government and economy. Although such integrated puritan communities existed as alternatives in New England, the puritan grandees of the Providence Island Company could never countenance such an overturning of good order.

One hurdle they were prepared to jump: the need for ample salaries to attract "able Ministers" to their project. Whereas Lewis Morgan had been offered £40 per year, they soon decided they would go as high as £100, a very substantial salary. The decision of where to place any applicant on this sliding scale would be made "according to the quality and desert of the person." Although they hated the idea of salaries paid in sterling in London, the adventurers determined to pay half the minister's salary; the other half to be levied on the island's inhabitants in commodities and sold for the minister's benefit by the company. To free the minister from "private Molestations" and uncertainty, the company would temporarily make up any deficiencies in the planters' half of the salary, but they expected to be repaid in future. A small committee – Lords Saye and Brooke, Sir Nathaniel Rich, and John Pym, or any two of them – was to interview prospective minister–colonists and make reasonable agreements with them.[40]

The Reverend Henry Roote traveled to Providence Island in 1633 after negotiating extremely specific and extensive terms with the company. That the adventurers were willing to enter into and record such terms of agreement shows how anxious they were to recruit this man of "Ability,

40. PIC Ct., 12–3–31; Gen. Ct., 2–9–32. A stipend of £100 was often mentioned as an ideal for ministerial income, but many, perhaps most, English clerics fell below this level in the 1630s. Pastors throughout England supplemented their incomes by farming, although this was frowned upon by the authorities. On actual and ideal incomes, see Christopher Hill, *Economic Problems of the Church* (Oxford, 1968), 108–24; Donagan, "Clerical Patronage of Warwick," *Proceedings of American Philosophical Society* 120 (1976), 402–5; Hirst, *Authority and Conflict*, 303. On the farmer–parsons of England, see Alan Macfarlane, *The Family Life of Ralph Josselin* (Cambridge, 1970), 34–9, 59–63; Underdown, *Revel, Riot, and Rebellion*, 90; and Clive Holmes, *Seventeenth-Century Lincolnshire* (Lincoln, 1980), 56.

gravity, and deserts." Henry Roote was born in 1590 and received a B. A. degree from Magdalene College, Cambridge, in 1611. At the time he was recruited, he had been preaching at Gorton Chapel in the parish of Manchester. Before and after his trip to Providence Island, he preached at Stockport, Cheshire.[41] The company's terms were very generous; all Roote's transportation expenses, as well as those of his entire family, were to be paid even if he returned to England to bring back his wife. His salary was computed in the ancient legal unit of 100 marks (£66 13s 4d) per year to be paid in England, as well as land in Providence Island; and the salary was to be paid until he actually landed back in England. If he were to die in the colony while his family was there, the family would have the choice of land on the island or free transportation home. If he died in the settlement before they came, his family was to have £100. If he or any of his family were taken prisoner, the company would pay their ransoms. As an added act of generosity, the investors forwarded him £10 to furnish himself for comfort on his voyage, and when they found later that he had actually spent more, they decided to make that sum a free gift.[42]

Edmund Calamy wrote of Roote: "In early life he was a considerable traveller," perhaps referring to this voyage to the Indies.[43] When he arrived in Providence Island, he did not like what he saw and, as the company may have hoped, joined himself with the substantial civilian puritans who were his natural allies. As a mature man in his forties, he was able to exert the type of influence that younger ministers, however learned, could not, and he set about to make the changes the colony needed. Samuel Rishworth wrote Sir Thomas Barrington that "for that short time he hath been here, he hath begun a Reformation, of many things which were amiss."

Roote apparently decided that more substantial changes would have to be ordered from London, especially ridding the island of undesirables, if the adventurers' hopes were to be realized, and he therefore returned to London with a plan fully endorsed by the civilian leadership to put before the company. If it was accepted, he promised the colonists, he would return to them. Rishworth wrote that Roote would explain "the whole state of the Island" to the investors, and on behalf of his fellow

---

41. On Henry Roote's background, see Venn, *Alumni Cantabrigienses*, I, vol. 3, 486; Matthews, ed., *Calamy Revised*, 417; and John Booker, "The History of Denton Chapel," in Chetham Society *Remains* XXXVII (1856) [Chetham *Miscellanies*, II], 71n.
42. PIC Ctee. 5–25–33, 6–28–33; PIC to Gov. and Coun., 7–20–33; and to Gov. Bell, 7–1–33.
43. Calamy, *The Nonconformists Memorial*, rev. ed. Samuel Palmer (London, 1803), III, 450–2.

substantial settlers, Rishworth begged Barrington to see that the terms were accepted "by one unanimous consent" and Roote returned to the island, "otherwise (we) I fear shall, be much discouraged for our hearts are set upon him."[44]

Hope Sherrard added his voice in another letter to Sir Thomas Barrington in which he dwelled on the colonists' fears of Spanish attack. Sherrard said that such fears had in part occasioned Roote's "so sudden departure from us." Because only God could protect the island, its colony must be made a godly settlement worthy of divine attention. Sherrard himself gave formal notice, "as I have also written to Mr. Pym more at large," that he would return by the next ship "if Mr. Roote cannot procure the settling of some businesses according to our desire." He acknowledged the great expenses of the undertakers and prayed that God would crown their efforts to plant the gospel on the mainland. "What glory thereby would accrue to God! how would it eternise their honours names to posterity! and how would the child unborn bless their honours."[45]

In sending Henry Roote, the grandees had been relying on the transforming power of a great preacher to turn their experiment onto the proper course. Stories abounded in England of the miracles wrought by one dedicated and powerful minister in sinful towns.[46] The remigrating Roote and the letters that accompanied him revealed that much more, even structural change, was required to make Providence Island a godly society. So far the experiment had been a failure. As Sir Benjamin Rudyerd wrote in his letter defending his brother, "We well hoped (according to our Intentions) That we had planted a Religious Colony in the Isle of Providence, instead whereof we find the root of bitterness plentifully planted amongst you, an industrious supplanting one of another, and not a Man there of Place (a strange thing to consider) but he doth both accuse, and is accused; these are uncomfortable fruits of Religion."[47]

Soon after his return on the *Falcon*, Henry Roote laid his terms before the company. If they would take steps toward reform, "he hoped to procure 100 persons to go over at their own charge." In short, he expected to attract the same kind of substantial men and women who were going to Massachusetts Bay and to import a critical mass of godly

44. Rishworth to Barrington, Dec. 1, 1633, B. L., Egerton MS 2646, fol. 52.
45. Hope Sherrard to Sir Thomas Barrington, 1–6–34, B. L., Egerton MS 2646, f. 58–59v.
46. When Samuel Clarke came to be preacher in Alcester, "the Town, which before was called Drunken Alcester, was now Exemplary, and eminent for Religion all over the Country." Clark, *Lives of Sundry*, 7.
47. Rudyerd to Gov. Bell, 1633, Bermuda Archives, Acc. 51.

settlers. Never before had the adventurers had such a prospect. The company was willing to consider the plan despite its large demands: "[O]ne main thing he looks for is the removal of some persons now resident in the Island." Those present at the general court of May 19, 1634, agreed that such removal could be done legally, perhaps by offer of a role in company enterprises on the mainland.

Captain William Rudyerd, already back in England, may have been one object of the Reverend Roote's demands. Rudyerd had continued to stir up controversy; the company wrote that an unspecified scandal he had cast on Henry Halhead was "without ground, by which we find that the captain was much to blame." The adventurers present on May 19 (including Sir Benjamin Rudyerd) "promised to submit their own private respects, and relations to the public good and reformation of the Island." Pym's relative Lieutenant William Rous may have been another. Both men had been allowed to remain in places of dignity on Providence Island by the intervention of their powerful kin in the past; now their relatives promised not to interfere.

The other sweeping demand of Roote's plan, developed in conjunction with Hope Sherrard and the civilian leadership, concerned administrative change. These new substantial planters "would not undertake the voyage, but upon a promise to have the government in their own hand, which the Company are constrained to yield unto to preserve the Island from desertion." Roote and his allies demanded nothing less than a scrapping of the island's government, with godly civilians placed firmly in control. Roote and the experienced settlers who backed him must have looked for a system very like that being developed simultaneously in Massachusetts Bay, where the bond between approved godliness and the right to participate in government was just being cemented.[48]

Company members initially responded favorably to these terms because of their discouragement with Providence Island combined with their newfound hopes for trade on the Central American mainland. They judged 1634 an opportune time to divide the two ill-fitting halves of the enterprise. Let the military men develop the trade, using Providence Island as a safe storehouse and processing center, while the godly civilians built the kind of community the grandees hoped for.

Throughout their discussions in the summer of 1634, however, the investors were unable to find the resolve to settle on such a drastic redesign of their project. As they talked, the difficulties loomed larger. Roote's scheme was just one alternative the adventurers talked of in these weeks. Therefore, their response to the planters' demands was

48. PIC Gen. Ct., 5–19–34.

noncommittal. And, although the company promised to use "all convenient means to persuade him," they reported in their next letter that Roote's "own occasions" prevented him from returning just then. The *Long Robert* sailed with these letters in September 1634.[49] Company discussions during the preceding summer had focused on disappointed hopes for development of a marketable commodity on the island and on rapidly growing and unanticipated expenses. Economic failure was directly tied in adventurers' minds to lack of religious development; godly men and women would not emigrate until the island's future was secure.[50] They agreed among themselves that for the time being "they may make a civil commodity of it, upholding the profession of religion, moral duties, and justice till God shall please to plant amongst them a more settled Church." They also acknowledged in their letters that an unruly element in the colony, calling for "mixed dancing and other vanities," was outspokenly defiant. Their letter to Governor Bell lamely concluded on this issue: "We forbear as yet to send more particular directions, for preventing the abuse of God's creatures, but refer it to you at present to take the best course you shall be able, and to advise the Ministers to second your Authority with their public exhortations, wherein we wish you to give them all encouragement, as having therein received direction from us."[51]

The godly residents of Providence Island had looked for much more in the *Long Robert*; the letters were long and full of detail but almost entirely concentrated on new plans for economic development, particularly of new trades with the mainland. Henry Roote never returned to Providence Island. In 1639 he preached at Honiley, Warwickshire, in a living belonging to close associates of Lord Brooke. During the early 1640s, he moved to Northenden, Cheshire, and then to Halifax in Yorkshire. In 1645 he gathered a congregation at Sowerby Chapel, Yorkshire, where he remained until ejected in 1662.[52]

Meanwhile, ever mindful of the link between a sound economic base and the establishment of a settled godly society, the company did not want to jeopardize the former by premature and risky enhancement of the latter. Some of the colonists to whom the godly party objected were the very ones whose expertise was necessary to development of new Central American projects and to the island's defense. Nicholas Goodman, the workmaster, was an example of the kind of man whose

---

49. PIC to Gov. and Coun., to Gov. Bell, and to Hope Sherrard, 9–34.
50. See the negotiations with Mr. Samuel Symonds, Gen. Ct., 7–2–34.
51. PIC Prep. Ct., 6–13–34; PIC to Gov. Bell, 9–34.
52. Calamy, *Nonconformists Memorial*, rev. ed., III, 450–2; Matthews, ed., *Calamy Revised*, 417; Hughes, *Politics, Society, and Civil War*, 79n.

skills were essential but whose presence was disruptive. He was brought before the company while they were discussing the demands of Roote and the colonists. The long list of charges justifying his expulsion from the colony was headed by (1) "Stubbornness and contentious words against the Governor and Council," and (2) "Quarreling against religion." After hearing his claim that he had been provoked by "ill language," company members decided not to punish him.[53] The company was not willing to risk alienating such a valuable man, regardless of his quarrelsomeness and irreligion.

Captain Rudyerd would later return to Providence Island as a privateering captain. William Rous remained until he, too, left the island to command a privateer. The *Long Robert*, which carried word that Roote would not return, also concluded the charges against Nicholas Goodman and brought the company's (apparent) reinstatement of William Rous to the council table over the council's objections.[54] The company made it clear that life was to continue as usual on Providence Island.

Just as the investors were reluctant to remove colonists to whom the godly party objected, so they were loath to accede to demands for congregational control over life in Providence Island. They continued to believe that only minutely detailed scrutiny by themselves could ensure that their experiment would not go awry. As tensions in Massachusetts Bay between the claims of tender consciences and the powers over even civil rights claimed by the gathered congregations there erupted into open conflict in the antinomian crisis in 1636, the grandees of the Providence Island Company became ever more convinced that only control by leaders such as themselves promised successful creation of a just godly society. All the company needed was time to establish their settlement securely, and they hoped that the colonists and the Spanish would give it to them.

The status quo could not be maintained, however; the situation rapidly deteriorated for the godly congregation on Providence Island. Hope Sherrard wrote to Sir Thomas Barrington in despair in February 1635 of his grief and humiliation:

> [H]aving been publicly affronted by Capt. Hooke and some others that joined together to foment a faction against me in the church: having been publicly opposed and disgraced by the Governor in the open congregation: having had such witnesses come in against me upon oath, that upon my certain knowledge have sworn to many

53. PIC Prep. Ct., 5–13–34; Gen. Ct., 5–15–34, 5–16–34, 5–17–34; Ctee., 5–30–34; Prep. Ct., 6–16–34; PIC to Gov. and Coun., 9–34.
54. See Chapter 3.

falsehoods, which I shall be able to prove by the testimony of twenty or thirty men of understanding and good reputation, upon their corporal and solemn oaths whensoever they shall be lawfully called having had the lewdest persons in the Island to abuse, slander and vilify me; whom I wish that they had not been countenanced and supported by the Governor who in the most of my Causes hath showed himself a party with them against me: not to speak of the great wrong and indignity he together with those that have joined with him have offered me upon Record, by their manifold virulent speeches and invectives: he hath added courses of injustice as I conceive (I speak it under correction of your worships Judgement together with the rest of the Honourable Company to whose noble determinations I shall always stand as it is fit in the Lord, and therefore would not be thought to be so presumptuous as to go about to forejudge anything) and how can it be otherwise, seeing he maintains this rotten principle that whatsoever he Commands be it either lawful or unlawful yet we must yield an absolute and active obedience to the same without any questioning power I wish that he had not as well (or rather as ill) exercised as Claimed: but if this principle may stand good what are we in this Island, else but his absolute slaves and vassals. Furthermore he hath imprisoned me now also above this quarter of a year, and most of that time he hath committed me close prisoner, for that, which my conscience (so far as it is enlightned) telleth me was my duty to do in the course of my Ministry; but the one Comfort I have amongst many in the holy Scriptures, that in the beatitudes Matt. 5: as our Savior makes poverty of spirit the first steps to true blessedness, so he makes persecution for righteousness sake to be as it were the complement of it in this life.[55]

The causes of Sherrard's disgrace are obscure; his long letter to the company does not survive. Sherrard was evidently using his one weapon, excommunication, with increasing frequency and for maximum effect. Opponents found themselves suspended from the sacrament suddenly and without warning, being simply passed by in the service.[56]

Mr. or Captain Hooke, one of his chief antagonists, appeared before a company committee in June 1635. The "original" of his quarrel with Sherrard had been his excommunication; excommunication had "encouraged his servants to neglect him" and this, combined with his own sickness, had caused the failure of his plantation. He offered to bring in

55. Hope Sherrard to Sir Thomas Barrington, 2–35, B. L., Egerton MS 2646, ff. 76–77v. Coincidentally, at exactly the same time, the company was writing to Governor Bell that they "utterly dislike" his use of the term "Absolute power" and "therefore would not have it once named"; PIC to Gov. Bell, 2/3–35.
56. PIC to Sherrard, 3–36.

witnesses to explain the circumstances and aftermath of his excommunication, but the company declined for the moment. More broadly, he charged Sherrard with "negligence in his function (the same being so observable that Mr. Roote had given him a reprehension for it) and with debility of memory, whereby he was made unfit for the ministry."[57]

Hope Sherrard had earlier excommunicated another key man, gunner Philip Trippett. Before they heard of Hope Sherrard's censure of Mr. Hooke and the minister's imprisonment, the company had directed Governor Bell to look into Trippett's situation "and as you shall see occasion to give him relief." The investors hoped that the colonists "well considered how high a censure excommunication is." It should be "tenderly used" but also not lightly removed.[58]

Few ships went to Providence Island in this period; it would be a long time before the company took official notice of Sherrard's situation. At the time he was writing, early in 1635, the company struggled to come to terms with their own discouragement. In March 1635 Sherrard's friend, a minister named Moorton, asked that Sherrard be sent servants because the minister had voluntarily assigned the two servants formerly sent him to the company's service. He also asked that Sherrard be assured of his stipend even if the company were to sell their interest in the island. Denying any intention to sell, the company paid what was due on Sherrard's salary of £50 a year and agreed that he might have four servants if his friends provided them but that the company could not be expected to replace them if they died. The company was especially interested in settling Sherrard firmly into the island's ministry and were making arrangements to send his intended wife to him.[59]

Other evidence of the polarization of Providence Island's religious life had come to the company's attention by 1635. Samuel Rishworth particularly had taken up uncompromising positions that put him in direct confrontation with Captain Daniel Elfrith and Governor Bell as well as with many of the planters. Rishworth fought the island's increasing turn to slave labor and promised slaves to work for some

57. PIC Ctee., 6–24–35. Roote's doubts about Sherrard may have added to his decision not to emigrate. Captain Hooke was related to John Pym through Pym's wife, Anna Hooke; see Newton, *Colonising Activities*, 73n.
58. PIC to Gov. Bell, 2/3–35.
59. PIC, Ct., 3–9–35. Mr. Moorton may have been Nicholas Morton, who had been ejected from the rectory of Blisland in Cornwall and had moved to St. Mary Overy's in Southwark. He was the father of Charles Morton, scientist and theologian, who emigrated to Massachusetts and became a fellow of Harvard College. See the biographies of Charles Morton in Edmund Calamy, *The Nonconformist's Memorial*, 2nd ed. rev. by Samuel Palmer (London, 1775–77), I, 273–4; and Zaller and Greaves, ed., *Biographical Dictionary of British Radicals*.

termination to their servitude. He also used his position as councilor to challenge Bell and Elfrith over the conduct of the company stores.

Rishworth saw himself as standing in defense of true religion against the disorderly and ungodly faction. In 1635 the company was unsympathetic, seeing his "continual wrangling in the face of the country" as a source of disorder and defeat for their larger plans. But this stance was softened in Secretary Jessop's simultaneous private letter to Rishworth. Jessop urged him to bear his suffering, "the cost of your Christian profession," in such a way that "God's enemies" would be confounded.[60] The godly sort in Providence Island were already on the path that would lead to formation of a separate gathered congregation. Their party was strengthened by the return of their ally Mr. Richard Lane, whose departure Governor Bell had attempted to forestall, with the rank of councilor.[61]

At the same time, the company was furiously seeking another minister. They had approached George Burdett, who, like Roote before him, promised that he could bring substantial godly settlers with him, including some who had been intending to return to New England. Burdett was offered the same terms as Hope Sherrard. In addition, because of his large number of children, he was to have a house built for him in a location of his choice, with land sufficient for twelve servants, three of whom were to be sent with him. At Burdett's insistence, the company offered his followers abatement of the system of tenancy at halves to one in which colonists kept everything they raised for their own sustenance and two-thirds of their marketable crops. Again the company was confronted by the unpalatable fact that godly settlers required independence through control of their own livelihood; only by promising the means of competency could Providence Island compete with New England for such men and women.

Despite these inducements, George Burdett declined the offer two weeks later. At the same time, company husband William Woodcock reported that he had recruited a Mr. Pruden to go as minister. A month later the investors were looking at a man whose status was so dubious that they required him to be ordained a deacon before embarking and then to return on the same ship so that they could judge his performance. All these men ultimately declined to go.[62]

The adventurers' wooing of such clergymen is symptomatic of the low ebb their confidence had reached by the middle of the decade.

60. PIC to Gov. Bell, 2/3–35; Jessop to Rishworth, 4–9–35, B. L., Add. MS 10615, no. 70.
61. See Chapter 4.
62. PIC Ctee., 2–20–35; 3–5–35; Ct., 4–14–35.

Burdett was an unlikely shepherd for the troubled flock in Providence Island. Censured at Trinity College, Dublin, for profanity, he had become a puritan at Sidney Sussex College, Cambridge, after which he obtained the lectureship at Great Yarmouth in Norfolk. He attracted criticism wherever he went. His lectures at Great Yarmouth were said to have been characterized by "coarse invective" against the vicar and those who conformed to the extent of taking communion. In June 1635, shortly after his negotiations with the Providence Island Company, he fled to New England, allegedly leaving his wife and children in poverty. After about a year in Salem with Hugh Peter, he found Massachusetts too confining and traveled north to Dover, which had been settled by a company of gentlemen of which Saye and Brooke were members. There he was accused of repeated acts of adultery and breaches of the peace. His impassioned preaching attracted followers wherever he went, but he was always a thorn in the side of authority. Burdett, "the dishonour of his profession & monster of nature," left New England in 1641 amid rumors that he intended "to turn Jesuit."[63]

By 1635, then, the Providence Island Company adventurers had reason for fears about the future of their experiment in constructing a new puritan society. Friction was growing between the godly party and other colonists whose skills and experience made them invaluable. Substantial men and women in their thousands were pouring into New England while the Providence Island investors searched in vain for good Christians to go to their island in the required numbers. Prospective colonists were put off by the island's problems: its religious wrangles, its failure to find a good source of economic returns, and the ever-present danger of Spanish attack.

All this seemed to change in 1635 with the repulsion of the Spanish. So unprepared were the planters for such a challenge that nothing short of God's strong arm could have brought success; he had moved the settlers' hearts to seek him in a "special ordinance" before the assault. At last God had given a sign.[64] Moreover, the Spanish attack gave the company the grounds they needed to ask for a grant of letters of reprisal; privateering could now solve the settlement's economic problems, freeing the settlers of the crushing burden of paying off the investors and allowing them to focus on their own society.

63. On Burdett's career, see Moody, ed., *Letters of Thomas Gorges*, 5–6n; and Thomas Gorges to Richard Bernard, August 21, 1641, ibid., 35. See also Robert Stansby to John Wilson, April 17, 1637, *Winthrop Papers* III, 390; Thomas Dudley to John Winthrop, Dec. 11, 1638, ibid., IV, 86; and Thomas Gorges to John Winthrop, Feb. 23, 1641, ibid., 322–3; Joseph B. Felt, *Annals of Salem*, 2nd ed. (Salem, 1849), II, 572–3; and Clark, *The Eastern Frontier*, 40.
64. PIC to Gov. and Coun. by the *Blessing*, 5–36.

Great new plans were laid. Governor Bell was replaced by the godly Captain Robert Hunt, who came armed with instructions to end the conflict between the congregation and others in the island's elite. Hunt had close associations with the New England puritans, who noted his decision to emigrate to the southern colony. He delayed his departure for a few months so that he could gather substantial men – Frederick Johnson, Matthew Downes, and John Francis – to go with him and support the reconstruction of the island's life. All three were to be added to the council.[65] The company directed Hunt to give his first attention to restoring Hope Sherrard to freedom and his place of dignity. The Reverend Mr. Moorton (or Moreton) had again come to the company on behalf of his friend in May 1636, saying Sherrard was imprisoned and destitute in the island, the cost of his imprisonment having consumed all his income for the preceding year.[66]

In the batch of letters sent with Robert Hunt in 1636 in the *Blessing*, the company regretted their lack of time to deal with all the reports previously sent from the island, but they insisted on taking up Sherrard's case. On examination they found that he had been punished because of the way he exercised his ministerial function, which was expressly forbidden by the company's instructions and their agreement with the minister. Promising to look closely at the disagreements that led to the problem, they directed that in the meantime Sherrard be freed and encouraged to resume his ministry. Furthermore, they "utterly" forbade that he or any other minister be disrupted in performing his function: "The breach of which order we shall interpret as one of the highest contempt and disrespect to our authority, and as a very great affront which we shall punish in a severe way."[67]

The accompanying letter to Hope Sherrard and Governor Hunt's instructions refined this order and stipulated a role for the civil arm, commending consultation between the minister and governor when excommunication was in question. Hunt was directed to "advise with Mr. Sherrard in private how some differences in the Island about Ecclesiastical censures may be composed, divers having complained to us that they find themselves much aggrieved for the same." The letter to Sherrard offered condolences for his tribulation and gave assurances that no minister would suffer in that way again, but the company urged

65. Samuel Reade wrote to John Winthrop, Jr., of Hunt's decision for Providence Island just two weeks after Hunt agreed; Reade to Winthrop, March 5, 1636, *Winthrop Papers* III, 233–4; PIC to Gov. and Coun. by the *Blessing*, 5–36.
66. PIC, Gen. Ct., 5–30–36. See the Gen. Ct of 2–26–36 and the Ctee. of 3–26–36 for evidence that Sherrard had been advanced money by colonists, including Henry Halhead.
67. PIC to Gov. and Coun., 5–36.

"care and consideration" in matters of excommunication. They asked that "in cases of eminent importance" he consult with Hunt, "who we assure ourselves is a discreet and godly man, and will concur with your self in all just ways for the suppression of sin, and encouragement of godliness." No one was to be suspended from the sacrament without warning and a chance to give satisfaction, "that so he may not be passed by in the church, not expecting it." Excommunications already pronounced were to be reviewed with "all the Christian moderation that may stand with a safe conscience." Finally, Sherrard was urged to go on in his labors, offering "a pattern of holiness, meekness, and peaceableness," to silence those "that may otherwise seek advantage against you." Again the investors promised to do all in their power to send "some faithful fellow laborers" to help in the ministry.[68]

Through February and March 1636, company members had negotiated with two ministers, Mr. Jackson and Mr. Partridge, after hearing them preach. Although the company wrote in June that an unnamed new minister actually was sailing in the *Happie Return*, neither Jackson nor Partridge agreed to emigrate. Ralph Partridge, whose "intellectual abilities" Cotton Mather compared to a soaring eagle, went to Duxbury in Plymouth colony. As the investors had written in May, "[I]f we cannot send such as we desire, you must blame your selves and not us, the unhappy discontents that have fallen out betwixt the minister and the Government being so public and offensive that all other argument which may be offered can very hardly balance with that discouragement." In 1637 the investors wrote again that their negotiations with yet another unnamed minister had failed "just upon the ship's departure, through a necessity which neither of us could decline."[69]

Providence Island, as so often, lost out in competition with Massachusetts Bay; yet from the standpoint of English puritans, the northern colony had embarked on a far more dangerous course, which, as Stephen Foster points out, looked like "straightforward apostasy" to "most English observers."[70] The other puritan experiment, rent by open

---

68. PIC Instructions to Gov. Hunt, 3–36; PIC to Sherrard, 3–36. Captain Elfrith was told that the company had not had time to scrutinize his quarrel with Sherrard but hoped that the minister would make peace with him; PIC to Elfrith, 3–36.

69. PIC Ct. 2–20–36, 3–8–36; Ctee. 3–14–36; PIC to Gov. and Coun. by the *Blessing*, 5–36, by the *Happie Return*, 6–36, and by the *Mary Hope*, 3–37. On Ralph Partridge see Cotton Mather, *Magnalia Christi Americana* (1702; rpt. Hartford, 1855), I, 404–5; Walker, *Creeds and Platforms*, 175, 184; and George F. Willison, *Saints and Strangers* (New York, 1945), 357–9. Jackson's identity is unknown.

70. Foster convincingly demonstrates how the New England Way, with its tendency to withdraw into the company of the godly, grew out of developments within English puritanism; see *The Long Argument*, 94–8, 155–66.

rebellion within the Boston congregations, moved to solidify congregational control of the colony's political life. By the middle of the 1630s, church membership was increasingly available only to "visible saints," those in whom a congregation saw clearly evidenced "the work of God's grace," and only church members could vote or hold office.[71] In the eyes of the lords and gentlemen, this elevation of the religious sphere over the state laid the foundation for a new "popish tyranny," the very development they deplored in England. To give congregations decision-making power over who would have civil rights in the society was to recreate the intolerable situation in which bishops' authority extended to the country's political life. Such confusion of spheres would only lead to disaster.[72]

Providence Island Company member Sir Nathaniel Rich had written enquiring about Massachusetts Bay's organization in 1633. John Winthrop's answer, after affirming the healthfulness of New England,

71. Edmund S. Morgan, *Visible Saints: The History of a Puritan Idea* (Ithaca, NY, 1965), 99–101. On the conception of the "New England Way" see Harry S. Stout, *The New England Soul: Preaching and Religious Culture in Colonial New England* (Oxford, 1986), 13–23.

Although this step made Massachusetts a genuinely radical polity, according to Stephen Foster, Philip Gura argues that the requirement of evidence of conversion for church membership and civil rights may have been instituted to head off even more radical demands from those who sought an order based solely on the Bible. John Cotton's rejected code of laws, called *Moses his judicialls*, was part of this campaign for a true Bible commonwealth. Foster, *Their Solitary Way*, 46–7; Gura, *A Glimpse of Sion's glory*, 127–8, 133, 140, 162–3. For Cotton's legal code, see Worthington C. Ford, "Cotton's 'Moses his judicials,'" *Massachusetts Historical Society Proceedings* 2nd ser., XVI (1902), 274–84; and Anon., *An Abstract of the lawes of New England as they are now established* (London, 1641). See also J. F. Maclear, "New England and the Fifth Monarchy: The Quest for the Millennium in Early American Puritanism," *William and Mary Quarterly* 3rd ser., 32 (1975), 231–40. Gura points out that only the Indian praying towns of John Eliot were true biblically based commonwealths; ibid., 134, 136, 140. As Maclear argues, Eliot saw his "Indian theocracy" as a model to be extended to Europe; ibid., 247.

72. See Saye to John Winthrop, July 1640, *Winthrop Papers* IV, 263–8, esp. 266–7. Lord Brooke wrote about the inevitable increase of light in his own times, perhaps thinking of New England, "And yet some went from us lately with a candle burning, brighter perhaps than ours; though it were lighted here." He went on to wonder why Christians feared "quick actings of the Spirit," which were censured by "those who forget that Text, Judge not lest ye be Judged."

Brooke compared the relationship between church and state to a happy marriage: "(Both keeping their bonds whilst the Husband hath the supremacy)." The state had, he argued, care of the Ten Commandments, "and yet the Church preserving to her self Her rights." *Discourse on Episcopacie*, 48, 116.

For full discussion of the issues involved, see Karen Ordahl Kupperman, "Definitions of Liberty on the Eve of Civil War: Lord Saye and Sele, Lord Brooke, and the American Puritan Colonies," *Historical Journal* 32 (1989), 17–33. Lord Saye's nephew and close associate Henry Parker, in his *Discourse on Puritans*, wrote, "God sees not as man sees, and yet he that will judge uprightly ought to see as God sees, and not as Man," 56–7.

described the evolving plan of civil and church government in a few terse sentences covering emotion-laden debates. Winthrop called the civil plan of governance "mixed," with freemen choosing magistrates and three representatives to the quarterly courts. He did not mention that freemanship rested on church membership. He wrote that the churches were governed by "Pastors, Teachers, ruling Elders and Deacons, yet the power lies in the whole Congregation...."[73]

As news of events in Massachusetts filtered back to England in 1635, Lords Saye and Brooke sought further understanding of the New England Way. Sir Henry Vane the younger, the puritan son of a leading gentleman and an associate of the Providence Island investors, had already decided to join the New England venture; Saye and Brooke also contemplated possible emigration to New England.[74] Saye and Brooke, who began an outpost at Saybrook in Connecticut in 1635 with John Winthrop, Jr., as governor, sent a series of questions to the Boston leaders. The answers convinced them that the northern colony had deviated from the proper English puritan course, and they gave up any idea of moving to Massachusetts.[75]

Even in New England, not all puritan leaders were comfortable with the relationship between church and state that had evolved in Massachusetts

73. Winthrop to Rich, May 22, 1634, *Winthrop Papers* III, 166–8. Winthrop wrote just one week after a revolt of the freemen had wrought massive changes in the Massachusetts Bay system of governance and had turned him out of the governor's office. At the general court of May 14, 1634, the freemen, led by Israel Stoughton, demanded to see the charter, which as they suspected gave the freemen the right to make the colony's laws, a function hitherto assumed by the governor and assistants. At this general court, the system Winthrop described was instituted. He would not be reelected governor until the crisis of the antinomian challenge in 1637. Stoughton wrote a long letter about the grievances to his brother John, rector of the puritan parish of St. Mary Aldermanbury in London, in which the Earl of Warwick was a communicant. On these events see Winthrop, *Journal*, ed. Hosmer, I, 122–5; Israel Stoughton to John Stoughton, 1635, Massachusetts Historical Society *Proceedings* 58 (1925), 446–58; and Andrews, *Colonial Period*, 441–4.

It was in this letter to Sir Nathaniel that Winthrop reported that the Indians were "near all dead of the small Pox, so as the Lord hath cleared our title to what we possess." *Winthrop Papers* III, 167.

74. Sir Henry Vane the younger, a follower of Anne Hutchinson, was elected governor of Massachusetts Bay in 1636. He was turned out of office the next year and returned to England in August 1637.

75. The proposals of Lords Saye and Brooke are printed, along with John Cotton's answer written in 1636, in Thomas Hutchinson, *The History of the Colony and Province of Massachusetts-Bay*, ed. Lawrence Shaw Mayo (Cambridge, MA, 1936), I, Appendices II and III, pp. 410–13. The point at issue is blurred in B. Katherine Brown, "The Puritan Concept of Aristocracy," *Mississippi Valley Historical Review* 41 (1954–55), 105–12. For discussion of the Massachusetts Bay polity and its theoretical underpinnings, see Breen, *Character of the Good Ruler*, and Edmund S. Morgan, ed., *Puritan Political Ideas, 1558–1794* (New York, 1965), "Introduction."

Bay. Access to civil rights only through the approbation of the congregation disturbed the Reverend Thomas Hooker, who left Massachusetts in 1636 with his followers to found Hartford in Connecticut. Reports reached England that there were divisions over religious issues in the Bay and that before he left there Hooker had preached against excessive strictness in gathering congregations.[76] Hooker wrote to John Winthrop in 1638 specifically rejecting any system in which the religious arm had decision-making powers over civil affairs; he, like Saye and Brooke, argued that only clearly defined law can protect the subject's liberty with "a general council [counsell] chosen by all to transact businesses which concern all."[77]

Roger Williams, expelled from Massachusetts soon after Hooker left, also argued strongly that any mixing of the civil and religious functions

76. Baird Tipson argues that Hooker did not require conversion relations for church membership. See his introduction in "Samuel Stone's 'Discourse' against Requiring Church Relations," *William and Mary Quarterly* 3rd ser., XLVI (1989), 793–94 and fn. Charles Cohen argues that such relations were required by Hooker in *God's Caress*, 143 fn.

77. Thomas Hooker to John Winthrop, December 1638, *Winthrop Papers* IV, 75–84, esp. pp. 80–2; R. Stansby to John Wilson, April 17, 1637, Massachusetts Historical Society *Collections* 4th ser., VII (1865), 10–11; Andrews, *Colonial Period of American History*, II, 78, 87–90. In his *Vindiciae Veritatis* Lord Saye praised New England's 1648 Cambridge Platform of church organization, which ordained a congregational system with provision for synods in cases of larger issues but singled out the writings of the "learned godly Mr. Hooker of New England" against usurpation of power by one congregation over another, 123, 127–32. See also Gura, *Glimpse of Sion's glory*, 165, 173.

For a review of the controversy over whether Hooker was more democratic than the Massachusetts Bay leaders, see Sydney E. Ahlstrom, "Thomas Hooker – Puritanism and Democratic Citizenship: A Preliminary Inquiry into Some Relationships of Religion and American Civic Responsibility," *Church History* 32 (1962–63), 415–31; and Perry Miller, "Thomas Hooker and the Democracy of Connecticut," in his *Errand into the Wilderness* (Cambridge, MA, 1956), 16–47. Hooker had been fellow of Emmanuel College, Cambridge, from 1609 to 1618 and had been lecturer and catechist in the college.

Thomas Gorges, puritan governor of a small Maine colony, was also disturbed. He wrote to his clergyman in England, the puritan divine Richard Bernard, who had written against the practice of the Bay, and to his uncle Sir Ferdinando Gorges and others about his misgivings; Robert E. Moody, ed., *The Letters of Thomas Gorges, Deputy Governor of Maine, 1640–1643* (Portland, ME, 1978), 7, 17–18, 36–7, 57, 109; the Reverend Richard Bernard of Batcomb in Somersetshire sent two manuscript copies of his book against the New England way of gathering churches to Boston in 1636, to which a reply was returned in 1638 and published in *Church-Government and Church-Covenant Discussed. In an answer of the Elders of the severall Churches of New-England to two and thirty Questions, sent over to them by divers Ministers in England, to declare their judgments therein. Together with an Apologie of the said Elders in New-England for Church-Covenant, sent over in Answer to Master Bernard in 1639. As Also in an answer to nine Positions about Church-Government. And now published for the satisfaction of all who desire resolution in those points* (London, 1643). See Winthrop, *Journal* I, 279, 293.

could only result in the corruption of both. Williams, far more radical than Hooker, later believed that he had seen his predictions come true in Boston in the 1630s and in the England of the 1650s.[78]

Saye and Brooke were, then, in good puritan company when they rejected the Massachusetts practice of making approved godliness a prerequisite to citizenship. Nor was the question a matter of mere abstract debate. As they corresponded with Saye and Brooke, the Bay Colony leaders were in the process of purging magistrates and other Boston church members for holding unorthodox opinions.[79] In Stephen Foster's words, the purge was conducted with "a fury approaching outright sadism."[80]

Such actions caused immense concern among English Puritans; increasingly, Massachusetts came to be characterized as a center of persecution where, as Nathaniel Ward proudly proclaimed in 1647, the only liberty available to "Enthusiasts" was "free Liberty to keep away from us."[81] In the wake of the challenge by the followers of Anne Hutchinson, the ministerial synod drew up a list of eighty-two erroneous opinions, hardening New England orthodoxy and symbolically closing their eyes to any further unveiling of the light.

Sir Richard Saltonstall, a charter member and assistant of the Massachusetts Bay Company, grieved over what he saw as the perversion of the colony's mission. Although he returned to England, his sons remained in New England, and he was closely associated with Providence Island Company members in plans to colonize along the Connecticut River. In 1652 he wrote to John Cotton and John Wilson about his concerns, blaming the ministers as the sources of persecution:

> Reverend and dear friends, whom I unfeignedly love and respect, It doth not a little grieve my spirit to hear what sad things are reported daily of your tyranny and persecutions in New England, as

78. Williams, *The Hireling ministry none of Christs,* 1652, ed. Perry Miller, in *Complete Writings of Roger Williams,* VII, 189–90; and *The Examiner defended,* in *A Fair and Sober Answer to Two and twenty Questions,* 1652, ed. Miller, ibid., 218.

79. Emery Battis, *Saints and Sectaries: Anne Hutchinson and the Antinomian Controversy in the Massachusetts Bay Colony* (Chapel Hill, 1962), chapter 17, esp. 258–68. See Delbanco, *Puritan Ordeal,* 154–60, for the argument that John Davenport left Massachusetts to found New Haven as a dissent from the Bay Colony's hardening orthodoxy; Cotton also considered emigrating to New Haven.

80. Foster, *Their Solitary Way,* 53, 55. In the Long Parliament debates over the disestablishment of episcopacy, John Pym said, "[W]hat pity is it that ministers should be prosecutors." John Moore notes of Pym speech, February 26, 1640, in Notestein, ed., *Journal of Sir Simonds D'Ewes,* 413.

81. Theodore de la Guard [Ward], *The simple cobler of Aggawam in America.* Fifth edition repr. in Peter Force, comp., *Tracts and Other Papers* (1844; repr. Gloucester, MA, 1963), III, no. 8, 6.

that you fine, whip, and imprison men for their consciences. . . . Truly, friends, this your practice of compelling any in matters of worship to do that whereof they are not fully persuaded, is to make them sin, for so the apostle (Rom. 14 and 23) tells us, and many are made hypocrites thereby, conforming in their outward man for fear of punishment. We [who] pray for you and wish you prosperity every way, hoped the Lord would have given you so much light and love there, that you might have been eyes to God's people here, and not to practice those courses in a wilderness, which you went so far to prevent. These rigid ways have laid you very low in the hearts of the saints. . . . I hope you doe not assume to yourselves infallibility of judgment, when the most learned of the Apostles confesseth he knew but in part and saw but darkly as through a glass, for God is light, and no further than He doth illuminate us can we see, be our parts and learning be never so great.[82]

Roger Williams and Sir Henry Vane, both banished from Massachusetts, were welcomed and honored in England. The radical spiritist Samuel Gorton, similarly expelled, was given the powerful sponsorship of the Earl of Warwick in founding a new settlement out of the reach of Boston at Shawomet, renamed Warwick, in Rhode Island. English puritans even deplored the expulsion of the Socinian William Pynchon, founder of Springfield, Massachusetts, as improper treatment for a man of such stature.[83] All these returnees were seen as men of substance, men who should have been given a hearing. They were united in their rejection of concentration on outward forms of worship rather than the inward truth of the Christian's spirit; all felt that Massachusetts Bay's test of visible sainthood risked forcing the consciences of Christians who sought the light with a true heart. They naturally found a sympathetic ear among leading puritans such as the Providence Island investors.

From the returnees' stories English puritans extracted lessons, terrible traps to be avoided as England embarked on its own course of experimentation with godly government.[84] They began to realize the full

82. Sir Richard Saltonstall to John Cotton and John Wilson, 1652, in Robert E. Moody, ed., *The Saltonstall Papers, 1607–1815* (Boston, 1972), 148–9. John Cotton's point-by-point reply, which chided Saltonstall for credulously accepting the critics' words, was printed in Thomas Hutchinson, *Collection of Papers Relative to Massachusetts-Bay* (repr. Boston, 1865), II, 129–34. Saltonstall's letter is in the same collection, 127–9.

83. Blair Worden explains why Socinianism, antitrinitarian in doctrine, was despised, but also its attraction for thinkers such as Milton, Locke, and Newton; "Toleration and the Cromwellian Protectorate," in Sheils, ed., *Persecution and Toleration*, 203–4.

84. Sir Henry Vane was already closely connected to Providence Island Company members when he emigrated. He acted as agent for Lords Brooke and Saye in New

meaning of John Winthrop's claim, delivered in his 1634 letter to Sir Simonds D'Ewes, that New Englanders had "clearer light and more Liberty" to set up a novel order in America.[85] As events unfolded in 1637, Sir Edmund Moundeford informed D'Ewes that the Providence Island Company expected to divert "a great part of the Stream" to "this plantation instead of new England."[86]

Providence Island Company members would ultimately turn decisively against the sects of the Interregnum years. What they argued for was an erastian settlement with toleration; none favored what they saw as the unrestrained explosion of sectarian enthusiasm that respected no limits and often reintroduced Arminianism. Quakers and Anabaptists particularly elicited their scorn. Lord Saye's last book was an attack on the Quakers, *Folly and Madness Made Manifest*, in which he wrote that the spirit within could be used to justify any action, regardless of how destructive or wild. Like many others Saye, who accused the Quakers of using witchcraft to attract proselytes, thought that they were allied with or at least similar to the Jesuits. Saye was cited by the Quakers in their chronicle of sufferings for his persecution of them in Banbury. Other Providence Island Company members reacted similarly to the sects.[87] All this was far in the future in the 1630s; none then thought that toleration would have any but a beneficial effect.

England; see Maclear, "Making of the Lay Tradition," *Journal of Religion* XXXIII (1953), 128. For acceptance of Roger Williams as an ally by puritan thinkers such as Thomas Goodwin, William Walwyn, and John Wilton, see Strider, *Lord Brooke*, 218–30; and Delbanco, *Puritan Ordeal*, 167–8. On Gorton and Pynchon, see Hambrick-Stowe, *Practice of Piety*, 94–5; Gura, *Glimpse of Sion's Glory*, 20, 85, 88–9, 116–17, 167, 194–6, 288, 298, 307–10, 318; Wall, *The Crucial Decade*, chap. 4; and Kenneth W. Porter, "Samuell Gorton, New England Firebrand," *New England Quarterly* 7 (1934), 405–44. See also Hubbard, *General History of New England*, 335.

85. Winthrop to D'Ewes, July 21, 1634, *Winthrop Papers* III, 171–2.
86. Moundeford to D'Ewes, 1637? [date obliterated, but internal evidence suggests 1637], B. L., Harleian MS 287, f. 265.
87. Saye, *Folly and Madness Made Manifest* (London, 1655), 2, 4–8, 19–20, 31; Joseph Besse, *A Collection of the Sufferings of the People called Quakers* (London, 1753), I. 563–65. Several members of the Halhead family as magistrates assisted the prosecution of Quakers, but Henry Halhead wrote against those who "seek to root out and destroy any of the people of god, under the Notion of Sectaries, and Disturbers of the State; though many of them adventured their lives to do them good!"; see Halhead, *Inclosure Thrown Open*, 3; Barrie Trinder, "The Origins of Quakerism in Banbury," *Cake and Cockhorse* 7 (1979), 263–72; Blankenfeld, "Puritans in the Provinces," 308–16.

The Earl of Manchester also became disturbed by sectarian diversity, as did Oliver Cromwell. See Adamson, "The Peerage in Politics," (unpub. Ph.D. diss., Cambridge University, 1986), 107; Pearl, "Royal Independents," *Transactions Royal Historical Society* 5th ser., XVIII (1967), 89–91; Hirst, *Authority and Conflict*, 321–2, 342–5; Seaver, *Wallington's World*, 66; and Worden, "Toleration and the Cromwellian Protectorate," in Sheils, ed., *Persecution and Toleration*, 212.

As English puritans looked at the colonies in 1636 and 1637, the religious problems of Providence Island, troubling as they were, must have seemed more hopeful of settlement than those of the northern colony. Men and women who saw the danger in New England could leave and found new societies, as Williams and Hooker did, but within Massachusetts the course was already set. The investors continued to believe that on Providence Island renewal could come with the infusion of sufficient numbers of sober and right-minded people.

In fact, for many reasons Massachusetts Bay was to be far more successful than Providence Island because rank-and-file colonists were less interested in the theoretical issues of political lessons and far more interested in ensuring personal and religious security through ownership of property and control over their own economic lives than the adventurers had realized. Only with such independence could godly colonists believe themselves safe from interference in pursuing their own religious goals. The challenge of Anne Hutchinson and her supporters, the first of many such challenges to Massachusetts Bay orthodoxy, convinced colonists of the dangers of too much openness and toleration of dissent.[88] The emphasis of the English puritan leadership, as represented by the Providence Island Company investors, on allowing the widest possible opening to those who sought the light of God's truth, was unwelcome in the Bay.

Moreover, the Boston leadership had hit on the avenue to successful re-creation of the relationships that made the system of county government function well in England. The greatest difficulty in creating new societies overseas lay in the fact that, as John Murrin and Gary Kornblith have pointed out, it was impossible to import the supporting web of relationships and obligations that made regional government work in England. Anthony Fletcher and John Stevenson argue that the hierarchical system in England was "mediated by the vertical ties of patronage and clientage and softened by additional horizontal ties of kin and neighbourhood." Massachusetts Bay's stroke of genius was to substitute the web created by the bond of church membership and the mutual esteem of the certified godly for that other set of ties.[89]

The Providence Island investors in the later 1630s renewed their

---

88. Gura, *A Glimpse of Sion's Glory*, is the best description of these several challenges and their sources.
89. John Murrin and Gary Kornblith, Paper delivered to conference on Anglo-American social history, Williamsburg, VA, September 1985, 11–12, 16; Fletcher and Stevenson, eds., *Order and Disorder in Early Modern England*, "Introduction," 2–3, 15–16. See also T. H. Breen and Stephen Foster, "The Puritans' Greatest Achievement: A Study of Social Cohesion in Seventeenth-Century Massachusetts," *Journal of American History* LX (1972), 5–22; and Foster, *Long Argument*, 148–68.

endeavor to send godly settlers and painful ministers to their island. These efforts forced the grandees to confront the truth they found so difficult to accept: No settlers of the right sort would emigrate without complete security of land tenure and control of government in their hands. Increasingly through the Laudian repression of the 1630s, puritan emigration took the form of congregations led by their ministers; thus company members found clergymen interposed between themselves and the right kind of colonists. Whether it offended their commitment to lay control or not, they found themselves repeatedly negotiating with ministers about the church and government relationships that settlers demanded in America.

Renewed recruitment efforts from 1638 put the Providence Island investors in direct competition for colonists and ministers with New England. They treated with the lawyer Thomas Lechford and two key ministers, Charles Chauncy and Ezekiel Rogers. Lechford, who had defended William Prynne in his 1637 trial, wrote that the Providence Island investors had offered him "a place of preferment."[90] The records first indicated in February 1638 that Chauncy and Rogers might be willing to consider Providence Island as a destination; they were promised that members of the company had firmly committed themselves to go. In their negotiations with Ezekiel Rogers, the adventurers finally offered the kind of independence and security that Massachusetts Bay had meant for individual colonists all along:

> That men of quality shall be admitted to places of council and magistracy. That every man that can transport himself and family with six men servants shall be a free holder and have land assigned him sufficient to maintain him and his family paying for every servant xx lb. of tobacco a head, or of the like value, and four days work for every servant in a year to the public works. That those freeholders shall have a voice in choosing the Governor and making of laws. That they shall have the naming of their own ministers, and ordering all church affairs. That tobacco and other commodities shall be sent home in the Company ships for a reasonable freight.[91]

Ezekiel Rogers asked for time to consider; his reply was never recorded. He, Chauncy, and Lechford went to Massachusetts in 1638

90. Lechford to Hugh Peter, March 11, 1638/9 in Lechford, "Notebook," ed. Hale, *American Antiquarian Society Transactions*, 7 (1885), 48. Lechford's continuing relationship with the Providence Island investors is indicated by his copying into his notebook in New England the oath refused by Lords Saye and Brooke in 1639 when Charles I called for support against the Scots. Saye and Brooke were briefly imprisoned for this refusal. Lechford, ibid., 105.
91. PIC Ctee. 3–1–37/8.

despite the Providence Island Company's enticements. Lechford was ultimately dissatisfied and returned to England, where he published his book *Plain Dealing* (1641) as an attack on the New England Way.[92] Chauncy, whom Samuel Eliot Morison describes as "easily the most distinguished of the Cantabrigians who emigrated to New England," and a former fellow of Trinity College, stayed on to become the second president of Harvard in 1654.[93]

Ezekiel Rogers, son of the great Elizabethan preacher Richard Rogers, was a client of company member Sir Thomas Barrington. After a period as chaplain to the Barrington family, he had been appointed by the Barringtons as rector of Rowley St. Peter in Yorkshire, where he chafed under the requirements of his clientage. Rogers was suppressed by Archbishop Laud, Bishop Richard Neile's two-year effort to "reclaim" him having been a failure.[94] He and members of his congregation founded the town of Rowley in Massachusetts in 1638. In New England he argued strongly for a campaign to root out remnants of antinomianism and other "foul errors."[95] Like others wooed by the Providence Island Company, he would have made an uncomfortable religious presence in the island.

In their disappointment, the investors first attempted to recruit a Mr. Saunders, and then just before the ship sailed in April 1638, they engaged John Ward. The investors' letter to the governor and council assured them that Ward "will be painful and fruitful among you." Unfortunately, the letter was obsolete before it left England. Two days after it was written, Ward's wife had urgently asked the company to

92. On Lechford's experience of Massachusetts, see Cohen, *God's Caress*, 138–57; and Gura, *Glimpse of Sion's Glory*, 130–2.
93. Morison, *The Founding of Harvard College* (Cambridge, MA, 1935), 89–91. John Winthrop referred to Chauncy as "a great scholar, and a godly man," *Journal*, ed. Hosmer, I, 332.
94. Henry Jacie to John Winthrop, Jr., *Winthrop Papers* III, 58–9; *Calendar of State Papers, Domestic*, 1638–39, 431.
95. On the life of Ezekiel Rogers, see Mather, *Magnalia Christi Americana*, I, 408–13; Stephen Foster, "English Puritanism and the Progress of New England Institutions, 1630–1660," in Hall, Murrin, and Tate, eds., *Saints and Revolutionaries*, 16–23; Gura, *Glimpse of Sion's Glory*, 22, 106, 165–6. On the founding of Rowley, Massachusetts, see Allen, *In English Ways*, 165–9. Once in Massachusetts Rogers accepted and then was released from an invitation to lead his followers to settle at Quinnipiac in New Haven colony; Isabel MacBeath Calder, *The New Haven Colony* (New Haven, 1934), 68–70.
   In Massachusetts Rogers continued his spirited defense of the economic independence of his parishioners, attempting to break the economic monopoly of the Boston merchants. See Foster, *Solitary Way*, 118; and *Long Argument*, 27–9. He carried on an acrimonious transatlantic campaign to get Sir Thomas Barrington to pay him money he believed he was owed for improvements to the parsonage of the Barrington living he had held in Yorkshire. See Cliffe, *Puritan Gentry*, 136.

release her husband from his contract. The reluctant adventurers sent a letter to Nathaniel Butler, who was going as governor in the same ship, giving permission for Ward to "desert the voyage. If he shall think fit to recede from his contract upon those grounds which his wife alleged which ground the Company apprehended to be altogether mistaken and false." The terms of her objections were never specified. Cotton Mather wrote that John Ward's wife had received a legacy giving her the revenue of a parsonage worth £200 a year if she married a minister. Ward managed to conform sufficiently to draw this stipend for one more year but emigrated to New England in 1639.[96]

Only a handful of colonists were persuaded to divert their destination from New England to Providence Island in 1638 despite the company's willingness to go so far in relinquishing control over the settlers.

In late summer of 1638, a second ship was sent out. The first item taken up in the company's letter of instructions to the governor and council concerned the island's desperate need for ministers. Failure to send new ministers stemmed, the adventurers insisted, not from their "forgetfulness," but from the discouragement bred in the minds of recruits by reports from the island. The investors particularly blamed the colonists for their refusal to contribute to the minister's maintenance. Still, they were prepared to offer sizable stipends and were in treaty with two ministers whom they hoped to send in August.

Hope Sherrard still lived under a crushing burden of debt stemming from his period of imprisonment. He even complained about the expense involved in the company's initiative in sending his intended wife to him. His salary was mortgaged well in advance of each payment by the company's honoring of the bills he sent home by every ship.[97] In April 1638 the adventurers raised his salary to £60 a year and arranged for him to have two new servants. In the August letters, they advanced

---

96. PIC Gen. Ct., 4–5–38; Ctee., 4–12–38; Ctee., 4–25–38; PIC to Gov. and Coun., 4–23–38. There were at least three ministers named John Ward and several Nathaniel Wards in East Anglia in the 1630s. This John was probably the cousin of Nathaniel Ward (who preached in Bermuda and whom the original Bermudian settlers of Providence Island had wanted instead of Lewis Morgan), and son of Nathaniel Ward, who held the Rich family living of Standon Massey in Essex until 1634 when ejected by Laud he went to New England. John Ward occupied the Warwick living at Hadleigh in Essex. On Nathaniel and John Ward, see Mather, *Magnalia Christi Americana*, 521–4; K. W. Shipps, "Lay Patronage of East Anglian Puritan Clerics in Pre-Revolutionary England," unpub. Ph.D. diss., Yale University, 1971, 271–2; Donagan, "Clerical Patronage of Warwick," *Proceedings of the American Philosophical Society* 120 (1976), 392; Wilkinson, *Adventurers of Bermuda*, 2nd ed., 222–4.
97. PIC to Sherrard by the *Mary Hope*, 3–37; William Jessop to Sherrard, 3–25–35; and 4–37, B. L., Add MS 10615, no. 132, 162. Sherrard had sent Jessop an armadillo and a turtle shell in recompense for his efforts on his behalf.

additional money to help him pay his bills, and they recommended to the settlers that they also augment his allowance if they ever hoped to receive additional ministers.[98]

In 1638 as in 1636, company members saw grounds for hope in the continuing struggle to build a godly community in Providence Island. The company decided to replace Governor Robert Hunt, who had become wholly identified with Sherrard's congregation, but to encourage him to remain and support the island. The new governor, Captain Nathaniel Butler, was an experienced colonial hand. Like Captain Bell, he was a former governor of Bermuda, of which he had written a long history.[99] He was a fortifications expert, which answered one of Providence Island's needs, and he was committed to making the island securely prepared for attack.

Not only had Butler gotten the Bermuda settlers moving on their own defense, but he had succeeded in calming the religious passions that had raged on the islands. By his own account, Butler was able to forestall "all the infectious heats and dangerous breaches" in Bermuda by introducing the order of worship used "within His Majesty's dominions in Jersey and Guernsey, being one and the very same with that of the French Protestants, those of the united provinces, and even Geneva itself." Both Bermuda ministers, including the puritan Lewis Hughes, promised cooperation, whereupon Butler himself translated the service "verbatim into English, out of a French Bible which he brought over with him." Butler allowed no variation, and Bermuda settled into religious peace. Captain John Smith's version of the story pointed out that this service omitted "all those particulars they so much stumbled at" in the Book of Common Prayer.[100] The Providence Island

---

98. PIC to Gov. and Coun. in the *Swallow* and *Spy*, 7–38; PIC to Sherrard in the *Swallow*, 7–3–38.
99. Butler's *History of the Bermudaes or Summer Islands*, was published by the Hakluyt Society in an edition edited by J. H. LeFroy (London, 1882). LeFroy erroneously attributed the work to Captain John Smith, who had used Butler's manuscript as the basis for Book V of his *Generall Historie of Virginia, New-England, and the Summer Isles* (London, 1624).
100. Butler, *History of the Bermudaes*, ed. LeFroy, 172–3; Smith, *Generall Historie*, in Barbour, ed., *Complete Works*, II, 377; Lewis Hughes to Sir Nathaniel Rich, January 1619, Manchester Papers, H.M.C., 8th *Report* (1881), no. 265. On the religious settlement in Jersey and Guernsey, see A. J. Eagleston, *The Channel Islands under Tudor Government, 1485–1642: A Study in Administrative History* (Cambridge, 1949), 38–42, 54–62, 128–45, and Russell, *Causes of English Civil War*, 51. On Bermuda see Craven, *An Introduction to the History of Bermuda*, 141–3. For the religious opinions of Lewis Hughes and his cooperation with Butler, see "Lewis Hughes' 'Plaine and True Relation of the Goodnes of God Towards the Sommer Ilands'," ed. Wesley Frank Craven, *William and Mary Quarterly* 2nd ser., 17 (1937), 56–89.

adventurers must have considered the acquisition of Butler a great coup. His practical spirit, firm yet sensitive to the religious scruples of his colonists, combined with his determination, gave new grounds for hope. Butler was not destined to replicate his Bermuda success in Providence Island. The diary in which he recorded his daily activities for most of his stay documents the steady withdrawal of the self-styled godly party into a completely separate congregation, a process that was already well advanced when Butler arrived in September 1638. The governor came to feel that all resistance to his policies stemmed from secret cabals among those he styled the "Old Councilors," members of Sherrard's congregation who opposed privateering and the military preparedness that inevitably accompanied it. As he wrote to Lord Saye, "I never lived amongst men of more spleen nor of less wit to conceal it."[101]

Meanwhile, the company once more repeated its fruitless attempts to draw new ministers. Negotiations were resumed with Paul Amyraut (called Amirant in the Providence Island Records), an Oxford-educated preacher of German birth. The company had first approached Amyraut in 1636 after he had been suspended by Bishop Matthew Wren of Norwich for refusing to bow at the name of Jesus. Although he had apparently accepted their terms, he went instead to Holland, where he was an army chaplain as well as minister to the Presbyterian church in Utrecht. He was in Essex when the adventurers again attempted to recruit him in 1639; again he accepted their terms (£50 per year, £30 of which to go to his wife in England, one servant, and diet at the governor's house) but failed to emigrate. Again the company had to write that their hopes had been disappointed.[102]

The adventurers' urgency in 1639 stemmed from Hope Sherrard's refusal to administer the sacraments, leaving all the island's inhabitants bereft of the most fundamental Christian experience. In their disappointment over losing Amyraut, the adventurers asked Governor Butler

---

101. B. L., Sloane MS 758. Butler was writing a book of seamanship during his period on Providence Island. He kept his diary in the back pages of the same notebook, and he wrote notes of his letters in the notebook's spare front pages. The diary indicates that he was involved in writing letters to be sent back to England in April and May of 1639, but there is a great discrepancy between the tone of the letter notes and the tone of the diary for April and May 1639. Internal evidence indicates that the letter notes were written in very late 1639 or early 1640. The notes may be for letters that were never written because Butler decided to return and put his case before the company in person.

102. PIC Ct. 6–14–36, 5–23–39; PIC to Butler by the *Mary*, 7–39; PIC to Hunt by the *Mary*, 7–39. Calamy reported that Amyraut was "ancient" when ejected from Mundesley, Norfolk; Calamy, *Nonconformist Memorial*, 2nd ed. rev. by Palmer (1775), II, 196. On his career see Zaller and Greaves, ed., *Biographical Dictionary of British Radicals*.

to "give Mr. Sherrard and his particular congregation all liberty and favor in the way wherein they are." As they had argued in so many other settings, company members averred "that God makes no difference between them that do faithfully and heartily seek him though there be in the appearance of men some difference between them in opinion and practice concerning outward things." Part of their concern was "to maintain correspondency with New England which we hope to make very beneficial both to that colony and to ours."[103]

To the displaced governor Robert Hunt and "the company that are joined with you in church government," they promised "all freedom which you can desire." They hoped that Sherrard would assume a double role, that he would continue to preach to the entire island and not "yet so to impropriate yourself to your own congregation as that others should lose the benefit of your ministry." The company commended Sherrard's "moderation" in refusing to administer the sacraments of communion and baptism, "to avoid the discontent of others." They only wished they could supply someone else to baptize children for those who desired it. They promised to favor "those that join with you" as much as was fitting but asked Sherrard to take care not to offend "others that are not fully of your judgement and practice."[104]

Sherrard's decision to suspend the sacraments could be characterized as moderate because the alternative would have been administration to his gathered congregation alone, leaving out all who had not joined in church covenant with him. Such was the practice in New England's congregations. Ministers such as John Cotton had organized separate circles of the godly within their congregations even in the England of the 1610s and 1620s; those within this association had received communion in special ceremonies. In New England only those who participated in the covenant were welcomed to the monthly or bimonthly communion.[105]

Suspension of the sacraments became a common solution in the England of the 1640s and 1650s after the breakdown of ecclesiastical discipline. Ministers who did not wish to preside over a "promiscuous" sacrament, one offered to all comers regardless of their spiritual state, but who did not want to take the risk of open division considered abeyance the safest course. Some ministers did exclude those they con-

103. PIC to Butler, 7–39.
104. PIC to Hunt, 7–39; PIC to Sherrard, 7–39.
105. On Cotton see Holmes, *Seventeenth-Century Lincolnshire*, 95–6. On Cotton and other prospective New Englanders, see Foster, "English Puritanism and New England Institutions," in Hall, Murrin, and Tate, eds., *Saints and Revolutionaries*, 9–10, and *Long Argument*, 142–3. On translation to the New England situation, see Cohen, *God's Caress*, 160–1, and Hambrick-Stowe, *Practice of Piety*, 123–5.

sidered sinners. The returned New Englander Thomas Weld was accused of admitting only eight women and two men at Gateshead in the 1650s; those excluded numbered above a thousand.[106]

Against this background, the Providence Island Company could consider Sherrard's suspension of the sacraments a moderate policy, but many colonists chafed under it, including Governor Nathaniel Butler. Butler went to hear Sherrard preach twice each Sunday throughout most of the period covered by his diary. In the early months he either recorded his attendance without comment or remarked that the sermons were good. He was angry in February 1639 when Sherrard held a special thanksgiving for the rescue of a shipwrecked man after his silence on the deliverance of Captain Axe from the enemy, but overall his judgments were favorable.

In this early period, Butler attempted to solve the problem of the sacraments with his customary practicality. A second minister, Nicholas Leverton, had come to the island. Leverton, educated at Oxford, had gone to Barbados and thence to Tobago, intending to help found a settlement sponsored by the Earl of Warwick.[107] The reduced company, shipwrecked and suffering from Indian attacks, had left Tobago and made for Providence Island, the only land in English hands that the winds and currents would let them reach. Leverton was greeted there by those who wished to worship according to the Book of Common Prayer, and unbeknownst to the company in London, he began a ministry on the other side of the island. Butler met with Leverton on February 19, 1639, and asked him to administer the sacrament of communion on the following Sunday, to which Leverton agreed. Butler then traveled over on the Saturday to be ready and heard Leverton preach twice that Sunday.

This experiment was never repeated. Edmund Calamy wrote that Leverton had distinguished himself rather by his frivolity than by his seriousness at Oxford and had never really thought much about religious issues. "But now, being made very serious by the remarkable providences he had met with, and finding Mr. Sherwood [Sherrard] a pious person, he was disposed to hear his reasons for Nonconformity; which

---

106. Hirst, *Authority and Conflict*, 282, 324; Roger Howell, "Thomas Weld of Gateshead: The Return of a New England Puritan," *Archaeologia Aeliana* 4th ser., XLVIII (1970), 323, 328–9. Hugh Peter had earlier been as restrictive in his gathered congregation in Rotterdam; see Perry Miller, *Orthodoxy in Massachusetts, 1630–1650* (orig. pub. 1933; repr. New York, 1970), 112.

107. See Bennett, "Peter Hay, Proprietary Agent in Barbados," *Jamaican Historical Review* V (1965), 20–5, on attempts to settle Tobago from Barbados after Trinidad and Tobago were acquired by the Earl of Warwick in 1638.

induced him heartily to fall in with him in the same way."[108] Leverton and Sherrard were henceforth allies.

By spring 1639 criticisms of Sherrard's sermons began to creep into Butler's diary entries. On Easter Sunday, April 14, Butler went to church twice; Sherrard's second sermon, he wrote, was more a narration than a sermon. On May 5 Sherrard sent word that he was "so ill at ease, as not able to discharge his ministerial function."[109] Butler stayed home and prayed and read the Scriptures with his household, "but many of the people and most of the Council coming in were partaking with us." The following Sunday at the close of the afternoon service, after preaching "very well," Sherrard announced the "admission of a new Proselyte."[110]

At the same time, Butler had acted in ways calculated to offend his puritan colonists. He pressed Hope Sherrard for a catalogue of the books he held from the company. On April 13, Easter eve, he received two Spanish Dominican friars held prisoner on Providence Island who "came to me this Evening, to give me the Bueña Pasca, according to their custom." Next day he entertained the friars at dinner. At a time when the island's population was rent over the issue of worshipping with unregenerate Protestants, to receive the blessing of Papists must have seemed outrageous. There matters stood at the end of May when Butler embarked on a privateering voyage of several months' duration.

When Captain Butler returned in September 1639, the separation of the congregation had progressed. On September 22 Sherrard crossed over the line. He "made a short sermon but a long preamble touching his intention to administer the Sacrament of Supper to all those that would enter into his Covenant; and gave rules, rather than reasons, why he would exclude all others." In the event, Butler pointed out, he broke his own rules by admitting Captain Hunt, "who being of a church of Holland, was not (by their professed Tenets) to be received without leave of the church." On October 6 Butler stayed home from church because Sherrard had announced he would again serve communion but only to those who had entered into covenant with him, "the which I finding no ground to do, kept from the church of purpose to exclude myself."

108. Calamy, *Nonconformist's Memorial*, 2nd ed. rev. by S. Palmer (1777), 290–5; Matthews, *Calamy Revised*, 323–4.
109. Ministers in New England also agonized over the state of their own souls in connection with preaching; see Stout, *New England Soul*, 35.
110. Butler's Diary is B. L. Sloane MS 758. In March Sherrard had altered his principles sufficiently to baptize the child of "an especial favorite of his." Butler remarked that he had never before seen him do this.

From September on, Butler's comments on Sherrard's sermons were mostly negative. He often wrote that Sherrard had preached "Suo modo." On October 20 he "found him strangely possessed with a strain of [vile] [crossed out] uncharitable and dangerous suggestions out of the pulpit." He recorded with satisfaction that two of Sherrard's English servants ran away that day; two of his slaves had run away the previous Sunday. The sermons were increasingly expositions of controversial points. On November 24 Sherrard excused himself for giving expositions on two chapters, "but for my part; they seemed as strong to me, as any of his sermons." Butler began to go only once a Sunday and sometimes skipped altogether. On Christmas he "wished an invitement to go to church, but our ministers held it superstition to preach on Christmas day." On the following Sunday they had two "angry" sermons.

Early in January 1640, Governor Butler received a petition said to be on behalf of "all the Masters of the Families" and in the name of "the Inhabitants in General." The petition, whose presentation Butler had encouraged, complained of their deprivation of the sacrament and asked Butler to go to England to present their case to the company. Next day, "Mr. Sherrard made a very wild and spleenative sermon." In his letter notes, Butler described the minister as the instigator of resistance to him and to the company's orders in alliance with the "Old Councilors." He wrote Lord Brooke that his administration of justice was styled persecution from the pulpit, and that "if any thing be debated in the Council of the Island: the next sermon will have a glance at it; or a Jerk, or a censure."[111]

Captain Butler described Sherrard as falling ever more deeply into a kind of wild anger that rent even his own congregation. On February 9 Butler stayed home but heard that the minister "fell very foul upon one of his own flock; giving out furious and very unbeseeming words in respect of the time and place, though (perhaps) not, in respect of the person." Next Sunday Butler again stayed home, seeking to avoid "such malicious Invectives" that ruined the spirit of the day but reported "some of his flock Councilors were with me, about the taking up, of a challenge of Dispute which they were afraid to answer: as plainly appeared by the Lie, that he told out of the pulpit to that purpose, the very same afternoon." Butler, who was beginning his last week in Providence Island must have taken satisfaction in seeing members of the congregation turn to him for help.

At his departure on February 24, 1640, Nathaniel Butler left Providence Island under the temporary governorship of Captain Andrew

---

111. A jerk is a witty or sarcastic speech.

Carter, an avowed enemy of Sherrard's congregation. Within two months Carter had dispossessed and banished Robert Robins, sending him to hard labor on a privateering ship, in an irregular proceeding over the protests of the minister and his allies on the council.[112] Robins's account pictured the island as devoid of law, "the Land being daily up in arms." Far worse was to come.

At the end of May 1640, Providence Island was again attacked by Spanish forces; after furious and desperate fighting, the enemy was repelled. Halhead, Lane, Sherrard, and Leverton wrote a long letter home describing the fight and including an extensive list of the many divine providences, which showed that despite all that had happened, God still favored the colony. They closed with the hope that the adventurers, too, would renew their attention. In the course of the account, the writers told of Captain Carter's execution of Spanish prisoners who had been promised fair quarter, a report that filled company members with indignation.[113]

Edmund Calamy wrote of the ensuing events in his *Nonconformist's Memorial*. The colonists, pointing to the charter, claimed the right to appoint their own governor in the case of the incumbent's leaving the island. They appointed Richard Lane. "But the other privately arming some of the ruder sort, seized Lane and both the ministers, and sent them prisoners to England, with an information against them to Archbishop Laud, that they were disaffected to the liturgy and ceremonies of England." Laud was himself in custody when the four men (including Henry Halhead) arrived late in 1640, and the prisoners were welcomed by the Providence Island Company. The investors endorsed their view but expressed chagrin that the four leaders had not acquiesced rather than leave the island bereft of a minister.[114]

Nicholas Leverton attempted to return to Providence Island, but Hope Sherrard had had enough. He held a series of livings in England, where his relationships were apparently as turbulent as they had been in the Indies. He was placed as interim at Sandwich in Kent. He served the

---

112. See Chapter 9.
113. Halhead, Lane, Sherrard, and Leverton to the Providence Island Company, June 17, 1640, Finch Manuscripts, Leicestershire Record Office. The letter is excerpted in the Hist. Man. Com. Seventeenth *Report*, 51–8.
114. Calamy, *Nonconformist's Memorial*, 2nd ed. rev. by S. Palmer (1777), I, 292–3; PIC Ct. 1–4–41, 2–13–41, 3–25–41; PIC to Gov. and Coun. 3–29–41.
    Calamy wrote that Sherrard and Leverton were reunited many years later. Both had the mark of the Indies. Leverton was identified by an ostler at Sandwich who remarked, "you are somewhat like our minister; I believe you have lived in the hot countries as well as he." Sherrard, minister at Sandwich, and Leverton were then reunited "to their mutual joy." Ibid., 294.

garrison at Kenilworth in Warwickshire as chaplain in 1644 and 1645, after which he apparently returned to Sandwich. The parishioners of St. Clement's parish there petitioned the House of Lords in 1647, alleging that Sherrard had obtained the living through secret manipulation, "knowing himself (by reason of his Inabilities, in his public preaching, and of the ill affections, which the well affected and honest people of the Town do bear unto him) no way able to gain the consent of any Considerable part of the parish." The issue came before the Lords because the parishioners had been able to gain "the favor" of the Earl of Manchester, who promised to acquaint the Earl of Warwick "(who well knew many of the parishioners)" with the facts of the case. Shortly thereafter the Lords placed Sherrard in the parish of Melcombe in Dorsetshire.[115]

After the expulsion of the ministers from Providence Island, the little remnant of Sherrard's congregation, five in all according to John Winthrop, appealed to New England for aid against their persecution.[116] At the same time, company members, led by Lords Saye and Brooke, renewed their campaign to recruit colonists of the solid puritan sort, and this time their efforts focused on New England, where economic depression was making many doubt the providential status of the northern settlements. In the event, remigration to the Indies was forestalled by the fall of Providence Island to the Spanish.

The New England historian Edward Johnson was contemptuous after the fact of the would-be Caribbean migrants from Massachusetts, portraying them as weak-minded people seeking novelty and license: "[T]hey wanted a warmer country, and every Northwest wind that blew, they crept into some odd chimney-corner or other, to discourse of the diversity of Climates in the Southern parts, but chiefly of a thing

---

115. For Sherrard's career, see Petition of Henry Forstale, Mayor of Sandwich in Kent, and John Elgate, Churchwarden of St. Clement's Parish there, October 28, 1647, House of Lords Record Office; House of Lords *Journal*, X (1647/48), 32; Matthews, ed., *Walker Revised*, 216; Venn, *Alumni Cantabrigiensis*, part I, vol. 4, 63; William A. Shaw, *A History of the English Church during the Civil Wars and Under the Commonwealth, 1640–1660*, 2 vols. (London, 1900), II, 344, 347, 351; and Anne Laurence, *Parliamentary Army Chaplains, 1642–1651*, Royal Historical Society *Studies in History* 59 (London, 1990), 173.

Sherrard's eldest son John, born in Providence Island, entered Trinity College, Dublin, in September 1658 as a Scholar Commoner. He had been at school with "Mr. Cromlaham" in Dorchester. See George Dames Burtchaell and Thomas Ulick Sadleir, *Alumni Dublinienses*, new ed. (Dublin, 1635), 750. Samuel Cromleholme (Crumlum) revitalized Dorchester Grammar School as headmaster from 1651 to 1657 before returning to St. Paul's School as High Master; see J. M. Fletcher, "A Trio of Dorchester Worthies," *Proceedings of the Dorset Natural History and Antiquarian Field Club* XLVII (1926), 134–40.

116. Winthrop, *Journal*, ed. Hosmer, II, 33–5.

very sweet to the palate of the flesh, called liberty, which they supposed might be very easily attain'd, could they but once come into a place where all men were chosen to the office of a Magistrate, and all were preachers of the Word, and no hearers, then it would be all Summer and no Winter."[117]

This caricature was the epitaph of the Providence Island adventurers' dream of a society in which godly men and women could be free to seek the truth of God's revelation and by their efforts contribute to the great cumulative unveiling of the light that they hoped and believed was imminent. In their final letter to the governor and council, the adventurers wrote that Mr. Leverton was returning to be their minister. And they wrote, as they had so often, that attempts to get other ministers had foundered "by reason of discouragements entertained through the great differences that have fallen out in the Island." Hope remained, and they believed that their negotiations with another man of "moderation, piety, and abilities" might bear fruit, in which case he would go on the next ship in about six weeks.[118] By the time these words were written, the lords and gentlemen of the Providence Island Company were diverting their attention to the reconstruction of England's ecclesiastical and civil polity. Their hopes were to be dashed in this as they had been in their American isle.

117. J. Franklin Jameson, ed., *Johnson's Wonder-Working Providence, 1628–1651* ([1654] New York, 1867), 207–8.
118. PIC to Gov. and Coun., 3–29–41.

9

Governing Puritan Privateers: The Governorships of Robert Hunt and Nathaniel Butler

THE PROVIDENCE ISLAND EXPERIMENT began in a spirit of renewal in 1636 following the providential repulse of the first Spanish attack on the little colony and the company's receipt of letters of reprisal. Captain Robert Hunt, Lord Brooke's protégé and a godly man, was selected to replace Governor Philip Bell. Whereas Bell's experience was largely West Indian, Hunt had served with Protestant forces in the Netherlands and at the siege of La Rochelle. Careful plans were laid for the orderly handing over of power and the stifling of those elements that had proved so unruly. At the same time, company members took on the responsibility of creating a large new joint stock to supply the plantation.

Captain Hunt made his acceptance of the governorship contingent on his taking some godly company with him, particularly Mr. John Francis, Mr. Matthew Downes, and a Mr. Knight. Francis, a man "eminent in religion and versed in Arms," was designated commander of Trippett's Fort, now renamed Brooke Fort, and made responsible for training colonists on the north side of the island. He, Downes, and Mr. Frederick Johnson, who also went in 1636, were to be added to the council, of which Johnson was to be secretary. Knight was encouraged to emigrate by the personal testimony of former planters who attended the company meeting. Although Knight was "much commended" by Hunt, the investors, "being informed that he was naturally passionate and plyable" as well as inexperienced, declined to make him lieutenant of Fort Henry under Captain Rous. The entire council was to assemble to greet the new governor when he landed and to witness the publication of his commission. The company respited the oath of office because Captain Hunt had asked for some changes to make it closer to oaths used in England.[1]

---

1. PIC Gen. Ct., 2–15–36, 2–22–36, 2–29–36, 3–8–36, 3–9–36; PIC to Gov. and Coun. on reception of Hunt, 5–36, PIC to Gov. and Coun. by the *Blessing*, 5–36.

The revised oath was sent in a letter to the governor and council the following month. Acknowledging God's knowledge of the heart and the powerful vengeance he took on false swearers, officers were to swear to maintain the true religion, to "abhor" and oppose the "Authority and superstition" of Rome. They were also required to swear that the Providence Island Company were "the only true owners of this island." All officers swore to dedicate themselves to the company's rights and to the administration of "right and justice."[2]

Robert Hunt's bargain with the investors was not very different from Philip Bell's. His agreement promised him 100 acres to be attached to the office, and twenty servants. The colonists were to provide him two or three experienced servants to train his own inexperienced men, and they were directed to build a home for him sufficiently spacious for entertainment befitting his office and for the public business of the island. In the meantime, the investors suggested that the governor be billeted with Ensign Fitch. The new secretary and the clerks of the stores were to have as much land as they needed near the governor. Hunt's tenure was to be at the pleasure of the company. Should he leave office, he was to have fifty acres and fourteen of his servants; he would also be offered command of one of the best forts. If he chose to return to England, the company agreed to pay the passage of himself and his family.[3]

The company's key concern was for an orderly handing on of power. Secretary Johnson carried secret orders calling for government by the majority of the council if Captain Hunt were to die at sea. If the island were threatened, Captain Rous, if he was present, was to command until the danger was over. The new governor and council were commanded to treat Captain Bell with all courtesy and respect and to maintain him on the council. Steps were taken to make sure he did not attempt to organize a party in his interest to oppose Hunt's takeover.[4]

Privateering offered new opportunities to make the island colony a financial success, but every ship using its harbor as a base would increase the danger of another Spanish attack. Therefore, the adventurers included a hefty contingent of new military specialists in their 1636 ships. Company members interviewed a wide variety of gunners, sergeants, and lieutenants, offering them inducements to emigrate and servants to free them for greater attention to training the settlers and

2. PIC to Gov. and Coun. by the *Happie Return*, 6–36.
3. PIC Agreement with Hunt, 3–1–36, Commission to Hunt sent in the *Blessing*, PIC to Gov. and Coun. in the *Blessing*, 5–36.
4. PIC Gen. Ct., 3–2–36; PIC to Gov. and Coun. by the *Blessing*, 5–36, Instr. to Hunt, 5–36, Secret Instr. to Johnson, 5–36.

bolstering the island's preparedness. They also shipped ammunition and small cannon, and Governor Hunt was directed to watch carefully for any embezzlement of the ammunition. The colonists need not fear as the island became a privateering base.[5]

The adventurers promised the speedy supply of 500 to 600 men, which would still the complaints of planters already in the island. They set right a few specific cases of men who had been erroneously placed in servitude or who had been detained in the settlement. Samuel Rishworth was restored to the council until the company had time to investigate charges against him. They promised to arrange for the shipment of further magazines of supplies but also commanded Governor Hunt to make sure that the stores were handed out fairly and with due regard for the debts owed the investors. Supplies could not be sent unless the colonists were willing to deal honestly with the company, saving their commodities for company ships and satisfying their debts before they attempted to leave. The governor was also to view the plantations regularly, dispossessing planters who were negligent.[6]

Unfortunately, Robert Hunt was a dismal failure as governor of Providence Island. He was sent as a godly man, but his religious priorities caused him to become allied too strongly with Hope Sherrard's congregation, and his policies served to increase factionalism within the leadership. He entertained all complaints against the now-defenseless Philip Bell, allowing some deponents to testify without oath, which the company absolutely forbade. The adventurers wrote that the persecution of Bell smacked of the use of public justice for private ends and warned Hunt that they considered the council's censure of Bell to be a censure of the company.[7] At Hunt's departure from England, the company had acknowledged the many differences already seething in Providence Island, disputes they had not had time to consider, as well as "foul aspersions" against some colonists. Robert Hunt was not the man to control vice and bring factions together, a truth investors were soon forced to confront.[8]

In 1637 the stunned adventurers received the colonists' "mutinous"

5. PIC Gen. Ct., 2–18–36, 2–29–36, 3–2–36; Ctee., 3–1–36, 3–11–36, 3–14–36; PIC to Gov. and Coun. by the *Blessing*, 5–36, and by the *Happie Return*, 6–36; PIC Agreements with Edward Hudson, John Riche, Francis Lofthouse, John Adcock, and Edward Staunton, 3–9–36.
6. PIC to Gov. and Coun. by the *Blessing*, 5–36, by the *Happie Return*, 6–36, Instr. to Hunt, 5–36.
7. PIC Gen. Ct., 6–22–37; PIC to Gov. and Coun. by the *Mary Hope*, 3–37. The company was also indignant over proceedings against Captain Rous that resulted in his removal from the council, which were so incompletely reported that they could not follow them; PIC to Gov. and Coun. by the *Mary Hope*, 3–37.
8. PIC, Gen. Ct., 3–2–36, Instr. to Hunt, 5–36.

petition, a document Samuel Rishworth's return to England was meant to amplify. The hint of blackmail involved in rumors that the colonists had set a date by which they would desert Providence Island if the investors did not meet their demands further soured company dispositions. Even deeper controversy was implied by the revelation of two versions of the petition, one transmitted by the governor and council and the other by Captain Bell. Investors inferred that the discrepancy stemmed from Governor Hunt's favoring of the petitioners, which investors considered "fit to be reprehended." They wanted to interview Captain Rous, leader of the party opposing the petition, as well as Rishworth. The investors remarked sarcastically that they were surprised nothing had been transmitted to them of the events leading to the mutiny and petition because those involved had had plenty of time to write to their particular friends all about it.

Company instructions outlined a course for Captain William Rudyerd, returning as commander of the *Mary Hope*, should he arrive to find the island in a state of mutiny. The investors warned colonists that they could never return to England without facing prosecution if they should desert a venture in which the royal government had taken a strong interest.[9]

Not only had Hunt proven to be a weak reed, but other hand-picked men failed to achieve investors' expectations. Matthew Downes, charged with many instances of "bad carriage," was ordered from the council. He had charged enormous and unjustified bills on company members, £50 on Lord Brooke and £70 on Mr. Woodcock, as well as a £50 debt owed to Captain Rous, and the company ordered sale of his assets to satisfy his debts.[10] Captain Francis, soon to join the core of the opposition to Nathaniel Butler, was accused of malfeasance in the operation of the store; pending investigation the company decided to keep him in his post, while assuring him that they would not "be easily led into an evil opinion of any man so well disposed as we hope he is."[11]

Richard Lane, whose return caused a bitter fight among company members, also disappointed them. Not only had he sold the servants sent him by the company rather than using them in profitable enterprises,

9. PIC Ctee., 2–11–37, 6–14–37, 6–24–37, 6–26–37; Gen. Ct., 6–22–37; PIC to Gov. and Coun. by the *Mary Hope*, 3–37, Instr. to Rudyerd for the *Mary Hope*, 1–37. Clerk Thomas Jenkes, whom Samuel Rishworth accused of malfeasance in keeping the stores' books, wrote William Jessop privately that he had not been involved in the petition; see Jessop to Jenkes, Summer, 1637, B. L., Add. MS 10615; PIC Ctee., 6–26–37.
10. PIC to Gov. and Coun. by the *Mary Hope*, 3–37. See the order to investigate the imprisonment of Downes, PIC, Instructions, Commission for Grievances, 7–38.
11. PIC to Gov. Butler by the *Mary*, 7–39.

but he refused to render a "tolerable account" for the large and valuable magazine entrusted to him by Lord Brooke. In 1638 a special commission, consisting of the new governor Nathaniel Butler, Henry Halhead, Samuel Rishworth, and Elisha Gladman, was set up to investigate. The commissioners were authorized to seize all Lane's assets to pay his debt to Lord Brooke.[12]

Everything led to the conclusion that a new, firmer, and more experienced hand was needed at the helm. Although the company letter of March 1637, punning on the island's name, said that Hunt had been called to the governorship by Providence itself, he was out in 1638. In the end the investors concluded that his errors had stemmed from "want of experience" rather than any willingness to offend.[13]

Investors now believed they had found the ideal governor in Captain Nathaniel Butler, sixty-one years old, a close associate of the Earl of Warwick, and an experienced soldier and colonial governor.[14] Butler, who commanded ships in expeditions to Cadiz, the Isle of Rhé, and La Rochelle during the 1620s, had preceded Philip Bell as governor of Bermuda (1619–22) and had written a classic history of the island. Butler's book formed the basis of Captain John Smith's treatment of Bermuda in his *Generall Historie of Virginia, New England, and the Summer Isles.* Butler had arrived to find the Bermuda colonists exercised about the same issues of religious controversy, public works obligations, and divided hopes and responsibilities that disturbed Providence Island. By his own account, he managed to bring peace to a badly divided settler population and turned them to productive work, regulating their tobacco so that only worthy leaves were sent home. The forts, which were like "scarecrows" when he arrived, were rebuilt; in procuring settlers' cooperation he was sensitive to their seasonal crop needs.[15]

12. PIC to Gov. and Coun. by the *Swallow* and *Spy*, 7–38; Commission for Lane's Acct., 4–16–38. See PIC to Gov. Butler by the *Mary*, 7–39, where the company pleads lack of time to consider Mr. Lane's letter on Lord Brooke's account.
13. PIC Ctee., 6–24–37; PIC to Hunt by the *Mary Hope*, 3–37, and by the *Mary*, 6/7–39.
14. Butler's experience showed in his bargaining with the Providence Island Company. He told Lord Brooke that he thought twenty servants, the compensation accepted by Captains Bell and Hunt, would "produce small profit" and therefore wanted a salary paid in London. The investors asked Brooke to bargain for the lowest possible salary and in any case not to exceed £100. Lord Brooke reported back that Butler had settled for £60 to be paid to his wife in London and £20 for his journey, PIC Ctee., 3–26–38.
15. On the life of Nathaniel Butler, see W. G. Perrin, *Boteler's Dialogues* (London, 1929), vii–xxix. On Butler's governorship in Bermuda, see Craven, *Introduction to the History of Bermuda*, 20–40, 131–40; Wilkinson, *Adventurers of Bermuda*, 2nd ed., 130–45; Butler, *History of the Bermudaes*, ed. LeFroy; and Smith, *General Historie*, in Barbour, ed., *Complete Works of Captain John Smith*, II, 375–89.

Nathaniel Butler was no "yes man." Company members knew they were attracting a man with strong convictions and the assurance to carry out his own agenda. Shortly after his arrival in Bermuda, he had informed the Bermuda Company through his patron Sir Nathaniel Rich that he needed a free hand, suggesting that the company should tear up all its own orders for three years past and make no new ones for the next three years until he had sufficient experience to see what should be done. He stressed that receipt of constant and contradictory orders from England only frustrated good order because nothing but experience on the ground would allow anyone to understand what was needed. He pointed out to Sir Nathaniel the perpetual colonial problem of settlers who defied the government in the island and relied on their contacts at home to protect them from discipline. Butler wrote that after only two months in the colony, taunting planters told him they had already written home that "I am become a Sabbath-breaker, a rioter, a ravisher of other mens wives, an Extortioner, a Tyrant, a what not!" Only a company that sent out men in whom it had faith to govern and who then trusted those men and backed them up deserved to succeed. Butler's rendition was a classic of the problems of company-sponsored colonies.[16]

Like Captain John Smith, Nathaniel Butler both served in the colonies and offered extensive analyses of their problems and prospects. Butler left Bermuda in 1622 and spent several months in Virginia, whose English colony had recently been shattered by the great Powhatan attack of March 1622. When he returned to England in 1623, he offered "The Unmasked face of our Colony in Virginia as it was in the Winter of the yeare 1622," a devastating indictment of the colony's poor condition, as part of the campaign to discredit the Virginia Company administration.[17] Butler carried on his habit of writing about his experiences. His diary of Providence Island offers the only picture of daily life in the colony; like his history of Bermuda, it illustrates the difficulties of establishing a new English society in a strange environment and separated by thousands of miles of water from ultimate authority in England.[18]

16. Butler to Sir Nathaniel Rich, October 23, 1620, in Ives, ed., *Letters from Bermuda*, 188–98; see also Butler to the Somers Islands Company, in his *History of the Bermudaes*, ed. LeFroy, 215–24. The *Oxford English Dictionary* defines "rioter" as "one who leads a disorderly or licentious life, or who indulges in debauchery."
17. Butler's "Unmasked Face" is printed in Kingsbury, ed., *Records of the Virginia Company* II, 374–7. On the struggle between the Rich family and Edwin Sandys and his associates over the Virginia Company, see Craven, *Dissolution of the Virginia Company*. Nathaniel Butler, a client of the Riches, was a member of the council of the Virginia Company in London.
18. Butler's diary was kept in the spare pages of the notebook in which he was writing his book on seamanship, B. L., Sloane MS 758. The book on seamanship is published as *Boteler's Dialogues*, ed. W. G. Perrin by the Navy Records Society.

Nathaniel Butler was a sophisticated man with wide experience of the European continent. In his government of Providence Island, he emulated as far as possible the style of a Renaissance princely court. While he was governor of Bermuda, Butler had built a state house for the conduct of public business, and Captain John Smith included an engraving of it in his account of Bermuda. The drawing shows not the crude shed expected in a frontier outpost but a small Venetian palace, elegant in its simplicity. Butler wrote that he built the statehouse "after the fashion which he had seen in other countries in parallel with this," with a flat roof, and thick stone walls for coolness and strength against hurricanes "as most proper for the place and climate" in hopes others would emulate him.[19]

The Bermuda statehouse is a key to the assumptions and personality of Nathaniel Butler. His continental experience and the use he made of it put him in the cultural vanguard at a time when Inigo Jones was introducing the Italianate style of architecture into England. Moreover, the Renaissance "mirror for princes" literature argued that liberality and magnificence were key attributes in a ruler and that creating noble buildings exemplified these traits.[20] Butler knew that style mattered, and he was determined to live in a manner calculated to elicit obedience and admiration.

On Providence Island Governor Butler lived in the manner of a grandee. He typically spent his mornings hearing disputes between colonists, of which there was apparently a never-ending supply, or having himself rowed in his "gundeloe" to view the fortifications or the militia exercises. He always dined in company, usually at his own house, and on occasion he entertained as many as 100 of his colonists. When his duties permitted and there was a lull in the "wonted paroxysms" of public business, he wrote his book on seamanship. To the extent possible, he lived as the Renaissance theorists recommended.

Lewis Hughes, the puritan minister on Bermuda, described Butler as a model governor: "In his time the Kings Laws were established in the Islands, and the Assizes kept orderly as they are in England. Before his

19. Butler, *History of the Bermudaes*, ed. LeFroy, 231–32. In this section he also described the building or rebuilding of the forts, powderhouses, and gun carriages that had been so badly neglected before him. During Butler's governorship on Providence Island, the adventurers wrote that they would like to have a "convenient house" built for council meetings, but "cannot as yet send tile and bricks to that purpose," PIC to Gov. and Coun. by the *Swallow* and *Spy*, 7–38.
20. Skinner, *Foundations of Modern Political Thought*, I, 127. One argument Providence Island Company members advanced against the bishops was that because they were not born to nobility they could never exhibit the liberality their positions called for.
    On Inigo Jones and the "sensational" effect of his introduction of Italianate architecture, see John Summerson, *Georgian London*, 3rd ed. (Cambridge, MA, 1978), 27–9: "Taste in architecture reached London about 1615."

time, ever since Capt. Mores time, the Governors will went for law, and some of the Kings Subjects were hanged contrary to the Kings law, and some condemned and censured to perpetual slavery."[21] Because Butler had won the admiration of Hughes and had settled Bermuda's religious controversies, the investors had reason to hope he could perform the same miracle in Providence Island with Hope Sherrard and the disgruntled colonists.

Butler was not without critics in Bermuda, however, and the main source of tension was the issue of privateering. Captain Butler had long been associated with the Earl of Warwick in the latter's privateering.[22] In Providence Island much of Captain Butler's time as governor and admiral was taken up with the needs of the privateers and preparations for an attack on the island that their activities seemed bound to attract. His diary shows him welcoming ships and their officers regularly; while Butler was in residence, three or four ships came in almost every month, and as many were sent out. Some were ships from England, some belonged to Providence Island men, and many were Dutch. Many outgoing small ships were commissioned to go to the Moskito Coast to fish or turtle, or to cut wood on one of the islands, but often these vessels, although not labeled men of war, would return with a prize in tow. Each returned ship occasioned days of activity in judging prizes and settling disputes, and each of these incoming vessels when first sighted had occasioned an alarm that kept the colonists in turmoil. When privateers were in port, Butler spent his time with their captains, discussing the state of the Caribbean and dealing with their cargoes and provisioning needs.

The letters and instructions sent with Captain Butler demonstrated the investors' awareness of how much their venture had changed its character. In announcing the change of governor, again accompanied by a revision of the oath of office, the company praised Butler's "very good parts and experience, being an ancient soldier at sea and land" and remarked that the island's defense now particularly required "a man of ability in regard of the danger from the Spaniard." Early in 1638 the

---

21. Lewis Hughes, "To the right honourable, the lords and others of his majesties most honourable privie councell," 1625(?), B. L., Add. MS 12496, photostat #219, Massachusetts Historical Society, Americana series, 1928.

22. The Somers Islands Company wrote Governor Butler of calls from Bermuda to defy the Spanish antichrist, that they were "the common objections of our modern thieves when they mean to rob the Spaniard." See Butler, *History of the Bermudaes*, ed. LeFroy, 212–14 for this letter and Butler's professed confusion over its contents. See the proposal for privateering in large fleets drawn up by Butler for Warwick in 1626; B. L., Add. MS 41616, ff. 29v–35v. For the larger context, see Craven, *Dissolution of the Virginia Company*, 254–5.

company had taken note of "great preparations in Spain for the West Indies" which led them to expect an attack on Providence Island that year. Captain Hunt was to be offered command of Black Rock Fort in place of Captain Elfrith, who was now invited to come home. Captain Axe, the new vice admiral, had made Elfrith's removal a condition of his return to Providence Island. Captain William Woodcock was returned to the island as lieutenant governor. The commissions of all three men made clear the company's expectation that they would spend time away from the island on privateering expeditions. When present on the Island, Butler was to oversee the fortifications and military training as his "principal care." Presumably New England's Captain Underhill, had he agreed to emigrate, would have had prime responsibility in readying the island for defense.[23] To mollify the planters, the adventurers informed them that when the island was sufficiently prepared for attack, they would be allowed to send out privateering ships from whose gains the company would take 20 percent, and the admiral and vice admiral 2.[24]

In sending Nathaniel Butler, the Providence Island Company restructured the island's government. The council was revitalized by the return of Samuel Rishworth who, the investors wrote, had "acknowledged before us his offence about the petition," and had promised to argue against it back in the island. His son Samuel was now to be clerk of the council. New clerks of the stores were going out, John Peck and Elisha Gladman, in addition to Mr. Woolsey, with strict instructions to see that colonists honored their obligations and paid fairly for goods sent from England. Gladman was also added to the council.[25]

The council's role and authority were drastically undercut by the creation of a council of war, which was to consist of Captains Butler, Robert Hunt, Samuel Axe, and Andrew Carter. In addition to his roles as councilor and pricer of store goods, Elisha Gladman was to have charge of all maritime and military supplies, which he was to give out under the direction of the council of war. Now all decisions concerning public works and the colonists' militia obligations were removed from the council and placed under the captains on the council of war. In so doing, the Providence Island Company deviated from the example of all successful English colonies, where success was accompanied by lodging

23. PIC to Gov. and Coun. by the *Expedition*, 4–23–38; PIC, Commission to Captain Axe, 7–38, and agreement with Captain Woodcock, 6/7–38; PIC Ctee., 1–31–38, 3–24–38, and 3–26–38; PIC, Instructions to Butler, 4–23–38.
24. PIC to Gov. and Coun. by the *Expedition*, 4–23–38; PIC Instructions to Butler, 4–23–38, and to Council of War, 7–38.
25. PIC Ctee., 4–18–38; PIC, Agreement with John Peck, 6/7–38; PIC to Gov. and Coun. by the *Expedition*, 4–23–38.

such issues firmly under civilian control. In the threatening world of the western Caribbean, such amateurism was not seen as possible.[26]

The council of war was authorized to levy obligations for the construction of a powderhouse, and the company slaves were to be given over to the captains' direction. Even new servants sent from England could be set to labor on the public works for a period before they were distributed among their new masters. The council of war was also to decide on the distribution of military officers among the forts. They were to recycle ships taken as prizes back into privateering, constantly enlarging the fleet, and the council of war was to oversee the certification and division of prize cargoes. Captain Axe, who was on both councils, was not required to attend either if other matters seemed more important to him.[27]

In addition to the two councils, the Providence Island Company also set up a special commission composed of Governor Butler, Captain Axe, and Mr. Gladman to hear the colonists' accumulated grievances and to attempt to wipe the slate clean. This commission's instructions included a great many specific complaints from individuals, but most fell into one of several large categories. Colonists had complained about food shortages; they also complained, as they had throughout the colony's life, about the availability and distribution of store goods from England and about the company's standard markup of 25 percent. As before, settlers asked for more servants, and many complained that they had been forced to remain on the island although they should have been allowed to leave.

Many of these complaints could be dealt with from London or relatively easily by the new commissioners. Some, such as the complaints of scarcity of provisions, were explained by investors as the result of "riotous feasting" by some families, and lack of industry in others. Saying that they never intended the island to be a prison, the adventurers authorized Governor Butler to use his own discretion in allowing discontented settlers to leave.[28] Other complaints, such as those about the

26. Company members took the advice of Mr. John Francis on the construction of an armory but did not put him on the Council of War; PIC to Gov. and Coun. by the *Swallow* and *Spy*, 7–38.

27. PIC to Gov. and Coun. by the *Swallow* and *Spy*, 7–38; Instructions to Butler, 4–23–38; Commission and Instructions to Coun. of War, 7–38; Agreement with Capt. Axe, 7–38.

28. PIC to Gov. and Coun. by the *Expedition*, 4–23–38; and by the *Swallow* and *Spy*, 7–38; PIC to Butler by the *Swallow*, 7–3–38; Instructions for Commission for Grievances, 7–38. In their April 1638 letter the investors wrote that they had received testimony in London from an experienced man, John Briggam (or Brigham), who offered to raise food for 200 people by the labor of twenty; see also PIC Ctee.,

supply of magazines, were blamed on the planters' refusal to meet their obligations to pay for what they took from the stores.

Underlying many of the complaints, however, was the hint of something far more sinister and disturbing: actual malfeasance on the part of councilors, their acts "savoring of spleen or partiality." Settlers had been victimized in various ways. Some were punished for violating company instructions of which they had never been informed. According to information received, the council was charging planters 5 percent of the proceeds if they sold their plantations. Some officers had enlarged their own plantations beyond the intended fifty acres at the expense of other settlers. Councilors took the best of the store goods sent from England, so the poorer planters were forced to buy elsewhere at higher price.

Councilors also defrauded the company. Investors sent servants to officers, "that they may live comfortably and suitably to those several trusts wherein they are employed." Instead, councilors sold their servants and used the company slaves on their private pursuits. They had favored their friends by the creation of many officers, creating a burden on the company, but had excluded other men from being jurors. The company had reason to believe that a great many commodities had been paid in for the public works, yet somehow the costs remained unsatisfied. This was linked in investors' minds to the mishandling of the magazines and officers' failure to account properly for the goods sent. The investors specifically accused Mr. Jenkes of having engineered a fraudulent judgment on Mr. Downes's assets in an attempt to deprive company members of money Downes owed them.[29]

So badly had the government deteriorated and factionalization progressed, according to reports, that the Providence Island Company saw no hope except in sending new officers who were unrelated to any faction and were experienced in military and colonial affairs to try to reestablish order and harmony. Their strenuous attempts to recruit Ezekiel Rogers and Charles Chauncy show that the investors had by no means given up on their mission to create a godly community on Providence Island. Attempts to foster new commodities continued apace, and attempts to lure ministers of stature were renewed. As a token of

3–26–38. On February 6, 1640, Butler attended a "great feast, made by all the Welshmen in the Island." B. L., Sloane MS 758.
29. PIC to Gov. and Coun. by the *Expedition*, 4–23–38; and by the *Swallow* and *Spy*, 7–38; PIC to Butler by the *Swallow*, 7–3–38; PIC Instructions to Commission for Grievances, 7–38. In the July 1638 letter to the governor and council, the company specified that officers' salaries and public works were to be paid for by a tax of twenty pounds of tobacco per head for servants and forty pounds for slaves. Magazines from England were *not* to be used in this way.

future success, some free planters emigrated with Butler, including a small group of skilled men and their families who were diverted from New England. The essential problem remained: how to solve the venture's economic problems through Caribbean ventures without perverting the colony's religious and social mission.

According to reports, Nathaniel Butler had come into a Bermuda run by a tyrannical and exploitative government, producing poor quality tobacco, and rent by religious conflict, and three years later he had left a well-fortified and productive settlement that had a fair degree of harmony. What he had accomplished in Bermuda at the end of the 1610s could be replicated in Providence Island at the end of the 1630s.

Governor Butler began as the company expected. From his arrival in early February 1639 and throughout his governorship, he held a grand council meeting early in each month, a meeting often followed by dinner with the councilors. He apparently succeeded in conveying a sense of purpose to the planters. In late March 1639 he met with the council and the masters of the families to urge faster progress on the fortifications, which everyone agreed to, whereupon Butler promised they could look forward to a relaxation of the work in six weeks. In many months, however, he met far more frequently with the council of war, particularly as he planned his own privateering voyage that began at the end of May 1639. When he announced his intention, following as he said the company's instructions, to "visit and view the Maine about Cape Gracias a Dios," as well as "for a design in the Bay of Honduras," most of the people were "well satisfied; only some of the old counsellors would need be of another mind." Nonetheless, the entire council came aboard his ship to wish him farewell.[30]

Butler's privateering voyage was frustrating and fruitless. His fleet stopped briefly on the Moskito Coast, where they met a Providence crew sent out on a turtling expedition and were informed that Captain William Jackson, a privateer financed by London merchant Maurice Thompson under a commission issued by the Providence Island Company, had recently captured a slave ship at the Honduras port of Trujillo. The town's citizens had paid Jackson handsomely for the ship's return, giving him, according to Butler, "eight thousand weight of Indigo, two thousand pieces of Eight, and two chains of Gold." Butler's own expedition proceeded to Trujillo, which they captured easily "but found it most miserably poor and utterly empty ... having all of them run away one way and conveyed their goods out another way." Butler prevented his disgruntled men from burning the town. All they captured

30. Butler Diary, B. L., Sloane MS 758, 3–28–39; 5–21–39; 5–30–39.

was one frigate, and in exchange for the sail belonging to that ship, Butler gave the town's representatives "a worser boat from us."[31]

Butler's expedition, minus two ships found unfit for the voyage, left the coast of Honduras and made for Cape San Antonio at the western tip of Cuba. Then began a series of miscalculations that robbed them of any hopes of success and almost brought the crew to dehydration and starvation. Captain Nicholas Roope, brother-in-law of the Reverend Arthur Rous and commander of the *Warwick* in which Butler sailed, died two weeks into the voyage. His successor was Lieutenant James Riskinner, brother or son of Captain Nicholas Riskinner (or Reiskimmer), who had died shortly after arriving to take up the governorship of Association Island under the Providence Island Company in 1635. By Captain Butler's account, Riskinner was utterly ignorant of the Caribbean or good sailing techniques and completely under the control of his two Mates.

This trio, whose orders Butler was powerless to countermand, set out on a tragicomic "mad course," involving wild misidentifications of their locations and the islands they sighted, that took the expedition fruitlessly around the western Caribbean as their supplies ran dangerously low. Only once in two months did they actually make landfall "according to expectation."

When their calculations were consistently proven wrong, the master and mates first blamed the ship, which they said was foul and therefore did not go well, and then they began to suspect something far more sinister. Butler's rendition of their litany of excuses gives modern readers some insight into how distasteful the presence of the mariners and the mental universe they represented must have been to the puritan colonists. In their "arrogant Ignorance" these "Heathens in the Roundhouse" claimed that only witchcraft could have thrown off their calculations so completely and caused them to mistake their locations. When for the third time the company sighted a sail that then disappeared when they

---

31. Butler Diary, B. L., Sloane MS 758, 5–31–39; 6–6–39 to 6–20–39. Captain Jackson took his cargo to New England, where John Winthrop recorded that he sold sugar and indigo for £1,400, with which he bought supplies for renewed privateering, *Journal*, ed. Hosmer, I, 309–10.

    Persistent rumors dogged Butler, alleging that Trujillo had compounded with him for 16,000 pieces of eight; the Providence Island Company examined him on this issue when he returned to England. See PIC Gen. Ct., 5–27–40. Modern sources continued this rumor. A. P. Newton's *Colonising Activities*, 257, asserts that Butler acquired 16,000 pieces of eight in gold and indigo as a result of capturing Trujillo, and W. G. Perrin in his introduction to *Boteler's Dialogues*, xviii, says he exacted a ransom of 16,000 pieces of eight. All apparently confused Jackson's success with Butler's disappointment.

tried to approach the ship, "the superstitious seamen began to talk of conjuring, and ill presages."

Butler's experience is revelatory, not only of the superstitious cast of the mariners' minds but also of the woeful state of ignorance in English seamanship despite the knowledge gained in the Elizabethan sea war against Spain. Butler was humiliated when they encountered a Dutch ship in Jamaica. The Providence Island party was desperate for fresh water, and the Dutch told them where it could be had conveniently near at hand. Had they not met the Dutch ship, the English "might have missed of it we having no one man amongst us, that knew where to look for it nor scarce how." Again and again the English company's ignorance of Caribbean locations was revealed, and Butler found that his map had even mislocated Jamaica. In a period when life was so precarious, English privateers could not rely on the knowledge of just one man such as Captain Roope.[32]

Nathaniel Butler did attempt in his voyage to lay the groundwork for future plans of development. He wrote a brief appraisal of Cape Gracias a Dios as a site for a plantation and assiduously fostered good relations with the Indians along the Moskito Coast, emphasizing the persistent belief that these natives hated the Spanish and loved the English. He allowed several Indians to join his ships at the Cape; the Indians he met there were "very loving people; but the poorest Indians that ever I saw." Others from the Moskito Coast also accompanied him. In the 1670s Alexander Exquemelin wrote of the Cape natives: "These Indians are a great asset to the rovers, as they are very good harpoonists, extremely skilful in spearing turtles, manatees and fish. In fact, an Indian is capable of keeping a whole ship's company of 100 men supplied with food, when he is in a place where there's something to catch." The hospitality of these Indians made the coast a place of refuge for English mariners from the later sixteenth century.[33]

The Providence Island Company had already begun an outpost in the Bay of Honduras with their grant to William Claiborne for Ruatán. Butler also made contact with Indians of Guanaho (or Guanaco) Island,

32. Butler Diary, June–September 1639, quotes from 7–24, 7–29, 8–3, 8–9, 8–11, 8–14. Captain Riskinner, Butler later discovered, had cost the company the capture of rich prizes through cowardice, ibid., 10–15–39. Even as tensions increased between the Spanish enemy and the English colonists, the company was forced to continue to counsel its captains to rely on captured Spanish pilots; see PIC Instr. to Axe for the *Swallow*, 7–38; Instruct. to Dell for the *Advantage*, 7–39; and Ct., 6–19–40.

33. Butler Diary, B. L., Sloane MS 758, 6–2&3–39, 8–25–39; A. O. Exquemelin, *The Buccaneers of America* (1678), trans. Alexis Brown, intro. Jack Beeching (Harmondsworth, 1969), 220. Exquemelin described the life of the Cape Indians in his chap. 8, 219–26.

seven leagues from Ruatán off the coast near Trujillo, who were "subjects or rather slaves to the Spaniards of Truxilla" and, he said, loved them accordingly. After Butler's return to Providence Island, Indians of Guanaho sent letters with Captain Morgan asking, according to Butler, "to be brought off from thence from the cruelty of the Spaniards: and to be placed either at the Cape or in any of our other Islands; and to pay for their own transportation, or to become Tributaries to the Honorable Company where they are provided that they may be defended from the Spaniards." Butler laid their request before the council of war.[34]

As prospects for a wider English role in the western Caribbean began to seem better, conditions in Providence Island became more tense; the two processes were related. As soon as he returned to the colony in mid-September 1639, Butler learned that the *Robert*, one of the two unfit ships eliminated from his little fleet, had been captured and its crew imprisoned in Spain. He also learned that the Spanish governor of Cartagena was campaigning to get a strong force sent out to attack the English pirates' nest. The commander of the 1639 treasure fleet had refused his pleas, but it was clear that the drive would not end there. The planters were justifiably alarmed by the consequences they would suffer as privateering prospered.[35]

Butler found that conditions on the island had deteriorated markedly during his absence. In July 1639 the adventurers had sent letters in Maurice Thompson's ship *Mary* with instructions telling the planters that they were "weary" of their great expenditures without return and so would send no more magazines or servants. Thompson had been persuaded to send a magazine with the most needed supplies, and the colonists were authorized to pursue free trade with all comers. They were again urged to plant "great store" of provisions so that many ships could be supplied.

Company members had hurriedly pulled together letters of instruction in the summer of 1639 because they believed that good silver ore had been discovered within the area of their patent. Such hopes had existed since 1638 when a Mr. Donington came to the company with news that he had tested ores from Providence Island and had found them promising. In response the investors decided to enlarge their investments and to send 150 men in July 1638 shortly after the ship that had carried Nathaniel Butler. The *Swallow* and *Spy* that carried commissions for the council of war and the commission for grievances also brought

34. Diary, 6–9 and 10–39, 10–15–39, 11–8–39.
35. Governor Butler had also heard complaints of Captain Axe's activities in Cuba, Diary, 5–2–39.

instructions to Captains Butler, Hunt, and Axe about the search for ore, a topic barely mentioned in the company's general letter to the governor and council.[36]

The 1638 instructions about ore were concerned above all with secrecy. "Finers" were sent with the instructions; they were to return with the ore as soon as their work was done. They were to be directed to look for ore in all likely places in the island, particularly "in a place where now or lately stood Michael Archer's kitchen." The tests, three on each sample, were to be conducted in the presence of at least two of the captains, but no other person was to be admitted unless his labor was absolutely necessary. Everyone involved was to be bound by an oath of secrecy. Once the tested ore, carefully packaged and labeled, was dispatched to England, no one was to be allowed to do any digging or refining until word was received from the company. Meanwhile, all colonists could rest assured that they would share in the general prosperity when it came.[37]

In 1639 the instructions sent in the *Mary* were fuller and more expansive. Genuine silver (or gold) ore had been discovered in the Bay of Darien on a neck of land 150 leagues from Providence that became an island at high tide, and the company had entered into partnership with Maurice Thompson for development of the mine. Mr. Samuel Border had revealed the ore's existence to the investors; he and Captain John Brent discovered the mine, which measured twelve miles long and two miles wide. The company proceeded cautiously. Knowledgeable men in England said that the ore could be worth as much as £60 a ton, but they had decided to move slowly "because we will not make ourselves subject of men's scorn and derision as heretofore some of our countrymen have done who sent out many ships upon small trial and brought home nothing but dirt."

Despite their anger that company employees, including Governor Butler, believing the mine was outside the company's patent, had thought of developing it themselves, the investors entrusted the management of it to Captains Butler, Axe, and Brent, and to Lewis Morris and Mr. Samuel Border. John Butler was sent from England; along with Maurice Thompson's agent, he was to supervise the digging. As in 1638, the ore was not mentioned in the company's general letter to the governor and council, and secrecy was enjoined. Ore was to be brought to Providence Island as long as supplies held out, but the last cargo was to be sent directly home. If it proved good, they were to dispatch a ship to New

36. PIC Gen. Ct., 3–3–38; 3–10–38; 3–16–38; 3–20–38.
37. PIC, Instructions on the Search for Ore, 7–38. "Finers" refers to refiners.

England, where vessels could be hired to transport ore back to England. In the Indies, investors were dependent on their agents who were frustratingly slippery. They believed reports that Nathaniel Marston, returned to the island with the new project of 1638, had embezzled a "wedge of gold" and some gold dust from Captain Axe's ship; they also thought that he had informed some Dutch mariners of the location of their mine. Furthermore, they had been informed that Captain Axe had applied for a ship and privateering commission in Holland, although the company preferred to believe that Axe's application was only in case Providence Island failed completely. In their instructions to Captains Butler, Axe, and Carter, the adventurers promised they would not be "strait and scant handed to you." Anyone else trying to exploit the mine was to be arrested.[38]

In the event, none of the company's 1639 plans and promises, either for allowing greater liberty for free trade to the planters or for development of the Darien mine, were revealed to the colonists, as the *Mary* was seized by Algerian pirates on its outward voyage. The colonists carried on it, including Mr. John Symons who was returning to his wife on Providence Island, endured a far harsher captivity than those who were captured by the Spanish. Symons's November 1639 letter to Lord Mandeville appealing for assistance spoke eloquently of the despair afflicting the nearly 2,000 English held in Algiers. Symons humbly said he knew that the company did not have the funds to ransom him and his fellows and asked them to appeal to the king for support.[39]

During the summer of 1639, the king had raised his standard and commanded the nobility of England to help him meet the challenge posed by Scotland's militant refusal to conform to the Church of England's order of worship. Lords Saye and Brooke were briefly imprisoned for their refusal to sign the oath Charles required.[40] The challenge was

38. PIC Ct., 5–8–39, 5–15–39; Gen. Ct., 5–23–39; PIC Agreement with Na: Marston, Chirurgeon, 6/7–38; PIC to Butler by the *Mary*, 7–39; PIC to Parker, ibid., 7–39; PIC to Brent, ibid., 7–39; PIC Instructions to Butler, Axe, and Carter, ibid., 7–39; PIC Instructions to John Butler, 7–39.
39. John Symonds to Lord Mandeville, Nov. 1639, Manchester Papers, 423, photostat in Library of Congress. On February 20, 1640 a meeting attended only by John Pym and the Earl of Warwick advanced £50 for the ransom of John Butler, company agent sent in the *Mary* to oversee the mining operation; PIC Ctee., 2–20–40.
    K. R. Andrews describes how the organization and skills of the Algerian pirates were transformed in the 1620s, making them a major threat to Atlantic shipping; *Ships, Money and Politics*, 160–1.
40. For the refused oath, see A. B. Grosart, ed., *Lismore Papers*, 2nd ser. (London, 1888), IV, 19–23. News of the lords' imprisonment traveled quickly. Sir Edmund Verney criticized the committing of Lord Saye as "weak" in a letter to his son, Ralph; and Brilliana Harvey wrote her son Edward of her hope that they had both been freed. Thomas Lechford in Massachusetts copied the oath into his notebook. See

284   *Providence Island, 1630–1641*

sidestepped in 1639, but the problems remained, forcing Charles I to call his first parliament in eleven years in April 1640. Providence Island Company members were deeply involved in all these events. Inevitably, the colony and its problems receded in their attention. At the very end of 1639, the Earl of Warwick wrote on behalf of the company to his "assured friend" Mr. Webster in Amsterdam asking him to investigate the possibility of Providence Island's sale to the Dutch West Indies Company.[41]

Meanwhile, the settlers, whose last set of full instructions and supplies had arrived in the fall of 1638, were forced to carry on as best they could. The miscarried 1639 letters had said confidently that the investors understood Providence Island was well supplied with provisions. In fact, when Nathaniel Butler returned from his privateering voyage, he found his colonists beset by dearth occasioned by drought. In September 1639 ships were sent out to search for food, and Governor Butler ordered all privateers to make provisions part of their quest, especially because poor colonists were beginning to suffer. Early in October, rains came and the settlers began planting. In early November ships returned with corn, and on November 7 the colonists held a combined day of thanksgiving to God "for the deliverance from the Gunpowder Treason; for his merciful sending to us of seasonable rains; and the safe return of our men of war from sundry places and parts." The governor invited the entire council and Hope Sherrard and his wife to dine with him.[42]

This dinner may have been one of the last of such conviviality; Butler's diary entries for October and November 1639 began to reveal the depth of animosity separating the factions of Providence Island. In referring to his enemies, the governor called them the "Old Councilors," the "Congregation," and the "Sherrardian Councilors" interchangeably. On November 6, the day before the great thanksgiving and dinner, the monthly court had attempted to heal all breaches but "not without discoveries of the sinister practices of some, who were extremely unfit for the employments that they were entrusted withal, and the great professions they gloried themselves in."

Butler pictured the Old Councilors as enemies of the company and the poorer planters as well as of himself. They ridiculed the company's

John Bruce, ed., *Letters and Papers of the Verney Family*, Camden Society, O. S., 56 (London, 1852) 228–9; Thomas Taylor Lewis, ed., *Letters of Lady Brilliana Harvey*, Camden Society, O. S., 58 (London, 1853), 48–9; and Lechford, "Notebook," ed. Hale, *American Antiquarian Society Transactions* 7 (1885), 105.
41. Warwick to Webster, Dec. 9, 1639, PIC Records.
42. Butler Diary, B. L., Sloane MS 758, 9–21–39; 9–25–39; 10–2–39; 11–2–39; 11–4–39; 11–7–39; and notes for letters, pt. 8.

instructions, and led by Richard Lane and inflamed from the pulpit, they plotted resistance to the per-head tax that replaced the former sharecropping arrangement. Angry at being left off the council of war, they sought to bring its acts into contempt. While Butler was away from the island, the Old Councilors sent a ship, the *Queen of Bohemia*, to New England for support and, he said, plotted to replace him as governor and seize his goods. At the end of November Captain Hunt sailed with permission in his own frigate to the Moskito Coast. When Hunt's ship returned without him in February 1640, Butler concluded that he intended to sail to New England.

For their part the councilors accused Butler of persecution. Their side of the story does not survive, but the governor's first diary entry concerns his direction that the plantations of John Francis, Isaac Barton, and Richard Smithe (Henry Halhead's son-in-law) be surveyed to see if they exceeded the company's allocations. All were found to be within the guidelines. At their court of June 1640, the company seriously considered many complaints and charges against Butler sent by colonists. The investors also investigated whether they had been cheated of some of the cargo brought home by Captain Axe's ship in which Butler traveled.[43]

Nathaniel Butler, who referred to himself in a letter to the company as "your martyr," consistently portrayed all attacks as stemming from his efforts to carry out company instructions fairly and efficiently. He wrote that the faction against him "pride themselves" on being "the Tormentors of their Quondam Governors," and he constantly reiterated his theme that the adventurers must select a governor they believed in and then endow him with real power. He must especially have authority to select his own council if he was to carry out the company's wishes. Lack of progress on the fortifications, for example, was due to the obstruction of these "captious councilors." So seriously did he take these problems and so basic was the reorganization needed that Butler had decided to come home and argue the case in person; he brought the petition signed by the masters of families against their being deprived of the sacrament with him. Three "Sherrardian Councilors" refused to sign his records at his departure because he absented himself during their visit, but many other planters came to wish him farewell on his

43. Butler, Notes for letters, B. L., Sloane MS 758; and Diary, ibid., 2−9−39; 10−11−39; 11−6−39. Although Captain Hunt was a member of the congregational party, Butler maintained good relations with him. The shared military experience of the two apparently created a bond. See Diary, 4−27−39. For reference to charges against Butler, see PIC Ct., 5−7−40; 6−19−40; 6−20−40; 6−23−40.

last day, February 23, 1640, before he departed on the *Swallow* captained by Samuel Axe.[44]

Throughout Butler's tenure, the colonists had been out of direct contact with the company in London. By the time a new set of letters and a new magazine were sent out in Maurice Thompson's ship *Hopewell* in March 1640 Butler was already on his way home. By this time the company letters and meeting notes were recorded only very cryptically, and nineteen pages in the letterbook were left blank. Members' attention was obviously engaged in the gathering political storm in England. Without company authorization, Butler had left the government of Providence Island in the hands of Captain Andrew Carter, a man with no sympathy for the congregation and its hopes.[45]

Andrew Carter had been in the island since 1636. He had originally gone as the proposed governor of a small contingent sent to Henrietta (San Andreas) Island by company husband William Woodcock. When Woodcock abandoned the scheme as being too dangerous on the unfortified island, Carter settled on Providence Island and received marks of the company's favor in the form of servants and compliments. He informed the investors of embezzlement from cargoes of prizes taken by privateering Captains Axe and Parker. In their gratitude the investors attempted to send his wife to him at company charge in the ill-fated *Mary*.[46]

Carter, whom many of the colonists never recognized as a legitimate governor, lost little time in letting the planters know that things had changed. He and his sidekick Elisha Gladman began to run the island's government on their own authority. They denied some of the council their privileges and rank, allowing "many other particular affronts and indignities which were almost unsufferable being done by vile persons in the very face of the Country." According to the displaced councilors, Carter executed "the office of Government without oath, banishing some, imprisoning others without alleging any cause, or affording them the just privilege of a trial, and winking at horrible crying sins, which would have inforced any Magistrate indued with that power which he challenged to himself, to have drawn out the sword of Justice against them." He was unable to control such behavior because, "as some of the Common sort of people have vaunted it, saying that if he pleased

---

44. Letter notes, ibid., and Diary, 10–15–39; 1–11–40; 1–18–40; 2–3–40; 2–21–40; 2–23–40.
45. Captain William Woodcock had been designated lieutenant governor when Butler was appointed; PIC Agreement with Woodcock, 6/7–38.
46. PIC to Gov. and Coun. by the *Mary Hope*, 3–37; and to Carter by the *Mary*, 7–39; Jessop to Carter, 4–17–37, B. L., Add. MS 10615.

them not, as they had put him in, so they would thrust him out [margin: as it is reported]."[47]

One example of Carter's unjust dealing eventually came before the House of Lords. On April 20, 1640, Carter threw a gentleman "anciently descended' named Robert Robins (or Robyns) in jail, refusing to tell him the cause and without notifying the council or allowing Robins to send word to his friends. Robins was brought before Carter, "who pretended himself Governor of the Island but was not." The next day without hearing any evidence Carter pronounced a judgment of banishment on Robins. According to Robins's petition for redress to the House of Lords, Carter said he need not try Robins according to the laws of England, that "the cause of his banishment was his pleasure."

Despite the intervention of Hope Sherrard and councilors Henry Halhead, Richard Lane, and Captain John Francis, together with the Lieutenant General Captain William Woodcock, all of whom said they would be "bound body for body for the petitioner" to keep him on the island until his case was heard by the company in London, Robins was placed on board the privateer commanded by Captain William Jackson, where by his own account he was mistreated, forced to do demeaning work, and cheated out of the share of the voyage's proceeds that should have been his.

Jackson later returned to Providence Island, where he freed Robins, who tried unsuccessfully to recover his property. His debtors refused to pay what was due, and there was "no law to be had there for any the Land being daily up in arms." Carter gave Robins a release to return to England, and he took ship with "one Tompson." Edward Thompson, master of Maurice Thompson's *Hopewell*, carried Providence Island Company authorization for privateering. Thompson joined forces with Jackson after they met in the Gulf of Florida, and Robins again found himself on Jackson's ship. After another grueling voyage, including a period of imprisonment in Ireland, Robins, destitute, was back in England and attempting to seek redress for his losses from the House of Lords. Jackson himself arrived back in England at the very end of 1640, his ship "richly laden with Indigo."[48]

47. Henry Halhead, Richard Lane, Hope Sherrard, and Nicholas Leverton to the PIC, June 17, 1640, Finch MSS, Leicestershire RO, p. 1; calendared in Historical Manuscripts Commission, 17th *Report* (1913), I, 51–8.
48. There is a discrepancy in the various accounts of these events. Robins's petition gives April 20, 1639 as the date of his first imprisonment by Carter. A. P. Newton and V. T. Harlow follow him in assigning the events he describes to 1639, but at that time Captain Butler was still in Providence Island and was very much in control. He did not embark on his privateering voyage until the end of May, and his diary said nothing of leaving Carter in charge or of the imprisonment of Robins in April. Butler mentioned Captain Jackson as sailing from the island under a commission

Meanwhile, the situation in Providence Island had changed dramatically as a result of a second major Spanish attempt to dislodge the colony at the end of May 1640, the anniversary of the commencement of Captain Butler's privateering voyage. Councillors Henry Halhead and Richard Lane and the two ministers Hope Sherrard and Nicholas Leverton wrote a long description of the attack and its aftermath that was filled with indications of the providence of God seen in the successful repulsion of the enemy with almost no losses to the English. This document rings with the colonists' conviction that they lay under a special protection of God and their scorn for the imposters who had thrust themselves into positions of authority but who in the testing fire of battle showed themselves to be both cowards and incompetent. Indeed, according to their account, the island was nearly lost and the suffering of the colonists was compounded by the governor's utter lack of planning and provisioning for such an event, although he knew it must come.

In fact Don Melchor de Aguilera, Captain General of Cartagena, had renewed his pleas for concerted action against Providence Island, that "den of thievery," whose good harbors and close proximity to both Cartagena and Portobello were enabling English pirates so to lessen the flow of food and other supplies along the coast that real famine often threatened the Spanish cities, in addition to the loss of rich cargoes felt at home.[49] The captain general convinced Don Juan de Vega Basan and Don Rodrigo Lobo, generals of the Brazil fleet, to take on the challenge. The generals refused the governor's request that his son of twelve or thirteen might command the action and chose Cartagena's sergeant-

signed by him on March 19, 1639. Jackson next appeared in New England on August 27, 1639, where, according to John Winthrop, he "furnished himself with commodities, and departed again for the West Indies." Jackson spent another year privateering in the Indies before returning to England in the winter of 1640–41. All the evidence seems to indicate that the forceable recruitment of Robins occurred in April 1640 when Captain Carter was in the governor's seat. This hypothesis better fits the known facts, both of what transpired in Providence Island and of the timing of Jackson's return to England that carried Robins home.

The petition of Robert Robins, April 22, 1642, is in the House of Lords Record Office; see also *Lords' Journals* V, 10, for an order authorizing Lord Pagett, Lord Brooke, and Lord Robartes to investigate. On Edward Thompson, see PIC Ctee., 2–16–40. For discussion of this episode, see Newton, *Colonising Activities*, 267–8, and Harlow, ed., *Voyages of Captain William Jackson, Camden Miscellany*, XIII (1923), v–viii; B. L., Sloane MS 758; Winthrop, *Journal*, ed. Hosmer, I, 309–10. On Jackson's return, see PIC Ct., 1–4–41. The company took notice of Jackson's cargo and its contribution to the alleviation of their debt in PIC to Gov. and Coun., 3–29–41.

49. For earlier pleas, see Butler, Diary, B. L., Sloane MS 758, 9–13–39.

major Don Antonio Maldonado de Texeda. The galleon, with 200 infantrymen, was commanded by Captain Joan de Ibarra of the Portuguese army; Captain Nicolás Soza de Vasconcelos, accompanied by his brother the Count of Castelmayor, commanded a further 400. The count brought all the Portuguese noblemen in Cartagena with him at his own expense. Barely 100 Spaniards went from Cartagena; they were commanded by two captains, Don Pedro de Soto Altamirano and Melchor Nuñes de Rosas. There was also a small group of "Mulatoes and Black creoles." The force numbered about 700 soldiers in addition to the seamen, and the ships included the *Black Robin*, the Earl of Warwick's captured *Robert* now pressed into Spanish service.[50]

When news of thirteen Spanish ships lying in a position to attack was first brought to Providence Island, some "scoffingly" said "surely they were but so many boobies, so that it nothing moved them that had taken all the power upon themselves to be any whit more watchful or to bestir themselves in preparation." As the ships drew near and prepared to land their troops, Captain Carter proved himself a coward, lost the power to command, and took advice from all and sundry. When the Iberian soldiers drew near their landing place on a beach midway between Black Rock Fort and the mouth of the Black River, "singing with a dreadful and formal tone *pero, diabolo, cornuda, sa sa sa*," Carter was terrified; even the common soldiers were ashamed at his "ducking at every shot."

The forts so carefully rebuilt by Nathaniel Butler did good service; the invaders found the island formidable, "naturally fortified and more so by art." The information that had been given to them at Cartagena was faulty, so were forced to spend a day in dangerous sounding to determine a landing place. Fire from the forts forced the Iberians to attempt their landing at a disadvantageous place where they had to wade ashore and face slippery rocks and a sheer cliff, but Carter's negligence undercut the forts' benefit. A great gun just installed at Black River's mouth did good service in forcing the enemy away but had only five cartridges. The gunner was forced to spike it when he ran out of

50. "Account of the journey and Battle of Santa Catalina Island written by father friar Mateo de San Francisco, Chaplain major and administrator of the Armada of Portugal, under the command of Don Gerónimo Gomes de Sandoval, Royal Admiral of the Ocean and Captain General of Galleons and fleet in the city of Cartagena de Indias, the 29th of November of 1640," General Archive of the Indies, Seville, *Audiencia de Santa Fe, legajo* 223. On the damage done to Spanish colonial life by privateers from Providence Island, see the "Relation of Captain Don Torivio de Palacio y Sierra," n.d., ibid.; and "Don Alonso de Cardena's Complaint [to Charles I] and a Reference thereupon, 1640," in Robert Sanderson, comp., *Foedera*, 20 vols. (London, 1704–35), XX, 416.

powder just as the invaders were landing "so ill provided was she (although at a place so advantageous to annoy the enemy through the negligence of those that should have looked better to it)."[51]

The English force consisted of just about 100 soldiers, according to the councilors' and ministers' letter.[52] (Father Mateo de San Francisco's report to Spanish authorities said that they had been led to expect an island populated by 200 men, "all employed in working the land," but found instead they faced "more than 700 men with a chief who is very experienced in war.") The English colonists faced an invasion force of 300, the "Choicest and Stoutest Soldiers in the whole Fleet." The attack came about six in the evening of Saturday, May 30. Of those 300, the settlers later learned from a Frenchman who had been a Spanish captive, only two were spared death or wounding completely. The force was smaller than it should have been because several large boats, necessary to landing, had been destroyed in a storm while the fleet gathered off the appropriately named *Quitasueño* (lose sleep) reef northwest of Providence Island off Cape Gracias a Dios.

The man appointed Spanish governor of Providence Island was with the invasion fleet; he would have governed 600 settlers, with "Eleven Caballeroes to accompany him; who (as they told us) had vowed and taken the Sacrament upon it that he would either take the Island or leave his carcass there. Such preparation they had made to invade us that they had utterly unfurnished Carthagene, and all other places near adjoining of all Ships, frigates and boats. . . ." Among the English, only two men, servants, were killed, and both had marked themselves out for providential retribution. One had repeatedly attempted to run away, and the other had "a little before the fight belched out horrible oaths and desperate Imprecations against himself, proudly vaunting what great matters he would do against the enemy, in case he came on them."

The Iberian invaders had been assured by the governor of Cartagena that the English would "fly away like so many sheep at the very sight of an enemy approaching." Their faith introduced a note of pathos into the English account. "Some of our enemies coming on shore had their muskets fastened about their bodies, bringing with them bottles of

51. Halhead, Lane, Sherrard, and Leverton to the PIC, June 17, 1640, Finch MSS, Leicestershire R. O.; calendared in Historical Manuscripts Commission, 17th *Report* (1913), I, 51–8. The account of the action that follows is taken from this source.
52. Governor Butler had written that he could not carry out instructions for setting up trial juries because there were too few eligible men on the island; "Notes for my letters," B. L., Sloane MS 758. The company acknowledged the same reality in restructuring the government in 1641; PIC to Gov. and Coun., 3–29–41.

water, besides bread and cheese in the snapsacks, with pumpion [pumpkin] seed and pease to plant, and some of them had candles and linstocks in their hands (as if the day had been theirs before hand)."[53] Father Mateo de San Francisco's account said that the invading force was supposed to have carried provisions for forty days, after which they were to be supplied by the governor of Cartagena, but they were running out as they returned to Cartagena after fifteen days.

Whereas Father Mateo's account stressed the courage and gallantry of the Iberians, the English report repeatedly returned to its major theme: the cowardice and negligence of Captain Carter and his associates from which only God's special providence had delivered them. In the heat of battle many English cried out "for Gods sake powder and shot, which one of our Captains hearing charged them to be silent, fearing lest the enemy should be thereby encouraged, and so bid them that were thus destitute to do as he did who betook himself to the throwing of stones, for which service our Negroes thinking themselves to be as sufficient as others, presently put themselves forward, and did good Execution by this means." Carter's crony in command of Warwick Fort was supposed to supply powder and shot but neglected to do so and refused to supply even those who sent for it.

Another associate, made commander of Black Rock Fort, ordered, in Carter's presence and before his fort was assaulted, the spiking of the fort's two big guns. He also ordered all the powder and shot taken to Warwick Fort on the separate spit of land where the women and children were sheltered. His only reason: "that they might there die altogether." This plan was stopped by "the vehement outcries and importunities of some of the bystanders," and a gunner was able to unspike one of the guns that was soon to see good service, but Carter did flee to Warwick Fort. He also intercepted the food that the soldiers of the running army had arranged out of their own supplies to be sent to them; "[N]evertheless though they exceedingly needed it, being sore wearied by their painful march and their great toil in the fight, he little considered them, who whiles they were falling in on their enemies, he fell on their victuals, and in the very heat of the fight shewed his stomach which was not to fight but to feed." Carter also put some of the victuals on board a ship in the harbor, which led his critics to believe that he had intended to try to slip away.

53. For the English report of the battle, see Halhead, Lane, Sherrard, and Leverton to the PIC, June 17, 1640, Finch MSS, Leicestershire R. O.; calendared in Historical Manuscripts Commission, 17th *Report* (1913), I, 51–8. Linstocks are yard-long staffs, one end of which is pointed to stick in the ground and the other forked to hold a lighted match, a smoldering wick used to ignite matchlock muskets.

The very hand of God, seeking to protect the true reformed religion, was seen at every turn in the island's deliverance. The invaders had brought a great wooden cross to be their standard, "besides many other small crosses, pictures as Images which were found about the bodies of the slain. One of them was observed, having received a mortal wound, to tear his gods from about his neck and to throw them away with indignation; another of them was slain through the picture of their Lady Mary, which was shot twice through as it did hang about his neck." God protected the English colonists in such a way that they understood their own efforts were of no avail and all depended on divine aid; he surely could not allow such idolators to believe that their gods had given victory.

However touching the faith of the invading soldiers, in both their religion and their officers, the English had no doubt as to the grisly fate that would have awaited the vanquished colonists. The women, "amongst whom were some big with child, others with infants hanging upon the breast and little ones in their hands," who were gathered praying in Warwick Fort rightly feared the worst. Among the effects of slain soldiers, according to the report, were found "pardons... to lie with virgins and women, whom they might slay or keep alive at their pleasure, but as for the men they were all to have been put to the sword, as the prisoners confessed." Slaves were to be sent in the second supply to serve as executioners.

The English could not hold out their own example as superior, however. Company members in London were horrified to read that Captain Carter had ordered the execution of prisoners, even those who had given themselves up fully armed on the promise of free quarter. Whatever they thought about other details of the account, this was a transgression the adventurers could not allow. Carter was ordered home as soon as they knew of his violation of the standards of civilized warfare.[54]

Immediately following the repulsion of the invasion, the English colonists came together on Thursday, June 11, for a day of thanksgiving and rejoicing. All the inhabitants, "both English and Heathens," assembled on the place, formerly Knave's Acre and now renamed Bloody Beach, where the Spanish had landed. After a sermon and prayers, the colonists "made a fire of the Gods and idolatrous monuments of our enemies in the view and sight of the heathens, whom we did inform that the Gods

54. On the seventeenth-century "etiquette of belligerence," see Barbara Donagan, "Codes and Conduct in the English Civil War," *Past and Present* 118 (1988), 78–81.

whom our enemies trusted in and called upon could neither save their worshippers from slaughter, nor themselves from the fire."

Unity bought of common deliverance from danger did not last. The Reverend Nicholas Leverton recorded that "the people pleading a right by charter to choose their own governor," tried to oust Captain Carter from the governor's office and replace him with Mr. Richard Lane. For his part Carter, "privately arming some of the ruder sort," seized Lane, Halhead, and the two ministers and sent them home as prisoners, bypassing the company by including "an information against them to Abp. Laud, that they were disaffected to the liturgy and ceremonies of England."[55]

Lane, Halhead, Sherrard, and Leverton sailed on Maurice Thompson's *Hopewell*, the same ship that initially carried the unfortunate Robert Robins. When the investors heard of the ship's arrival at Bristol on January 4, 1641, they immediately ordered the prisoners' release and required them to attend the company to answer the charges against them. At this meeting, February 13, John Pym, the Earl of Warwick, and Lords Saye and Mandeville determined that the four prisoners' interpretation of the company wishes had in fact been correct: The instructions carried by the *Seaflower* early in the colony's history should have been followed. When Captain Butler left the island, which he had no right to do without first informing the company, the council and ministers should jointly have determined his interim successor. Despite earnest efforts by Elisha Gladman and Lieutenant Charles Whettenhall to argue the viewpoints of Captains Butler and Carter, the four men were released and held guiltless.[56]

Despite an early inclination to continue Carter in office until a new governor, Captain John Humphrey of New England, could be sent, the adventurers soon decided that Carter and William Wyatt, Ralph Leicester (or Lester), Maurice Morgan, and Lewis Powell, whose behavior was suffused with "their discontentful and mutinous spirit," should be ordered home. Moreover, Mr. Jenkes and Lieutenant Whettenhall were not permitted to return, although Jenkes was allowed to travel on Thompson's ship as far as Warwick's island of Trinidad if he wished. Jenkes's house in Providence Island was to be "set apart" for the new governor. Lieutenant, now Captain, Thomas Fitch, "a man of a quiet spirit and of approved integrity and not so engaged to either side as to put him upon any offensive or distasteful carriages," was sent back as deputy governor, and he was to govern until Humphrey arrived. Fitch was to have an

55. Calamy, *Nonconformist's Memoriall*, rev. ed. by Palmer, I, 292–3.
56. PIC Ct., 1–4–41; 2–13–41.

absolute veto over any person's desire to go to Providence Island. Nicholas Leverton and Richard Lane were induced to return, the latter to be on the council. Also appointed or reaffirmed councilors were Sergeant Major Robert Hunt, Captain Francis "(who is to have an admonition)" warning him "to avoid all offensive demeanor in time to come," Captain Axe, and Captain Woodcock. All other officers were to remain, and Aaron Butcher was to become sheriff or marshall.[57]

The adventurers' joy at the successful repulsion of the enemy, which gave "further arguments of hope that God hath reserved it for some special services to his own Glory and the honor of this Nation," was clouded by news of the killing of prisoners after quarter had been given. Richard Lane had affirmed to a meeting attended by Warwick, Saye, and Mandeville that Carter had put such captives to the sword, and the investors decided that act must be punished. Captain Fitch was to interrogate Andrew Carter, and if he judged the story to be true, Carter was to be sent home a prisoner, "it being a crime so heinous, so contrary to religion and to the law of Nature and Nations that it ought not to escape without punishment."[58]

With the commissions to Captain Fitch and to Captain Humphrey as governor, the correspondence of the Providence Island Company came to an end. Though they did not realize it, their godly experiment on the island had finished with the departure of Lane, Halhead, and the two ministers. Even in the spirit of renewal in which they moved to cleanse the colony of mutinous and dangerous spirits and to ensure leadership by godly and upright men as the 1640s opened, the company's attention was focused on the mainland. John Humphrey and the colonists attracted to the project at this late stage were promised that after a brief sojourn on Providence Island they would be in a position to found a great British colony in Central America, one that could realize all their hopes. The island named after God's guiding hand was no longer the focus of their plans for the Indies; the intentions of divine providence for their own island of Britain had already begun to unfold.

57. PIC Ct. and mtgs., 2–25–41; 3–2–41; 3–9–41; 3–24–41; 3–25–41. PIC to Gov. and Coun., 3–29–41; and Instr. to Dep. Gov. Fitch, 3–29–41.
58. PIC mtg. at Warwick House, 3–24–41; PIC to Gov. and Coun., 3–29–41; and Instr. to Dep. Gov. Fitch, 3–29–41.

10

The Business History
of the Providence Island Company

THE PROVIDENCE ISLAND COMPANY was organized in 1630 with a working capital of £3,800 promised from the twenty adventurers. (The Earl of Holland, perpetual company governor, was given a whole share without investing any money because the investors needed his court connections.) The size of each adventure, initially £200, was steadily increased as expenses mounted. By June 1632 it had reached £520, and by May 1633 it had reached the enormous sum of £1,025, at which the size of one whole adventure was frozen.

The investors were already involved in many ventures; they were seasoned veterans at organizing and running a colonial company. From the outset, they decided to conduct their affairs by the ballot box rather than by show of hands. The Virginia Company had turned to the ballot box when controversy threatened; it could also be useful as a way of allowing members to defy royal directives on election of specific officers. Elections of the key office of deputy governor (the effective head of the organization) were frequently contested in the Providence Island Company and were settled, without numbers being recorded, by ballot.[1]

Providence Island Company organizers had worked together in many other colonial schemes; they had shown their willingness to invest both their energies and their money in projects to advance the interests of themselves and the nation. Many were members of the Virginia Company and its offshoot, the Somers Islands (Bermuda) Company. The Earl of Warwick and his kinsman, Sir Nathaniel Rich, led the Bermuda Company for decades; they held the balance of power in

---

1. For first use of the ballot box, see PIC Gen. Ct. 5–10–31. On its use in other colonial companies, see Pearl, *London and Puritan Revolution*, 91–3; Craven, *The Dissolution of the Virginia Company*, 86–8; Wilkinson, *Adventurers of Bermuda*, 149, 161. The necessity of its introduction in the House of Commons in 1646 was seen as a mark of political failure; see Kishlansky, *Rise of the New Model Army*, 137.

both companies as tensions developed between the merchants and gentleman-investors. The Riches were leaders in the group that brought the plight of Virginia to royal attention in 1623, initiating the course of events that resulted in the revocation of the Virginia Company's charter.[2]

One of the issues in the Virginia Company's disputes was privateering. Warwick had been involved in privateering throughout his life, as was his father before him. During the sea war against Spain in the second half of the 1620s, Warwick, who became the second earl in 1619, fielded a very large fleet. Of all privateering ships set out by members of the aristocracy between 1626 and 1630, half sailed for the earl. Captain Nathaniel Butler, who had played a key role in the attack on the administration of Virginia by the Virginia Company, drew up a proposal for a new concept of privateering in large organized fleets that became the plan for Warwick's campaign. The earl personally led an expedition in 1627 that was unsuccessful in gaining prizes but enhanced his reputation.[3]

Warwick's father had been a guarantor of Ralegh's final expedition to Guiana, posting bond for his return. The second earl immediately took up the project for founding a colony on the South American mainland after Ralegh's execution. He attempted to recruit the separatists who founded Plymouth on Cape Cod for his new plantation on Guiana; the first colony went out in 1620.[4] When the Pilgrims went to New England instead, Warwick was able to help them get a patent, as he did the Massachusetts Bay Company, by virtue of his position in the Council for New England.

Warwick and Lords Saye and Brooke were investors from the 1620s in the East India Company, where they formed a clique with London merchant Matthew Cradock that was critical of the company's operation under the directors. Their campaign to curtail the company governors'

2. On these events, see Craven, *Dissolution of the Virginia Company*, chap. 9, and *Introduction to the History of Bermuda*, 156–8.
3. John C. Appleby, "English Privateering during the early Stuart Wars with Spain and France, 1625–1630," unpub. Ph.D. diss., University of Hull (1983), 206; Butler's proposal is B. L., Add. MS 41616, ff. 29v–35v. Warwick and the vice admiral of the expedition, William Ball, each wrote an account of the 1627 voyage; see Nelson P. Bard, ed., *The Earl of Warwick's Voyage of 1627*, in N. A. M. Rodger, ed., *The Naval Miscellany* V (1984), 15–93.
4. For the Guiana colony and Warwick's role as head of the company, see Joyce Lorimer, *English and Irish Settlement on the River Amazon, 1550–1646* (London, 1989), 60–8, 192–4, 197. On the recruitment of the Pilgrims, see Bradford, *Of Plymouth Plantation*, ed. Morison, 28, 39; and Frank Thistlethwaite, *Dorset Pilgrims: The Story of Westcountry Pilgrims who went to New England in the 17th Century* (London, 1989), 17.

power was carried on throughout the 1630s, the period during which the Providence Island Company was active.[5]

Thus, the leaders of the Providence Island Company were seasoned veterans of colonial ventures and knew the pitfalls, having seen many failures and few successes; they especially knew the ins and outs of company organization. Two interrelated characteristics immediately set off the Providence Island Company from its contemporaries: The membership was strictly limited to a handpicked small clique, and the sums invested by the adventurers were far larger than those hazarded in other early seventeenth-century colonial ventures. Yet John Pym, who managed the company finances, never had enough money to meet expenses, and despite early resolutions to the contrary, the company borrowed again and again just to keep operating. One reason for the arrears was that some adventurers were notoriously slow in paying up; on occasion special embassies were dispatched to try to pry money out of delinquents.[6]

A more serious problem grew out of the rhythm of ship departure and return, especially as each returning vessel carried complaints of inadequate supplies from the colonists. Each time a ship was sent out or reentered English waters, several thousand pounds were required to stock it or pay off its charter agreement. These sums, often required without warning, had to be raised quickly and the only way to do that was to borrow. Haltingly at first and then on an ever-larger scale, the adventurers borrowed large sums of money at interest rates ranging between 7 and 9 percent.[7] The loans were usually for six months or less, but they were often rolled over, with only the interest payments being kept up. Bonds were signed by company members with the stipulation that the entire company, or the investors in the particular joint stock making the commitment, were responsible.[8]

The Providence Island Company could not have functioned without borrowing, and many people, men and women, came forward to lend. Through such experiences these national leaders were led to reflect on the way in which the economy functioned and the need for a more modern system. In 1641 Lord Saye wrote a manuscript called "A defense of Usury," arguing that the provision of money available for

---

5. Pearl, *London and Puritan Revolution*, 92, 97, 170, 286–8.
6. For one such delegation to the Earl of Warwick, see PIC Ct. 11–17–34.
7. G. C. A. Clay, *Economic Expansion and Social Change: England, 1500–1700*, 2 vols. (Cambridge, 1984), II, 281, says that in the 1630s "favoured private borrowers could raise money at 7 percent or even less."
8. On bonds and the ways in which they functioned in early seventeenth century England, see Eric Kerridge, *Trade and Banking in Early Modern England* (Manchester, England, 1988), 39–42.

borrowing at interest was essential to the operation of the national economy. Following John Calvin, Saye sought to overturn "that odd whimsical conceit . . . that money doth not bring forth money. But to this I answer, neither doth corn bring forth corn, unless it be sowed, and if money be employed it will bring forth money, and that with a larger return than any thing else, because it answereth all things." Saye believed that a return of 8 percent was reasonable for the lender and compared it to the rent a landowner would collect.[9]

Experience of investment in overseas ventures clearly placed men such as Saye far ahead of their peers in understanding what it would take to establish England on a more modern financial footing. Conventional gentry opinion condemned usury or the taking of interest at all. Popular theater and, despite Calvin, puritan sermons portrayed takers of interest as bloodsuckers. Lord Saye was castigated as the "White Jew of the Upper House" because of his "defense of Usury."[10]

Had the company been able to develop a valuable cash crop, investors' borrowing would have been beneficial in just the way Saye outlined. But the burden was very great. At times the adventurers borrowed money just to pay interest due; therefore, the company debt constantly grew, and merely keeping it up formed a large financial burden. With clocklike regularity, John Pym laid out the company's financial picture and forced the adventurers to confront their indebtedness.

Borrowing was one solution to recurring financial pressures. Investors discussed and rejected the possibility of opening the company's membership, fearing the pollution of purpose that would come with the presence of merchants more interested in profits than in building a godly society.[11] Another acceptable solution was to encourage adventurers to form special joint stocks for limited purposes. The *Long*

9. Saye's manuscript is in the Cambridge University Library, Add. MS 44/20. Another copy is in the library of Queen's College, Oxford. For Calvin on usury, see John T. Noonan, Jr., *The Scholastic Analysis of Usury* (Cambridge, MA, 1957), 365–7; and Jesper Rosenmeier, "John Cotton on Usury," *William and Mary Quarterly* 3rd ser., XLVII (1990), 548–57. On theories about usury generally, see R. H. Tawney, "Introduction," to Thomas Wilson, *A Discourse Upon Usury*, 1572 (1st. pub. 1925; repr. London, 1963).

10. The "White Jew" is not named; the phrase occurs in Anon., *A Letter to the Earle of Pembrooke Concerning the Times, and the sad condition both of Prince and People* (London, 1647), 12. John Adamson identifies its target as Lord Saye in "The English Nobility and the Projected Settlement of 1647," *Historical Journal* 30 (1987), 602. On popular opinion see Butler, *Theatre and Crisis*, 211, and Cliffe, *Puritan Gentry*, 114–17. On the technical difference between interest and usury, see Kerridge, *Trade and Banking*, 34–9. See also Stone, *Crisis*, 142, 165, 178, 183–4.

11. John Pym's extensive analysis of the company's financial situation occurred at a General Court, 12–2–34. The discussion of enlargement of the company of adventurers took place 5–17–34 and 5–19–34.

Robert, a ship sent out in 1634, was financed by a special stock; this became common for the company ships, most of which were financed by separate stocks. In 1635, when the investors were granted a patent to develop trade on the Central American mainland, they decided that proceeds from this venture would accrue only to those who shared in its financial undertaking.[12]

Lord Brooke signified his willingness to take on the entire burden of funding, provided direction of the enterprise was wholly entrusted to him. Brooke had owned two whole shares since 1633 and consistently put in larger sums than other adventurers. John Pym led those who were unwilling to turn over their project entirely. The increasing strain within company councils over the direction of the project had already surfaced in an explosive dispute over the issue of allowing Mr. Richard Lane to return to Providence Island.[13] Lane, Lord Brooke's protégé, had originally gone to the Indies in 1633 to supervise the growing of madder and to act as company agent in setting up trade on the mainland at Darien. Lane returned to England in 1634, having accomplished nothing, in defiance of Governor Bell's attempt to detain him. Lane and Sherrard had engaged in a bond of £200 to make good all Lane's agreements with the adventurers.

When asked if he would return to the island, Lane said there was "no great encouragement" to do so "unless there might be a reformation of some miscarriages in the government there" that injured both the company and the planters. When the company promised changes and invited him to draw up a list of acts "that seemed to swerve from Justice and the Company's instructions" to guide them, Lane agreed to return. He was promised a place when the company moved to plant a settlement on the mainland or the right to return home at will if such settlement did not take place. Lane was to go with his own family and Sherrard's intended wife, whose presence would bind the minister to the colony. Soon Lane was back in the company courts, asking for economic concessions in the colony and £40 to furnish himself for the voyage. The general court on February 16, 1635, promised to consider his demands. At its adjournment, the court, as it often had before, authorized all company members remaining in town "or such number of them as shall be at any time assembled to be a standing committee for ordering of all businesses concerning the company's affairs."[14] This simple formula covered a dangerous constitutional issue.

12. For this patent, see P.R.O., Signet Office Docquet Book 11, 1634–38, March 1634/35.
13. See the General Court of 7–1–34.
14. PIC Ord. Ct., 2–5–35; 2–9–35; Gen. Ct., 2–16–35.

Four days later a committee consisting of Lords Saye and Brooke, Sir Nathaniel Rich, Sir Thomas Barrington, Sir Benjamin Rudyerd, John Pym, Henry Darley, and William Woodcock entered into an extensive commitment to Lane to ensure his "cheerfulness" in undertaking the voyage and the encouragement of "other honest persons" to enter the company's service. He was to be made a councilor in Providence Island and was offered a loan of £20 for his preparations. The committee also carried on negotiations for an additional minister. And they agreed to a further payment by the adventurers to cover new costs.[15]

On February 22, two days later, the general court was to meet again, but the absence of company deputy governor Sir Gilbert Gerard meant that those present – Saye, Brooke, Rudyerd, Barrington, Pym, Darley, and Woodcock – met instead as a committee. The issue of Lane's membership on the council was again debated, and Pym launched a heated attack. He argued that the council should not be allowed to grow too large and that therefore councilors' places should be reserved for men with military training, especially as some of the forts lacked captains. He pointed to the factionalization of the island and implied that Lane would add fuel to the fires of conflict. Furthermore, on the basis of his reading of the company's instructions, Bell had tried to prevent Lane from leaving. If Lane, having defied the governor, were now returned in glory, "the dispeopling of the Island may be endangered." Pym was angry that Lane had stipulated such expensive conditions before he would return after deserting his post; he also mentioned charges that Lane had been drunk in the island.

Lord Saye, Brooke's constant friend and ally, answered Pym on behalf of Brooke's client. He argued that if the council grew too big or had unfit members, the company was always at liberty to remove some. He asserted his belief that Lane was "ingenuous" and that his role on the council would be to "help to oversway the worser party." Moreover, the charges brought against Lane were ambiguous in the records. Lord Saye concluded: "[I]t will be a good encouragement to good people when such as Mr. Lane shall be put into places of authority he being reputed godly."

Other adventurers were asked to give their opinions. Brooke, Barrington, and Woodcock concurred with Saye. Pym refused to give his opinion formally, saying that the committee was not empowered to "determine" such questions.[16] Pym pursued this line when the company next met formally in an ordinary court with Gerard in the chair. Pym asserted that not only had the committee exceeded its authority but,

15. PIC Ctee., 2–20–35.   16. PIC Ctee., 2–22–35.

when the general court failed to meet on its appointed day, the committee's warrant lapsed. He feared a precedent whereby two or three members could bind the whole company "to their great prejudice." Despite his arguments, the majority of those present – Gerard, Brooke, Rudyerd, Rich, Pym, Darley, Graunt, and Woodcock – determined that the committee had acted within its powers and that Lane was legally elected to the Providence Island Council.[17]

When the ordinary court reassembled in the afternoon, Pym again rehearsed all his arguments against Lane, pressing even harder on the charge of drunkenness and on Lane's extortion of the office of councilor from the company. He also warned again of the dangers of too-powerful committees. Nonetheless, he now agreed to the appointment on the condition that Lane be given a stern admonition to "carry himself indifferently" as a councillor and to give "an example of a wise, a sober conversation." To this the company quickly agreed. Lane was called in and charged to avoid occasions of scandal and to do "equal right to all without being swayed, by by-respects or affections in matters of Council."[18] After the transaction of much business, the court concluded with a motion by Sir Nathaniel Rich that Oliver St. John study the company's patent and rule on the general court's power to appoint and empower committees.[19]

The adventurers' letter to Bell accompanying the returning Lane merely said that, although they appreciated Bell's effort to carry out their orders as he saw them, they approved Lane's returning home and now sent him back, "he being reputed honest and industrious," and authorized Lane to choose any unoccupied land to raise any commodity he could procure. Several pages later, after a long discussion of the many disputes that rent the council and the necessity for unity of purpose, appears the bare statement: "We have chosen Mr. Lane to be of the council in Providence, and therefore would have him admitted presently on his arrival, he taking his oath according to our former instructions."[20]

The greatest stress within the company stemmed from financial

17. The Long Parliament came to rely on committees for much of its specific policy formulation and administrative capacity. See Kishlansky, *New Model Army*, 5, 132, 162–8.
18. PIC, Ord. Ct., 3–9–35.
19. The standing committee set up by the General Court on February 9, 1637, was given a long and detailed list of matters it was empowered to decide.
20. PIC to Gov. Bell, 2/3–35. Richard Lane had a terrible outward voyage on the *Expectation* under the command of Captain Nicholas Riskinner, appointed governor of Association Island (Tortuga). Lane wrote the company that Riskinner took his goods by force and threatened to shoot or hang him, "and to make it a bloody day." See PIC Gen. Ct., 2–26–36.

problems. By the end of 1635 the company's entire debt, including debts for ships' hire and interest payments, was £4,599.09.08, a figure large enough to bring profound discouragement.[21] Just when the undertaking was at its lowest ebb, news was returned at the beginning of 1636 of the island's repulsion of a Spanish attack. This providential event confirmed investors' faith that they were involved in a godly enterprise, and it opened the door to privateering with government consent, which promised to give the company the financial backing it needed to keep the plantation alive. Everything was now changed; the royal government took notice of the colony and expected the company to carry on "or else to put it off to others that will not let it fall." The amount required to pay off old debts and to continue was computed at £10,000. Again Pym forced a full-dress debate: "It was now considered what great sums had been disbursed, and that still the Company remain in debt, and it was thereupon propounded by Mr. Treasurer that the Company would consider how to go on, or else in what way to rid themselves fairly of it." Pym strongly urged continuance.

The company discussed Lord Brooke's offer to finance and run the operation. They also considered bringing in new investors or turning it over completely to a different set of backers. Finally, they thought of "delivering it over to the state" but realized that that course would not free them of all responsibility. Some members were extremely reluctant to put in more money on any terms, and, none of the propositions winning support, decision was postponed.[22]

But the company had to act; every week that passed increased the danger in which the colony stood. Therefore, in February 1636 the adventurers created a new joint stock to raise the necessary money. Investors were invited to subscribe, one full share being £500, and to pay in their subscriptions within the coming two years. The new undertakers were to send 500 new settlers out to the Indies. This new joint stock would reap all profits during the ensuing nine years, after which this new investment would be considered an addition to the original stock. Sources of profit included not only returns from the island and the mainland trade but also prizes from the golden source the Spanish attack had opened: privateering. The adventurers turned down Lord Brooke's offer to take on the entire responsibility but welcomed his offer to make up any of the needed £10,000 not subscribed by the others. On these terms Sir Nathaniel Rich, Lord Saye, John Pym, William Woodcock, Sir Thomas Barrington, and the Earl of Warwick each agreed to pay in £500. The sum of £250 was promised by Richard

21. PIC, Ct., 11–13–35.   22. PIC, Ct. 1–29–36, 2–1–36.

Knightley, Sir Benjamin Rudyerd and Rudyerd's partners, Sir William Waller and John Upton together. The company also moved to clear up arrears, deciding that those with outstanding debts would have to make them good. Gerard, Pym, Darley, and Woodcock were appointed a committee to oversee this process.[23]

As they reorganized their company, the investors also planned a new relationship with the colonists, giving them some of the control and assurances planters in other colonies now took for granted. Settlers were promised that the land would soon be divided up with certainty of tenure and rents would be lowered. Promising commodities discovered on the mainland fueled hopes of rich returns from planting. And of course privateering seemed to guarantee an end to financial problems. Privateering commissions were issued for the ships *Blessing* and *Expectation*. Pym noted that the Earl of Holland, who normally signed whatever was put before him, actually perused these commissions, "reading every whit himself" at Pym's request before he signed them. "And for more caution Mr. Pym intreated Lucas to remember that his Lordship had read it before he signed it."[24]

None of this was sufficient to solve the venture's problems quickly enough to make the company solvent. Lord Brooke soon began to retreat from his commitment, although he continued to contribute much more than any other adventurer. He argued that his offer to make up the deficit of the needed £10,000 had been contingent on the promise that 500 settlers would be sent and that many substantial people would go at their own expense.[25] Resurgence of the plague had prevented members from gathering the necessary emigrants; no one knew whether they could have done so in any case.

Intractable problems plagued the project. John Pym began to complain that he had been put to enormous expense and trouble by his efforts to superintend company business, which required that he remain in London. He repeatedly asked for recompense in the form of an increase

23. PIC, 2–12–36, 2–13–36. Doubts remained despite the renewal of purpose; the adventurers stipulated that if a "fair opportunity" of selling the island were to emerge in the next three months, the new joint stock would sell and the proceeds would be divided up fairly between old and new investors.

24. PIC Gen. Ct. 5–23–36. Mr. Lucas may have been John Lucas, an associate with Sir Christopher Neville and others in an English colony on the Amazon founded in 1629; this group had been issued letters of marque in March 1629. See Lorimer, *English and Irish Settlement on the River Amazon*, 93–101, 321–8. Or he may have been Nicholas Lucas, purser and part owner of the *Constant Warwick* with the Earl of Warwick and others, including William Jessop in 1649; see A. W. Johns, "The *Constant Warwick*," *Mariner's Mirror* 18 (1932), 254–66.

25. PIC Ord. Ct. 4–14–36.

in his adventure. Finally, at the annual election in May 1636, he refused to stand again for treasurer; he argued that because the new joint stock was under Lord Brooke's control no treasurer was needed. The office was left empty; members hoped Pym would continue informally to oversee their affairs. Company Secretary William Jessop, who was paid a salary of £40 per year, took over many of these responsibilities.

In 1636 there was another major change in company operation. Sir Nathaniel Rich, whose dedication to Providence Island was capped by his service as company deputy governor in 1635–6, died several months after leaving office. Rich willed his share to Lord Mandeville, his executor, who soon became one of the most committed and active investors.[26]

No investor was absolutely unwavering in support of the project. Throughout its life, company members were receptive to possibilities of selling the entire venture to Dutch entrepreneurs. Sir Edmund Moundeford wrote that "the States of Holland" offered £70,000 for it but that the king dissuaded the adventurers from selling. The Earl of Holland reported to the company in February 1637 that, although Charles I had finally given permission for the sale, the Dutch ambassador had indicated "their unwillingness to part with so great a sum as might be expected by the company." Late in 1639 letters from "Mr. Andries Van Haard" of Amsterdam reopened the possibility of sale, this time to the Dutch West India Company; Providence Island Company representative Mr. Webster in Amsterdam was directed to investigate. A Spanish report of the 1641 fall of the English colony said that the company had repeatedly refused a Dutch offer of 600,000 pieces of eight for the island.[27] Certainly the temptation was never sufficient to make the core group give up their claims despite intractable problems.

The relationship between the company and the government was a fertile source of problems. Customs charges played a large role in the company's financial woes. When the royal government took an interest in Providence Island after 1636, investors began to hope for some relief. In probing this concern, they were delving into one of the key issues of

26. At the General Court of 5–21–36, Lord Mandeville was admitted to half Sir Nathaniel's share in the original company stock. The general court of 2–9–37 admitted Mandeville to Rich's shares in all ventures. A year later Mandeville promised to invest £1,000 in his own right; PIC Gen. Ct., 3–20–38.
    Sir Nathaniel Rich's will is printed in Waters, *Genealogical Gleanings* II, 871–873; see also Wilkinson, *Adventurers of Bermuda*, 238–239.
27. PIC Ct. 1–29–36; Gen. Ct. 2–12 & 13–36, 5–26–36; 2–9–37; 12–9–39. Moundeford to Sir Simonds D'Ewes, n. d., B. L., Harleian MS 287, f. 265; "Relation of Captain Don Torivio de Palacio y Sierra," n.d., General Archive of the Indies, Seville, *Audiencia de Santa Fe, legajo*, 223.

the period: the government's need for money and the few sources available to it.

Historians agree that the early Stuart monarchs were starved for money. John Nef estimates that the income of Louis XIII of France was ten times that of Charles I in the 1630s.[28] Customs were a crucial part of the English king's revenues, the only part that was inflation-linked. Customs payments made up at least half the royal income by the 1630s; moreover, the customs farmers, who actually operated the system, were the only source of credit available to the king. Reliance on customs was destructive to the economy, particularly because duties were charged on exports as well as imports. Therefore, the king leased to the customs farmers the right to plunder the national economy.

Ironically, it was future Providence Island Company members, men who wanted a strong national government capable of leading England into its proper role at the head of the Protestant nations, who had tried to put the king's finances on a sounder footing in the parliaments of the 1620s in return for royal power-sharing with parliament. All taxation was rooted in feudal relations, dues to the chief feudal lord in the nation. What was needed was a modern tax like the excise, which would be imposed by Pym in the Civil War years. In the 1630s the government limped along with the inadequate customs and resorted to the extraparliamentary taxation that helped bring on its downfall.[29]

Despite royal reliance on customs duties for income, colonies typically were exempted from these payments in their early years. Both Virginia and its spin-off, Bermuda, were exempted from customs duties for the first seven years and were to have reduced payments for a further twenty-one years. Massachusetts Bay, the puritan colony founded simultaneously with Providence Island, received the same exemption.[30]

28. John U. Nef, *Industry and Government in France and England, 1540–1640* (Philadelphia, 1940), 129.
29. On taxation and the royal income, see Conrad Russell, "Parliament and the King's Finances," in his *The Origins of the English Civil War* (London, 1973), 99–100, 105–7, 111–14; Russell, *Parliaments and English Politics*, 31, 228, 398, 413–15; Russell, *Causes of the English Civil War*, 173–4; Adams, "Spain or the Netherlands?", in Tomlinson, ed., *Before the English Civil War*, 81; Clay, *Economic Expansion and Social Change*, II, 256, 264–5; Hirst, *Authority and Conflict*, 4, 29, 149; Hunt, *The Puritan Moment*, 187; G. E. Aylmer, *The King's Servants: The Civil Service of Charles I, 1625–1642* (New York, 1961), 64, 248. Professors Russell and Hunt particularly point to the activities of future Providence Island Company members toward giving the crown an assured income in return for a guaranteed parliamentary role.
30. Craven, *Dissolution of the Virginia Company*, chap. 8; Wilkinson, *Adventurers of Bermuda*, 78; Andrews, *Colonial Period*, I, 155–6, 323, 357–8, 368–9. Providence Island founder Sir Nathaniel Rich took the lead in constructing a settlement with the king, the Tobacco Contract, after the exemption ran out; see Craven, ibid.;

Captain John Smith, Virginia veteran and New England promoter, wrote in his final book, *Advertisements, For the Unexperienced Planters of New-England, Or Any Where* (1631), "Now as his Majesty hath made you custom-free for seven years, have a care that all your Country men shall come to trade with you . . . there is nothing more inricheth a Commonwealth than much trade, nor no means better to increase than small custom."[31]

The Providence Island Company was stunned to discover, therefore, that "through a defect in their letters patent," they had no such exemption and customs were charged on supplies they sent to the island "contrary to His Majesty's intention." While considering alternatives such as carrying their goods to Holland or elsewhere for sale, the company moved their governor, the Earl of Holland, to apply for an exemption on exported goods and for "easing" of customs on imports of tobacco. Holland was also to apply for the farm of customs on goods other than tobacco imported from company possessions.[32] Unanswered petitions dragged on until finally in 1636 the investors, confident in their belief that the king recognized the value of their undertaking, saw real grounds for hope.

The king's answer was disappointing and demonstrates the constricting quality of the national reliance on customs. Charles I refused to allow the company an abatement because he had learned that the farmers of the customs would deduct from his own revenues the amount abated. He did promise to do the company good in some other way. The adventurers then decided to apply for permission to sell their tobacco in Holland or other places where the market was good. They also resolved to deal privately with the customers, hoping for a twopenny reduction in the rate.[33]

The plague drove members from London shortly after this meeting; they were not to assemble again until early in 1637 at Warwick Castle, Lord Brooke's seat. Negotiations for sale of the island to the Dutch had again fallen through. The king continued to promise some tangible support but remained vague. And the *Hopewell* had just arrived from the Indies carrying a petition from the colonists that the company labeled mutinous. So dire was the situation that the Earl of Holland actually attended a meeting. He carried word of the king's strong desire

Wilkinson, ibid., 152–3, 163–70, 194–6, 203–5; Russell, *Parliaments and English Politics*, 33, 47, 98. See *By the King. A Proclamation concerning Tobacco* (London, 1624), issued Sept. 29.

31. Smith, *Advertisements*, in Barbour, ed., *Complete Works*, III, 298–9.
32. PIC Mtg. 9–6–31; Prep. Ct. 11–21–32; Gen. Ct. 11–24–31, 2–9–32, 11–26–32.
33. PIC Gen. Ct. 5–18–36.

to keep Providence Island in English hands. Charles I was now prepared to offer either a sum of money or means to secure the island; the investors sat down with Holland to draw up a list of proposals.

On June 24, 1637, following the personal testimony of returned colonists Philip Bell and Samuel Rishworth on the state of the colony, the adventurers held a full-dress discussion of what should be done. The committee of June 24th decided that despite their "great discouragements" the effort must go on. The first reason cited was: "The strength and opportunity of that Island to become the foundation of very great enterprises by annoying the Spaniard and intercepting his treasure whereby he hath troubled and endangered most of the states of Christendom and doth foment the wars against the professors of the reformed Religion." Next was the island's proximity to the "Maine continent of America," where "by the industry of many hands" English men and women could produce "the richest drugs and merchandise which come from America." Their third reason was his majesty's expressed willingness to enlarge their privileges, allowing them exemption of customs "outward and homeward," from charges on powder and ordnance, and from admiralty duties on goods taken from the Spanish. Moreover, all English subjects were to be prohibited from operating within the area of the company's patent.

Now a further joint stock was authorized and opened to the "Nobility and Gentry of the Kingdom; and others his Majesty's Subjects" to raise a stock of £100,000. Each share was to be £1,000, with four votes; investors who put in £250 could have one vote. The adventure was to be paid in two annual installments over five years; thus, the company would have £20,000 per year. And payments would stop once the venture became self-supporting, which investors thought would probably happen "within a year or two." Adventurers were to have benefits proportional to those who had subscribed to the new joint stock the previous year; they would share proceeds for nine years before the first adventurers were reimbursed.[34]

A technicality prevented their royal grant of privileges from going through immediately, but company members were buoyed up by their new prospects. Sir Edmund Moundeford wrote two letters to Sir Simonds D'Ewes, urging him to join these "men fearing God, desirous to enjoy and advance true religion . . . in these Last, worst backsliding times." In September 1637 Moundeford wished "they had your advice and society, I know they would be glad of your company," and he was sure the grant of expanded privileges would come soon. In his undated letter

34. PIC Gen. Ct. 2–9–37; Ctee. 6–24–37.

he laid out the requested privileges from memory and promised to send an exact copy as soon as it arrived. Moundeford thought it likely that the renewed effort would divert attention from New England. Sir Thomas Barrington also preserved the notice of the new joint stock offer among his papers.[35]

Ultimately, the king referred the company's petition to the Lords and Commissioners for Plantations, who also conferred with the judge of the Admiralty Court and the Attorney General. After all this, the company's standing was still murky because the commissioners referred many things back to the king's pleasure.[36] The company's great reorganization was stalled.

When John Pym presented the grievances of the nation to the parliament in April 1640, these frustrating experiences must have been in his mind as he lamented the great impositions imposed by the government: "[E]specially they have been insupportable to the poor plantations, whither many of his Majesty's subjects have been transported, in divers parts of the Continent, and Islands of America, being a design tending to the honour of the Kingdom, and the enlargement of his Majesty's dominions: The Adventurers in this noble work, have for the most part, no other support but Tobacco, upon which, such a heavy rate is set, that the King receives twice as much, as the true value of the commodity to the owner." If merchants sought to sell their wares elsewhere, the king tried to tax this trade also "to the great discouragement of such active and industrious men."[37]

Parliament's renewal was still two years in the future when company members realized that they would get no exemptions written into their patent by Charles I. Whatever abatement they achieved would be ad hoc, through negotiations and appeals on individual cargoes. In the face of this discouragement, however, the company vowed to carry on and even to invest their own persons. When in January 1638 Pym reminded investors that the two years during which the money pledged in 1636 was to have been paid in were almost up and that the promised 500 colonists had not been sent, investors again renewed their commitment and eventually decided to extend the 1636 order. The adventurers in this stock had expended about £10,000 and had sent 300 men; more could not be gathered because of the plague. The new joint stock was

35. Moundeford to D'Ewes, Sept. 2, 1637, B. L., Harleian MS 386, f. 156, and undated, ibid., MS 287, f. 265. I thank Christopher Thompson for calling this correspondence to my attention. Barrington's copy of the offering is in Essex R. O., Hatfield Broad Oak MS D/DBa 02/21.
36. PIC Gen. Ct. 11–27–37.
37. Pym, *A Speech Delivered in Parliament . . . Concerning the Grievances of the Kingdome*, 17–18.

endorsed but without the grand hope of assembling a joint stock of £100,000 from the nobility and gentry of the nation. Provision had to be made for those who had subscribed in 1636 but did not wish to subscribe now.

At this point some company members volunteered to go out to the colony; the adventurers believed the venture would never prosper without such a presence. Charles I had promised "encouragement to those men of quality" who went in person, and investors had been toying with this idea ever since 1636 when John Pym had made the suggestion that the company be empowered to choose "by plurality of voice" those who should go out "and that to the same election every member of the company may be tied to submit." Moundeford wrote D'Ewes that the investors had determined to send three of their number, "no man to refuse, whom the company should choose.... Some of the Lords and others of great quality are resolved to go."[38]

In discussion of the new joint stock in 1637, the adventurers decided that before any company member went a good ship and pinnace with 100 fighting men and "proportionable" ammunition would be sent to prepare the fortifications and plant victuals. Those with pressing reasons could be excused, and no investor would be expected to go without at least one other member. They would be accompanied by "at the least" three good ships, two pinnaces, 250 seamen, and 300 landmen carrying sufficient ordnance and ammunition and a full year's supply of food. The ships and pinnaces would spend several months privateering, and henceforth company ships would not go out under the master alone "but that some Gentleman of experience, and courage shall be appointed captain of every such ship."[39]

In January 1638 Lord Saye offered to go to Providence Island "if a body of adventurers be joined" and if other company members agreed to accompany him. Two weeks later the Earl of Warwick, Lord Brooke, and Henry Darley agreed to go to the island "in their own person." The new joint stock was drawn up and subscribed on March 20. The Earl of Warwick, Lords Saye and Mandeville, and John Pym each now promised £1,000 to be paid in when a new supply was sent out; Lord Brooke promised £2,000 on the same terms. They decided to approach the king again for rectification of their privileges.[40]

The intractable problem of customs continued to plague the Provi-

---

38. PIC Ord. Ct. 5-14-36; Moundeford to D'Ewes, n.d., B. L., Harleian MS 287, f. 265. John Pym settled his will in 1637; see Russell, *Parliaments and English Politics*, 321.
39. PIC Ctee. 6-24-37; Gen. Ct., 11-27-37.
40. PIC Ctee. 1-31-38; Ct. 2-14-38; Ctee. 3-1-38; Ct. 3-3-38; Ct. 30-20-38.

dence Island Company throughout its existence. As the decade went on, other problems increasingly emerged to mar even their few successes. The mechanics of maintaining and supplying a settlement in the western Caribbean and operating in European markets forced investors to place their trust in men who knew those worlds and acted comfortably within them. Inevitably, some of these men proved to be irresponsible or inept, and investors lost by their mistakes. John Hart, first company husband, died, leaving his books in disarray; it took a year or more to clear up the problems he left the company. The death in 1638 of William Woodcock, trusted company husband and member, also cost the investors dearly because ownership of their goods was unclear. A cargo worth over £1,500 had recently arrived in the *Mary Hope* and in the ship of New Englander William Peirce, and most of that was now in question. Debts left from this debacle still plagued survivors in 1650.

Cargoes from Providence Island ended up in Europe without company permission. Braziletta wood sent from their second island of Association (Tortuga) to France in 1633 was claimed to have been in bad condition; this dispute, in which the company had been misled either by their colonists or by their agent in France, Abraham Chamberlain, dragged on for years. Other problems were caused when the *William and Anne* was wrecked off the coast of Brittany early in 1635. A year later the company was still trying to settle issues surrounding its cargo. When company member Henry Darley went to Holland in 1634, he was asked to investigate whether ships from Association were going there to sell their cargoes.[41]

Some agents actively cheated the company. Gabriel Rudd, merchant of Amsterdam, made off with £600 advanced to him for purchase of two pinnaces early in 1638. Earlier, the investors were so incensed at the dilatoriness of Giles Merch, who had taken command of the *Expectation* when the master died of a fever that raced through the crew, that they instituted a suit in the Admiralty Court. His actions cost them, they believed, thousands of pounds. Captain Thomas Newman had been authorized, like all company privateers, to enter into consortship agreements. He allied with the notorious captain Diego el Mulato, who, the company was informed, took a very rich prize they had captured to Holland. A Mr. Gossage was sent as company agent to recover what he could.[42]

41. PIC Gen. Ct. 2–14–34, 6–19–34; Prep. Ct. 6–13–34; Ctee. 7–18–34, 3–5–35; Ord. Ct. 3–9–35.
42. PIC Ct. 6–21–37, 1–28–39, 2–15–39; Gen. Ct. 4–2–38. A suit over tobacco shipped on the *Expectation* by John Florey who died on the voyage is in P. R. O., H. C. A. 24/100, 158–9.

Successful privateering provoked attacks in return, and captures of their ships forced the adventurers to confront this reality as they discussed their obligation to their captains who languished in foreign prisons. Captain William Rous, Pym's kinsman, required substantial payments to escape imprisonment in Spain in September 1639; he had been captured in the *Blessing* in 1636.[43] In 1639 London merchant Maurice Thompson's ship *Mary* was captured by Algerian pirates en route to Providence Island with settlers and a minerals expert. The sufferings of the crew and settlers cost further pain and expense and left Providence Island unsupplied at a crucial moment.[44]

Thus, even though some returns began to come in toward the end of the decade, company members could never feel in control. The leakage was immense, and their quest for control was doomed. Most members ceased taking an active part in company affairs. From 1638 on, the five investors who had subscribed to the 1638 stock – the Earl of Warwick, Lord Mandeville (the Earl of Manchester from 1642), Lords Saye and Brooke, and John Pym – carried on virtually alone. Rarely did any other member attend a meeting. Every few months these five were called on to contribute to meet company expenses, usually interest payments coming due. They entered into agreement with Maurice Thompson to carry on the business of supplying the island and helping develop its possibilities.

Some rich prizes were taken by company ships, but their fate sometimes reinforced the adventurers' sense of the fragility of the enterprise. A Spanish account of the colony's fall in 1641 alleged that in 1638 Providence Island privateers seized twenty frigates with 300,000 pounds of indigo, thirty cases of which were found on the island in 1641.[45] Edmund Moundeford's September 1637 letter to Sir Simonds D'Ewes wrote of "news of a ship of ores returning with ample booty from the Spanish." Two months later George Garrard wrote to Thomas Wentworth that "the traders also into the Isle of Providence...have taken a Prize sent home worth £15,000." Records of company meetings for these months refer to "intimations received" of Captain Thomas Newman's return with a rich cargo, and the Earl of Holland applied for

---

43. See Richard Fanshawe to Mr. Secretary Coke from Madrid, June 12, 1638, P. R. O., S. P. 94/40, f. 85; PIC Ct. 1–29–38; Ctee. 2–20–40.
44. PIC Ct. 5–15–39; Mtgs. 2–20–40, 2–25–40, 3–24–40. A naval expedition two years before had succeeded in freeing many English men and women held captive in Algiers; see John Dunton, *A True Journall of the Sally Fleet* (London, 1637).
45. "Relation of Captain Don Torivio de Palacio y Sierra," n.d., General Archive of the Indies, Seville, *Audiencia de Santa Fe, legajo* 223.

permission for Pym to remain in London to deal with it when it came in.[46]

But the company's great hopes were dashed. Captain Newman's ship *Providence* was captured in December 1638 off the coast of England two leagues from Dungeness by a Dunkirk pirate. Mariners testified in the Admiralty Court that the cargo, which included four diamonds and many bags of pearls – as well as bags of gold and silver, two huge lumps of gold so heavy a man could barely lift them, and a long gold chain – was worth £30,000. Because Newman had been captured in "English seas" and was held for actions "beyond the tropic line," the adventurers petitioned Charles I for assistance in getting both Newman and his cargo released. Secretary of State Coke wrote urgently to the king's representative in Brussels, Sir Balthazar Gerbier, of "this Extravagant wrong." Gerbier's reply indicated his difficulty in arguing the English case: The Dunkirkers held Newman to be "the greatest Pirate this day on the Seas." He wrote that the case would "prove a very intricate process."[47]

A decade later the company was still trying to get some satisfaction for this seizure and the expenses of getting Newman and officers who traveled with him released from prison. The outrage of their "barbarous and uncivil Usage" figured in Oliver Cromwell's 1654 declaration justifying the Western Design.[48] The *Happie Return*, one of Newman's ships, did come in, in April 1638, with a cargo of which the company's share was worth £2,000; some of the goods seized by Newman filtered in on other ships, but much of that value was lost in the tangled affairs following William Woodcock's death.[49]

Captain Samuel Axe's *Swallow* came into Plymouth richly loaded with gold, silver, jewels, indigo, and cochineal in May 1640. The few

46. Moundeford to D'Ewes, Sept. 2, 1637, B. L., Harleian MS 386, f. 156; Garrard to Wentworth, Dec. 16, 1637, *The Earl of Strafforde's Letters and Dispatches*, ed. W. Knowler, 2 vols. (London, 1729), II, 141; PIC Gen. Ct., 12–9–37, 2–11–37; Holland to Attorney General John Bankes, Jan. 2, 1638, Bod. Lib., Bankes MS bundle 65, piece 16.

47. Sir John Coke to Gerbier Jan. 9, 1639, Gerbier to Coke Jan. 22 and 31, 1639, P. R. O., S. P. Flanders, S. P. 77/29, ff. 19, 21, 51–4; Gerbier's remonstrance to the Cardinal Infante about Captain Thomas Newman, Jan. 26, 1639, ibid. ff. 46–9; mariners' depositions, P. R. O. CO 1/10; and Warwick to Windebank, Sept. 1639, ibid. John Winthrop noted Newman's capture in his *Journal*, ed. Hosmer, II, 11.

48. PIC Ct. 1–29–38, 2–12–39, 2–14–39, 5–15–39; Mtgs. 2–20–40; *A Declaration of His Highness*, in Patterson et al. eds., *Works of John Milton*, XIII, 543–5. Parliament took up the problem of the Dunkirk pirates and their support by the Brussels authorities in the 1640s; see H. M. C. Appendix to the 4th *Report* (London, 1874), House of Lords Manuscripts, 60, 79–80, 83. See also Craven, "Warwick, A Speculator in Piracy," *Hispanic American Historical Review* 10 (1930), 468–72.

49. PIC Gen. Ct. 4–2–38; Ct. 5–30–38, 12–13–38; Ctee. 4–12–38, 6–17–38.

investors present issued a blizzard of orders and commissions in May and June attempting to forestall or correct the seamen's embezzlement of the cargo's riches and get them safely up to London. The island's governor, Captain Nathaniel Butler, came home on the *Swallow*. The company investigated and apparently dismissed reports that Butler had taken the Spanish port of Trujillo and ransomed it for 16,000 pieces of eight.[50]

Shortly after, according to Spanish ambassador Alonso de Cárdenas, Captain James Riskinner successfully completed the voyage begun with Captain Butler, arriving at the Isle of Wight in the *Warwick* "very richly laden with silver, gold, Diamonds, Pearls, Jewels, and many other precious commodities." Riskinner testified that he had seized four Spanish ships. Suit was brought in the High Court of Admiralty against the master Edmund Grove, who was accused of embezzling "bags, boxes, and cabinets" of gold and jewels worth at least £1,000 from its cargo.[51]

In January 1641, after an extended period in the Indies, Captain William Jackson brought in indigo worth £2,000. Captain Jackson sailed from Providence Island on March 19, 1639. As we have seen, he captured a rich prize at Trujillo on the Bay of Honduras, which was redeemed by the inhabitants for 8,000 pounds of indigo, 2,000 pieces of eight, and two chains of gold. Jackson next appeared in New England on August 27, 1639, where, according to John Winthrop, he "brought much wealth in money, plate, indigo, and sugar. He sold his indigo and sugar here for £1,400, wherewith he furnished himself with commodities, and departed again for the West Indies." Jackson spent another year in the West Indies before returning to England in the winter of 1640–1, bringing a rich cargo for the Providence Island Company.[52]

In addition to the big strikes, there is also evidence that ships from Providence Island were capturing many smaller vessels engaged in coastal commerce and making life in the Spanish settlements very difficult. These ships would have been carrying humble products, such as the

50. PIC Ct. 5–17–40, 5–11–40, 5–27–40, 6–2–40, 6–9–40, 6–19–40, 6–20–40, 6–23–40, 6–26–40, 12–26–40. On the taking of Trujillo, see Chapter 10.
51. Don Alonso de Cárdenas to Charles I, July 11, 1640, P. R. O., S. P. 94/42, f. 1. On Cárdenas's complaints, see Craven, "Warwick, Speculator in Piracy," *Hispanic American Historical Review* 10 (1930), 472–3. Testimony on *Warwick and Secretary con Grove*, including the statement from Riskinner, is in P. R. O., H. C. A. 24/102, f. 9; H. C. A. 13/56, ff. 504–5, 512–13. I thank Joyce Lorimer for calling these documents to my attention.
52. On Jackson's return, see PIC Ct., 1–4–41, 2–10–41; Winthrop, *Journal*, ed. Hosmer, I, 309–10. The company took notice of Jackson's cargo and its contribution to the alleviation of their debt in PIC to Gov. and Coun., 3–29–41.

hides and tallow sold in New England from a "small Spanish frigate" captured by Captain Thomas Newman in 1638; Winthrop recorded that Newman had taken "many of their small vessels."[53] Shortly before his petition about James Riskinner, Spanish ambassador Don Alonso de Cárdenas had complained to the king about the "Ships of War" sent "with express order to infest the Coasts of the Indies, and to disturb the quiet and freedom, with which the Subjects of the King his Master, do sail and traffic peaceably in those Seas." Whatever losses the adventurers had sustained had, according to Cárdenas, been "abundantly satisfied." How much of this booty remained in Providence Island or was traded in the Indies is impossible to determine;[54] some may have found its way into the cargoes recorded in the company records. Individual investors may have made money off of these activities as adventurers in separate joint stocks. Such continuing depredations caused the Spanish authorities finally to decide that they must rid themselves of the English colony altogether.[55]

At the end of the colony's life, the adventurers also believed that they had discovered several rich mines whose development would enrich the company.[56] In their instructions for locating and testing ore, the investors showed their suspicion, probably justified, that colonists would siphon off proceeds before they were reported to London. The adventurers in most colonial ventures believed that some sleight of hand occurred in the keeping of accounts that allowed settlers to escape their obligations.

Providence Island Company members who had remained with the project were not prepared to pull out of their commitment as the decade neared its end; they had no foreknowledge of the great events soon to begin in England. In 1638 they petitioned the government for an enlarged grant that would allow them to create a settlement on the mainland or "some of the larger Islands of the West Indies." Although they had not yet had an answer by the end of March 1639, the Earl of Holland reported that the king had expressed "his most gracious

53. Winthrop, *Journal*, ed. Hosmer, I, 277, 283.
54. The Spanish claimed to have found many rich jewels and other commodities on Providence Island when it was taken in 1641; see "Relation of Captain Don Torivio de Palacio y Sierra," n.d., General Archive of the Indies, Seville, *Audiencia de Santa Fe, legajo*, 223.
55. "Don Alonso de Cárdena's Complaint and a Reference thereupon, 1640" in Sanderson, *Foedera* XX, 416. Captain John Smith saw privateering in much the same terms; he wrote bitterly of investors' seeking "Letters of Mark to rob some poor Merchants" instead of putting their money into building colonies; *The True Travels, Adventures, and Observations of Captaine John Smith*, 1630, in Barbour, ed., *Complete Works*, III, 223.
56. See Chapter 9.

approbation of the Company desire and intention." The members hoped
that those among them who were interested "will be pleased not to
dispose of themselves to any other plantation . . . and to assure themselves that the hearts of divers of the Company are really set upon the
prosecution of this enterprise."[57]

This hope may have been directed at the Earl of Warwick. While
the Providence Island Company sought an enlarged patent, Warwick
bought the patent for the islands of Trinidad and Tobago, and he
made an offer of £12,000 for Barbados, with "the intention to set up
sugar works." The Barbados deal had fallen through by 1639. The
next year he was accused of attempting to lure planters and servants
from Barbados to Trinidad and Tobago; he also tried to drain settlers
from Bermuda through his kinsman by marriage, Bermuda governor
Captain Thomas Chaddock (or Camock), brother of Sussex Camock.
Chaddock, who went to Trinidad in 1640, died there. Throughout the
1640s, Warwick repeatedly tried to populate these islands, which were
described as being rich in materials for ship building and commodities
in demand in Europe: "[T]he Tobacco of Trinidada is the best in the
known World."[58] Warwick, who became Lord Admiral under the parliament in 1642, also sent out privateering fleets throughout the 1640s,
including the enormously successful three-year voyage of Captain William
Jackson that culminated in the capture of the island of Jamaica.[59]

Warwick remained active in the Providence Island Company in the
late 1630s, and these other activities may have been perceived as
complementary to its economic success. At the same time, Lords Saye,
Brooke, and Mandeville redoubled their efforts on behalf of Providence
Island as a godly settlement. Lord Saye in particular sought settlers
from New England, and the company acquired an experienced and
godly governor, Captain John Humphrey, from Massachusetts. Although
their attention was increasingly diverted to events at home, they were in
the midst of renewing their commitment when the Spanish conquest
ended their hopes.

57. PIC Ct. at Fawsley 3–29–39.
58. On Barbados, see Bennett, "Peter Hay, Proprietary Agent in Barbados," *Jamaican
Historical Review* V (1965), 20–5. On Trinidad and Tobago, see "The Discription of
Tobago," and "The Discription of Trinidada," B. L., Sloane MS 3662, in Harlow,
ed., *Colonising Expeditions to the West Indies and Guiana*, 114–31, quotation on p.
120. For the Bermuda connection, see Warwick to Captain Chaddock, December 18,
1641, B. L. Add. MS 10615, no. 184; Wilkinson, *Adventurers of Bermuda*, 2nd ed.,
89 n., 400.
59. Harlow, ed., *Voyages of Jackson, Camden Miscellany* XIII; P. R. O., H. C. A.
24/106, f. 233; Craven, "Warwick, Speculator in Piracy," *Hispanic American
Historical Review* 10 (1930), 474–7; Christopher Thompson, *Two Puritan Commonwealths: Providence and New England* (Wivenhoe, Essex, 1987), 19–20.

Meanwhile, the company's debt steadily mounted; it was at its highest when the settlement fell to the third Spanish attack in 1641. In 1642 William Jessop drew up a list of the debts and distributed the obligation among the investors according to the various stocks to which they owed responsibility. At that time the company had thirteen bonds outstanding, the principal ranging in size from £100 to £1,500; the total debt represented by these bonds was £9,221.03.01. In addition, the Earl of Manchester and John Pym owed three bonds of £500 each; Lord Saye was a cosigner on one of those. Jessop also laid out the debts owed by the members as a share of this sum. Most owed less than £300; several were indebted for under £100. The five major investors owed much more: The Earl of Warwick owed £975; Lord Mandeville £453; Lord Saye £1,190; Lord Brooke £1,879; and John Pym £1,739.[60]

The English colony on Providence Island was "extinguished" shortly before the outbreak of civil war at home. John Winthrop, who resented the recent efforts to recruit settlers in New England, recorded the event: "... Providence was taken by the Spaniards, and the lords lost all their care and cost to the value of above £60,000."[61] Company affairs were in confusion throughout the 1640s. Problems inevitably grew out of the nature of joint stock companies, in which there was no limitation on liability; any member could be held liable for the entire debt.[62] Members of parliament and their servants were immune from prosecutions for debt; with the Long Parliament in operation, most Providence Island Company members were thus beyond the reach of creditors.[63]

Sir Thomas Barrington, like John Pym, Lord Brooke, and Sir Edmund

60. These reckonings were contained in a deposition made by Jessop in 1644 at the request of Alexander Pym when Jessop was going abroad. Copies of the deposition, with the names of Jessop and Warwick at the bottom, are in the Essex R. O., Hatfield Broad Oak MS D/DBa 02/26; and in the Warwickshire R. O., Warwick Castle MS BB 841, Box 457, CR 1886. See Appendix III.
61. Winthrop, *Journal*, ed. Hosmer, II, 12. Winthrop made another estimate of the company's losses. He carried on an indignant correspondence with Lord Saye over the company's attempts to lure settlers from New England at the end of the 1630s. Notes on the back of a letter from Lord Saye obviously made in haste and anger contained several questions, the last of which was: "What is become of their 1200001?" See Massachusetts Historical Society *Collections* 5th ser., I (1871), 303.
62. On the rules under which joint stock companies operated, see Craven, *Introduction to the History of Bermuda*, 26, 32–3.
63. In 1641 a merchants' committee testified that MPs' immunity had already cost London merchants £1,000,000; see Hirst, *Authority and Conflict,* 212. One example was privateer Captain William Jackson, who in 1641 claimed immunity from prosecution for debts owed London merchant Thomas Frere for an expedition before his Providence Island Company service. The Earl of Warwick testified that Jackson was "his menial Servant, and took Wages of his Lordship"; Frere was briefly imprisoned for contempt. See Harlow, "Introduction," *Voyages of Captain William Jackson, Camden Miscellany* XIII, vii.

Moundeford, died in 1643; his heir Sir John Barrington petitioned parliament in 1645 for relief from company creditors who hounded him, as one who did not have the immunity of a member of parliament, for the entire debt. Barrington recalled the zeal for the nation's good and for religion that motivated the Providence Island Company, and the great sums they invested, but "the said Island was by the hard and undue dealing of such as then swayed the Affairs of this Realm exposed to the rapine of the public enemy, by means whereof the said Adventurers... were greatly prejudiced." He asked for immunity from all but his father's own debt, "whereby your Lordships shall preserve from ruin a family that hath been (and he hopes shall remain) serviceable to the State, without injustice to the Creditors." The reply, pointing to lands allocated to John Pym's estate for the purpose of paying his debt, granted Barrington's plea for immunity.[64]

A few last meetings of company members or their heirs took place in 1649 and 1650. After the unsettled Civil War years, creditors were pressing for their money. Now the debts were again laid out, and everything was included. Some members with lower indebtedness had already paid off much of their obligation, but the high totals remained high. Added to the sums from Jessop's distribution of 1642 were amounts still owing from the first adventure. In addition, William Woodcock's debt was distributed among various investors. Several adventurers acceded to Lady Brooke's demand for a reduction in Lord Brooke's account, and a portion of his debt was also distributed among several adventurers. The total debt was £18,898.19.3.[65] The company petitioned for a share of the ransom of the *Santa Clara*, a Spanish ship seized in English waters in the early 1640s, as recompense for their loss in the capture of Captain Newman's ship in 1638. Company members placed great hope on this source of funds, but their suit dragged on without result.[66]

Private papers bear witness to families' struggles to pay off these

64. Essex R. O., Hatfield Broad Oak MSS D/DBa 02/28, 30; *Journals of the House of Lords* VII, 506, July 24, 1645, calendared in Historical Manuscripts Commission Sixth *Report*, 71. On Pym's estate, see B. L. Add MS 31116, f. 99v. On Moundeford, see R. W. Ketton-Cramer, *Norfolk in the Civil War: A Portrait of a Society in Conflict* (London, 1969), 145–6.
65. A copy of these debts is in Essex R. O., Hatfield Broad Oak MS D/DBa 02/25. For a complete listing, see Appendix III. The estimates presented in William Robert Scott, *The Constitution and Finance of English, Scottish and Irish Joint-Stock Companies to 1720* (Cambridge, 1912), II, 327–37, are not reliable on these issues.
66. On the *Santa Clara* suit, see PIC Mtg. 4–17–49, 2–5–50; Hist. Man. Com. 4th *Report* (London, 1874), April 20, June 28, July 6, 1641; 5th *Report* (London, 1876), Oct. 12, 1643. Suits concerning the *Santa Clara* run through the records in H. C. A. 24/105, 106, 108. I thank Joyce Lorimer for bringing this material to my attention.

debts during the 1650s. Lord Saye went into retirement after the execution of Charles I in 1649; his son Nathaniel Fiennes acted for him in the 1650s. Lady Brooke, left to speak for her husband's interests with the assistance of his solicitor, Colonel John Bridges, was able to secure release from her son's wardship and to deal with the creditors. She wrote anxiously to Nathaniel Fiennes in 1652 or 1653 that the sheriff was lying in wait to arrest her brother-in-law William Greville "for the debts which Mr. Pym should discharge, his [William Greville's] lying in prison for the Company's Debt will much reflect upon them he never having been one of the Company."

In the 1650s Nathaniel Fiennes took on some of the role John Pym had played in the Providence Island Company in the 1630s. He wrote several long letters to the Earl of Manchester in 1652 outlining his attempts to contact company members and get their assurances of willingness to pay their portion of the company debts. Like Lady Brooke, he complained frequently of Alexander Pym's failure to fulfill his promises. He wrote that he was "almost weary of the business, for that I find no body almost mindeth it but myself, and it is too great a burden for one man, and besides, as I always feared so now by what your Lordship writeth concerning Sir John Gore's debt I begin to find that transacting business for others in their absence and at a distance my actions would be subject to mistakes, and yet I thought I had writ plainly enough." So intricate were the settlements that unless all agreed to pay, no one would. After describing his many complicated negotiations, Fiennes wrote: "That which giveth all the stop in the business is Mr. Pym's not performing what he undertook." Some of the actual process of settlement can be followed in the papers of Brooke's estate, which show the bonds slowly being canceled throughout the 1650s and into the 1660s.[67]

Those members of the Providence Island Company who survived into the 1650s and the heirs of those who did not must have wondered whether the venture could have been designed differently for success. When the colony was founded, no one could have foreseen the events of the 1640s, nor could they have predicted what would become possible

---

67. Lady Brooke's letter to Nathaniel Fiennes is in the Huntington R. O. DD M 28/7/15. Parliament settled £5,000 on her youngest son Fulke, born after his father's death, and granted her the London house of Lord Digby, the Earl of Bristol, in recompense for damage done to Brooke's estate while Bristol, a royalist, was guardian; see Strider, *Lord Brooke*, 76–7. Letters of Nathaniel Fiennes on settlement of the company's debts are in the same collection, DD M 28/7/16–20. The Brooke papers are in the Warwick R. O., Warwick Castle MS, BB 841, Box 457, CR 1886. I thank Christopher Thompson for bringing these manuscripts to my attention.

for the adherents of the reformed religion at home. When Oliver Cromwell was persuaded to embark on the Western Design, the fate of Providence Island figured heavily in his advisors' thinking, and the founders' conception took on a renewed vitality.

11

The End and Persistence of Providence Island

NEITHER PROVIDENCE ISLAND'S DESERTION by Nathaniel Butler nor the 1640 Spanish attack and its aftermath, even when combined with heady and demanding events in England as Charles I was forced to call parliament after an eleven-year hiatus, led the core among the investors to abandon their commitment to their venture in the Indies. Rather than being a time to shelve their plans in favor of other more immediately pressing problems, the changed environment made the adventurers once again optimistic about the realization of their hopes. In 1640 and 1641 the company turned in a new direction in the search for godly colonists and the stability they would bring: They urged the remigration of settlers already in New England who would consider moving south.

From the perspective of hindsight, this seems a ludicrous proposition. In 1640 the little island colony had less than a year of life left; New England was on the brink of a career of unprecedented colonial growth and strength. Yet, what is so clear after the fact was not apparent at the time. Rapid political change in England brought a dramatic drop in the flow of colonists to New England, which, without the influx of money the emigrants had brought, suffered a calamitous economic depression. From the viewpoint of 1640, it was a propitious time to convince colonists to move to a more promising location, and many New Englanders were prepared to listen.[1]

The Providence Island adventurers had always seen the American puritan colonies as one great interlocking venture. Their eyes were focused on England and on the good that colonies might do for their country and for the reformed religion. New England was both too far from the fight against the potent enemy of both, Spain, and too cold

---

1. John Winthrop described the beginning of the depression in his *Journal*, ed. Hosmer, II, 19, 31.

and barren of rich commodities to help England in the momentous struggle. By 1640, as the pace of events suddenly quickened and with it the grandees' sense that providential forces were coming to their culmination, it was time to bring the country's resources together and realize the potential God had given them.

When parliament convened, John Pym pointed to the weakness of the Spanish empire and the large numbers of English men and women in America: "There are now in those parts . . . at least Sixty thousand able persons of this Nation, many of them well armed, and their bodies seasoned to that Climate, which with a very small charge might be set down, in some advantageous parts of these pleasant, rich and fruitful Countries, and easily make his Majesty Master of all that treasure, which not only foments the War, but is the great support of Popery in all parts of Christendom."[2]

By 1640 John Winthrop's perspective was less English and more New English, and he responded to such suggestions with outrage. In a famous exchange of letters, Lord Saye answered Winthrop's charge that Saye was unfairly denigrating New England. Saye accused Winthrop of misapplying Scripture by arrogating to his colony those passages in the Bible in which God chose the land of Canaan for Israel. He correctly predicted New England's economic decline as immigration fell off, leaving colonists with nothing but the cold, barren land, in which "rich men grow poor and poor men if they come over are a burden," and suggested that colonists had a free choice.

Lord Saye did not deny that emigration to New England had been a work of God, but he suggested that God had meant to gather people in Massachusetts "until you were grown unto such a body as were able to do him service, and sit down in safety in such places as may be most fit for the work he hath in hand." And, lest there be any confusion over what God's work consisted of, he reminded Winthrop of the necessity of "the advancement of the gospel and putting down the great adversary thereof that man of sin, whereunto as you are now you neither are able nor are likely to be to put your hands to the least wheel that is to be turned about in that work otherways than by well wishing thereunto." Those who remained in New England would sit out the culminating events of God's great drama.[3]

2. Pym, *A Speech Delivered in Parliament . . . Concerning the Grievances of the Kingdome*, 38.
3. Saye and Sele to Winthrop, July 9, 1640, *Winthrop Papers* IV, 263–268, quotations from 265–6. Giles Firmin wrote to Winthrop from Ipswich on February 12., 1640, reporting that he had "heard a Conclusion gathered against these Plantations, because the Lord hath so sadly afflicted the founders of them in their estates; that therefore it

Lord Saye struck a raw nerve because, as Winthrop wrote, "many men began to inquire after the southern parts." Thomas Gorges, the young puritan governor of his uncle Sir Ferdinando's colony in Maine, visited Boston in 1641 and "found the place in a distracted condition, men unresolved in their minds what to do, some for the West Indies, some for Long Island, some for old England."[4]

Captain John Humphrey, who had expressed doubts about the success of the Massachusetts colony in such a northerly location as early as 1630, was selected to succeed Nathaniel Butler as governor of Providence Island and of the company's projected colony on the Central American mainland. Captain Humphrey was married to the sister of the Earl of Lincoln, whose own wife was Lord Saye's daughter. Humphrey, a lawyer, was treasurer of the Dorchester Company, the antecedent of the Massachusetts Bay Company. At the founding, he remained in England to oversee the company's affairs there. When he emigrated in 1634, he immediately became an assistant and played a very active part in the colony's life, culminating in his appointment as "serjeant-major general," the highest military post in Massachusetts Bay, in 1638.[5]

Humphrey collected 200 to 300 people "(at least)" willing to go with him to Providence Island, leading to a bitter argument with John Endecott "in the open assembly at Salem" over his recruitment efforts.

was not a way of God, to forsake our Country," ibid., 191. See Andrew Delbanco, *The Puritan Ordeal* (Cambridge, MA, 1989), chap. 3, for a description of the profound unease felt in New England over the colonists' failure to participate in the Civil War.

4. Winthrop, *Journal*, ed. Hosmer, I, 333–5; Thomas Gorges to Sir Ferdinando Gorges, Sept.?, 1641 in Moody, ed., *Letters of Thomas Gorges*, 52. See Gura, *Glimpse of Sion's Glory*, 220–5, and Frank Strong, "A Forgotten Danger to the New England Colonies," American Historical Association, *Annual Report for the Year 1898* (1899), 79–94. On the depression in Massachusetts, see Bernard Bailyn, *The New England Merchants in the Seventeenth Century* (New York, 1955), chap. 3.

   Hugh Peter so despaired for the future of New England that he seriously considered emigrating to Providence Island; ultimately he returned to England where he became an influential preacher with the parliamentary army; Peter to John Winthrop, April 1638, in "The Winthrop Papers," Mass. Hist. Soc. *Collections* 4th ser., VII (Boston, MA, 1865), 200–1. See Raymond Phineas Stearns, *The Strenuous Puritan: Hugh Peter, 1598–1660* (Urbana, IL, 1954), 149–50. Stearns assigns the date of April 1639. On the widespread fears of New England's failure as indicating a misreading of God's will and the remigration it occasioned, see Cohen, *God's Caress*, 229–33, and Cressy, *Coming Over*, 194–203. Cressy argues that *New England's First Fruits*, written by Henry Dunster and/or Thomas Weld and published in London in 1643, was intended partly as counterpropaganda.

5. Humphrey to Isaac Johnson, December 9, 1630, *Winthrop Papers*, II, 327–9; Humphrey to John Winthrop, December 12, 1630, ibid., 331–4. On the appointment of Humphrey as governor of Providence Island, see PIC Ct., 2–25–41, and Winthrop, *Journal*, ed. Hosmer, II, 25–6. For the career of John Humphrey, see Frances Rose-Troup, "John Humfry," *Essex Institute Hist. Colls.*, LXV (1929), 293–308.

The future Fifth Monarchist Thomas Venner was reported to have amassed a company in Salem ready to transfer; Venner was "zealous for emigrating to Providence, W. I." Thomas Lechford also reported the gathering of a large group for the "Lords Isle of Providence" and the adjacent mainland, which many thought to have a better climate and soil than New England.[6]

So poor had Massachusetts become, Humphrey advised the investors in a letter to Lord Mandeville, that prospective remigrants were selling their assets at a third or a fourth of their value. Their transplantation would have to be funded from London, and repayment must be out of commodities raised in the south. Humphrey counted on the grandees' support, "for I know the deep dye of Christ's blood which you have received will not suffer you to let any of his causes to die & languish in your hands."

Humphrey warned the Providence Island adventurers against laying "any clogs or burdens" upon the New Englanders, "more than they have here been acquainted with either in civil or Ecclesiastical matters."[7] The investors, finally seeing within their grasp a massive immigration of the right kind of seasoned settlers sufficient to begin the second phase of their colonization, that of the Central American mainland, acceded to the New Englanders' demands. They finally offered the outright land ownership and control over governance that Providence Island's planters had asked for all along.

In late February 1641, within days of clearing the charges laid by Andrew Carter against Henry Halhead, Richard Lane, Hope Sherrard, and Nicholas Leverton, the investors decided that "to carry on the affairs of Providence" Captain Humphrey "now in New England" be commissioned as governor and that Maurice Thompson be allowed £100 for sending out a ship with 100 men and supplies, especially the cordage and shot necessary for the privateers. Humphrey was to begin as governor of Providence Island, a post the investors wrote him was "below your merit," but would become governor of a much greater enterprise at Cape Gracias a Dios as soon as the colony had attracted sufficient people. When Humphrey's absence was required, Captain Thomas Fitch, the new deputy governor returning directly from England,

6. Humphrey to Earl of Manchester, March 27, 1641, Hist. Man. Com. *Eighth Report, Manchester Papers,* 424; Felt, *Annals of Salem,* II, 577; Lechford, *Plain Dealing,* 113–14; Endecott to John Winthrop, 1639, in "Winthrop Papers," Massachusetts Historical Society *Collections* 4th ser., VI (Boston, 1863), 138–41; Winthrop, *Journal,* ed. Hosmer, II, 25–6.
7. Humphrey to Lord Mandeville, March 27, 1641, Historical Manuscripts Commission, Eighth *Report,* Manchester Papers, 424, original in Bermuda Archives.

would function in his place. Humphrey would have complete freedom to come and go as developments warranted. As token of their faith in the new leadership, the investors disbanded the council of war. Letters and commissions were sealed throughout March 1641.[8]

In all their deliberations and letters, the company promised every encouragement to the new settlers. Early in March a Mr. Goose approached the Providence Island Company with a proposition for settling a large company of New Englanders on the mainland. An agreement was finally settled with Emmanuel Truebody for the transport of Humphrey and his colonists in two ships of 140 tons each, the *Swallow* and the *Salutation*, in return for twenty-five slaves. William Truebody, father of Emmanuel, was to receive 400 acres of land anywhere within the company's patent outside of Providence; William was to become captain of a fort when such was built and was also to be a councilor of the new settlement. Truebody agreed to transport a further 100 persons from New England within a year of receiving his reward. Former planters were promised the right to remove property, slaves, and servants from Providence Island as soon as such actions would not endanger the colony.

To the intending settlers, the company promised that Captain Humphrey would be their governor and that his tenure would be such as both the company and "the principal Members of such Colony, shall from time to time" agree. Colonists were promised "all reasonable conditions and encouragements for the freedom, comfort and prosperity of the said Plantations," and the company promised to listen carefully to all propositions. The Massachusetts Bay general court had tried to dissuade intending migrants by pointing out the danger of the West Indies and also "Their subjection to such governors as those in England shall set over them, etc." To attract these planters, the Providence Island Company was finally willing to give up their control.[9]

Humphrey had been making preparations in New England for some time. Some of his recruits could have sailed in 1640 but were prevented by lack of shipping. He wrote that many discontented people in New England were currently thinking of going to Florida instead, a voyage that could be accomplished in small barks, and asked the grandees to

8. PIC Ct. 3-9-41, 3-10-41, Mtg. 3-24-41; PIC Commission to Capt. Humphrey, 3-1-41; Commission to Captain Fitch, 3-41; PIC to Capt. Humphrey, 3-31-41; PIC Instr. to Fitch, 3-29-41.
9. PIC Ct. 3-9-41, 3-15-41, 3-24-41, 3-25-41, 6-28-41; PIC Inst. to Fitch, 3-29-41; PIC to Gov. and Coun., 3-29-41; PIC Agreement with Truebody, 6-29-41; Winthrop, *Journal*, ed. Hosmer, I, 333-4.

send shipping as quickly as possible. Winthrop, watching all these preparations with dismay, was gratified by Humphrey's reverses, seeing the judgment of God in the fire, started by arson, that burned all his stored corn and hay in 1640. The captain persevered, however, and in 1641 the first contingent of thirty men, five women, and eight children set out for the Caribbean in two tiny ships of the New England merchant William Peirce.[10]

Providence Island Company members' relationship with New England went back before the founding of either colony. The Massachusetts Bay Company had won its original patent through the intervention of sympathetic Providence Island Company members, including the Earl of Warwick, who was at that time president of the old and virtually moribund Council for New England, the heir of the original western merchants' Virginia Company.[11] John Humphrey wrote to Massachusetts leader Isaac Johnson, also brother-in-law to the Earl of Lincoln, "We are all much bound to my Lord Saye for his cordial advice and true affections. As also to my Lord of Warwick. Sir Nathaniel Rich deserves much acknowledgement of his wise handling Sir Ferdinando Gorge...."[12]

In 1632 Warwick made a further New England grant to men who shared his vision of England's colonial future. Lands along the Connecticut River were granted in joint tenancy to a group of patentees including Providence Island Company members Lords Saye and Brooke, Sir Nathaniel Rich, Richard Knightley, John Pym, Henry Darley, company husband William Woodcock and, as clerk, company secretary William Jessop.[13] As early as 1630, patentee John Humphrey wrote of this patent to be arranged by Warwick, "My lord of Warwick will take a Patent of that place you writ of for himself, and so we may be bold to do there as if it were our own." In reality, the patent was never properly

10. Winthrop, *Journal*, ed. Hosmer, I, 333–5, II, 11–12.
11. See Andrews, *Colonial Period*, I, 354–9, 365–8 for the ambiguity of this grant.
12. Humphrey to Johnson, December 9, 1630, *Winthrop Papers*, II, 329. John Masters in Watertown, Massachusetts, wrote in 1631 to Sir Thomas and Lady Barrington and other gentry that the land was fit for ladies and gentlemen as soon as more accommodations were built, apparently indicating that Barrington had floated the idea of emigrating as the Great Migration began; B. L., Egerton MS 2645, f. 245.
13. Also included were associates of the company members: Sir Richard Saltonstall, Sir Arthur Haslerig (Brooke's brother-in-law), John Hampden, John Humphrey, George Fenwick, Henry Lawrence, Sir Matthew Boynton, Edward Hopkins, Herbert Pelham, Philip Nye, as well as a member of the Barrington family, and sons of Warwick and Saye. Charles J. Hoadly, *The Warwick Patent* (Hartford, 1902), 6–10; Newton, *Colonising Activities*, 83–4.

sealed because Sir Ferdinando Gorges, a founding member, reasserted his authority in the revived Council for New England and ousted Warwick. The patentees believed the grant was legal, however, and acted accordingly.[14]

In 1633 a group of lords and gentlemen, including many of the same people, acquired rights to land along the Piscataqua River in New Hampshire including the site of Dover.[15] The Connecticut River grant was not pursued immediately, but the Piscataqua patentees did attempt to enter the fur trade, which brought them into collision with stations already set up by Plymouth colony. John Winthrop, writing of an incident on the Kennebeck River between Saye and Brooke's men and Plymouth agents with loss of life on both sides, warned Sir Nathaniel Rich, saying that the Plymouth colonists had "engrossed all the Chief places of trade in N: E: viz: Kenebeck, Penobscott, Narigancet, and Conecticott." Windsor on the Connecticut River was also a Plymouth trading post site.[16] At the same time, Winthrop recorded receipt of a letter from the Earl of Warwick congratulating Massachusetts Bay on its success and offering "his help to further us in it."[17]

In 1635 the Connecticut River patentees began to act on their grant. Many reasons coincided to encourage action. Sir Nathaniel Rich had written to John Winthrop in 1633 inquiring about the religious and civil polity in Massachusetts Bay, as had Lords Saye and Brooke in 1634. The unsatisfactory replies, indicating blurring of civil and religious jurisdictions, may have inspired the gentlemen to set up

---

14. Humphrey to Johnson, December 9, 1630, *Winthrop Papers*, II, 329; Andrews, *Colonial Period*, I, 403–4.
15. These patentees included Providence Island Company members Lords Saye and Brooke, and Brooke's half-brother Godfrey Bosville. Saltonstall and Haslerig were patentees, as were the Reverend Ephraim Huitt, George Wyllys, William Whiting, and Edward Holyoke. Charles E. Clark, *The Eastern Frontier: The Settlement of Northern New England, 1610–1763* (Hanover, NH, 1983), 39–41; Thomas Hutchinson, *The History of the Colony and Province of Massachusetts-Bay*, ed. Lawrence Shaw Mayo, 2 vols. (Cambridge, MA, 1936), I. 92; Edward Howes to John Winthrop, Jr., March 25, 1633, *Winthrop Papers* III, 114–15; Lemuel A. Welles, "Introduction," *The Wyllys Papers, Collections of the Connecticut Historical Society* XXI (1924), xxii–xxiii; and Martin, *Profits in the Wilderness*, 102.
16. Winthrop to Rich, May 22, 1634, *Winthrop Papers* III, 166–8. Both Winthrop and Bradford wrote about this incident in their histories: Winthrop, *Journal*, ed. Hosmer, I, 111, 123–9; Bradford, *Of Plymouth Plantation*, ed. Morison, 262–8. Lords Saye and Brooke borrowed five pieces of ordnance from the Providence Island Company for their New England venture in 1633, for which they paid £25 10s in 1634; PIC Ct. 7–9–33; 12–2–34.
17. Winthrop, *Journal*, ed. Hosmer, I, 130. Captain Thomas Wiggin, the investors' agent in New Hampshire, testified on behalf of Massachusetts Bay to the privy council committee investigating attacks by Ferdinando Gorges and his allies on the puritan colony's charter in 1633; see Andrews, *Colonial Period*, I, 408–9.

alternative puritan communities along the river, a prime location for both agriculture and trade. As the royal government moved to collect an irregular tax in ship money and the celebrated trial of John Hampden occurred in England, the idea of an acceptable American refuge seemed more imperative. The creation of a Commission for Regulating Plantations under the chairmanship of Archbishop Laud in April 1634 promised novel scrutiny and control of future settlements. Moreover, Sir Ferdinando Gorges, edged out of power in the Council for New England by the Earl of Warwick, had begun to attempt to reassert control over some of the regions ceded by the earl, and largely as a result of his effort, the royal government had instituted quo warranto proceedings against the Massachusetts Bay charter. Such proceedings had resulted in the forfeiture of the Virginia Company's charter a decade before, with the conversion of Virginia to a royal colony, and supporters in England feared the same fate for Massachusetts. The activities of Dutch traders along the Connecticut also made action imperative.[18]

The Connecticut River was a natural location for settlement. Unlike inland Massachusetts, it offered excellent farmland with ready access to prime trading locations. Its origination in the far north made it a natural conduit for the fur trade as well as a highway for the colonists' trade in their own commodities. John Underhill, who had been in conference with the Providence Island investors, wrote in 1638 of the natural riches of Saybrook and the fertile meadows lining the river, which was navigable for sixty miles by pinnaces: "[P]ity it is so famous [excellent, splendid] a place should be so little regarded."[19]

In 1635 the Massachusetts Bay colonists also began to move across country to plant along the Connecticut River at Springfield, Windsor, Wethersfield, and Hartford. Sometimes, as at Windsor, clashes occurred between these remigrants and settlers sent directly from England by the lords and gentlemen, but relations between Massachusetts Bay and the patentees in England remained cordial. Both sides saw their activities as complementary rather than adversarial. In the uncertainty of the times, colonization in Connecticut by the lords and gentlemen was "most advantageous both for the securing of our friends at the bay and our own personal accommodations."[20]

John Winthrop, Jr., son of the Massachusetts Bay governor, accepted

18. See Andrews, *Colonial Period*, I, 411–22. On events in England and the involvement of the puritan grandees in them, see Cust, *Forced Loan*.
19. Underhill, *Newes from America*, 18–19.
20. Henry Lawrence to John Winthrop, Jr., September 22, 1635, *Winthrop Papers* III, 212–13.

a call in 1635 to govern the settlement at the mouth of the Connecticut River named Saybrook for its principal founders.[21] Henry Vane, puritan son of Charles I's secretary of state and governor of Massachusetts Bay in 1636–7, acted as agent for the lords and gentlemen interested in planting settlements on the river to the west, as did Hugh Peter. Peter recruited Lion Gardiner, whom he had known as a godly soldier in the Netherlands when Peter preached in exile there, to be the colony's engineer and military expert. Both Vane and Peter spent time in Saybrook.

The investors strongly indicated their intention to emigrate personally. Henry Lawrence wrote in September of 1635, "[W]e are peremptory for Connecticut, it being as you know and so continuing, the joint resolution of us all that nothing but a plain impossibility could divert us from that place," and he warned Winthrop to get ready for many emigrants the next summer. Two leading Yorkshire puritans, Sir Matthew Boynton and Sir William Constable, determined to remove to Saybrook, Boynton with a "great family." They were recruited by Providence Island Company member Henry Darley of Buttercrambe in Yorkshire. Constable, chronically in debt, actually sold his estates and moved to London. Boynton, also in London, was more cautious; he enjoined absolute secrecy on Winthrop. Their activities attracted attention despite their best efforts, and according to the Reverend Philip Nye, "when they came down found the Country full of the reports of their going." They abated their efforts for the time, but, he assured Winthrop, "our gentlemens minds remain the same, and are in a way of selling off their estates with the greatest expedition." Ultimately, however, these "Gentlemen of the North" gave up plans of going to Connecticut; in 1637 they went with Nye to a gathered church at Arnhem in Holland that also included fellow Yorkshireman Sir Richard Saltonstall. Boynton's son Francis stayed behind; he had just married Constance, daughter of Lord Saye. In the event, only George Fenwick of all the investors went to Saybrook.[22]

The Saybrook venture is well known, as is the apparent early decline

---

21. See the agreement between the younger Winthrop and the Saybrook Company, July 7, 1635, *Winthrop Papers* III, 198–9. See Martin, *Profits in the Wilderness*, 53.
22. Philip Nye to John Winthrop, Jr., September 21, 1635, *Winthrop Papers* III, 211; Henry Lawrence to same, September 22, 1635, ibid., 212–13; Sir Matthew Boynton to same, February 23, 1636, ibid., 226–7; J. T. Cliffe, *The Yorkshire Gentry, From the Reformation to the Civil War* (London, 1969), 123, 306–8; Greaves and Zaller, ed., *Biographical Dictionary of British Radicals*, "Sir William Constable"; Foster, *Long Argument*, 29–31, 163.
The new Laudian commission for plantations meant strict controls on emigration

of commitment by its sponsors despite the urgency expressed by them in its founding. The demands of the renewal of the Providence Island venture in 1636 combined with the exigencies of the Pequot War in Connecticut to cause the adventurers to keep Saybrook a fort rather than a full settlement. Thus, the Warwick Patent has appeared to be little more than a flash in the pan. But historians have overlooked the simultaneous spreading of influential Providence Island Company associates all along the Connecticut River and along the shore. In many cases evidence of these other settlements has been erroneously assigned to Saybrook. Thus, evidence of a large and ambitious plan to plant an English-sponsored puritan presence in Connecticut to balance the Massachusetts-based westward swarming has been lost.

In June 1635 Francis Styles and his two brothers, London carpenters, arrived in Boston on their way to the site of Windsor with a party of eighteen indentured servants. They were sent by Sir Richard Saltonstall, original member of the Massachusetts Bay Company and emigrant in the *Arbella* fleet, and Providence Island Company husband William Woodcock to build a settlement with accommodation for gentlemen on the river above Hartford.[23] Plymouth already had a trading post at Windsor, and a party was moving there at the same time from Dorchester, Massachusetts. Massachusetts claimed that the land was freely available as the "Lord's waste" and bolstered that claim by purchase from Indians. The Plymouth men replied that if it was waste land, they should have it by right of prior settlement, but only the Warwick patentees claimed a commission to settle that was recognizable under English law. Nonetheless, to the dismay of both Plymouth and Saltonstall, the Dorchester men "greedily snatched up all the best grounds upon that River," and forced the others out. Stiles and his men finally accepted land at Warehouse Point to the north. John Winthrop wrote his son of a "very loving letter from my Lord Saye" in which, referring to "those up the River [who] have carved largely for themselves," Saye wrote that "he thinks they will after repent when they see what helps they have deprived themselves of."[24]

and colony building; Andrews, *Colonial Period*, I, 411–14. See the coded letter to John Winthrop, Jr., from Sir John Clotworthy, April 1635, *Winthrop Papers* III, 195–6.

23. Saltonstall returned to England in 1631 but remained intimately involved in Massachusetts Bay affairs; several of his children continued to live in the colony and he defended its charter in England. In 1640 he married Martha, daughter of Thomas Camock. For his biography, see Robert E. Moody, ed., *The Saltonstall Papers, 1607–1815*, Massachusetts Historical Society *Collections* 80–81 (1972), I, 4–24.

24. Bartholomew Greene to Sir Richard Saltonstall, December 30, 1635, *Winthrop Papers* III, 217–18; Lord Brooke to John Winthrop, Jr., 1636, ibid., 218–19; Sir

The Connecticut River was perceived as an economic unit. The settlement of both Saybrook and the Windsor region in 1635 would have given the patentees control of the Connecticut River from its mouth to the falls. The younger Winthrop's good friend Edward Howes advised that as soon as John had fortified the mouth of the Connecticut "meanly well," he should leave a garrison there and "go farther up," even as far as seventy miles, observing and learning from the Indians where the best place, "commodious for trade and husbandry," would be.[25] Hartford, Wethersfield, and Springfield were also settled in 1635, each by a small party of remigrants from Massachusetts.

Wethersfield was founded from Watertown; its leading planters had come with Sir Richard Saltonstall from Halifax in Yorkshire in the original migration. Among the other settlers were the same James Cole who had found the worship services sponsored by Lords Brooke and Saye in Warwickshire so inspiring, and a member of Providence Island Company secretary William Jessop's family.[26]

In 1636 two groups came to bolster the plantation at Hartford. Thomas Hooker, a grateful client of the Earl of Warwick and correspondent of many Providence Island Company members, led a migration from Newtown (Cambridge) in Massachusetts. Hooker transplanted partly because, like the investors, he had serious doubts about the Massachusetts way of admission to church membership and of restricting civil rights to church members.[27] Early in 1636 Sir Richard Saltonstall wrote that when he came back to New England, he intended to settle at Hartford and "Join with Mr. Hooker," rather than at Windsor.[28]

At the same time, George Wyllys, a close associate of Saye and Brooke, sent a party of indentured servants from England under William Gibbins to begin a plantation suitable for a gentleman at Hartford. Gibbins and his men built a grand house of two stories with an attic; his land contained the now-famous Charter Oak. Wyllys, lord of the manor of Fenny Compton in Warwickshire, appointed as trustees

Richard Saltonstall to same, February 27, 1636, ibid., 229–30; John Winthrop to same, June 10, 1636, ibid., 268. The Plymouth men would have preferred to deal with representatives of the lords and gentlemen than with the Dorchester men. For events as seen by the Plymouth traders, see Bradford, *Of Plymouth Plantation*, ed. Morison, 280–4.

25. Howes to Winthrop, September 3, 1636, *Winthrop Papers* III, 292–3.
26. On Wethersfield's founding and the early settlers, see Henry R. Stiles, *The History of Ancient Wethersfield*, 2 vols. (New York, 1904).
27. See Chapter 8. John Winthrop denied that any disagreement between Hooker and John Cotton on ecclesiastical matters motivated that move; Winthrop to Sir Simonds D'Ewes, July 20, 1635, *Winthrop Papers* III, 200.
28. Saltonstall to John Winthrop, Jr., February 27, 1636, *Winthrop Papers* III, 230.

over his substantial English estate two sons of Lord Saye, James and Nathaniel Fiennes, Richard Wyllys, and William Sprigge, Lord Saye's steward, when he emigrated to Hartford in 1638. His wife Mary was the cousin of Hannah Dugard, wife of Lord Brooke's client Thomas Dugard. By 1641 Wyllys was governor of Connecticut. Sir Nathaniel Rich's nephew Nathaniel Browne was also in Hartford in 1636.[29]

Also in 1636 William Pynchon led a small party to found Agawam, later named Springfield, on the east bank of the Connecticut River above the river's highest navigable point. Pynchon was already heavily involved in the fur trade; his location high up on the river would give him first access to pelts being traded south from colder regions. Nonetheless, good relations continued between Agawam and the patentees' associates along the river. Long Island Sound was the source of the best wampum shells, and Pynchon, who wrote to the younger Winthrop as "your most loving friend," fueled his fur trade with wampum supplied from Saybrook. Pynchon's son John, who was a close friend of the younger Winthrop, married Amy, the daughter of Governor George Wyllys of Hartford.[30]

Nor was the Windsor project given up by the patentees. In 1639 another substantial Warwickshire party emigrated under the leadership of the Reverend Ephraim Huitt, another client of Lord Brooke. Huitt was a highly regarded preacher in Warwickshire; Simeon Ashe and Thomas Dugard took turns attending Huitt's sermons and shared their notes. He was welcomed by the Windsor minister, John Warham, and Huitt became teacher of the church there. This wave of new settlers was welcomed into the community. John St. Nicholas, a Warwickshire

29. *Wyllys Papers*, Conn. Hist. Soc. *Colls.* XXI (1924), xxiii–xxvi; Ann Hughes, "Thomas Dugard and His Circle in the 1630s – A 'Parliamentary–Puritan' Connexion?" *Historical Journal* 29 (1986), 771–93, and *Politics, Society, and Civil War in Warwickshire*, 77; Cressy, *Coming Over*, 214. Nathaniel Browne is mentioned in Rich's will, reprinted in Waters, *Genealogical Gleanings* II, 872–3.
30. William Pynchon to Winthrop, Jr., June 2, 1636, *Winthrop Papers* III, 267; for the correspondence between John Pynchon and John Winthrop, Jr., see Carl Bridenbaugh, ed., *The Pynchon Papers* I, *Letters of John Pynchon, 1654–1700*, Colonial Society of Massachusetts *Publications* 61 (Boston, 1982). On the founding of Springfield, see Samuel Eliot Morison, "William Pynchon, The Founder of Springfield," Massachusetts Historical Society *Proceedings* 64 (1930–32), 67–81. On the marriage of John Pynchon and Amy Wyllys, see *Wyllys Papers* 83. Stephen Innes, *Labor in a New Land: Economy and Society in Seventeenth-Century Springfield* (Princeton, 1983) describes the economic development of Springfield under William Pynchon and his son John; for the friendship of John Pynchon and John Winthrop, Jr., see especially pp. 23–5. See also Lynn Ceci, "Native Wampum as a Peripheral Resource in the Seventeenth-Century World-System," in Laurence M. Hauptman and James D. Wherry, eds., *The Pequots in Southern New England* (Norman, OK, 1990), 48–63.

gentleman also frequently in Brooke's company, acquired land in Windsor at this time but ultimately failed to emigrate; he was to be an important member of parliament in the Protectorate.[31]

The Warwick patentees may have seen the Hartford–Windsor pattern, with Massachusetts remigrants and substantial settlers from England settling together, as the most desirable model. Their letters stressed the good that would flow to all from their commitment to the project of populating and developing the rich river and its lands, and colonists' letters echoed this theme.[32] The leading role taken by English gentlemen such as Wyllys would have been seen as only natural to all concerned. The migrants from Massachusetts to the Connecticut River formally recognized this principle. After months of negotiation between the migrating Massachusetts men and the younger Winthrop representing the Warwick patentees, in the course of which Thomas Hooker had solicited the opinion of the lords and gentlemen through a letter to Lord Saye, the Massachusetts General Court issued on March 3, 1636, a commission recognizing the claims of the Warwick patentees and accepting John Winthrop, Jr., as governor of Connecticut. It specified that Winthrop acted on behalf of "certain noble personages & men of quality interested in the said river." The commission was for one year only because, as no reply had yet been received to Massachusetts Bay's letters, "the minds of the said personages . . . are as yet unknown." In return the right of the Massachusetts people to settle on the river was accepted. The commission went on to set up a temporary form of government by the consent of the inhabitants (a principle quite different from that established in Massachusetts), which would be replaced when the wishes of the patentees in England were known.[33] Thus, the Connecticut River settlers generally agreed with the principle of church–state relations endorsed by the lords and gentlemen in England and accepted their leading role.[34]

In 1661 the Connecticut application to Charles II for a formal charter referred to the colony leaders' belief that the patent of the lords and gentlemen "was derived from true royal authority." To bolster its

31. On the Warwickshire connections, see Hughes, *Politics, Society, and Civil War in Warwickshire*, 72–9. On the Huitt party's migration, see Thistlethwaite, *Dorset Pilgrims*, 144–5, 155, 170–2, 191, 200–1.
32. John Winthrop to John Winthrop, Jr., June 1636, *Winthrop Papers* III, 268–9; Henry Lawrence to Winthrop, Jr., September 22, 1635, ibid., 212–13.
33. The commission for government of Connecticut is printed in *Massachusetts Bay Records* I, 170–1 and in William DeLoss Love, *The Colonial History of Hartford* (Hartford, 1935), 65–7.
34. See Foster, "English Puritanism and the Progress of New England Institutions," in Hall, Murrin, and Tate, eds., *Saints and Revolutionaries*, 14.

claims, the colony wrote to Lord Saye, then seventy-nine years old, asking for his support in their application. His reply, lamenting his weak and sick condition, referred them to the Earl of Manchester, "a noble and worthy lord, and one that loves those that are godly. And he and I did join together, that our godly friends of New-England might enjoy their just rights and liberties." When visited by John Richards, Saye remembered the patentees as Warwick, Manchester, Brooke, Pym, Rich, and Fenwick. He suggested that William Jessop, who was "our Clerk," would be the best source of information about the original Warwick patent.[35]

Other Connecticut settlements, founded by settlers directly from England, were also associated with the lords and gentlemen. Lord Brooke had been granted the land on which New Haven was founded in 1638 by a congregation from St. Stephen's church, Coleman Street, in London. Brooke was closely associated with London puritan radicals, including the pastor of St. Stephen's, John Davenport.[36] Coleman Street Ward was a prosperous merchant community that included many interested in overseas expansion; Sir Richard Saltonstall was a parishioner. During an earlier exile in Holland, John Davenport had worked with Hugh Peter to recruit Lion Gardiner for the Saybrook venture. Thomas Fugill, first secretary of New Haven and one of the seven pillars of the church, had served with the family of Providence Island Company member Henry Darley.[37] In 1639 in his second voyage to New England, George Fenwick brought a group of eminent settlers to found Guilford, up the coast from New Haven. This party was led by Fenwick's friend Reverend Henry Whitfield.[38]

35. John Richards to Winthrop, December 18, 1661, and Lord Saye to same, December 1661, Winthrop MSS, Massachusetts Historical Society. The application and the correspondence with Saye are reprinted in Benjamin Trumbull, *A Complete History of Connecticut* (New Haven, 1818), I, 511–15. See also Andrews, *Colonial Period*, II, 76–79. Lord Saye was restored to the privy council at the Restoration.
36. Pearl, *London and Outbreak*, 169, 229; Tolmie, *Triumph of the Saints*, 26, 49; Calder, *New Haven*, 50; and *Biographical Dictionary of British Radicals*, ed. Greaves and Zaller.
37. Alexander Young, *Chronicles of the First Planters of the Colony of Massachusetts-Bay, 1623–1636* (Boston, 1846), 525 n.
38. Hoadly, *Warwick Patent*, 25; Andrews, *Colonial Period*, II, 145–62. New Haven and Guilford departed from the Connecticut pattern and followed the Massachusetts practice of church admission and limitation of political participation; in some areas they were stricter than the Bay Colony. Stephen Foster argues that, whereas the Connecticut River towns reflected the sentiments of the earliest migrants and were moderate on issues of church admission and civil rights, New Haven was settled exclusively by later 1630s migrants and reflected the radicalism infused by experience of Laudian repression in England. He does not, however, take account of the influx of migrants directly from England into the river settlements; see *Long Argument*, 156–7.

So substantial and so threatening were the migrations to Connecticut in the later 1630s that, according to Thomas Hooker, Massachusetts propagandists were spreading lies about the region in England in an attempt to divert intending settlers, a charge John Winthrop answered with ridicule, saying it "makes me a little merry."[39] Clearly, the Providence Island Company investors retained a substantial interest in New England throughout the 1630s and were intimately involved in the network of settlements that mushroomed in Connecticut during the decade. If the 1640s had not opened with signs of great changes to come in England, these leading men might have built personally on the foundation they and their associates had laid.[40]

The Earl of Warwick became head of the Commission for Plantations in 1643. During his tenure, the panel rejected Massachusetts Bay's claims to the Narragansett country, giving a patent for that region to Roger Williams and authorizing the return of the radical spiritist Samuel Gorton to Shawomet, renamed Warwick. Both had been banished by the Boston government for erroneous opinions; thus the Warwick Commission firmly "checkmated Winthrop's plan to extend his orthodoxy throughout New England." These actions implicitly rejected any claim by Massachusetts to extend its control into areas not covered by its patent and left open the question of future settlement and development.[41]

No dichotomous thinking is necessarily implied by the English puritan grandees' program. They viewed as open questions about the future of the colonies that we now see as closed; maintaining the broad spectrum of colonies in health and relative independence was their goal. Warwick introduced legislation favoring Massachusetts at the request of Edward Winslow at the same time he was checking that colony's expansionist schemes. Thomas Hutchinson recorded that the intervention of the Earl of Manchester and Lord Saye secured the confirmation of the Massachusetts Bay charter at the Restoration.[42]

---

39. Hooker to Winthrop, December 1638, *Winthrop Papers* IV, 75–84; Winthrop to Hooker, March 1639, ibid., 99–100. Winthrop's merriment can be contrasted with his righteous anger when he believed that Providence Island investors were denigrating Massachusetts in attempts to attract colonists from there; *Journal*, ed. Hosmer, II, 11–12.

40. Young George Wyllys explained to his father in Connecticut on April 8, 1640, that he was delaying his emigration because, with the times so unsettled, he could not sell land "except for an extreme under value; but the parliament which is to begin the 13th of April gives many hopes of better times . . ."; *Wyllys Papers*, 8–11.

41. Dunn, *Puritans and Yankees*, 45–9. John Winthrop copied each man's passport letter into his *Journal*, ed. Hosmer, II, 197–8, 282–3.

42. On Warwick, see Adamson, "Peerage in Politics" (unpub. Ph.D. diss., Cambridge University, 1986), 106; Hutchinson, *History of Massachusetts-Bay*, ed. Mayo, II, 3.

Above all, they saw their interests in Providence Island and in New England as complementary, each region supporting and improving the other.

Ties were strengthened by substantial commercial contacts between Providence Island and the puritans to the north that grew stronger as the decade neared its end. Maurice Thompson, on whom the adventurers relied increasingly for shipping, regularly traded with New England. New England merchants traded with Providence Island, and the southern colony sent cargoes, both of their own tobacco and of captured prize goods, to be sold in the north. Whereas the company wrote Nathaniel Butler that the best goods for sale in New England were hides, tallow, and sarsaparilla, John Winthrop recorded in his diary the arrival of New Englander William Peirce with "some cotton, and tobacco, and negroes, etc., from thence." Winthrop said that the only commodities for the West Indies were dry fish and strong liquors. Captain William Jackson's entry into Boston harbor with his rich prize in 1639 made a great impression.[43]

Some cargoes found less welcome. In 1640 Providence Islanders Samuel Barton, John Baynes, Richard Beaton, Thomas Jenkes, and John Wills set out their ship *Providence* under master and part owner John Pinckard for New England loaded with tobacco and cotton; if they failed to sell the tobacco for 10 pence per pound there, they planned to take it to Newfoundland and then to Ireland. The journey was cut short by inability to acquire supplies in New England at reasonable rates, while the tobacco could fetch only four pence at most. Leaving the passengers there, the crew sailed on to Ireland and eventually to Bristol, where the ship was sold.[44]

In 1641 the company thought that the Spanish Dominicans held prisoner on Providence Island should be sent to New England; they made embarrassing prisoners yet knew the island too well to be released in the Indies. Pequot captives from the north had been deposited on Providence Island by Peirce in 1638 on the first voyage of the Salem-built *Desire*.[45]

When, in the later 1630s, Providence Island colonists found themselves with cargoes of ore or of captured booty that were too great to carry to

---

43. PIC to Butler by the *Mary*, 7–39; Winthrop, *Journal*, ed. Hosmer, I, 260, 309–10; Coldham, *English Adventurers and Emigrants*, 109.
44. The tangled outcome of this voyage produced several suits in the High Court of Admiralty. See P. R. O., H. C. A. 24/100 f. 322, 24/101 f. 326; 24/102 f. 51–52; H. C. A. 13/56 ff. 416–417, 421–422. I thank Joyce Lorimer for calling these documents to my attention.
45. PIC to Gov. and Coun., 3–29–41; Stearns, *Strenuous Puritan*, 139.

England in the ships they possessed, they were instructed to send to New England, where they were sure to be able to hire vessels.[46] The Providence Island Company also hired ships of New Englanders, such as William Tinge's *Expedition*, which went to Providence Island in 1638.[47] All these commercial contacts laid a solid foundation for further exchanges, extending even to transfer of populations such as Captain John Humphrey and his associates contemplated in 1640–1. Had these New Englanders emigrated in 1640 as planned, the history of Providence Island, and of the ties between the West Indies and New England, might have been quite different. As it was, the move came too late.

Spanish leaders knew of the planned major migration from New England to Providence Island; such news may have added a sense of urgency to the project of ousting the English colony there. General Francisco Díaz Pimienta, admiral of the Plate Fleet, wrote to King Philip IV that Sergeant-Major Robert Hunt, leader of the island's puritans, had secured 300 New Englanders who were resolved to remove to the Caribbean and eventually to settle near Cape Gracias a Dios.[48]

Meanwhile, Spanish colonists chafed in helpless anger at the depredations made on their lives by English corsairs from Providence Island. General Pimienta was outraged at hearing of the second failed attack in 1640 and resolved to avenge the insult. On special royal orders, he assembled a massive fleet of seven large ships and four pinnaces with attendant boats, manned by 1,400 soldiers and 600 seamen in Cartagena; the armada arrived off Providence Island on May 19, 1641.[49]

This force learned from the mistakes of the previous offensive. Pimienta scouted carefully, having split his commanders up into several reconnoitering parties, each reporting to the general meeting at which the plan of attack was formulated. Pimienta decided to focus the offensive on the relatively unfortified east side of the island. Many of his advisers argued for the half moon bay on the southwest, which would allow the artillery of their ships to cover the assault; but Pimienta, who

46. PIC Ct., 3–29–39; PIC to Butler by the *Mary*, 7–39; Instructions to Butler, Axe, and Carter, 7–39.
47. The company's lengthy and intricate negotiations with Tinge stretched over many meetings from March 5, 1638, to April 20. On William Tinge and his sons, see Martin, *Profits in the Wilderness*, 20–2.
48. Nathanial Butler recorded Hunt's departure at the end of November 1639 for an expedition to the Moskito coast; his ship returned to Providence Island without him next February 18; B. L., Sloane MS 758.
49. General Francisco Díaz Pimienta to Philip IV, September 11, 1641, Archive of the Indies, Seville, *Audiencia de Santa Fe, legajo 223*.

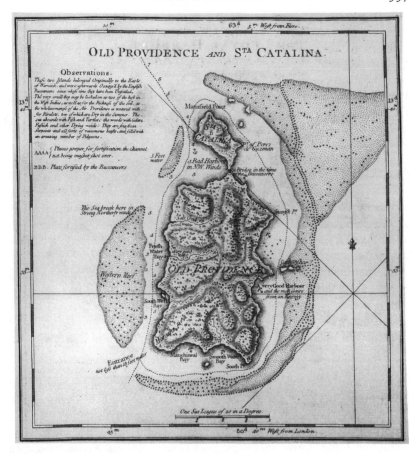

Old Providence. (Thomas Jeffreys, *The West-India Atlas*, London, 1783; courtesy of the John Carter Brown Library at Brown University.)

had noticed the English colonists furiously digging two trenches from the hills to the beach and their placement of two cannon to rake the invaders, rejected that advice. His opinion was confirmed after the fact by Governor Andrew Carter, who confided that he had pinned his hopes on being attacked there.

The invasion was delayed by foul weather so severe that Pimienta feared loss of the shallops. The entire company was dispirited by this sign and by the strong winds that made the eastern attack impossible. Now Pimienta decided to focus boldly on the main harbor at New

Westminster, thinking that the strong winds would bring his pinnaces in faster than the English could move their main force over land. The artillery of the pinnaces would answer that of the heavily fortified harbor defenses. The great warships were ordered out of the fight; they would be needed undamaged later to transport silver back to Spain. Pimienta heard out his captains' protests but decided to go ahead with the plan on May 24.

Pimienta, with his 1,400 soldiers, attacked at dawn. He found the fortifications impressive and commented favorably on the courage of the force of English and Africans that ran to confront them.[50] Despite these defenses, Pimienta's strategy quickly succeeded, and he moved to occupy the governor's house on the hill, sending men to occupy the fortifications and the small island across the neck of land where many of the colonists had taken refuge.[51] Others fanned out into the brush and hills to find any pockets of resistance. When the English defenders saw the Spanish flag flying over their governor's house, they lowered their own English flags on the forts and sent their captive Spanish friars with a white flag to offer their surrender. Pimienta decided to spare the lives of the English and to send the men to Cádiz, where they could pay their own way home. On May 25 he took possession of the island formally with all solemnity, and a Roman Catholic mass was celebrated in Hope Sherrard's church.

The Spanish found Providence Island well provided with arms and ammunition, including sixty pieces of heavy artillery and a great deal of equipment stockpiled for the attempt to colonize the Moskito Coast. The island was inhabited by 381 slaves who were sold at Cartagena and Portobello by order of the king and about 350 English settlers, including some formerly on San Andreas and elsewhere who had consolidated on Providence Island after the 1640 attack. The number of slaves was much lower than the Spanish expected; they learned that the English, fearful of rebellion, had dispersed many of their slaves to St. Christopher's and Bermuda. Eighteenth-century accounts of the Moskito Coast hold that a ship manned by rebelling slaves was wrecked south of Cape Gracias a Dios in 1641. These memoirs differ on the escapees' origin. One theory is that they were fleeing from Providence

50. Cromwell's declaration against Spain denigrated the colonists' efforts, saying that they had fallen into dissension, and "did not think so much of making a good Defence, as of making good Conditions for themselves, which upon the Delivery up of the Island, with little or no opposition they obtained"; *A Declaration of His Highness*, in Patterson et al., eds., *Works of Milton*, XIII, 543.
51. Nathaniel Butler moved into a new governor's house on May 14, 1639; B. L., Sloane MS 758.

Island as it fell to the Spanish. All accounts agree that the newcomers melded into the native population.[52]

Pimienta respectfully disobeyed royal orders to dismantle the island's defences. He pointed out its impregnability and the tremendous damage done by corsairs based on it. The Dutch had already expressed interest in acquiring it; if they spent 100,000 ducats on it, he wrote, no power on earth could take it away from them. Corsairs from Providence Island had made life impossible along the Spanish coast; more merchant ships had entered the port of Cartagena in the two months since the English fell than in the previous two years. Festivities greeted the news among all the coastal Spanish. Nor would Providence Island be expensive to maintain. Pimienta reported that he had found the island well provided with corn, beans, bananas, and thousands of pigs. He envisioned a small, self-sustaining garrison, and he left behind a force of 150 gunners and infantrymen under the command of Don Geronimo de Ojeda. His actions were endorsed by a royal cédula in 1643, and his enterprise was rewarded with a knighthood of the Order of Santiago.[53]

John Winthrop considered it a special providence that Hope Sherrard and Nicholas Leverton had been expelled from Providence Island before the fall, as he thought that the ministers would have been killed in retribution for the slaughtered Spaniards of 1640.[54] The island's English residents — even Andrew Carter, who had ordered the execution — were spared by order of General Pimienta. Some scattered to the Moskito Coast and the islands of St. Christopher's, Tobago, and

52. One stumbling block for intending immigrants from New England had been information from "some among us, that came from Providence" about "how ill the island is manned"; Humphrey to Mandeville, H.M.C. Eighth *Report*, Manchester Papers, 424. Further military equipment, including twenty-four barrels of gunpowder to replace "old powder," was on its way to the island as the attack came; PIC Ct. 3–9–41, 3–15–41; PIC to Gov. and Coun. 3–29–41. On reports of the 1641 shipwreck of fleeing slaves, see Eduard Conzemius, *Ethnographical Survey of the Miskito and Sumu Indians of Honduras and Nicaragua*, Smithsonian Institution, Bureau of Ethnology *Bulletin* 106 (Washington, DC, 1932), 16–18; Linda A. Newson, *Indian Survival in Colonial Nicaragua* (Norman, OK, 1987), 38–9, 201–2; and Mary W. Helms, *Asang: Adaptation to Culture Contact in a Miskito Community* (Gainesville, FL, 1971), 15–18. I thank Cynthia Van Zandt for bringing this to my notice.

53. General Francisco Díaz Pimienta to Philip IV, September 11, 1641, Archive of the Indies, Seville, *Audiencia de Santa Fe, legajo* 223; Donald Rowland, "Spanish Occupation of the Island of Old Providence, or Santa Catalina, 1641–1670," *Hispanic American Historical Review* 15 (1935), 299–302. The events were reported from the English point of view in an anonymous newsletter, *A Letter from the Low Countries* (1642), which carried the running head "Avisos from severall places" (pp. 5–6), Thomason Tracts, E. 141.10, British Library. The Spanish governor soon found that the island was more difficult to maintain than Pimienta envisioned.

54. Winthrop, *Journal*, ed. Hosmer, II, 35.

Ruatán, and many returned to England.[55] One, Samuel Young, who had been in the colony from the beginning, wrote to Lord Mandeville out of his "great misery and distress" for aid. Hope Sherrard had encouraged him to write, about "a sore and long captivity under the hands of a tyrannical and Cruel enemy, occasioned by the loss of Providence." Not only had Young suffered in captivity; he had also lost all the estate built up in ten years' work on the island. Sick and friendless, he had been driven to "miserable and extreme poverty." His last hope was that Mandeville would "look upon me with an eye of pity and Compassion." His letter carried an endorsement by Sherrard attesting to Young's piety and honesty and his great need. Young's letter must stand for many other such pleas now lost.[56]

During the summer of 1641, unsuspecting English immigrants continued to converge on Providence Island. Deputy Governor Thomas Fitch and the Reverend Nicholas Leverton, together with Richard Lane, had set out from England in April 1641. When they arrived at Providence Island to find it taken, Leverton's biographer avows that at the minister's insistence, the newcomers "ventured a brush" with the Spanish conquerors, "wherein they killed a great many of their men, and forced their armed longboats ashore."[57] A note of a case in the High Court of Admiralty reports examination of Captain Thomas Fitch, August 12, 1642. The ship in which he was passenger, the *William and Sarah*, was driven onto the rocks as it sailed toward Virginia and was lost twenty to thirty leagues from Providence Island and four or five leagues from the Moskitos; fifty or sixty souls were saved from the shipwreck.[58]

Captain Fitch chose to return to England after the repulsion of the 1641 returnees. Lane and Leverton, however, careered around the Indies for a further two years, during which they "had many preservations (almost miraculous) from famine, from the Spaniards, and in violent storms." Leverton ultimately returned to England after preaching for a year in Bermuda. After his reunion with Hope Sherrard, he traveled to London, where, according to Calamy, "he was received with great honour and respect by the lords proprietors of the island of Providence." He was settled in the ministry at High Henningham in Suffolk, where he named his son Gershom because, like Moses, "I have been a stranger in a strange land." He then moved to St. Tudy in Cornwall, where he

55. Burns, *British West Indies*, 2nd ed., 210. The English contingent on Ruatán was overrun by Spanish attackers in 1642.
56. Samuel Young to Lord Mandeville, n. d., Huntington R. O., DDM 32, 9/13.
57. Calamy, *Nonconformist's Memorial*, rev. ed. by Palmer, I, 292–5.
58. P. R. O., H. C. A. 13/58, f. 205v.

became a valued member of the classis that included Charles Morton, the future Harvard fellow. Ejected at the Restoration, he accepted an invitation to minister to the English colony in Surinam, where he died shortly after his arrival.[59]

The little fleet of colonists from New England in two small ships also arrived too late. On a stop at St. Christopher's they heard "a great fleet of Spanish ships was abroad." William Peirce, "a godly man and most expert mariner," urged his passengers to return to New England. When they insisted on going on, he replied, "Then am I a dead man." Peirce read the Bible to the entire company each morning; as they approached Providence Island, he read a passage from Genesis "(as it fell in course)": "Lo I die, but God will surely visit you and bring you back." As Peirce's ship neared the island, the company were surprised to see no flag over the fort and no approaching boat. It was not until they were very close that they saw the cannon aimed at them. Peirce and Samuel Wakeman, a merchant of Hartford who had come to buy cotton, were mortally wounded by the first shot, after which the Spanish fruitlessly rained shots on the first ship. The second vessel had providentially lagged behind and so was completely unscathed. Although the migrants escaped harm, they were, according to John Winthrop, so racked by guilt and shame that they asked to be left at Cape Gracias a Dios or in Florida or Virginia, but all were returned to New England by the sailors. Winthrop recorded with satisfaction their return to Boston. Some of the defectors acknowledged "their error...in the open congregation, but others were hardened." He wrote of the foolishness of Humphrey and his band for leaving "a place of rest and safety, to expose themselves, their wives and children, to the danger of a potent enemy, the Spaniard."[60]

John Humphrey himself apparently never went to Providence Island; he sailed for England on November 21, 1641, a few months after the return of his would-be settlers. Three years later Philip Bell was warned that Warwick was planning to prepare the way for his replacement as governor of Barbados by "one Mr. Humphrey (a New England

---

59. Calamy, *Nonconformist's Memorial*, rev. ed. by Palmer, I, 292–5; Matthews, ed., *Walker Revised*, 97, 271, 345; Shaw, *History of the English Church*, II, 425. On the Cornwall classis to which Morton and Leverton belonged, see Coate, *Cornwall in the Great Civil War*, 338–41, 346–7. The classis minutes are printed in Chetham Society *Remains Historical and Literary*, n.s., 41 (1898), 175–88.
60. Winthrop, *Journal*, ed. Hosmer, I, 334; II, 11–12, 33–5. William Hubbard treats the challenge in the same manner as Winthrop; *A General History of New England*, 2nd ed., 1682 (Boston, 1848), 375–85. See also John Endecott to John Winthrop, February 1641, *Winthrop Papers* IV 314–15; Strong, "Forgotten Danger," 79–83.

man)."[61] Humphrey was chosen to bear the sword of state before John Bradshaw, Lord President of the High Court that tried Charles I.[62]

Meanwhile, the culmination of their hopes neared for English puritan leaders as parliament took up the grievances of the people and the Civil War loomed ever closer at home. The crisis called for all the talents the grandees had to offer. John Pym and Lord Saye took up leadership roles in the two houses of parliament, and Sir Gilbert Gerard was treasurer of the army. Warwick became admiral of the parliamentary fleets. Lord Mandeville, now Earl of Manchester, headed the Eastern Association armies. Oliver Cromwell and Sir Thomas Barrington served under him, and Gregory Gawsell was the association's treasurer. Lord Brooke commanded the combined armies of Warwickshire and Staffordshire. These military commanders were praised for filling their armies with men who fought willingly for the cause, and for raising good men from the ranks. Brooke apparently contributed to his soldiers' upkeep from his own pocket.[63]

Providence Island returnees served parliament's cause. Sussex Camock had been the governor of Landguard Fort since 1636. Other names match those of former colonists. Captain Thomas Fitch joined Lord Brooke's regiment of foot as the Civil War began. He served the Protector faithfully and lost public office when he conspired to prevent the return of Charles II. Captain Benjamin Hooke was captain in Lord Rochford's regiment. A Captain Hunt was wounded at Lord Brooke's capture of Stratford; Captain Robert Hunt later served in the regiment of Colonel Sir Henry Cholmley.[64] The godly Captain Hunt, like so many former Providence Islanders, found himself drawn back to the colonies after the war. He was named governor of a proposed

61. Philip Bell wrote and asked for godly colonists and ministers from New England to aid him in restoring order to his "distracted" colony of Barbados, which was disturbed by the presence of "divers sects of Familists," but the Massachusetts authorities rejected his request; Hubbard, *General History of New England*, 346–7.
62. On the life of John Humphrey, see Frances Rose-Troup, "John Humfry," *Essex Institute Historical Collections* LXV (1929), 293–308; on the rumors about the Barbados governorship, see Puckrein, *Little England*, 97.
63. *A Worthy Speech made by the Right Honourable the Lord Brooke, at the election of his Captaines and Commanders at Warwick Castle* (London, 1643), 7; Thomas Johnson, *Some Special Passages from Warwickshire. concerning the proceedings of the Right Honourable the Lord Brooke* (London, 1642), 3. See Holmes, *Eastern Association* and Hirst, *Authority and Conflict*, 244–5. Lord Brooke was involved in the navy commission with Warwick as well as commanding in the armies; Strider, *Lord Brooke*, 45, 66.
64. Edward Peacock, *The Army Lists of the Roundheads and Cavaliers*, 2nd ed. revised (London, 1874), 32, 34, 38; Zaller and Greaves, ed., *Biographical Dictionary of British Radicals*; Anon., *The Last Weeks Proceedings of the Lord Brooke* (London, 1643), 4.

settlement on Assada near Madagascar; investor Maurice Thompson was his connection to this effort. Hunt wrote a book, *The Island of Assada*, projecting the great wealth that would flow to investors in the venture, which he compared favorably to Barbados. He explained that he was prepared to leave wife, friends, and comfort in England because his Providence Island experience had convinced him of the importance of such expeditions both to the nation and to God. Captain Hunt died shortly after his arrival in Assada in 1650.[65]

As their attention increasingly was diverted to domestic concerns, Providence Island Company members made desperate attempts to keep a remnant of their claims alive in the Indies and to make their goals national aims. In September 1641, following the capture of Providence Island and Spanish harassment of shipping at Calais, a parliamentary committee proposed action against Spain, and calls for a West India Company, first heard in the 1620s, were renewed. Sir Benjamin Rudyerd's 1626 speech in favor of such a company was printed several times in the 1640s. Pointing to Spanish sweeping away of English planters, the committee envisioned a privately financed company to attack Spanish shipping and colonies, for which £300,000 would be needed for three years. The committee pointed to the enrichment of Holland through its own West India Company. As in the 1620s, many Providence Island investors were involved in promoting this scheme; the company's March 1641 letter to John Humphrey (the final item in the company's correspondence) mentioned "some public undertakings which may shortly come to a resolution here touching the West Indies" that would "further improve and advance your beginnings," especially on the mainland.[66]

65. Hunt, *The Island of Assada, Neere Madagascar* (London, 1650). Notice of his death is in the journal of Charles Wilde, February 4, 1650, to July 28, 1652, B. L., Sloane MS 3231, 26–27; and in Ethel Bruce Sainsbury, ed., *A Calendar of the Court Minutes Etc. of the East India Company, 1650–1654* (Oxford, 1913), ix–x, 10–12, 292–3.

The campaign for an outpost on Madagascar was begun by Prince Rupert and his circle around Henrietta Maria; Davenant's poem *Madagascar* (1638) celebrated this notion of Rupert's heading a conquering fleet; A. M. Gibbs, *Sir William Davenant: The Shorter Poems, and Songs from the Plays and Masques* (Oxford, 1972), 1–21; and Butler, *Theatre and Crisis*, 34. See also Walter Hamond, *A Paradox. Prooving, That the Inhabitants of the Isle called Madagascar, or St. Laurence, (In Temporall things) are the happiest People in the World* (London, 1640); and Richard Boothby, *A Breife Discovery or Description Of the most Famous Island of Madagascar of St. Laurence in Asia neare unto East-India* (London, 1646).

66. Newsletter of Lord Scudamore, end of August 1641, B. L., Add MS 11045, f. 141; B. L., Harleian MS 5047, f. 79; Proceedings in Parliament, Sept. 1641, B. L., Sloane MS 3317, ff. 25–26; *Commons Journals*, II, 1640–42, September 9, 1641, 288; PIC to Humphrey, 3–31–41. A book published anonymously, *A Little True Forraine Newes: Better Than a greate deale of Domestick spurious false Newes, published*

As events came to a head in the early 1640s, the grandees saw their predictions coming true. The Irish rebellion, according to Nicholas Canny, was seen as "part of an international conspiracy aimed at universal overthrow of Protestantism."[67] Parliament dealt with this crisis by extending the colonizing principle of private enterprise. Saying that the English treasury was "wonderfully exhausted," early in 1642 parliament authorized creation of a body of adventurers who would suppress the Irish rebellion with government-supplied weapons and English soldiers, pressed if necessary. In return the adventurers were to have "satisfaction" from the "many millions of acres of the rebels lands of that kingdom which go under the name of profitable lands," and the Providence Island investors were intimately involved. A total investment of £1,000,000 was envisioned; Warwick wrote that it was expected 2,000 Londoners would invest £500 each. In the event, although London did predominate, the subscription was sold throughout the country; a flood of propaganda pamphlets focusing on the suffering of Irish Protestants accompanied the offer. Urged on by John Pym, more than 100 members of parliament subscribed, but the total subscription was far less than the envisaged £1,000,000.

Lord Brooke was appointed commander of the forces for Ireland; Lord Wharton, staunch puritan and close associate of the Providence Island group, was authorized to raise a brigade. An expedition, to be paid for by a separate subscription for which Maurice Thompson was treasurer, was soon authorized, and preparations began for a fleet of twelve ships and six pinnaces. This expedition was led by Alexander, Lord Forbes, with New Englander Hugh Peter as chaplain and Captain John Humphrey as sergeant major over the land troops. Humphrey tried to convince John Winthrop, Jr., to accompany the campaign: "Good dear loving Sagamore, let us have your company if possible."

The invading force waged a very destructive campaign of terror, especially in the southwest and in the area around Galway, but it was inconclusive. In the end the troops, who had arrived at Kinsale in July, left for England in September 1642. Suppression of the Irish rebellion quickly became entangled with growing tensions between king and

daily without feare or wit (London, 1641), gave news of lucrative Dutch exploits in Brazil. On the scheme of the 1620s, see Chapter 1; for the reprinting of Rudyerd's speech, see Appleby, "English Plans for a West India Company, 1621–1629," *Journal of Imperial and Commonwealth History* 15 (1987), fn 31.

67. Nicholas Canny, "The Marginal Kingdom: Ireland as a Problem in the First British Empire," in Bernard Bailyn and Philip D. Morgan, *Strangers Within the Realm: Cultural Margins of the First British Empire* (Chapel Hill, 1991), 55. Ambassador Cárdenas complained to Charles I on November 11, 1641, that his mail from Dublin was being opened and read; P. R. O., S. P. 94/42, ff. 242–4.

parliament at home; money raised for Ireland was diverted to the parliamentary cause, as was the brigade raised by Lord Wharton, which saw action at Edgehill.[68] Ultimately the adventurers emerged again as Cromwell made his plans for Ireland.

Even in the midst of all these events some evidence suggests that Providence Island investors also strove to send new colonists to the Moskito Coast in order to maintain their patent claims even as civil war broke out in England. A small pamphlet was published, probably in 1643, lacking both title page and any indication of either its authors or its intended audience. It may have been sent to clients or distributed by agents of Providence Island Company members. Its offers carried a note of desperation that comported well with the times. *Certain Inducements To well minded People* began with a call to bring the light of true religion to Indians in the Indies, who, according to the pamphlet, abhorred the Spaniards and their religion, seeking English names, as the Moskito Indians were reported to have done, and hoping that English Christians would come to live among them. The pamphlet quickly moved on to the many foods, vegetable and animal, available to prospective colonists in that supremely healthy environment.

Much internal evidence indicates that the Moskito Coast was the area described in *Certain Inducements*. Dette "(which is an excellent perfume, growing naturally, and there is some probability it would be much better transplanted)" was one of the plants offered as an inducement. Dette, from the Moskito Indian word for vanilla, *diti*, was promoted by the Providence Island Company in 1636.[69] It was not mentioned in connection with any other colony and does not appear in lists of commodities from the Indies. Among the animals, the pamphlet

68. Karl S. Bottigheimer, *English Money and Irish Land: The "Adventurers" in the Cromwellian Settlement of Ireland* (Oxford, 1971), 39–53, chap. 3, 76–82; Brendan Fitzpatrick, *Seventeenth-Century Ireland: The War of Religions* (Totowa, NJ, 1989), chap. 7; Patrick J. Corish, "The Rising of 1641 and the Catholic Confederacy, 1641–5," in *A New History of Ireland*, III, *Early Modern Ireland, 1534–1691*, ed. T. W. Moody, F. X. Martin, F. J. Byrne (Oxford, 1976), 303; Hugh Hazlett, "The Financing of the British Armies in Ireland, 1641–9," *Irish Historical Studies* I (1939), 24–27; J. R. MacCormack, "The Irish Adventurers and the English Civil War," ibid., X (1957), 21–58; Richard Bagwell, *Ireland Under the Stuarts*, II, 1642–60 (London, 1909), 36–44; Andrews, *Ships, Money and Politics*, 60, 195–7; Raymond Phineas Stearns, "The Weld–Peter Mission to England," Colonial Society of Massachusetts *Publications* (1934), 201–11; Stearns, *Strenuous Puritan*, 188–218; John Humphrey to John Winthrop, Jr., July 21, 1642, *Winthrop Papers* IV, 352–3. In 1638 the Providence Island Company had briefly treated with Lord Forbes through Lord Brooke about engaging his brother for the government of their island; PIC Ctee. 2–20–38.

69. Sir William Dampier, using the Spanish-derived name, later wrote: "There grow on this Coast *Vinelloes* in great quantity, with which Chocolate is perfumed," *A New Voyage Round the World* (1st pub. 1697; repr. of 1729 ed., London, 1937), 35–6.

describes a wide variety of turtles, the qualities of which the Providence Island colonists knew expertly. The author refers to information on the interior from English informants, also pointing to the Moskito Coast, which was far better known to the English than to the Spanish in the 1640s.[70]

Internal evidence also indicates that puritan leaders of the Providence Island Company stripe had authorized the pamphlet: It was addressed specifically to those "many thousands" who were suffering "by the plundering and utter ruin of their Estates, by the cruelty of the Cavaliers, or through the decay of Trading...." To those willing to emigrate, the investors held out the prospect of life in a land where plenty would allow "a godly people" to be "more liberal to God in public and domestic duties" and "more free to each other, in acts of hospitality, courtesy, relief, and commerce."

The times dictated the extreme pressure under which the offering was made. Colonists who landed within two months after the first arrival were promised six acres within four miles of the proposed town and sixty acres "in some other place" for every person brought over. All allotments were to be in freehold tenure guaranteed to heirs forever. Those who arrived between two and six months after the founding were to have the same except that the large grant was to be fifty acres; and emigrants arriving within the second six months were to have four acres in the town area and thirty acres outside. Every family was to have a house and garden lot in the town. The offer applied to every immigrant, and servants were to be guaranteed the same when their terms were up. Those who invested £100 would receive 500 acres, and the investment would be repaid out of profits; other investments would be repaid proportionally. Investors who chose to send servants would receive land as if they had gone themselves, and their servants would also get land when out of service.[71]

These terms offered the same kind of private development possibilities that the mainland colonies had offered as much as two decades before. If combined with self-government, they were also the route to successful colonization. Had the Providence Island Company been prepared to move in this direction earlier, the fate of their colony might have been

---

70. Pimienta was outraged that he had no one capable of guiding his ships on the Moskito Coast and that he therefore had to rely on an English pilot; General Francisco Díaz Pimienta to Philip IV, September 11, 1641, Archive of the Indies, Seville, *Audiencia de Santa Fe, legajo* 223.

71. Anon., *Certain Inducements To well minded People, Who are here straitned in their Estates or otherwise: or such as are willing out of Noble and publike Principles, to transport Themselves, or some Servants, or Agents for them into the West-Indies, for the propagating of the Gospel and increase of TRADE.* (np, 1643?).

different. Their colonists had forged ties with Central America and its inhabitants that would thrive in the future. If *Certain Inducements* was a Providence Island Company effort to maintain its claims, it failed for lack of follow-up.

As the Civil War and problems of governance consumed all their attention and, for Pym, Brooke, Moundeford, and Barrington, their lives, only small efforts were made to keep an English presence alive on the mainland, although the Earl of Warwick, through his headship of the Commission for Plantations added to his main office of Lord Admiral, continued his party's strong identification with the American colonies. Many fellow company members served on his committee for plantations.[72] William Jessop and Maurice Thompson moved into key roles in government. K. R. Andrews says that Jessop was "effectively Secretary to the Admiralty from 1643." Thompson headed a committee that controlled the navy and the customs from January 1649 and became "the architect of commercial and maritime policy, the prime mover behind the Navigation Act of 1651."[73]

Some activities continued in the West Indies. Acting on a Providence Island Company commission secured through his patron the Earl of Warwick and backed by Maurice Thompson, Captain William Jackson embarked on a second long privateering voyage in the West Indies that lasted from 1642 to 1645. Prominent in his fleet were Providence Island veterans Captains Samuel Axe as vice admiral and William Rous as commander of the almost 900 land troops raised in Barbados and St. Christopher's, as well as Lewis Morris, master of the *Dolphin*. Jackson's triumph, the capture of Jamaica with his small force, fed the notion that the Spanish empire was corrupt and weak, ripe for conquest by a morally superior English force: "The veil is now drawn aside, & their weakness detected by a handful of men." Jackson's quest for treasure to repay the investors precluded settlement of the island with English, but his men were impressed with the beauty and fecundity of the place. The message conveyed by Jackson's voyage was conserved and put into operation when Oliver Cromwell was in a position to realize the long-standing goals of English puritans for the West Indies.[74]

72. *Two Ordinances of the Lords and Commons Assembled in Parliament. Nov. 2, 1643 and March 21, 1645. Whereby Robert Earle of Warwick is made Governor in Chief, and L. high Admirall of all those Islands and other Plantations ... upon the Coasts of America* (London, 1645) gave lists of the committee members.
73. Andrews, *Ships, Money and Politics*, 58, 195.
74. On Jackson's voyage, see *Mercurius Americanus*, ed. V. T. Harlow, *Camden Miscellany* XIII, 1–35, quotation from p. 35; and Harlow's "Introduction," v–xxvi. A New Englander, Captain Cromwell, brought two prize vessels from this expedition into Boston in October 1646, where he presented Governor Winthrop with a sedan

As English leaders looked at America during the 1640s, the West Indies seemed the obvious focal point; rumors abounded that many already in America were prepared to move south. The mainland colonies looked marginal: The Chesapeake, struggling along with its cyclical tobacco economy, faced economic depression throughout the 1640s.[75] And cold, rocky New England entered a severe depression with the dropping off of immigration, making its earlier prosperity seem artificial indeed and feeding the notion that New England had outlived its usefulness.

Nor was it obvious to English leaders that the West Indies was unsuitable for the grand national effort they envisaged. The puritan colony on Providence Island had failed, but, as puritans assumed national leadership in England, the lessons of that failure were unclear. Many argued that it had failed because of its small size and because the British government had treated it as peripheral. Thomas Gage, a former member of the Dominican order who had traveled with the Spanish in Mexico and Central America, wrote in 1648 that Providence Island, "though but little, might have been of a great, nay greater advantage to our Kingdom, than any other of our plantations in America."[76]

As Oliver Cromwell moved into leadership of the nation, the goals of Providence Island Company investors finally became the goals of the national government.[77] Shortly after the failure of the Western Design, some participants and observers criticized Cromwell's foreign policy as anachronistic and shortsighted for lavishing money on a project to defeat declining Spain, which actually enhanced the strength of a rising power, France. Historians have continued this line of attack ever since.[78]

chair "which (as he said) was sent by the viceroy of Mexico to his sister" and was said to be worth almost £50. Winthrop gave it to pacify Charles d'Aulnay, who was furious with Massachusetts Bay for aiding his rival claimant to Acadia, Claude La Tour. See Winthrop, *Journal*, ed. Hosmer, II, 272–3, 284–6.

75. Menard, "British Migration to the Chesapeake Colonies," in Carr, Morgan, and Russo, eds., *Colonial Chesapeake Society*, 104.

76. Gage, *The English-American*, 77–8, 199–203. See Oliver Cromwell to Maj. Gen. Richard Fortescue, October 1655, in Wilbur Cortez Abbott, ed., *The Writings and Speeches of Oliver Cromwell* (Cambridge, MA, 1945), III, 857, and *A Declaration of His Highness*, in Patterson et al., eds., *Works of John Milton*, XIII, 509–63, esp. 537–45, 559.

77. Cromwell, although not an investor himself, was related to and associated with many of the Providence Island Company members.

78. Slingsby Bethell, "The World's Mistake in Oliver Cromwell" (1668), *Harleian Miscellany* VII (1810), 348–53, 356; C. H. Firth, ed., *The Memoirs of Edmund Ludlow . . . 1625–1672* (Oxford, 1894), II, 2–3. For modern versions of this indictment, see Menna Prestwich, "Diplomacy and Trade in the Protectorate," *Journal of Modern History* XXII (1950), 110–21, and G. M. D. Howat, *Stuart and Cromwellian Foreign Policy* (New York, 1974), 7, 88. Roger Crabtree, "The Idea of a Protestant Foreign Policy," in Ivan Roots, ed., *Cromwell: A Profile* (London, 1973),

Cromwell saw his policies, not as an anachronistic throwback to the days of Elizabeth, but as the logical culmination of thirty years of development and struggle. The civil wars began in an atmosphere of crisis, in the belief that Laudian policies aimed at reinstating popery in England. This sense of the precariousness of the Calvinist establishment pushed people into open war, and they sought a conclusion that would end threats to it now and in the future.[79] It was given to the Protector to make the reformed religion so secure that no future developments could threaten it. To accomplish that goal, he had to protect England from foreign invasion and from the activities of enemies within. Cromwell and those around him believed that, until Spain was severed from its sources of riches in the Indies, the danger of attacks on England would remain.[80]

The weakness of Spain was not an argument *against* attacking it; God had brought that country low just at the time when true Protestants were victorious in England so that the final blow could be struck and the power of Antichrist eliminated once and for all.[81] New England clergymen argued vigorously for this interpretation of events. Through the Reverend William Hooke of New Haven, Cromwell initiated a correspondence with John Cotton, who was considered to be

160–89; Charles P. Korr, *Cromwell and the New Model Foreign Policy: England's Policy toward France, 1649–1658* (Berkeley, 1975), chap. 11; and John F. Battick, "A New Interpretation of Cromwell's Western Design," *Journal of the Barbados Museum and Historical Society* XXXIV (1972), 76–84, argue that the Western Design was a policy based on rational calculation of risks and gains.

79. See Morrill, "Religious Context of English Civil War," Royal Historical Society, *Transactions* 5th Ser., XXXIV (1984), 155–78; Hibbard, *Charles I and Popish Plot*, chaps. 1, 2; Foster, "The Godly in Transit," in Hall and Allen, eds., *Seventeenth-Century New England*, 194, and "English Puritanism and the Progress of New England Institutions," in Hall, Murrin, and Tate, eds., *Saints and Revolutionaries*, 5–6; Robin Clifton, "The Popular Fear of Catholics during the English Revolution," *Past and Present* no. 52 (1971), 43, 54; and Michael G. Finlayson, *Historians, Puritanism, and the English Revolution: The Religious Factor in English Politics before and after the Interregnum* (Toronto, 1983), 106, 115–18. For fuller discussion of the Western Design and the thinking surrounding it, see Karen Ordahl Kupperman, "Errand to the Indies: Puritan Colonization from Providence Island through the Western Design," *William and Mary Quarterly* 3rd ser., XLV (1988), 70–99.

80. As Battick points out, the Western Design, as a direct activity of the government, represented a sharp break from the Elizabethan policy of "free-booting, private, or semi-private ventures" ("New Interpretation of Cromwell's Western Design," *Journal of the Barbados Museum and Historical Society* XXXIV [1972], 82).

81. The flow of treasure from the West Indies to Spain, which had remained great from its peak in the late sixteenth century through the 1630s, slowed dramatically by the middle of the seventeenth century. See Earl J. Hamilton, *American Treasure and the Price Revolution in Spain, 1501–1650* (Cambridge, MA, 1934), 32–8, and D. A. Brading and Harry E. Cross, "Colonial Silver Mining: Mexico and Peru," *Hispanic American Historical Review* LII (1972), 569.

one of the foremost interpreters of the Bible's prophetic passages. In 1651 he asked Cotton to help him interpret events: "What is the Lord a doing? What prophesies are now fulfilling?" Cotton's answer, according to Samuel Sewall, was "that to take from the Spaniards in America would be to dry up Euphrates," thus fulfilling the prophecy in Revelation 16:12 that heralded the last days: "And the sixth angel poured out his vial upon the great river Euphrates; and the water thereof was dried up, that the way of the kings of the east might be prepared."[82] Cotton argued that the attack on episcopacy in England was the pouring of the fifth vial and that the entire process, the culmination of history, was speeding up. His interpretation carried great weight with the Protector.[83]

Debate in the Council of State over plans to attack the Spanish West Indies centered on the questions of feasibility and justification. Major General John Lambert argued strongly that success was "improbable," but Cromwell had many other advisers who contended that Spain was now so weak and its territories so ill protected that a strong English fleet could take land at will, even sweep Spain from America.[84] Now governmental leaders lamented the parsimonious shortsightedness of Charles I and pointed to the advantage England might have reaped from keeping control of Providence Island. Veterans of that colony joined the force attacking Spanish possessions. Andrew Carter, with the rank of colonel, commanded a regiment. Lewis Morris, now in Barbados, raised a regiment there, and Kempo Sabada, a Dutch mariner who had served Providence Island as a pilot, functioned in that role for the Western Design.[85] In a letter to Major General Richard Fortescue at

82. This passage was often linked to Jer. 51:36–37, which prophesies a time when God will plead the cause of his people "and take vengeance for thee; and I will dry up her sea, and make her springs dry. And Babylon shall become heaps, a dwellingplace for dragons, an astonishment, and an hissing without an inhabitant." Cromwell to Cotton, October 2, 1651, in Hutchinson, comp., *Collection of Original Papers Relative to the History of the Colony of Massachusetts-Bay*, 1, 266; "Diary of Samuel Sewall, 1674–1729," Massachusetts Historical Society, *Collections* 5th Ser., VI (Boston, 1879), 437.

83. John Cotton, *The Pouring Out of the Seven Vialls* (London, 1642), esp. 85–97; Cotton to Cromwell, August 25, 1651, in Thomas Hutchinson, comp., *Collection of Papers*, 1, 262–65.

84. The debate in the Council of State is recorded in C. H. Firth, ed., *The Clarke Papers* (Camden Society, *Publications* N. S. [LXI London]), 1899, III, 203–8.

85. Andrew Carter showed a remarkable ability to recover from disgrace. Commissioned a lieutenant colonel in Lambert's regiment, he was forced to leave the parliamentary armies in Scotland in 1651 because of his drunkenness. Lewis Morris asked the government to settle his debts so that his family would not be left destitute if he were killed; when Morris was refused, he decided not to participate in the fighting. Kempo Sabada was associated with Albertus and William Blauvelt, who had been active on Providence Island and the Moskito Coast. He lived in New England during the

Jamaica, Cromwell announced that his government would "strive with the Spaniard for the mastery of all those seas" and went on, "therefore we could heartily wish that the Island of Providence were in our hands again" because its location made it perfect for attacking the mainland and for "the hindrance of the Peru trade and Cartagena."[86]

When a formal justification was issued, the Protector demonstrated that his policy was the culmination of thirty years of thinking on the part of leading English puritans. Cromwell's manifesto was written by a committee headed by Nathaniel Fiennes, second son of Lord Saye and Sele and a member of the Lord Protector's council of State; Providence Island Company secretary William Jessop served as clerk to the council. The fate of the Providence Island colony, failing after repeated assaults, formed the centerpiece of the declaration's recital of the cruelty and lawlessness of the Spaniards in the Indies. The document took great pains to argue that the island had been unoccupied and that its settlement by English colonists had not, as the Spanish alleged, taken place in time of peace. In fact, English occupation dated from Christmas Eve 1629, just before the peace of 1630. Arguing that, as in 1588, the issue was the independence of England, the manifesto concluded that it was the Spanish who had repeatedly broken the peace: "We must have War, where the Spaniards will not let Us have Peace."[87]

For men who saw divine purpose in all events, the sailing of the expedition was a heady experience. Cromwell wrote to Admiral William Penn, commander of the fleet, that if it was, as they thought, God's business, then all would see his hand in it. Roger Williams was ecstatic, writing that the sailing of the ships was the beginning of

1650s. For information on participants in the Western Design, see *The Narrative of General Venables*, ed. C. H. Firth, Camden Society *Publications* n. s., 60 (London, 1900), esp. xxi, xxvi, 20. On Kempo Sabada, see PIC Ct., 6–19–40; J. Franklin Jameson, ed., *Privateering and Piracy in the Colonial Period: Illustrative Documents* (New York, 1923), 14 n., and Lion Gardiner to John Winthrop, Jr., April 5, 1652, Massachusetts Historical Society *Collections* 4th ser., VII, 63–4.

86. Cromwell to Fortescue, October 1655, in Abbott, ed., *Cromwell Writings and Speeches*, III, 857–8. See S. A. G. Taylor, *The Western Design: An Account of Cromwell's Expedition to the Caribbean* (Kingston, Jamaica, 1965); Dunn, *Sugar and Slaves*, 151–5. Korr places the Western Design in the context of European politics; *Cromwell and the New Model Foreign Policy*.

87. *A Declaration of His Highness*, in Patterson et al., eds., *Works of Milton*, XIII, 509–63, esp. 537–45, 559. In 1738 Thomas Birch attributed this declaration to John Milton, and this attribution has been accepted until recently. The Yale edition of *The Complete Prose Works of John Milton*, gen. ed. Don M. Wolfe (New Haven, 1971), V, Part II, 711–12, finds no evidence to support it. When Cromwell's expedition took Jamaica, the victors forced the Spanish there to sign the same terms given the Providence Island colonists. Robert Venables and Gregory Butler to Oliver Cromwell, June 4, 1655, in *Thurloe State Papers*, III, 511.

"greater & greater Revolutions approaching" and that thousands in England now wished to crown the Protector with gold.[88]

New Englanders were intimately involved in the entire conception. Cromwell was as convinced as the earlier Providence Island investors that God had gathered upright English citizens in New England so that when the time came they could answer the call to do his work elsewhere. According to Roger Williams, John Cotton's "interpreting of Euphrates to be the West Indies" was all the Protector needed. Together with that interpretation of prophecy, "the supply of gold, (to take off taxes), & the provision of a warmer Diverticulum & Receptaculum then N. England is, will make a footing into those parts very precious & if it shall please God to vouchsafe success to this fleet, I look to hear of an invitation at least to these parts for removal from his Highness, who looks on N. E. only with an eye of pity, as poor, cold & useless." Thomas Gage, trading on his presumed experience of America, had told the council that New England and Virginia "are even worn out" and would provide many colonists for Panama and elsewhere.[89]

Many New England colonists found the summons attractive, but others pointed to rumors of sickness and suffering in Jamaica, arguing that the sufficiency of the north was preferable to riches at such a price.[90] The Massachusetts Bay leadership was right to urge caution. The great expedition of the Western Design, after failing miserably in an attempt to conquer Hispaniola, limped on to take Jamaica, where disease, exacerbated by inadequate and inappropriate supplies, mowed the forces down. New Englander Edward Winslow died on the voyage from Hispaniola to Jamaica, some said of a broken heart, and

---

88. Cromwell to Penn, December 20, 1654, in Abbott, ed., *Cromwell Writings and Speeches*, III, 551; Roger Williams to John Winthrop, Jr., Feburary 15, 1654, Massachusetts Historical Society *Collections* 4th Ser., VI, 289; Williams to Winthrop, Jr., February 21, 1656, in Bartlett, ed., *Letters of Williams*, 298.

89. Williams to John Winthrop, Jr., February 15, 1654, Massachusetts Historical Society *Collections* 4th Ser., VI, 291; Gage declaration in Birch, ed., *Thurloe State Papers*, III, 60–1.

90. Daniel Gookin to Secretary Thurloe, Boston, January 21, 24, 1656, in Birch, ed., *Thurloe State Papers*, IV, 440; William Goodson and Robert Sedgwick to Cromwell, March 12, 1656, ibid., 601; Cromwell to Maj. Gen. Fortescue, October 30, 1655, in Abbott, ed., *Cromwell Writings and Speeches*, III, 858; Leverett to Gov. Endecott, London, December 20, 1656, in Hutchinson, *History of Massachusetts-Bay*, ed. Mayo, I, 163n–4n. See Frank Strong, "The Causes of Cromwell's West Indian Expedition," *American Historical Review* IV (1898–99), 228–45, and "Forgotten Danger," 84–94.

The idea that colonists from the North American mainland would move farther south persisted. The Nicholas Papers contain a 1662 report to the king that "New England is a very poor country," and arguing that the settlers there and in Virginia will go to Guiana; B. L., Egerton MS 2543, f. 123.

one by one the other leaders either died or gave up. As letters from Massachusetts Bay made clear, the news of the reproof God had given England, laying it "low in the dust," was soon known all over the Atlantic world.[91]

Moreover, the newly wise commanders now informed Cromwell that it was not so easy to encounter the Spanish treasure fleet at sea or to besiege a mainland city like Cartagena. In fact, before that disastrous attack English planters on Barbados had tried to dissuade the fleet even from attempting Hispaniola.[92]

The New Englander Robert Sedgwick, commander of the land forces, knew what the problem was: "God is angry." As he wrote to John Winthrop, Jr., "What God will do with this design I know not. I was willing some time to believe God was in it, but he yet seems to disown us." In a long letter to the Protector, Sedgwick wrote that unless God stayed his hand the entire army would die "and shall be as water spilt upon the grass, that cannot be gathered up again." He concluded that "this generation" might simply be destined to "die in the wilderness."[93]

Sedgwick contended that the army sent in the Western Design had not been of the godly and upright stamp necessary to such a great work, but he perceived a more fundamental problem that reached right down to the basic conception of the enterprise. As in Providence Island, preying on the fortunes of others, however unworthily gained, could not be the foundation of a godly society. Analyzing the problems of Jamaica, Sedgwick made his case to Cromwell: It was not "honourable, that your highness's fleet should follow this old trade of West-India cruisers and privateers, to ruin and plunder poor towns, and so leave them." He reiterated this judgment in a later letter to Secretary John Thurloe, saying that the practice gave the English a bad name among the very Indians and slaves they said they were coming to protect, making them seem to be merely spoilers and ruining the grand design for which they had embarked.[94] Oliver Cromwell was forced to

91. For reports of bad conditions on Jamaica, see Birch, ed., *Thurloe State Papers*, III, 157–8, 505, 508, 510–11, 646–7, 650–1, 674, 682, 689; IV, 30, 451–8, 602, 605; and Firth, ed., *Ludlow Memoirs*, I, 416–17.

92. Adm. William Goodsonn to Secretary Thurloe, January 24, 1655, in Birch, ed., *Thurloe State Papers*, IV, 453; Maj. Robert Sedgwick to Thurloe, January 24, March 12, 1656, ibid., 454–5, 604–5; J. Berkenhead to Thurloe, February 17, 1654, ibid., III, 158.

93. Sedgwick to Cromwell, November 5, 1655, ibid., IV, 151–5; Sedgwick to Thurloe, March 12, 1656, ibid., 605; Sedgwick to Winthrop, November 6, 1655, in "The Winthrop Papers," Massachusetts Historical Society *Collections* 5th Ser., I (Boston, 1871), 381.

94. Sedgwick to Cromwell, November 5, 1655, in Birch, ed., *Thurloe State Papers*, IV, 153; Sedgwick to Thurloe, March 12, 1655, ibid., 604.

acknowledge what the Providence Island Company had already learned: A godly settlement could not be erected by a military expedition, and it could not pay its own way in the short run. Cromwell was shattered by the defeat at Hispaniola. He never accepted that the failure of the Western Design signaled God's endorsement of Spain, but he was forced to see it as a rebuke of England. The goals advocated over thirty years by the puritan grandees were not God's goals after all.[95]

Robert Sedgewick was right: A godly and stable settlement could not derive its income from privateering, however authorized or justified. How the money was amassed did matter, and the means inevitably affected every aspect of life. With Providence Island's godly settlers dispersed, only its privateering tradition lived on in the Caribbean.

From the 1650s the West Indies became a theater where bands of pirates, amalgamations of men from many nations, careered around the seas, plundering and bringing terror to Spanish communities. They were known as buccaneers for the wooden grills, *boucans*, over which they grilled the meat of animals they hunted. The pirates, led by such men as Henry Morgan, were legendary for the cruelty and rapacity with which they assaulted their hapless victims; their reputation alone was enough to terrify. Providence Island was seized by privateers several times, and Tortuga was their base for a time. Their favorite base was Port Royal, Jamaica, where Morgan enjoyed the patronage of the governor Thomas Modyford, who had urged the Western Design on Oliver Cromwell.

Modyford's encouragement of Henry Morgan, like the Providence Island Company's plan to fund their colonial activities through privateering, shows the ambiguous meaning of the Elizabethan legacy. England could sponsor an empire and reap its benefits without paying the costs by relying on private enterprise for its military arm. Even the government in London, which eventually conferred a knighthood and the lieutenant governorship of Jamaica on Henry Morgan, was prepared for a time in the later seventeenth century, like Queen Elizabeth, to underwrite private warfare that it could not control. John Evelyn recorded his reaction when Modyford's letters describing Morgan's sacking of Panama City were read to the Council for Foreign Plantations in 1671. He wrote that the exploit was "very brave; they

95. See Blair Worden, "Oliver Cromwell and the Sin of Achan," in Derek Beales and Geoffrey Best, eds., *History, Society and the Churches: Essays in Honour of Owen Chadwick* (Cambridge, 1985), 127, 135–41. Worden argues that Cromwell's refusal of the crown, which he calls perhaps his most disastrous decision, sprang in part from this sense of sin and failure.

took, burnt, and pillaged the town of vast treasures. . . . Such an action had not been done since the famous Drake."[96]

Like the exploits of Drake, Hawkins, and Ralegh, Providence Island continued as a potent symbol of England's potentially great empire and of the cruelty of the Spaniards. Its story was told at times when leaders cast their eyes on the Spanish-controlled mainland and dreamed of accomplishing the goal of a great British presence there. Refugees and associates of the Providence Island venture continued to live along the Moskito Coast, and the notion that the puritan colony had cemented a firm friendship with its Indians beckoned to those who saw in the decline of Spain an invitation to British activity.

When England went to war against Spain in 1739, the loss of Providence Island again figured in public discussion. Sir Benjamin Rudyerd's speech for a West-Indies Association was reprinted, as was Cromwell's declaration against Spain, with its concentration on Providence Island's fate, and magazine and pamphlet discussions of the war recalled Cromwell's aims and justifications.[97] As the power of Spain faded in England's consciousness, however, Providence Island also faded away to the point that many historians confused it with New Providence in the Bahamas.[98]

In 1835 the British Royal Navy made a survey of the East Coast of Central America, and C. F. Collett, a member of the survey team, sent a description of Providence Island to the Royal Geographical Society. Collett wrote that the island was called St. Catharine in the English translation of Exquemelin, but "from whom, or when, it received its

---

96. John Evelyn, *Diary of John Evelyn*, ed. William Bray and Henry B. Wheatley (London, 1906), II, 264. The classic account of the buccaneers is Exquemelin, *Buccaneers of America*. For modern treatments, see Dunn, *Sugar and Slaves*, esp. chap. 5; Burns, *British West Indies*, 313–321; and Robert C. Ritchie, *Captain Kidd and the War against the Pirates* (Cambridge, MA, 1986), chap. 1.
97. Rudyerd's speech was printed with *Sir Thomas Roe his Speech in Parliament* (1641) as *A Speech Delivered in Parliament By a Person of Honour* (London, 1739). Anon., *A True Copy of Oliver Cromwell's Manifesto Against Spain, Dated October 26, 1655 Containing Authentick Accounts of many Pyracies, Robberies, Murders, and Cruelties committed by the Spaniards upon the English, during the pacifick reign of James I and perplext Reign of Charles I* (London, 1741), 19–21; A Gentleman of the Middle Temple [John Banks], *A Short Critical Review of the Political Life of Oliver Cromwell*, 3rd ed. (London, 1647), 200–3. On the war of Jenkins' Ear, see Philip Woodfine, "The Anglo-Spanish War of 1739," in Jeremy Black, ed., *the Origins of War in Early Modern Europe* (Edinburgh, 1987), 185–209. I thank David Armitage for calling to my attention the revival of interest in the Providence Island project in service of the Darien Company and in the Anglo-Spanish War.
98. See Newton, *Colonising Activities*, 7–9.

present name of Old Providence it is not easy to say." That name, once so evocative of England's aspirations both for the nation and for empire, elicited only puzzlement from these men of the modern British navy.[99]

99. C. F. Collett, R. N., "On the Island of Old Providence," *Journal of the Royal Geographical Society* 7 (1837), 203–210, quotation from p. 204. The 1831 novel by Jane Porter, *Sir Edward Seaward's Narrative of his Shipwreck, and consequent discovery of certain islands in the Caribbean Sea . . . From the year 1733 to 1749, as written in his own diary,* was set in Providence Island. Seaward and his wife discovered hidden treasure – forty bags each holding 500 gold doubloons bearing the date 1670 together with crucifixes and a Spanish brass belt buckle – and this treasure ultimately poisoned the idyllic pleasure of their Eden; Porter, *Sir Edward Seaward's Narrative,* 3 vols. (London, 1831), I, 120, 217–22, 228.

Providence Island Company Members

William Ball
1/2 of Sherland's share, 1633.

Gabriel Barbor (d. 1633)
Hesitant Charter Member, left company 1632.
Companies: E. Ind., Va., S. I., French, Feoffees for Impropriations.

Thomas Barnardiston
1/4 share, 1634; refused permission to leave company, 1634.
First cousin of Knightley.
Companies: E. Ind., Levant.

Sir Thomas Barrington, M.P. (1589–1644)
Full share, 1631, elected deputy 1632.
Brother-in-law of Gerard; cousin of Oliver Cromwell and John
    Hampden; niece and cousin married to Oliver St. John.
Companies: French, Va.

Godfrey Bosvile, M.P. (1596–1658)
1/4 share, 1634.
Half-brother of Lord Brooke, father-in-law of Roger Harlakenden of
    Earl's Colne, who emigrated to Massachusetts Bay in 1635.
Companies: Piscataqua.

Sir Thomas Cheeke, M.P. (d. 1659)
1/4 of N. Rich share, 1632.
Brother-in-law of Warwick, father-in-law of Mandeville.
Companies: Va., Guiana, S. I.

Henry Darley, M.P. (c.1596–c.1671)
2/3 of Gerard share, 1632; elected deputy 1636 and 1637.
Companies: Ct. River, Mass. Bay.

John Dyke, company husband
Charter Member; elected deputy 1630 and 1631; left company 1632.
Companies: S. I., Va., E. Ind.

James Fiennes, M.P. (d. 1679)
1/4 share, 1633.

William Fiennes, Lord Saye and Sele, M.P. (1582–1662)
Charter Member
Daughters married Earl of Lincoln and heirs of Sir Matthew Boynton
and Sir Walter Erle.
Companies: French, S. I., Ct. River, Piscataqua, E. Ind.

Gregory Gawsell
Charter Member
Brother-in-law of Saltonstall, estate agent for Earl of Warwick.
Companies: French.

Sir Gilbert Gerard, M.P. (1587–1670)
Charter Member, elected deputy 1634.
Brother-in-law of Barrington.
Companies: Va., S. I.

John Graunt
Charter Member.
Companies: French, S. I.

Robert Greville, Lord Brooke, M.P. (1608–1643)
Charter Member.
Brother-in-law of Sir Arthur Haselrig, half-brother of Bosvile.
Companies: French, E. Ind., Ct. River, Piscataqua.

John Gurdon, M.P. (1595–1679)
Charter Member.
Nephew of Herbert Pelham; brother-in-law of Sir Richard Saltonstall.
Companies: French.

Sir Edward Harwood (d. 1632)
Charter Member.
Companies: French, Va., S. I., Feoffees for Impropriations.

Richard Knightley, M.P. (d. 1639)
Charter Member.
Companies: French, Va., S. I., Ct. River.

John Michell, Machell
  1/4 of Sir N. Rich's share, 1633.
  Cousin of Rich.
  Companies: E. Ind.

Edward Montague, Lord Mandeville; Earl of Manchester 1642, M.P.
    (1602–1671)
  1/2 share, 1636; inherited Sir N. Rich's share, 1637.
  Son-in-law of Warwick (1st wife) and of Cheeke (3rd wife); 4th wife
    was widow of Warwick.
  Companies: S. I.

Sir Edmond Moundeford, M.P. (1595–1643)
  Charter Member.
  Companies: French.

John Pym, M.P. (1584–1643)
  Charter Member, elected deputy 1638 and 1639.
  Companies: French, S. I., Ct. River.

Henry Rich, Earl of Holland, M.P.
  Charter Member, company governor.
  Cousin of Sir Nathaniel, brother of Warwick.
  Companies: French, Guiana, Va., S. I.

Sir Nathaniel Rich, M.P. (1585–1636)
  Charter Member, elected deputy 1635.
  Cousin of Warwick and Holland.
  Companies: French, New Eng. & Mass. Bay, Va., S. I., Ct. River.

Robert Rich, Earl of Warwick, M.P. (1587–1658)
  Charter Member.
  Cousin of Sir Nathaniel, brother of Holland; father-in-law of
    Mandeville and Robartes; Mandeville also married Warwick's
    widow; brother-in-law of Cheeke; heir married Cromwell's
    daughter, 1657.
  Companies: Africa, Guiana, Guinea, E. Ind., New Eng. and Mass.
    Bay, S. I., Va., French.

John Robartes; Lord Robartes 1634, Earl of Radnor 1679, M.P.
    (1606–1685)
  Charter Member.
  Son-in-law of Warwick; sister married into Rous family.
  Companies: French.

Sir Benjamin Rudyerd, M.P. (1572–1658)
  Charter Member.
  Companies: French, S. I.

Oliver St. John, M.P. (c. 1598–1673)
  Charter Member.
  Married Joan Altham; Elizabeth Cromwell, 2nd wife, was niece and
    cousin of Sir Thomas Barrington.
  Companies: Guiana, Va.

Christopher Sherland, M.P. (d. 1632)
  Charter Member.
  Companies: French, Feoffees for Impropriation.

Thomas Symons
  1/4 of St. John share, 1632.
  Companies: E. Ind., Levant [?].

John Upton, M.P.
  1/4 of Dyke's share, acquired from Pym, 1632; partner with Waller
    and Rudyerd in separate stocks. Company agent in Devon.
  Brother-in-law of Pym.

Sir William Waller, M.P. (1598–1668)
  1/4 share from 1636 (partnered with Upton and Rudyerd in separate
    stocks).

William Woodcock, company husband (d. 1638)
  1/4 share, 1634, introduced by Lord Brooke.
  Companies: Ct. River.

William Jessop, company secretary, d. 1675.

Creditors of the
Providence Island Company

Bonds are posted for double the amount loaned. Variations in spellings of names have been preserved.

1632

Mr. Edmund Bruster (Brewster), £1,500 (three bonds of £500 each, reduced to one of £500)   5–3, 7

1633

Mr. Richard Spitty and John Pym bound for £100 taken up by Mr. Dyke   3–19

Mr. Brewster, Mr. Richard Blower (Blore)
  £1,000 (£523.6s.8d to be paid in 6 months at Gray's Inn Hall, 9 1/3 percent)   3–28

Lord Viscount Wimbledon
  £800 (£416 to be paid in 6 mo, 8 percent)   4–15

Debts outstanding: Sir William Cope (£1,500), Mr. Graunt (£200), Lord Gray (£500), Mr. Blore (£500), Lord Wimbledon (£400) all to be paid off by adventurers bringing in their last £200   7–8

1634

Mr. [John] Alured, procured by Mr. Darley, £300   5–17

Mr. John Browne of Middle Temple, £800 (in one month) to discharge bond to Earl of Lincoln   5–20

Lord Brooke lends £500 to pay Mr. Alured, other bills   6–9

Mr. Blore says Mr. Bruster dropped out, wants bond to him alone (£500)   7–2

Pym asks company to give security for £100 bond to Mr. Spitty, granted (see 3–13–33)   7–30

Old debts reviewed: Mr. Blore, Mr. Gray, Mr. Bagshaw, Lord Wimbledon, Lord Brooke remain, £650 to undertakers of last voyage, £2,700 in all. Mr. Sprigg acts as agent for Mr. Bagshaw, Mr. Bridges for Lord Brooke.   12–2

Bridges asks for his £500. Company borrows in two bonds, £50 and £700, of Mr. Thomas Hewyett (Hewitt), dated Dec. 6, payable June 7. This was added to the £650 already decided on.   12–8

1635

Mr. Bridges pledges £200 from Lord Brooke until next term   2–22

Mr. Blore wants £500 now due; Secretary to ask Mr. Bridges to find the money   5–2

Mr. Jessop had £250 entrusted to him by friends, borrowed for Mr. Woodcock's "present occasions," to be secured by money owed by the Earl of Warwick   5–16

Pym lays out debts due (£782.4.0): Mr. Bridges £200 and £4 interest; Mr. Gray £400 in full of £500; interest to Hewitt for 6 months on £1,200, £42 (7 percent); interest to Mr. Browne for 6 months on £800, £32 (8 percent); to Mr. Woodcock £104.4.0. Company decides all to be paid by borrowing.

With this £800 borrowed, company debts will be:
    Blore, £500
    Hewytt, £1,200
    Browne, £800
    Lord Wimbledon, £400
    Mrs. Smith and Mrs. Collins, £250
In all: £3,950.
With Subtraction of amounts for setting out of the *Long Robert* and the *Expectation*, debt is £2,584.

Mr. Blore wanted his debt renewed but wanted Sir Thomas Barrington added to the security. Company said present security was sufficient, would prefer to pay off debt.   6–8

Bond sealed by Brooke, Rudyerd, Pym, Darley for £1,600 to Lord Saye for payment of £821 in four months, per order of 6–8.   6–29

Bond sealed by Warwick, Saye, Rudyerd, Pym, Darley, Woodcock, Graunt for £1,000 for payment of £511.13.4 in four months to Mr. Garret at Mr. Alyes shop, for seamen in the *Long Robert*; to be repaid by Warwick for debt owed company.   7–1

Pym lays out debts coming due in 1635 (all with interest):

Blore	10–30–35	520	0 0
Wimbledon	10–16–35	416	
Browne	12–35	828	
Hewyt	12–6–35	1,242	
Collins	11–14–35	156	
Mrs. Smith	12–21–35	104	
Interest due 5–13 to 6–20:		16	4
Garrett	11–6–35	511	13 4
Saye	11–1–35	821	

Total: £4,599.9.8 (principal £4,450; interest 149.9.8)   11–13

Garrett loan on Warwick debt renewed to May 6.   11–21

Bond sealed to James Borrage (sealed December 1, 1635 for payment of £517.10.1 in six months) for part payment of £1,200 due Mr. Hewytt, now called in. Another bond sealed for payment of £416 to Mr. Bevill in six months for same.

Mr. Garrett's bond for £517.10 renewed to June 6, but James Borrage to be creditor rather than Mr. Garrett.   12–7

1636

Lord Saye partially paid off by new loan from Mrs. Jone Gerrard, £517.10.0 due in six months   2–11

Bond for loan from Alderman Cambell, £208 for next August 24, to pay remainder owed Lord Saye.   2–22

Bond to Lady Cambell, for paymt of £621.13.4 on September 2, to pay Mr. Woodcock for the voyage.   2–29

Bond to Sir William Acton, for payment of £526.13.4 on November 12 to pay Mr. Woodcock for present voyage.   3–3

Sir Benjamin Rudyerd demands his name be taken off the bonds to Lady Campbell and Mr. Acton for the new joint stock.   3–19

William Jessop acts as broker for loan, £160, has money from friends.

5–28

Bond sealed to Gregory Gawsell for payment of £166.8.0 December 1 at Warwick House, to pay off Mrs. Collins £150 and interest.   5–30

Bond for payment to Mrs. Heling in Woodstreet, £1,037.6.8 on December 10, for expenses of various voyages.   6–1

Bond for payment to Mr. Stone of Coleman Street, £500 with interest (left blank), to be paid within ten days. William Greville one of the guarantors.   6–16

Bond for payment of £205?.6.8 to Thomas Colwall at his shop in Bartholomew Lane ult October; Bond for payment of £310 ult November to Peter Calfe, both guaranteed by Brooke, Pym, and Edward Bass. Brooke, Pym, William Greville bound to pay £520 Dec. 29 to Abraham Corcellis.

These bonds are ultra £1,037.6.8 to Mrs. Heling; £500 with interest to Mr. Stone.   6–28

1637

Bond of £3,000 to pay Mrs. Heling £1,560 on September 3 at her house in Wood Street.   2–24, 26, 27

Bond to Mr. Holman for £1,600 for payment of £800 with interest on October [left blank]. Of this £460.11.5 for account of Saye, Brooke, and Pym for charges for voyage of *Mary Hope*; £339.8.7 for account of whole company to pay interest and bills.   3–17

Bond to Sir Thomas Aston for payment of £208 on September 18, taken up to pay off £200 with interest to Sir James Cambell.   3–18

Bond to Dr. Winston for £1,000 for payment of £520 November 13, taken up for payment of £500 with interest to Mr. Richard Blore.

5–12

Mrs. Crane calls in £800 part of debt. Bond sealed June 9 for £1,200 for payment of £624 December 11 to Mrs. Anne and Mrs. Elizabeth Chester [?] at Mr. Stone's house in Coleman Street. £500 to be used to pay off two bonds by undertakers of the *Mary Hope*, £300 to Peter Calfe and £200 to Mr. Colwall. £100 for Brooke's own use, to be paid by Jessop.   5–18

Bond for £2,000 paymt of £1,033.6.8 November 25 to Mr. Bigmon at his shop in Cheapside. £800 to go to pay off Mrs. Crane; £200 for Pym's own use.   6–22

Bond for payment of £517.10.0 December 27 to Sir Matthew Boynton for seamen's wages in *Expectation*. 6–26

Bond for £200 for payment of £104 January 8 to George Evelin of Grass Inn Esquire at Mr. Rhetorick's shop. 7–7

Bond for payment of £515.8.0 to Mr. Frances Theobalds of Gray's Inn May 4. 12–11

Bond for payment of £1,035 [unclear who lender was] to pay off Sir Matthew Boynton and for discharge of first 6 months' freight for *Happie Return*; Bond for paymt of £208 [day left blank] to Mr. Hollyoke. 12–16

1638

Bond for payment of £832 August 16 to Mr. John Fountain for the second 6 months of *Happie Return* wages and interest. 2–15

Bond for payment of £520 to Sir William Acton at his house in Bishopsgate Street August 24 on the account of the new under-takers. 2–21

Bond for payment of £520 September 16 to Mr. William Rosse of St. Martin's in the Fields on the account of the new undertakers. 3–14

Bond for payment of £624 September 23 to Mr. Richard Woodward for new adventurers. 3–20

Bond for payment of £624 October 3 to Mr. Hugh Hubbert of London, Gent. on the account of the new undertakers. 3–31

Bond for payment of £624 October 13 to John Gore Esq. in St. Martin's Lane on the account of the new undertakers. 4–6

Mr. Borrage demands his money, two bonds of £500 each. Pym to take up same elsewhere. 5–30

Bond for payment of £300 plus £10 interest May 15 to Mr. Harris upon the general account (8 percent). 12–13

1639

Arrangements made to pay off Lord Wimbledon, Lady Cambden, Dr. Winston, Mr. Hubbard, Mr. Theobalds, Mr. Hollyock, and Mr. Winwood. 6–6

Money called in by Sir Marmaduke Langdale, Sir Henry Reeve, Mr. Heydon, Mr. Fonntayne, Lord Camden, Mr. Smith. Amount to £3,500.

Michaelmas term

1640

Company owes interest payments in Michaelmas term to:

		£	
Lady Bevill 18 mo. int for		£400	£48
Mr. Smith "		100	12
Sir Thomas Acton	6 mo.	200	8
Sir Wm. Acton	6 mo.	500	21.13.04
Mr. Bigmon	6 mo.	800	34.13.04
Mr. Evelyn	6 mo.	100	4.05.0
Mrs. Heyling	6 mo.	1,500	60
Mrs. Heyling		1,000	40
Mrs. Chester		600	26
Mr. Stone		500	21.10
Mr. Holman	12 mo.	800	64
Sir Henry Reeve		800	34.13.04
Alderman Cordell		1,000	43.06.08
Mr. Gore		600	26
Mr. Harvey		700	30.06.08
Mr. Frannell		500	21.13.04
Mr. Harris		300	13

Total interest due: £509.01.08

Principal called in: Lady Bevill £400; Mr. Smith £100; Sir Thomas Aston £200; Mr. Holman £800; Mr. Stone £500.

Total: £2,000.

Also due £74.09.10 for wages.

8–25

1641

June 28, account of money due. List of creditors grouped by agents who dealt for the creditors, with interest due.

Through Mr. Colwall:

Mr. Gore	£600	£26
Mr. Bigmon	800	36 [money called in]
Sir Wm Acton	500	22.10.0
Sir Henry Reeve	800	36
Mrs. Chester	600	27 [money called in]

Alderman Cordell	1,000	45

Interest due

Mr. Holman	800	128 (for 2 yrs) Money called in if interest not paid or bond received.
Mrs. Heyling	1,000	40
	1,500	60 £100 due

Through Mr. Lukins:

Mr. Harvy	700	30.6.8

Through Mr. Long:

Mr. Stone	500	21.10.0

Through Mr. Shalcrosse:

Mr. Harris	100	16 [Called in, in full of £300]

Through Mr. Rhetorick

Mr. Evelyn	100	4.5.0

Adds up to £492.11.8 in interest, £1,500 in money called in (excluding Mr. Holman) = £1,992.11.8.

In addition Saye, Mandeville, and Pym share £67.10.0 responsibility for interest due to:

Mr. Honywood	1,000	45
Mr. Harvey	500	22.10.0

1642

Reckoning of bonds owed (presented in Jessop deposition, 1644)

Mr. Gore principal	£ 600
Mr. Binion	800 (part of £1,000, remainder due on Pym's particular account.)
Sir Wm Acton	500 prin.
Sir Henry Reeve	800 prin.
Mrs. Chester	600 "
Alderman Cordell	1,000 "
Mr. Harvy	700 "
Mr. Stone	500 "
Mr. Evelyn	100 "
Mr. Holman	800 "
Mrs. Heyling	1,000 " [£1,500 of Heyling debt
Mrs. Heyling	1,500 account of William Woodcock]
Mr. Parkall	300 "

Also due to Moundeford £19.00.7 and Graunt £2.02.6 on accounts.

Total = £9,221.03.1

Also particular bonds: To Sir John Evelin and Sir John Gore, two bonds for £1,000 to pay off £1,000 to Mr. Honywood by the Earl of Manchester (Lord Mandeville) and Pym; and to Mr. Harvy for £500 by Manchester, Saye, and Pym.

William Jessop's Final Reckoning of Investors' Debts

The Earl of Warwick of the distribution	£975.06.02 1/2
for his part taken off from the first Adventurers	138.18.06
for his part taken off the Lord Brooke's	231.05.02
for his part of Mr. Woodcock's debt	108.15.08
Total charge	£1,454.05.6 1/2
Lord Saye and Sele on the distribution 1642	1,190.04.11 1/2
for his part taken off from the first Adventurers	138.18.06
for his part of Mr. Woodcock's debt	108.15.08
Total charge	£1,437.19.01 1/2
The Earl of Manchester on the distribution	£453.05.0 1/4
for his part taken off from the first Adventurers	138.18.06
for his part of Mr. Woodcock's debt	220.10.01
Total charge	£812.13.07 1/4
Lord Brooke on the distribution after the Additional Charges	
	£849.07.0
for his part taken off from the first Adventurers	277.17.0
for his part of Mr. Woodcock's debt	217.11.04
Total charge	£1,344.15.04
Lord Robartes the remainder on the distribution	2.06.09
Sir Thomas Barrington on the distribution 1642	76.01.0 1/2
for his part taken off from the first Adventurers	138.18.06
qu: for his part taken off the Lord Brooke's	231.05.02
for his part of Mr. Woodcock's debt	108.15.08
Total charge	£555.00.04 1/2
Sir Benjamin Rudyerd on the distribution	£114.07.7 1/4
for his part taken off from the first Adventurers	69.09.03
for his part taken off the Lord Brooke's	115.12.07
for his part of Mr. Woodcock's debt	54.07.10
Total charge	£353.17.03 1/4

Mr. Pym on the distribution	£1,739.19.03 3/4
for his part taken off from the first Adventurers	138.18.06
for his part of Mr. Woodcock's debt	108.15.08
Total charge	£1,987.13.05 3/4
Mr. Henry Darley on the distribution	£361.05.05
Mr. John Upton on the distribution	£44.07.09 3/4
	61.14.06
for his part taken off from the first Adventurers	34.14.07 1/2
for his part taken off the Lord Brooke's	57.16.03 1/2
for his part of Mr. Woodcock's debt	27.03.11
Total charge	£225.17.01 3/4
Sir William Waller on the distribution	£44.07.09 3/4
for his part taken off from the first Adventurers	34.14.07 1/2
for his part taken off the Lord Brooke's	57.16.03 1/2
for his part of Mr. Woodcock's debt	27.03.11
Total charge	£164.02.07 3/4
Mr. Gawsell the remainder on the distribution	£24.17.06
My Symons the remainder on the distribution	£3.17.0
Lord St. John remainder on the distribution	£2.15.0
Mr. Bossevile for the ship *Robert*	£169.16.06
Mr. Machell for the ship *Robert*	£40.01.06
Mr. John Gourden for his Additional Adventure with Capt. Newman	
	£63.05.0
Sir Gilbert Gerrard the remainder on the distribution	£13.10.06
Mr. Knightley on the distribution	£192.00.04
for his part taken off from the first Adventurers	69.09.03
for his part taken off the Lord Brooke's	115.12.07
for his part of Mr. Woodcock's debt	54.07.10
Total charge	£431.10.0
Total indebtedness on Jessop's reckoning	£9,949.09.07

NB: The manuscript indicates that Gerrard and Knightley should have been inserted between Rudyerd and Pym.

Source: Essex Record Office, Hatfield Broad Oak MS D/DBa/o2/25.

Bibliographical Essay

The *Records of the Providence Island Company*, two large folio volumes, were copied after the colony's failure by company secretary William Jessop when surviving members attempted to clear up the debts remaining from the venture. Volume I contains copies of all letters sent from London to the colony, as well as those sent to Association Island. Volume II contains detailed minutes of company meetings. These volumes are in the Public Record Office at Kew, CO 124/1,2. Informal letters sent to individual clients on behalf of particular investors were preserved in a shorthand notebook kept by Jessop. This notebook is in the British Library (Add. MS 10615) together with a transcription prepared by Mr. K. L. Perrin in 1968–9 with the aid of funds provided by the History Faculty Board of Oxford University and with the help of Professor Hugh Trevor-Roper (Lord Dacre of Glanton) and Dr. Valerie Pearl.

Few letters and reports from the colony survive. The first notice of the island's discovery sent by Philip Bell from Bermuda is in Vernon A. Ives, ed., *The Rich Papers: Letters from Bermuda, 1615–1646* (Toronto, 1984), 319–21. A set of letters sent home shortly after the first colonists from England arrived was excerpted and circulated among investors. One set of excerpts is in the manuscripts of Sir Thomas Barrington, Hatfield Broad Oak MS D DBa 02/8, Essex Record Office. This collection also contains other documents preserved by Sir Thomas that deal with his investment in Providence Island. A few other sources survive from the project's early years. The island's admiral made a survey of the western Caribbean; "Daniell Ellffryth's Guide to the Caribbean, 1631," ed. Stanley Pargellis and Ruth Lapham Butler is printed with notes in the *William and Mary Quarterly* 3rd ser., I (1944), 273–316. The Bermuda Archives, Accession 51, contain letters from Captain William Rudyerd, Lieutenant William Rous, and Sir Benjamin Rudyerd concerning events in the island.

A report of the 1640 Spanish attack prepared by Henry Halhead, Richard Lane, Hope Sherrard, and Nicholas Leverton and sent to the company June 17, 1640, is in the Finch MSS, Leicestershire Record Office, Box 4982, ff. 4–14, and calendered in Historical Manuscripts

Commission, Seventeenth *Report* (1913), I, 51–8. The Manchester Papers contain several Providence Island letters; photostats are in the Library of Congress and they are calendared in the Historical Manuscripts Commission, Eighth *Report* (1884), nos. 416, 420, 423, 424.

The only systematic picture of daily life in the colony occurs in the diary kept toward the end of the decade by Governor Nathaniel Butler; this manuscript, for which he used the back and front pages of a book on seamanship he was writing, also contains notes for letters to company investors. Captain Nathaniel Butler's "A Diary, from February 10th 1639 of My Personal Employments," is in the British Library, Sloane MS 758.

After the first Spanish attack in 1635, the royal government considered its response; a set of documents prepared for this discussion, including a report by Secretary of State Sir John Coke, is in the Public Record Office, CO 1/8: Providence Island Company, "A Declaration made the 21st of December 1635 To the right Honorable the Earle of Holland," 81; Sir John Coke, Draft Memorandum, December 1635, 83; Declaration at Whitehall, December 21, 1635, 86.

Company efforts to manage their business and to attract new investors survive in letters from Sir Edmund Moundeford to Sir Simonds D'Ewes, September 2, 1637, B. L. Harleian MS 386, f. 156, and undated, ibid., MS 287, f. 265; and in the Earl of Holland's request to Attorney General John Bankes that John Pym be allowed to remain in London, January 2, 1638, Bodleian Library, Bankes MS bundle 65, piece 16.

All these primary sources emanating from Providence Island colonists and investors are in the collection *Papers Relating to the Providence Island Company and Colony, 1630–1641*, ed. Karen Ordahl Kupperman, in the series *British Records Relating to America in Microform*, gen. ed. W. E. Minchinton (Microform Academic Publishers, 1989).

"Don Alonso de Cárdena's Complaint [to Charles I] and a Reference thereupon, 1640," in Robert Sanderson, comp., *Foedera*, 20 vols. (London, 1704–35), XX, presents evidence of the damage done by privateers from Providence Island to Spanish colonies. Spanish accounts of the 1640 and 1641 attacks on Providence Island are in the Archivo General de Indias, Seville, *Audiencia de Santa Fe, legajo 223*. They include the "Relación de Meritos" of Captain Don Torivio de Palacio y Sierra; an "Account of the journey and Battle of Santa Catalina Island written by father friar Mateo de San Francisco, Chaplain major and administrator of the Armada of Portugal, under the command of Don Gerónimo Gomes de Sandoval, Royal Admiral of the Ocean and Captain General of Galleons and fleet in the city of Cartagena de Indias, the 29th of

November of 1640"; and General Francisco Díaz Pimienta to Philip IV, September 11, 1641.

The conquest was reported from the English point of view in an anonymous newsletter, *A Letter from the Low Countries* (1642), which carried the running head "Avisos from severall places" (pp. 5–6), Thomason Tracts, E. 141.10, British Library. The indictment of the Spanish was again detailed in *A Declaration of His Highness, by the Advice of His Council; Setting Forth, on the Behalf of this Commonwealth, the Justice of their Cause Against Spain*, 1655, in *The Works of John Milton*, gen. ed. Frank Allen Patterson (New York, 1937), XIII, 509–63.

After the fall of Providence Island, an offering was apparently made to attempt to keep the project alive. This was in Anon., *Certain Inducements To well minded People, Who are here straitned in their Estates or otherwise: or such as are willing out of Noble and publike Principles, to transport Themselves, or some Servants, or Agents for them into the West-Indies, for the propagating of the Gospel and increase of TRADE* (n.p., 1643?).

Primary information about the Providence Island project can also be found in the *Winthrop Papers* published by the Massachusetts Historical Society, Vols. II–IV (Boston, 1931–44) and in John Winthrop, *Winthrop's Journal: History of New England, 1630–1649*, ed. James Kendall Hosmer, 2 vols. (New York, 1908). Captain John Smith presents much of the background on which company members drew in *The Complete Works of Captain John Smith*, ed. Philip L. Barbour, 3 vols. (Chapel Hill, 1986). In addition to his Providence Island diary, Nathaniel Butler wrote a *History of the Bermudaes or Summer Islands*, ed. J. Henry Lefroy, (London, 1882). Lefroy erroneously attributed this work to Captain John Smith, who used it as the basis for the Bermuda section of his *Generall Historie*.

Company investors Lords Brooke and Saye wrote books that offer valuable insights into their thinking. Lord Brooke wrote *The Nature of Truth* (London, 1640), facs. ed. with intro by V. de Sola Pinto, n.p. 1969, and *A Discourse Opening the Nature of That Episcopacie, Which is Exercised in England*, 2nd ed. (London, 1642), facs. repr. William Haller, ed., *Tracts on Liberty in the Puritan Revolution, 1638–1647*, II (New York, 1934). Lord Saye wrote *Vindiciae veritatis. Or, an answer to a discourse intituled, truth it's manifest* (London, 1654). On the authorship of this tract, see J. S. A. Adamson, "The *Vindiciae veritatis* and the political creed of viscount Saye and Sele," *Bulletin of the Institute of Historical Research* 60 (1987).

The most important secondary source about Providence Island, and the only previous book-length treatment, is A. P. Newton, *The Colonising Activities of the English Puritans* (New Haven, 1914). A midnineteenth century survey resulted in two publications: C. F. Collett, R. N., "On the Island of Old Providence," *Journal of the Royal Geographical Society* 7 (1837), 203–10; and Captain Richard Owen, *A Nautical Memoir, Descriptive of the Surveys made in H. M. Ships "Blossom" and "Thunder," from 1829 to 1837* (Dublin, 1840?), 101–5. Modern treatments of the island are Peter J. Wilson, *Crab Antics: The Social Anthropology of English-Speaking Negro Societies of the Caribbean* (New Haven, 1973); and James J. Parsons, *San Andrés and Providencia: English-Speaking Islands in the Western Caribbean* (Berkeley, 1956). On the rivalry between Providence Island and Massachusetts Bay, see Karen Ordahl Kupperman, "Errand to the Indies: Puritan Colonization from Providence Island through the Western Design," *William and Mary Quarterly* 3rd ser., XLV (1988), 71–99, and Frank Strong, "A Forgotten Danger to the New England Colonies," American Historical Association, *Annual Report for the Year 1898* (1899), 79–94. Subsequent Spanish attempts to occupy the island are the subject of Donald Rowland, "Spanish Occupation of the Island of Old Providence, or Santa Catalina, 1641–1670," *Hispanic American Historical Review* 15 (1935), 298–312.

A limited number of studies on men connected to the project have been done in recent years. On Henry Halhead, see D. E. M. Fiennes and J. S. W. Gibson, "Providence and Henry Halhed, Mayor of Banbury 1630/31," *Cake and Cockhorse* 7 (1978), 199–210. On company members, see Wesley Frank Craven, "The Life of Robert Rich, second Earl of Warwick, to 1642," unpub. Ph.D. diss., Cornell University, 1928; Nelson P. Bard, Jr., "William Fiennes, First Viscount Saye and Sele: A Study in the Politics of Opposition" (unpub. Ph.D. diss., University of Virginia, 1973); Robert E. L. Strider, *Robert Greville, Lord Brooke* (Cambridge, MA, 1958); Conrad Russell, "The Parliamentary Career of John Pym," in *The English Commonwealth, 1547–1640*, ed. Peter Clark, Alan G. R. Smith, and Nicholas Tyacke (New York, 1979), 147–65; Barbara Donagan, "A Courtier's Progress: Greed and Consistency in the Life of the Earl of Holland," *Historical Journal* 19 (1976), 317–53, and "The Clerical Patronage of the Earl of Warwick," *Proceedings of American Philosophical Society* 120 (1976), 388–419; D. R. Barcroft [David L. Smith], "The Political Career of Sir Benjamin Rudyerd" (unpub. undergrad. diss., Cambridge University, 1985). The investors figure prominently in J. T. Cliffe, *The Puritan Gentry: The Great Puritan Families of Early Stuart England* (London,

1984), and biographies of many of them can be found in Richard L. Greaves and Robert Zaller, eds., *Biographical Dictionary of British Radicals in the Seventeenth Century*, 3 vols. (Atlantic Highlands, NJ, 1983).

The social and intellectual milieu in which the grandees operated can be understood through Mervyn James, *English Politics and the Concept of Honour, 1485–1642, Past and Present Supplement 3* (Oxford, 1978); Quentin Skinner, *The Foundations of Modern Political Thought*, 2 vols. (Cambridge, 1978); Lawrence Stone, *The Crisis of the Aristocracy, 1558–1641* (Oxford, 1965); Anthony Fletcher, *Reform in the Provinces: The Government of Stuart England* (New Haven, 1986); and "Honour, Reputation and Local Officeholding in Elizabethan and Stuart England," in Anthony Fletcher and John Stevenson, eds., *Order and Disorder in Early Modern England* (Cambridge, 1985), 92–115. A broader constituency for new ideas is seen in Edmund S. Morgan, *Inventing the People: The Rise of Popular Sovereignty in England and America* (New York, 1988).

Company members figure heavily in debates over the causes of the English Civil War. Conrad Russell presents the case for seeing the war as the result of a breakdown in the political process in *The Fall of the British Monarchies, 1637–1642* (Oxford, 1991); *The Causes of the English Civil War* (Oxford, 1990); and *Parliaments and English Politics, 1621–1629* (Oxford, 1979). On longer-term causes, see the essays in Richard Cust and Ann Hughes, eds., *Conflict in Early Stuart England: Studies in Religion and Politics, 1603–1642* (London, 1989); Richard Cust, *The Forced Loan and English Politics, 1626–1628* (Oxford, 1987); and L. J. Reeve, *Charles I and the Road to Personal Rule* (Cambridge, 1989). The local political role taken up by company members in Essex and in Warwickshire is shown in William Hunt, *The Puritan Moment: The Coming of Revolution in an English County* (Cambridge, MA, 1983), and Ann Hughes, *Politics, Society and Civil War in Warwickshire, 1620–1660* (Cambridge, 1987). Their centrality in national politics is delineated in Christopher Thompson, "The Origins of the Politics of the Parliamentary Middle Group, 1625–1629," *Transactions of the Royal Historical Society* 5th ser., 22 (1972), 71–86; and R. M. Smuts, "The Puritan Followers of Henrietta Maria in the 1630s," *English Historical Review* XCIII (1978), 26–45.

On company members' Civil War roles, see J. H. Hexter, *The Reign of King Pym* (Cambridge, MA, 1941); Valerie Pearl, "The 'Royal Independents' in the English Civil War," *Royal Historical Society Transactions* 5th ser., XVIII (1968), 69–96 and "Oliver St. John and the 'Middle Group' in the Long Parliament," *English Historical Review*

LXXXI (1966), 490–519; Clive Holmes, *The Eastern Association in the English Civil War* (Cambridge, 1974); J. S. A. Adamson, "The Peerage in Politics, 1645–49," (unpub. Ph.D. diss., Cambridge University, 1986); and Mark A. Kishlansky, *The Rise of the New Model Army* (Cambridge, 1979). They also figure in Valerie Pearl, *London and the Outbreak of the Puritan Revolution: City Government and National Politics, 1625–43* (Oxford, 1961), and Anthony Fletcher, *The Outbreak of the English Civil War* (London, 1981).

On the religious issues that led to war, see Simon Adams, "The Protestant Cause: Religious Alliance with the West European Calvinist Communities as a Political Issue in England, 1585–1630" (unpub. D. Phil. diss., Oxford University, 1973); John Morrill, "The Religious Context of the English Civil War," *Transactions of the Royal Historical Society* 5th ser., 34 (1984); Caroline Hibbard, *Charles I and the Popish Plot* (Chapel Hill, 1983); and Blair Worden, "Providence and Politics in Cromwellian England," *Past and Present* CIX (1985), 55–99.

The Providence Island investors and colonists were deeply committed puritans. For recent treatments of what this meant, see Nicholas Tyacke, *Anti-Calvinists: The Rise of English Arminianism, c. 1590–1640* (Oxford, 1987); Patrick Collinson, *The Religion of Protestants: The Church in English Society, 1559–1625* (Oxford, 1982) and *Godly People: Essays on English Protestantism and Puritanism* (London, 1983); Charles Lloyd Cohen, *God's Caress: The Psychology of Puritan Religious Experience* (Oxford, 1986); Stephen Foster, *The Long Argument: English Puritanism and the Shaping of New England Culture, 1570–1700* (Chapel Hill, 1991) and *Their Solitary Way: The Puritan Social Ethic in the First Century of Settlement in New England* (New Haven, 1971); and Charles E. Hambrick-Stowe, *The Practice of Piety: Puritan Devotional Disciplines in Seventeenth-Century New England* (Chapel Hill, 1982). On relations between lay and clerical puritans, see Karen Ordahl Kupperman, "Definitions of Liberty on the Eve of Civil War: Lord Saye and Sele, Lord Brooke, and the American Puritan Colonies," *Historical Journal* 32 (1989), 17–33, and Barbara Donagan, "Puritan Ministers and Laymen: Professional Claims and Social Constr: ints in Seventeenth Century England," *Huntington Library Quarterly* 47 (1984), 81–111.

The great classic work on the process of colonization is Charles M. Andrews, *The Colonial Period of American History*, 4 vols. (New Haven, 1934–38). Wesley Frank Craven, *Dissolution of the Virginia Company: The Failure of a Colonial Experiment* (New York, 1932), is also a classic and treats many of the issues that would become important in the English Civil War. John J. McCusker and Russell R. Menard in *The Economy of British America, 1607–1789* (Chapel Hill, 1985) present a modern overview. On merchant leadership in colonization, see David Harris Sacks, *The Widening Gate: Bristol and the Atlantic Economy, 1450–1700* (Berkeley, 1991).

On the English West Indies, see V. T. Harlow, ed., *Colonising expeditions to the West Indies and Guiana, 1623–1667* (London, 1925); Gary A. Puckrein, *Little England: Plantation Society and Anglo-Barbadian Politics, 1627–1700* (New York, 1984); Richard S. Dunn, *Sugar and Slaves: The Rise of the Planter Class in the English West Indies, 1624–1713* (Chapel Hill, 1972); and Carl and Roberta Bridenbaugh, *No Peace Beyond the Line: The English in the Caribbean, 1624–1690* (New York, 1972). The changing environment is treated in David Watts, *The West Indies: Patterns of Development, Culture and Environmental Change Since 1492* (Cambridge, 1987) and *Man's Influence on the Vegetation of Barbados, 1627–1800*, University of Hull Occasional Papers in Geography 4 (1966). English activities in Central America are treated in Robert A. Naylor, *Penny Ante Imperialism: The Mosquito Shore and the Bay of Honduras, 1600–1914* (Cranbury, NJ, 1989) and Narda Dobson, *A History of Belize* (London, 1973). For the psychological impact of colonization in the south, see Karen Ordahl Kupperman, "Fear of Hot Climates in the Anglo-American Colonial Experience," *William and Mary Quarterly* 3rd ser., XLI (1984), 213–40. On the key role of the Dutch, see Jonathan I. Israel, *Dutch Primacy in World Trade, 1585–1740* (Oxford, 1989).

On servitude, see Russell R. Menard, "From Servants to Slaves: The Transformation of the Chesapeake Labor System," *Southern Studies* XVI (1977), 355–90; Hilary McD. Beckles, "Plantation Production and White 'Proto-Slavery': White Indentured Servants and the Colonisation of the English West Indies, 1624–1645," *The Americas*, 41 (1985) and *White Servitude and Black Slavery in Barbados, 1627–1715* (Knoxville, TN, 1989); and David Galenson, *White Servitude in Colonial America: An Economic Analysis* (Cambridge, 1981).

Wesley Frank Craven and Kenneth R. Andrews have written extensively on the imperial context within which these events were set. For Craven see "The Earl of Warwick, A Speculator in Piracy," *Hispanic American Historical Review* 10 (1930) and *An Introduction to the History of Bermuda* (Williamsburg, VA, 1940). Kenneth R. Andrews's books include: *Ships, Money and Politics: Seafaring and Naval Enterprise in the Reign of Charles I* (Cambridge, 1991); *Trade, Plunder, and Settlement: Maritime Enterprise and the Genesis of the British Empire, 1480–1630* (Cambridge, 1984); *The Spanish Caribbean; Trade and Plunder, 1530–1630* (New Haven, 1978); and *Elizabethan Privateering: English Privateering during the Spanish War, 1585–1603* (Cambridge,

1964). On privateering in the 1620s, see also J. C. Appleby, "English Privateering during the Spanish and French Wars, 1625–1630" (unpub. Ph.D. diss., University of Hull, 1983). On plans for a West Indies Company throughout the 1620s, see John C. Appleby, "An Association for the West Indies? English Plans for a West India Company," *Journal of Imperial and Commonwealth History* 15 (1987), 213–41. Investment in imperial activities is the subject of Theodore K. Rabb, *Enterprise and Empire: Merchant and Gentry Investment in the Expansion of England, 1575–1630* (Cambridge, MA, 1967); K. R. Andrews, N. P. Canny, and P. E. H. Hair, eds., *The Westward Enterprise: English ·Activities in Ireland, the Atlantic, and America, 1480–1650* (Liverpool, 1978); and Henry C. Wilkinson, *The Adventurers of Bermuda*, 2nd ed. (Oxford, 1958).

Recent work on the Chesapeake and New England has begun to demonstrate more similarity in their early organization and aspirations than previous historiography has allowed for. On the colonies generally, see Jack P. Greene, *Pursuits of Happiness: The Social Development of Early Modern British Colonies and the Formation of American Culture* (Chapel Hill, 1988). For new work showing the dynamism of the New England puritan settlements, see Virginia DeJohn Anderson, "Migrants and Motives: Religion and the Settlement of New England, 1630–1640," *New England Quarterly* 68 (1985), 339–83, and *New England's Generation: The Great Migration and the Formation of Society and Culture in the Seventeenth Century* (Cambridge, 1991); Daniel Vickers, "Competency and Competition: Economic Culture in Early America," *William and Mary Quarterly* 3rd ser., XLVII (1990), 3–29; John Frederick Martin, *Profits in the Wilderness: Entrepreneurship and the Founding of New England Towns in the Seventeenth Century* (Chapel Hill, 1991). This work was prefigured by Stephen Innes, *Labor in a New Land: Economy and Society in Seventeenth-Century Springfield* (Princeton, 1983).

Whereas New England is coming to be seen as having been organized along principles allowing economic individualism and maximizing family security, studies of the Chesapeake are emphasizing the development of community values in that region. Thus, the overdrawn contrast between the two regions is giving way to convergence. On the Chesapeake, see Lois Green Carr, Russell R. Menard, and Lorena S. Walsh, *Robert Cole's World: Agriculture and Society in Early Maryland* (Chapel Hill, 1991); Lois Green Carr, Philip D. Morgan, and Jean B. Russo, eds., *Colonial Chesapeake Society* (Chapel Hill, 1988); and James R. Perry, *The Formation of a Society on Virginia's Eastern Shore, 1615–1655* (Chapel Hill, 1990).

Index

Abbreviations: *col.*, colonist in Providence Island; *cred.*, creditor of Providence Island Company

Acton, Mr. (col.), 154, 160–1
Acton, Sir William (cred.), 363, 365–7
Adcock, John (col.), 269 fn. 5
admiralty courts, 78–9
Africa Company, 359
Aguilera, Don Melchor de, 288–9
Algiers, pirates capture the *Mary*, 283, 311
Altham, Joan, 360
Alured, Mr. John (cred.), 361
Alyes, Mr., 363
Amyraut (Amirant), Reverend Paul, 137 fn. 45, 259
Andrews, K. R., 347
Archer, Michael (col.), 282
Arminianism, 10–13, 181, 253
Arrat, John (col.), emigrates with family, 165
Ashe, Simeon, 331
Assada, Island of, 343
assemblies, as necessary to colonial success, 125–31, 140–3, 206–8, 211
Association Island, *see* Tortuga
Aston (Acton), Sir Thomas (cred.), 364, 366
Axe, Captain Samuel (col.), 33, 49, 60, 203, 216, 281 fn. 35; accused in deaths of Indians, 212; applies for Dutch letters of marque, 191, 197, 283; background, 190; compensation, 58; directs mainland trade, 104; friendship with Nathaniel Butler, 212, 216, 285; later career, 99; on commission for grievances, 214–20, 276; on committee to deal with ore, 282–3; on council of war, 214–20, 275–6; move to mainland, 73, 96, 191, 196; plat of mainland, 199 fn. 48; privateering captain, 286, 312–13; quarrel with Gov. Bell, 62, 73, 195–6; quarrel with Daniel Elfrith, 72–3, 195–6, 212, 275; reappointed to council 1641, 294; report to Providence Island Company 1638, 108–9; return to

Providence Island 1638, 211–12, 275; voyage with Jackson (1642–5), 347; work on fortifications, 28, 31, 41, 72–3, 191–7

Bagshaw, Mr. (cred.), 362
Bahamas, New Providence, 355
Ball, William, 357
Banbury, Oxfordshire, 6; colonists from, 46–9, 118, 147, 154; great fire, 46–7, 186–8; puritanism of, 47; Quakers in, 253
Barbados, 19, 84–5, 99, 136, 261, 343, 347, 353; density of slave population compared with Providence Island's, 172, 175–6; development, 110–17, 124–5; economy, 83, 102; Warwick offers to buy colony, 315
Barbor, Gabriel, 357
Barnardiston, Thomas, 357
Barrington, Sir John, 317–18
Barrington, Sir Francis, 8
Barrington, Sir Thomas, 1, 357–8; correspondence with colonists, 65 fn. 37, 120, 131, 196, 237–8, 241–2; death of, 316; debt to company, 316–17; interest in emigration to Massachusetts, 325 fn. 12; political activities, 7–14; religious convictions, 3, 222–5; recruits colonists, 47, 139, 186, 256; role in English Civil War, 342; role in Providence Island Company, 300–1, 308, 362; subscribes to new joint stock 1636, 302–3; ties to Connecticut River settlements, 325
Bartlett, John (col.), 103
Barton, Isaac (col.), 285
Barton, Samuel (col.), 335
Bass, Edward, 364
Baxter, Richard, 10
Baynes, John (col.), 335
Bazelie, Luke (col.), 156
Beaton, Richard (col.), 335

379

drive for military preparedness, 181–90; economy, 12, 17, 48, 84–6; government compared with colonial government, 50–3, 142, 181–5, 208, 254; plague in, 205

Erastianism, 223, 252–3

Erle, Sir Walter, 185, 358

Essex, John (col.), 36, 38, 47

Essex, colonists from, 47–8; Braintree, 47–8; Witham Affray, 186

Evelin (Evelyn), Mr. George (cred.), 365–7

Evelin, Sir John (cred.), 368

Evelyn, John, on buccaneers, 354–5

Eversten, Richard, *see* Pagett

Exquemelin, Alexander, 280

Fawsley, Northamptonshire, 4

Feild, Richard (col.), 159 fn. 34

Fenwick, George, 145, 325–9, 333

Feoffees for Impropriations, 357

Fiennes, James, 331, 358

Fiennes, Nathaniel, 318, 331; and Western Design, 351

Fiennes, William, *see* Saye and Sale

Fitch, Ensign (later Captain) Thomas (col.), 103, 154, 156, 191, 268; attempted return to Providence Island 1641, 340; deputy governor of Providence Island, 175, 293–4, 323–4; investment in privateering, 139 fn. 52; role in English Civil War, 342

Fletcher, Anthony, 254

Florida, as destination for emigrants from New England, 324, 341

Floud (col.), 157–8

Floude, Roger (col.), 87

Fonseca, 94

Forbes, Alexander, Lord, 344–5

Forbes, John, 345 fn. 68

forced loan, 1626, 8, 22, 141–2

Forman, Thomas (col.), 70

Fortescue, Sir John, 207–8

Fortescue, Major General Richard, 350–1

fortifications on Providence Island, 31, 39, 41, 109, 181, 190–7, 204–8, 288–93, 338; Black Rock Fort, 72, 194, 211, 275, 289–91; Brooke Fort, 194, 267; Darley's Fort, 194; Fort Henry, 31, 36, 59, 69–70, 194, 211, 267; Warwick Fort, 28, 31, 194, 291; primary focus of Butler governorship, 211, 258, 275, 285, 289; report by William Rudyerd, 197; responsibility of Samuel Axe, 28, 31, 41, 72–3. See map, 193

Foster, Ensign John (col.), 211

Foster, Nicholas, 111

Foster, Stephen, 21, 247, 251

Fountain (Fonntayne), Mr. John (cred.), 365

France, financial situation, 305; policy toward, 200; war with, 181, 183–5, 267, 271

Francis, John (col.), 217, 246, 267, 276 fn. 26, 285, 287–8; commander of Brooke Fort, 267; malfeasance, 270; reappointed 1641 with warning, 294

Francis, Robert (col.), 159

Frannell, Mr. (cred.), 366

free trade, 64; colonists' demands for, 42–3, 45, 113, 121, 133–4; company allows, 140–1; demands from other colonies, 134–5; granted, 281

French Company, 357–60

Fugill, Thomas, 333

Gage, Thomas, 70–1, 169 fn. 70, 191, 215; adviser to Cromwell, 348, 352

Gardiner, James (col.), 156

Gardiner, Lion, 333

Garrard, George, 311

Garrett, Mr. (cred.), 363

Gates, Edward (col.), 38, participation in government 46, 75, 121

Gates, Peter (col.), 174

Gates, Sir Thomas, 45

Gawsell, Gregory, 358, 364; role in English Civil War, 342

Gerard, Sir Gilbert, 1, 357–8; religious position, 222 fn. 3; role in English Civil War, 342; role in Providence Island Company, 300–3

Gerbier, Sir Balthazar, 312

Gerrard, Mrs. Jone (cred.), 363

Gibbins, William, 330

Gladman, Mr. Elisha (col.), 214, 271; on council of war and commission for grievances, 275–6; ally of Andrew Carter, 286, 293

Goodman, Nicholas (col.), 73 fn. 57, 96, 195–6; expulsion from Providence Island, 241

Goose, Mr., 324

Gore, Sir John (cred.), 318, 365–6, 368

Gorges, Sir Ferdinando, 322–7

Gorges, Thomas, 135, 177 fn. 91, 250 fn. 77, 322

Gorton, Samuel, 252, 334

Gossage, Mr., 310

Gracias a Dios, Cape, 39, 87, 99, 169, 278, 280, 290, 323, 336, 338, 341; trade expedition to, 94, 104

Granajo Island, *see* Guanaho

386 *Index*

340–1; role on Providence Island,
261–4, 288
Ligon, Richard, 22; on Barbados sugar
revolution, 112–14
Lincoln, Theophilus Clinton, 4th Earl of, 8,
70, 322, 358
Lobo, Don Rodrigo, 288–9
Lofthouse, Francis (col.), 269 fn. 5
Long, Mr., 367
Low Countries, 15, 192, 199, 214, 259,
267, 306, 310
Lucas, Mr., 303
Lukins, Mr., 367

Machiavelli, Niccolò, 209–10
Madagascar, 343
magazines of supplies, 30, 42, 269;
colonists' debts to, 90, 133, 136, 164;
complaints of poor distribution, 73–4,
130–3, 140, 276; end of, 281; irregular
arrival, 121–2, 129–30; prices, 88, 132,
276; complaints in other colonies,
134–5; malfeasance of clerks, 73–4,
138, 140
Maldonado de Texeda, Don Antonio, 289
Manchester, Edward Montague, Earl of,
see Mandeville
Mandeville, Edward Montague, Lord, Earl
of Manchester from 1642, 1, 4, 265, 357,
359; activities in Providence Island
Company, 79, 147, 293–4, 304, 318,
323, 367–8; clients, 283, 340;
Connecticut River settlements, 333–4;
debt to company, 316; on slavery, 168
fn. 65; political activities, 9–14; religious
convictions, 3, 222 fn. 1 and 3; role in
English Civil War, 342; subscribes to
new joint stock 1638, 309–11, 315
Markham, Gervase, 184
Marston, Nathaniel (col.), 95–6, 100, 283
Marten, Sir Henry, 186, 188
martial law, 188–90
Maryland, 124–6, 213
Massachusetts Bay colony, 1, 25, 34, 47;
appeal for help by Providence Island
colonists, 265, 285; assistance from
Providence Island Company members,
296; challenges in, 69–70, 241, 245,
247–54; conflict over public works in,
207–8; criticism by Providence Island
Company members, 221–2, 228, 236,
247–54, 321–7; customs exemption,
305–6; depression in, 320–5, 348;
economy, 101, 116, 321–5; government
of, 54, 247–54; grounds of success, 21,
44, 82, 116, 125–9, 139–46, 245, 254;

problems over magazines, 135;
Providence Island slaves exported to,
172, 174; providential explanation of
King Philip's War, 177–8; as puritan
refuge, 16–17; as radical puritan
experiment, 18, 51, 221–2, 225–6, 236,
247–54, 260; source of settlers for
Providence Island, 175, 253, 265–6,
320–5, 334, 336, 341; unruly colonists
in, 54, 161
Massachusetts Bay Company, 51, 251, 322,
324, 357–9; quo warranto proceedings
against, 327
Mateo de San Francisco, Father, 290–1
Mather, Cotton, 192, 247, 257
Maymouth, Jeffrey (col.), 155
Maynard, Thomas (col.), 48
mechoacan, *see* medicines
medical practitioners, demand for, 165
medicines, 97; jallop, 88; mechoacan, 86,
88, 92, 93 fn. 34, 164; rhubarb, 85;
scorzonera, 85
Merch, Giles, 310
Michell (Machell), John, 359
military needs, 181, 195, 199, 203,
208–20, 268–9, 274–6; armaments,
194–9, 214, 269, 309, 323, 338; neglect
of armaments, 196, 204–5, 289–91
military training, civilian control necessary
to success, 217–19, 275–6, 285; in
England, 182–5, 208–10, 218–19; in
Virginia, 217; in New England, 217–18;
on Providence Island, 29, 31, 70, 181–2,
189–90, 195–9, 203–5, 212, 267;
primary focus of Butler governorship,
211, 275–6
military veterans, 2, 31, 39, 44, 49, 203–5;
disruptive influence of, 59–60, 69–75,
189–93, 198, 203–6; ignorance,
288–92; in England, 184–9; influx
1638, 210–11; gunners, 164, 243, 268,
291
Millner, Goodman (col.), 154
ministers, as leaders of colonists' demands
for independence, 33–8, 129, 139–40,
229–36, 239, 244, 255; competition
with New England for, 135, 139–40,
210, 229–30, 238–9, 244–7, 254–5,
277; elimination from government,
221–2, 230–1; poor quality in
Providence Island, 228–30 (*see also*
individual ministers' entries); roles,
229–31; salaries for, 236, 243, 244,
257–9
modern "new lands" development, U.S.
AID analysis of, 114–15, 133